THE LORE OF THE CHINESE LUTE

Chinese scholar, with attendant carrying his lute
(Ming Dynasty drawing)

The Lore of the
Chinese Lute

An Essay in the Ideology of the *Ch'in*

R.H. van Gulik

Orchid Press

THE LORE OF THE CHINESE LUTE: An Essay on the Ideology of the *Ch'in*
R.H. van Gulik

First published, Monumenta Nipponica, Tokyo, 1940.
Second edition, Monumenta Nipponica and Charles E. Tuttle Co., Tokyo & Rutland, 1969.
Third edition copyright © Orchid Press, Bangkok 2011.

ORCHID PRESS
P.O. Box 1046,
Silom Post Office,
Bangkok 10504,Thailand
www.orchidbooks.com

Front cover image: Detail of a scroll-mounted painting in ink and colours on silk, in memory of lute master Ye Shimeng (業詩夢); China, Republican Period. Overall painting size 266 x 68 cm. Collection of the Museum Volkenkunde, Leiden, Netherlands, inventory number 5263-1. Reproduced by kind permission of the Museum Volkenkunde.

Rear cover image: The Minggang ("singing hill") *qin* (*ch'in*), from the collection of Mr. Shum Hing-shun; Chinese fir and red lacquer; China, Southern Song dynasty, Xianchung period (1265-1274 CE). Length 122.5 cm., width (at shoulder) 23 cm. Previously published in *Gems of Ancient Chinese Zithers: Shum's Collection of Antique Qin from the Last Millennium*, The Department of Music and the University Museum and Art Gallery, University of Hong Kong, 1998. Reproduced by kind permission of Mr. Shum Hing-shun.

ISBN: 978-974-524-236-4

This essay is respectfully dedicated
to the memory of
my first teacher of the lute
YEH SHIH-MENG

葉 詩 夢

[OBIIT 1937 AETATE 74]

a gifted musician
and
a great gentleman

PREFACE

琴　琴　'*Although the tones of the lute*
意　聲　　　*may be featured,*
誰　雖　*When listening to them*
可　可　　　*who shall be able to fathom their significance?*'[1]
聽　狀

THIS ESSAY *is an attempt to describe the cultural significance of a Chinese musical instrument, the seven-stringed lute.
Commonly called* KU-CH'IN[2] *or 'the lute of antiquity', it was played
more than two thousand years ago as it is still today. It is chiefly
used as a solo instrument, producing a subdued and highly refined
music.*

*But rather than its imposing age or its charming tones, it was
the unique place it holds in Chinese culture that prompted this
study. For from a remote time the lute was set apart as the inseparable companion of the literatus, that engaging combination of
official, poet, painter and philosopher, till gradually it became in
itself a symbol of literary life, with all of its elegant and tasteful
pleasures. The musical properties came to be accessory to the instrument as center of a special system of thought, an ideology fitly
encompassing the eclectic tendencies characteristic of the old-
fashioned Chinese scholar.*

*Although it is with this ideology—its origin, development and
final formulation—that the present essay is concerned, there must be
frequent references to the music itself. The author, merely a dab-
bler in musical science, had to take into consideration various
aspects of it, withal aware that he encroached upon ground more
properly reserved for musicologists. Among these, the author would*

---

1 From the poem 'Chiang-shang-chang-ch'in' 江上張琴, 'Playing the
Lute on the River', by the Sung scholar Ou-yang Hsiu (歐陽修, 外集, ch. 1).
2 古琴

be most gratified to find readers, although he addresses himself primarily to Orientalists, in the hope of drawing attention to one of the lesser known aspects of Chinese culture. Musicologists will discover here a veritable treasure house of ancient Chinese music in general, a rich source which might, with scientific analysis based on historical musicological principles, revolutionise the opinions on ancient Chinese music current now both east and west. This music of the lute may truly and proudly call itself T'AI-KU-I-YIN,[3] *'tones bequeathed from high antiquity'.*

It has seemed desirable to include a more or less exhaustive list and a critical discussion of the sources where these musicological materials are found, and it is hoped that they may serve musicologists in the further study of problems which could be but briefly treated here. Then, should one among them compile a complete handbook of lute music, the author would feel at least discharged of part of the large debt he owes it. Many were the joys the lute gave him. Old melodies enlivened weary summer evenings, and playing some light prelude often heartened him to attack again knotty passages in many a musty Chinese volume. During the writing of the following pages about the ideology of the lute, its music was an invariable inspiration.

Here a few remarks may be added on the use of the word 'lute' as a translation of the Chinese word 'CH'IN'. In selecting for Oriental musical instruments equivalents in a Western language one must choose between those which would suggest the outer form, and others of closer cultural reference. In the former respect 'cither'[4] would seem most appropriate for the CH'IN, *but because of the unique position it occupies in Chinese culture the author has preferred to follow the latter way, adopting the word which since olden times in the West has been associated with all that is artistic and refined, and sung by poets. Therefore 'CH'IN' is translated 'lute', and the word 'cither' is kept for such instruments as the* sê

---

3 太古遺音

4 In English the word *cither* is rather loosely applied to various kinds of stringed instruments. I use it in the sense of the cither played in Tyrol and Austria: a flat, wooden sounding box, over which about thirty strings are strung. It is set upon a table, and played with both hands.

and chêng, *the construction of which, in any case, comes nearer that of the Western cither.*[5]

The body of this essay appeared in four successive issues of the semiannual periodical MONUMENTA NIPPONICA, *published at Tokyo. The author wishes to express his gratitude to the editor of that journal, through whose kindness it was made possible that this essay appears now in book form. Since part of it was printed from the moulds of the original type, it could not be made to answer to high typographical standards, and while a few misprints could be corrected, many page references had to be cancelled. The reader is requested to refer frequently to the index, to which much care has been given.* [*sic.*]

To the original two appendices, both bibliographical, there have been added two more. Appendix III, *'The Lute as an Antique', is the revision of an article 'On Three Antique Lutes', which appeared in the* TRANSACTIONS OF THE ASIATIC SOCIETY OF JAPAN, *second series, no.* XVII. *The author's thanks are due to the Society for kind permission to reprint the illustrations that accompanied the said article. Appendix* IV, *'The Chinese Lute in Japan', is based upon an article entitled 'Chinese Literary Music*

---

5 *Ch'in* rendered as 'lute'. Dr. Curt Sachs wrote to me stating that, in his opinion, the rendering 'lute' is incorrect, since this term gives the Western reader a wrong impression of the shape and structure of the *ch'in;* he recommends the term *psaltery*. It is quite true that the shape of the psaltery resembles that of the Chinese *ch'in*, while our Western lute rather resembles the Chinese pear-shaped mandolin, the *p'i-p'a*. In my opinion, however, the shape of an Oriental musical instrument should not constitute the first consideration when selecting an English equivalent; the spirit of the music produced by an instrument and the place it occupies in the culture of its native country are as important factors as its shape and structure. This point holds true especially in the case of the Chinese *ch'in*, which occupies so unique a position in antique and modern Chinese life. In selecting 'lute' as translation of *ch'in*, my object was to convey to the general reader something of the cultural significance of this instrument and its music. Since the word 'lute' is associated by West-erners with poetry and refined enjoyment, it adequately suggests the atmosphere that surrounds the *ch'in*, while 'psaltery', on the other hand, suggests an instrument doomed to obsolescence since many centuries; moreover many readers would have been unfamiliar with this term. For these reasons I still prefer to render *ch'in* as 'lute', giving the inner meaning precedence over the physical form.

It should be noted that in Western literature considerable confusion reigns with regard to the translation and identification of Chinese and Japanese musical instruments. I am presently working with the Japanese historian and musicologist Kishibe Shigeo 岸邊成雄 on a list of Chinese and Japanese musical instruments—a list intended for reference use by Western students of Far Eastern music. Each item will consist of an illustration of the instrument, a brief description, and a proposed English rendering of its name. It is hoped that this list will assist the student in correctly identifying the instruments mentioned in various Western sources.

and its Introduction into Japan', which was contributed to the commemoration volume offered Prof. Chōzō Mutō, in 1937. Since the publication of these two studies a number of new materials have been found, necessitating a change in several of the statements made. Needless to say, the present essay supersedes all the author's earlier publications on the subject.

Finally, the writer has been induced by friends to add a Chinese preface wherein he has tried to summarise the significance of the lute. It is presented with diffidence, in the knowledge that a Westerner's excursions into Chinese composition must remain forever hazardous.

*   *   *

The author would have it understood that these pages are, most literally, an essay: an approach to the subject, an attempt to describe it, nothing more. The field being almost untouched, its materials had to be collected in originali and one by one, sometimes more than a year passing by before a rare item was at last found in the dim corner of some Chinese or Japanese bookstore. The argument which grew with the investigation of these texts led by frequent, unmarked cross-roads where the best direction may not always have been chosen. Moreover, official duties prevented sustained application; it is feared that along the way not a few errors or misstatements have escaped detection. In the end the author presumes to claim only the credit attendant on an honest effort: original sources are quoted in full, and each translation is accompanied by the Chinese text. The aim was to lay the full materials before the reader, at once enabling him to trace mistakes and supplying him with guideposts to further research.

*   *   *

Quite apart from scientific aspects, the description of beauty must always be an invidious undertaking, whether it be the beauty of form, thought, colour, or of tones. In endeavouring to write of things elusive as these one experiences perforce a feeling of frustration; one searches out words, only to realize their insufficiency to express the inexpressible.

Yet the exercise is restful to the mind, bringing as it does the happy thought that however inadequate and imperfect the description of it, beauty itself is perfect and shall last forever. As the Sung scholar Su Tung-p'o says in his celebrated poetical essay on the Red Wall: 'There remain only the clear breeze over the river, and the moon shining over the mountains. The ear catches the wind, and it is sound. The eye sees the moon, and it becomes colour. These things no one can forbid us to take in: they shall be forever with us, for they are part of the never exhausted fullness of the creation.'[6] It was such considerations that influenced the author to publish this study, feeble though be the effort it represents; for when his bones and these pages shall be mouldering, the wind will still rustle in the pines, and the rivulet murmur among moss-grown stones. And ultimately it may be said that perhaps the sole design of this essay was to show that lute music in its simplest essence is the echo of these undying voices of living nature.

*   *   *

In the forty-first year of the Wan-li period, A.D. 1613, the Ming scholar Lin Yu-lin published a book on stones and rocks.[7] A year later[8] he wrote a treatise on the lute, in the introductory remarks to which he says: 'First I published a book on stones, in four chapters; it distracted my mind from the worries of daily life and made me dwell among mists and coloured hazes. Now I follow it up with this "Elegance of the Lute"... For there exists a close harmony between stones and the silk strings. Always when

---

[6] 惟江上之清風，與山間之明月，耳得之而爲聲，目遇之而成色，取之無禁，用之不竭，是造物者之無盡藏也.

[7] *Su-yüan-shih-pu* 素園石譜, by Lin Yu-lin 林有麟; the original Ming edition is now very scarce. In 1924 a reprint was published by the Zuhon-sōkaṇkai 圖本叢刊會, at Tokyo.

[8] *Ch'ing-lien-fang-ch'in-ya* 靑蓮舫琴雅, cf. Appendix II, no. 6.

I sit confronting the many-hued rocks and mountains, and play a tune on my antique lute while the moon shines through the spreading pines, I feel greatly elated and my thoughts are borne away to unearthly regions. Therefore, having published my book on stones, I felt it incumbent upon me also to write this treatise on the lute.'[9]

The present writer in 1938 published an essay on Chinese inkstones.[10] When now in 1939 he ventures to send forth this other on the lute, he feels somewhat reassured, notwithstanding its many shortcomings; for he hopes that at least he adheres to the old approved principle of 'treading in the footsteps of the ancients'.

Netherlands Legation　　　　　　　　　　*R. H. van Gulik*
Tokyo, 22 Dec. 1939

---

[9] 余先梓石譜四卷，烟霞一洗塵俗，琴雅繼出，蓋絲與石原自作合，每當山石璘瑉，疏松月上，奏瑤琴一曲於其間，飄々欲仙矣，故有石譜，似不可無琴雅.

[10] *Mi Fu on Inkstones*, Orchid Press, Bangkok 2006 [Peking 1938].

後　序

夫此者內也、彼者外也、故老子曰、去彼取此、蟬蛻塵埃之中、優遊

忽荒之表、亦取其適而已、樂由中出、故是此而非彼也、然眾樂琴爲

之首、古之君子、無間隱顯、未嘗一日廢琴、所以尊生外物養其內也

、茅齋蕭然、值清風拂幌、朗月臨軒、更深人靜、萬籟希聲、瀏覽黃

卷、閑鼓綠綺、寫山水於寸心、欵宇宙於容膝、恬然忘百慮、豈必虞

山目耕、雲林清閟、蔭長松、對白鶴、丙子秋莫、於宛平得一琴、殆明清

曲非必多、手應乎心、斯爲貴矣、乃爲自適哉、藏琴非必佳、彈

間物、無銘、撫之鏗鏘有餘韵、弗敢冒高士選雅名、銘之曰、無名、

非欲以觀眾妙、冀有符於道德之旨云

余既作琴道七卷、意有未盡、更申之如右、然於所欲言、未罄什

一云

和蘭國笑忘高羅佩識於芝臺之中和琴室

EDITOR'S NOTE

FOR this revised edition, the parenthetic material which so cluttered the text in the first edition has been transferred to footnotes, so that the text now can be read more smoothly. Dates have been checked in H. A. Giles's *A Chinese Biographical Dictionary*, the *Nihon rekishi daijiten* 日本歴史大辞典 (20 vols., Kawade Shobō 1964), and the *Daijimmeijiten* 大人名事典 (10 vols., Heibonsha, 1962); a number of incorrect readings of Japanese proper names have been revised; page references in footnotes and index have all been checked and corrected when necessary. Since translation of the ancient measurements of 尺 and 寸 by *foot* and *inch* respectively, is not entirely satisfactory, the Chinese terms have been retained. Finally, the author's own corrections and additions found in *MN* VII (1951) have been incorporated fully.

CONTENTS

CHAPTER ONE: General Introduction   *page* 1

Characteristics of lute music—twofold function of the lute: orchestral and solo instrument—the solo lute as the special instrument of the literary class—description of the lute, and of the way it is played—origin and development of the lute and SÊ—place of the lute and lute music in Chinese cultural life—lute music in Japan

CHAPTER TWO: Classical Conceptions of Music   23

Chinese classical conceptions of music according to the YÜEH-CHI—*twofold aspect of music, cosmological and political—music belongs to heaven, and corresponds to what is heavenly in man—it is a means for perfecting the government, and for improving the individual—music as a source for pleasure not recognized*

CHAPTER THREE: Study of the Lute   29

§1 SOURCES
(from p. 29)

More materials on the significance of the lute than on lute music—three groups of materials: scattered references to the lute, special treatises on the lute, and CH'IN-PU, *handbooks for the lute—reasons for the rarity of* CH'IN-PU—*their contents—recent Chinese books on the study of the lute*

§2 ORIGINS AND CHARACTERISTICS
(from p. 35)

The establishment and evolution of CH'IN *ideology due chiefly to three factors: Confucianist (social), Taoist (religious), and psychological—Buddhist influences: a Mantrayanic magic formula as lute tune, a Lamaist hymn adapted to the lute—a summary of the history of* CH'IN *ideology*

LIST OF ILLUSTRATIONS

Note: The presence of an asterisk * prior to an illustration number indicates the illustration is following the page number quoted.

A NOTE ON THE VIGNETTES

FACING PAGE 1: The lute master Hsü Shih-ch'i 徐時琪, putting on the strings. After the frontispiece of his lute handbook *Lü-ch'i-hsin-shêng* 綠綺新聲, pub. in the Wan-li period.

PAGE 22: Playing the lute in the intimacy of the library; from an illustrated Ming edition of the play *Hsiu-ju-chi* 繡襦記.

PAGE 27: The *p'ai-hsiao* 排簫, Pandean pipes used in the ceremonial orchestra; from the *Chih-shêng-shih-tien-li-yüeh-chi* 直省釋奠禮樂記, preface 1891.

PAGE 100: The *hsüan* 壎, ancient ocarina; from the *Chih-shêng-shih-tien-li-yüeh-chi*.

PAGE 105: Young nobleman playing the lute; from an illustrated Ming edition of the play *Hsi-hsiang-chi* 西廂記.

PAGE 139: Talking with the lute on one's knees; from the well-known handbook for painters, *Chieh-tzŭ-yüan-hua-ch'uan*.

PAGE 161: The lute as played in the ceremonial orchestra; same source as the preceding item.

PAGE 198: Lute inscription, reading *i-ch'in-shuo-fa* 以琴說法, 'promulgating the Dharma by means of the lute'; from the *K'u-mu-ch'an-ch'in-pu* (see p. 53).

CHAPTER ONE

General Introduction

Characteristics of lute music—twofold function of the lute: orchestral and solo instrument—the solo lute as the special instrument of the literary class—description of the lute, and of the way it is played—origin and development of the lute and sê— place of the lute and lute music in Chinese cultural life—lute music in Japan

THE MUSIC of the ancient lute as a solo instrument is widely different from all other sorts of Chinese music: it stands entirely alone, both in its character and in the important place it occupies in the life of the literary class.

It is easier to describe this music in negative than in positive terms. It may be stated at once that it is not like that of any of the better known stringed instruments to be found in present-day China, as, for instance, the two-stringed violin or *êrh-hu*, the four-stringed mandoline or *p'i-p'a*, or the moon guitar or *yüeh-ch'in*.[1] The music of these instruments being highly melodical, it can be appreciated by anyone who possesses some capacity for musical adaptation. At first hearing their music may seem a little strange, but the ear soon adjusts itself to the quaint chords and unusual movements, and this music is easily understood.

The lute, on the contrary, is not so easy to appreciate, chiefly because its music is not primarily melodical. Its beauty lies not so much in the succession of notes as in each separate note in itself. 'Painting with sounds' might be a way to describe its essential quality.

Each note is an entity in itself, calculated to evoke in the mind of the hearer a special reaction. The timbre being thus of the utmost importance, there are very great possibilities of modifying the colouring of one and the same tone. In order to understand and appreciate this music, the ear must learn to distinguish subtle nuances: the same note, produced on a different string, has a different colour;

---

1 二胡, 琵琶, 月琴

the same string, when pulled by the forefinger or the middle finger of the right hand, has a different timbre. The technique by which these variations in timbre are effected is extremely complicated: of the vibrato alone there exist no less than 26 varieties. The impression made by one note is followed by another, still another. There is thus a compelling, inevitable suggestion of a mood, an atmosphere, which impresses upon the hearer the sentiment that inspired the composer.

Playing the lute is therefore entirely a question of touch, necessitating complete mastery of the finger technique of both hands.[2] This is the reason why it takes a fairly long time before one can play the lute. Anyone with an ear for music may, in a month or so, become a tolerably efficient performer on the *êrh-hu*, or, in a few months, on the *p'i-p'a*. But studying the lute is like playing the violin or piano: it takes years of assiduous and regular practice. The results, however, reward the labour, as the best of China's past has found its expression in the music of the lute.

The origins of the lute and lute music lie hidden in the mist of China's remotest past.

According to literary tradition, from the most ancient times the lute had two essentially different functions. In the first place it was a part of the orchestra, played at ceremonies in the ancestral temple and on other solemn occasions, and further at banquets, for entertaining guests. On the other hand the lute in itself was used as a solo-instrument by the individual player, for his own enjoyment and whenever he liked.

It is in this twofold function that the lute occurs through all the dynasties, up to the present day.

The orchestral lute is essentially the same as the solo instrument, the only difference being in the way it is played. Whilst the music of the solo lute, as I pointed out above, is exceedingly complicated, the technique of the orchestral lute is very simple, the left hand being hardly used at all. In the orchestra for Confucian ceremonies six lutes are used, three on the left and three on the right. As its sounds are low, its music is drowned in the din of the percussion instruments, and playing the lute in the ceremonial orchestra is not a very gratifying task. However, according to a dissertation on music dating from the Sung period,[3] there existed during the Chou dynasty other or-

---

[2] Cf. *Wu-chih-chai-ch'in-pu* (Appendix II, 15), ch. 1, p. 63: 音韻之妙，全賴乎指法之細微.

[3] *Yüeh-shu* 樂書 by Ch'ên Yang 陳暘, eleventh century, ch. 130.

chestras, where the lute played a more prominent part: thus the court music called *t'ang-shang-yüeh*[4] consisted chiefly of chant, accompanied by stringed instruments. In this orchestra there were 48 singers, accompanied by, inter alia, 12 lutes. Still, in Chinese books on music, and in literature generally, the orchestral lute is only occasionally mentioned, and is not distinguished especially among the other instruments of the orchestra.

The solo lute, however, has been fixed by tradition as the special instrument of the literary class, and as such since time immemorial has enjoyed a privileged position. The solo lute is called the 'Instrument of the Holy Kings', its music 'Tones bequeathed by High Antiquity'.[5]

Father Amiot, whose treatise on Chinese music was published in 1780, was much impressed by the deep significance which the Chinese literati attached to the lute. He says: 'In short, the Chinese say that the construction of the lute, its shape, everything about it, is doctrine, everything expresses a special meaning or symbolism. They add that the sounds it produces disperse the darkness of the mind, and calm the passions; but in order to obtain these precious benefits from it, one must be an advanced student of wisdom. Only sages should touch the lute: ordinary people must content themselves with contemplating it in deep silence and with the greatest respect.' And in a note he adds: 'Our Emperor [Ch'ien-lung, 1736–95] himself has several times consented to be painted in the attitude of a man profoundly absorbed in playing the instrument that in his Empire is considered as belonging by right to those whose studies are concentrated on literature and wisdom.'[6]

Around the solo lute has gathered a rich and varied lore, which has given rise to a special class of literature. It is this system of thought that surrounds the lute, this *ch'in* ideology, that forms the subject of these pages. Therefore the orchestral lute is mentioned only for the sake of comparison, and especially when discussing

---

4 堂上樂
5 聖王之器　太古遺音
6 Cf. *Mémoires concernant les Chinois*, vol. VI: *Mémoires sur la musique des Chinois tant anciens que modernes*, pp. 56–7: '[En] un mot, la construction du Kin, sa forme, disent les Chinois, tout en lui est doctrine, tout y est représentation ou symbole. Les sons qu'on en tire, ajoutent-ils, dissipent les ténèbres de l'entendement, et rendent le calme aux passions; mais pour en recueillir ces précieux fruits, il faut être avancé dans l'étude de la sagesse. Les seuls sages doivent toucher le Kin, les personnes ordinaires doivent se contenter de le regarder dans un profond silence et avec le plus grand respect.' Also, p. 58, footnote: 'Notre Empereur lui-même n'a pas dédaigné de se faire peindre plusieurs fois dans l'attitude d'un homme profondément occupé à tirer des sons d'un instrument, qui passe dans son Empire pour être dévolu de droit à ceux qui font leur principale étude de la littérature et de la sagesse.'

historical problems, where the orchestral and the solo lute must be considered together. Before touching these questions regarding the history of the lute I will first give here a short description of the instrument itself, and of the way in which it is played.

According to literary tradition the lute has undergone hardly any changes during the period of more than two thousand years when it was the favourite instrument of the literary class. The only fact that all sources agree upon is that the number of strings was originally five, representing the five tones of the Chinese pentatonic gamut. Later, two more strings giving two halftones were added, bringing the number of strings up to seven; this modification is said to have been introduced in the Chou period.

The body of the lute, which functions as sounding-box, consists of two boards of a special kind of wood, superimposed one upon the other (cf. fig. 1). The upper part, made of *t'ung* wood, is concave, while the lower part, made of *tzŭ* wood, is flat, with two openings for transmitting the sound.[7] Over this sounding box the seven silk strings are strung. They are all of different thicknesses: that farthest from the player and giving the lowest tone is the thickest, while that nearest the player and giving the highest tone is the thinnest of all. On the left the strings, in two groups of three and four, are fastened to two wooden knobs driven into the bottom board. On the right side each string ends in a peculiar knot. It passes through a loop of silk, which can be twisted by turning a tuning peg made of wood, ivory or jade. The knot prevents the string from slipping when it is tuned by twisting the loop. On the right side, where the loops pass through holes in the body of the sounding box, a bridge is set up, made of a special kind of hard wood (usually red sandalwood, *tzŭ-t'an*),[8] glued to the upper board. A little to the left of this bridge the fingers of the right hand, except the little finger, pull the strings. The four fingers of the left hand stop the strings at various places, the hand being guided by thirteen studs made of some precious metal or of mother-of-pearl, and embedded in the varnish along the front side of the sounding box. In playing, the performer lays the lute on a special table, so that the side where the tuning pegs are is at his right. He sits on a comparatively high seat, preferably without elbow rests, since these might interfere with the free movement of the arms (cf. fig. 3).

As to the method of playing, I have already pointed out above that the timbre of a note, and therefore the finger technique, is of the

7 桐, 梓   8 紫檀

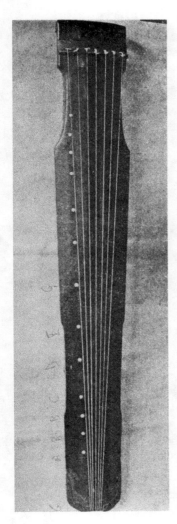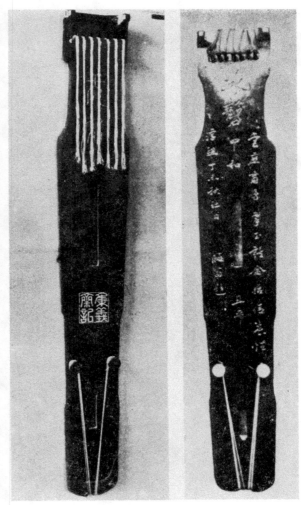

#1a: A lute dating from the end of the Ming period. Author's collection. Note the 13 studs inlaid along the left side, and the bridge on top, where the strings are fastened to the silk loops.

#1b: Bottom board of the same lute. Note the two apertures for transmitting the sound, and the silk loops hanging down, coming out of the tuning pegs. Name (covered by the silk loops) *Wu-ming* 無名; seal: *Chi-i-chai-chi* 集義齋記.

#2: A Sung lute, dated 1187. Collection of Mr. Cheng Ying-sun 鄭穎孫, at Peking. Bottom board, showing inscriptions, and the two jade knobs, to which the strings are fastened.

♯3: Playing the lute: from the *Ch'in-hsüeh-ju-mên*,
cf. Appendix II no. 19.

highest importance. This appears clearly from the way in which lute
music is noted down. The lute has a peculiar system of notation of its
own, the most striking feature being that no notes are indicated,
but only the way a string is played. Each note is thus represented
indirectly by a complicated symbol, consisting of a combination of
abbreviated Chinese characters, which indicate precisely: (a) the
string to be played; (b) which finger of the right hand should pull
the string, and whether inwards or outward; and (c) with regard to
the left hand, which finger should touch the string, at what place and
in what way. This system of notation, for which more than two
hundred special signs are used, is called *chien-tzŭ*, 'abbreviated characters.'[9] Literary sources are vague as to the date of its invention,
but it seems to go back at least to the first centuries A.D.

At first sight this notation seems complicated and confusing, but

9 减字. For a description of the *chien-tzŭ*, see below, Chapter
v, section 3, *Symbolism of the Finger Technique*.

after a little practice it becomes quite easy to use it. Besides, since it is so explicit in its directions, after this system came into use lute music could during many centuries be transmitted with a fair amount of accuracy.

Literary tradition asserts that the original function of the lute was as a solo instrument; as such it was played by its inventor, one of the ancient Chinese mythical Emperors, said to have ruled in or about the third millennium B.C. Some sources say it was the Emperor Fu Hsi,[10] others Shên-nung,[11] others Shun.[12]

We may leave aside the question which claim for priority is justified; in any case literary tradition asserts that the lute in general is a very ancient Chinese instrument, existing already in the beginning of the Shang[13] period, for which the dates 1766–1122 B.C. are given.

But when we investigate reliable documents of this ancient period, such as inscriptions on fragments of oracle bones and tortoise shell, and on bronze sacrificial vessels, the truth of this tradition regarding the high age of the lute appears very questionable.

An investigation of these ancient documents seems to point to the fact that the earliest Chinese music consisted chiefly of percussion instruments, like drums, bells and sonorous stones.[14] The character for music, *yüeh*,[15] itself suggests a wooden standard with bells or drums attached to it.[16] The next stage seems to have been the addition of bamboo flutes. In the *Book of Odes, Shih-ching*,[17] there is preserved an interesting hymn, called *No*,[18] which describes music and is attributed to the Shang (Sung State, 7th or 6th century B.C.); various kinds of drums, sonorous stones and flutes are mentioned, but not a single stringed instrument. I have looked through several works on inscriptions on bone and tortoise shell, consulting also the convenient index *Chia-ku-wên-pien* published in 1934 by Sun Hai-po.[19] But I have not yet found any indication of the existence of a stringed instrument,

---

10 Cf. *Ch'in-tsao* (App. II, 1), opening line: 'Formerly Fu Hsi made the lute' 昔伏羲氏作琴.

11 *Fêng-su-t'ung-i;* see below, p. 70.

12 Cf. *Li-chi, Yüeh-chi.* See below, Chap. II.

13 商

14 The fact that the character *ku* 鼓, occurring frequently in inscriptions on oracle bones and representing a drum beaten by a stick, has the general meaning of producing music (出音曰鼓 cf. *Chou-li,* ch. 23, commentary), also points to the priority of percussion instruments. From ancient times to the present day this word *ku* is used for 'playing the lute' 鼓琴; expressions like *t'an-ch'in* 彈琴 and *chang-ch'in* 張琴 are of later date.

15 樂

16 Cf. fig. 5, no. 23, the character for *yüeh* as it appears on oracle bones, and no. 24, as it appears in the small-seal script.

17 詩經

18 那

19 甲骨文編, 孫海波

while there are numerous references to bells, drums and sonorous stones.

The old trustworthy references to the lute occur in other songs of the *Book of Odes*, e.g. *Lu-ming*,[20] which is ascribed to the Western Chou period (1122–770 B.C.). It is a 'festal ode, sung at entertainments to the king's ministers, and guests from the feudal states'.[21] The host says: 'I have elegant guests, the *sê* is played, the reed-organ is blown'; and in the third strophe: 'I have elegant guests, the *sê* is played, the lute is played.'[22] The ode *Kuan-chü* (the first ode of the *Shin-ching*) describes the music played at the homecoming of a bride: here *ch'in* and *sê* are mentioned, besides bells and drums.[23] Another ode, *Ch'ang-ti*, uses the harmony of lute and *sê* being played together as a symbol: 'Happy union with wife and children is like the music of *ch'in* and *sê*.'[24]

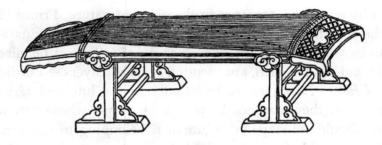

\#4: The *sê*, ancient cither with 25 strings.

Here the lute is mentioned together with the other ancient stringed instrument, the *sê*. In literature the lute is nearly always connected with the *sê*, *ch'in-sê* being in constant use.[25]

---

20 鹿鳴

21 This is the affirmation of Legge.

22 我有嘉賓，鼓瑟吹笙；鼓瑟鼓琴

23 關雎；琴瑟友之，鐘鼓樂之

24 常棣；妻子好合，如鼓瑟琴 (Legge, II, 1, Ode IV). By allusion to this line the harmony of the *ch'in* and *sê* is used in later literature as a fixed symbol for conjugal love. Cf. expressions like *ch'in-sê-chih-hsien* 琴瑟之絃 'husband and wife', *ch'in-sê-pu-hsieh*, 琴瑟不叶 'conjugal discord', etc.

25 琴瑟. Purposely I have left out of consideration here the passage of the *Book of History* (*Shu-ching* 書經 ch. *I-chi* 益稷), where the lute and *sê* are mentioned. Here the music master K'uei (in some later texts exalted as the creator of all music) praises the power of the music directed by him: 'K'uei said:

"When the sounding stone is tapped or strongly struck; when the lutes [i.e. *ch'in* and *sê*] are swept or gently touched to accompany the singing: the [imperial] progenitors come to the service, etc." ' 夔曰戛擊鳴球，搏拊琴瑟，以詠祖考來格 (Legge, *Book of History*, p. 87). The fortunes of the text of the *Shu-ching* are well known (cf. P. Pelliot, 'Le Chou-tching en caractères anciens et le Chang-chou-che-wen', in: *Mémoires concernant l'Asie Orientale*, II, Paris 1816). Although the chapter *I-chi* belongs to the so-called 'text in modern writing', which was noted down by Fu Sheng shortly after the burning of the books in 213 B.C., the text shows evident signs of having been remodeled by later scholars. We must remember that inscriptions on oracle bones*

For the purpose of historical investigation it is impossible to consider the lute apart from the *sê*. I will therefore give here a brief description of this other stringed instrument of antiquity.

The *sê* is considerably bigger than the lute, but much simpler in construction. It has 25 strings, all of equal length and thickness. Each string runs over a separate, moveable bridge, the tuning being adjusted by pushing this bridge to the left or to the right. When all strings are tuned, the moveable bridges are seen to run in an oblique row over the surface of the instrument, a figure which is compared with a flight of wild geese.[26] The *sê* is played with both hands, touching the strings two at a time to the right of the bridges. As it is a heavy and rather unwieldy instrument, it is placed on a couple of low trestles (cf. fig. 4).

During the latter half of the Chou dynasty, besides their orchestral function, both *ch'in* and *sê* were played as solo instruments. This is shown by numerous passages in the older literature. Prince Hsiang had the lute taught to his favorite concubine.[27] Confucius also is said to have played the lute as well as the *sê*[28]. Two of his disciples, Tzû-lu and Tsêng Tien, are mentioned as *sê* players.[29] Further, the *Book of Rites*, *Li-chi*, refers repeatedly to the lute and *sê* as solo instruments: they may not be played by a man whose parents are ill; one should not step over a lute or *sê* belonging to one's master; an official should always have both instruments near at hand, etc.[30]

Already during the Chou dynasty the lute seems to have been preferred to the *sê* for serious music. Many references are made to famous masters of the lute,[31] whilst the *sê* is mentioned only occasionally. Beginning with the Han period the *sê* as solo instrument is hardly mentioned at all. It is said that the Han Emperor Kao-tsu[32] had two concubines, T'ang-shan fu-jên and Ch'i fu-jên, who were both experts on the *sê*, but other references are rare.

---

*show that the ancient ceremonial orchestra was much simpler than one would conclude from this passage. I suspect that it was mixed up somehow or other with the next one: 'K'uei said: "Oh! when I strike the stone or tap the stone, all kinds of animals lead on one another to gambol, etc." ' 夔曰於予擊石拊石，百獸率舞. Perhaps the former longer passage is an elaboration of this shorter second one, which mentions only sonorous stones, and bears a more archaic character.

26 雁陣

27 a) 襄公 571–54 B.C. b) Cf. *Ch'un-ch'iu*, ed. Couvreur, Book IX, 14th year.

28 *Chuang-tzû* 莊子 ch. 31, Yu-fu 漁父; *Chia-yü* 家語 ch. 15, ch. 35. *Lun-yü* 論語 Book XVII, ch. XX, 1.

29 Tzû-lu: *Lun-yü*, Book XI, ch. XIV, 1; Tsêng Tien: *ibid.* Book XI, ch. XXV, 7.

30 a) 禮記. Ed. Couvreur, I, I, 4; I, I, 3; I, II, 1.

31 E.g. in *Chuang-tzû*: Chao Wên 昭文; in *Lieh-tzû*: Ku Pa 瓠巴, Master Wên 師文, Master Hsiang 師襄, Po Ya 伯牙.

32 高祖 206–195 B.C. 唐山夫人，戚夫人

That the *sê* as a solo instrument fell into disuse is probably due to the rise of a new instrument, the *chêng*,[33] in construction not unlike the *sê*, but smaller and much easier to handle. The *chêng* is said to have been invented by Mêng T'ien, who is also credited with the invention of the Chinese writing brush.[34]

Chinese sources assert that the tradition of the *sê* as a solo instrument was entirely forgotten from the Eastern Chin period[35] (317–420 A.D.). Later efforts at reviving the solo *sê* appear to have been more or less of an archaeological nature: the famous musician and poet of the 12th century, Chiang K'uei, studied the *sê*, and during the Yüan dynasty (1280–1368) the scholar Hsiung P'êng-lai composed a *sê-pu*.[36] Only in comparatively recent times have serious efforts been made to reconstruct the methods of playing the *sê* as a solo instrument or together with the lute.[37]

---

33 箏

34 蒙恬, died 210 B.C.

35 E.g. the preface to the *Sê-pu* by Hsiung P'êng-lai. 東晉

36 姜夔, 熊朋來, 瑟譜

37 At Canton there was published in 1870 a *Ch'in-sê-ho-pu* 琴瑟合譜, 'Handbook for Playing *ch'in* and *sê* Together', written by the scholar Ch'ing Jui (慶瑞, pen-name Hui-shan 輝山). Having studied the lute for several years, he became interested in the *sê*, but could find nobody to teach him this instrument. Then he set to work with the handbook of Hsiung P'êng-lai (see above), but came to the conclusion that Hsiung's method was not in accordance with the rules of ancient music. As his wife, a lady called Li Chih-hsien 李芝仙, was an able musician, he made her accompany on the *sê* his lute playing, and on the basis of these experiments he fixed a tuning for the *sê*, and composed the notation for eight old melodies, set to be played by the lute accompanied by the *sê*; these tunes are published in his handbook. I have tried out his system, using instead of the *sê* a so-called *fu-ch'in* 拊琴, a variant of the *chêng* 箏 which is used in Kiangsu province and is exactly the same as the small *sê* (小瑟, 15 strings), but easier to handle since it has tuning pegs. I find that he aims at a complete unison effect, each note of the *ch'in* being the same as the corresponding note on the *sê*. He introduces a vibrato for the *sê*, to be effected by pressing down a string left of the bridge, as is done while playing the Japanese *koto*. The results of his method are not very interesting. When unison is aimed at, it is much better to play a *ch'in* duo, as is often done by Chinese lute players. Moreover I doubt very much whether Ch'ing's method gives any idea of the way the *sê* was played in ancient days.

In 1838 Ch'iu Chih-lu (邱之稑; his biography is to be found in *Kuo-ch'ao-ch'i-hsien-lei-chêng* 國朝耆獻類徵 ch. 422) published a book called *Lü-yin-wei-k'ao* 律音彙考, in which he tries to fix the orchestral music for a great number of ancient ceremonial songs. He devotes a detailed discussion to the *sê*, which had an important function in the ceremonial music at district feasts and archery contests (cf. *I-li* 儀禮, ch. Hsiang-shê-li 鄉射禮). His observations are based on a careful investigation of the correct dimensions and tunings of instruments according to the standards of the Chou period.

In 1923 Yang Tsung-chi published a *Ch'in-sê-ho-pu* 琴瑟合譜 as a part of his *Ch'in-hsüeh-ts'ung-shu* (cf. App. II, 7); he examines various systems for playing and tuning the *sê*, and gives with annotations some tunes to be played by a duo of lute and *sê*. I regret that, having no *sê* in my collection, and my spare time in which to pursue these studies being limited, I have not yet had any chance to verify the theories set forth in the latter two books. It is not sufficient to work out the theories of the authors; one should make practical experiments. What looks perfectly all right on paper often proves to be quite wrong when applied in practice. As both books are the results of serious studies, I recommend them for a closer investigation.

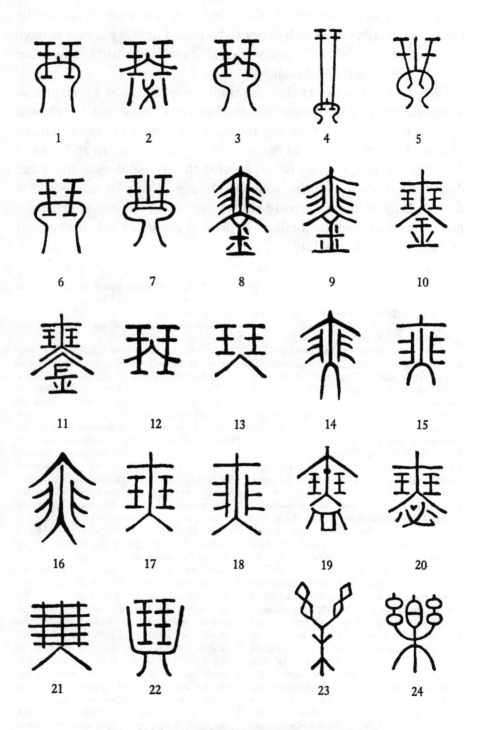

#5: Old forms of the characters for *ch'in* and *sê*.

Whilst the *sê* as a solo instrument fell into oblivion at an early date, the lute, on the contrary, has firmly maintained its position as a solo instrument during more than two thousand years—up to the present day.

Now we can return to the problem, touched upon above, of the origin of the lute. Although, as I pointed out, stringed instruments appear to have come into use later than instruments of percussion and flutes, still the origin of the lute dates from ancient times, let us say from the latter part of the Shang dynasty, about 1400 B.C. For investigating this question literary data are insufficient; besides, such data are misleading because they were artificially made to conform to the literary tradition of the Confucianist school of thought.

The only method for obtaining at least some vague idea about the oldest history of the lute, is, as far as I can see, to leave literary tradition aside, and to concentrate upon palaeographical data, comparing the various old forms of the two characters used to represent *ch'in* and *sê*, which in the modern script are 琴 and 瑟.[38]

In their modern form both characters are composed of an upper and a lower part. They both have the upper part in common; this element is explained as pictorial. The lower parts 今 and 必 are explained as phonetics.

These modern forms are derived from the shapes the characters show in the 'small' seal script (*hsiao-chuan*);[39] these forms I reproduce in fig. 5, no. 1: *ch'in*, no. 2: *sê*. The small seal was drawn up in 213 B.C. by Li Ssû, the minister of the First Emperor, Ch'in-shih-huang-ti, notorious for his burning of the books.[40] About A.D. 100 these characters were collected and recorded by the famous scholar Hsü Chên in his epoch-making dictionary *Shuo-wên*.[41] Although Li Ssû took as his basis the old characters which he found, he modified them to a considerable degree, so that this writing, as Karlgren observes, 'to a very large extent was an entirely new script'.[42] The *Shuo-wên* again is separated by more than 300 years

---

[38] Mention must be made of an archeological source, a *sê* of the Yin dynasty, found in a tomb in Ch'ang-sha, Hunan Province. This important archeological find has been described by Umehara Sueji 梅原末治 in the periodical *Tōyōshi kenkyū* 東洋史研究, vi, no. 2. The instrument is made of hardwood and measures about one foot by three feet. It seems to have had 23 strings (cf. Kishibe Shigeo, *Tōyō no gakki to sono rekishi* 東洋の樂器とその歷史, Tokyo 1948, p. 153).

[39] 小篆

[40] 李斯. An excellent critical summary of occidental discussions of the old forms of the Chinese script is to be found in O. Franke, *Geschichte des Chinesischen Reiches*, iii, pp. 137–8; cf. also the publication by D. Bodde, *China's First Unifier* (Leyden 1938), the chapter on the unification of writing.

[41] 許愼, 說文

[42] B. Karlgren, *Analytic Dictionary of Chinese and Sino-Japanese*, p. 3.

from the time of Li Ssû, and during that interval several modifications were introduced, as is shown by the study of inscriptions on stone from the early Han period. During later dynasties the *Shuo-wên* was published in numerous editions, and lengthy commentaries were added, the standard one being the edition by Tuan Yü-tsai.[43]

The rudimentary text of Hsü Chên was faithfully reprinted, but with regard to the reproduction of the sealscript various editors introduced all sorts of modifications mostly motivated by calligraphic considerations.[44] We must not forget that the sealscript became a branch of calligraphy, and that consequently several styles for writing these characters exist. Thus there are hardly any two editions of the *Shuo-wên* which give exactly the same seal form of a character. For this reason I have reproduced five different forms of the character *ch'in* (fig. 5, nos. 3–7), taken from various editions. As will be seen from these, however, the essential parts of the character were in this case left unchanged.

In the *Shuo-wên* the character for *ch'in* is made into a separate heading, and also the character for *sê* is classified thereunder.

Chinese palaeographers have gone to much trouble to explain these *Shuo-wên* forms. Generally they are of the opinion that the character for *sê* (no. 2) is a derivation from that for *ch'in* (no. 1). As regards no. 1, the consensus of opinion is that it must be taken as a pictorial ideograph, representing the shape of the lute. A work of the Ming period, the *Liu-shu-ching-yün*,[45] preface dated 1567, says that this picture is made after the head of the lute, seen from the side, showing the tuning pegs and the two knobs for fastening the strings; it follows the heading *chio* 珏, two jade tablets, because the tuning pegs were made of jade. A work of the Ch'ing period, the *Shuo-wên-hsieh-tzû-chien* by Hsü Ching[46] gives the form shown in no. 4, and adds the remark that it is easy to see in this character a picture of the lute seen from above: one has only to pull it out lengthwise! These are but mild examples. The Ch'ing scholar Wang Chün in his *Shuo-wên-shih-li*,[47] pub. 1844, goes into more detail, and says that the picture was drawn after the bottom of the lute. The curved line rep-

---

43 段玉裁, style: Jo-ying 若膺, 1735–1815

44 Therefore for Chinese palaeographic studies it is advisable to consult as many different editions of the *Shuo-wên* as one can lay hands on. The labour involved is much reduced by the monumental work of Ting Fu-pao 丁福保, the *Shuo-wên-hsieh-tzû-ku-lin* 說文解字詁林, Shanghai, 1928; in it, under each character choice passages culled from 182 works on the *Shuo-wên* are reproduced in facsimile, permitting the reader to make comparisons and draw his own conclusions.

45 六書精蘊
46 說文解字箋, 徐灝
47 王均, 說文釋例

resents the shoulders of the lute, the two lowest strokes of *chio* stand for the two knobs, the two perpendicular strokes represent the strings fastened to the knobs, and the four upper horizontal strokes stand, *mirabile dictu*, for the bridge which is seen on the *upper* side of the lute. Other scholars think that *chio* must be taken as a significant, meaning something precious and indicating that the lute is a precious instrument. Still others think that *chio* must be taken in its literal sense of 'tablets of jade': the curved line is a cord on which they are suspended. They assume that the lute originally was a percussion instrument, something like the present-day *pa-ta-la*,[48] an instrument introduced from Burma. This interpretation is followed by Takata in his *Kochūhen*,[49] who therefore does not give the character a separate heading but classifies it under *yü*, 'jade'. Wieger, in his *Caractères chinois*, p. 216, gives the same explanation.

I have quoted the above opinions to show that such speculations, being based entirely on the small seal characters, are valueless. In order to be able to make more likely guesses we have to go farther back than the small seal, and refer to the older forms, known by the convenient Chinese term *ku-wên*,[50] 'ancient shapes'. *Ku-wên* stands for all the old forms of characters dating from before Li Ssû's re-organization of writing. They are taken from sacrificial vessels of the Chou period, inscriptions on bone, and various other archeological remains.

Nos. 8 and 9 reproduce two *ku-wên* forms of the character for *ch'in*; the style of the strokes of no. 8 points to its being taken from an inscription on bronze. The upper part of these two characters shows clearly that the element later written as 玨, has nothing at all to do with jade, but forms part of an independent pictorial element. The lower part *chin* 金 is the phonetic. These two forms given here are apparently the prototype of the two variants of the modern character for *ch'in*, given in current editions of *K'ang-hsi-tzû-tien*[51] (cf. nos. 10, 11). If we compare nos. 8 and 9 with no. 13, which is another old form, I think we may agree with many commentators on the *Shuo-wên*, who assert that this form no. 13 is a simplification (*shêng-wên*)[52] of the complete type reproduced in nos. 8 and 9: of the phonetic *chin* 金 only the upper part is taken over, which looks like *jên* 人. In the *li* script of the Han period this character was still further simplified

---

48 把打位; cf. *Ch'ing-hui-tien-t'u* 清會典圖.
49 高田，古籀篇
50 古文

51 康熙字典
52 省文

by writing the element 人 not under, but over, the pictorial element; cf. no. 12, form taken from an inscription on the tombstone of the lute player Lu Chün (died A.D. 172).[53] This is the form we recognize in the small seal character from which we started, reproduced in no. 1. Some scribe felt it necessary to add again a complete phonetic element, and chose 今 as an abbreviation for 金, 今 being originally the phonetic element of the character 金; for this modification there are many parallels, e.g. 淦, later written 汵. This is the type shown in the modern character 琴.

When we turn now to the character for *sê*, we observe that in the small seal (cf. fig. 5, no. 2) the character for *sê* is derived directly from the character for *ch'in*, by adding to the pictorial element a phonetic that later scribes represented as 必; that this representation is very arbitrary is evident from phonetic reasons. How this phonetic element is constructed is difficult to say, as its seal form, which is taken over from the *ku-wên* script, cannot be identified with other phonetics. That it was a phonetic and not a pictorial element becomes evident when we turn to the *ku-wên* forms of the character for *sê*, reproduced in nos. 14, 15 and 16 (17 and 18 are the forms as printed in current editions of *K'ang-hsi-tzŭ-tien*): here the phonetic element is missing, and we see only a figure which can hardly be anything else than a pictorial representation. Now if we compare this *ku-wên* form for *sê*, nos. 14–16, with the *ku-wên* form for *ch'in*, nos. 8, 9, we find that the *ku-wên* for *sê* is exactly the same as the upper, pictorial part of the *ku-wên* character for *ch'in*.

Thus, while from the small seal forms of both characters we would assume that *sê* was a derivation from *ch'in* ('an instrument not unlike the *ch'in*, and called *sê'*), from the *ku-wên*, on the contrary, we would conclude that *ch'in* was derived from *sê* ('an instrument not unlike the *sê*, but called *ch'in'*). To make the problem still more complicated we also find *ku-wên* forms for *sê*, which show under the pictorial element the enigmatic phonetic which we find in the small seal (cf. nos. 19, 20). Chinese commentators go no further than to state that apparently in ancient times there existed a constant interchange between the two characters.

In my opinion we can go one step further: this interchange of the forms for *ch'in* and *sê* admits of but one conclusion, viz. *that originally there was but one character*, resembling the upper part of the *ku-wên* forms of *ch'in* (and occasionally of *sê*), which was neither *ch'in* nor *sê*,

[53] 隸書, 魯峻

but some archaic Chinese stringed musical instrument. This instrument was used together with the drums, bells, sonorous stones and flutes of the ritual orchestra, and also as a solo instrument. From a musical point of view these two functions are essentially different: whilst the orchestral instrument had only to produce music that was simple but of strong volume (not to be drowned by the loud sounds of the percussion instruments), the solo instrument on the contrary was meant to be played alone, or as an accompaniment for the human voice. Thus it was not necessary that the solo instrument should produce a great volume of sound, but on the other hand it had to answer much more complicated musical needs. The orchestral and the solo instrument thus followed different ways of evolution: while the orchestral instrument remained almost unchanged, the solo instrument was gradually more and more developed in a technical sense. After some lapse of time the difference between the orchestral and the solo varieties of this instrument became so great that the necessity was felt for a distinctive nomenclature. This having been established, the pictorial character was not sufficient for indicating which instrument was meant, so phonetics were added. That this was done so irregularly must be due to the scribes, who no longer knew that both characters were originally the same, and considered one a derivation of the other.

Finally there remains the question of how the pictorial character that represented the archaic instrument was constructed. On the basis of my experience with several lute-like oriental instruments I may remark that the most striking aspect of such an oblong stringed instrument in a picture is to draw some horizontal lines indicating the strings, and cross these by some vertical lines indicating some sort of bridges,[54] finally adding some element expressing the action of playing, or a stand to lay the instrument on. On the basis of this reasoning I drew the entirely hypothetical character reproduced in no. 21. This hypothetical character may be compared with an old form of the character *ch'in* (no. 22) recorded in the *Fu-ku-pien*,

---

[54] It seems probable that the thirteen *hui* are remnants of vertical lines, or possibly bridges. An old quotation, cited by Ch'ên Yang (陳暘, Sung period) in his *Ch'in-shêng-ching-wei* 琴聲經緯 seems to point in this direction: 'The Ancients said about the tones of the lute that they are divided into vertical and horizontal sounds' 古人之論琴聲有經有緯.

The seven strings pulled with the right hand only give the 'vertical' tones (緯 *wei*, literally *woof*), and the tones produced when the left hand presses a string down on the place indicated by one of the *hui* while the right hand pulls it, are called 'horizontal' (經 *ching*, literally *warp*). These terms could refer to the fact that the archaic lute offered an image resembling the texture of a woven*

by the scholar Chang Yu of the Sung dynasty.[55] One might explain by technical reasons the fact that the horizontal lines are cut up, and the vertical lines stressed, it being easier to engrave a long vertical line than a horizontal one, as anybody knows who has tried his hand at carving Chinese seals.

The above digression on the oldest history of *ch'in* and *sê* is not more than a hypothesis. The only advantage it has over other explanations is that it seems less far-fetched and a little more logical. Yet it has often appeared that historical truth runs counter to all logic, and explanations that seem far-fetched sometimes prove to be true ones. So I give this hypothesis here for what it is worth: only one of many possibilities.

There remains one remark to be added. In the above discussions I have relied exclusively on the pictorial element of the ancient script, leaving the phonetic side of the question untouched. Though agreeing with the opinion that the study of Chinese epigraphical problems in general must include also the phonetic aspect,[56] in this particular case I have refrained from doing so, since here it seems unlikely that it could shed some more light on the oldest history of lute and *sê*. For the sake of convenience I have used throughout my discussion the names of both these instruments as they are at present pronounced in Peking. But in ancient Chinese *ch'in* must have been pronounced something like *k'ièm*, and *sê* something like *shièt*.

* * *

Finally I have to add a few words on the place occupied by the lute in the daily life of the Chinese.

The lute has never been an instrument of the multitude, both theoretical and practical factors preventing it from ever becoming popular. The theoretical factor I have already referred to above in the quotation from Father Amiot: the lute was reserved for a small class, its study 'belonging by right to those whose studies are concentrated on literature and wisdom', i.e. the literati. And this does

---

*fabric, the seven strings being crossed vertically by thirteen lines or some sort of bridges. It might be worthwhile to investigate historically the terms for the thirteen studs, 徽 and 暉, together with this word 緯. Phonetically all three belong together.

55 復古編，張有

56 Recently again stressed by P. Boodberg in his important article 'Remarks on the Evolution of Archaic Chinese', in *Harvard Journal of Asiatic Studies*, II, p. 329. With regard to *ch'in* and *sê* I would draw attention to the fact that since ancient times both words have been combined with an explanatory character, which at the same time roughly indicates their pronunciation, viz. *ch'in* is coupled with *chin* 禁 'restraining', and *sê* with *sê* 嗇, meaning 'sparing'. Old literature gives many of these couplets, like 音 and 飲, 笙 and 生, 德 and 得, 朔 and 蘇. It might be worthwhile to make a list of such couplets, and investigate them phonetically.

not apply only to the Ch'ien-lung period (1736–95), during which the learned Father was writing, but also to the two thousand years preceding. Among the practical factors I may mention the paucity of competent teachers, the difficulty of the technique, the high price and the rarity of good instruments. So the lute remained reserved for the small circle of the happy few, an exquisite treasure jealously guarded by the literati.

The lute is one of the indispensable paraphernalia of the library of the Chinese scholar. In a country like China, where literature is held in so high an esteem, and where until recent years (1905) the only way to an official position was through the gate of the literary examinations, the library has a deeper meaning than anywhere else. It was the sanctum where the literatus passed the greater part of his life, writing and reading, firmly convinced that the outer world could give nothing that was not to be found described and analyzed in choice language in the many volumes that were piled upon the shelves around him. The saying of the *Tao-tê-ching*, 'Without going outdoors I know the world, without looking out of the window I see the Way of Heaven',[57] might well be written as a motto over the door of each Chinese library.

In the course of time there was formed a fixed tradition regarding the library, which minutely described the things a literatus should always have near at hand. On his desk should lie the inkslab, a stick of ink on a special stand, a vase containing some thoughtfully chosen and well arranged flowers, an antique vessel to wash his writing brushes, a stand to lay the wet brush on, paper weights, seals, etc. On a small table there should be a chess board, and on another an incense burner. In all available corners bookstands should be arranged, while the remaining parts of the walls should be covered with scrolls showing graceful lines of characters or a famous painting. And in a dry corner, far from the window and not reached by the rays of the sun, there should be hanging one or more lutes.

The lute, symbol of literary life, enhances by its very presence the special atmosphere of the library, and at the same time is an elegant ornament. Its graceful, slender shape is pleasing to the eye, and the deep colour of its lacquer and its charming patina harmonizes with the antique appearance of its surroundings. Its venerable age suggests the wisdom of the sages of bygone times, and is it not said that

[57] *Op. cit.* ch. 47.

the scholar, though living in the present, should in his thoughts dwell with the Ancients?[58]

Like the old bronze sacrificial vessels often found in the abode of the scholar, the lute is an object for appreciative study by cultured connoisseurs. For the bottom board of antique lutes is covered with inscriptions and seals, engraved in its coat of lacquer.[59] For instance the valuable lute reproduced in fig. 2, shows an inscription engraved by the famous philosopher Chu Hsi.[60] Its special name is *Ping-ching*,[61] 'Icicle Sonorous Stone'; the inscription reads: 'The tone Kung corresponds to the tone Shang. The sonorous stones are tapped, the bells are struck. With calmed emotions nurturing one's nature, the music is harmonious and even. Written by Hui-wêng (literary name of Chu Hsi), in the ninth month, autumn 1187.'[62] After the lapse of some time the lacquer of old lutes shows tiny cracks (*tuan-wên*),[63] by the shape of which connoisseurs fix the age and genuineness of antique specimens.

But the lute is more than other antique objects, because it is at the same time a musical instrument. 'Of the most precious antiques none equals the lute. Bronze tripods of the Hsia dynasty, and sacrificial vessels of the Shang period, old autographs and famous paintings, all these are valuable. But tripods and sacrificial vessels can only be displayed as decoration, they cannot be used. They cannot be compared with the lute, which sings if its strings are touched, giving an impression of meeting the ancients in person, in the same room, and talking with them.'[64] These lines were written by a scholar who himself was an expert performer on the lute. But this is an exception: even among the literati consummate lute performers were always rare. The so-called requisites of the library became in large part mere conventions: the presence of a chess-board does not imply that the master of the library is a devotee of the Royal Game, nor does the presence of a lute necessarily mean that he can actually play it.

A knowledge of the special system of thought belonging to the lute is a part of the education of every literatus, but only a small number among them have mastered its music. Still it was considered

---

58　*Li-chi*, ed. Couvreur, ch. xxxviii, 11.

59　For more details, cf. App. iii, *The Lute as an Antique*.

60　朱熹, 1130–1200.

61　冰磬

62　宮應商鳴，擊玉敲金，怡情養性，中和且平，淳熙丁未秋社日晦翁題.

63　斷文

64　*Ch'in-hsüeh-ts'ung-shu;* cf. App. ii, no. 7, in the treatise *Ch'in-yü-man-lu* 琴餘漫錄: 古器中最可寶者，莫如琴，夏鼎商彝，古書名畫，非不貴也，然鼎彝祇能陳設，不適於用，非若琴按弦則鳴，如與古人晤談一室.

a sign of elegant taste to express some well-known principles of *ch'in* ideology in a new form, or to extoll in a poem the special merits of a lute one happened to possess—and could not play! A good example of a mass of literary productions centring round one famous lute is the collection *Hsieh-ch'in-shih-wên-ch'ao* published in 1815 by Wu Ching-ch'ao; one day he bought the favourite lute of the well-known loyal Sung scholar Hsieh Fang-tê.[65] Literary friends and acquaintances composed essays and poems in praise of this lute, and this collection, filling five volumes, was privately published by the happy owner of the instrument.

For his not playing a scholar might quote numerous elegant excuses. He might cite the old Taoist paradox that curiously resembles the famous line in Keats' *Ode on a Grecian Urn:* the unheard tones are the most beautiful. Or he might point to the great poet of the Chin period T'ao Ch'ien who, according to tradition, had a lute without strings or studs hanging on the wall, and who in one of his poems said: 'I have acquired the deeper significance of the lute; why should I strive after the sound of the strings?'[66] This attitude, though it may be well founded from a philosophical point of view, discouraged scholars from aspiring to become accomplished performers on the lute. Therefore this attitude was sharply criticised by real lute players. It is said in the *Ch'in-sê-ho-pu*:[67] 'In the houses of the wealthy there may sometimes be seen lutes hanging on the wall as a decoration, richly adorned with precious stones;[68] but they are only meant to dazzle people's eyes. If one asks (the owner) about music, he stands dumbfounded, and does not know about what one might be speaking. Then there are also those perverted and vainglorious people who do not attach strings and tuning pegs to their lutes, thus injustly using the Master of the Five Willows (fancy name of T'ao Ch'ien), and hoping thus to conceal their own worthlessness; those people are especially ridiculous!'[69]

Such protests by discerning connoisseurs of lute music are rare: the great majority of the literati, if they played the lute at all, contented themselves with being able to play only two or three of the simpler tunes or even but a few bars. The view stated by Ou-yang

---

65 謝琴詩文鈔；吳景潮；謝枋得，1226–89.

66 陶潛，365–427. 但得琴中趣，何勞弦上聲.

67 See n. 37 above.

68 For a discussion of such richly decorated lutes refer to App. III, *The Lute as an Antique.*

69 富家整飾或有琴懸諸壁間裝璜點綴，亦不過輝人目而己，詢其音律懜然不識爲何物，更有矯情干譽而絃軫不備，謬借五柳先生爲掩醜計，尤可笑也. (ch. 1, p. 8)

Hsiu,[70] the great scholar of the Sung dynasty, in his essay *The Three Lutes* (dated 1062), may be taken as representative of the general attitude of Chinese scholars to the lute. He says: 'From my youth I did not relish vulgar music, but loved the sounds of the lute. I particularly liked the tune *Flowing Streams*, in its simpler version. During my life I often was in distress, and I roved over the country from north to south. All the other tunes of the lute I entirely forgot, only this one tune *Flowing Streams* remained in my memory during dream and sleep. Now I am old, and I play it only occasionally. For the rest I only know some smaller tunes; yet this is sufficient for my own enjoyment. One need not know many tunes; in studying the lute the most important point is to learn to find satisfaction in playing.'[71]

Notwithstanding the fact that the music of the lute was transmitted only by a few masters scattered over the Empire, officially the instrument itself was held in universal respect. I have come across only very few books where the position of the lute as the unique representative of the music of the ancients is challenged.[72] Often, it is true, the lute was used to accompany vulgar music. Occasionally one will see on a painting a scholar playing the lute while a singing girl accompanies him on the four-stringed guitar or some other frivolous instrument. And, though playing the lute should restrain all passions, Chinese novels and theatre pieces more than once mention a young scholar who by playing the lute conquers the heart of his beloved.[73] But such misuse of the lute, though doubtless frequent, was never officially approved.

During the latter half of the Ch'ing dynasty it appears that the lute was played in only a few circles of musical scholars, some in

---

70 歐陽修, 1007–1072.

71 三琴記 (外集, ch. 14)：余自少不喜鄭衞,
獨愛琴聲, 尤愛小流水曲, 平生患難, 南北奔馳,
琴曲率皆廢忘, 獨流水一曲夢寐不忘, 今老矣,
猶時能作之, 其他不過數小調, 弄足以自娛,
琴曲不必多, 學于于自適.

72 For instance, a work on music in general, dating from the nineteenth century, called *Mien-ch'in-hsieh-hsüeh-yüeh-lu* 眠琴榭學樂錄, by Shên Wên-ying 沈文熒. In ch. 4 he says that it is wrong to call the lute the special instrument of the ancients, for it is not better than the *p'i-p'a*. Moreover the lute has no less than five defects; among others, its finger technique is so complicated that one cannot sing while playing, its tones are not pure, its rhythm is confused. Notwithstanding these statements, which must seem

terrible heresy to the old-fashioned lute connoisseur, this book contains a mass of valuable information, especially because the author also discusses in detail the tuning, finger technique and notation of some popular instruments like the *yüeh-ch'in* 月琴. I possess only a very fine manuscript copy of this book; I do not know whether it was ever published.

Further I also refer to the *Hsüeh-chai-chan-pi* 學齋佔畢, by Shih Shêng-tsu (史繩祖, 13th century), where the second chapter starts with a discussion entitled 'The *sê* comes before the lute' 瑟先於琴; there the lute is called inferior to the *sê*, and also to the mouth-organ, *shêng*.

73 See, for example, the *Hsi-hsiang-chi* 西廂記, part II, act IV.

Chekiang province, some in Fukien, others in Szuchuan : a negligible minority when compared with the vast number of scholars who devoted themselves to literary pursuits, and brought fame to Ch'ing letters. Lute music, a drooping flower, too much sheltered in the dimness of the library, was gradually withering away. It grew to resemble too much the *chih*[74] fungus, the agaric symbolizing longevity, dried specimens of which decorate the desk of the scholar; they are graceful to look at, but dry and lifeless.

Fortunately, since the establishment of the Chinese Republic interest in lute music has revived.[75] Unhampered by the old exclusionist tendencies, the study of the lute spread to broader circles. Younger Chinese scholars who have studied musicology abroad are investigating lute music on modern scientific principles.[76] Many pupils flock round the few old teachers, books and manuscripts on the lute are eagerly sought for, and in the near future we may confidently look forward to a renaissance of lute music in China.

Next to China the only other country where the lute was played and studied is Japan.

Japanese tradition mentions as the father of lute music in Japan a Chinese Ch'an priest, Shin'etsu.[77] Fleeing the troubles that marked the early years of the Ch'ing dynasty, he came to Japan (1677), and was invited to Mito by the feudal lord Mitsukuni,[78] a great patron of learning. Shin'etsu could play the lute, and soon a great number of devoted pupils gathered round him. According to Japanese sources this was the beginning of lute playing in Japan.[79]

Western scholars in several books on Chinese music in general have paid due attention to the lute.[80] In 1911 G. Soulié gave a general description of the lute, devoting some space to a description of the

74 芝

75 How enthusiastically the lute is still studied appears from the book *Hui-ch'in-shih-chi* 會琴實紀, published in 1920 in one volume by the well-known lute player Yeh Chang-po (葉璋伯, called Hsi-ming 希明). This book is a collection of documents and pictures relating to a reunion of lute experts, organized in 1919 by Mr. Yeh. In this book one also finds a list of about fifty contemporary lute players, with their addresses. Further, I refer also to R. Taki, *Ongaku shiryō no chōsa*, in: *Tōhō gakuhō (Journal of Oriental Studies)*, Tokyo, July 1935, p. 254.

76 For instance, Wang Kuang-ch'i 王光祈, who attempted to transcribe *ch'in* notation with European symbols; cf. his *Fan-i-ch'in-*

pu-chih-yen-chiu 翻譯琴譜之研究, Shanghai 1931. Also Chang Yu-ho 張友鶴, who in the Peking periodical *Yin-yüeh-tsa-chih* 音樂雜誌 published a series of articles on the lute, entitled *Hsüeh-ch'in-ch'ien-shuo* 學琴淺說, in which several examples of lute tunes transcribed in European notes are given *(op. cit.* 1).

77 Chinese: Hsin-yüeh 心越, better known by his literary name Tōkō Zenji 東皐禪師, 1639–95.

78 光圀, 1628–1700.

79 For a discussion of the study of the lute in Japan, I refer to App. IV of this essay, *The Chinese Lute in Japan*.

80 For a more complete list of references to the lute in Western literature, see App. I.

way it is played.[81] M. Courant discussed the instrument and its tuning *in extenso*,[82] whilst L. Laloy dwelt more upon its significance.[83]

The lute, however, has occupied since ancient times so unique a position in Chinese musical life, and its special literature is so extensive, that I think it well deserves to be treated separately. For the lute is the only instrument forming the center of a special system of thought; it is the only instrument the playing of which has been considered from ancient times as a means for reaching enlightenment.

In the following pages I propose to discuss the ideology of the lute, and its place in Chinese history, leaving aside as much as possible all questions directly relating to musical theory. I hope that some day a musicologist shall write a practical handbook for the lute player. For the time being these pages may suffice as a general introduction. According to the Chinese tradition on the study of the lute this is the correct order, for is it not said in the rules for the lute player that one may not touch the strings of the lute before its significance is clearly understood?

81 G. Soulié, *La Musique en Chine;* cf. App. I, no. 3.

82 M. Courant, *Essai historique sur la musique classique des chinois;* cf. App. I, no. 6.

83 L. Laloy, *La Musique chinoise:* cf. App. I, no. 5.

CHAPTER TWO

Classical Conceptions of Music

Chinese classical conceptions of music according to the YÜEH-CHI—
*twofold aspect of music, cosmological and political—music
belongs to heaven, and corresponds to what is heavenly in
man—it is a means for perfecting the government, and for
improving the individual—music as a source for pleasure not
recognized*

THE ideology of the lute is a separate system of thought, which was
gradually evolved in the course of the many centuries that the
Way of the lute was cherished and cultivated by the literati. Various
factors promoted the establishment of this ideology, and manifold
influences determined its evolution. In the following chapters I shall
endeavour to give a sketch of this development. As the rules of *ch'in*
ideology were never assembled and canonized in one basic text, we
shall have to collect our data from various literary sources, and with
these materials on hand, try to form for ourselves a more complete
picture of the system.

Before embarking upon this rather complicated task, we first must
obtain an idea of Chinese conceptions of music in general. Fortunately
there exists a special text, which gives a good survey of the classical
conceptions. This is the *Yüeh-chi*, 'Annotations on Music', a part of
the *Li-chi*,[1] usually called *Book of Rites*, one of the classics of the
Confucianist school. The *Li-chi* was composed at a comparatively
late date, viz. about the beginning of our era. The *Yüeh-chi* was drawn
up by the scholar Ma Yung.[2] Yet a comparison with older data, such
as passages relating to music scattered in the works of the various
philosophers that flourished in the latter part of the Chou dynasty,
shows clearly that although the formulation of the *Yüeh-chi* is late,
the ideas which it contains are elaborations of considerably older
conceptions. But the materials are cast in a Confucianist form, and as
such this text is authoritative for literary musical ideals. As moreover

[1] 樂記, 禮記   [2] 馬融, style: Chi-ch'ang 季長, 79–166.

in Chinese literature it remained until quite recently the standard text on music, extensively quoted in nearly all later books on music or musical theory, I think we may well take this text as basis for our discussions of Chinese music in general.[3]

This treatise contains a great variety of information, not only on the significance of music, but also on the ceremonial orchestra, and the ritual dances that were executed to its music. Statements on the meaning of music in general are scattered throughout the work; I shall try to arrange the most important references of this kind more systematically and discuss them in order.

The significance of music appears to be twofold, depending on whether it is viewed in its universal, cosmological and superhuman aspect, or, on the other hand, in its specialized, political, human aspect.

In its universal aspect music is the harmony inherent in all nature, embracing heaven and earth. In its specialized aspect it is applied to man, both as an individual and as a member of the political unity, the State.

In the *Yüeh-chi* both the universal and the specialized aspects of music are discussed extensively. As this text belongs to the Confucianist school, however, it is only natural that the latter aspect is stressed.

Throughout this treatise music is considered as inseparable from rites (*li*):[4] both are indispensable to the proper government of the State. In more than one passage, however, it is pointed out that music is superior to rites, mainly because music consists of heavenly harmony, rites of earthly harmony. 'Music is the harmony of heaven and earth, rites constitute the graduation of heaven and earth. Through harmony all things are brought forth, through graduation all things are properly classified. Music comes from heaven, rites are modelled after earthly designs.'[5] 'Music aims at harmony, it belongs to the higher spiritual agencies, and it follows heaven. Rites aim at the distinction of differences, they belong to the lower spiritual

---

[3] For musical materials of a more archaic character I may refer to a work of Taoist coloring dating from the third century B.C., the *Annals of Spring and Autumn of Lü Pu-wei* 呂氏春秋. In ch. v are embodied four sections on music, especially important because they quote ancient myths, indicating the role of music in archaic totemistic ceremonies. This book has been translated by R. Wilhelm: *Frühling und Herbst des Lü Bu-we*, Jena 1928. I may refer also to the works of the philosopher Huai-nan-tzû; cf. L. Laloy's discussion in *T'oung-pao*, May 1913, pp. 291–8.

[4] 禮

[5] *Yüeh-chi*, ch. I, paragraph 23: 樂者天地之和也，禮者天地之序也，和故百物皆化，序所群物皆別，樂由天作，禮以地制.

agencies, and follow earth. Therefore the Holy Sages composed music in order that it might correspond to Heaven, and they instituted rites so that they might correspond to Earth. When rites and music are manifest and perfect, Heaven and Earth will be regulated.'[6]

Music and man are closely connected, because music corresponds to what is Heavenly in man. 'When man is born he is serene: this is the nature of Heaven. Experiencing contact with outer things, he is moved, and in his nature desire is created. . . If man cannot regulate his likes and his dislikes, the outer things will lead him astray, he will grow incapable of introspection, and the Heavenly nature in him disappears.'[7] 'For this reason the Kings of olden times instituted rites and music in order to regulate human emotions.'[8] 'Music points to what all beings have in common; rites point to that in which all beings differ. What is common leads to mutual love, what is different leads to mutual respect.'[9] 'Music is based on the inner life of man, rites on outer appearances. Music comes from within, therefore it is serene; rites come from without, therefore they are elegant.'[10]

As music is a direct manifestation of Heaven, the wise ruler shall utilize it to assist him in governing the State properly. 'In Music the Holy Sages took delight, because music can improve the heart of the people. Music has a profound influence on man, it can improve customs and ameliorate morals. Therefore the kings of olden times promoted the teaching of music.'[11] 'Therefore, when music flourishes, human relations are clarified, eyes and ears are made more susceptive, body and mind are in balanced harmony, good customs prosper and morals are improved, and peace reigns everywhere under Heaven.'[12]

Thus music appears as one means for transferring the Heaven-inspired virtues of the Wise Ruler to his subjects.

'Music is formed in the heart. Tones are the shape in which music is expressed. Elegance and rhythm are the decoration of the tones. The Superior Man takes the feelings in his heart as basis, he gives

6 *Ibid.* ch. I, par. 29: 樂者敦和率神而從天，禮者別宜居鬼而從地，故聖人作樂以應天，制禮以配地，禮樂明備，天地官矣.

7 *Ibid.* ch. I, par. 11: 人生而靜，天之性也，感於物而動，性之欲也……好惡無節於內，知誘於外，不能反躬，天理滅矣.

8 *Ibid.* ch. I, par. 13: 是故先王之制禮樂，人為之節.

9 *Ibid.* ch. I, par. 15: 樂者為同，禮者為異，同則相親，異則相敬.

10 *Ibid.* ch. I, par. 15: 樂由中出，禮自外作，樂由中出，故靜，禮自外作，故文.

11 *Ibid.* ch. II, par. 7: 樂也者，聖人之所樂也，而可以善民心，其感人深，其移風易俗，故先王著其教焉.

12 *Ibid.* ch. II, par. 8: 故樂行而倫清，耳目聰明，血氣和平，移風易俗，天下皆寧.

them shape in music, and then he gives this music its final form.'[13] But, in performing, because of this deep meaning of music, stress should not be laid on superficial beauty of melody and specious notes; above all the spiritual, the transcendental significance of music must be made manifest. 'The greatness of music lies not in perfection of tone'[14] for: '(In rites and music) virtue is more than art.'[15]

This principle was already recognized by the Ancient Rulers: 'The kings of olden times instituted rites and music, not to satisfy the mouths and stomachs, the ears and eyes, but in order to teach the people to balance their likes and dislikes, and to bring them back to the Right Way.'[16]

Besides stating these lofty views on the general meaning of music —music in the universe and music in the State—the *Yüeh-chi* also devotes several lines to the meaning of music to the individual. 'A wise man has said: "Not for one single moment may one separate oneself from Rites and Music." When one perfects oneself in music with the aim of regulating the heart, then as a matter of course the heart shall be calm, straight, tender and pure.'[17] 'Therefore, during a musical performance in the Temple of the Ancestors, prince and statesman, high and low listen together, and an atmosphere of harmony and respect prevails. During a musical performance on the occasion of clan festivals or village festivals, old and young listen together, and an atmosphere of harmony and compliance prevails. During a musical performance in the household, parents and children, elder and younger brothers listen together, and an atmosphere of harmony and affection prevails.'[18]

And finally I may quote a passage describing the attitude towards music of the *Chün-tzû*, the ideal man of the Confucianist school: 'The Superior Man returns to his original heavenly nature, and thereto he conforms his thoughts. He distinguishes between good and bad, and in accordance therewith regulates his conduct. He does not perceive lewd sounds or indecent spectacles, he keeps his heart undefiled by lascivious music or unbecoming rites. His body is free

---

13 *Ibid*. ch. ɪɪ, par. 23: 樂者心之動也，聲者，樂之象也，文采節奏聲之飾也，君子動其本，樂其象，然後治其飾.

14 *Ibid*. ch. ɪ, par. 9: 是故樂之隆非極音也.

15 *Ibid*. ch. ɪɪɪ, par. 5.: 是故德成而上，藝成而下.

16 *Ibid*. ch. ɪ, par. 10: 是故先王之制禮樂也，非以極口腹耳目之欲也，將以教民平好惡

而反人道之正也.

17 *Ibid*. ch. ɪɪ, par 23: 君子曰，禮樂不可斯須去身，致樂以治心，則易直子諒之心油然生矣.

18 *Ibid*. ch. ɪɪɪ, par. 28: 是故樂在宗廟之中，君臣上下同聽之，則莫不和敬，在族長鄉里之中，長幼同聽之，則莫不和順，在閨門之內，父子兄弟同聽之，則莫不和親.

from laziness and negligence, falsehood and depravity. He makes his ears and eyes, nose and mouth, all the functions of perception of his entire body conform to what is right, and so achieves righteous conduct. Then he expresses his sentiments in chant: he accompanies them on lute and *sê*, moves the shield and the axe, and uses as decoration the pheasant feathers and the ox tails, and finally he lets the flutes sound. The splendour of complete virtue makes the four seasons revolve in harmony, and establishes the right order of all things.'[19]

From the above quotations it will be clear that according to classical ideas there is but one sort of music deserving that name: that of the ceremonial orchestra. Its music and its dances are not meant for relaxation and for diversion, they are sacred institutions, established by the Holy Kings of old for the purpose of regulating the State and perfecting the individual. As for solo instruments, they are only recognized as music when they have also a function in the ceremonial orchestra, like the lute and *sê*.

In the well-governed Confucianist State music meant for pleasure does not exist. Occasionally, when the government is decaying, and the end of a state is approaching, there will arise tones not conforming with these high musical principles. But this music is usually not referred to as such, it is called 'lewd notes' or 'vulgar sounds'; these incite people to depravity, confuse the proper relations between men and women, ruler and subject, and sap the foundations of the State. They have nothing to do with what is called music.

19 *Ibid*. ch. II, par. 15–16: 是故君子反情，以和其志，比類以成其行，姦聲亂色不留聰明，淫樂慝禮不接心術，惰慢邪僻之氣不設於身體，使耳目鼻口心知百體，皆由順正以 行其義，然家發以聲音，而文以琴瑟，動以干戚，飾以羽旄，從以簫管，奮至德之光，動四氣之和，以著萬物之理.

CHAPTER THREE

Study of the Lute

§1 SOURCES

More materials on the significance of the lute than on lute music—three groups of materials: scattered references to the lute, special treatises on the lute, and CH‘IN PŪ, *handbooks for the lute—reasons for the rarity of* CH‘IN-PU—*their contents—recent Chinese books on the study of the lute*

IT must be considered fortunate, at least for the subject of this essay, that materials for investigating the ideology of the lute are more extensive and reach much farther back in history than those for studying lute music itself.

To illustrate this I may mention the fact that whereas the oldest *ch‘in* tune preserved in notation[1] dates from the T‘ang period (618–907), references to the significance of the lute may already be found in the old Classical Books. And while the earliest printed handbooks for the lute date from the Ming dynasty (1368–1644), essays on the meaning of the lute date from the beginning of our era.

Thus for the study of *ch‘in* ideology we have rich materials at our

---

[1] The tune preserved is the fifth chapter of a well-known old Chinese melody, called *Yu-lan* 幽蘭, 'The Orchid in the Profound Vale', and was found in Japan. This text is especially important because it gives, not the ordinary notation in abbreviated characters *chien-tzû* (see Chap. I, n. 9), but uses an apparently older system, where as a rule every movement is described in full. It was copied out by the famous Japanese Confucianist Ogyū Sorai (荻生徂徠, 1666–1728, also known as Mononobe Mokei 物部茂卿), after a T‘ang manuscript, allegedly reproducing a text from the Sui period dated 590. When the Chinese scholar and bibliophile Yang Shou-ching (楊守敬 1835–1915) stayed in Japan in 1880–4 and searched everywhere for old Chinese books and manuscripts, he also purchased a copy of this manuscript. It was reprinted in the *Ku-i-ts‘ung-shu* (古逸 叢書, cf. Pelliot, *Notes de bibliographie chinoise*, *BEFEO*, II, page 315); in 1911 it was again reprinted by Yang Tsung-chi (see below) in his *Ch‘in-hsüeh-ts‘ung-shu*, who endeavored to transcribe the tune in the usual *ch‘in* notation. In the same *ts‘ung-shu* Yang Tsung-chi reprinted an article on this tune by Li Chi 李濟. It would appear that the prolix method of notation used in this manuscript represents an early stage of the system. Still I hesitate to attach much value to this text for a study of the development of *ch‘in* annotation. Ogyū Sorai's manuscript was copied out again and again. I recently purchased an old copy, with Japanese commentaries and explanatory illustrations. The question arises whether Ogyū Sorai faithfully followed the Chinese original, or whether he wrote out in full a manuscript originally in *chien-tzû*, for his own purposes.

disposal. For the sake of convenience I shall divide them into three groups.

In the first place there are materials of a more or less casual nature, to be found in all kinds of books on various subjects. The oldest references occur in the Classical Books, mentioned above. The writings of the philosophers of various schools that flourished about 300 B.C. also often contain valuable materials on the significance of the lute. I mention especially Huai-nan-tzû and Lü Pu-wei (see p. 24, n. 3).[2] The former so often uses musical conceptions to illustrate his ideas, that he might well be called the 'musical philosopher'. Further, in historical and encyclopaedic compilations stories about famous lute players are often related; such anecdotes indirectly shed much light on ancient Chinese conceptions of the lute.

Secondly there were also composed special treatises on the lute. The oldest that has been preserved seems to be the *Ch'in-ch'ing-ying* by the Confucianist philosopher Yang Hsiung.[3] During the Han dynasty there were written several of such books on the lute: the bibliographical section of the History of the Han Dynasty mentions four,[4] that of the Sui period seven items. Unfortunately these books are all lost, and were so already in the Sung dynasty.[5] We still have, however, scores of books on the lute dating from the end of the Han to the beginning of the Ming period. And thereafter the literature on the lute increases rapidly: not only were there published a great number of special books on the lute, but also works on music in general devote entire chapters to the lute and its connotations. The mass of this literature is so vast that one can hardly hope to survey it all.

Thirdly there are the so-called *ch'in-pu*,[6] handbooks for the lute player. Since because of their rarity these are the least known, I shall describe this category here more fully.

Although hundreds of *ch'in-pu* have been published since the beginning of the Ming dynasty, most of them are difficult to obtain. A collector of the 19th century observes: 'The so-called handbooks

---

2 准南子; 呂不韋

3 琴清英; 揚雄, 53 B.C.–A.D. 18

4 *Han-shu-i-wên-chih* 漢書藝文志, by Pan Ku (班固 A.D. 32–92). Some of the items mentioned here may have contained some sort of notation. I mention: *Ya-ch'in-chao-shih-ch'i-p'ien* 雅琴趙氏七篇 'Compositions for the Solo Lute, by Mr Chao, 7 parts', with the remark added: 'Tunes that were played by Wei Hsiang, minister under the Emperor Hsuan' (73–49 B.C.) 宣帝時丞相魏相所奏. Another commentator adds that Chao and a few other authors of similar treatises were granted an audience by the Emperor, and played the lute in the august presence.

5 Cf. *Ch'in-shih* 琴史, the passage quoted on p. 56 below.

6 琴譜

of the lute are not very much sought after by bibliophiles: they content themselves with just collecting a few items, so as to have also this sort of book represented on their shelves. As bookshops cannot sell them at a high price, they do not value them much; as moreover these books were very rarely reprinted, they were easily lost. During eighteen years I was able to collect only 41 specimens, which were bought by me or presented to me by my friends.'[7] I may add to this that generally *ch'in-pu* were published in very limited editions, printed from badly cut wood blocks, and on inferior paper. The reason for this state of affairs is that they were usually published by lute teachers, for the use of their pupils. So the printing and editing were done as cheaply as possible, and only a small number of copies were made. An exception is formed by those *ch'in-pu* that were published by scholars of name and high official standing, who could afford to have a handbook published without regard to the cost.

For the present subject, the study of the ideology of the lute, the latter class is the more important, because the authors had a wide knowledge of the literature on the subject, and could easily express their thoughts in writing. It goes without saying, however, that from a purely musical point of view, the value of a *ch'in-pu* rests entirely in the quality of the tunes given in notation: this depends upon the musical gifts of the editor, and has nothing to do with his scholarship. Often the most enticing melodies will be found in the cheapest editions.

Of course melodies in notation form the main part of a *ch'in-pu*.[8] But apart from that they contain introductory chapters, and it is here that the principles of *ch'in* ideology are to be found.

The contents of a *ch'in-pu* are generally arranged according to one fixed model. As is usually the case with Chinese books, they open with one or more prefaces, by the author and his pupils or friends,

---

7 See the *T'ien-wên-ko-ch'in-pu-chi-ch'êng* (Appendix II, 18), vol. I: 琴譜參考. 琴譜一書, 藏書家不甚購求, 隨收數種以備一類, 書坊店無善價可售, 故亦不重之, 而此書又少翻刻, 故最易亡滅, 余至今十有八年, 所購及諸公所贈止此四十一種. At present nearly all early Ming handbooks are rare, and often known to exist only in two or three copies. If one is lucky enough to find one, it is usually either incomplete, or else fetches a prohibitive price. During the last four years I have combed the bookshops in China and Japan for *ch'in-pu*, and copied out some very rare specimens in libraries. But still I have not yet been able to obtain many Ming *ch'in-pu* mentioned in old catalogues, and I fear that some are irretrievably lost.

8 The only exception is the *Yü-ku-chai-ch'in-pu* 與古齋琴譜; published in 1855 by Chu Fêng-chieh 祝鳳喈; in this *ch'in-pu* not a single tune is given, the whole book being filled with minute directions for building lutes, and with discussions on the theory of lute music.

and thereafter give the *fan-li*[9] or 'introductory notes'. The prefaces are important, because they not only furnish the reader with biographical details about the author and his circle of musical friends, but because they also often mention where he obtained the versions of the tunes given in his book. In the *fan-li* the author often states his views on the significance of the lute and its music.

Then follow chapters on the history of the lute; names of famous instruments are enumerated, sometimes accompanied by drawings showing their various shapes, and reproducing their inscriptions. Often there are also inserted some practical discussions as to how lutes should be built, how the strings should be made, etc. Then come rules defining what might be called the discipline of the lute player: where and to whom the lute may be played, in what costume etc.; I shall discuss these rules in detail in the third section of this chapter. Also explanations of the technical terminology are given, and suggestions as to how lutes should be stored away, how to repair them, and how to make the table on which the lute is laid. Lists of tunes, of famous lute players, and of lute builders of succeeding dynasties are also added.

Thereafter come lengthy dissertations on the musical theory of the lute. Sometimes they confine themselves to the practical aspects, as fixing the correct tuning and the various modes, at other times they lose themselves in abstruse speculations on the absolute pitch and the correct dimensions of the twelve sonorous tubes.[10] In these pages I do not quote from this part of the *ch'in-pu*, since it contains no information on the ideology peculiar to the lute.

Of greater importance to our present subject is the section on the significance of the tones: each tone has its special association, and should evoke a certain emotion. Below I devote a special chapter to this question.[11]

Finally there comes a special chapter on the finger technique, and the system of annotation used in describing this technique. This chapter is called *chih-fa*[12] and it forms, so to say, the key to the handbook, for without it the player would find in the notation of the tunes many obscure passages, since editors often use all kinds of variants

---

[9] 凡例
[10] The *Ch'in-sê-ho-pu* very justly observes that the greatest musical theoreticians are usually not the best musicians: 'In ancient times the people who excelled in playing the lute did not bother themselves (cf. *Lun-yü*

XIX, 4) with the laws of musical theory; those who did so were not good performers on the lute' 凡例, 12: 古之善鼓琴者必不泥於律呂, 泥律呂者必不善於鼓琴.
[11] Chapter v, § 2: 'Symbolism of Tones'.
[12] 指法

of the signs of the *chien-tzŭ* system. Unfortunately this chapter has often been torn out, to prevent the handbook from being used by unqualified people. The best edited *ch'in-pu* illustrate these directions regarding the finger technique with drawings of the correct positions of the hand, sometimes further explained by symbolical pictures.[13]

In addition to these introductory chapters the main body of a *ch'in-pu*—the tunes in notation—also contains materials for studying the ideology of the lute. The tunes are accompanied by prefaces, colophons and commentaries, which give the name of the composer and explain the meaning of the tune; sometimes they even go so far as to explain the special significance of each part of a tune, and of each bar.[14]

These handbooks of the lute differ considerably in quality. Not only does the make-up vary, as mentioned above, but also the quality of the contents. Generally speaking they may be divided into two groups which I propose to call *basic* and *secondary*. In the first group I would classify that small number of *ch'in-pu* that combine well-written and logically arranged introductory chapters, with original and carefully edited versions of the tunes. As one wrong stroke in the notation will cause a tremendous confusion, the verifying of the characters (of the cut blocks)[15] with regard to the *ch'in-pu* is even more important than with ordinary books, where a wrong character may usually at a glance be detected by referring to the context.

Already an author of the Ming dynasty complains of the many mistakes in the notation of the *ch'in-pu*. He says: 'Those who excelled among the lute masters transmitted [the doctrine of] the lute and the handbooks. Thus the compiling of the handbooks rested with the lute masters. Still there are mistaken ones; if one stroke is wrong, then the finger technique fails because of this false tradition. And if this false tradition continues for a long time, the mistakes cannot be corrected any longer, and the true spirit of the lute melodies is lost.'[16] Many *ch'in-pu* boast in their prefaces that not a single stroke or dot in the notations is wrong, but those that measure up to this standard are rare.

The majority of the *ch'in-pu* still extant belong to the secondary group; their introductory chapters are a medley of passages taken from the basic handbooks and various other sources, clumsily patched

---

13 For a discussion of these, see Chapter v, § 3: 'Symbolism of the Finger Technique'.

14 In Chapter IV, 'The Significance of the Tunes', I shall often have to refer to these remarks added to the tunes.

15 In Chinese: *hsiao-tzŭ* 校字.

16 琴譜取正. 琴師之善者傳琴傳譜, 而書譜之法在琴師亦有訛者, 一畫之失指法即錯以訛傳, 訛久不可正, 琴調則失眞矣 (Appendix II, 4, *Tsun-shêng-pa-chien*).

together. The tunes given in notation are copied after those of the basic handbooks, with but few alterations. But even the editors of these secondary *ch'in-pu* often added some new materials of their own: a new way of expressing rhythm, adding ordinary notes to the *chien-tzû*, etc. Cases of absolute plagiarism are rare; I have so far been able to discover only one.[17]

It is only since the establishment of the Chinese Republic in 1911 that Chinese scholars have tried to collect and critically investigate these various materials on the lute. I may mention here the work of two lute players, who devoted many years to these studies.

In the first place is Yang Tsùng-chi, who died around 1929, having during a long time taught the lute in Peking.[18] He was an enthusiastic collector of rare *ch'in-pu* and antique lutes, and, although not an eminent scholar or brilliant stylist, he still had had a suitable literary education. The result of his studies on the lute and its literature are collected in his *Ch'in-hsüeh-ts'ung-shu*,[19] which contains not less than 32 original treatises. Unfortunately he did not work according to a fixed plan, but, *more sinico*, he jumps from one subject to another, giving the most heterogeneous items of information under one and the same heading. As no index or detailed list of contents has been added, one has to work through the entire work in order to locate a passage. But notwithstanding these shortcomings it is a valuable book, as yet the only one that tries to treat all aspects of the study of the lute.

His friend Chou Ch'ing-yün was a great collector of *ch'in-pu*, and he diligently studied their prefaces and colophons, comparing different editions of the same work. On the basis of what must have been a marvellous collection he compiled two books. In 1914 he published the *Ch'in-shu-ts'un-mu*,[20] a *catalogue raisonné* of all *ch'in-pu* he either possessed himself, or the titles of which he found in old and new catalogues. These items are all arranged chronologically, and in many cases he reprints their prefaces. It is to be deplored, however, that he did not add to each item a note as to whether he had actually seen the book or not. Therefore it is not always possible to know whether or not he relies on secondary information. The famous

---

[17] Namely, the *Chiao-an-ch'in-pu* 蕉庵琴譜, published in 1877 by Ch'in Wei-han 秦維翰, in which are given exactly the same versions as printed in the well-known *Wu-chih-chai-ch'in-pu* (Appendix II, 15). The editor has, however, made up for this to a

certain extent by giving in the introductory chapters a particularly good survey of the various tunings.

[18] 楊宗稷, style: Shih-po 什百.

[19] Appendix II, 7.

[20] Appendix II, 8.

bibliophile Miao Ch'üan-sun[21] wrote a preface. In 1917 he supplied these bibliographical materials with biographical data, publishing a *Ch'in-shih*,[22] in which notes are given on the lives of famous editors of *ch'in-pu* and of lute players; Yang Tsung-chi added a preface to this book.

Notwithstanding their shortcomings these three books are indispensable works for the student of the lute. The materials which the authors used are hardly obtainable in the libraries of Europe or America, and even in China and Japan most of the rare items are found together only in some private collections.[23]

§2 ORIGINS AND CHARACTERISTICS

The establishment and evolution of CH'IN *ideology due chiefly to three factors: Confucianist (social), Taoist (religious), and psychological—Buddhist influences: a Mantrayanic magic formula as lute tune, a Lamaist hymn adapted to the lute— a summary of the history of* CH'IN *ideology*

CH'IN ideology may be called a separate system in so far as every time that one meets the lute in Chinese literature, it is found to be associated with a special system of thought.

In minor details this system is differently described by various authors, but its characteristic points remain the same. One would look, however, in vain for a special standard text, in which this system is clearly formulated, and its elements systematically arranged, so as to form a canon for the significance of the lute.

Since early times there is found the term *ch'in-tao*,[24] literally: the Way of the lute, meaning: the inner significance of the lute and how to apply this in order to find in the lute a means for reaching enlightenment. The literatus and lute player Huan T'an[25] wrote a treatise entitled *Ch'in-tao*; this title is registered in the *Yü-hai*,[25] but it has not been preserved. This book may have been an attempt to give a summary of the principles of *ch'in* ideology. This term *ch'in-tao* might be translated as 'the doctrine of the lute'; but as we

---

21 繆荃孫, 1844–1919.

22 Appendix II, 9.

23 For materials on the lute in Western books I may refer to Appendix I, while a description of the Chinese books on the lute and of the *ch'in-pu* quoted in these pages may be found in Appendix II.

24 琴道

25 桓譚 (he lived about the beginning of our era); 玉海

do not possess a special text where the principles of this doctrine are set forth, I think a vague term like 'ideology of the lute' is the more suitable translation.

In the long course of its development *ch'in* ideology benefited by its lack of delimitation; because of the absence of a fundamental text, *ch'in-tao* was able to absorb a great wealth of various conceptions. Below I shall try to sketch an outline of this ideology, at the same time making an attempt to analyze the factors that caused its establishment, and influenced its further evolution.

In Chapter II, I discussed the classical conceptions of music in general, as expounded in the *Yüeh-chi*. We are not justified, however, in taking that discussion as a final basis when embarking upon an investigation of historical problems, although till recent days the *Yüeh-chi* was looked upon by Chinese scholars as having unquestionable authority. In order to be able to make a discreet use of this text, we shall first have to consider it critically.

Chinese historical records are unique in so far that they cover an unbroken line, reaching from high antiquity to the present day. But we must always bear in mind that the cement of this imposing edifice is formed by the continuity of the written language. And this literary language, although extremely flexible and highly expressive, is yet too much a special product of a limited circle, a comparatively small group of writers, all belonging to the same class and having a similar trend of thought, not to strain a correct representation of the actual facts. History was, until recently, a section of the vast field of Chinese letters; it was, like most other Chinese sciences, kneaded and remoulded until it became literature. This fact becomes evident when one tries to study some subject in its historical frame; when comparing archaeological and ethnological data with their descriptions as transmitted in literary documents, we cannot fail to realize that these describe life and its phenomena from a particular and narrow angle: the point of view of the literary class. We are constantly confronted with what might be called a revolving process, something like the following. A certain phenomenon is observed and recorded. This record is written in the highly polished literary idiom, and by this mere process of recording, the actual facts are already modified to some extent. In this form it finds its way into some book or essay. Other literati quote the passage, but before doing so they test it by literary traditions, and make the necessary alterations to harmonize it with these. Moreover they will link it up with some appropriate classical quotation, and add that this was the phenomenon as it has appeared since ancient times. Now, when after the lapse of some centuries or so, another observer finds this same phenomenon in actual life, before writing about it he consults the records drawn up by former observers, and finds these to be rather different from what he actually sees. But as a rule his reaction is not to question the correctness of these records, but on the contrary he will accept them as the absolute truth, and in connection with the present condition of the phenomenon he will sadly point out the decadence of the times, deploring that a phenomenon that formerly was in such perfect accordance with literary ideals has come to be so vulgar. And this process repeats itself any number of times, till the discrepancy between the actual phenomenon and its description becomes so wide that a later writer treats them as two entirely different things.

It goes without saying that this theoretical example is far too simplistic and general, and that real cases are infinitely more complicated. Further, as a rule, such a development applies especially to subjects lying outside the direct domain of the literatus—which were many. Still I think it is as true as generalizations can be. It may serve as one explanation for the fact that there is inherent in Chinese literature what might be called a paradisaical complex: a tendency to reverse the natural course of the evolution of culture, to make it start with a summit of perfection, after which there is a steady decline. Of course there are numerous other and more potent factors underlying this tendency; factors based upon a trend of thought common to all human beings, and which explain the fact that this paradisaical complex occurs in many other civilizations. But in China the force of the literary tradition must certainly be counted as one of them.

When we consider the pronouncements of the *Yüeh-chi* in the light of the foregoing observations, it becomes evident that they are not to be taken as a faithful description of the opinion of the ancient Chinese on music in general. The views quoted are a production of literary tradition. For the literati ceremonial music was the apex of all music, and consequently they expected all other musical manifestations to be in accordance with these ideals. What deviated from this fixed canon had to be remoulded till it fitted in; then and then only could it be officially accepted. That this ceremonial music itself is in many respects an artificial production stands to reason. When the *Yüeh-chi* speaks of the music of the clan festivals, it depicts them as decorous celebrations, ignoring their origin. Comparative ethnology teaches us that the actual songs sung at clan festivals were far more archaic, though their meaning and portent was certainly not less deep or mystic than that of any classical text. The ancient terminology was maintained, but the interpretation was biased to the extent of giving a false representation of the real facts.

In some cases the materials that had to be remodeled by the literati set them some difficult problems. For instance, the songs of the *Book of Odes* so clearly showed their original character of folksongs, that the literati needed all their ingenuity to force them into the classical mould. Some of them, the odes of Chêng and Wei,[26] ancient love-songs, they had to give up as being impossible to remould. Therefore the literati labelled them irrevocably with their *hic niger est*, and in Chinese literature they are, quite wrongly, always used to denote lewd and vulgar music. I need not discuss this question further here, since it has already been analyzed by M. Granet in his pioneer researches on the *Book of Odes*.

Thus the conceptions of music as expounded in the *Yüeh-chi* did not answer real conditions; neither the music at the court, nor the music of the people could pass the muster set by these literary standards. This is only natural, since music is a very human art that develops spontaneously, unhampered by moral or philosophical considerations.

Even though we can hardly see conditions of the pre-Han period except through the documents drawn up and refashioned by the literati, indirect information definitely points to the fact that popular music, theoretically designed as the 'lewd notes of Chêng',[27] was much in favour at the court and among the populace. Prince Wên of Wei[28] expressed his preference unequivocally when he said: 'When in full ceremonial dress I must listen to the Ancient Music, I think I shall fall asleep, but when I listen to the songs of Chêng and Wei, I never get tired.'[29] Thus in the period preceding the Han dynasty the Ceremonial Music was forced to the background by the ever-waxing influence of secular music. To use the words of the great historian Ssû-ma Ch'ien:[30] 'The right way of government decayed, and the music of Chêng prospered. The feudal lords and hereditary princes made their names famous in neighbouring states, and vied with each other in power. Since Confucius could not cope with the

---

26 鄭, 衞; *Shih-ching*, Books VIII and IX.
27 See *Lun-yü*, Book XV, ch. 10; Book XVII, ch. 18.
28 426–387 B.C.
29 See *Yüeh-chi*, ch. III, 6.
30 司馬遷, born in 145 B.C.

singing girls sent by Ch'i,[31] and had to give up his position in Lu, although retiring he rectified the music in order to lead people to the right path, he composed the Wu-chang music in order to criticise the trend of the times, but none heeded his counsels. The decay went on and in the period of the Six States the feudal lords indulged in dissipation and idleness. Then it was impossible for them to return to the right path, they lost their lives and their families were exterminated and all the states were unified under Ch'in.'[32]

Official recognition of popular music came under the reign of Emperor Hui[33] when a special bureau for this was established. This bureau was called *yüeh-fu*, and its task was to collect and record popular songs. Later these songs themselves were also called *yüeh-fu*.[34] When the Emperor Wu fixed the rites for the sacrifices to Heaven and Earth,[35] this bureau was reorganized, and considerably widened in scope. Well-known poets like Ssû-ma Hsiang-ju and Li Yen-nien[36] were ordered to investigate and correct the popular songs assembled, in order that charming melodies might be properly harmonized, and the accompanying texts polished, to make them more enjoyable for a cultivated and refined audience.

In later literature it is stated that the *yüeh-fu* was instituted in order to choose and put on record such folksongs as were considered to be of an edifying and elevated character, to ameliorate the morals of the people. But in my opinion this is clearly the distorted point of view of the Confucianist school of thought. The original function of the *yüeh-fu* was certainly not to restrain popular music, but on the contrary to encourage it, and to assemble as many gay songs fit for entertainment as possible. This is shown, e.g., by a passage from the *Account of Rites and Music of the Han History*,[37] where the endeavours of Emperor Ai[37] to curb the rampancy of popular music are described; a commentator adds: 'Although the Emperor Ai stopped

---

[31] This incident is referred to in *Lun-yü*, Bk. XVII, ch. 4. Legge adds the note: 'In the 9th year of the duke Ting, Confucius reached the highest point of his official service. He effected in a few months a wonderful renovation of the state, and the neighbouring countries began to fear that under his administration Lu would overtop and subdue them all. To prevent this, the duke of Ch'i sent a present to Lu of fine horse and of 80 highly accomplished beauties. The sage was forgotten, government neglected. Confucius, indignant and sorrowful, withdrew from office

and, for a time, from the country too.'

[32] 史記, 樂書, 治道虧缺, 而鄭音興起, 封君世辟, 名顯隣州, 爭以相高, 自仲尼不能與齊優, 遂容於魯, 雖退正樂以誘世, 作五章以刺時, 猶莫之化, 陵遲以至六國, 流沔沈佚, 遂往不返, 卒於喪身滅宗, 并國於秦.

[33] 惠帝, r. 194–188 B.C.

[34] 樂府

[35] 武帝, 140–87 B.C.; *chiao-ssû* 郊祀

[36] 司馬相如, 179–117 B.C.; 李延年, 2nd cent. B.C.

[37] 漢書禮樂志; 哀帝, r. 6–1 B.C.

the songs of Chêng and Wei, and restricted the number of officials of the *yüeh-fu*, he did not succeed in establishing elegant music on the basis of the Classics and the ancient rules.'[38] If the *yüeh-fu* was intended to control popular music, the Emperor would have enlarged, and not restricted, the number of officials.

Equally abortive were the efforts at a reform in favour of music conforming to literary standards made by Ho-chien Hsien-wang, the son of the Han Emperor Ching.[39] The growth of secular music was further encouraged when Central-Asiatic music, the so-called *hu-yüeh*,[40] became increasingly popular in China. The class of palace music called *huang-mên-ku-ch'ui-yüeh*[41] (music for entertaining the guests at Palace festivals and banquets) occupied a much more important place than Ceremonial Music, and its influence grew with every succeeding dynasty.

This light music reached its zenith during the Sui (590–618) and T'ang (618–907) periods.[42] In those times it did not, however, any longer derive its inspiration from Chinese popular music; the *yüeh-fu* genre had become a literary style, cultivated by scholars as an archaizing[43] sort of poetry cut off from its living root, the folk-song. Foreign modes and instruments prevailed, and an enormous amount of Indian and Central-Asiatic music was adopted.[44] And these foreign airs were not even in accordance with the twelve sonorous tubes, on which all Chinese musical theory has been based since times immemorial. We read in the *Account of Music of the Liao History*: 'The 28 foreign modes are not fixed by means of the Chinese sonorous tubes, but by the strings of the *p'i-p'a*.'[45] Even songs belonging to a semi-popular, but essentially Chinese class of music, were reset on Central-Asiatic modes.[46]

When the highest social circles set such an example, it can be easily understood that the music that was heard in the streets and at social

---

38 哀帝雖有放罷鄭衛之言, 減樂府之員, 然不能據經做古制爲雅樂.

39 河間献王, 景帝, r. 156–140 B.C.

40 胡樂

41 黃門鼓吹樂

42 See the fundamental study by K. Hayashi: *Sui-t'ang-yen-yüeh-tiao-yen-chiu* 林謙三, 隋唐燕樂調研究, Shanghai 1935 (appeared only in Chinese).

43 *ni-ku* 擬古

44 In the *Account of Music in the Dynastic History of the Sui Period* 隋書音樂志, we find the following amazing enumeration of seven

musical departments instituted by the Emperor Yang (煬帝, r. 605–17): 國伎, 清商伎, 高麗伎, 天竺伎, 安國伎, 茲龜 (＝屈支) 伎, 文康伎.

45 二十八調, 不用黍律, 以琵琶絃協之. According to Chinese tradition the size of each of the twelve sonorous tubes (黍律 *shu-lü*) was determined by the number of grains of millet it could contain; the basic tube, *Huang-chung*, should contain exactly 1200 grains.

46 Note the remarks of Hayashi (*op. cit.* p. 61) regarding *ch'ing-shang-yüeh* 清商樂.

gatherings was still further removed from the literary standards fixed by tradition. Still it formed a part of the daily life of the literati and of the common people. We have but to read through essays and poems of the T'ang period to see how immensely popular this so-called 'vulgar' music was with the gay and pleasure-loving people of that time. Yet, when one leafs through the scores of voluminous works on music referring to that period, one finds involved speculations on the absolute pitch of the ground-note, and other abstruse questions of musical theory, but not a word about popular, let alone about foreign, music. For this music was contrary to established literary principles, and there was no recognized precedent for it; so it was simply ignored. This is one of the many cases where the records drawn up by the literati give a biased representation of the actual conditions.

Returning now to the *Yüeh-chi* we can, after the above discussions, state that already about 400 B.C., when these conceptions were formulated, they were neither in accordance with the conditions prevailing at the time, nor did they give a good idea of the situation during past centuries. Still less could they be applied to the evolution of music during subsequent dynasties. Notwithstanding, the *Yüeh-chi* was, and remained, the only standard text on music recognized by the literati, and thus by official historians.

This digression into the history of music in general was necessary, because in my opinion the discrepancy between actual musical conditions and the standard set by literary tradition was one of the factors that caused the creation of the ideology of the lute, and strongly influenced its further evolution.

Although the literati ignored what they called 'vulgar' music in their learned musical dissertations, they were of course perfectly aware of its existence, and moreover liked it immensely. This is sufficiently shown by an inspection of the many old paintings which depict the life of the literary class: there one sees gatherings of literati, assembled on a beautiful spot in the open, and enlivened by a bevy of fair damsels, who play the three-stringed violin, the cither and a great variety of other instruments, all introduced from foreign countries. This popular music was in fact the only kind of music that the greater part of the literati could in reality hear. For the Ceremonial Music was only performed on special occasions, and for a limited audience. Yet, although known often only from books, the Ceremonial Music and literary musical standards had officially to be kept intact. For if popular music were allowed to invade also the sacred domain of literature, classical ideals might become endangered, and therewith the very foundations of the State.

It is here that the significance of the lute becomes apparent; it was the only instrument that, although properly belonging to the ceremonial orchestra and boasting of a venerable age, pure Chinese origin, and constant association with the most holy Sages of Confucianism, could still be played in private life as a solo instrument, and still demonstrate all the high musical ideals fixed by literary tradition.

Since ancient times notions that perfectly harmonize with classical ideals were associated with the lute. For instance, in the *Yüeh-chi* it is said that music belongs to Heaven, and as such may assist man to regain his original heavenly nature. Now, as the philosopher Huai-nan-tzû observes, the lute was created in mythical times to provide man with an instrument to regain his original serenity: 'to make man return to his divine origin, to restrain his low passions, and make him revert to his heavenly nature'.[47] In the *Ch'in-tsao*[48] this idea is formulated as follows: 'Fu Hsi made the lute, whereby to restrain falsehood, to guard the heart against low desires, that man might be cultivated and his nature regulated, to make man return to what is truly heavenly in him.'[48]

Further, the *Yüeh-chi* says that music was used by the Ancient Sages to regulate the Realm. Now in the *Book of History*, in *Huai-nan-tzû*, and several other philosophical texts of the period, the following line is quoted: 'When Shun was Emperor, he played the five-stringed lute, and sung the song *Nan-fêng*, and the Realm was regulated.'[49] Wise men of later times should also cultivate lute music, to illustrate the benevolent rule of the Ancient Sovereigns: 'to play the lute in order to sing the way of the Ancient Kings'.[50]

Already the Chinese word for lute in itself pointed to this high destiny. As is well known, a favourite Chinese way of explaining a word is to couple it with a homonym. So in the *Book of Rites*, *Li-chi*, the word for 'virtue', *tê* 德, is explained as *tê* 得, 'possessing (rectitude)'. In the same way the *Fêng-su-t'ung-i*[51] explains the word *ch'in* 琴 (lute), by coupling it with the homonym *chin* 禁, which means 'restraining'. The text reads: 'Lute means restraining. With this instrument licentiousness and falsehood are restrained, and the

---

47 以歸神杜淫，反其天心 (*op. cit.* 泰族訓).

48 Appendix II, 1. 所以禦邪僻，防心淫，以修身理性，反其天眞也.

49 舜爲天子，彈五絃之琴，謂南風之詩而天下治.

50 彈琴以詠先王之風 (韓氏外傳, Ch. 2).

51 風俗通義

human heart is rectified.' This phrase makes, according to Confucianist teachings, the lute an instrument for 'nourishing the heart': *yang-hsin*.[52] The philosopher Mencius observes: 'To nourish the heart there is nothing better than to make the desires few. Here is a man whose desires are few—in some things he may not be able to keep his heart, but they will be few. Here is a man whose desires are many—in some things he may be able to keep his heart, but they will be few.'[53] Thus the lute, through its capacity for restraining human passions, was a suitable instrument for everyone desiring to become the ideal statesman and ruler of the Confucianist school of thought, the Superior Man, the *Chün-tzû*.[54]

So the lute became one of the indispensable implements belonging to the outfit of the scholar; it became a symbol of literary life. As an old text says: 'The Superior Man does not suffer the lute to be separated from him during one single moment.'[55] Also, from a practical point of view it was suitable for solitary enjoyment. Scholars with musical inclinations could, when reciting the songs of the *Book of Odes, Shih-ching*, or some famous old essay, accompany this on the lute, as an elegant enjoyment sanctioned by tradition. Literati who, despite the trend of the times, clung to a strict observance of ancient principles also with regard to music, considered the lute as the stronghold of the music of the ancients, since here in one instrument were combined all the elevated conceptions expressed by the Ceremonial Music. Therefore they deepened its significance, in order to remove it farther from ordinary music and to consolidate its position as the treasure house of true music and the only officially recognized musical instrument of the literary class.

So we see that the very fact that music in general became the opposite of literary musical ideas, caused these conceptions to be ever more withdrawn into the narrow circle centring round the lute. The more that popular and foreign music advanced, the more the system of ideas connected with the lute was enlarged and elaborated on the basis of ancient classical passages. It was in the course of this process of emphasizing the difference between the lute and secular music that the ideology of the lute was established and developed till it became a separate system of thought.

This tendency to stress the isolated position of the lute as the one instrument of the true Confucianist scholar, appears constantly in

---

52 養心   53 See Legge, *Mencius*, Book VII, 35.
54 君子   55 *Fêng-su-t'ung-i;* see below, p. 72.

the tenets of *ch'in* ideology. Efforts are made to keep lute music for the use of the literary class only that it may not be tainted with vulgar or foreign influences. Already for purely practical reasons the lute lay outside the reach of the common people, since good instruments were expensive, the technique of playing extremely difficult, and teachers rare. The lower classes could afford to buy a guitar or a violin and play popular tunes on it, relying on the ear; but the lute had its own complicated system of notation, incomprehensible for those not specially educated in literature. In addition, artificial barriers were drawn up: explicit rules defined the classes of people to whom the lute may be played or taught. These lists are highly instructive. They mention, for example, that merchants and vulgar people are unqualified for occupying themselves with the lute, thus underlining the tendency to keep the lute reserved for the small circle of the elect.

Many of these rules can only be appreciated in their real significance by comparing them with the actual conditions of music which I described above. We find among the people who are forbidden to touch the lute, for instance, singing girls and actors. That this group was included is evidently in protest against the fact that at the more intimate parties at the court the lute was also played to execute *yüeh-fu* songs. This kind of music is even registered as a special class, the so-called *ch'in-ch'ü-ko'-tz'ŭ*.[56] That many handbooks for the lute also exclude Buddhist priests from lute music, and sharply denounce the music of foreign countries as 'barbarian', is doubtless to be interpreted as a reaction against the ascendency of the Indian and Central-Asiatic elements in secular music. In the next section of this chapter I shall discuss these rules in more detail. The examples given here may suffice to show that the break between real musical conditions and Confucian literary musical ideals was one of the factors that promoted the evolution of *ch'in* ideology.

Next to this social factor, which for convenience sake may be called Confucianistic, there was also a second, that might be called the Taoistic, lying in quite another domain of culture, viz. that of religion.

This second factor, which promoted the coming into being of *ch'in* ideology, is also slightly involved, and makes a detailed explanation necessary.

As mentioned above, the lute was considered as a means for regaining man's original purity by restraining low desires and banish-

---

[56] 琴曲歌詞. For a collection of poems sung to this music., see *Yüeh-fu-shih-chi* 樂府詩集, by Kuo Mao-ch'ien (郭茂倩, Sung period), chapter VIII.

ing evil thoughts. This belief in the original purity of human nature, doubtless one of the fundamentals of Chinese thought, is one of the most important links that connect Taoism and Confucianism. But the Taoist and Confucianist explanations and appreciation of this conception differ considerably.

In Taoism, however, speculations regarding the original purity of human nature rise far above the very earthly teachings of Confucianism; human nature is considered from a cosmic point of view. For the Taoist the universe is a manifestation, one peculiar aspect, of an all-pervading, supernatural agency, indicated by the term *tao*, which gave its name to the system. It is difficult to find for this term one entirely satisfactory equivalent; the Way seems most convenient. This *tao* is present in all things, in the most elevated as well as in the most base. The aim of Taoism is to learn to see one's own self as a part of this *tao*, so as to reach a complete reunion with it. Taoist writings constantly mention, as a condition for reaching this state of highest bliss and delivery from all earthly bonds, a regaining of the original purity. This original purity may be reached by returning to the utmost simplicity, both in mental and physical aspects. One must do away with all the superfluous things with which man has surrounded himself, thereby better to be able to concentrate upon the essence of *tao*, and by such introspection attain the primordial serenity. In the *Tao-tê-ching* this is called 'returning to the root, and so regaining serenity.'[57]

Taoist writers give several descriptions of this state of complete reunion with *tao*. Lieh-tzû describes this blissful condition as follows: 'After nine years [of meditation under the guidance of a master] I gave up speaking and thinking, I did not know the difference between benefit and damage, I did not know whether my master was really my master, nor yet that another was my friend. Outer and inner life had completely melted together. Thereafter the five senses also melted together, I could not determine whither sensations came. My mind was frozen, my body free, flesh and bones seemed to have become rarefied. I did not know on what my body rested, nor did I know what was under my feet. I was borne hither and thither, like a leaf that falls from a tree, or like dry chaff, without knowing whether the wind was riding on me, or I on the wind.'[58]

---

57 Ch. 16: 歸本曰靜.

58 *Ibid.* ch. 黃帝: 九年之後，橫心之所念，橫口之所言，亦不知我之是非利害歟，亦不知彼之是非利害歟，亦不知夫子之爲我師，若人之爲我友，內外進矣，而後眼如耳，耳如鼻，鼻如口，無不同也，心凝形釋骨肉都融，不覺形之所依倚，足之所履，隨風東西，猶木葉幹殼，竟不知風乘我，我乘風乎.

Another description of this state of detachment from earthly bonds is given in a passage in the works of the philosopher Chuang-tzû: 'Formerly I dreamt that I was a butterfly, freely fluttering about, just as it liked. I did not know that it was I. Suddenly I awoke, and realized that I was I. Now I wonder whether I dreamt that I was a butterfly, or whether I now am a butterfly, dreaming that it is I.'[59]

For the method of meditative self-culture, Chuang-tzû coined the term *yang-shêng*[60] 'nurturing (the spiritual life)'. In the chapter that has this title as its heading he says: 'If one takes *tao* as standard, then one may preserve one's body, complete one's life, and exhaust one's term of years.'[61] This *yang-shêng* is to be compared with *yang-hsin*, mentioned above with regard to Confucianist teachings: for *yang-shêng* also, a restraining of desires is obligatory.

These early Taoist conceptions are the foundation on which the most imposing monuments of Chinese thought are built. It seems, however, that these teachings were taken in their literal sense already at a fairly early date. Especially in the first century A.D., when Taoism was reorganized after the example of Buddhism, the accent fell more and more on the materialistic aspects of meditation. Meditation was no longer exclusively considered as a means for salvation, but chiefly as a means for obtaining occult powers, to perform all kinds of magical feats. So the passage of Lieh-tzû quoted above was interpreted as a description of a method of accomplishing levitation, while Chuang-tzû's definition of *yang-shêng* was taken to refer to the art of prolonging life. The lofty teachings of Taoism degenerated into alchemy, aiming at transmuting metals and finding the elixir of immortality.

Returning now to the lute, we see that the fundamentals of *ch'in* ideology described above fitted in exactly with Taoism, both with its philosophical and with its alchemistic aspect.

Playing the lute purifies one's nature by banishing low passions, therefore it is a sort of meditation, a means for communicating directly with *tao*. Its rarefied notes reproduce the 'sounds of emptiness', and so the music of the lute tunes the soul of the player in harmony with *tao*. Further, as we shall see below, the measurements and the construction of the lute all stand for cosmic elements, so its contemplation is conductive to a realization of eternal truths and cosmic harmony.

---

[59] Ch. II, last passage: 昔者莊周夢爲胡蝶, 栩栩然胡蝶也, 自喻適志與, 不知周也, 俄然覺則蘧蘧然周也, 不知周之夢爲胡蝶, 胡蝶之夢爲周與.

[60] 養生

[61] 緣督以爲經, 可以保身, 可以全生 . . . . 可以盡年.

Therefore it is only natural that the passages of Lieh-tzû and Chu-ang-tzû quoted above were taken as subjects for lute compositions. During the Sung dynasty Mao Chung-wêng composed the tune '*Lieh-tzû-yü-fêng*'[62] (Lieh-tzû riding on the wind), and in the Yüan period Mao Min-chung composed the tune '*Chuang-tzû-mêng-tieh*'[62] (Chuang-tzû dreaming of the butterfly). The latter in particular is a very delicate composition, with striking passages entirely in harmonics, which suggest the detached state of mind indicated by the subject.

Seen from the more materialistic angle, playing the *ch'in* was a means for purifying the body, thus bestowing upon the performer freedom from sickness, and longevity. To obtain these blessings neo-Taoistic writers recommend, in addition to fasting, etc., exercises[63] for learning to regulate breathing, *lien-ch'i*.[64] Now playing the lute is said to harmonize the circulation of the blood, thereby regulating the breathing. In this way the vital Yang essence in the body is cultivated, and evil influences are driven away. As the philosopher Kuan-tzû observes: 'to regulate the blood and the breath, in order to obtain longevity'.[65]

Therefore the lute is allotted a very special place amongst the Treasures of the Library: playing the lute can not be mentioned in one and the same breath as playing chess, or other literary pursuits. In the *Questions and Answers on the Study of the Lute*,[66] we read: 'Question: Which is superior, the lute or chess?—Answer: The quadruplet lute-chess-calligraphy-painting has been used since the time of Hui-tsung of the Sung dynasty. But in reality the lute is an instrument that embodies *tao*, and as such it is entirely different from chess. The lute is near to Taoism, it teaches one how to subdue the scheming mind. To illustrate this the tune *Ou-lu-wang-chi*[67] was made. But

---

[62] 毛仲翁, 列子禦風; 毛敏仲, 莊子夢蝶

[63] A most detailed description of all these exercises is given in the *Tsun-shêng-pa-chien* (Appendix II, 4), the section *Ch'ing-hsiu-miao-lun* 清修妙論. Also confer the excellent article by Henri Maspéro, 'Les procédés de "nourrir le principe vital" dans la religion taoiste ancienne' (*Journal Asiatique*, CCXXIX, 1937). A convenient summary of the materialistic side of Taoist teachings is given in O. S. Johnson, *A Study of Chinese Alchemy*, Shanghai 1928; see also M. Chikashige, *Alchemy and Other Chemical Achievements of the Ancient Orient*, Tokyo 1936, and A. Forke, *Geschichte der mittelalterlichen chine-*

sischen Philosophie, Hamburg 1939, pp. 131 ff.

[64] 鍊氣

[65] 管子, 導血氣以求長年

[66] *Ch'in-hsüeh-ts'ung-shu*; see Appendix II, 7: 問, 琴與棋孰優. 答. 琴棋所畫四者並稱自宋徽宗時始, 實則琴爲載道之器, 與棋爲絕對反比例, 琴與道家爲最近, 宜戒機心, 是以有鷗鷺忘機之曲, 棋則專用機心, 精者常有嘔血傷生之事, 琴則以却病爲收效之初基, 此所以相反也.

[67] A famous lute tune, composed during the Sung period by Liu Chih-fang 劉志方. Most *ch'in-pu* explain this song as follows: There was an old fisherman who used to take delight in long trips on the sea. The*

for playing chess one needs just such a scheming mind. Chess experts often suffer from hemophtysis and general decline in health. The lute, on the contrary, driving away sickness, is a first basis for attaining prosperity. Therefore it is quite the opposite of chess.'

In this connection I may also quote an anecdote about the Sung poet Lin Pu:[68] he excelled in playing the lute and in calligraphy, but he was not very good at playing chess. He used to say: 'All things of this world I can generally understand; only I cannot bear myself to be defiled by playing chess.'[69]

Lute amateurs indignantly protest against the designation of lute music as an art, for it is far more than that, it is a Way, a path of wisdom, *tao*.[70]

From the above it will be clear that next to the influence of Confucianist literary tradition, Taoist conceptions also contributed to the formation of *ch'in* ideology, and promoted its further development. As was also pointed out above, the lute was, however, played only by a comparatively small number of the literati. Therefore, to explain the wide divergence of *ch'in* ideology, to the above-mentioned factors a third one must be added, viz. the psychological one.

This psychological factor can be described in a few words. Few scholars were expert on the lute, but on various occasions in official and private life they enjoyed popular music. Now the lute supplied a means of self-justification for these scholars, both to other people and to themselves. In all sorts of mixed company the scholar could listen with delight to performances of popular music, and from time to time lustily chime in with some gay song; but when asked about his views on music, he could gravely point to the lutes hanging up in his library, and thereby definitely remove all doubts that might exist with regard to his elevated disposition. On the other hand, returning from a noisy banquet with some old friends, enlivened by the presence of some charming singing girls, the scholar could, in the silence of his library,

---

*flocks of gulls were so used to him that he could pat them. His wife knew of this, and one evening when he came home, she said to him: 'I like gulls. Why not bring one or two with you, so that I may enjoy looking at them?' At dawn the fisherman went out. But the flocks of the gulls flew high, and did not come down to him. 鷗鷺忘機, 有海翁者, 常遊海上, 群鷗習而狎焉, 其妻知之, 抵暮還家, 謂翁曰, 鷗鳥可娛, 盍攜一二歸玩之, 至且往, 則群鷗高飛而不下矣. This parable is an elaboration of a passage of *Lieh-tzŭ*, II, 11; its meaning is that as long as man is without desire,

without a 'scheming mind', he shall live in complete harmony with nature.

[68] 林逋, better known by his posthumous name Ho-ching 和靖, 967–1028.

[69] Lin Pu shows the typical mentality of the lute player: he did not care for worldly things, did not marry or adopt sons, but spent his days in a secluded abode, where he cultivated plum trees and reared cranes. People therefore used to say of him: 'The plum trees are his wife, the cranes his sons' 梅妻鶴子.

[70] 藝 as opposed to 道. See below, p. 82.

take the lute from its brocade cover, burn incense, and touch a few strings, thereby convincing himself that, although he might temporarily amuse himself with vulgar music in order to while away some moments of leisure, in reality he only appreciated the sacred music of the Ancients.

There could be mentioned also other reasons for the coming into being and further evolution of *ch'in* ideology, but in my opinion the three factors mentioned above must be considered as the decisive ones. I have discussed these three factors here separately, but it goes without saying that in the literature on the lute it is impossible to make such clear distinctions, and various views are found woven together.

Only in a few cases are the Confucianist and Taoist spheres of thought clearly differentiated as, for instance, in the two characteristics that should mark lute music, viz. *chin*, 'restraining', and *hsün*,[71] 'following', defined in this way: 'Restraining means driving away the false nature constituted by wantonness and low desire. Following means nurturing the Right Essence of balanced harmony.'[72]

Both views are also summarized in the two fixed epithets of the lute, viz. *ya*, 'accomplished, elegant' and *miao*, 'wonderful'.[73]

The question arises which of the two factors mentioned above had most influence on the development of *ch'in* ideology. As far as I can see, the answer must be that it was Taoistic ideas that predominated in the evolution of this system of thought. One might say that the formulation of the fundamental thoughts of *ch'in* ideology is Confucianistic, but that their contents are typically Taoistic. The literati, being as a rule of an eclectic disposition, accepted these Taoist teachings, since they did not clash with classical ideals, nor detracted from the special high position of the lute.

Herewith we must also take into consideration the fact that the Taoist considerations mentioned above corresponded directly with the most archaic, the pre-classical, Chinese notions. Taoism was the receptacle in which archaic Chinese thoughts were preserved. For instance, cultivating the Yang principle, the essence of light and vitality, is a very old conception; hence jade, cowry shells and other objects, credited with possessing a great amount of Yang power, were deposited in the tomb together with the deceased, to guard the

---

71 禁, 順
72 禁則去慾淫之絃心，順則養中和之正氣 (Liu Yü, preface to Yang Piao-chêng's *ch'in-*

pu; see App. II, 13).
73 雅, 妙

corpse, and thereby the earthly spirit *p'o*,[74] against decay. Thus the notion that playing the lute strengthens the Yang essence and thereby prolongs earthly life, fits in with the most archaic conceptions.

Through this preponderance of the Taoist element, *ch'in* ideology, notwithstanding the Confucianist tendency to keep the lute as purely Chinese as possible, still remained open for foreign influences, as long as these were not detrimental to the sacred character of the lute. These foreign elements are mainly Buddhist, and through Taoism some later schools of Mahayanic Buddhism, which might be comprised under the general name of Mantrayana, had some influence on the lute. The alchemist teachings of neo-Taoism show too many striking affinities with Mantrayanic magical practices for there not to have existed much interaction between them. Just as Taoist sorcery aims at prolonging life, levitation, subduing devils and other magical powers, so the Mantrayana teaches that the devoted practitioner may acquire the *aṣṭasiddhi*, the eight magical powers, i.e. levitation (*laghimā*), becoming invisible (*adṛçyā*), etc. To obtain these *siddhi*, Mantrayanic texts describe in detail complicated rituals, different according to the special deity worshipped and the aim desired. But the preliminaries remain the same: the practitioner must bathe, put on new clothes, then choose a clean place in a quiet abode, and burn incense. Only then may he go on to the drawing of the magic circle (*maṇḍala*), and in the center thereof imagine, or actually build, the altar. After these preparations he may start on the execution of the ritual.

Now when we read in the handbooks for the lute player the elaborate rules describing where and how the lute may be played, we cannot fail to notice their striking resemblance with Mantrayanic magical rites. To begin with, the table with the lute on it is constantly referred to as *ch'in-tan*,[75] 'lute altar'. This altar should be erected preferably on a beautiful spot in nature; it must be far from all worldly noise, pure, and surrounded by exquisite scenery. In the next section of this chapter I shall give more particulars. This short description may suffice to show the affinity with the rules given in, for instance, the *Mahāvairocana Sūtra* for *tsê-ti*,[76] 'choosing the place (for erecting the altar)'; there it is said that one should select a mountainous landscape, with trees and rivulets; borders of streams, frequented by wild geese and singing birds; a pure and secluded abode.[77] The other rules also resemble the Mantrayanic ritual: before touching the lute the player must don ceremonial dress, wash his hands, rinse his mouth, and purify his thoughts. After having burned incense he may take the lute from its cover, and place it on the lute table. Then he should sit down before it in a reverent mood, and regulate his breath and concentrate his mind. His body should be kept steady and erect, 'unmoving and imposing like the T'ai shan'. Yet his mental attitude must be humble, 'as if he were standing before a superior'.

That thus playing the lute became a magical act, a ritual for communicating with mysterious powers, is, in my opinion, doubtless due to this indirect Mantrayanic influence.

Further, the lute underwent Buddhist influences directly. There were many lute players among famous monks, such as, during the T'ang period, Master Ying, and, during the Sung dynasty, I-hai and Liang-yü.[78] When some Indian priests came to China they also brought lute-like instruments with them, and Chinese scholars studied these foreign instruments in connection with the Chinese lute. We find, e.g., that Ou-yang Hsiu, famous poet and scholar of the Sung period, praised in a poem the performance of the monk Ho-pai on an Indian stringed instrument (probably the *vīṇā*).[79]

A curious result of this direct Buddhist influence is the fact that among the better known *ch'in* tunes there is one entitled *Shih-t'an* 'Buddhist Words', which is nothing but a Mantrayanic magic formula, a *dhāraṇī*.[80] The music of this tune is decidedly Indian, vibratos and glissandos reproducing the frequent melismas used in Buddhist polyphonic chant in China and Japan up to this day. The words are also given, for the greater part in transcribed bastard Sanskrit, the usual language of *dhāraṇī*, and starting with the stereotyped opening formula 'Hail to the Buddha! Hail to the Law! Hail to the Community!'[81]

As far as I know, the first printed text of this tune was published by

---

[77] *Taishō-issaikyō* 大正一切經, No. 848, translated by Śubhākarasiṃha 施無畏, T'ang period. Cf. *Hōbōgirin, dictionnaire encyclopédique du Bouddhisme d'après les sources chinoises et japonaises*, 1937, s.v. *chakuji*. These Indian ideas fitted in with Chinese conceptions of the salutary effect of contemplating beautiful scenery; see below, section 3 of this chapter.

[78] See *Ch'in-shih* (Appendix II, 9), ch. 2. 穎師, 義海, 良玉.

[79] 歐陽修, 1007–1072; 和白. See the collected works of Ou-yang Hsiu, 外集 ch. 3, the poem *Sung-ch'in-sêng-ho-pai*.

[80] 釋談. Curiously enough this tune seems rather popular: it is included in the repertoire of the *p'i-p'a*, and in 1929 a version for the *san-hsien* was published (cf. *Yin-yüeh-tsa-chih* 'Music Magazine', vol. I, 5, Peking, 1929).

[81] Namo buddhāya namo dharmāya namaḥ saṃghāya 南無佛陀耶南無達摩耶南無僧伽耶.

Yang Lun in his *ch'in-pu, Po-ya-hsin-fa*.[82] The editor added a commentary, which is an interesting example of the scanty knowledge that the literati in general possessed of Buddhist texts. He says: 'I find that this tune is a magic formula by the Ch'an Master Pu-an, which later people set to music. Originally Sanskrit has the sounds *êrh-ho, san-ho* and *ssû-ho*,[83] each represented by a letter. In Chinese script only the notation for the lute has these letters. Therefore the Mirror of the Rhymes of the Seven Sounds[84] originated in India, answering to the seven strings of the lute. This is the origin of them [i.e. of the Seven Sounds]. Those tones which formerly were sung by the monks in the garden of Anāthapiṇḍada,[85] are now adapted to the lute. The music wherewith Gautama Buddha could subdue a mad elephant and cure the bites of venomous snakes, can now be used to make cranes dance and for taming pheasants. Although Confucianism and Buddhism fundamentally originate from different sources, their music mysteriously forms a true bond between them, although at first sight one would be inclined to dismiss this idea with a laugh.'[86]

The priest Pu-an lived from 1115–69, and was famous for his magical powers. He is said to have been able to heal maladies, command rain and drought, and to perform other magical feats. He left a book in three chapters, entitled *Pu-an-yin-su-ch'an-shih-yü-lu*.[87] It would seem that Yang Lun connects the seven kinds of sounds distinguished by Indian grammarians (guttural, palatal, etc.) with the seven notes of the Chinese scale (*kung, shang, chiao, chih, yü, pien-*

---

[82] Preface dated 1609; see Appendix II, 14.

[83] *Erh-ho, san-ho* and *ssû-ho* are technical terms used in Chinese transcriptions of Sanskrit texts, indicating that the two, three, or four characters preceding the sign should be contracted; e.g. 里波二合 is to be read *rva*, and not *riva*, 悉恒里三合 is to be read *stri*, and not *sitari*, etc. The author connects these signs with the same indications used in *ch'in* annotation, where they mean: make this note sound together with the preceding one (*êrh-ho*), or with the two preceding ones (*san-ho*); for instance one plucks the fourth string, while the sound of a vibrato produced on the second string has not yet died away. From this queer association one would conclude that Yang Lun misunderstood entirely the meaning of *êrh-ho* etc. in Sanskrit transcriptions. For a detailed discussion of the system the Chinese used for transcribing Sanskrit texts I may refer to my book *Hayagriva, the Mantrayanic Aspect of Horse Cult in China and Japan*, Leyden 1935, p. 48: 'The reading of the magic formulae'.

[84] *Ch'i-yin-yün-chien*: these four characters look like the title of a book, though I could not identify it as such.

[85] 給園, abbreviation of 給孤獨園, Sanskrit: *Anāthapiṇḍadā-syaramaḥ*, the estate in which the Jetavana, the favorite abode of Buddha, was located. It was presented to the community by the rich merchant Anāthapiṇḍada, a fervent worshipper of the Enlightened One. Fa-hsien has given a description of this sacred place (see Beal's translation, p. 75).

[86] 按斯曲，即普庵禪師之咒語，後人以律調擬之也，盖緣梵有二合三合四合之音，亦有其字，華書惟琴譜有之，故七音韻鑑，出自西域，應琴七絃，斯之所由出也，昔作僧梵于給園，今付徵音于百納，瞿曇氏，所爲調狂象，制毒龍者，玆可以舞鶴而馴雉矣，雖儒釋固自異源，而音韻微有冥契，聊寄一時之笑傲云耳.

[87] 普庵印肅禪師語錄

kung, pien-chih).With regard to this amazing statement I may draw attention here to the fact that Chinese scholars with Buddhist interests often were very well read in the Buddhist Canon, but seldom showed any knowledge of the real conditions depicted in those texts; further it is worth noticing that they were firmly convinced that Indian civilization was a kind of far-off and deteriorated Chinese culture.

Ch'in-pu of the Ch'ing period usually include this tune *Shih-t'an*, always adding the remark that the musical notation was drawn up by the poet and lute expert Han Chiang.[88] I have tried to find out where Han Chiang obtained this formula and its music, but without result; even for a lute player he was an extremely eccentric and cantankerous fellow, who never married but spent his days roaming up and down the vast Ch'ing Empire, always dragging along his lute and a couple of padlocked coffers with the manuscripts of his poetical works.[89] As the music of the tune *Shih-t'an* is doubtless of Indian origin, I am inclined to believe that he heard it somewhere in a Lamaist temple.

It was in this way that the other Indian tune among the lute tunes originated. In 1893 the Ch'an priest K'ung-ch'ên published a handbook for the lute, entitled *K'u-mu-ch'an-ch'in-pu*.[90] To the usual repertoire of lute tunes he adds some of his own composition, amongst others a lute version of a chant sung by Lamaist monks, called *Na-lo-fa-ch'ü*.[91] He added a colophon which says: 'In the autumn of the year 1888 I visited a friend in Peking. Wandering aimlessly about, I came to the Chan-t'an-ssû,[92] and there heard the lamas sing in chorus a Sanskrit chant, in clear and harmonious tones. I asked the people there what it was and learned that it was the old *Na-lo-fa-ch'ü*. The next day at noon I went there again, bringing my lute with me, and asked the lamas to sing the chant once more. Then I accompanied it on my lute. Having thus obtained the whole tune in notation, I

88 韓晶, style: Ching-chêng 經正, literary name Shih-kêng 石耕; he lived in the beginning of the Ch'ing period.

89 See Han Chiang's detailed biography in the *Ta-ch'ing-chi-fu-hsien-chê-chuan* 大清畿輔先哲傳, ch. 27.

90 空塵禪師; 枯木禪琴譜

91 那羅法曲. *Na-lo* 那羅 may mean the deity Nārāyaṇa 那羅延那, or it may stand for Nārada 那羅陀, or again for Naropa, 那羅巴祖師, the Indian Vajra-teacher, who in the eleventh century came to Tibet and there acquired great fame; the last alternative

seems the most probable. *Fa-ch'ü* must mean here 'Buddhist (Dharma)-hymn', although Chinese dictionaries only give it as a Taoist chant, much in vogue at the court of the T'ang emperors (cf. *Tz'ŭ-yüan* 辭源, s.v.).

92 'Temple of the Sandalwood Buddha', destroyed by the Allied Forces in 1900 as it was one of the centers of the Boxers; it stood near the present National Library. Cf. Arlington and Lewisohn, *In Search of Old Peking*, 1935, pp. 134–5. As is shown above, K'ung-ch'ên visited this temple only twelve years before the Boxer troubles broke out.

gave it this title, that it may be put on record, at the same time following the example set by Shu Hsi in writing his *Pu-wang-shih*, requesting all high-minded connoisseurs to correct it.'[93]

I think it must have been in a similar way that Han Chiang obtained his version of the tune *Shih-t'an*.

Be this as it may, these two examples will perhaps suffice to show to what extent Buddhism influenced lute music, notwithstanding the Confucianist tendency to keep the lute as purely Chinese as possible.

*   *

Summing up the remarks in Chapter I about the oldest history of the lute, and the above discussions about the various elements of *ch'in* ideology, we may state that the lute from the end of the Shang period appears as a part of the orchestra for sacred music. During the latter half of the Chou dynasty the lute appears also in the orchestra of more worldly music, and at the same time as a popular solo instrument of the cultured class. Some of its features made the lute particularly suited for retaining, more than any other instrument, certain ancient conceptions of a magical character, properly belonging not only to the lute, but to music in general. The lute being more widely used in daily life than the complete orchestra, the virtues ascribed to the orchestra and to music generally were gradually all transferred to the lute.

When the Confucianist school of thought was established, and actual musical conditions were found not to answer to the theoretical principles, the literati connected the archaic conceptions associated with the lute with their secondarily evolved dogmas of a paradisaical antiquity, and they praised the lute as the favourite musical instrument of the Holy Kings of olden times.

Especially during the Han period, which was marked by a tendency to return to the glorified images of mythical antiquity, the position of the lute as the unique symbol of all correct and accomplished music was further consolidated. Several special treatises on the lute and its significance appear: the *Ch'in-ch'ing-ying*, by Yang Hsiung, the *Ch'in-tao* by Huan T'an, and the *Ch'in-tsao* by the famous writer Ts'ai Yung.[94]

---

93 戊子秋訪友京都, 間步旃檀寺, 聽喇嘛齊歌梵唄, 音聲清和, 詢之左右, 知其為那羅法曲之遺音, 翌午携琴復往, 乞其反之而後撫絃和之, 得譜成曲, 即題斯名以紀之, 亦效束晳補亡之意, 祈諸高明正之. Shu Hsi, style Kuang-wei 廣微, third century A.D. He wrote six poems in the style of the *Book of Odes* in order to complete their number, which according to tradition was 311. These poems he called *Pu-wang* 補亡, 'supplements of what has been lost'; they are to be found in the *Wên-hsüan* 文選, ch. 19.

94 琴清英, 揚雄, 53–18 B.C.; 琴道, and above, ch. 3, note 25; 琴操, and App. II, 1.

During the subsequent Chin and Wei periods, when Buddhism spread over China, and neo-Taoism flourished, the magical virtues of the lute as being conducive to meditation, and prolonging life, were again stressed. From this period dates the celebrated *Ch'in-fu*, 'Poetical Essay on the Lute', by Hsi K'ang.[95] Here the mysterious virtues of the lute are celebrated in exquisite language, and the materials suited for constructing lutes are described. This essay may be called the best-known literary production relating to the lute, and quotations from it will be found in nearly every treatise on this subject; it may be found in the *Wên-hsüan*.[96]

Protected alike by Confucianism and Taoism, and being also in accordance with Buddhist principles, the lute was firmly established in its privileged position. During the Sui and T'ang periods, when popular music was prospering, the lute was cultivated especially by the literati. It is at this time that we hear the names of famous lute makers; for instance, some members of the Lei[97] family.

During the Sung dynasty it seems that the lute was played in broad circles of literati; the literature of this period shows hundreds of poems and essays on the lute. It was at this time that the scholar Chu Ch'ang-wên composed his *Ch'in-shih*,[98] from which I shall quote below.

When, after the Yüan dynasty, China was again united under a pure Chinese dynasty, the Mings, there appeared a conservative tendency similar to that of the Han Period: a return to ancient Chinese standards. The Ming dynasty saw the heyday of lute and lute music; the standard handbooks for the lute were published, and endeavours were made to assemble the various elements of *ch'in* ideology and arrange them more systematically. In the refined social milieus of the period, where the tea ceremony, flower arrangement, genre painting and other arts were enthusiastically practised, the lute found congenial surroundings.

As pointed out above, during the Ch'ing period the interest in the lute waned gradually, to grow again in recent times.

I may end this chapter with translating a passage from the *Ch'in-shih* of Chu Ch'ang-wên, from which one may see how the development of the lute and lute ideology appeared to a scholar of the Sung period.

'The music of the lute prospered under the Emperors Yao and

---

95 琴賦; 嵇康 style: Shu-yeh 叔夜, 223–262.

96 文選 ch. 18.

97 雷

98 琴史 cf. App. II, 2.

Shun, and during the Three Dynasties [i.e. Hsia, Shang and Chou]. But since the beginning of the period of the Warring States, the accomplished tones decayed and lewd music arose: people liked meretricious and decadent notes and were averse to harmonious and serene music. Prince Wên of Wei[99] was a good ruler of those times, but he said: "When in full ceremonial dress I must listen to the Ancient Music, I think I shall fall asleep." [If a man of such an exalted position showed so little understanding,] how much worse then the ordinary people of those times must have been. Later the cither from Ch'in, the barbarian flute, the harp, the *p'i-p'a* and other similar instruments rose in succession and spread, while the lute fell into oblivion. When the Hans came to rule, they had no time for restoring the ancient customs, but Hsien-wang[100] devoted much time to a study of the accomplished music. During the reigns of the Emperors Hsiao and Hsüan, lute players like Mr Chih, Mr Lung, Mr Chao and Mr Shih for the first time used in their books on the lute the expression *ya-ch'in*, 'accomplished lute', to distinguish it from vulgar music. Moreover, Huan T'an and K'ung Yen[101] collected tunes of the lute, and great Confucianist scholars of that time, such as Ma Yung[101] and Ts'ai Yung, especially loved this art [of playing the lute]. Therefore all the people of those times held the lute in high esteem. Thereafter Yüan Chi[102] and Hsi K'ang promoted the lute. With the beginning of the Wei and Chin periods, famous literati and high-minded scholars studied the lute in ever increasing numbers; I cannot set down here all their names which are recorded in history. Coming to the Sui and T'ang periods, there were many officials who cultivated this doctrine, but poets and artists who occupied themselves with the lute were rare. Still there were some virtuous and wise men who wrote about the lute, like Lü Wei, Li Liang-fu, Ch'ên Cho, Chao Wei-ch'ien, Li Yo, Chai Sung, Wang Ta-li, Chên K'ang-shih and others. They are all said to have written books on the lute, and their titles are registered in the bibliographical accounts of the histories of those periods, but I have not seen them, and neither have I heard whether they really understood the lute or not.'[103]

99 426–386 B.C.

100 Son of Ching-ti, r. 156–140 B.C.

101 Style: Shu-yüan 舒元, 268–320; style: Chi-ch'ang 季長, 79–166.

102 阮籍, famous poet and lute player, 210–263.

103 *Ch'in-shih*, ch. 6: 琴之爲樂，行於堯舜三代之時，至戰國時，雅音廢而淫樂興，尚鏗鏘

墜靡之聲，而厭和樂深靜之意，魏文侯當時之賢君，猶云吾端冕而聽古樂，則惟恐臥，況其下者乎，於是秦箏羌笛筌篌琵琶之類，迭興而並進，而琴亡矣，漢興猶未暇復古，由河間漢王留神雅樂，孝宣時制氏，龍氏，趙氏，師氏之家，始於琴書謂之雅琴者，以別於俗樂也，又桓譚，孔衍，皆集琴操，乃馬融，蔡邕，以大儒名當時特好斯藝，時人翕然宗尚，阮嗣宗，嵇叔夜紹而倡*

*The lute should be played amidst charming scenery, or in the library, before flowers, during a moonlit night in autumn, while burning incense—rules defining the classes of people for whom the lute may be played, and for whom not—occasional sectarian views, excluding Buddhists—correct way of carrying the lute, lute pages—*CH'IN-SHIH, *the lute chamber—*CH'IN-SHÊ, *spiritual community of the lute*

MOUNTAINS and water (*shan-shui*)[104] is the name by which in artistic treatises the Chinese designate a landscape, thereby determining its two most essential elements; in mountains and streams, vast and imposing, the eternal *tao* shall reveal itself to the contemplative observer.

Under an old pine tree, sitting on a steep bank overhanging a flowing stream, absorbed in the contemplation of far mountain tops severed from the earth by floating mists, such is the scenery with which Chinese painters love to surround the lute player.

When, borne on the unworldly and serene tones of the lute, the mind of the player is purified and elevated to mystic heights, his soul may commune with the essence of the rugged rocks and vast stretches of water confronting him, and so he may experience a complete reunion with *tao*. This atmosphere of wide, open nature should always accompany the lute player; 'though his body be in a gallery or in a hall, his mind should dwell with forests and streams.'[105]

It was not only aesthetical considerations, however, that caused this custom of preferably representing the lute player as confronted with an impressive mountain landscape. Doubtless here the function of the lute as an instrument to strengthen the vital essence of the player also was an important factor. Further, in painting, mysticism and magic

---

*之，自魏及晉，名儒高士，學者益多，而史册之間，豈遑徧述，迨乎隨唐，搢紳多以是道爲務，而清言雅伎，罕嘗攻之，間有賢智有所論著，如呂渭，李良輔，陳拙，趙惟謙，李約，齊嵩，王大力，陳康士之徒，皆云有書，其名載於藝文

志，然余所未覩，亦不聞其果精於琴與否.

104 山水

105 *Ch'in-sê-ho-pu, fan-li*, p. 8: 雖身列廊廟必意在林泉.

lie closely together. The contemplation of the beauty of streams and mountains may impart to the observer the vital forces that are inherent in nature, and thereby prolong his earthly life. 'The people of old say that landscape painters often live to an old age, because they feed upon mist and clouds. The entire scenery which they have before their eyes is one spring of life.'[106] This statement about the landscape painter may also be applied to the lute player, for the conception of the magical salutary influence of contemplating mountains and streams fits in exactly with some of the more materialistic aspects of *ch'in* ideology.[107]

The same double interpretation may be attached to the direct surroundings of the lute player when performing on the lute in the open: one should be near an old pine tree, admiring its gnarled, antique appearance. In the shade of the pines some cranes should be stalking, and the lute player should admire their graceful movements, modeling on them his finger technique. Since ancient times both pine tree and crane have been credited with possessing a special amount of vital essence, and therefore both are symbols of longevity.[108]

After some beautiful spot in the open, the abode of the scholar is the most suitable place for playing the lute. The ideal dwelling of the scholar should breathe an atmosphere of secludedness; it is surrounded by a garden, fenced off by pine trees or bamboos; narrow footpaths should meander among miniature rocks of interesting shapes and lotus ponds, leading to a small pavilion of rustic appearance, where the scholar may compose poetry or read his books. 'Where Ni Tsan dwelt there was the Ching-pi pavilion, breathing an atmosphere of profundity and remoteness from earthly things. There he had assembled several thousand books, all of which he had corrected with his own hand. On all sides there were arranged antique

---

106 The Ch'ing painter Wang Yü 王昱, in his *Tung-chuang-lun-hua* 東莊論畫, 5th paragraph: 昔人謂山水家多壽, 蓋煙雲供養, 眼前無非生機.

107 I may remark in passing that in other respects also we find the same notions connected with both painting and lute playing. In the same passage of the authoritative treatise on painting quoted above, it is said: 'Studying painting is a means for nurturing one's nature and emotional life —— it may elevate one to serenity' 學畫所以養性情 . . . . 迎靜氣.

Like the lute player when about to touch the strings of the lute, the painter too first has to make his mind pure and detached from all earthly desires: 'Before the painter takes up his brush, his mind must be aloof and his thoughts elated; when he starts painting, his spirit must be serene and his soul frozen' 未動筆前, 湏興高意遠, 已動筆後, 要氣靜神凝. (par. 8) This 'frozen' mental condition is a typical Taoist notion; see the passage of Lieh-tzu, quoted above on page 45. Finally it is said: 'Although painting is but one of the arts, it still is a manifestation of Tao' 畫雖一藝, 其中有道. (para. 10)

108 Below, in ch. VI, I shall discuss these associations in more detail.

sacrificial vessels and famous lutes, and the abode was surrounded by pine trees, cinnamon trees, orchids, bamboos, etc. It was fenced off by a high paling of poles and bamboo, suggesting aloofness and refined delicacy. Every time the rain had stopped and the wind had abated, Ni Tsan used to take his staff and wander about, just going where his steps led him. When his eye met with something which particularly struck him, he played his lute, thus finding aesthetic satisfaction. Those who saw him then knew that he was a man who dwelt outside this world.'[109]

Cultivating and arranging flowers, a favourite occupation of the retired scholar, also harmonizes with the lute player. 'One should play the lute for the cinnamon of the mountains, prune blossoms of the waterside, jasmine, gardenia, orchids from Fu-chien, mimosa, magnolia and similar flowers. Those with a pure fragrance but without loud colours are the best.'[110]

A moonlit night is dear to the lute player: 'In spring and autumn, when the weather is limpid and harmonious, even during the night people are often awake. Then the ten thousand sounds of emptiness are all silent, and moonlight fills the sky. When one lays the lute on his knees, and plays some small tunes, this also shall elate the feelings.'[111]

The moonlight makes the thirteen studs glitter, and so guides the hands of the player. Therefore these studs are often called *chin-hsing*, brilliant stars. 'But one should play after the first watch [after nine o'clock in the evening], and before the third watch [before 1 o'clock]; for before nine the noise of daily life has not yet become quiet, and after 1 o'clock one is too tired and sleepy.'[112]

Playing the lute on the knees is a favourite literary theme; it is more poetical to represent the musician sitting within the circle of his friends, or in a shaded valley, with the lute on his lap, than to have him seated behind the lute table. Still this position is not very suitable for executing the complicated finger technique. As a Ming scholar observes: 'When people play the lute on their knees, they can only

---

109 Ni Tsan 倪瓚, style: Yün-lin, 1301–1374, famous painter and poet. This passage is taken from the *Ho-shih-yü-lin* 何氏語林, compiled by Ho Liang-chün 何良俊, sixteenth century. 倪雲林所居, 有清閟閣, 幽迥絕塵, 中有書數千卷. 皆手自校, 古鼎彝名琴陳列左右, 松桂蘭竹之屬敷舒繚繞, 其外則高木修篁蔚然深秀, 每雨止風收, 携杖履自隨逍遙容與, 遇會心處, 鼓琴自娛, 望之者識其爲世外人也.

110 *K'ao-p'an-yü-shih* (App. II, 3): 對花,

宜共岩桂, 江梅, 茉莉, 簷葡, 建蘭, 夜合, 玉蘭等花, 清香而色不艷者爲雅. Orchids from Fu-chien are praised for their pale yellow and green colors.

111 *Ibid.*: 對月, 春秋二候, 天氣澄和, 人亦中夜多醒, 萬籟咸寂, 月色當空, 橫琴膝上, 時作小調, 亦可暢懷.

112 *Ch'ing-lien-fang-ch'in-ya* (App. II, 6) ch. III. 但湏在一更後, 三更前, 蓋初更人聲未寂, 三更則人倦欲眠矣.

perform smaller tunes, such as they know very well. Otherwise it is impossible.'[113] From my own experience I would add that the only passages which can be executed correctly in this position are some preludes and codas, these being as a rule in the so-called 'floating sounds', that is to say the left hand does not press down the strings, but only touches them lightly, so as to produce harmonics.

When not rambling through the mountains to observe wild streams and gushing waterfalls, the scholar may still find by the quiet waterside in his own garden a congenial atmosphere for playing the lute. 'When a breeze floats through the pines, or when there is the rippling sound of a rivulet, then especially one should play the lute. For all these three things have natural tones, therefore they are in perfect harmony with each other. Or again by the pond near the library window where one smells the fragrance of the water lilies, or in the wood by the waterside, where the redolent waves wash the islets; when the light breeze is refreshing, and the swimming fish come to the surface to listen: what joy can exceed this?'[114]

As we saw in the foregoing chapter, when the lute is played incense must be burned. The handbooks for the lute recommend incense that gives a fine, crinkling smoke. Its subtle fragrance contributes to the exalted mood necessary for playing and appreciating lute music. For, 'The use of incense gives manifold benefits. When retired scholars, detached from the world, are sitting together discussing *tao* and its application, they burn incense to purify their hearts and rejoice their spirits. At the dead of night, when the morning moon is in the sky, artistic and sad poetical folk burn incense, and their hearts are elated and they whistle carelessly. By the bright window copying old famous scrolls, or leisurely humming, flywhisk in hand, or when reading at night under the lamp, incense is burned to drive away the demon of sleepiness. Therefore incense may be called the "Old Companion of the Moon."'[115]

The disposition of the lute player must be very much like that of a priest before sacrificing: he should be purified physically and mentally, freed from all earthly thoughts, and ready for communication with the deepest mysteries of life.

To attain to this, beside the more general rules to be found scat-

---

113 *Tsun-shêng-pa-chien* (App. II, 4): 人膝上鼓琴，惟純熟小操，則可，否，亦不能.

114 *K'ao-p'an-yü-shih* (App. II, 3)：臨水. 鼓琴偏宜於松風，澗響之間，三者皆自然之聲，正合類聚，或對軒窗池沼，荷香撲人，或水邊林

下，清漪芳沚，微風洒然，游魚出聽,此樂何極.

115 *Ibid.*：香之爲用，其利最溥，物外高隱坐語道焚之，可以清心悅神，四更殘月與味蕭騷焚之，可以暢懷舒嘯，晴窗榻帖，揮塵閒吟，籌燈夜讀，焚以遠辟睡魔，謂古伴月.

tered in the texts quoted in the foregoing chapter, the handbooks of the lute also prescribe a certain discipline. The rules of this discipline are summed up in various numerical categories. For instance, a handbook of the Ming period gives fourteen rules, decreeing when the lute may be played.

1 Meeting someone who understands music.
2 Meeting a suitable person.
3 For a Taoist recluse.
4 In a high hall.
5 Having ascended a storied pavilion.
6 In a Taoist cloister.
7 Sitting on a stone.
8 Having climbed a mountain.
9 Resting in a valley.
10 Roaming along the waterside.
11 In a boat.
12 Resting in the shadow of a forest.
13 When the two essences of nature are bright and clear.
14 In a cool breeze and when there is a bright moon.[116]

In nearly all other handbooks of the lute dating from the Ming and Ch'ing dynasties, these rules are given in about the same form. They are not very stringent, since by inserting the second rule the decision of for whom to play is practically left to the discretion of each individual performer. It should be noted that half of the items refer to playing the lute in the open air, and that two items especially mention Taoism.

The corresponding set of rules as to when the lute may not be played is much more precise and severe, and therefore the least observed. The same source gives these rules as follows:

1 When there is wind and thunder, and in rainy weather.
2 When there is a sun or moon eclipse.
3 In a court room.
4 In a market or shop.
5 For a barbarian.
6 For a vulgar person.
7 For a merchant.
8 For a courtesan.

---

116 Yang Piao-chêng his in handbook of the lute (App. II, 13); 琴有十四宜彈. 遇知音, 逢可人, 對道士, 處高堂, 升樓閣, 在宮觀, 坐 石上, 登山埠, 憩空谷, 遊水湄, 居舟中, 息林 下, 值二氣清朗, 當清風明月.

9 After inebriation.

10 After having had sexual intercourse.

11 In dishevelled and strange clothes.

12 When flushed and covered with perspiration.

13 Not having washed one's hands and rinsed one's mouth.

14 In loud and noisy surroundings.[117]

For rule 3 other books give: 'Near a prison',[118] which seems more likely. With regard to rule 5, which forbids the playing of the lute for barbarians, the *ch'in-pu* urge especially strict observance of this. Another handbook of the Ming period explains this rule as follows: 'Outside China there are people who jabber barbarian tongues. As the sounds of their language are not correct, how can they ever harmonize with the correct words of the Holy Sages? Therefore one should not play the lute for them. The lute is fundamentally an instrument by the music of which the Sages and Superior Men of China nurture their nature and cultivate their persons. Such a thing is unknown in barbarian countries, therefore it is not allowed.'[119]

Rule 7, forbidding playing for a merchant, is amplified as follows: 'The lute is an instrument whereby the Holy Sages cultivate their persons and nurture their nature; [this includes] being contented in poverty, knowing moderation, and restricting luxury. But merchants have sharp appetites and strong desires. Therefore a tradesman's disposition runs counter to the Way of the Holy Man.'[120] This point is, however, subject to controversy. The merchant class is defended in these words: 'Bartering and trading are fundamentally not low and despicable things. The people of old often knew how to demonstrate holy truths by means of low things. Tzû-kung[121] accumulated great wealth; Fan Li[121] three times divided his wealth after having assembled it. When among the greatest of merchants are men like Tzû-kung and Fan Li, why then should they not be allowed to play the lute? It is far better to look only at the character.'[122]

---

117 琴有十四不宜彈. 風雷陰雨, 日月交蝕, 在法司中, 在市塵, 對夷狄, 對俗子, 對商賈, 對娼妓, 酒醉後, 夜事後, 毀形異服, 腋臊臭嗅, 不盥手漱口, 鼓動喧嚷.
118 Yang Lun's *T'ai-ku-i-yin* (App. II, 14): 近囹圄.
119 *Ch'in-ching* (App. II, 5) ch. 8: 非中土有鄉譚番語者, 以其語音不正, 安能合聖人之正音, 故不宜也, 琴本中國賢人君子養性修身之樂, 非蠻貊之邦所有也, 故不宜.
120 *Ibid*. 琴本聖人修身養性, 甘貧知止戒盈之樂, 商賈乃利欲慳貪, 市井之人反於聖人之道.

121 The style of Tuan-mu Tzû 端木賜, famous disciple of Confucius who became a high official. Fan Li was a man from the Ch'un-ch'iu period, who three times accumulated great wealth and three times gave it away, as he preferred a life in retirement; cf. *Shih-chi* 史記, ch. 129, *Han-shu* 漢書 ch. 91.
122 *Ch'in-ching*, ch. 8: 貿遷原非鄙賤事, 古人每以鄙賤事而發神奇, 子貢貨殖, 范蠡三遷致富商賈之魁者以賜與蠡, 撫琴豈有外之者哉, 顧品格何如耶.

Rules 8 and 9 were taken least seriously. It is true that *courtesan* is a very elastic term, but considered in the light of the general principles there can be no doubt that it was meant to be interpreted very strictly. In practice, however, we find that this rule is made to apply only to the lowest kind of courtesan. Singing girls who brighten literary gatherings on old paintings are seen playing the lute, and novels cite lute playing as one of the accomplishments of the perfect courtesan. Other handbooks read for 8: 娼優, or 娼妓優伶, meaning: 'courtesans and actors'. As I have pointed out already, on p. 44 above, this exclusion of the actors was meant as a protest against the great numbers of actors from foreign countries who found employment at the Court.

Rule 9 also involved a delicate question, many of the most famous scholars being great wine-bibbers. The Ming scholar T'u Lung has found a mild and convenient explanation of this rule. He says: 'The disposition of people who play the lute is refined, they ought only to sip tea. Occasionally, however, they may use wine to stimulate their feelings, but only just sufficient to make them feel slightly exhilarated and no more. If one tries to play the lute when one is really dead drunk, then this is a great shame that cannot be tolerated.'[123]

The attitude which the *ch'in-pu* take regarding Buddhism is interesting. As I mentioned above, the lute was very popular with Buddhist monks, and several are cited in the lists of famous lute performers. Still, occasionally there appear in Taoist quarters sectarian views, and some handbooks of the early Ming period include an item 'Buddhist priests' in the list of people to whom it was not allowed to play or to teach the lute.[124] Naturally this rule met with much opposition, and as an extreme reaction some Buddhists tried to prove that the lute originated in India, since it is mentioned in the Buddhist sutras![125] Generally, however, lute amateurs were of too

---

123 *K'ao-p'an-yü-shih* (App. II, 3): 飲酒. 彈琴之人風致清楚, 但宜啜茗, 間或用酒發興, 不過微有釀意而已, 若堆體酩羅葷膻蕩情狂, 飲致成醉者之狀, 以事琴此大醜最宜戒也.

124 E.g., *Ch'in-ching:* 沙門子不宜鼓琴.

125 The passage is taken from the 31st paragraph of the *Ssǔ-shih-êrh-chang-ching* (四十二章經, cf. *Taishō-issaikyō* 大正一切經 No. 784). The original obviously means some Indian stringed instrument, in Chinese translations of Buddhist texts always indicated by transcriptions of Sanskrit words. For more details I may refer to the useful essay by K. Hayashi: 'On Musical Terms in Chinese Buddhist Scriptures', in: *Tōyō ongaku kenkyū,*

I, 1937 東洋音樂研究, 林謙三, 佛典に現れた樂器, 音樂, 舞踊.

That in the present case *ch'in* is used, is to be explained by the fact that this particular sutra was translated at a very early date (first century A.D.), when the correct renderings of Sanskrit technical terms had not yet been determined. The passage runs: 'Buddha asked a monk: "How do you occupy yourself when at home?" The monk answered: "I love to play the lute." Then Buddha asked: "What happens when the strings are strung too loose?"—"They give no sound."— "What happens when the strings are strung too tight?"—"Then they snap."—"What*

eclectic a disposition to be much impressed by either the extreme Taoist or Buddhist view, and they contented themselves with placidly quoting the two views together. A couple of extreme cases may here be cited: 'There was a monk called Chüeh (Enlightenment), who wished to study the lute under Master Pai-ho (White Crane). Master White Crane did not like the idea, and did not teach him. The monk was sad. Master White Crane said: "This is strange indeed! The study of a certain Śākyamuni originated from the doctrines of barbarians in western countries. But the lute represents the *tao* of the Holy Men of the Middle Kingdom, so it is not suitable for you. And he persisted in not teaching him." '[126]

'Master Huang-fu chose as literary name Tung-hsü-tzû (the Master of the Emptiness of the Cave). He explained the doctrines of Lao-tzû and Chuang-tzû by teaching lute Music, and his disciples were many. Among them there were also Buddhist monks. The Master said: How can bald pates and black robes fold in their arms the instrument of the Holy Men? And pointing with his flywhisk he told them to go away.'[127]

'To fold in the arms'[128] is the traditional term used for carrying the lute. Literature and art love to represent the ideal scholar roaming through the mountains or along the sides of streams, taking his lute with him, to play an appropriate melody when moved by a beautiful sight. Old paintings mostly show him accompanied by a boy servant, who carries the lute in its brocade cover in his arms. Also at home this boy was entrusted with the care for his master's lutes, and therefore such a boy is called *ch'in-tung*,[129] 'lute page'.

The handbooks give minute instructions as to how the lute is correctly carried. A Ming handbook[130] distinguishes two methods, the old and the new. Fig. 6, left, shows the old way: the ancients carried their lute with the upper board turned outwards and with the head in front and the tail, a little lower, behind. During the Ming dynasty

---

*happens when the strings are strung not too loose and not too tight?"—"Then all sounds come forth harmoniously."—Then the Buddha said: "The study of Truth is the same: if the heart is tuned correctly, one may obtain the Truth" ' 佛問一僧, 汝處家爲何業, 對曰愛彈琴, 佛問緩絃如何, 曰不鳴矣, 絃急如何, 曰聲絕矣, 緩急得中如何, 曰諸音普矣, 佛曰學道亦然, 心須調適, 道可得矣. This text, taken from the *Ch'in-ching*, differs slightly from that given in the Buddhist Canon.

126 *Ch'in-ching* (App. II, 5): 有僧名覺者,

學琴於道人白鶴子之門, 鶴子惡而不受, 僧不悅, 鶴子曰怪哉, 釋氏之學, 出於西方, 夷狄之教, 琴乃中國聖人之道, 非爾所宜也, 竟不傳.

127 *Ibid.*: 皇甫先生號洞虛子, 講老莊之學, 以傳琴鳴, 弟子甚眾, 而沙門雜然, 先生曰豈有髡髮緇衣而抱聖人之器乎, 悉麾去之.

128 抱

129 琴童

130 *Yang-ch'un-t'ang-ch'in-pu* 陽春堂琴譜, by the same authors who composed the *Ch'in-ching*.

people followed the new way (fig. 6, right) turning the bottom board outwards, a position which was said to ensure a firm hold.

Next to Buddhism, there is another question connected with the discipline of the lute player which has given rise to some controversy in the *ch'in-pu*, viz. whether one is allowed to accompany one's lute play with singing or not.

♯6: Carrying the lute, from the *Yang-ch'un-t'ang-ch'in-pu*.

In the handbooks of the lute this question is discussed as *chan-wên*[131] (to cut out the words), *wên* standing here for both the text of the tunes and for prefaces and colophons added to them.

The Ming prince Tsai-yü says, in his standard work on music, *Yüeh-lü-ch'üan-shu*,[132] that music on stringed instruments in general is impossible without the accompaniment by the human voice. In the chapter *Tsao-man-ku-yüeh-pu* he devotes a special section to this question, entitled: 'Discussing how the ancients did not sing without accompanying the words on the strings, nor played a stringed instrument without singing to it.'[133] This he calls a 'fixed custom'[134] of the ancients; singing without accompaniment, or playing stringed instruments without singing he calls an 'exception'.[135] Then he ob-

---

131 刪文
132 朱載堉, 樂律全書
133 操縵古樂譜；論古人非弦不歌,非歌不弦

134 *chang-shih* 常事
135 變

serves: 'People today when reciting poetry cannot accompany these songs on the lute; that is because the tradition of the lute is lost.'[136]

Some among the composers of *ch'in-pu* are of the same opinion as Tsai-yü: in their notation of the tunes, they print the *chien-tzŭ*[137] and the corresponding words of the tune in parallel vertical columns. This method is followed by, e.g., Yang Piao-chêng.[138] Others add the text of the tune separately, before or after the notation. On the other hand there were also many lute players who maintained that to sing when playing the lute did not conform to the sacred character of this music.

The most sensible attitude seems to be that taken by Kuo Yü-chai in his *Tê-yin-t'ang-ch'in-pu*.[139] In his prefatory remarks he says: 'The lute stands for the original harmony of what is truly from Heaven in man; its tones rise from the serenity of the soul. Therefore I do not like to restrict this music with words. For then the tones become confused, and the melody and rhythm are impeded. Therefore as a rule I have kept to the music, and left out the words. Still there are also cases where, if the words are left out, it is impossible to get the tones right. Therefore, where the text should be cut out, I cut it out, and where it should not be left out, I preserved it to show the meaning of the melody to the player.'[140]

In this *ch'in-pu* all old melodies which have not from ancient times been connected with a special poem or essay, are given in notation only, whilst such as have always been associated with a definite text (as, e.g., some odes in the *Book of Odes*), are given together with the words. This system seems very commendable. When playing through the various tunes of the lute repertoire, one finds that they show a considerable difference in style: the music of some is evidently nothing but the accompaniment of a song, whilst others could hardly be accompanied by the human voice, and are apparently meant as instrumental music only. Two good examples may be found in the *Kao-shan-liu-shui* and *Lu-ming*.[141] The former is a highly expressive composition, impossible to accompany with the voice; the other, on the contrary, is simple and more melodical, and is doubtless a reproduction of one of the tunes to which this ancient ode was sung. In other cases it is more difficult to decide to which category a given tune

---

136 今人歌詩與琴不能相入，蓋失其傳耳.
137 減字
138 Appendix II, 13.
139 郭裕齋，德音堂琴譜, published in 1691.
140 琴乃天眞元韻，音出自然，不喜以文拘

之，拘之則音雜，滯其高下抑揚，故取音而棄文，然亦有舍文而不能成音者，故可刪者刪之，不可刪者存以備觀焉.
141 高山流水；鹿鳴

belongs: the decision must be left to the taste of each individual player.

In view of the present condition of lute music I hardly think it advisable to use the lute for the accompaniment of songs, since its music, for practical reasons, is not suited for this. Already during the Sung dynasty the finger technique had become so complicated that the lute could not be used for accompaniment. 'The lute players of the present age do not sing while playing, but try to obtain beauty by complicated sounds.'142

#7: Playing the lute in ideal surroundings. A painting by the famous Ming artist Shên Chou (沈周 1427–1509).

Often in the house of a lute amateur a special room or bower is set apart for playing; such a place is called *ch'in-shih*143 (lute chamber). A Ming treatise144 sets out the following conditions for such an abode: 'It should truly reproduce the tones, and not sound hollow. The best is a room in a storied building; there the boards of the ceiling ensure that the tones are not dispersed, and the empty space beneath makes the tones ring through. If one chooses a high hall or a spacious chamber, then the tones are dispersed and thin. And when one plays in a narrow room or in a small house the tones cannot ring

142 近世琴家所謂操弄者，皆無歌辭，而繁聲以爲美; *Ch'in-shih*, in App. II, 2.
143 琴室
144 *K'ao-p'an-yü-shih* (App. II, 3): 琴室. 宜實，不宜虛，最宜重樓之下，蓋上有樓板則聲不散，其下空曠則聲透徹，若高堂大厦，則聲散漫，斗室小軒，則聲小達，如平屋中，則於地下埋一大缸，缸中縣一銅鐘，上用板鋪，亦可，幽人逸士或於喬松修竹，岩洞石室，清曠之處，地清境寂，更有泉石之勝，則琴聲愈清，與廣寒月殿何異哉.

through. If the building consists of only one floor, a big jar should be buried underneath. In this jar a bronze bell should be suspended, and then the jar should be covered by boards. Wise men living in retirement also take for their lute chamber tall pines and high bamboos, or a cavern in the rocks; in such a pure and airy abode in the serenity of nature and quiet surroundings, and especially when there is the impressive sight of a rivulet babbling over stones, the tones of the lute shall gain in clearness. Is not such a place like the Moon Palace of Wide Coolness?'[145] It seems difficult to justify the suggestion for burying a jar with a bell by the laws of acoustics, but it must have appealed to the imagination of the lovers of lute music. Other Ming authors[146] criticize this statement, which seems to be based on a story told about the Han poet Ssû-ma Hsiang-ju:[146] he used to play the lute on a special terrace called *ch'in-t'ai*. When later the state Wei attacked Shu, and soldiers camped on that place and dug trenches, they found more than twenty big jars, which had served to make the music resound.[147]

Finally we have to consider in greater detail the tendency to keep the study of the lute reserved to a small circle of the elect.

Above I quoted some rules which restrict the number of persons to whom the lute may be taught. With regard to this group of qualified persons the expression *ch'in-shê*[148] is often met with in the literature on the lute. This literally means: 'lute association'. When the term is used for a group of amateurs of the lute who happen to live in the same district, and who are in regular contact with each other, this translation suffices. But generally the word *shê* in this expression has a much wider meaning; as this special significance is not indicated in dictionaries, I will treat it here in some detail.

Especially since the latter half of the Ming dynasty, in circles of scholars of elegant interests and cultivated taste who were connoisseurs of raising chrysanthemums, of flower arrangement, of appreciating incense, of nursing orchids, etc., there came into existence a fixed tradition, canonizing the right methods for pursuing

---

[145] Refers to a story told in the *Lung-ch'êng-lu* 龍城錄 (ascribed to the T'ang poet Liu Tsung-yüan 柳宗元, 773–819): 'Once the Emperor Ming-huang together with one of his Taoist masters made a journey to the moon on a full-moon night, where he found a palace called "Abode of Wide Coolness and Pure Emptiness."' 廣寒清盧之府 This magic journey is the subject of a well-known lute melody. See below, pp. 89 ff.

[146] *Ch'ing-lien-fang-ch'in-ya* (cf. Appendix II, 6), ch. 3: 前輩理琴處, 或埋甕于地下, 此說恐妄傳 (2nd century A.D.):

[147] *Ch'ien-ch'üeh-chü-lei-shu*. 潛確居類書 (pub. 1630), ch. 79: 司馬相如好鼓琴, 有琴臺在浣溪正路, 金花寺北, 魏伐蜀, 于此下營, 掘塹得大甕二十餘口, 蓋以響琴也

[148] 琴社

these hobbies, and especially the right mental attitude to be adopted towards them. Some scholars noted down these traditions, which were called *yo* 約 (covenants, or rules). So the well-known essayist Chang Ch'ao wrote a *Wan-yüeh-yo*[149] (Rules for Enjoying the Moon), Chiang Chih-lan wrote a *Wên-fang-yo* (Covenant of the Library).[150] A *Ch'in-yo* (Covenant for the Lute) will be found below.[151] Such treatises on various subjects dear to the literatus bear a very personal character, and are mostly written in a chatty vein, contrary to those called *pu or shih*, which strive to be more scientific.

Now the term *shê* may be considered as being an expansion of *yo*; *shê* denotes the total of all people who know and faithfully observe the rules fixed by tradition for the pursuance of some elegant hobby. It does not imply any social or local unity; anyone who raises chrysanthemums in the correct way is a member of the *Chü-shê*[152] (Spiritual Association of Lovers of the Chrysanthemum), whether he lives in Peking or in Canton, or anywhere else. In such cases *shê* is perhaps best translated as 'Spiritual Community'. We find, e.g., a booklet entitled: *Chü-shê-yo*[153] (Covenant of the Spiritual Community of the Chrysanthemum Lovers) and another called *Ku-huan-shê-yo* (Covenant of the Spiritual Community of the Booklovers).[154] Books of this class form a special branch in Chinese literature, important because, next to the novels, they are sources of valuable data on the private life of the literary class.

As the lute was so highly valued by the literati, it goes without saying that in the handbooks for the lute the *ch'in-shê* is repeatedly referred to. In the *Ch'in-ching* the rules indicating to whom and where the lute may be played are prefaced by a short notice, entitled *ch'in-shê*, saying: 'In a modest dwelling[155] there should be a stand for laying the lute on, and a case for storing it away. There should be a flywhisk, a sonorous stone, brushes and ink to keep the lute company

---

149 張潮, style: Shan-lai 山來, 17th cent.; 玩月約

150 江之蘭, style: Shê-chêng 舍徵; 文房約. This and the *Wan-yüeh-yo* are to be found in the *T'an-chi-ts'ung-shu* 檀几叢書, a collection of the works of various minor authors of the Ch'ing period, published in 1695 by Wang Cho 王晫. All the books reprinted in it are important for the study of the domestic life and leisurely pastimes of the literati.

151 琴約. See pp. 82 ff.

152 菊社

153 菊社約

154 古歡社約. The *Chü-shê-yo* was written by Ti I 狄億, the *Ku-huan-shê-yo* by Ting Hsiung-fei 丁雄飛; both books are to be found in the *T'an-chi-ts'ung-shu*, mentioned above. The latter contains some very sane suggestions for bibliophiles: If a book is borrowed it may not be kept longer than a fortnight; one should not entrust a borrowed book to someone else to return it. 借書不得踰半月, 還書不得托人轉到.

155 *huan-tu*; cf. *Book of Rites, Li-chi*, Ch. XXXVIII, 10.

and there should be lustrous flowers and cranes to be its friends. All these things belong to the domain[156] of the lute. Those who are not in this class do not belong to the Spiritual Community of the lute.'[157]

The same book on the next page describes which people are qualified for being considered as members of the *ch'in-shê*; in conclusion I translate this passage.

'All who study the lute must be accomplished scholars, and they must be good at reciting poetry.

Their appearance should be pure and detached, suggesting antique originality; they may not be coarse and vulgar.

Their minds should be benign and tender, they should be virtuous and righteous, able to be content even in poverty, and always firmly clinging to their principles.

Their words should be true and reliable, they should not strive after superficial beauty or after obtaining a thin varnish of culture.'[158]

§4 SELECTED TEXTS

THE five texts relating to *ch'in* ideology translated below are purposely taken from sources that in both date and quality differ widely.

The first is the section on the lute taken from the chapter on music of the *Fêng-su-t'ung-i*,[159] a miscellaneous collection of encyclopedic character, compiled by Ying Shao.[160] This text furnishes us with a good example of the pure Confucianist view.

The second text is a small treatise by a well-known Confucianist scholar of the Yüan dynasty, Wu Ch'ên,[161] author of many learned books on the Classics. These two texts are both written in a polished literary style, as befits the high scholarly standing of their authors.

Their style contrasts sharply with that of the clumsily written third text, one of the introductory chapters of a handbook for the

---

156 *t'ung-chi* 通籍, lit. a signboard hanging near the gate of the Palace, on which were written the name and full description of those people who were allowed to go in and out freely; *i-yang* 嶧陽, lit. 'on the southern slope of I Mountain', the place of origin of the lute—a mythical emperor was said to have found there the right sort of wood for making the first lute.

157 琴社. 環堵蕭疊以受桐, 猊磐翰墨以侶

桐, 瓊葩偓禽桐之侑也, 江風山月桐之供也, 此皆通籍于嶧陽者也, 非此族也不在社黨.

158 凡學琴必須要有文章能吟咏者, 貌必要有清奇古怪不粗俗者, 心必要有仁慈德義能, 甘貧守志者, 言必要有誠信無浮華薄飾者.

159 風俗通義, chapter VI.

160 應劭, style: Chung-yüan 仲遠, second century A.D.

161 吳澄, style: Yu-ch'ing 幼清, 1249–1331.

lute dating from the Ming dynasty.[162] This book was compiled by Yang Piao-chêng, a professional lute expert of very low scholarly standing; evidently he has difficulty in expressing his thoughts freely in the literary medium, and often relapses into colloquial expressions. Still, as he was a clever musician, who knew how to recast the famous old tunes in a simpler but yet charming form (such as might be executed even by mediocre lute players), and because of the extraordinarily great number of copies in which his book was printed, it was one of the most popular handbooks of the Ming period. Even now copies can be easily purchased in Chinese and Japanese bookshops.

The chapter that I have chosen here for translation is interesting because it shows the quaint admixture of heterogeneous elements that *ch'in* ideology had come to be.

The same general remarks hold good for the fourth text, one of the introductory chapters of the *Wu-chih-chai-ch'in-pu*, a handbook which may be called the most popular guide for lute players during the Ch'ing dynasty. The editor of this book was also a mediocre scholar, but an excellent musician. The versions of the tunes given here are very attractive, and rich in subtle nuances. Moreover there have been added to the notation special marks, indicating the rhythm. It is still the handbook most widely used by lute players today, and may be obtained at very little cost in China and Japan.

The book of Yang Piao-chêng was an individual production; this handbook, however, is a typical example of a *ch'in-pu* that was composed by a group of students gathered round a famous master.[163] The editor was not a great stylist: he patched together several passages from other sources without being able to produce smoothly running prose. In his preface, printed in his own handwriting, he tries to cover the meagre contents by using all kinds of strange and antiquated characters, instead of the ordinary forms, a process which, when indulged in too much, is condemned as vulgar by Chinese literati.

The fifth text is *Covenant for Transmitting the Lute*, a treatise of the type discussed above, page 69. The author is Ch'êng Yün-chi, who is also the compiler of a *ch'in* handbook, the *Ch'êng-i-t'ang-ch'in-pu*.[164,165]

---

162 For characters and further particulars, see App. II, 13 and 15.

163 For more details see App. II, 15.

164 程允基, style: Yü-shan 寓山, 18th century; 誠一堂琴譜, preface dated 1705.

165 For other texts from various sources which illustrate the principles of *ch'in* ideology, the reader is referred to Chapter VI, § 4: 'Some Famous Stories and Much-quoted Passages Relating to the Lute'.

THE LUTE

BY YING SHAO, SECOND CENTURY A. D.

REVERENTLY I read in the '*Shih-pên* :[166] 'Shên-nung made the lute.' In the *Book of History* : 'Shun played the five-stringed lute, and sang the song "Southern Wind", and the Realm was regulated.' In the *Book of Odes* it is said : 'I have elegant guests, the *sê* is played, the lute is played.'

The accomplished lute includes all music, it embraces all of the eight sorts of sounds.[167] Of those things the Superior Man always has around him, he loves the lute best, and he does not suffer it to be separated from him.

The lute need not necessarily be displayed in the Ancestral Hall or during the clan festivals, it is not like bells and drums that must needs be suspended on carved standards. Though [the lute be played] in a poor dwelling or a desolate street, deep in the mountains or in a profound valley, it will lose nothing [of its true meaning].

The lute is considered to hold the mean between great and small music, and its tones are harmonious. Its heavy sounds are not boisterous so as to be confusing, its light sounds are not too weak so as to be inaudible. It is suited for harmonizing the human mind, and may move man to the improvement of his heart. Therefore, the word 'lute' means 'restraining', and the word 'accomplished' means 'rectifying', indicating that the Superior Man keeps to the right by restraining himself. By right and accomplished sounds, right thoughts are instigated, therefore the good heart is victorious, and falsehood and wickedness are repressed. Therefore the Holy Sages and Superior Men of ancient times carefully watched over their emotions ; and when falsehood arose they restrained it ; when they met with something good they made it their own. When they had leisure they could act freely because they had perfected their thoughts. When there was something that oppressed them, when their Way was obstructed, so that they could not practise it, or again when they could not execute their teachings when serving the State, then [all these things] they expressed in the lute, in order to give vent to their thoughts, and proclaim them to posterity. The songs they composed when they

---

166 A treatise by Liu Hsiang (劉向, 77–6 B.C.), lost since early times.
167 That is, the sounds of the instruments made of stone, metal, silk, bamboo, wood, skin, gourd, and clay.

were able to practise their Way they called hymns, by this term expressing the beauty and elevatedness of the Way they practised. They did not grant themselves one moment rest, they were neither overbearing nor effusive, they loved rites, but they did not try to exalt their own thoughts. The songs they composed when oppressed and melancholic they called elegies, by this name indicating that even when meeting with disasters or falling into danger, when being oppressed and reduced to necessity, although steeped in sorrow and unable to reach their aims, they still kept to the rites and right-eousness, without fear and without misgivings, rejoicing in the Way and not loosing their consistency.

When Po Tzû-ya[168] played the lute, Chung Tzû-ch'i listened. When Tzû-ya in his thoughts dwelt on high mountains, Tzû-ch'i said: 'How excellent! Impressing like the T'ai-shan!' When a moment later Tzû-ya in his thoughts dwelt by flowing streams, Tzû-ch'i again said: 'How excellent! Broad and flowing like rivers and streams!' When Tzû-ch'i died, Po [Tzû]-ya broke his lute and tore the strings, and all his life did not play any more, since he now deemed the world not enough to play for.

At present the length of the lute is four *ch'ih* five *ts'un* [*c.* 4½ feet, ed.], thus featuring the Four Seasons and the Five Elements. The seven strings symbolize the Seven Stars.[169]

TEN RULES FOR PLAYING THE LUTE

BY WU CH'ÊN, 1249–1331

1 When laying the lute on the table one should see that it sticks out on the right side a hand's breadth, so that one may easily turn the tuning pegs. If one seats oneself exactly opposite

---

168 One of the most famous lute players of antiquity; for more details, see Chapter IV: 'The Significance of the Tunes', pp. 97–8.

169 琴. 謹按世本, 神農作琴, 尚書, 舜彈五絃之琴, 歌南風之詩, 而天下治, 詩云, 我有嘉賓, 鼓瑟鼓琴, 雅琴者, 樂之統也, 與八音並行, 然君子所常御者, 琴最親密, 不離於身, 非必陳設於宗廟鄉黨, 非若鐘數羅列於庭懸也, 雖在窮閻陋巷, 深山幽谷, 猶不先琴, 以爲琴之大小得中, 而聲音和, 大聲不譁人而流漫, 小聲不湮滅而不聞, 適足以和人意氣, 感人善心, 故琴之爲言禁也, 雅之爲言正也, 言君子守正以自禁也, 夫以正雅之聲, 動感正意, 故善心勝, 邪惡禁, 是以古之聖人君子, 慎所以自感, 因邪禁之, 適故近之, 間居則爲從容以致思焉, 如有所窮困, 其道閉塞, 不得施行, 及有所通達而用事, 則著之於琴, 以舒其意, 以示後人, 其道行和樂而作者, 命其曲曰暢, 暢者, 言其道之美暢, 猶不敢自安, 不驕不溢, 好禮不以暢其意也, 其遇閉塞憂愁而作者, 命其曲曰操, 操者, 言遇菑遭害, 困厄窮迫, 雖怨恨失意, 猶守禮義不懼不懾, 樂道而不失其操者也, 伯子牙方鼓琴, 鍾子期聽之, 而意在高山, 子期曰善哉乎, 巍巍若泰山, 頃之間而意在流水, 鍾子又曰善哉乎, 湯湯若江河, 子期死, 伯牙破琴也絃, 終身不復鼓, 以爲世無足爲音聲也, 今琴長四尺五寸, 法四時五行也, 七絃者, 法七星也.

the fifth stud, then one can freely execute all the movements of the left and right hand.

2 The right hand when attacking the strings should not go farther to the left than the fourth stud; when one attacks the strings near the bridge, the tones produced will be true. The finger technique should not be floating, nor should it be heavy and confused. The right hand should touch the strings lightly, but the left hand should press them down firmly.

3 When one plays the lute, regardless of whether there are other people present or not, one must always behave as if one were in the presence of a superior. The body should be erect and straight, the spirit should be clear, the mind at rest, the look concentrated, the thoughts serene. Then the touch of the fingers naturally is correct, and the strings emit no wrong sounds.

4 When producing sounds one should aim at simplicity, and also at naturalness. Its wonderfulness lies in the correct shifting over from the light touch to the heavy, and in applying correctly ritardando and accelerando. When the finger technique is applied clumsily and wrongly, the measure is not rigidly observed, and when one is striving after specious effects, the melody is spoilt and confused. These are all deficiencies, which should fundamentally be corrected.

5 The basis of the lute consists in simplicity and serenity. Therefore one should not try to add extra sounds, but rigidly observe the indications for the finger technique; then one shall get a solemn, controlled style of playing, worthy to be seen. If one does not take care in attacking the strings to discriminate between flesh sounds and nail sounds, if the various movements are not linked up correctly, and if, moreover, while executing the attack with the thumb, the chords, and the upward and downward harpeggio, the hand and arm are stiff and not correctly adjusted, then one has not yet achieved the wonderful finger technique.

6 The quality of the lute tends to loftiness. Therefore, if while playing one changes one's mien and allows the eyes to wander, or worse, if the body is stooping, the feet put one atop the other, the head shaking, and the shoulders moving up and down, then an atmosphere of unelegance is created. Knowing these deficiencies one should correct them. Moreover, when

the sentiments are not elated, all kinds of flaws and short-comings arise, and one had better give up the lute altogether.

7 When the ancients composed tunes for the lute, they some-times aimed at expressing leisurely and satisfied feelings, but sometimes they wished to express their melancholy. Therefore one must understand the meaning of a tune. If one just plays the music as it is written, one will not be able to express the sentiments of the composer. And how then shall the mood of the ancients be found in the wood and the silk?

8 In studying the lute, getting down to the essence is the most important. If one tries to learn too much [at one time], how then shall one be able to grasp the essence? Therefore, if one has succeeded in getting an eminent Master to teach some tunes, one should play these same tunes through again and again, lest one forget the significance inherent in them. Moreover, wonderful music arises from constant practice. This is what is meant by the saying that only by incessant application can one derive satisfaction from the strings. If not, then because one studies too many different tunes, the shortcomings shall be many, and it shall be as if thorns grew on one's fingers.

9 The saying 'Rigidly observe the rites by respecting the Way' means, when applied to lute playing, not to play when there is wind or rain, or in a common atmosphere. But if one meets someone who understands the deeper meaning of music, or having ascended a storied building, or a mountain, if one rests in a valley, sits on a rock, or tarries by a stream, or when the two original principles are in harmony, then all these conditions are to be called excellent and suited for the lute. On the contrary, the presence of a vulgar man, a cour-tesan, an actor, a drunken and noisy atmosphere, these all are bad conditions for playing the lute. Therefore one should be discreet in choosing the time and place to play the lute.

10 Playing the lute is meant for nurturing one's nature, therefore one should not aim at acquiring fame by it. If one meets a kindred spirit, then one should play; if not, then one had better put the lute in its cover, and reserve it for one's own enjoyment. If one plays the lute before people who do not

like it, or before disorderly and vulgar persons who boast of their qualities, how can one not be ashamed? In such a case one cannot but hastily conceal the fact that one plays the lute.[170]

MISCELLANEOUS REMARKS ON PLAYING THE LUTE

BY YANG PIAO-CHÊNG, SIXTEENTH CENTURY

THE meaning of the lute is restraining the false and bringing back to the right, in order to harmonize the heart of man. Therefore the Holy Sages made the lute for regulating their persons and for nurturing the harmony of their emotions. Restraining wanton extravagance, and rejecting excessive luxury, one should cherish the music of the Holy Sages, that thereby one may learn the mysterious wonder of their souls, and so rejoice in their thoughts.

Whosoever plays the lute must choose a pure dwelling or a spacious hall; or he must ascend a storied building; or he may tarry by trees and rocks, or climb a steep cliff; or again he may ramble along the verdant bank of a stream, or he may dwell in a monastic abode.

---

[170] 琴言十則. 一. 置琴案上軫前須容掌許，以便轉軫，身坐正對五徽，則左右手往來通便

一. 彈絃不得過四徽，蓋近岳則聲實故也，下指不得浮漂，亦不得重濁，入絃欲淺，按絃欲實

一. 鼓琴時無間有人無人，常如對長者在前，身湏端直，且神解，意間，視專，思靜，自然指不虛，下絃不錯鳴

一. 取聲欲淡，又欲自然，其妙在於輕重切當緩急得宜，若布指拙惡節奏疏懶與艷巧多端聲調煩雜，皆琴之疵纇，不可不戒

一. 琴資簡靜，無增容聲，然須理會手勢，則威儀可觀，若按絃不間甲肉，前指不剛後指，而且攣撮拂歷掌腕蹲探無法，是尙未得妙指，雖在彈，奚以爲哉

一. 琴品欲高，若撫琴時，色變，視流，甚至偃身疊足，搖首，舞屑，氣象殊覺不雅，即知而禁之，則又神情不暢瑕釁叢生，不如己之可也

一. 古人製曲，或怡情自適，或憂憤傳心，須要識其意旨，若徒取聲，則情與製違，古人風調，何有於絲桐之間

一. 琴學貴精，多則便不能精，如從明師學得數曲，當時時調弄，旣不失其遺意，而且妙音出於熟習，所謂密爾自娛於斯絃也，不然多學多廢，寧免手生荊棘何

一. 曰盡禮以得其道，如風雨市廛不彈是也，至遇知音，升樓閣，登山，憩谷，坐石，遊泉，值二氣之清朗，皆際勝而宜於琴者，反是而對俗子，娼優，與夫酒穢塵囂，皆惡景也，自當善藏其用

一. 彈琴養性，非取必於人知，故有好而邀者，宜爲一鼓，不則囊琴自適而已，若奏曲不好之前，與誇能流俗之士，亦幾無恥，亟須韜晦

'Wooden sounds' refers to the vibrato and other graces, produced by rubbing the string on the surface of the sound-box. *Yin* and *jou* are described below in Chapter v, § 3, nos. 41 and 42. Master Ch'i-yen was a lute player from Szuchuan Province (cf. *op. cit.* ch. XI, page 7 *verso*); Yeh-lü-ch'u-ts'ai in his later years adopted Ch'i-yen's classical style, and abandoned the technique taught by his earlier masters Mi-ta 弭大 and Wan-sung 萬松 (cf. *op. cit.* ch. XII, page 2).

I add in passing that Yeh-lü-ch'u-ts'ai was especially interested in the melody *Kuang-ling-san*. This melody I discuss in some detail in my book *Hsi K'ang and his Poetical Essay on the Lute* (Monumenta Nipponica Monographs, Tokyo 1941 (rev. ed., 1969) ch. 3[4]). There a reference should be added to the excellent article by Tai Ming-yang 戴明揚, entitled *Kuang-ling-san-k'ao* 廣陵散考, and published in the *Fu-jên-hsüeh-chih* 輔仁學志, Peking 1936, vol. v, nos. 1 and 2.

When the two essences of nature are balanced, lofty and clear, on a night when there is a cool breeze and a brilliant moon, he must burn incense in a quiet abode. He must steady his heart, introvert his thoughts, so that soul and body are in complete harmony. Then only shall his soul communicate with the spirit of Nature, and he shall be in harmony with the wonderful Way.

If there is not present a man who understands [the inner meaning of] music, one had better play to the cool breeze and to the brilliant moon, to the dark-green pines and quaintly-shaped stones, to an ape of the mountain tops or to an old crane. Then one naturally grasps the inner meaning of this music. When one knows its meaning, one understands its tendency; when one understands its tendency, then one may [truly] understand the music. Though the music be technically well executed, if its tendency is not understood, what benefit shall it give? It is nothing more than a big noise that avails nothing.

In the first place one's personality should be aloof [from all material things], and still elegant, and one's bearing must be pure. Further, the finger technique should be correct, the touch should be correct, the mouth should be bearded and the belly full of ink [i.e. one should be a mature literatus]. Only when these six qualities are all provided for may one take part in the Way of the lute.

If one wishes to play the lute, one should first see that one is dressed correctly: either a gown of crane-feathers, or a ceremonial robe. [For] only if one knows the appearance of the Holy Sages shall one be able to appreciate their instrument [i.e. the lute]. Next one should wash the hands, burn incense; then one should approach the table and lay the lute on its stand. One should be seated opposite the fifth stud, in such a way that this stud faces the heart of the player. Then both hands should be lifted. The heart is regulated, the body is steadied, it does not incline to right or left, or sway forward or backward. The feet should be planted on the earth like the stance of an archer.

One should take care that the right hand touches the correct string, and that the movements of the left hand are correct. The hands should be kept low and evenly balanced; they should not be raised unduly high. Left and right hand should touch the strings on the places indicated by the studs [in such a way that] the right hand is near the bridge; the nails of the hand should not be long, but just about the breadth of one grain. The strings should be touched half by the flesh and half by the nail; then the sound is not dry, but clear and rich. [The left hand] should press the board as if it would penetrate the wood. The outward and inward touch of the thumb, index and middle finger of the right hand, the vibrato, vibrato ritardando of the left hand, and the quick movements of the right hand over one or more strings, all these touches should be fully expressed, they should not be executed loosely and hastily, to give the impression of a light and flowing style. If one aims at specious dexterity and playing to the eye of the public, one had better leave the lute alone and take to acting; if one aims at producing ornate tones that captivate the ear, one had better drop the lute and take to the cither.[171]

The greatest emphasis must be laid on [distinguishing between] the light and heavy, the swift and slow touch, and between the decrescendo and crescendo.

When one's self is naturally aloof and earnest, then one shall correspond to the Mystery of the Way, and one's soul shall melt together with the Way. Therefore it is said that successfully executing music is not caused by the hands, but by the heart, that music is not produced by notes, but by the Way. When one does not strive to express music in tones, but lets it come naturally, then one may experience the Harmony of Heaven and Earth, then one may be in communication with the virtue of the Universal Spirit.

Also it is said: The vibrato, the vibrato ritardando, the ascending and the descending attack of the left hand, the light or the heavy, the swift or the slow touch of the right hand, all these things can hardly be explained in words. They can be understood only by a man of learning.[172]

171 In connection with this plea for a simple style of lute playing I cite the following poem by the great statesman and scholar Yeh-lü-ch'u-ts'ai (耶律楚材, 1190–1244), who besides his many other accomplishments also was an expert lute player. This poem is found in his collected works, the *Chan-jan-chü-shih-wên-chih*湛然居士文集 (*Szu-pu-ts'ung-k'an* edition, ch. xi, page 7 *recto*).

愛棲巖彈琴聲法二絕
須信希聲是大音. 猱多則亂吟多淫.
世人不識棲巖意. 祇愛時宜熱鬧琴.
多著吟揉熱客耳. 強生取與媚俗情.
純音簡易誰能識. 却道棲巖無木聲.

Two poems on my loving the lute-technique of Master Ch'i-yen.

I

I firmly believe that rarefied tones constitute the real great music,

Frequent use of vibrato ritardando confuses the melody, frequent use of other vibrato leads to a lax style.

People of the present day do not understand the meaning of Master Ch'i-yen's music,

They only love the fashionable style, and play the lute so as to produce a rude noise.

II

Frequent application of vibrato grates upon the ears of the listener,

This style is aimed only at captivating the common fancy.

The pure tones are simple—but who can appreciate them?

People only say that Ch'i-yen does not use the wooden sounds.

172 彈琴雜說. 琴者禁邪歸正以和人心. 是故聖人之制將以治身育其情性和矣, 抑乎淫蕩,*

ON THE LUTE OF HIGH ANTIQUITY

FROM THE WU-CHIH-CHAI-CH'IN-PU, PUB. 1721

IN olden times when Fu Hsi[173] ruled all under Heaven, he looked upwards and contemplated, he looked downwards and investigated. Through his supernatural influence he made the map rise from the Yung river [cf. *Shu-ching*, ch. 'Ku-ming', 19],[174] and accordingly he drew the Eight Triagrams. Then listening to the winds of the Eight Directions he made the sonorous tubes.[175] On I Mountain[176] he selected a lonely dryandra tree, and making the Yin principle complete the Yang principle, he created Elegant Music, calling it Lute.

Lute means 'restraining', that is to say restraining falsehood and guarding against wantonness. It further implies bringing to the fore benevolence and righteousness, and causing the return to the Way; it is a means for cultivating the person and regulating the mind; it makes man return to what is truly of Heaven in him;[177] it makes him forget his earthly shape and reunites him with Emptiness. The spirit becomes concentrated, and melts into the Great Harmony.[178]

The lute is made to measure three *ch'ih* six *ts'un* and five *fên*. This symbolizes the 365 degrees of the celestial sphere, and the 365 days of the year. Its breadth is six ts'un, symbolizing the six harmonies.[179] It has an upper and a lower part, which symbolize the

*去乎奢侈，以抱聖人之樂，所以微妙在得夫其人而樂其趣也，凡鼓琴必擇淨室高堂，或升層樓之上，或於林石之間，或登山嶺，或遊水湄，或觀宇中，值二氣高明之時，清風明月之夜，焚香靜室坐定心不外馳，氣血和平，方與神合靈，與道合妙，不遇知音，寧對清風明月，蒼松、怪石巔猿老鶴而鼓耳，是爲自得其樂也，如是鼓琴須要解意，知其意則知其趣，知其趣則知其樂，不知音趣，樂雖熟，何益，徒多無補，先要人物風韻標格清楚，又要指法好，取音好胸次好，口上要有髯，肚裏要有墨，六者兼備，方與添琴道，如要鼓琴，要先須衣冠整齊，或鶴氅，或深衣，要知古，之像表，方可稱聖人之器，然後盥水焚香，方纔就揚以琴，近案，座以第伍徽之間，當對其心，則兩方舉指法，其心身要正，無得左右傾欹前後抑合其足履地若射步之，宜右視其手，左顧其絃，手腕宜低平，不宜高昂，左右要對徽，右手要近岳，指甲不宜長，只肉要相半，其聲不枯，清潤得宜，按令入木，劈托抹桃勾踢吟猱鎖歷之法，皆盡其力，不宜飛撫作勢輕薄之態，欲要手勢花巧以好看，莫若推琴而就撫，若要聲音艷麗而好聽，莫若棄琴而彈箏，此爲琴之大忌也，務要輕重疾徐卷舒，|| 若體態骨重，方能與道妙

會神與道融，故曰德不在手，而在心，樂不在聲，而在道，興不在音，而自然，可以感天地之和，可以合神明之德，又曰左手吟猱綽綿注，右手輕重疾徐，更有一般難說，其人湏要讀書.

173 One of the mythical emperors, said to have lived in the third millennium B.C. The map is said to have shown the eight triagrams *pa-kua* (the base of the *Book of Changes*), and some other mystic drawings; it was drawn on the back of a dragon-horse which rose from the waves.

174 See *Shu-ching*, ch. *Ku-ming*, 19.

175 The twelve *lü* 律呂, bamboo tubes of various dimensions, which were said to produce the 12 chromatic semitones of the octave, and which since ancient times have formed the basis of Chinese musical theory.

176 A mountain in Shantung province.

177 Quoted from the opening lines of the *Ch'in-tsao* 琴操; see App. II, 1.

178 Quoted from Lieh-tzû; see above p. 45.

179 Heaven, earth, and the four cardinal points.

interchanging breath of Heaven and Earth. The upper part of the bottom is called pond, the lower part pool. Pond means water; water is even. Pool means to submit, [the two thus meaning] if the people on high are even [i.e. just] the people below will be obedient. The front is broad, the backpart is narrow, symbolizing the difference that exists between the venerable and the common. The upper board is concave, symbolizing Heaven, the lower board is flat, designating Earth.

The Dragon Pond[180] measures eight *ts'un*, to let pass the winds of the eight directions. The Phoenix Pool[181] measures four *ts'un*, to unite in it the four seasons. There are five strings, to correspond to the five tones, and to symbolize the five elements. The thick strings are the Prince; they are slow, harmonious, and unobtrusive. The thinner ones are the Statesmen; they are pure, unselfish, and obedient. The two strings that were added later are called *wên* and *wu*, and by their elegance they express the decorous feelings between Prince and Statesman; *kung* is the Prince, *shang* is the Statesman, *chiao* is the People, *chih* stands for affairs, and *yü* for things in general.[182] When these five tones together depict the Right, then the realm will be well regulated, and the numerous people will be peaceful.

Thus is the influence of the Accomplished Music on man: his nature is made to return to the Right, Prince and Statesmen shall be righteous, parents and children shall love each other, falsehood and low desires disappear, and man returns to his true heavenly nature.

The [licentious] music of Chêng brings doubt to man; in his nature, which is [originally] serene, false and wanton thoughts are born, the difference between man and woman is confused, and a propensity to licence is instigated.

Therefore, by contemplating the lute and by listening to its music [in a certain place or time] one may behold the disposition of the people and the condition of government [in that place or at that time], and one may know whether in the world the Way flourishes or is decaying.

Shun played the five-stringed lute, and sang the song *Nan-fêng*, and in order to give peace to the minds of all under heaven he composed the T'ai-p'ing music. It is said in the *Ch'in-shu*: The lute is an instrument that was created by Fu Hsi, and completed by Huang-ti. It symbolizes Heaven and Earth, and its use is to promulgate the wonderful Way. It contains the Spirit of Great Holiness, and produces

---

the ninety sorts of sounds. First it was made with five strings; later, during the reigns of King Wên and King Wu respectively, two more strings were added, to establish the chant of the Dragon and the Phoenix, and to penetrate the mystery of lower and higher spiritual agencies. Its tones are right, its essence harmonious; although its size is small, its significance is great.

When the inner meaning of the lute is understood, one may derive benefit from it. Through its influence people who are hasty shall become quiet, those who are quiet shall become harmonious. When the heart is harmonious and even, one is affected neither by sorrow nor by joy: one becomes in complete harmony with what is truly from heaven in one's nature. When this heavenly nature is clearly recognized, then the difference between human nature troubled by emotions, and original serenity, shall be made clear again, one shall not be confused any longer by life and death, nor shall one be affected by earthly laws.

The ancient Emperors and Enlightened Kings all understood profoundly [these mysterious qualities of the lute]. It has not yet been known for a man to hear the Right Music without being influenced by it. When formerly Master Hsiang[183] pulled the lute, the swimming fish rose from the water to listen, and [hearing the lute music of Po Ya][184] the six horses looked up from their fodder. Things that have a shape, and animals that have no speech, they all are influenced by the music of the lute; how much more then human beings! So it was until the Right Music was lost and [people] turned away from the Way of the lute.

The lute may establish fortitude and harmonize the primordial spirit. Only Yao understood this, therefore he composed the hymn *Shên-jên*. Further the lute may complete the Way, thereby establishing the minds of the weak and timorous. This is the meaning of the elegy *Ssû-ch'in*,[185] composed by Shun, of the elegy *Hsiang-ling*,[186] composed by Yü, and of the elegy *Hsün-tien*,[187] composed by T'ang.

---

183 *Shih-hsiang* was a famous lute player of old, mentioned in *Lieh-tzû*, ch. *T'ang-wên* 湯問. This passage, however, gives the credit for making the fish come out of the water to another lute expert, Ku Pa: When Ku Pa played the lute, birds started to dance and fish jumped out of the water.

184 I have inserted the reference to Po Ya, since the final words are a quotation from *Hsün-tzû* 荀子, ch. *Ch'üan-hsüeh* 勸學, where it is said: 'When Po Ya played the lute, the

six horses looked up from their fodder' 伯牙鼓琴, 而六馬仰秣.

185 The *Ch'in-tsao* (App. II, 1) says that the Emperor Shun composed this song to express his affection for his parents.

186 According to the *Shu-ching*, Yü composed this song when he had completed the task of regulating the waters.

187 Composed by Wu-wang of the Chou dynasty to train people in military arts. Cf. the Sung treatise *Ch'in-ch'ü-pu-lu* 琴曲譜錄:習武事.

Since the Ancient Emperors and the Enlightened Rulers, the heart
has been rectified and the person has been cultivated, the State has
been regulated and peace has been brought to the realm[188] by the
right sounds of the lute and by these alone. How then can one say
that the wonderful Way of the lute is but a small craft? To consider
the Way of the lute as one of the arts is a great mistake indeed.[189]

COVENANT FOR TRANSMITTING THE LUTE

BY CH'ÊNG YÜN-CHI, EIGHTEENTH CENTURY

1 The lute is the instrument of the Holy Sages: Superior Men
   therewith nurture the Essence of the Mean Harmony, cultivate
   their selves and regulate their nature. Playing the lute must
   therefore be called a Way to wisdom and not one of the arts.
   All who love the study of the lute should wait till they meet
   [a pupil who is] a scholar of cultured taste and correct conduct; only then may they teach him the lute. How could one
   speak about the lute to people of frivolous and ostentatious
   disposition?

2 As the various schools of lute players are not the same, so their
   traditions are different.[190] But the main point [which all

---

188 See *Ta-hsüeh* 大學, ch. I.

189 上古琴論. 昔者伏羲之王天下也, 仰觀
俯察, 感滎河出圖以畫八卦, 聽八風以製音律,
採嶧山孤桐, 合陰備陽, 造爲雅樂, 名之曰琴,
琴者禁也, 禁邪僻而防淫佚, 引仁義而歸正道,
所以修身理性, 返其天眞, 忘形合虛, 凝神太和,
琴製長三尺六寸五分, 象周天三百六十五度, 年
歲之三百六十五日也, 廣六寸, 象六合也, 有上
下, 象天地之氣相呼吸也, 其底上曰池, 下曰沼,
池者水也, 水者平也, 沼者伏也, 上平則下伏,
前廣而後狹, 象尊卑有差也, 上圓象天, 下方法
地, 龍池長八寸, 以通八風, 鳳沼長四寸, 以合
四氣, 其絃有五, 以按五音, 象五行也, 大絃者
君也, 緩和而隱, 小絃者臣也, 清廉而不亂, 迨
至文武加二絃, 所以雅合君臣之恩也, 宮爲君,
商爲臣, 角爲民, 徵爲事, 羽爲物, 五音畫正, 天
下和平, 而兆民寧, 雅樂之感人也, 性返于正,
君臣義, 父子親, 消降邪欲, 返乎天眞, 鄭聲之
惑人也, 正性邪, 淫心生, 亂男女之別, 動聲色
之偏, 故視琴聽音, 可以見志觀治, 知世道之興
衰, 故舜彈五絃之琴, 歌南風之詩, 以平天下之
心, 爲太平之樂也, 琴書曰琴之爲器, 創自伏羲,
成于黃帝, 治象乎乾坤, 用宣乎妙道, 含大靈
氣, 運九十種聲, 初製五絃, 加於文武, 建龍鳳
之號, 通鬼神之幽, 其聲正, 其氣和, 其形小, 其
義大, 如得其旨趣, 則能感物, 志躁者, 感之以
靜, 志靜者, 感之以和, 和平其心憂樂不能入,

任之以天眞, 明其眞, 而返照動寂, 則生死不能
累, 方法豈能拘, 古之明王君子, 皆精通焉, 未
有閒正音而不感者也, 昔者師襄鼓琴, 則有遊
魚出聽, 六馬仰沫, 有形之物, 無語之獸, 尚能
感之, 況於人乎, 自正音失而琴道乖矣, 琴能制
剛, 而調元氣, 惟堯得之, 故堯有神人暢, 其次
能全其道, 則柔儒立志, 舜有思親操, 禹有襄陵
操, 湯有訓佃操者是也, 自古帝明王, 所以正心
修身, 齊家治國平天下者, 咸賴琴之正音是資
焉, 然則琴之妙道, 豈小技也哉, 而以藝視琴道
者, 則非矣.

190 There can be no doubt that originally
every single 'school' of lute playing goes back
to one famous master; he initiated a certain
style of playing the lute, and taught this to
his disciples, thus founding a 'school'. His
disciples transmitted his teachings to their
own followers, and so the circle grew wider
and wider. In the course of the centuries the
names of the original founders of the 'schools'
were lost, and the schools became a kind of
local tradition, associated with a geographical
location rather than with the name of a
particular lute master. Many minor schools
disappeared completely or were incorporated
into broader geographical divisions.

At present there still exist the following*

*'schools', named after the provinces where they were founded and where their tradition continued to flourish.

蜀派	吳派	浙派	閩派
Shu-p'ai	Wu-p'ai	Che-p'ai	Min-p'ai
(Szuchuan)	(Kiangsu)	(Chekiang)	(Fukien)

廣陵派	虞山派
Kuang-ling-p'ai	Yü-shan-p'ai

The Shu-p'ai or Szuchuan School retains many of the antique features of lute music, and seems to reproduce fairly accurately the style of lute playing popular during the T'ang period. This must be ascribed to the fact that Szuchuan Province, through its isolated position, has been less influenced by cultural developments in Central China. The Szuchuan style of playing the lute bears a robust character, and stresses those single notes and graces that constitute the melody of a tune; grace notes that do not affect the melodic pattern are either omitted or played in a casual way. On the other hand this school likes to use chords; in Szuchuan-notations of well-known tunes one often finds a chord where other lute handbooks only write a single note. This feature must probably be explained by the fact that during the T'ang dynasty the lute was often used together with other musical instruments of a greater sound volume, and also for accompanying the human voice; hence the tendency to emphasize the melody. It should be noted that even now in Szuchuan there exists a tradition of intoning ancient poetry, the singer accompanying himself on the lute.

The Chekiang School was greatly influenced by the popular music that flourished during the Yüan dynasty. The masters of this school often added verses in the fashionable style to older lute melodies, supplementing the original melodic pattern with many extra grace-notes. Hence this school is often criticized as being 'clever but common'. Probably Yeh-lü-ch'u-ts'ai's masters Mi-ta and Wan-sung (see n. 170) were members of this Chekiang School; this would explain his changing to the simpler style of the Szuchuanese master Ch'i-yen.

The Fukien School was established later than the others, probably during the thirteenth or fourteenth century. This school tried to adapt lute music to popular instruments such as the cither and the *p'i-p'a;* consequently it is not greatly esteemed by lute experts. Most musicians who, without ambition to become real lute players, still like to be able to play a few easy tunes, are followers of this school. They generally use the *Sung-fêng-ko-ch'in-pu* (see page 96),

a handbook that gives a great number of simple, short melodies, all accompanied by words. Although I quite agree that the Fukien School does not stand for the highest expression of lute music, it is still worth a closer study, for many of its tunes contain charming melodic patterns.

The Kiangsu School is without doubt the greatest, both as regards the quality of its music and the number of its members. Its origin lies buried in the distant past, for it already flourished in the third century. About 1600 this school split into two branches, the Kuang-ling-p'ai and the Yü-shan-p'ai. The most prominent representative of the Kuang-ling-p'ai was Hsü Ch'ang-yü (徐常遇, style Êrh-hsün 二勳, literary name Wu-shan-lao-jên 五人老人), a lute player from Yang-chou who flourished during the early years of the Ch'ing period. In 1702 his son published his lute handbook, which was reprinted in 1718; in 1773 it appeared in its final form, under the title of *Ch'ên-chien-t'ang-ch'in-pu* 澄鑒堂琴譜. The Yü-shan-p'ai, also called Ch'ang-shu-p'ai 常熟派, has its center in Ch'ang-shu near Soochow, where the great master Yen Chêng (see page 182) revived the ancient tradition of lute playing.

Hsü Ch'ang-yü and Yen Chêng are commonly called the 'founders' of the two branches of the Kiangsu School. This appellation, however, derives mainly from the veneration with which members of the two schools regard these two great lute masters. What they actually did was to give final form to a tradition that had developed long before in Yang-chou and Ch'ang-shu.

These two schools aim at a faithful reproduction of the melodic patterns of the antique tunes, including both the melodic and non-melodic graces. They stress the significance of the lute as a solo instrument and pay close attention to the 'color' of each particular note, at the same time attaching great value to the proper application of forte and piano, and to the correct rhythm. The Kiangsu School represents the highest form of lute music. One need not wonder, therefore, that most of the eminent lute players of the present either belong to the Kuang-ling-p'ai or the Yü-shan-p'ai; the best exponent of the former is probably Mr Chang I-ch'ang (張益昌, style Tzu-ch'ien 子謙) of Shanghai, while the latter is headed by Mr Ch'a Chên-hu (查鎮湖, style Fu-hsi 阜西) at Soochow. The two schools resemble each other closely, the only difference I could discover being that the Yü-shan-p'ai stresses the rhythm, while the Kuang-ling-p'ai insists so much on a correct rendering of all the*

schools have in common⌝ lies in their strict observance of the rules of harmony, and in giving special care to the finger technique. Students of the lute should ⌜first⌝ hear the style which the masters of various schools follow while playing, ⌜for once having chosen a master⌝ it is necessary that one wholeheartedly like his style and follow his precepts sincerely; then teaching and learning shall be well regulated. If the student reaches a complete understanding of these teachings, what shall prevent him from becoming even more proficient than his master?[191] Further, if a student receives one method of playing, but at the same time hears all kinds of different teachings,[192] he cannot concentrate his mind; then one should not trouble to teach him.

3 When Confucius studied the lute under Master Hsiang, ⌜after the first lesson⌝ he did not show himself for ten days; when Po Ya studied the lute under Ch'êng-lien, during three years he did not make progress. Therefore, those who start studying the lute must have a constant mind and a firm resolution, and they must be resolved to succeed in the end; only such people should be taught the lute. But if there are such that come with great enthusiasm but give up when they are halfway,[193] they are not worthy that a teacher occupy himself with them.

4 The lute is the instrument with which the Ancients nurtured their nature; they did not use it with the idea of making their livelihood by it. Now I often see lute masters of the present time, when about to teach somebody, immediately start talking about the salary; this is disgusting indeed, and drawing elegance through the mud. All who have the same attitude as I, should guard themselves against this. Drawn up by Yü-shan.[194]

---

*grace-notes that the rhythm is sometimes broken.

It will be clear from the above observations that the four 'schools' differ only in the *interpretation* of the lute melodies. They did not add to, nor materially alter the melodies of the lute repertoire.

191 *Ch'ing-ch'u-yü-lan*, from *Hsün-tzŭ*; the opening line of ch. I.

192 *Ch'i-ch'uan-ch'u-hsiu*, from *Mencius*, Book III, part II, 6.

193 *Pan-t'u-êrh-fei*; cf. *Chung-yung* 中庸, XI, 2.

194 傳琴約．一琴爲聖樂，君子涵養中和之

氣，藉以修身理性，當以道言，非以藝言也，習琴之友，必期博雅端方之士，方可傳之，輕浮佻達者，豈可語此

一派既不同，傳亦各異，首嚴音律兼重指法，習琴者須令聽過各家，務要心悅誠服，然後授受分明，苟會心明敏者，何妨靑出於藍，其或齊傳楚咻，志不專一，則亦不屑教誨之而已矣

一孔子學琴於師襄，十日不進，伯牙學琴於成連，三年未成，初學者須要心堅志決，必期有成，方可傳習，其或乘興而來，半途而廢，亦不足取也

一琴爲古人養性之具，非以資糊口計也，每見時師傳授，輒講酬儀，鄙穢難聞，風雅掃地矣，凡我同志，各宜戒之．寓山識

CHAPTER FOUR

The Significance of the Tunes

The Ming repertoire taken as the basis for a study of the significance of the tunes—significance of the modes—Chinese T I A O-I, and Japanese N E T O R I—the tunes divided into five groups—tunes describing a mystic journey (Taoistic)—tunes of a semihistorical character (Confucianist)—musical versions of literary productions—tunes descriptive of nature—tunes descriptive of literary life—summary

THE lute as a means of communing with Tao, the lute as the favourite companion of the scholar, the lute as the holy instrument of the Ancient Sages—all these various functions of the lute, and the tenets of lute ideology corresponding to them, are reflected in the repertoire: they find their expression in the subjects of the tunes.

Now, the lute repertoire is different for every period; the various elements, both Chinese and foreign, that in the course of time influenced lute music, to a large extent also determined its repertoire. In the heyday of Central-Asiatic influence (the Sui and T'ang periods), more than half of the repertoire consisted of musical versions of songs of a very worldly character. But during the Sung dynasty, when under the influence of the philosopher Chu Hsi and his powerful school a more severe attitude reasserted itself, lute tunes of a more classical character came to the fore. For our present subject, a consideration of the extent to which the tenets of *ch'in* ideology may be found reflected in the tunes, we must take as the basis the repertoire of the Ming dynasty. For, as we have seen above, it was during the Ming dynasty that the outlines of this special system of thought were more or less fixed.

It was during the Ming period that there were printed on a large scale handbooks for the lute with tunes in notation, accompanied by explicit commentaries as to their history and significance; thus from a study of the Ming repertoire we may obtain an idea not only of the melodies of these tunes, but also of what they meant to the people of those times.

Before studying the significance of the separate tunes, however, a few words must be said about the various modes (*tiao*)[1] and their ideological value.

The handbooks of the lute mostly divide the repertoire into the five modes, called after the old Chinese pentatonic scale (*kuang-shang-chüeh-chih-yü*), *kung-tiao*, *shang-tiao*, etc.[2] Next to these there exist scores of what might be called 'minor modes', partly of foreign origin; these are called together *wai-tiao*.[3] For each mode the tuning of the strings is different.

Now in the lute handbooks of the Ming dynasty each group of tunes belonging to the same mode is preceded by a short musical composition that bears as title the name of the mode, with the word *i*[4] (meaning) added. So the collection of tunes belonging to the *kung* mode opens with a short composition entitled *kung-i* (or also *kung-tiao-i*)[5] 'Meaning of the *kung* Mode'. These *tiao-i* contain a fixed tonal pattern, characteristic of the mode they indicate, and constitute the essence of all tunes composed in this mode. Short as they are, these *tiao-i* comprise a great variety of tones, especially some chords and other harmonical combinations which are typical for the mode the *tiao-i* introduces. Usually a *tiao-i* ends with a simple melodic pattern, entirely in harmonics ('floating sounds' *fan-yin*: while the right hand pulls a string, the left just touches it lightly, without pressing it down on the board).[6]

These *tiao-i* provide the player with a convenient check upon the tuning of his instrument. Playing through the *tiao-i*, he notices at once whether the tuning is correct or not. At the same time the *tiao-i* is a kind of finger exercise: it contains all the main grips necessary for executing tunes set to this mode.

In *ch'in* ideology, however, the *tiao-i* mean much more than just melodic patterns; they are called *i* (meaning), because they convey to the player and the hearer the peculiar atmosphere, the emotional and philosophical value of each mode. A lute expert of the Ming dynasty, Yang Lun,[7] in his handbook *T'ai-ku-i-yin*[8] adds to each *tiao-i* an introductory note. There he combines each mode with one

---

1 調
2 宮商角徵羽, 宮調, 商調
3 外調
4 意

5 宮意, 宮調意
6 泛音. See above, page 60.
7 意
8 楊倫. See App. II, 14.

of the five elements (*wu-hsing*) and with one of the five virtues (*wu-ch'ang*).[9] Then he connects each mode with a special manifestation of Tao, as they are explained in the *Book of Changes, Yih-ching*. So the whole scheme of the modes is placed in a cosmological frame. Playing the *tiao-i* may be called a preliminary ceremony: it prepares the player and the hearer for the real composition to come, it creates the correct atmosphere that belongs to the mode in which the composition is set.

The *tiao-i* are so intimately bound up with the tunes themselves, that in the Ming handbook *Shên-chi-pi-pu* most tunes end with the remark: 'Now add the harmonics of the *tiao-i* belonging to this mode.'[10]

During the Ch'ing dynasty the *tiao-i* seem to have been neglected; as a rule they are not printed in the handbooks of that period. But a survival is to be found in the codas (*shou-yin*, also called *wei*)[11] which in Ch'ing handbooks frequently are added to the tunes. These codas are entirely in harmonics, and for each mode closely resemble the passages in harmonics of the corresponding *tiao-i* of the Ming handbooks. The function of these codas is essentially the same as that of the *tiao-i*: while the *tiao-i* prepares the player and the hearer for the mode of the tune that is going to follow, the codas are retrospective, and, as it were, resume in one single passage the entire spirit of the mode to which the tune played belongs.

The *tiao-i* are doubtless very old. This may be concluded from the fact that although the tunes themselves as given in the early Ming handbooks differ greatly, the *tiao-i* are practically uniform. In Japan they are still used in the ceremonial Court music where they are called *netori* or also *torine*.[12] The *tiao-i* of the lute supply us with valuable materials for a study of ancient Chinese composition; in my opinion an investigation of the history of lute music should begin with a thorough analysis of the various *tiao-i* that are preserved.

For the study of the significance of the tunes themselves the handbooks of the lute supply ample materials. Usually to each tune given in notation there is added a preface, where the compiler of the handbook gives the name of the composer, and adds some remarks about the occasion that inspired him to compose the tune in question.

---

9 五行, 五常
10 入本調泛. See App. II, 11.
11 收音, 尾
12 音取, 取音. For more information about

the *netori*, see H. Tanabe, 田邊尚雄, *Nihon ongaku kōwa* 日本音樂講話, Tokyo 1921, pp. 515 ff.

Special care is given to describing the mood the composer was in when he created his music, and what thought he wished to express in his composition. It is the highest aim of the player in his execution of the tune to reproduce faithfully the mood of the composer. Each tune has its special significance, which must be done full justice by the player.

To help the player to realize the significance, often the various parts of a tune (*tuan*)[13] are given special titles, suggesting the meaning of that particular part of the melody.

As a rule these subtitles are not especially made for the lute melodies; they are fixed phrases, borrowed from a separate section of the Chinese artistic vocabulary, i.e. that of the *t'i-mu*[14] (superscriptions). A *t'i-mu* is a short, highly pregnant phrase, a conventionalized expression that describes a subject considered fit for inspiring an artist. A *t'i-mu*, such as for instance 'a waterfall descending from pine-clad rocks',[15] may inspire alike poets, painters and musicians. Looking through a catalogue of paintings[16] one finds hundreds of these *t'i-mu*. Because of their pregnancy these phrases are by no means easy to translate; in the examples given below my translation often is but one of many possible renderings. Many handbooks add to these subtitles some remarks about the style: whether the touch must be slow, energetic, delicate, etc. Further there are many stylistic indications, which correspond to our piano, legato, forte and so on.

Sometimes even to every bar there are appended explanatory remarks. For instance, we find in a tune describing a beautiful mountain landscape, under a bar in the first part, the remark 'Here one thinks of high mountains,' and under another: 'Here one thinks of flowing streams.'

The better-known tunes of the Ming repertoire number well over a hundred. From a musicological point of view, every one of these tunes constitutes valuable material for research. But for the study of *ch'in* ideology we need only consider a few of them. For a comparative study of the tunes shows that according to their subjects they may be conveniently divided into five groups, each group comprising a number of tunes of the same ideological type. Thus for our present subject it suffices to select for each group some representative tunes.

---

13 段
14 題目
15 松岩飛瀑

16 For example, the *Li-tai-cho-lu-hua-mu* 歷代著錄畫目, published in 1933 by John C. Ferguson.

The tunes here selected for discussion number about twenty. In some way or another all serve to illustrate the ideals of *ch'in* ideology. Some express Taoist principles, others celebrate antiquity, and all suggest the atmosphere that surrounds the lute and its music. Besides illustrating *ch'in* ideology, the tunes discussed below, as they form the nucleus of the *ch'in* repertoire, will at the same time give the reader a general idea about the subjects that inspired lute musicians. Most of the tunes mentioned here are often referred to in Chinese literature, and to this day are still the favourites of every Chinese lute amateur.

Above, in Chapter III, section 2, it was remarked already that in *ch'in* ideology the Taoist element predominates. A cursory inspection of the subjects of the tunes shows that there also the tunes with a Taoist colour top the list. Most prominent among these Taoist tunes are those of a type which I would call that of *The Mystic Journey*. The ethereal tones of the lute loosen the soul of the player from its earthly bonds, and enable him to travel to the mystic heights where the Immortals dwell, and to be initiated into the secrets of the Elixir of Life.

A good example is a tune called *Kuang-han-yu* (Traveling to the Palace of Wide Coolness) to be found in an early Ming handbook, the *Pu-hsü-t'ang-ch'in-pu*.[17] The various stages of the mystic journey described in this tune are indicated in the titles of its eight parts: the traveler ascends into the clouds, feasts with the Immortals, and finally again returns to earth.

1 Treading the cloud ladder.
2 Ascending into pure emptiness.
3 Feasting in the Pavilion of Wide (Coolness).
4 Cutting the cinnamon (used in preparing the elixir of immortality).
5 Dancing in rainbow garments.
6 Dancing with the Blue Phoenix. (In the middle of this part there occur some heavy chords, where the remark is added: 'The sound of the Jade Hare pounding the elixir of immortality.' According to Chinese popular belief, in the moon there lives a hare that prepares the elixir of life under a cassia tree.)
7 Asking about longevity.
8 Returning in the cloud chariot. (In the middle of this part

---

[17] 廣寒遊 (see p. 68, n. 145); 步虛堂琴譜 (App. II, 12).

there occur some high notes, with the explanatory remark: 'The sounds of laughing and talking of Chang-ngo, the Moon Goddess.')[18]

The tune *Lieh-tzû-yü-fêng* (Lieh-tzû Riding on the Wind) may serve as a second example; it refers to a passage in the old Taoist work connected with the name of this philosopher.[19] This tune is to be found in most *ch'in-pu*, and is generally ascribed to Mao Chung-wêng,[20] a composer of the Sung dynasty about whom little is known; only some of the more vulgar *ch'in-pu* ascribe it to the philosopher Lieh-tzû himself. The *Shên-chi-pi-pu*[21] gives the titles of its ten parts as follows.

1 Resting upon emptiness, riding on the wind.
2 Looking down on the earth.
3 The universe is spread out vast.
4 I do not know whether the wind is riding on me.
5 Or whether I am riding on the wind.
6 The mind dwells on mysterious plains.
7 The spirit roams in the great purity.
8 Whistling long in the vast azure.
9 Shaking one's clothes in the breeze.
10 Having attained the utmost ecstasy, turning back.[22]

Another well-known tune of this type, entitled *Ling-hsü-yin* (Song of Cool Emptiness) is also ascribed to Mao Chung-wêng.[23] This tune consists of three parts:

1 Ascending in the clouds with a crane as vehicle.
2 Riding on the wind up to the confines of heaven.
3 Treading the emptiness of the highest atmosphere.[24]

Besides the examples quoted here there exist scores of other tunes belonging to this same group. Under this group I would also classify another class of tunes that, though not exactly representing a mystic journey, still are closely related to it. These are the many tunes celebrating life in refined retirement.

Taoist lore often describes the abode of the Immortals and other paradisaical regions as being in a specified location, as, e.g. far in the

---

18 步雲梯, 登清虛, 宴廣亭, 折丹桂, 舞霓裳, 舞青鸞, 間長生, 囘雲車
19 列子禦風; see above, translation on p. 45.
20 毛仲翁
21 See App. II, 11.
22 凭虛馭風, 俯視寰壤, 渺焉六合, 不知風

乘我, 不知我乘風, 志在沖溟, 神遊太清, 長嘯空碧, 振衣天風, 興盡而還
23 凌虛吟; see the Ming handbook of Yang Piao-chêng, App. II, 13 (other handbooks give it as anonymous).
24 驂雲鶴駕, 乘風天表, 步虛太羅

western mountains, or high up in the sky. But at the same time the unseen world pervades ordinary life: we are living constantly in close proximity to it, and we would clearly perceive it could we but see with the soul instead of with the eyes. This idea has inspired countless Chinese writers: best known is the delicate essay by T'ao Ch'ien entitled 'The Plum Blossom Fountain'.[25]

In this essay (really the introduction to one of his poems), T'ao Ch'ien relates how a fisherman happened upon a grove of peach trees; exploring this beautiful spot he found the hidden entrance to a cave. Having entered it he found that it led into a strange country: people there were living happily and peacefully, wearing the garb of several centuries ago. The fisherman was kindly treated by them, and re-solved to return there. But once he had gone away he could never find his way back.

Tasting already during earthly life the joys of eternity is the privilege of the enlightened recluse, who, in his abode far from the loud world, returns to the simple life exalted by the Taoist writers. Thus the repairing of the sage to his mountain retreat, the scholar's rustic excursion which makes him realize the futility of worldly hopes, the ecstasy of the recluse who by contemplating the forces of nature beholds the eternal Tao; all these motifs may be classified under the group of the mystic journey.

In connection with this motif two persons, the Fuel Gatherer *ch'iao-jên* and the Old Fisherman *yü-fu* figure prominently.[26] They are the approved symbols of simple life in complete harmony with *tao*, as opposed to the cares and sorrows of the world. Above we saw that it was an old fisherman that discovered the Peach Blossom Foun-tain. Already the philosopher Chuang-tzû uses the Old Fisherman as a symbol of the sage who has realized truth; in the chapter entitled 'Yü-fu', the Old Fisherman appears: '. . . his beard and eyebrows were turning white, his hair was all uncombed, and his sleeves hung loosely down . . .' He points out to Confucius the Right Way, and then: 'He shoved off his boat, and went away among the green reeds.'[27] Also in later literature the Old Fisherman and the Fuel Gatherer are preferably chosen for delivering wise words about the meaning of

---

25 陶潛, 365–427; 桃花源記, translated by Giles in: *Gems of Chinese Literature, Prose*, Shanghai 1923, p. 104. Notice that Giles' footnote, 'The whole story is allegorical, and signifies that the fisherman had been strangely permitted to go back once again into the peach blossom days of his youth', entirely misrepresents the purport of this essay and should be disregarded.

26 樵人, 漁父
27 Legge.

life. The great Sung writer and artist Su Shih (Su Tung-p'o) wrote the *Yü-ch'iao-hsien-hua* (Leisurely Discourses of the Fuel Gatherer and the Fisherman), and the famous scholar Shao Yung of the same period chose this pair to deliver his philosophical principles.[28]

In the repertoire of the lute there occur many tunes that express this idea. As a first example I may mention the tune *Ch'iao-ko* (Song of the Fuel Gatherer), to be found in most handbooks and generally ascribed to Mao Min-chung, a composer of the end of the Sung period.[29] The *Shên-chi-pi-pu*[30] says that Mao Min-chung composed this tune when fleeing from the Mongol invasion of China. The eleven parts bear the following subtitles:

1 Flying from the world, without sorrow.
2 Proudly looking down on worldly affairs.
3 Settling down far on cloudy mountain tops.
4 Shouldering one's axe entering the wood.
5 Enjoying *tao* while reading one's books.
6 Shaking one's clothes on a steep cliff.
7 Whistling long in the echoing vale.
8 Singing the opportune wind.
9 Having obtained the true insight, whistling long.
10 Advanced in years like the long-lived pines.
11 In a drunken dance descending from the mountain.[31]

Secondly there is the *Yü-ko* (Song of the Fisherman),[32] the pendant of the tune mentioned above. This tune is ascribed to the great T'ang poet Liu Tsung-yüan.[33] In the handbook of Yang Piao-chêng this tune has not less than 18 parts, which bear the following subtitles:

1 Clouds over the rivers Hsiao and Hsiang (two rivers in Hunan province, famous for their beautiful scenery).
2 The autumn river glossy like silk.
3 Mist and rain over lake Tung-t'ing (the famous lake in the north of Hunan province).
4 The misty waves of the river Hsiang.
5 The brilliant moon in the broad heaven.
6 Antiphonal song of the fishermen.

---

[28] 漁樵閑話；邵雍，1011–1077 (cf. his *Yü-ch'iao-tui-wên* 漁樵對問 'Dialogue Between the Fisherman and the Fuel Gatherer').

[29] 樵歌，毛敏仲

[30] Appendix II, 11.

[31] 遯世無悶，傲睨物表，遠棲雲嶠，斧斤入林，樂道以書，振衣俹岡，長嘯谷答，詠鄭公風 (for the exact meaning of the expression *chêng-kung-fêng*, see *Hou-han-shu*, the biography of Chêng Hung 鄭宏)，豁然長嘯，壽倚松齡，醉舞下山

[32] 漁歌

[33] 柳宗元，773–819.

7 Cries of the wild geese.

8 At evening mooring near the western rock.

9 Evening song of the fishermen.

10 Lying drunk among the rushes.

11 Evening rain outside the weed-grown window.

12 The falling leaves of the *wu-t'ung* tree.

13 At dawn drawing water from the Hsiang river.

14 The fishing boats are rowed out.

15 Throwing the nets into the cool river.

16 The sun appears, the mists dissolve.

17 A splashing sound of the oars.

18 Highness of the mountains and eternity of the streams.[34]

All tunes belonging to this first group correspond to that part of *ch'in* ideology that I designated above as mainly Taoistic in character. Those tunes that belong to the next group, however, bear a more Confucianist character. They often treat of Confucius and other saints of antiquity, and celebrate the conduct of historical persons.

Tunes of a semi-historical character: under this group I classify all tunes that are connected with some famous person, or with a well-known historical theme. Among this category there must be mentioned in the first place the many compositions connected with Confucius. The Sage is said to have been a great lute player, and according to tradition he composed several lute melodies at critical moments of his eventful life. As a specimen I mention the famous old tune *I-lan*[35] (Alas, the Orchid!). This tune is already mentioned in a catalogue of *ch'in* tunes of the Han dynasty, the *Ch'in-tsao*,[36] the oldest list of *ch'in* tunes that exists. There it is said: 'The elegy *I-lan* was composed by Confucius. He had visited in succession all the Feudal Princes, but none of them could employ him. Returning from Wei to [his native state] Lu, he passed a hidden vale, and there observed a fragrant orchid flourishing alone. Heaving a sigh he said: "In truth, the orchid should be the perfume of kings, but now it is flourishing alone as a mate of common plants. It might be compared with the wise man, who finds that the times are not suited for practising his principles, and [consequently] associates with the common people." Having said this he halted his chariot, and drawing his lute near him, he

---

34 瀟湘水雲, 秋江如練, 洞庭烟雨, 楚湘烟波, 天濶月朗, 漁歌互答, 嗈嗈鳴雁, 夜傍西岩, 漁人晚唱, 醉臥蘆花, 蓬窓夜雨, 梧桐落葉, 曉汲湘水, 漁舟邐槳, 寒江撒網, 日出烟消, 欸乃一聲, 山高水長.

35 猗蘭

36 Appendix II, 1.

composed a tune on the orchid.'[37] The handbooks generally ascribe the tune to Confucius himself; the *Shên-chi-pi-pu* remarks: 'Wise men of olden times, taking this occurrence as an example, composed this elegy.'[38] The tune as preserved in early Ming handbooks does not show the characteristics of old melodies.[39]

Another tune of a semi-historical character that is found in nearly all handbooks is *Hu-chia*[40] (Barbarian Reed Pipe). This tune has 18 parts, and therefore is also often called *Hu-chia-shih-pa-p'o*[41] (Eighteen Blasts of the Barbarian Reed Pipe). This tune was composed by the T'ang musician Tung T'ing-lan.[42] The subject is the exile of Ts'ai Yen, daughter of the famous scholar and musician Ts'ai Yung,[43] round whom several lute stories center. The *Shên-chi-pi-pu* adds to this tune the following introduction: 'When the Han dynasty was in great confusion, Ts'ai Yen was abducted by Hu horsemen into the barbarian country, and there made the wife of their king. She stayed there twelve years, and bore the king two sons. The king held her in high esteem. Once in spring she ascended a barbarian chariot, and was moved by the sound of the reed pipes; she made a poem to express her feelings... Later the Emperor Wu, because of his friendship with her father Ts'ai Yung, despatched a general who redeemed her. She returned to China, but her two sons remained among the barbarians. Later, when the barbarians longingly remembered her, they rolled a reed into a pipe, and blew on it melancholy tunes. Thereafter Tung T'ing-lan of the T'ang dynasty, who excelled in the laws of music as expounded by Shên Yo and Chu Hsing-hsien,[44] transcribed this music of the barbarian reed pipe for the lute, and so made two tunes, called the Smaller and Greater Barbarian Reed Pipe.'[45] Evidently this story was made up to explain

---

[37] 猗蘭操者，孔子所作也，孔子歷聘諸侯，諸侯莫能任，自衞反魯，過隱谷之中，見薌蘭獨茂，喟然嘆曰，夫蘭當爲王者香，今乃獨茂，與衆草爲伍，譬猶賢者不逢時，與鄙夫爲倫也，乃止車，援琴鼓之.

[38] 古之哲人擬之而作是操.

[39] See the transcription of parts 1 and 2 by Courant, *op. cit.* page 170.

[40] 胡笳

[41] 胡笳十八拍

[42] 董庭蘭, who flourished during the K'ai-yüan period, 713–41.

[43] 133–192; see p. 177.

[44] *Shên-chia-shêng, chu-chia-shêng:* the meaning of these two terms is doubtful. Some sources give 汎 for 沈, and 枳 instead of 祝. It would seem that they refer to two schools

(*chia* 家) of musical theory, each called after the name of its chief exponent. I wrote Shên Yo and Chu Hsiang-hsien, because the first (沈約, 441–513) was a famous musical theorist, and the second (祝象賢, Liang dynasty) a well-known lute expert of about the same period. This, however, is a mere guess, and it does not pretend to settle the question. Modern Chinese scholars have given up the problem as hopeless; cf. Yang Tsung-chi in his *Ch'in-hsüeh-ts'ung-shu* (App. II, 7), *Ch'in-hua* 琴話 ch. 2, page 11, and also the relevant items in the *Yin-yüeh-tz'ŭ-tien* 音樂辭典 by Liu Ch'êng-fu 劉誠甫, Shanghai 1935.

[45] 漢室大亂，琰爲胡騎所獲，入番爲后，十二年生二子，王甚重之，春月登胡車琰感笳之*

a posteriori the presence in the *ch'in* repertoire of an obviously un-Chinese melody. The 16th part of this tune has been transcribed in western notation by Courant.[46] This tune is very popular in China, and is to be found also in the repertoire of the flute, *êrh-hu*, *p'i-p'a* and other instruments.

As a third example I may quote the highly attractive composition *Mei-hua-san-nung*[47] (Three Variations on the Peach Blossom). This melody was originally intended for the flute, and the famous flutist of the Chin period, the scholar Huan I, is mentioned as its composer.[48] Tradition asserts that he played this tune for Wang Hui-chih[49] when they happened to meet on the road. In the *Shên-chi-pi-pu* this tune has ten parts, which bear the following subtitles:

1 Evening moon over the mountains.
2 First variation: Calling the moon. The tones penetrate into the wide mist.
3 Second variation: Entering the clouds. The tones penetrate into the clouds.
4 The Blue Bird calls the soul.
5 Third variation: Trying to pass the Hêng river. The tones imitate a long-drawn sigh.
6 Tones of a jade flute.
7 Plaques of jade hit by a cool breeze.
8 Tones of an iron flute.
9 Peach blossoms dancing in the wind.
10 Infinite longing.[50]

The main melodic pattern of this tune is contained in parts 2, 3, and 5, which are transpositions of an extremely delicate and refined melody.

These three examples might be easily increased by scores of others. I mention only the *I-chiao-chin-li* regarding Chang Liang, the famous general of the end of the Ch'in period, the *Yen-kuo-hêng-yang*, said to have been made by the poet Su Wu during his captivity among the barbarians, and the *Ch'ü-yüan-wên-tu* ascribed to Ch'ü Yüan, the well-known poet of the 4th century B.C., etc.[51]

---

*晉, 作詩言誌, 後武帝與邕有舊, 勅大將軍贖文姬歸漢, 二子留胡中, 後胡人思慕文姬, 乃捲蘆葉爲吹笳奏哀怨之音, 後唐董庭蘭善爲沈家聲祝家聲, 以琴寫胡笳聲爲大小胡笳是也.

46 *Op. cit.* p. 171.
47 梅花三弄
48 晉, 桓伊

49 王徽之 son of the great calligrapher Wang Hsi-chih, 321–79.
50 溪山夜月, 一弄叫月聲入太霞, 二弄穿雲聲入雲中, 靑鳥啼魂, 三弄橫江隔江長歎聲, 玉簫聲, 凌風憂玉, 鐵笛聲, 風蕩梅花, 欲罷不能.
51 圯橋進履; 雁過衡陽, by 蘇武, died 60 B.C.; 屈原問渡

Musical versions of literary products: foremost among this group come musical versions of some odes of the *Shih-ching*.[52] *Kuan-chü*, the opening ode of this classic, which celebrates the virtues of the bride of King Wên of Chou, is, of course, famous.[53] Then the *Lu-ming*,[54] a festive ode, where a banquet for high guests is described. It would seem that these two odes are inserted in the *ch'in* repertoire because both mention the lute.[55] These tunes are transmitted in greatly varying versions. Still they show some archaic features, and therefore deserve a special study; they may contain some old musical motifs.

The other tunes belonging to this category can be described in a few words; most of the better-known literary products which mention the lute and its music, or generally correspond to the tenets of *ch'in* ideology, have been made subjects for lute melodies. Most handbooks contain musical versions of the *Li-sao*, of *Kuei-ch'ü-lai-tz'û*, *T'êng-wang-ko*, *Nan-hsün-ko*, etc.[56] Many examples of poems and essays set to lute music may be found in the handbook *Sung-fêng-ko-ch'in-pu* compiled by Ch'êng Hsiung.[57] The reverse process is followed when new words are made to existing melodies; this is called *t'ien-tz'û*.[58] Examples of tunes with *t'ien-tz'û* may be found in the handbook *Shu-huai-tsao*,[59] the sister volume to the *Sung-fêng-ko-ch'in-pu*.

Tunes descriptive of nature: tunes of this type, together with those describing a mystic journey, occupy three-quarters of the entire *ch'in* repertoire. After the remarks made above (Chapter III, section *3*), this connection of the lute with scenic beauty needs no further commentary.

Ts'ai Yung is mentioned as the composer of *Ch'ang-ch'ing*,[60] a solemn melody that describes winter and the coming of spring. The *Shên-chi-pi-pu* remarks: 'This tune takes its inspiration from the snow, describes snow's purity and freedom from all earthly stains, and expresses contempt for the world and elevation to empty clearness.'[61] The nine parts of this tune are entitled:

1 Heaven and earth breathe purity.
2 A clear, snowy morning.

---

52 詩經
53 關雎
54 鹿鳴
55 See above, p. 7.
56 離騷, 歸去來辭, 滕王閣, 南薰歌
57 松風閣琴譜; 程雄. His preface is dated

1677.
58 填詞
59 抒懷操
60 長清
61 取興於雪, 言其清潔而無塵滓之志, 厭世途超空明之趣也.

3 Snow and sleet fall together.

4 Mountains and water merge in each other.

5 The brilliant sun in the sky.

6 The wind blows through the luxuriant forest.

7 River and mountain are like a picture.

8 The snow melts on cliffs and in vales.

9 Spring returns to the world.[62]

Further, Kuo Mien[63] composed a tune on the rivers Hsiao and Hsiang entitled *Hsiao-hsiang-shui-yün*[64] (Clouds Over the Rivers Hsiao and Hsiang). The ten parts bear the following subtitles:

1 Mist and rain over lake Tung-t'ing.

2 The rivers Chiang and Han are quiet and clear.

3 Shadows of the clouds cast down by the brilliant sky.

4 The water is one with the sky.

5 Rolling waves, flying clouds.

6 The rising wind stirs the waves.

7 Sky and water are of the same azure colour.

8 The cold river in the cool moonshine.

9 Limpid waves stretching for ten thousand miles.

10 The scenery contains all aspects of nature.[65]

And here of course must also be classified that most famous of all lute melodies, the tune called *Kao-shan-liu-shui*[66] (High Mountains and Flowing Streams). This composition is ascribed to Po Ya,[67] the paragon of all Chinese lute players. He is said to have been a man from Ch'u[68] who lived during the Ch'un-ch'iu period. The story about him and his friend Chung Ch'i[69] is related in *Lieh-tzŭ*, chapter 'T'ang-wên': 'Po Ya was a great lute player, and Chung Ch'i a great listener. Po Ya while playing the lute thought of ascending high mountains. Then Chung Ch'i said: "How excellent! Impressing like the T'ai-shan!" And when Po Ya thought of flowing streams, Chung Ch'i said: "How excellent! Broad and flowing like rivers and streams!" What Po Ya thought Chung Ch'i never failed to understand. Once Po Ya roamed on the northern flank of the T'ai-shan. Caught in a torrential rain, he took shelter under a cliff. Sad in his heart he drew his lute towards him, and pulled the strings. First he played the

---

62 乾坤清氣, 雪天清曉, 雪霰交飛, 山河一色, 日麗中天, 風鼓瓊林, 江山如畫, 雪消崖谷, 萬壑回春.

63 郭沔, Sung dynasty.

64 瀟湘水雲

65 洞庭煙雨, 江漢舒晴, 天光雲影, 水接天隅, 浪捲雲飛, 風起水湧, 水天一碧, 寒江月冷, 萬里澄波, 景涵萬象

66 高山流水

67 伯牙, also called Po Tzŭ-ya 伯子牙.

68 楚

69 鍾期, also called Chung Tzŭ-ch'i 鍾子期.

elegy of the falling rain, then he improvised upon the sounds of crumbling mountains. But as soon as he had played a tune, Chung Ch'i had already grasped its meaning. Then Po Ya pushed aside his lute, and said with a sigh: "Excellent, how excellent! Your hearing is such that you know immediately how to express what is in my mind. How could I ever escape you with my tones!'"[70] The *Lü-shih-ch'un-ch'iu* supplements this story as follows: 'When Chung Ch'i died, Po Ya broke his lute and tore the strings, and all his life did not play any more, as he deemed the world not worthy to be played to.'[71]

There is hardly any Chinese book or treatise on music that in some form or other does not quote this story; see for instance the quotation in Chapter III above, section 4, the last passage of Ying Shao's essay. In later times the story was elaborated further, and made into a novel.[72]

This story may be said to contain the essence of the system of *ch'in* ideology, stressing as it does the supreme importance of the *significance* of lute music: to express it while playing, and to understand it while listening. Although about Po Ya and Chung Ch'i nothing is reliably known, there can be no doubt that the motif itself is a very old one; perhaps it is en echo of the sacredness of music in ancient China.

The date of the composition which is transmitted under the name *Kao-shan-liu-shui*, however, must be placed comparatively late. It is not mentioned in the *Ch'in-tsao*, and appears only as late as the T'ang period. The author of *Shên-chi-pi-pu* divides the composition into two separate tunes, which he calls *Kao-shan* and *Liu-shui*. But in his preface to the former he says that originally they formed but one tune; during the T'ang period this tune was split up in two parts, each without further subdivision (*tuan*).[73] During the Sung dynasty the part *Kao-shan* was divided into 4 *tuan*, and the part *Liu-shui* into 8.[74] The Ch'ing handbook *Ch'un-ts'ao-t'ang-ch'in-pu*,[75] however, gives it as one tune, and asserts that it was during the Yüan dynasty that the tune was wrongly divided into two parts. Be this as it may, the tunes

---

70 伯牙善鼓琴，鍾子期善聽，伯牙鼓琴，志在登高山，鍾子期曰，善哉，峩峩兮若泰山，志在流水，鍾子期曰善哉，洋洋兮若江河，伯牙所念，鍾子期必得之，伯牙游於泰山之陰，卒逢暴雨，止於岩下，心悲，乃援琴而鼓之，初爲霖雨之操，更造崩山之音，曲每奏，鍾子期輒窮其趣，伯牙乃舍琴而嘆曰善哉善哉，子之聽，夫志想象猶吾心也，吾於何逃聲哉.

71 鍾子期死，伯牙破琴絕絃，終身不復鼓琴，

以爲世無足復爲鼓琴者. 呂氏春秋卷十四，本味.

72 爺伯牙捽琴謝知音 n. 19 of the collection *Chin-ku-chi-kuan* 今古奇觀.

73 段

74 高山流水二曲本只一曲，至唐分爲兩曲，不分段數，至宋分高山爲四段，流水爲八段.

75 Appendix II, 17.

transmitted in the handbooks under this name do not seem to represent very old music. Very late is a special version of the part *Liu-shui*, a kind of 'show piece', composed by Chang K'ung-shan.[76] It was published in the *T'ien-wên-ko-ch'in-pu-chi-ch'êng*,[77] and reprinted and analyzed by Yang Tsung-chi in his *Ch'in-hsüeh-ts'ung-shu*.[78] This tune is technically so complicated that the composer had to invent a dozen new signs to be able to record this music in notation. Although interesting as a proof of the many possibilities of lute music, it has no value for the study of Chinese music. But the ideological motif which it bears in its name doubtless goes back to many centuries B.C.

Tunes descriptive of literary life: most of the tunes belonging to this type are of later date, as a rule from after the Sung dynasty. They sing the joys of the leisure hours of the scholar, passed with refined pleasures. As an example the following tune, ascribed to the literatus Liu Chi, may suffice.[79] It is entitled *K'o-ch'uang-yeh-hua*[80] (Literary Gathering in the Evening). The handbook of Yang Piao-chêng gives the names of its ten parts as follows:

1 Bridling emotions, indulging in meditation.
2 Celebrating antiquity, deploring the present.
3 Composing poetry and drinking wine.
4, 5 Discussing current topics.
6 A song with clapping of the hands.
6, 7 Elevated talk in the quiet night.
8 Thousand miles, one square.
9 Half of this evening equals ten years.
10 Kindred spirits, kindred traditions.[81]

About ninety-five per cent of the tunes that are contained in the lute repertoire may be classified under one of the above five groups. The remaining five per cent are purely musical compositions, and some Buddhist chants.

It goes without saying that the above classification is in many respects very arbitrary: the tunes have been selected from various Ming handbooks, and give but a very general idea of their contents. Still the above will suffice to show that nearly all the tunes of the Ming repertoire have some special meaning or portent: they are

---

76 張孔山
77 Appendix II, 18.
78 *Ch'in-pu* 琴譜, ch. 3.
79 劉基, 1311–75.

80 客窗夜話
81 羈情旅思, 慨古傷今, 題詩酌酒, 時世問答, 抵掌一嘯, 清談良夜, 千里一方, 半夜十年, 同志同傳.

what nowadays would be called 'programme music'. The music is not used independently, but chiefly as a means for expressing an idea, for conveying an impression. Music is made subservient to motif.

CHAPTER FIVE

Symbolism

§1 SYMBOLISM OF TERMS AND NAMES

Symbolism of the technical names for various parts of the lute—preponderance of the dragon and phoenix elements—symbolism of special names given to lutes

THE construction of the lute in general I have already discussed in Chapter I, at the same time quoting the technical names of some of its component parts. This technical terminology is very old; references in literature tend to show that it was already more or less fixed during the Han dynasty. As these terms illustrate some aspects of *ch'in* ideology, I shall here discuss them in greater detail.

Figure 8 shows the upper side (on the right) and the bottom (on the left) of a lute, with the technical names of each part added. Observing first the upper side, we see that the narrow, low bridge where the strings pass over the sounding box is called *lung-yin*[1] (dragon's gums); this part of the lute suggests the roof of a dragon's mouth. The higher bridge on the other end, where the strings are fastened to the silk loops, is called *yo-shan*.[2] 'Yo' is another name of the famous mountain, the T'ai-shan in Shantung province, a symbol of immovability and aloofness.

The narrow space seen beneath this bridge is called *fêng-ê*[3] (phoenix forehead); like *lung-yin* mentioned above, this term is apparently chosen because the slightly bent surface suggests also the forehead of the phoenix. The two terms for the small and the larger indentation, *hsien-jên-chien* (shoulders of the Immortal) and *yao* (waist),[4] are self-explanatory.

The left extremity of the lute is called *chiao-wei*[5] (scorched tail). This term refers to an anecdote told about the famous scholar and lute amateur Ts'ai Yung.[6] *Ch'in* handbooks usually give this story as fol-

---

1 龍齦
2 岳山
3 鳳額

4 仙人肩，腰
5 焦尾
6 蔡邕，133–92.

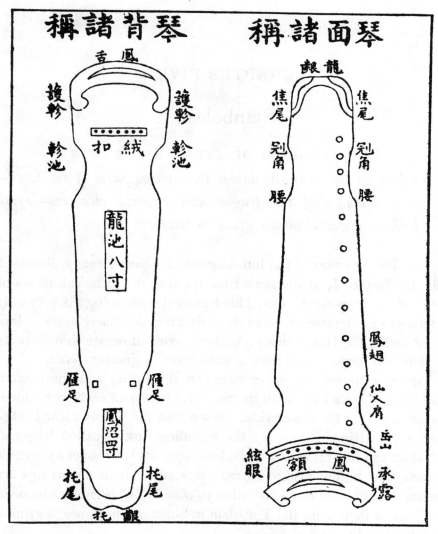

#8

lows: 'People from Wu were burning a log of *t'ung* wood for their cooking. Ts'ai Yung, when he heard its crackling sounds, said: "This will be the right material for making a lute!" He asked whether he might have the log, and made a lute from it. At one end, however, the marks of the burning still showed; therefore he called this lute Scorched Tail.'[7] In lists of lute names there occurs the appellation *I-hsin*[8] (left-over fuel); this name refers to the same anecdote.

The bulging part above the 'waist' is called *kuan-chüeh*[9] (cere-

---

[7] 吳人有燒桐以爨者，蔡邕聞其爆聲曰，此良材也，因請之，削以爲琴，而燒不盡，因名之焦尾.

[8] 遺薪

[9] 冠角

monial cap), since it shows the same outline as this type of headgear. Both sides are called *fêng-ch'ih*[10] (phoenix wings), because they resemble the straight wing feathers with which this mythical bird is usually represented.

Turning now to the bottom board, we see in the first place the two sound holes, to which I have already referred above in Chap. I. Usually the largest one is called *lung-ch'ih* (dragon pond), and the smaller *fêng-chao* (phoenix pool).[11] But from the *Ch'in-tsao* it would appear that during the Han period the upper hole was called simply *ch'ih* (pond), and the lower one *pin* (shore).[12] A Korean source of the Ming dynasty (*Ak-hak-kwe-pôm*) calls the upper hole *lung-ch'üan* (dragon fountain), and the other *fêng-ch'ih* (phoenix pond).[13]

The two pegs for fastening the strings are called *yen-tsu*[14] (goose feet) doubtless because of their suggestive shape. The lower part of the *fêng-ê* is called *fêng-shê*[15] (phoenix tongue). The remaining terms have no special connection with the lore of the lute.

The terms mentioned above show the preponderance of the two elements phoenix and dragon. The lore connected with these two mythical animals pervades the ideology of the lute; as will be seen below, many special names of lutes refer to the phoenix or the dragon, and not a few tunes celebrate their eminent qualities.

It is not only in lute music that these two fabulous animals occupy a foremost position; they are closely associated with Chinese music in general. They figure prominently in the decoration of the instruments of the ceremonial orchestra, and some instruments even derive their names from them (e.g. *Lung-ti*, and *Fêng-huang-hsiao*,[16] both names of flutes).

Chinese sources explain the close connection of phoenix and music by the fact that according to tradition it was the notes sung by the male and female phoenix that in hoary antiquity inspired man to construct the twelve *lü*, the sonorous tubes that form the basis of Chinese musical theory.[17] And with regard to the dragon they say that the lofty and awe-inspiring qualities of this mythical animal, and its rolling growlings when it roams through the clouds, suggest the solemn tones of ceremonial music. But the secondary character of

---

10　鳳翅
11　龍池，鳳沼
12　Appendix ii, 1；濱
13　樂學軌範, preface dated 1610；龍泉，
鳳池

14　雁足
15　鳳舌
16　龍笛，鳳凰簫
17　律；see *Han-shu* 漢書, *Lü-li-chih* 律曆志.

these explanations is evident: they represent endeavours to explain *a posteriori* an association, the real origin of which was no longer understood. The real origin must probably be sought in ancient Chinese beliefs, where the original forms of dragon and phoenix, i.e. *spirit of the waters* and *fire-bird*, played an important role, both being considered as granters of vitality and fertility. As such these animals figured prominently in the sacrifices and the ceremonial music connected therewith. This question, however, deserves a special investigation.

Next there are the special names borne by lutes. When a connoisseur obtains a lute the tones of which appeal to him, or which because of its colour, its shape or for some other reason captures his fancy, he will choose a special name for it. This name is carved in graceful characters in the bottom board (usually in the space above the Dragon Pond);[18] and henceforward the instrument is always referred to by this special name, which gives it something of a personal character and individual appeal.

Later connoisseurs may, and do, add laudatory inscriptions or other remarks, and so antique lutes are not infrequently covered with various inscriptions and seals, which make it a favourite object for the connoisseur's appreciation. For the carving of these inscriptions there exists a special technique, which I have discussed in Appendix III. For our present subject, however, it is only the names themselves that are of importance.

The happy owner of a beautiful instrument is free to choose any name for it that appeals to him. But usually it is selected from the existing lists of approved lute names. Such lists are to be found among the introductory chapters of most of the handbooks for the lute. A few were published separately. The best known is the *Ya-ch'in-ming-lu* compiled by Hsieh Chuang.[19] Just as in the titles of the tunes, also in these names of individual instruments various aspects of *ch'in* ideology are to be found reflected.

The greater part of the names describe the beautiful tones of the instrument. I mention, for instance, names like *Ling-lung-yü* (Tinkling Jade), *Hao-chung* (Singing Bell), *Yen-ying* (Echo of a Goose Cry), *Ch'un-lei* (Spring Thunder), *Ming-yü* (Singing Jade), *Lung-yin* (Dragon's Growling), *Lin-lang*, etc.[20]

---

18 See fig. II, in Chapter I of this book.

19 雅琴名錄 (謝莊, style: Hsi-i 希逸, 421–66); this text is to be found in the *Hsün-chih* 順治 edition of the huge *ts'ung-shu*, *Shuo-fu* 說郛.

20 玲瓏玉, 號鐘, 雁應, 春雷, 鳴玉, 龍吟, 琳琅.

Others refer to the fact that the lute is the repository of the correct music of the Ancient Sages: to this category belong such titles as *Ts'un-ku* (Preserving Antiquity), *Yu-shêng* (Befriending the Ancient Sages), *Huai-ku* (Cherishing Antiquity), *T'ai-ku-i-yin* (Tones Bequeathed by High Antiquity), *Ta-ya* (Great Elegance).[21]

Others again suggest the atmosphere that surrounds the lute and its music. Here I would classify for instance: *Ku-t'ung* (Lonely Dryandra Tree), *Han-yü* (Cool Jade), *Sung-hsüeh* (Snow on the Pines), *Yang-shêng-chu* (Master of Nurturing Life), *Hsüeh-yeh-chung* (Bells on a Snowy Night), *Ho-yu* (Friend of the Crane), *Ching-yu* (Friend of Serenity), *Fou-ch'ing* (Floating Sonorous Stone), *Sung-hsien* (Immortal of the Pine Forest), etc.[22] Some names of four characters evoke a picturesque scenery, suggesting refined aesthetic enjoyment, so dear to the artist and the connoisseur: *Shih-shang-ch'ing-ch'üan* (A Clear Stream Flowing over Stones), *Hsüeh-yeh-chung-shêng* (The Sound of a Temple Bell on a Snowy Evening), *Pi-t'ien-fêng-ming* (A Phoenix Singing in the Azure Sky), *Ch'ing-hsiao-ho-lei* (A Crane Crying in the High Air).[23]

The above are only a few examples; the lover of the lute may choose any name that pleases him from the vast field of Chinese literary allusion.

21 存古, 友聖, 懷古, 太古遺音, 大雅
22 孤桐, 寒玉, 松雪, 養生主, 雪夜鐘, 鶴友, 靜友, 浮磬, 松仙
23 石上清泉, 雪夜鐘聲, 碧天鳳鳴, 青霄鶴淚.

§2 SYMBOLISM OF TONES

*Great importance of timbre in lute music—Chinese attempts to define the various sorts of timbre—*LÊNG CHʻIEN'S *sixteen definitions, in text and translation*

Most handbooks for the lute player include among the introductory chapters a special section entitled *Chʻin-shêng*[24] (tones of the lute). There an attempt is made to express in words that extremely elusive element that constitutes one of the chief charms of lute music: the timbre, the colour of the tones.

Through the delicate structure of the lute, the strings respond to the most subtle nuances in the touch. The same note obtains a different colour when it is played with the thumb or with the forefinger of the right hand, and the timbre changes according to the force with which the string is pulled. This applies especially to the technique of the left hand: beneath the nimble and sensitive fingers of the expert player the strings show a wealth of unsuspected modulations. The high notes may either have a dry, almost wooden sound, or they may be sharp and metallic, and in another passage the same note may be clear and tinkling, like a silver bell. Low notes may be broad and mellow, or so abrupt as to be nearly rattling.

As the correct application of the various sorts of modulation is the basis of lute music, the Chinese have given much care to describe and define the various touches and the results they produce. In choosing the terminology they borrowed freely from the rich vocabulary of aesthetic appreciation, used by Chinese artists and connoisseurs.[25] Next to special musical terms like *chʻing* (light), or *sung* (loose),[26] we also find old appreciative adjectives, which are not easy to translate. We find for instance words like *yu, chʻing,* and *hsü,*[27] each of

---

24 琴聲

25 Both Chinese and Western dictionaries are sadly inadequate in their explanations of the hundreds of special terms that constitute this vocabulary. Yet an understanding of the scope of these terms, and of the subtle nuances in sentiment they imply, is absolutely necessary for a correct interpretation of the writings by Chinese art critics, whether their subject is fine art, belles-lettres, scenic beauty or music. It is to be hoped that some day a sinologue with artistic interest will undertake to compile a special dictionary of Chinese aesthetic terms, illustrated with appropriate quotations. A beginning on a small scale has been made by Lin Yu-tʻang in his *The Importance of Living,* New York 1937, Appendix B: 'A Chinese Critical Vocabulary'.

26 輕, 鬆

27 幽, 清, 虛

which suggests a definite atmosphere or mood. In most cases it is impossible to cover all the associations evoked by such a term with one single English word; their meaning must be understood through the context.

Not a few Chinese musicians have made endeavours to formulate such definitions for the various sorts of modulation. Well known, for instance, is a set of 24 articles, entitled *Ch'in-huang*, drawn up by the lute expert Hsü Hung and to be found in the *Ta-huan-ko-ch'in-pu*, a handbook for the lute connected with his name.[28] Universally approved, however, is the set of definitions formulated by Lêng-hsien, the 'Immortal Lêng', under the title of *Ch'in-shêng-shih-liu-fa* (Sixteen Rules for the Tones of the Lute).[29]

The 'Immortal Lêng' was a great musician of the beginning of the Ming dynasty; his real name was Lêng Ch'ien.[30] About 1370–1380 he occupied the position of Chief Musician in the *Yüeh-pu*,[31] the Board of Music. Besides music Lêng Ch'ien was deeply interested in Taoist magic; the *Imperial Catalogue* mentions a book by him entitled *Hsiu-ling-yao-chih* (Important Directions for Prolonging Life); apparently he lived to be a proof of the truth of his beliefs, for according to tradition he was over a hundred years old when he died.[32]

His *Ch'in-shêng-shih-liu-fa*, which I translate below, is reprinted in many of the later *ch'in-pu*, usually without quoting Lêng Ch'ien as the author. Therefore this essay is sometimes ascribed to other musicians. Besides the *ch'in-pu*, it is also to be found in the *Chiao-ch'uang-chiu-lu*[33] by Hsiang Yüan-pien and in the *T'an-chi-ts'ung-shu*.[33] For my translation I have used the text as published in the *Chiao-ch'uang-chiu-lu*.

This text presents various difficulties. The sentences are brief, and often ambiguous. It is often not clear whether descriptive adjectives apply to the finger technique or to the tones produced by it. In my translation I have taken all these adjectives to refer to the finger technique, in order not to confuse the reader.

The descriptive adjectives are not easy to render adequately:

28 琴況；徐谼；大還閣琴譜, first preface dated 1673. The second article has been translated by Laloy, on page 71 of his *La Musique chinoise*; see App. I, 5.

29 冷仙, 琴聲十六法

30 冷謙; style: Ch'i-ching 啓敬; literary name: Lung-yang-tzû 龍陽子. He died be-

tween 1403–24.

31 樂部.

32 In chap. 147, p. 10 *verso*; 修齡要指. For the tradition, see *I-nien-lu* 疑年錄, ch. 5.

33 蕉窗九錄；項元汴, 1525–90；檀几叢書.

they suggest rather than describe, they indicate but do not define. Many a sentence might in the translation have been spun out to a whole passage. I have aimed at brevity, leaving it to the reader to interpret the passages, and to elaborate their meaning. I do not pretend, however, that my translation is final; in many cases it is but one of a dozen different possibilities.

Often our text uses special terms referring to various parts of the finger technique; as those are discussed in the next section of this chapter, I have left them here without any special explanation.

SIXTEEN RULES FOR THE TONES OF THE LUTE

1 *Ch'ing*:[34] THE LIGHT TOUCH.

> Not light and not heavy are the tones of balanced harmony. When the melody starts,[35] one should aim at playing in these balanced tones. If, in applying the light and heavy touch, the rules of decrescendo and crescendo are adhered to, the sentiment of the tune appears of its own accord. The light touch is the most difficult of all. If not enough force is applied, then the tone is vague and not true, dim and not clear; though light, it is not elegant. The middle light tones are faultless, clear and true. [When applying the light touch] one should consider the string being as thin as one single silk thread of one ten-thousandth of an inch, the sound of which is spoilt when the finger as much as approaches it. Then these tones shall express a sentiment of infinite profundity. Sometimes one whole phrase or bar is played in the light touch, but there exist also the mixed, the higher and the lower light touches. Their tendencies vary, but, with regard to all, the main point lies in clearness and truth.[36]

2 *Sung*:[37] THE LOOSE TOUCH.

> The beauty of vibrato and vibrato ritardando lies in the loose touch. The left hand should move up and down over the string

---

34 輕

35 起周, in the handbooks often abbreviated to 己周; literally: 'beginning of the melody'. A tune usually opens with an introductory movement which has no melodic connections with the following parts. Then, mostly in the middle of the second movement, the chief melodic pattern of the tune appears for the first time. This passage is marked with the sign 己周.

36 一曰輕. 不輕不重者, 中和之音也, 起調當以中和爲主, 而輕重特 (read 持) 損益之則, 其趣自生, 蓋音之輕處最難, 力有未到則浮而不實, 晦而不明, 雖輕亦不嘉, 惟輕之中, 不爽清實, 而一絲一忽, 指到音綻, 幽趣無限, 迺有一節一句之輕, 有間雜高下之輕, 種種意趣, 皆貴於清實中得之.

37 鬆

in a rounded-off movement, light and freely, without any jerks or hitches. It should not be too hasty, nor too slow, but just right: this is what is called the loose touch. Heavy, thin, slow and quick vibrato and vibrato ritardando, all are based on the loose touch. Therefore, the wondrous music of the lute entirely depends upon touch. If the touch is rounded off, then the emotions are unified; if the loose touch is lively, then the thoughts are elated. The loose touch should evoke an impression as of water rising in waves, its substance should evoke an impression as of pearls rolling in a bowl; its sound should be like the resonance of intoning a text: this is what is called the loose touch.[38]

3 *Ts'ui:*[39] THE CRISP TOUCH.

The crisp touch is firm. Even for playing tunes of soft harmony and great elegance, both hands should attack the strings, firmly, so that the tones will not be turbid. For each hand this crisp touch is used, but it is hidden and does not come into sight, and it is not easy to express. When the right hand drags on the strings, then the tones will be turbid and dull. Therefore it is said: One should attack the strings with the tips of the fingers, touching them vertically from above. If one does not attack the strings smartly, then the tones will be sticky and irregular. Therefore it is said: The resonance should be like metal or stone, the movement of the fingers should be like the rising wind. For understanding the crisp touch, the swiftness of the fingers should first be known. The swiftness of the fingers is rooted in firmness. The firmness of the fingers is rooted in the arm. If the strength of the arm is applied, then the firm, crisp touch may be executed. Not until then can it be understood that the tendency to turbidity inherent in the strings does not annoy the true musician.[40, 41]

4 *Hua:*[42] THE GLIDING TOUCH.

Gliding means flowing: it is the opposite of halting. The tones

---

38 二曰鬆. 鬆即吟猱妙處, 宛轉動蕩無滯無礙, 不促不慢, 以至恰好, 謂之鬆, 吟猱之巨細緩急, 俱有鬆, 故琴之妙在取音, 宛轉則情聯, 鬆活則意暢, 其趣如水之興瀾, 其體如珠之走盤, 其聲如哦咏之有韻, 方可名鬆.

39 脆

40 The text reads: 在絃, 當爲知音厭聲耳, which does not seem to make sense. I follow the text as reprinted in the *Wu-chih-chai-ch'in-pu* (App. II, 15).

41 三曰脆. 脆者健也, 於冲和大雅中, 健其兩手, 而音不至於滯, 兩手皆有脆音, 第藏之不見, 出之不易, 右指靠絃, 則音滯而木, 故曰, 指必甲尖, 絃必懸落, 在指不勁, 則音膠而格, 故曰, 響如金石, 動如風發, 要知脆處, 即脂之靈處, 指之靈, 自出於健, 而指之健, 又出於腕, 腕中之力既到, 則爲堅脆, 然後識滯氣之在絃, 不爲知音厭聽.

42 滑

tend to be halting, and the fingers tend to be gliding. By nature the tones tend to be drawn out, and to follow each other in slow succession, like the bubbling sound of a stream, that goes on gurgling endlessly. Therefore this is called halting. If the finger technique is impeded, then it is not swift. The fingers should move up and down like gusts of wind, therefore this touch is called gliding. The most important point in the movement of the fingers is of course gliding. But sometimes also stopping is important. This stopping should be considered as a pause in the gliding. So that when in a tune there is halting, there must also be gliding; and if there is gliding, there must also be halting. Then both obtain their real significance.[43]

5 *Kao*:[44] THE LOFTY TOUCH.

Although the lofty touch resembles the antique touch,[45] they are essentially different. The antique touch is expressed by resonance, the lofty touch is modelled after melody. If the finger technique is serene and clear, and if moreover one can apply the lofty modulation, only then shall the meaning of the tones reach the mysterious wonder. Therefore this touch is of the utmost tranquillity, like a deep well that can not be fathomed, like a high mountain whose top is lost to the eye. It flows on, like streams that are never exhausted, and it is soundless like the threefold sound[46] of emptiness.[47]

6 *Chieh*:[48] THE PURE TOUCH.

If one wishes to attain perfection in tone, one should first attain perfection in the finger technique. The way of perfecting the finger technique passes from being to not-being, through multiplicity to simplicity. Not discoloured by one speck of dust, not defiled by one flaw, the secret of the finger technique dwells in the stage of the highest purity. But generally people do not

43 四曰滑. 滑者溜也, 又澀之反也, 音嘗欲澀而指嘗欲滑, 音本喜慢, 而緩緩出之, 若流泉之鳴咽, 時滴滴不已, 故曰澀, 指取走絃而滯則不驟, 乃往來之鼓動, 如風發發, 曰故滑, 然指之運用, 固貴其滑, 而亦有時平貴留, 所謂留者, 即滑中之安頓處也, 故有澀不可滑, 有滑不可無留, 意各有在耳.

44 高

45 See p. 113 below.

46 In *Chuang-tzǔ* 莊子, chapter *Ch'i-wu-lun* 齊爲論, are mentioned the sounds of Heavenly, of Earthly, and of Human Emptiness 天籟, 地籟, 人籟. *Lai* is the unheard harmony of the Universe, what the Greeks called the 'Harmony of the Spheres'.

47 五曰高. 高與古似, 而古實與高異, 古以韻發, 高以調裁, 指下既靜既清, 而又能得高調, 則音意始臻微妙, 故其爲甯謐也, 若深淵之不可測, 若喬嶽之不可望, 其爲流逝也, 若江河之欲無盡, 若三籟之欲無聲.

48 潔

realize this. If in the finger technique purity is perfected, then the tones become more and more rarefied.[49] The more rarefied the tones are, the more the spirit nears eternity. Therefore I say: if one wishes to perfect wondrous tones, one should first perfect the wondrous finger technique. In order to perfect the wondrous finger technique, one must necessarily start with cultivating purity in oneself.[50]

7 *Ch'ing:*[51] THE CLEAR TOUCH.

All tones are governed by clearness. If the place where the music is performed is secluded, clearness results; when the heart is serene, clearness results; when the spirit is solemn, clearness results; if the lute is true, clearness results; if the strings are clean, clearness results. Only when all these factors that affect clearness are assembled may one aim at clearness in the finger technique. Then left and right hand shall be like Male and Female Phoenix, chanting harmoniously together, and the tones shall not be stained with the slightest impurity. The movement of the fingers should be like striking bronze bells or sonorous stones. Slow or quick, no secondary sounds shall be produced, so that when hearing these tones one obtains an impression of purity—as of a pool in autumn; of brilliancy—as of the shining moon; of dim resonance—as of the babbling water in mountain gorges; of profundity—as of a resounding valley. These tones shall in truth freeze alike heart and bones,[52] and it shall be as if one were going to be bodily transformed into an Immortal.[53]

8 *Hsü:*[54] THE EMPTY TOUCH.

While playing the lute to express true tones, this is not very difficult. What is really difficult is to express emptiness. If asked 'The fingers move to produce tones; where does emp-

---

[49] *Hsi* 希, a typical Taoist adjective, difficult to translate. Together with the equally obscure terms *i* 夷 and *wei* 微, it is used in the 14th chapter of the *Tao-tê-ching* to describe Tao. There it is said: 'I listen to it but I cannot hear it, therefore I call it *hsi*' 聽之不聞,名曰希.

[50] 六曰潔. 欲修妙音者,必先修妙指, 修指之道, 從有而無, 因多而寡, 一塵不染, 一垢弗緇, 止於至潔之地, 而人不知其解, 指既修潔, 則音愈希, 則意趣愈永, 吾故曰, 欲修妙音者,

必先修妙指, 欲修妙指者, 又必先自修潔始.

[51] 清

[52] For this 'frozen' mental condition, see p. 58.

[53] 七曰清. 清者音之主宰, 地僻則清, 心靜則清, 氣蕭則清, 琴實則清, 琴潔則清, 必使群清, 咸集而後可求之指上, 兩手如鸞鳳和鳴, 不染纖毫濁氣, 應指如擊金戛石, 緩急絕無容聲, 試一聽之則澄然秋潭, 皎然月潔, 劃然山濤, 幽然谷應, 眞令人心骨俱冷, 體氣欲仙.

[54] 虛

tiness come in?' I would answer: It lies exactly in the producing of tones. If the tones are sharp, the player shows his precipitation; if the tones are coarse, then the player betrays his impurity; but if the tones are serene, then the player shows that he has achieved the expression of emptiness. This is the right way for appreciating music. The merit of the finger technique lies in two things; on the one hand in expressing the spirit of the melody, and on the other in refining its purity. When the spirit of the melody is expressed, then the heart will become serene as a matter of course, and when the purity is refined, the tones shall naturally be empty. Therefore though being quick they will not be disorderly, and though being many they will not be confused. The self-sufficiency of a deep well, an irradiating splendour, high mountains and flowing streams: with the spirit of these one's soul should harmonize.[55]

9 *Yu:*[56] THE PROFOUND TOUCH.

If tones are profound, then they come up to the standard of lute music. The quality of music depends upon the personality of the player; thus profundity comes from within. Therefore, when a high-minded and cultivated scholar executes a tune, then the resonance is profound. If one truly understands profundity as expressed by the fingers, the player can let himself go, whether the movement be slow or quick. The music will be broad and generous like the wind, and unstained by earthly dust. It will serve to show the elevated disposition of the player, and the fingers will depict the emotion that inspired each part of the composition. This is meant by the saying: Let the fingers express what the heart experiences.[57] When one hears his music one shall know the personality of the player. Such are the wonderful qualities of the profound touch.[58]

10 *Chi:*[59] THE RARE TOUCH.

The special quality of tone that is produced by the rare touch

---

55 八曰虛. 撫琴著實處, 亦何難, 獨難於得虛, 然指動而求聲, 烏乎虛, 余則曰, 政在聲中求耳, 聲屬則知躁, 聲粗則知濁, 聲靜則知虛, 此審音之道也, 蓋下指功夫, 一在調氣, 一在淘洗, 調氣則心自靜, 淘洗則聲自虛, 故雖急而不亂, 多而不繁, 深淵自居, 清光發外, 山高水流, 於此可以神會.

56 幽

57 Quoted from *Lieh-tzŭ*, chapter *T'ang-wên*.

58 九曰幽. 音有幽度, 始稱琴品, 品係乎人, 幽由於內, 故高雅之士動操便有幽韻, 洵知幽之在指, 無論緩急, 悉能安閒自如, 風度益溢, 些無塵染, 足覘瀟麗胸次, 指下自然寫出一段風情, 所謂得之心, 而應之手, 聽其音而得其人, 此幽之微妙也.   59 奇

appears in the vibrato and the glissando. If while playing it is applied in the right way, it should evoke an impression as if a thousand mountain peaks vied with each other in verdure, as if the ten thousand streams emulated each other's effervescence. It should impart to the hearer a sensation of flowing, of going on forever, an unbroken continuity. Where in a tune periods or bars are suddenly broken off, and at the end of a tune, care should be taken especially not to let the music end in a vague, careless way. For each part of a tune has its special sentiment that should be expressed by the performer. Moreover an expression should be given as if one were riding on horseback high in the mountains, amidst drifting clouds.[60] When every note is made to express the sentiment inherent in it, then only shall one know the wonder of the rare touch.[61]

11 *Ku:*[62] THE ANTIQUE TOUCH.

In studying the lute there are only two ways: either one follows the old methods, or one follows the methods that are in vogue at the time. Although the old music is obscured by its high antiquity, still if one tries to approach its meaning, its harmony and and simplicity may be reached as a matter of course. Therefore, when in playing one does not fall in with the tunes that are in vogue at the time, then the music breathes the spirit of the Emperor Fu Hsi. It should be grand, broad and simple, boldly moving over the strings, disdaining petty virtuosity. It should be unmoved like a profound mountain, like a cavernous vale, like an old tree or a cool stream, like the rustling wind, causing the hearer suddenly to realize the True Way. This is something that certainly is rarely seen or heard in this world; therefore it is called the antique touch.[63]

60 Quotation from the poem entitled *Sung-yu-jên-ju-shu* 送友人入蜀 (Collected Works, ch. 15), a poem by the great T'ang poet Li T'ai-po (季太白, 701–62). Lin Yu-t'ang translates these lines thus: 'Above the man's face arise the hills; beside the horse's head emerge the clouds' (cf. *My Country and My People*, New York 1936, pp. 246–7, where the rich imagery of these lines is aptly explained).

61 十曰奇. 音有奇特處, 乃在吟逗間, 指下取之, 當如千巖競秀, 萬壑爭流, 令人流連不盡, 應接不暇, 至章句頓挫, 曲折之際, 尤不可輕意草草放過, 定有一段情緒, 又如山從人面起, 雲傍馬頭生, 字字摹神, 方知奇妙.

62 古

63 十一曰古. 琴學祇有二途, 非從古則從時, 玆雖古學久淹而彷彿其意則自和澹中來, 下指不落時調, 便有羲皇氣象, 寬大純朴, 落落絃中, 不事小巧, 宛然深山邃谷老木寒泉, 風聲籟籟, 頓令人起道心, 絶非世所見聞者, 是以名曰古音.

12 *T'an:*[64] THE SIMPLE TOUCH.

The lute masters of the present time aim at charming the ears; they insist upon producing captivating sounds, thereby greatly sinning against refined elegance. This is because they do not know that the basis of lute music is simplicity. I, on the contrary, tune my lute to simplicity, therefore the great mass does not understand my music. Where is it that simplicity dwells? I love its sentiment, which is not extravagant nor contending. I love its flavour, which is like snow or ice. I love its echo, which is like the wind blowing over pines, like rain on bamboo, like the bubbling of a mountain stream, or like lapping waves. It is only with great musicians that one can talk about simplicity.[65]

13 *Chung:*[66] THE BALANCED TOUCH.

Balanced sounds occur in all music, but they are inherent[67] in the music of the lute. After the old music was lost, there were many that pulled the strings with ardent fervour, and carefully listened to the lute; but only the most excellent musicians[68] are able to transmit the echo of the empty vale. When, ignorantly, one rejoices in elaborating mellow and captivating tones, obliquity[69] results. When the finger technique is heavy and impure, obliquity results. When the resonance is strained and hasty, obliquity results. When the tones produced are coarse and sharp, obliquity results. When the strings are attacked hurriedly, obliquity results. When the personality of the player is unstable and casual, obliquity results. Rectifying this obliquity, returning to completeness, banishing the devious and aiming at the right, this is the way to obtain the tradition of the balanced touch.[70]

---

64 澹

65 十二曰澹. 時師欲娛人耳, 必作媚音, 殊傷大雅, 第不知琴音本澹, 而吾復調之以澹, 固衆人所不解, 惟澹何居, 吾愛此情, 不參不競, 吾愛此味, 如雪如冰, 吾愛此響, 松之風而竹之雨, 澗之滴而波之濤也, 故善知音者, 始可與言澹.

66 中

67 See *Chuang-tzǔ:* 因其固然, 'following its natural course'.

68 *Ying-jên-kua-ho*, lit.: 'The people of Ying play [*ho* in the 4th tone] songs that few are able to perform'; quotation from the

Sung-yü-chi 宋玉集. The meaning is as in the translation above.

69 *P'ien* is used as counterpart to *chung* 中, an allusion to the preface of the Doctrine of the Mean, *Chung-yung* 中庸, where it is said: 'Being without inclination to either side is called *chung*' (Legge) 不偏之謂中.

70 十三曰中. 樂有中聲, 惟琴固然, 自古音淹沒, 攘臂絃素而捧耳於琴者比比矣, 即有繼空谷之響, 未免郢人寡和, 不知喜工柔媚則偏, 落指重濁則偏, 性好炎鬧則偏, 發響局促則偏, 取音粗厲則偏, 入絃倉卒則偏, 氣質浮躁則偏, 矯其偏, 歸於全, 袪其倚, 習於正, 斯得中之傳.

14 *Ho*:[71] THE HARMONIOUS TOUCH.

Harmony is the basis of all tones: it means neither overdoing nor falling short.[72] It is modulated on the strings, it is experienced in the fingers, it is diversified in the notes. The strings have their own nature: if they are compliant, then they will be in harmony with each other. If they are recalcitrant, then they are false. When the movement of the fingers moving up and down, from one string to the other, is smooth like varnish, then the strings harmonize with the fingers. The tones are regulated by the gamut: sometimes they are to be produced exactly on the spot indicated by one of the thirteen studs, sometimes they are not. The numerical indications fix the notes. The important point is to make the vibrato smooth, and to make the chords harmonize precisely, in order to express the sentiment of the tune. Then fingers and tones will be in harmony. Every tone has its own special singificance; the significance comes first, for the notes adjust themselves to the significance. So all the wonders of this music are completed. Therefore, heavy and not vain, light but not floating, swift but not hasty, slow but not slack; with regard to vibrato and vibrato ritardando: smooth but not vulgar; with regard to glissandos: correct and not inaccurate; when all the movements are linked up together smoothly; when the crescendos and decrescendos are crisp and yet connected. . . then tone and significance shall be in harmony. Then the soul shall be free and the spirit at rest, fingers and strings melt together, and the pure harmony that leaves no trace shall be produced. These are the signs by which I recognize the great Harmony.[73]

15 *Chi*:[74] THE QUICK TOUCH.

In the finger technique both the slow and the quick touch are used. The slow touch is the basis of the quick, the quick touch is the echo of the slow. In the tunes both touches are alternating

---

71 和

72 Quoted from the *Lun-yü* 論語, Book XI, ch. 15. 3: 'The Master said: To go beyond is as wrong as to fall short.' (Legge)

73 十四曰和. 和爲五音之本, 無過不及之謂也, 當調之在絃, 審之在指, 辨之在音, 絃有性, 順則協, 逆則矯, 往來鼓動有如膠漆, 則絃與指和, 音有律, 或在徽, 或不在徽, 其有分數以位

其音, 要使婉婉成吟, 絲絲叶韻, 以得其曲之情, 則指與音和, 音有意, 意動音隨, 則衆妙歸, 故重而不虛, 輕而不浮, 疾而不促, 緩而不弛, 若吟若揉, 圓而不俗, 以綽以注, 正而不差, 紆廻曲折, 聯而無間, 抑揚起伏, 斷而復連, 則音與意和, 因之神間氣逸, 指與絃化, 自得渾合無迹, 吾是以知其太和.

74 疾

continually. Sometimes in the middle of a bar the touch is quick, but near its end it slows down; and a bar that ends on the slow touch sometimes is followed up immediately by a movement in the swift touch. Moreover there are two ways for executing the quick touch. The first is called the little swift touch, which must be brisk. It must be firm, yet the movement of the fingers should not spoil the elegance inherent in the swift touch; it should suggest floating clouds and flowing water. The second is the great swift touch. Its most important point lies in its precipitation, but one should make special efforts not to cause confusion by playing too quickly. Then as a matter of course one expresses a mood of tranquillity, and the sounds will come forth bubbling, like rocks crumbling down or like a cascade falling from a high place. Therefore the quick touch is regulated by the meaning of the tones. It is the meaning that lends tones their divine qualities.[75]

16 *Hsü:*[76] THE SLOW TOUCH.

The ancients used the lute to nurture their nature and their emotions; therefore they called its tones rarefied. This quality is to be expressed by the very slow touch. Tones are produced by the fingers, broadly roaming over the strings, but observing the right measure. The finger technique should be in accordance with the right measure, so that the music produced is in harmony with the gamut. Sometimes one entire bar is played calmly and slowly, sometimes also in the same bar slow and quick alternate with each other. Sometimes a bar breaks off in the middle and then goes on again, sometimes also while going on smoothly it suddenly breaks off. When this technique is executed correctly as each case requires, then naturally one produces the rarefied tones of antiquity, and gradually one penetrates the deepest mystery of this music.[77, 78]

---

[75] 十五曰疾，指法有徐，則有疾，然徐爲疾之綱，疾爲徐之應，嘗相間錯，或句中借速以落遲，或句完遲者以速接，又有二法，小速微快，要以緊，遞指不傷疾中之雅度，而隨有行雲流水之趣，大速貴急，務使急而不亂，依然安閒之氣象，而寫出崩崖飛瀑之聲，是故疾以意用，更以意神.

[76] 徐

[77] The last lines of this paragraph seem badly transmitted. *Yang-ch'un* is a famous old tune, said to have been composed by Sung Yu (宋玉, third century B.C.). It is not clear, however, whether *Yüeh-man-hsi-lou* is also the name of a tune, or a sentence in itself. Because such Chinese musicians as I have consulted could not solve the problem without making drastic changes in the text, I leave these lines untranslated.

[78] 十六曰徐，古人以琴涵養性情，故名其聲曰希，嘗於徐徐得之，晉生運指，優游絃上，節*

§3 SYMBOLISM OF THE FINGER TECHNIQUE

Postures of the hands, and their explanations—set of special pictures illustrating the finger technique; their various editions—technical terminology used in the lute handbooks— the abbreviated signs (CHIEN-TZÛ)—list of elementary CHIEN-TZÛ, their meaning and symbolism—examples of how the notation is read

WHEN the spirit of the various touches has been understood, then the lute player must devote his attention to their correct execution, and try to master the finger technique. Also with regard to this practical aspect of the technique of lute playing, the handbooks give explicit directions, illustrated by a rich symbolism. When the meaning of the abbreviated signs that constitute the lute notation has been understood, and when their spirit is recognized, then the student should be able to read and interpret correctly the tunes as they are recorded in the handbooks.

As has been stated above, lute music is written down not in notes, but in complicated symbols that indicate how a note is produced. These symbols are combinations of abbreviated characters, the so-called *chien-tzû*;[79] these shall presently be discussed in greater detail.

Among the introductory chapters of each lute handbook a special section, called *chih-fa*, or also *pu-tzû*,[80] is devoted to these *chien-tzû*. This section covers several pages; for as a rule in the handbooks no fewer than 150–200 special abbreviations are used, and each of these is carefully explained in this section. But the lute masters justly deem mere words inadequate for expressing all the subtleties of the technique described. When it is stated, for instance, that a certain sign means: 'Pull the third string inwards with the index of the right hand,' this explanation is not sufficient for the student who studies the lute without his master being present. For there are many ways to pull a string inwards with the index, but there is but one that is correct and that shall produce the desired timbre.

Therefore to the section *chih-fa* a second one is added, entitled

---

*其氣候，候至而下，以叶厥律，或章句舒徐，或緩急相間，或斷而復續，或續而復斷，因候制宜，自然調古聲希，漸入淵微，嚴道徹詩，幾回拈出

陽春調月滿西樓，下指遲，其於徐意大有得也.

79 減字

80 指法，譜字

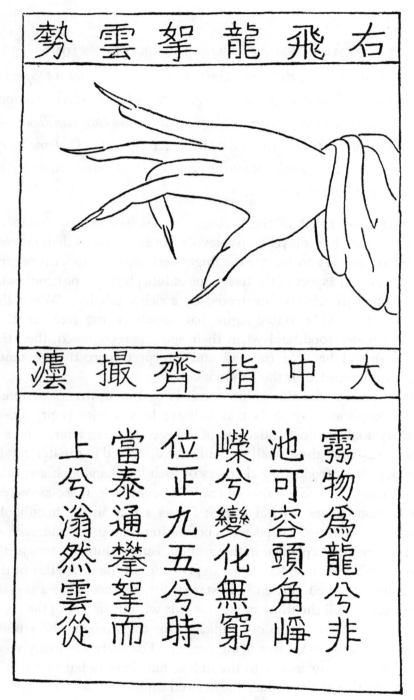

右飛龍挐雲勢

大中指齊撮灑

霧物為龍兮非
池可容頭角崢
嶸兮變化無窮
位正九五兮時
當泰通攀挐而
上兮滃然雲從

#9: Page from a lute handbook (Appendix II #18), showing a
posture of the right hand, with explanatory notes.

#10: Symbolic picture illustrating the finger technique (from a Japanese manuscript copy of the *Yang-ch'un-t'ang-ch'in-pu*).

#11: Symbolic picture illustrating the finger technique (same source as figure 10).

shou-shih (postures of the hands).[81] This section consists of a series of about forty drawings, showing in a schematic way the correct posture of right and left hand for each of the more frequently occurring touches. In some of the later handbooks these sketches are drawn so clumsily, that it is difficult to imagine how they could be of any use to the student of the finger technique. But the older handbooks often have more elaborate drawings, sketched with undeniable skill. To each drawing there is usually added a short sentence, which by means of comparison and symbol explains the spirit of each posture treated. Figure 9, for example, shows the correct posture of the right hand for executing a chord. This picture bears the legend: 'The right hand, suggesting a flying dragon grasping the clouds', and underneath is written: 'The way to produce a chord with thumb and middle finger.'[82] Thus the master tries to suggest to the reader that the touch should be broad and firm, the hand having more or less a clawing posture. Often the meaning is still further elaborated in a short explanatory note, called *hsing* (mood),[83] of the posture in question. The *hsing* of figure 9 reads: 'The dragon is a holy animal, a pond can not contain it. Its head and horns show a noble shape, its transmutations are inexhaustible. Having ascended the Throne [allusion to the fact that 'Dragon' is a fixed epithet of the Emperor], the world is prosperous. It ascends in the air grasping with its claws, the floating clouds follow it.'[84] Finally, to make the meaning clearer still, some handbooks add a picture representing the dragon grasping its way through the clouds (see fig. 10).

Tradition has fixed such a special symbol (*hsiang-hsing*)[85] for each of the elementary postures occurring in the finger technique. Vibrato is illustrated by a cicada creeping up the branch of a tree, three strings pulled at the same time are represented by sailing clouds, the plucking of one string with two fingers at the same time, by a wild goose carrying a reed stalk in its bill (see figs. 11, 12), etc. A full list of these symbols will be found below, where the abbreviated signs are discussed.[86]

---

81 手勢
82 右飛龍拏雲勢；大中指齊撮法
83 興
84 靈物爲龍兮，非池可容，頭角崢嶸兮，變化無窮，位正九五兮，時當泰通，拏拏而上兮，瀚然雲從.
85 像形
86 A brief note should be added to the discussion of the finger technique, concerning

artificial nails (*tai-chia* 代甲 or *ch'in-chia* 琴甲), which lute players sometimes use on their right hands.

As a rule the lute is played without artificial fingernails. The Chinese, and more particularly the members of the literary class, permitted their finger nails to grow longer than is customary in the West; thus Chinese lute players have to cut down the nails of the*

These symbolic explanations of the various postures of the hands are very old; they may already be found in literary sources of the third and fourth centuries A.D. The set of pictures (about 40 in all) belonging to these explanations, however, is of a later date. I could not trace them back further than the Ming period. As this set of pictures is not without artistic value, I may describe their history in a few words.

I found them in three publications of the Ming period; two of these give the pictures in a rather crude form, the third presents them in a more elaborate and artistic way. The two more primitive versions are found:

1 in the lute handbook published by the great musician Hu Wên-huan, entitled *Wên-hui-t'ang-ch'in-pu*.[87a]

*right hand, while we have to let them grow a little. The correct way of pulling a string is to use simultaneously half of the finger tip and the rim of the nail. If artificial nails are used, then the sound volume of a note increases, but at the same time it will lack that muted quality that is one of the characteristics of lute music. Hence most lute players condemn the use of artificial nails.

The oldest reference to artificial nails seems to be a note entitled *ch'in-chia* 琴甲, in the *Tzŭ-hsia-lu* 資霞錄, by the T'ang writer Li K'uang-i 李匡乂. 'At present,' he observes, 'lute players occasionally cut an artificial nail from bamboo, in order to strengthen the notes produced by the index pulling a string; this was first introduced by Ch'ien-kung' 今彈琴或削竹爲甲，以助食指之聲者，亦因汧公也. 'Ch'ien-kung' refers to the famous T'ang statesman and lute player Li Mien (李勉 717–88), author of the *Ch'in-shuo* 琴說 (cf. the *Ch'in-shu-ts'un-mu*, described below on p. 182, no. 8, note on the *Ch'in-shuo* ch. II, pp. 13 ff). A little farther, however, Li K'uang-i criticizes the use of artificial nails, which he condemns as 'rejecting the true for the false' 棄眞用假. According to Li, even when playing the harp or the cither no artificial nails should be used, 'for only if one is able to discard the false and return to the true, will their tones be of complete beauty 至如箜篌之與秦箏，若能去假還眞，其聲宛美矣. This aversion to the use of artificial nails is doubtless based on the ancient theory that the player should be in direct contact with his instrument, so that the vital essence may flow freely from the hands into the strings.

The *Wu-chih-chai* handbook (see p. 185, no. 15) gives in ch. I, in the section *Ch'in-chai-*

pa-tse 琴齊八則 ('Eight Rules for the Lute Chamber'), a brief note on artificial nails. This book recommends to make them from deer horn, ivory, tortoise shell, or the shaft of a goose feather. He also tells what glue should be used for attaching them to the fingers so that they will stay there for two weeks or so, without becoming loosened even by washing the hands in hot water.

87 a) 胡文煥，文會堂琴譜. Hu Wên-huan, style: Tê-fu 德甫 (or also: Tê-wên 德文), literary name: Ch'üan-an 全菴 (or also Chin-an 金菴), and Pao-ch'in-chü-shih 抱琴居士. This interesting personality, a typical Ming literatus, would be well worth a special study. He was a man of elegant tastes, who combined an ardent love for old books and antique lutes with interest in the theatre and its fair inmates and in the lighter genres of poetry. His collection of books and rare manuscripts was well known, and he enjoyed great fame as a lute expert. In addition he wrote numerous plays, and was considered one of the greatest dramatists of the Ming period. Most of his plays, however, are practically unknown; they probably slumber in forgotten corners of Chinese libraries. Hu Wên-huan showed his bibliophilic zeal by publishing an extensive collection of rare works acquired by him; this collection bears the name of *Ko-chih-ts'ung-shu* 格致叢書. It contained 346 items divided over 37 categories; 47 items were published separately. A list of the contents of this *ts'ung-shu* is given in the *Ts'ung-shu-shu-mu-wei-pien* 叢書書目彙編, Shanghai 1929, page 337. Complete copies of this collection, however, do not seem to exist; at least I myself never came across one. Occasionally, however, I obtained separate*

2 in the picture-encyclopedia *San-ts'ai-t'u-hui*.[87b]

The more elaborate version is to be found in a famous Ming handbook for the lute, the *Yang-ch'un-t'ang-ch'in-pu*.[88] It is not without interest to try to establish the relation between these editions.

The *Wên-hui-t'ang* handbook is the oldest source; the preface is dated 1596, according to its last sentence.[89] A specimen page of this handbook is reproduced in figure 12. As to the date of the *San-ts'ai* encyclopedia, its latest preface is dated 1609. The *Yang-ch'un-t'ang* handbook bears no date at all; still it is possible to fix approximately when it was published. This handbook was compiled by Chang Ta-ming,[90] a well-known lute master of the Ming period, who lived in Fukien province. His first great work on the lute was the *Ch'in-ching*, a work on the lute in general, without tunes in notation; it was published in 1609.[91] Now, in his preface to the *Yang-ch'un-t'ang* handbook, Chang Ta-ming states that after having published a work of a more general nature like the *Ch'in-ching*, he felt it necessary to supplement this with a handbook containing tunes in notation: 'The lute needs a handbook with tunes in notation, just as a cart needs its two thills.'[92] From this we may conclude that the *Yang-ch'un-t'ang* handbook was published sometime after 1609, the date of the *Ch'in-ching*. Further, the famous scholar and calligrapher Tung Ch'i-ch'ang[93] added an undated preface to this handbook. In this preface he says that he met Chang Ta-ming in Fukien when traveling there on official business.[94] Now it appears from Tung Ch'i-ch'ang's biography that he visited South China in official capacity in the year 1622: 'He was ordered to proceed to the south to collect documents and other historical materials relating to the former dynasty.'[95] Therefore we shall not be very wrong when we

---

*items. These show that Hu Wên-huan's reprints were fine specimens of Ming block prints, carefully collated and printed in graceful characters, editions in no way inferior to the celebrated *Chi-ku-ko* 汲古閣 reprints published by Mao Chin 毛晉 (1599–1659). It is to be regretted that no attempt has been made to collect all the writings of Hu Wên-huan, and to publish them together. Data about his life, too, are scattered over various sources. One shall look in vain for his biography in the *Ming-shih* 明史. Only the *Ming-tz'û-tsung* 明詞綜 gives, in ch. 10, a short biographical note.

b) 三才圖會. For a description of this interesting Ming encyclopedia, see S. Y. Teng & K. Biggerstaff, *An Annotated Bibliography of Selected Chinese Reference Works, Yenching Journal of Chinese Studies*, Monograph no. 12, Peking 1936, p. 124.

88 陽春堂琴譜

89 The last sentence of the preface running: 譜成於何時, 時蓋萬曆丙申下元也.

90 張大命

91 琴經; see App. ii, 5.

92 琴之必需夫譜猶車之不可廢兩轅也

93 董其昌, 1555–1636.

94 不佞客宦閩中與右衮張生有一日之知

95 *Ming-shih* 明史, ch. 288: 天啓二年命往南方採輯先朝章疏及遺事.

place the date of the *Yang-ch'un-t'ang-ch'in-pu* somewhere around 1625. Thus this publication is considerably later than the *Wên-hui-t'ang* handbook and the *San-ts'ai* encyclopedia. We may assume that Chang Ta-ming had the pictures of the *Wên-hui-t'ang* handbook redrawn by a skilled artist. The set of pictures as published by him offers a good example of the style of painting current during the

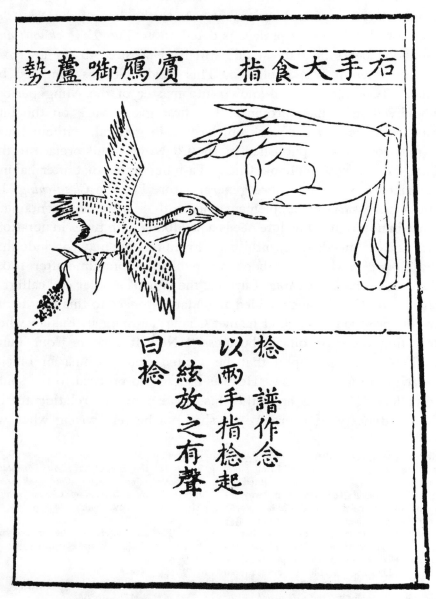

12: Symbolic picture illustrating the finger technique, from *Wên-hui-t'ang-ch'in-pu*. The photostat was kindly sent me by the Library of Congress, Washington.

Ming period (see figures 10 and 11). The reader may compare the *Wên-hui-t'ang* picture reproduced in figure 12, and the *Yang-ch'un-t'ang* version of the same picture in figure 11.

During the Ch'ing period the pictures were mostly left out, and the publishers of lute handbooks contented themselves with reproducing the sketches of the right and left hands in various postures, together with their explanations. The series of pictures, however, found its way to Japan. In 1746 Satō Itchō published an introductory handbook for the Chinese lute, entitled *Kokin seigi*.[96] This book reproduces the set of pictures of the *Yang-ch'un-t'ang-ch'in-pu*, in a slightly revised form.

Before proceeding on to a more detailed discussion of the various movements that constitute the finger technique, and the abbreviated signs by which they are indicated, a few general remarks about the terminology used are necessary.

First it must be remembered that when the player has his lute lying before him on the table, ready to be played, the end with the tuning pegs is on his right (see figure 3 in the first chapter of this essay). Then the thirteen *hui*, studs inlaid in the varnish, appear along the side farthest from the player; this side is called *wai* (outside).[97] The space between the *hui* varies greatly; each of these intervening spaces is theoretically divided into ten equal parts, called *fên*.[98] These *fên* are not indicated on the instrument: the player must learn to find them by practice. The *hui* are numbered 1–13, counting from right to left, and the *fên* are numbered 1–10. The player should see in his mind the *hui* and *fên* lengthened to lines running transversally over the whole breadth of the lute. Thus when the handbook says: 'Press with the left thumb the fifth string down on 9/3,' the player knows that he must choose the spot where a perpendicular line, starting from 9/3 along the outer side of the body of the lute, crosses the fifth string. It is along the row of *hui* that the thickest string, emitting the lowest note, is strung. This string is indicated by the number 1, the others by the numbers 2–7. Thus the string nearest to the player, on the inner side (*nei*),[99] is the thinnest and produces the highest note, and is indicated by the number 7.

In the notation the numbers indicating the strings are written in large characters; they form, so to speak, the marrow of the notation, and easily strike the eye when one looks over a passage of lute music in notation (see figures 14 and 15). The numbers indicating *hui*

---

96 佐藤一張, 古琴精義   97 徽, 外   98 分   99 內

♯13: Selected *chien-tzŭ*, abbreviated signs used in lute notation.

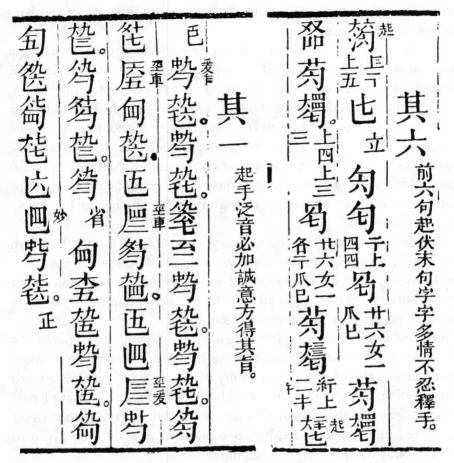

#14 & 15: Two passages from the *Wu-chih-chai* handbook.

and *fên* are written in smaller characters, easily distinguishable by their size and location (right top corner of a combination of *chien-tzŭ*) from those numerals that indicate the strings.

Needless to say, just as in ordinary Chinese writing, so also the *chien-tzŭ* of the lute notation are written in vertical columns, to be read from right to left. And just as in an ordinary Chinese text the commentary and notes are added between the text, but in smaller characters and in two columns; in the same way the columns of *chien-tzŭ* of ordinary size (called *chêng-wên*), are interspersed with *chien-tzŭ* in smaller type (called *fu-wên*).[100] The *chêng-wên* indicate the notes, the *fu-wên* various 'graces' and general indications such as vibrato, piano, etc. For a specimen passage of lute notation, see figs. 14 and 15. The small circles which in an ordinary Chinese text

100 正文, 副文

stand for commas and full stops, here have the function of the bars in our musical scores.

It must always remain an invidious undertaking to describe a musical technique in words. This applies *a fortiori* to Oriental music. Oriental and Western music show so many fundamental differences, that it is a hazardous task to translate Oriental technical terms by our own. Such renderings can never be accepted without considerable reserve. While describing the finger technique of the lute, I therefore have tried to avoid as much as possible the use of Western technical musical terminology; this method has made my explanations perhaps rather verbose, but I hope that a greater degree of accuracy has thereby been obtained.

Below I list 54 of the elementary *chien-tzŭ*. The only Western book wherein some of these abbreviations are discussed is the work on Chinese music by G. Soulié.[101] As, however, Soulié's informant was apparently not a competent lute expert, there occur many mistakes in the explanations. These are corrected below.

On the accompanying plate (figure 13) I have written out 54 abbreviated signs; those selected are the *chien-tzŭ* that occur most frequently in the lute notation. Many of the *chien-tzŭ* that remain are but combinations of those discussed here. My explanations are based on those given in the standard handbooks, and they have been verified by some lute masters in Peking. Special attention has been given to the symbolic explanations of each movement.

1 *San*:[102] this string should be played by the right hand only, the left hand not touching the string.

2 *T'o*:[103] the thumb of the right hand pulls a string outwards. Explained as 'A crane dancing in a deserted garden'.[104] Also as 'A crane dancing in the wind'.[105] The meaning is that the touch should be firm, but at the same time loose.

3 *Po* (sometimes read *p'i*):[106] the thumb of the right hand pulls a string inwards (with the nail). Explanation same as 2.

4 *Mo* (Soulié wrongly reads *mei*):[107] the index pulls a string inward. 'A crane singing in the shadow';[108] from the accompanying picture it appears that the shadow of a bamboo

---

101 Appendix I, 3.
102 散
103 托
104 虛庭鶴舞
105 風前鶴舞
106 擘, 劈
107 抹
108 鶴鳴在陰

grove is meant. The touch of the index should be as firm as that of the thumb, but less jerky; a smooth movement should be aimed at.

5   *T'iao*:[109] the index pulls a string outward. Explanation same as 4.

6   *Kou*:[110] the middle finger pulls a string inward. 'A lonely duck looks back to the flock.'[111] The curve of the middle finger should be modelled on that of the neck of the wild duck: curved but not angular. If the middle finger is too much hooked, the touch will be jerky.

7   *T'i*:[112] the middle finger pulls a string outward. Explanation same as 6.

8   *Ta*:[113] the ring finger pulls a string inwards. 'The Shang-yang bird hopping about.'[114] The Shang-yang is a fabulous bird, said to have only one leg. The idea is that, in contradistinction to the smooth movements of the index and middle finger, the touch of the ring finger should be short and crisp.

9   *Chai*[115] (Soulié wrongly reads *ti*) : the ring finger pulls a string outward. Explanation same as above.

10   *Ch'üan-fu*[116] (Soulié wrongly reads *ch'üan-mo*) : index, middle finger and ring finger each pull at the same time a different string, making the three strings produce together one sound. 'Light clouds sailing in the wind.'[117] The touch should be light and delicate, so that the three notes melt together.

11   *Li* (also explained as *tu*):[118] the index lightly passes over two or three strings in succession, in outward direction (Soulié says inward, which is wrong). Explanation same as 10.

12   *Ts'o*:[119] a chord; two fingers pull two strings at the same time, making them sound together. The strings to be pulled are indicated by their numbers, written on either side of the perpendicular stroke in the center of the abbreviated sign. The normal chord is a combination *t'o-kau*;[120] the opposite

109   挑
110   勾
111   孤鶩顧群
112   剔
113   打
114   商羊鼓舞

115   摘
116   全扶
117   風送輕雲
118   歷，度
119   撮
120   托勾

combination, *po-t'i*,[121] called *fan-ts'o*,[122] is indicated by adding the character *fan*[123] on top of the *chien-tzû* for *ts'o*.[124] 'A flying dragon grasping the clouds.'[125, 126]

13 *P'o-tz'û*:[127] index, middle and ring finger together pull two strings, once inward (*p'o*), and immediately after outward (*tz'u*). 'A swimming fish moving its tail.'[128] The illustration shows that a carp is intended. A measured, broadly sweeping touch should be aimed at.

14 *Ta-yüan*:[129] a movement consisting of seven sounds, played on two strings. First *t'iao*[129] on the string nearest to the body, and *kou*[129] on the string further away; a slight pause; then rapidly repeat the same movement twice; again a short pause, and end up with *t'iao* on the string one started with. This movement can be executed on any pair of strings, but usually it is found with regard to 1 and 4, 2 and 5, 3 and 6, 4 and 7. It is customary in the notation to write the first *t'iao* and *kou* in *chien-tzû*, and then to add underneath in a smaller character the *chien-tzû* for *ta-yüan*. 'A holy tortoise emerges from the water.'[130] The picture shows a tortoise climbing a small island in a pond. One should try to imitate the crawling movement of the legs of the tortoise: short, but determined touches, in absolutely the same rhythm.

15 *Pei-so*[131] (Soulié wrongly reads *pei-chao*): three sounds are produced on one and the same string, by a succession of *t'i-mo-t'iao*.[132] 'A wild fowl flapping its wings.'[133] Crisp touches in rapid succession.

16 *Tuan-so*,[134] one and the same string produces five sounds, first a slow *mo-kou*,[134] followed by *pei-so*. Explanation same as 15.

17 *Ch'ang-so*,[135] one and the same string produces seven sounds, first *mo-t'iao-mo-kou*,[136] then add *pei-so*. Explanation same as 15.

---

121 擘剔
122 反撮
123 反
124 撮
125 飛龍拏雲
126 Explained on p. 121 above. See also figure 10.
127 潑刺
128 游魚擺尾

129 打圓, 挑, 勾
130 神龜出水
131 背鎖
132 剔抹挑
133 鸧鶊鳥翔翔
134 短鎖, 抹勾
135 長鎖
136 抹挑抹勾

18 *Lun*[137] 'a wheel': this is a rapid movement, executed on one string, viz. *chai-t'i-t'iao*[137] in quick succession. It should be executed very lightly and delicately, so as to cause the three sounds to melt together. This term in itself is very aptly chosen: it implies that the three fingers should imitate the spokes of a wheel. When a wheel turns round swiftly, each separate spoke is no longer visible. 'A purple crab walking sidewards'[138]—the same idea, differently expressed. One should think of the rapid movement of the legs of small crabs when they scurry over the sand. Among the movements of the right hand, this is the only one that might be compared with the 'graces' executed by the left hand (vibrato, etc.); often lute players introduce *lun* when it is not written in the notation; for the movement is so rapid that it does not affect the rhythm. Therefore a simple *t'iao* or *mo*[139] may be replaced by a *lun*. A discreet appliance of *lun* may give a tune additional charm, but one should guard against overdoing it: avoiding cheap effects is one of the most important rules for the lute player. *Lun* is very much used in *p'i-p'a* music where its technical appellation is *ta-i-ko-lun-tzŭ* (to beat a wheel).[140]

19 *Pan-lun*,[141] 'half a wheel': the same movement as the preceding, but with middle and ring finger only.

20 *Ju-i*,[142] 'as one': two strings sound together. 'Female and male phoenix singing in harmony.'[143]

21 *Shuang-tan*,[144] 'double pulling': one string produces two sounds in rapid succession; usually *mo-kou*.[145] 'Cold ravens pecking at the snow.'[146] The picture shows a flight of emaciated ravens on a barren tree in a winter landscape: they peck at the snow that covers the dry branches, hoping to discover something to eat. The movement should be executed with the very tips of the fingers, a short, crisp, pecking touch.

22 *So-ling*[147] (properly the name of a musical instrument, consisting of several bells hung on a cord; when the cord is

---

137 輪, 摘剔挑
138 紫蟹傍行
139 挑, 抹
140 打一個輪子
141 半輪
142 如一

143 鸞鳳和鳴
144 雙彈
145 抹勾
146 寒鴉啄雪
147 索鈴

pulled, the bells ring together): the left hand glides lightly over several strings in succession, while the right index moves over the same strings in a light manner *(t'iao)*[148] simultaneously with the movement of the left hand; the movements of both hands should be strictly parallel. 'Bells hung on a cord being shaken.'[149] The aim is a subtle, tinkling effect. Properly this movement belongs to the 'floating sounds'.[150]

23 *K'un*,[151] 'welling up' (I do not know how Soulié obtained his reading *liao*): *t'i*[152] over several strings in succession, from 7 to 2, or from 6 to 1. 'A heron bathing in a whirlpool.'[153] One should think of a heron taking a bath in the small eddies of a stream in the shallow places along its banks: the whirling movement of the water, together with the flapping of the wings should suggest the character of the movement. Mostly played on the free strings, with the right hand only; occasionally, however, one string must be pressed down with the left hand. When executed correctly, this movement, together with the next item (its opposite), constitutes a very attractive motif. A later, and technically extremely difficult version of the tune *Liu-shui* (Flowing Streams),[154] has one part consisting of practically nothing but variations on this *k'un*. When it is played by a virtuoso (ordinary players would hardly dare to touch this tune!), one hears the babbling of water all through the melody: now the melody dominates, then the sounds of water, a fascinating effect.[155] The lute master Chêng Ying-sun[156] is a well-known player of especially this tune.

24 *Fu*,[157] 'to brush': the opposite of the preceding item, played over strings 1–6 or 2–7.

25 *Tsai-tso*,[158] 'repeat the preceding movement'. This and the following ten items do not represent notes: they are indications of a general character.

26 *Ts'ung-kou-tsai-tso*,[159] 'repeat the preceding passage, from the

148 挑
149 振索鳴鈴
150 *fan-yin* 泛音
151 滾
152 剔
153 鷺浴盤渦
154 流水

155 However, see my remarks on this tune, on p. 99 above.
156 鄭穎孫
157 拂
158 再作
159 從勾再作

place indicated by the bracket'. Instead of *ts'ung-kou*[160] one may also find *ts'ung-t'ou*,[161] meaning *da capo*.

27 *Shao-hsi*,[162] a short pause.

28 *Ju-man*,[163] *ritardando*.

29 *Chin*,[164] '(up) to'; for instance: '*k'un* from the 6th to the 1st string.'[165]

30 *Lien*,[166] *legato*.

31 *Ch'ing*,[167] *piano*.

32 *Chung*,[168] *forte*.

33 *Huan*,[169] *lente*.

34 *Chi*,[170] *presto*.

35 *Ta-chih*,[171] the left thumb. This and the following items all regard the finger technique of the left hand.

36 *Shih-chih*,[172] the left index.

37 *Chung-chih*,[173] the left middle finger.

38 *Ming-chih*,[174] the left ring finger.

39 *Ch'o*:[175] a finger of the left hand, before pressing down a string on the spot indicated by *hui* and *fên*, starts about 5 mm. to the left of that place, and quickly glides to the right, till the place indicated is reached. The result is a rising, prolonged note. 'A wild pheasant ascending a tree.'[176] The sound produced should resemble the cry of the wild pheasant, who sings in the morning. Soulié's explanation of this and the following item is mistaken.

40 *Chu*,[177] the opposite of the preceding item: One starts about 5 mm. to the *right* of the spot indicated, and then glides down to the left, till the spot is reached. Explanation as in no. 39. Both *ch'o* and *chu* are produced *simultaneously* with the pulling of the string by the right hand. They should be distinguished from *shang* and *hsia*[178] (cf. below, no. 45), which are executed *after* the right hand has pulled the string.

41 *Yin*,[179] *vibrato*. A finger of the left hand quickly moves up

160 從勹
161 從頭 (abbreviated into 叾).
162 少息
163 入慢
164 至
165 滾六至一
166 連
167 輕
168 重
169 緩

170 急
171 大指
172 食指
173 中指
174 名指
175 綽
176 野雉登木
177 注
178 上，下
179 吟

and down over the spot indicated. 'A cold cicada bemoans the coming of autumn.'[180] The plaintive, rocking drone of the cicadas (well known to all foreigners living in China and Japan!) should be imitated. Of this *yin* there exist more than ten varieties. There is the *ch'ang-yin*,[181] a drawn-out vibrato, that should recall 'the cry of a dove announcing rain';[182] the *hsi-yin*,[183] a thin vibrato, that should make one think of 'confidential whispering';[184] the *yu-yin*,[185] swinging vibrato, that should evoke the image of 'fallen blossoms floating down with the stream',[186] etc. Remarkable is the *ting-yin*[187]—the vacillating movement of the finger should be so subtle as to be hardly noticeable. Some handbooks say that one should not move the finger at all, but let the timbre be influenced by the pulsation of the blood in the fingertip, pressing the string down on the board a little more fully and heavily than usual.

42 *Jou*,[188] *vibrato ritardando*. A vibrato somewhat broader and more accentuated than *yin*.[189] Properly the character should be pronounced *nao*, meaning 'monkey'; but lute players pronounce it *jou*. Doubtless the character *jou*[190] meaning 'to twist, to rub' is the proper one. It was replaced by that read *nao* because, for use as *chien-tzŭ*, the 94th radical is more distinct than the 64th one. And, further, the symbolic association may also have played a role: for the vibrato ritardando should suggest 'the cry of a *monkey* while climbing a tree'.[191]

43 *Chuang*,[192] 'to strike against': after the right hand has pulled a string, the left makes a quick, jerky movement, up and down to the right of the spot indicated.

44 *Chin-fu*,[193] 'advancing and returning': after the right hand has pulled the string, the left glides upwards to a certain point indicated, then glides down again till it reaches the point where it started, or another spot, as indicated in the notation.

---

180 寒蟬吟秋
181 長吟
182 鳴鳩喚雨
183 細吟
184 喁喁私語
185 遊吟
186 落花隨水

187 定吟
188 猱
189 *yin*
190 揉
191 號猿升木
192 撞
193 進復

45 *Shang*[194] (ascending), and *hsia*[195] (descending): properly an elaborate form of the preceding item, but often interchangeable with it. *Shang* is gliding to the right, in stages. For instance, a string is pulled while the left hand presses it down on the spot indicated by the 9th *hui*. The notation adds the remark: 'glide upwards till 8/4, then till 7/8.'[196] *Hsia* is the same movement, but in opposite direction. Often *shang* and *hsia* count as many as three or four stages, and form part of the melody. Therefore movements like these properly should not be called 'graces': they do not 'grace' the original note, but are notes in themselves.[197]

46 *Fên-k'ai*,[198] 'divide and open': a peculiar movement, which makes one and the same string produce four sounds in succession. For instance, the right hand pulls a string while the left presses it down on the 9th *hui;* when the tone is still resounding, the left hand glides to the right in a resolute and bold movement till the next *hui* is reached, stays there for an infinitesimal moment, then glides back to the initial spot, and just when it arrives there, the right hand again pulls the string.

47 *Yen*,[199] 'to cover': the thumb, middle or ring finger of the left hand taps a string, producing a low, dull sound; the right hand does not touch the string. This touch is mostly executed with the left thumb; e.g., the ring finger presses a string down on the 9th *hui*, and the right hand pulls this string: thereafter one leaves the ring finger on the same spot, but taps the string with the left thumb, on the place indicated by the 8th *hui*. 'The woodpecker picking a tree.'[200] As many others, this symbol is remarkably well chosen from an acoustic point of view.

48 *Wang-lai*,[201] 'coming and going': a combination of *chin-fu* (no. 44) and *yin* (no. 41). A finger of the left hand, after the right has pulled the string, moves one *hui* to the right, produces 'vibrato', then returns to the original *hui*, and produces 'vibrato' there; and repeats this movement. After

---

194 上
195 下
196 上八四, 七八
197 Cf. the very pertinent remarks about the 'graces' in Indian music, in A. H. Fox Strangeways, *The Music of Hindostân* (Oxford

1914), ch. VII.
198 分開
199 罨
200 幽禽啄木
201 往來

the first vibrato, the sound caused by the pulling of the string by the right hand will have died away: the difficulty is to revive the sound by moving to the right and to the left with a strong jerk. 'A phoenix, having alighted on a branch, combs its tail feathers with its bill.'[202] Anyone who has observed a bird combing its feathers will recognize how cleverly this image is chosen: one sees the broad movement with which the bird first arranges the feathers (*chin-fu*), occasionally interrupted by short, tugging movements for discarding the down (vibrato).

49   *T'ao-ch'i*,[203] 'pulling up and raising': a movement peculiar to the left hand only, executed with the thumb. When the ring finger is pressing a string down, for instance on the 9th *hui*, the left thumb pulls the string. The same note would be produced if the thumb of the right hand pulled the string, while the left ring finger pressed it down on the 9th *hui*; but the timbre is entirely different. The accompanying explanation, 'Two immortals transmitting the Way,'[204] seems enigmatical. It was explained to me as follows. An adept who really understands 'the Way' (*tao*), knows that words are of no use in explaining it; cf. the opening sentence of the *Tao-tê-ching*: 'The *tao* that can be explained is not the eternal Tao.'[205] Therefore, when two adepts discuss *tao*, they just utter a short abrupt sound, which is said to comprise the cosmic function of *tao*. This idea Taoism has borrowed from the Ch'an[206] school of Buddhism; in Ch'an technical terminology this sound is called *ho*.[207, 208] Zen Buddhism, in its turn, doubtless borrowed this idea of the all-embracing magical power of a single sound from Mantrayana teachings, where, for instance, the vowel *a*[209] is considered as the receptacle of all the deepest mysteries. The utterance of such a single magic syllable may move all the spiritual agencies of the entire universe.[210] But to return to our present subject: the sound produced should be abrupt and dry.

---

202 栖鳳梳翎
203 搯起
204 二仙傳道
205 道可道非常道
206 禪, Jap. *Zen.*
207 喝, Jap. *katsu.*
208 For a good description of the all-important role of this sound in Ch'an Bud-

dhism, cf. D. T. Suzuki, *Essays in Zen Buddhism,* first series (London 1927), pp. 279–80.

209 阿

210 Cf. the article '*a*' in the *Hōbōgirin. Dictionnaire encyclopédique du Bouddhisme,* Tokyo 1929.

50 *Hu*,[211] 'a sloping bank': the right hand has pulled a string, pressed down by the thumb of the left hand on the 10th *hui*; one waits a moment, then glides with the left thumb to the right, till the 9th *hui* is reached. This gliding movement is called *hu*. It should be slow and emphatic, like dragging something up the sloping bank of a river. After the pause, the sound produced has lost most of its volume; the aim is to utilize the last echo of the sound for the *hu*.

51 *Kuei*,[212] 'to kneel': often it will prove inconvenient to press down a string with the tip of the left ring finger, especially when a *t'ao-ch'i* (no. 49) must be executed on the places indicated by the lower *hui*. In such cases the difficulty is solved by pressing down the string, not with the tip of the left ring finger, but with the back of its first joint. Thus that finger must assume a crooked posture. 'A panther grasping something.'[213] The idea is to suggest a firm, determined pressure. Soulié's explanation: *pao-chih*, 'little finger', is of course entirely erroneous, since the little finger of either hand is never used in lute music. For this reason in lute terminology the little finger is called *chin-chih*,[214] 'forbidden finger'.

52 *Fan-ch'i*,[215] 'here the floating sounds start': a sign warning the player that the succeeding notes are all in 'floating sounds', i.e., harmonics. As has been explained above, the harmonics are produced when the left hand, instead of pressing down a string on the board, just lightly touches it. The delicate touch of the fingers of the left hand is aptly described as 'white butterflies exploring flowers'.[216] Where the floating sounds should end, there occurs a sign read *fan-chih*;[217] the *chien-tzu* consists of the upper part of no. 52 added on top of the character *chih*.[218] Soulié's reading *fa* must rest on some mistake. It should be added that floating sounds are only possible on the places indicated by the *hui*, not on the intervening spots.

53 *Fang-ho*,[219] 'let go and unite': this touch especially applies to the ring finger of the left hand, and implies a kind of chord.

211 滘
212 跪
213 文豹抱物
214 禁指
215 泛起

216 粉蝶探花
217 泛止
218 止
219 放合

Suppose the right hand has pulled the 3rd string, while the ring finger of the left hand was pressing it down on the 9th *hui*. The next note is pulling the 4th string, free. Now, while the 4th string is being pulled, the left ring finger pulls the 3rd string, causing both strings to sound together. 'Echo in an empty vale.'[220] The accompanying picture shows two recluses standing in a vale, and clapping their hands.

54   *T'ui-ch'u*,[221] 'pushing outwards': a touch executed by the middle finger of the left hand. Suppose that the right hand has pulled the first string, while the left middle finger pressed it down on the 13th *hui*; while the next note is being played, the middle finger is left in its position on the *hui*. Then, when the next sound has been produced by the right hand, the left middle finger makes the 1st string sound by pushing it outward. 'A silver pheasant dancing.'[222]

In illustration of the above, I shall now explain two passages in lute notation, taken from the *Wu-chih-chai* handbook,[223] and reproduced in figures 14 and 15. To save space the strings are indicated by roman, the *hui* and *fên* by arabic numerals. Both passages are taken from the well-known lute melody *Mo-tzû-pei-ssû*[224] (the philosopher Mo-tzû sorrowing over the silk). The significance of this tune is understood by reading Mo-tzû, I, 3: *So-jan*,[225] the opening passage: 'Our Master Mo-tzû said with a sigh, when he saw silk being dyed: When silk is dyed with a dark colour, it becomes dark, when dyed with a yellow colour it becomes yellow: its colour changes according to the dye in which it is dipped, etc.'[226] The philosopher regrets the fact that man, originally pure, becomes soiled by contact with material life.[227]

Figure 14 shows the first part of this tune, an extremely attractive prelude, written entirely in harmonics. The gloss says: 'The harmonics of this first part must be played with sincerity, only then the meaning will be fully expressed.' The first line opens with the sign for 'start harmonics' (above, item no. 52); to the right an abbreviation for *huan-tso*,[228] 'slowly'.

---

220 空谷傳聲
221 推出
222 白鷳騰踏
223 Appendix II, 15.
224 墨子悲絲
225 所染

226 子墨子言見染絲者而歎曰，染於蒼則蒼，染於黃則黃，所入者變，其色亦變云云.
227 See A. Forke, *Mê Ti, des Sozialethikers und seiner Schüler philosophische Werke*, Berlin 1922, p. 166.
228 緩作

The left middle finger touches I on 9, while the right middle finger pulls the string inwards.

The left thumb touches VI on 9, while the right thumb pulls it outward.

The left middle finger touches II on 9, the right middle finger pulls it inward.

The left thumb touches VII on 9, the right thumb pushes it outward.

The left index moves lightly over VII-II, the right middle finger simultaneously executes *k'un* (no. 23).

The left middle finger touches I on 9, the right middle finger pulls it inward.

The left thumb touches VI on 9, the right thumb pushes it outward. The following two signs being the same as the second bar, they need no explanation.

The left index touches VI on 9, the right middle finger pulls it inward.

The left ring finger touches VII on 10, the right index pushes it outward.

The right index glides lightly over VI and V, connecting them (*ch'ing lien*[229]), while the left ring finger touches them on 10. It should be noted that if no *hui* is indicated, and if the sign *san*,[230] 'free strings', is missing, the position of the left hand remains unchanged.

The right middle finger pulls IV inward, the left ring finger still touching it on 10.

The left thumb touches VI on 9, the right index pushes it outwards. Etc.

Near the end of this passage we find the direction, *miao*,[231] indicating that especially that note is important. The passage ends with the sign *fan-chih*,[232] 'here the harmonics end'.

Figure 15 shows the beginning of the sixth part of the same tune. As here no harmonics are employed, the notation is slightly more complicated. The note says: 'The earlier six bars show a rising and subsiding tendency. Every note of the last bar is full of passion, it should not end up in a sloppy way.'

The left thumb presses VI down on 6, with the introductory gliding *chu* (no. 40); the right middle finger pulls it inward. Then the left thumb executes a protracted vibrato on 6, subsequently gliding up to 5.

229 輕連   230 散   231 妙   232 泛止

The left thumb presses VII down on 5, the right index pushes it outwards, the left thumb adds the jerk *chuang* (no. 43).

The right middle finger pulls VI inward, thereafter VII, the left thumb pressing down these strings on 5. Then the left thumb vibrates on 5, and glides up to 4/4. The right middle finger pushes VII outwards, and immediately afterwards pushes outward the free sixth string, making VII and VI sound together (*ju-i*[233]). Then the left thumb lightly pulls the nail up from the board, producing a light sound (*chao-ch'i,*[234] not given in my list).

The right middle finger pulls the free VI inwards.

The left thumb presses down VII on 4/4, the right middle finger pulls it inwards. Add *shuang-tan* (no. 21).

The right middle finger pulls the free VI.

The left thumb presses down VII on 4/4, the right middle finger pulls it inwards. Then the left thumb glides up to 4, thereafter to 3/3.

The left thumb remains on 3/3, the right middle finger pushes it outwards, immediately afterwards pushing the VI free (*ju-i*); after a slight pause, vibrato (*lo-chih-yin,*[235] a sort of protracted vibrato, not given in my list), then the left thumb lightly pulls up this same VII.

The right middle finger pulls the free VI.

The left thumb presses down VII on 3/3, the right middle finger pulls it inwards. A thin vibrato (*hsi-yin*),[236] and the thumb glides up to 2/5 (*êrh-pan*).[237]

The left thumb presses VII on 2/5, the right index pushes it outwards. The *ch'i*[238] in the margin indicates that here again there is a 'rise' in the melodic pattern.

This system of noting down lute music may seem too complicated and cumbersome to be practical. Yet some regular practice will prove it to be as convenient as our Western musical score. Lute experts have no difficulty in playing a new tune at first sight; I actually saw a Chinese lute master hum a tune he had never seen before, while looking over the notation.

It will be observed that no real notes are indicated. As the various tunings of the lute are minutely fixed, and all instruments are built on the same pattern (even the number of single silk threads that form one string is fixed), this omission presents the player with no seri-

---

233　如一
234　爪起
235　落指吟

236　細吟
237　二半
238　起

ous difficulty. The pitch is left to individual taste; some like it high, others low. But the pitch proportion between the strings must of course be correct.

More serious is the lack of any sign indicating measure. This is partly made up for by the distribution of the small round circles functioning as bars, and further by such indications as 'slow down', 'accelerate', etc.

In later times lute experts have felt these two shortcomings of the *chien-tzû* system. In the 19th century we find some handbooks where the musical note is added to each *chien-tzû* combination in symbols of the *kung-ch'ih*[239] system. These handbooks indicate the measure by a line of dots, running parallel to the *chien-tzû* columns. The distribution of these dots suggests the measure: if the dots are dense, the measure is slow; if sparse, the measure should be accelerated. Yet these systems never won universal approval. Yang Tsung-chi evolved a most elaborate system of *chien-tzû*, with a running explanation alongside;[240] in his *Ch'in-hsüeh-ts'ung-shu* he published several of the better known tunes in this notation. For reading this system some special study is necessary, but it is so explicit (both notes and measure being recorded), that I can recommend his handbook to everyone who wishes to study lute music without a master.

In 1931 the musician Wang Kuang-ch'i[241] made an attempt at transcribing the *chien-tzû* in a semi-Western way. He used our stave and notes, but of course had to add a great number of special signs.[242] The result was a system far more complicated than the original *chien-tzû*, and his method was never adopted by other workers in the field. Where typically Chinese things are concerned, it will as a rule be very difficult to improve upon the methods the old Chinese devised for dealing with them.

239 工尺. Soulié, *op. cit.* p. 36, reproduces a page from such a handbook.

240 Appendix II, 7.

241 王光祈

242 See his publication, *Fan-i-ch'in-pu-chih-yen-chiu* 翻譯琴譜之研究, Shanghai 1931.

CHAPTER SIX

Associations

§1 LUTE AND CRANE

LITERARY tradition has surrounded the scholar with numerous attributes, which have come to be considered as the symbols of literary life. Among this group the lute occupies a prominent place. Of the others, those that are constantly mentioned in connection with the lute are the crane, the pine and the plum tree, and the sword.

The origin of these associations dates from far before the establishment of any literary tradition; what their exact beginnings were, we shall probably never know. Yet it is not impossible to make a fairly accurate surmise as to at least the direction in which the solution must be sought. Later literary tradition suggests that the reasons were of a purely aesthetic character. It says that the crane was dear to the scholar because of its graceful movements and dignified behaviour, that the plum blossoms delighted his eye with their exquisite colour, that the gnarled shape of the pine tree taught him antique beauty, and that the sword reminded him of the straightness and purity of the Superior Man. Now these explanations hold true for later times, but they do not bring us any nearer to an understanding of their origin. For in that remote past the literatus did not yet exist.

There did exist, however, the head of the family, who, during the sacrifices to the ancestors, officiated as priest, and whose duty it was to see that by a proper appliance of magical ceremonies evil influences were warded off, and that by a strengthening of the vital essences, the family line was continued and crops were plentiful. Now, as we shall see below, crane, plum tree, pine and sword are all, just like the lute, credited with a great amount of Yang power, and for that reason give protection against evil forces. It would seem probable that these objects, in later times praised as the faithful companions of the scholar, originally surrounded the head of the family, and played some part in magical ceremonies, whereby their vital forces were transferred to the officiant. Literary tradition tried to ignore these ancient magic beliefs; but they are firmly rooted in popular religion, and time and again evidence of their existence also appears in literary sources.

The crane is one of the traditional Chinese symbols of longevity. Just like the tortoise, it is said to live to more than a thousand years. *Ho-ling*, 'crane age', is a much-used metaphor for advanced years[1]. The idea of old age, when carried through logically, leads to that of immortality. Therefore the crane is associated with the *hsien-jên*,[2] the Immortals: the crane is their favourite mount, and many a holy recluse is said to have disappeared from human sight riding on a crane.[3] The *Ch'ing-lien-fang-ch'in-ya*[4] tells the following story about Chang Chih-ho.[5] 'Chang Chih-ho loved to drink wine, and when inebriated used to play his lute all night long without resting. One evening there suddenly appeared a grey crane, which danced round about him. Chang then took his lute, and riding on its back, disappeared in the sky.'[6] There are also many stories of Taoist recluses and priests who transformed themselves into cranes; the *Shên-i-ching*[7] relates that the Taoist recluse Hsü Tso-ching,[8] having taken the shape of a crane, was wounded by an arrow of the Emperor Ming Huang; the *Hsü-sou-shên-chi*[9] tells the story of a Ting Ling-wei[10] who long after his death revisited his native town in the shape of a crane; and the *Lieh-hsien-chuan* says that Su-hsien-kung[11] after his death visited the earth in the shape of a white crane. Because of its constant association with the Immortals the crane is called *hsien-ch'in*.[12] Then we find the crane as soul bird, the bird that conveys the soul of the deceased to the upper regions; cf. the Chinese custom of placing the figure of a crane with spread wings on the coffin in a funeral procession.

The *hsüan-ho*,[13] or dark crane, is especially credited with a fabulously long life. The *Ku-chin-chu*[14] says: 'When a crane has reached the age of one thousand years, it turns a dark blue colour; after another

---

[1] 鶴齡 (See the book entitled *Ho-ling-lu* 鶴齡錄 by the Ming author Li Ch'ing 李清: biographies of people who attained to old ages).

[2] 仙人

[3] See, for instance, the story about Hsün Huan 荀瓌 in the *Shu-i-chi* 述異記 (18th century).

[4] Appendix II, 6.

[5] 張志和, 8th century.

[6] 張志和好飲酒, 醉則鼓琴, 終夜不休, 一夕忽有雲鶴旋繞, 張遂携琴跨鶴以昇.

[7] 神異經, 6–7th centuries.

[8] 徐佐卿

[9] 續搜神記, ascribed to the Chin writer T'ao Ch'ien 陶潛, but evidently a much later production.

[10] 丁令威

[11] 列仙傳 (about the beginning of our era: see the remarks by P. Pelliot, *Journal Asiatique*, June-August 1912, p. 149).

[12] 仙禽

[13] 玄鶴

[14] 古今注 (by Ts'ui Piao 崔豹, Chin 晉 period).

thousand years it turns black, and then it is called dark crane.'[15] Since olden times especially this dark crane has been associated with music. The *Jui-ying-t'u-chi*[16] says: 'A dark crane shall appear at a time when there is a Ruler who understands music. When in olden times, Huang Ti executed music on the K'un-lun mountain for all the Spirits to dance, on his right side there flew 16 dark cranes.'[17]

Sixteen dark cranes also appear in a story related by the great historian Ssû-ma Ch'ien in his *Shih-chi*.[18] This story exists in more than one translation already;[19] because of its great importance for our subject, however, I may be allowed to quote it here once more. 'When Duke Ling of Wei[20] was travelling to Chin, he halted on the bank of the river Pu. In the middle of the night he heard the sounds of a lute being played. He asked the members of his suite, but all respectfully said that no one had heard the sounds. Then the Duke summoned Master Chüan, and said to him: "I have heard the sounds of a lute being played, but when I asked my suite no one had heard it. Thus it seems that it is caused by a spirit or a ghost. Write this tune down for me." Master Chüan assented and, seating himself in the correct position, having placed his lute before him, he listened and noted down the tune. The next morning he said: "I have obtained the tune now, but I have not yet learned it. I beg you for one more night to learn it thoroughly." The Duke agreed, and yet another night passed. On the following morning he reported that he had mastered the tune. Then they left that place, and proceeded to Chin. They were received by Duke P'ing of Chin[21] who gave a banquet for them on the Shih-hui Terrace. When all had come under the influence of the wine, Duke Ling said: "When on my way here I heard a new tune; permit me to let you hear it." When Duke P'ing agreed, Duke Ling made Master Chüan sit down by the side of Master K'uang, place his lute before him and play it. But before he was half through, Master K'uang put his hand on the strings [to deaden the sounds], and said: "That is the music of a doomed state; one must not listen to it." Duke P'ing asked: "What is the origin of this tune?" Master K'uang answered: "It was made by Master Yen, to please the tyrant Chou. When Wu-wang had defeated Chou, Master Yen fled to the east, and drowned himself in the river Pu. Therefore it must

15 鶴千載變蒼, 又千載變黑, 所謂玄鶴也.

16 瑞應圖記 (ascribed to Sun Jou-chih 孫柔之, of the Liang period).

17 玄鶴王者知音樂之節則至,　昔黃帝習樂崑崙以舞衆神, 有玄鶴二八翔其右.

18 史記, ch. 24.

19 See Chavannes, *Mémoires historiques,* part III, p. 287: M. Courant, *op. cit.* pp. 4–5.

20 534–493 B.C.

21 557–532 B.C.

have been on the bank of that river that this tune was heard. Who first hears this tune, his state will be divided.'' Duke P'ing said: ''I have a great love for music. I wish to hear this tune to the end.'' Then Master Chüan played the entire tune. Then Duke P'ing said: ''Are there no tunes that are still more sinister than this one?'' Master K'uang said: ''There are.'' ''Could you play them for me?'' The Master answered: ''My lord's virtue and righteousness are not great enough for that. I may not play them for you.'' But the Duke said again: ''I have a great love for music; I wish to hear them.'' Then Master K'uang could not but draw his lute unto him, and play. When he had played once, there appeared sixteen dark cranes that alighted on the gate of the hall. When he played the second time, they stretched their necks and cried, they spread out their wings and started to dance. Duke P'ing was overcome with joy, and leaving his seat he drank the health of Master K'uang. Having returned to his seat, he asked: ''Are there no other tunes that are still more sinister than this one?'' Master K'uang said: ''Yes, there are those by which in olden times Huang Ti effected a great reunion of ghosts and spirits. But my lord's virtue and righteousness are not great enough to allow you to hear this music. And if you hear it, you will perish.'' Duke P'ing said: ''I am advanced in years, and I have a great love of music. I want to hear these tunes.'' Then Master K'uang could not but draw his lute unto him, and play. When he had played one, white clouds rose in the north-west. And when he played another, there was a storm wind, followed by a torrent, that made the tiles fly from the roof. All that were present fled, and Duke P'ing, in a great fright, threw himself down near the entrance of the hall.[22] Thereafter Chin was beset by a drought that scorched the earth for three years in succession.' This story, which bears a most archaic character (note that in the text of the story above, instead of '16' we find 'twice

---

22　衞靈公之時，將之晉，至於濮水之上舍，夜半時聞鼓琴聲，問左右皆對曰不聞，乃召師涓曰，吾聞鼓琴音，問左右皆不聞，其狀似鬼神，爲我聽而寫之，師涓曰諾，因端坐援琴聽而寫之，明日曰臣得之矣，然未習也，請宿習之，靈公曰可，因復宿，明日報曰，習矣，即去之晉，見晉平公，平公置酒於施惠之臺，酒酣靈公曰，今者來聞新聲，請奏之，平公曰可，即令師涓坐師曠旁，援琴鼓之，未終，師曠撫而止之，曰，此亡國之聲也，不可聽，平公曰，何道出，師曠曰，師延所作也，與紂爲靡靡之樂，武王伐紂，師延東走，自投濮水之中，故聞此聲必於濮水之上，先聞此聲者國削，平公曰，寡人所好者音也，願遂聞之，師涓鼓而終之，平公曰，晉無此最悲乎，師曠曰，有，平公曰，可得聞乎，師曠曰，君德義薄，不可以聽之．平公曰，寡人所好者音也，願聞之，師曠不得已，援琴而鼓之，一奏之有玄鶴二八集乎廊門，再奏之延頸而鳴，舒翼而舞，平公大喜，起而爲師曠濤，反坐問曰，晉無此最悲乎，師曠曰，有昔者黃帝以大合鬼神，今君德義薄，不足以聽之，聽之將敗，平公曰，寡人老矣，所好者音也，願遂聞之，師曠不得已，援琴而鼓之，一奏之有白雲從西北起，再奏之大風至而雨隨之，飛廊瓦，左右皆奔走，平公恐懼伏於廊屋之間，晉國大旱，赤地三年．

8'), not only furnishes a good example of the relation of the dark crane to lute music, but also illustrates in a striking way the awe-inspiring qualities with which the ancient Chinese credited this music.[23] Something of the ominous atmosphere of this old tale has been preserved in a number of ghost stories connected with the lute of later date. For some specimens of these see below, the fourth section of this chapter.

It is only occasionally, however, that we find faint echos of the oldest magical character of the association between lute and crane. In later times literary tradition has entirely overgrown these old beliefs; they are replaced by considerations of a purely aesthetical character. When the scholar is playing the lute in his garden pavilion, a couple of cranes should be leisurely stalking about. Their graceful movements should inspire the rhythm of the finger technique, and their occasional cries direct the thoughts of the player to unearthly things. For even these cries of the crane have a special meaning. They are said to penetrate unto Heaven: 'The crane cries in the marshes, its sound is heard in the skies,'[24] and the female crane conceives when it hears the cry of the male.[25]

The crane is described as having a great love for lute music. The *Ch'ing-lien-fang-ch'in-ya*[26] says: 'Lin Pu[27] greatly enjoyed playing the lute; whenever he played, his two cranes would start dancing.'[28] And the same source says about Yeh Mêng-tê:[29] 'Yeh Mêng-tê loved the lute, and would play for a whole day without resting, the tones of the lute mingling with the sounds of a brook. Later Yeh returned to mount Lu and sang songs, accompanying himself on his lute. On one occasion there suddenly appeared a pair of cranes that gamboled about and danced in his garden. Yeh kept them, and they did not go away, but started to dance every time he played.'[30]

---

[23] I may remark in passing that this tale contains some interesting data regarding the history of lute music. It appears that as early as the fifth century B.C. there existed some system for noting down lute music; for our text says explicitly that Master Chüan 'wrote down' (*hsieh* 寫) the ghostly tune he heard. His method of recording the tune is not different from that used by present-day lute players: first the melody in general is noted down, but then several more hearings are necessary to record the exact timbre of the tones, and to add the various 'graces'. Then the tune should be played through many times (*hsi* 習), for only when the music has been memorized can the player in his performance do full justice to it. The terms *i-tsou* 一奏 and *tsai-tsou* 再奏 are not very clear; I follow Chavannes' translation.

[24] See *Shih-ching* 詩經, *Hsiao-ya* x: 鶴鳴 于九皋, 聲聞于天.

[25] See the *Ch'in-ching* 禽經, authorship uncertain: 鶴以聲交而孕.

[26] Appendix II, 6.

[27] 967–1028.

[28] 林和靖喜琴, 每一鼓則二鶴起舞.

[29] 葉夢得, style: Shao-yün 少蘊, 1077–1148.

[30] 葉少蘊素好琴, 終日不倦, 泉聲與琴聲相亂, 後歸廬山, 倚琴而歌, 忽見二鶴翩躚飛舞庭中, 少蘊卽蓄之, 不去, 每一鼓未嘗不起舞.

Several lute tunes sing the excellent qualities of the crane. The *Pu-hsü-t'ang-ch'in-pu*[31] contains one tune that describes the crane in the scholar's garden; it bears the title 'Song of a pair of cranes listening to the babbling of a brook'.[32] Another tune celebrates the soaring flight of the crane: 'Cranes dancing in the sky'.[33] The *T'ien-wên-ko-ch'in-pu-chi-ch'êng*[34] has a tune entitled 'A pair of cranes bathing in a brook'.[35] The introductory note added to this tune is not without interest for our subject. 'Late in spring I visited a friend in Kuan-k'ou (Szuchuan Province). A pair of cranes were dancing in a clear rivulet. I observed their feathers white as snow, and the top of their heads red like vermilion. They fluttered up and down, and took their bath while dancing. Then they spread their wings and flew high up in the sky, and cried in harmony in the azure vault, making me doubt whether they were not Immortals. Then I drew my lute unto me, and composed[36] this tune.'[37] The Ming handbook *Shên-chi-pi-pu*[38] has a tune entitled 'Cranes crying in the marshes'.[39] The second half of the introductory remark says: 'The crane is a sacred bird. Its cries are most clear; they are heard at a distance of more than 8 miles. The meaning of this tune is to compare the tones of the lute with the cries of the crane. I kept two cranes in the bamboo grove surrounding my lute hall. Sometimes, in a shadowy place, they would dance together, other times they would fly up and cry in unison. But they would always wait for the appropriate time: they did not dance unless there was a cool breeze to shake their feathers, and they did not cry unless they could look up to the Milky Way as if they saw the gods. When the time was not propitious they would neither sing nor dance. Recognizing the spiritual qualities of these cranes, I composed this tune.'[40]

Various books give directions as to the proper way of rearing cranes and of recognizing birds of superior qualities. The qualities and outer marks of good cranes are described in the *Hsiang-ho-ching*;[41] this

---

31　步虛堂琴譜; see Appendix II, 12.
32　雙鶴聽泉吟.
33　鶴舞洞天
34　Appendix II, 18.
35　雙鶴沐泉
36　This statement does not conform to facts; when playing this tune, one soon discovers that it is nothing but a variation on the tune 'Song of a pair of cranes listening to the babbling of a brook' of the Ming handbook mentioned above.
37　暮春之初，訪友灌口，雙鶴沐於清泉，則見白翰欺雪，丹頂凝硃，以頡以頏，旋舞旋浴，

即而奮翮於霄漢之間，和鳴於蒼冥之際，意殆其仙歟，因援琴而作是操.
38　神奇祕譜; see Appendix II, 11.
39　鶴鳴九皋; see the *Shih-ching* quotation cited above.
40　鶴為仙靈之禽，其鳴亮亮聞八九里，此曲之義蓋以鶴鳴喻琴聲焉，予嘗畜二鶴於琴院竹林之間，或離影而對舞，或雙飛而交鳴，必有時焉，其舞也感涼風則舞，以振其羽，仰見霄漢如有神物則鳴，非時則不鳴，非時則不舞，故知其鶴之靈而有是操.
41　相鶴經

book, though of doubtful authenticity, seems fairly old, and is found in many *ts'ung-shu*. Ming treatises especially abound in discussions on the keeping and rearing of cranes, and on how to make them dance: one may train them to dance when one claps the hands.[42] Ch'ên Fu-yao[43] in an article on the rearing of cranes[44] says that from the thigh bone of a crane excellent flutes can be made: their sound is clear, and in harmony with the sonorous tubes.[45]

Finally I may quote a remark on the crane found in the *Tsun-shêng-pa-chien*: 'While staying in a country house in an empty wood, how could one do a single day without the company of this refined friend that makes one forget all worldly things?'[46]

§2 LUTE AND PLUM TREE,
LUTE AND PINE TREE

CHINESE poets and painters have never tired of the delicate beauty of the plum blossom, and the robuster grace of the gnarled pine tree. Poets celebrate the subtle colour and subdued fragrance of the plum blossom, and they admire the intriguing contrast of the tender flowers and the crooked and rough branches of the tree. And for more than a thousand years painters have chosen as their subject an old pine tree, standing lonely among steep rocks. The ideal of the lute player is to possess a little cottage somewhere in the mountains, surrounded by a grove of prunes. When there is a light breeze, the falling plum blossoms shall suggest to him the spirit of the more delicate touches of the finger technique. But if he can not afford that, when the right season has arrived he will take a flowering branch of the plum tree, and place it in a vase on his desk (see fig. 16). If one can have a house where some hoary pines guard the gate, they will lend dignity and style to one's mansion. And contemplating their antique appearance, the scholar shall

---

[42] Consult the *Tsun-shêng-pa-chien* (Appendix II, 4), ch. 15, pp. 80 ff., and the *K'ao-pan-yü-shih* (Appendix II, 3), ch. 3.

[43] The real name of Ch'ên Fu-yao 陳扶搖 is Ch'ên Hao-tzu 陳淏子; he was born in 1612, a native of Hangchow. Cf. B. Laufer, *T'oung-pao*, 1917, no. 4; Merrill and Walker, *Bibliography of East Asiatic Botany*, p. 552; A. Wylie, *Notes on Chinese Literature*, p. 150; L. Carrington Goodrich, *Monumenta Serica*, II, p. 407.

[44] Ch. 6 of the *Hua-ching* 花鏡, a charming small book on the cultivation of trees and flowers, published in 1688. The *Hua-ching* was in 1773 reprinted in Kyoto, in 6 vols. The Chinese original has been provided throughout with Japanese reading marks, and the pictures have been reproduced with much care. The Japanese editor of the text was a certain Hiraga 平賀.

[45] 又鶴腿骨爲笛, 聲甚清越, 音律更準.

[46] 空林別墅, 何可一日無此忘機清友.

recognize once more the antique atmosphere that hovers about the lute and its lore. But the appreciation of the stern beauty of the pine tree is not only a privilege of the rich: the poor recluse may derive enjoyment from growing a dwarf pine tree in a flat basin.

A study of the origin and subsequent evolution of the Chinese love for plum tree and pine (together with the bamboo) would fill a bulky volume. Below only a few of the most striking features are outlined.

When one observes the place occupied by the plum tree in Chinese

♯16: A scholar playing the lute before beautiful scenery.
Note the vase with plum blossoms, and the incense burner on the lute table.
From a rare illustrated Ming print, the *T'ang-shih-hua-pu* 唐詩畫譜.

culture, it will be clear that here, just as with the crane, magical conceptions play an important role. The plum tree is closely associated with creative power and fertility. Because of the fact that the black and seemingly lifeless branches of an old plum tree still produce tender blossoms, the Chinese ascribe to this tree an unusual amount of Yang power, of vital energy, and have made it a symbol of longevity. Blossoming when winter has barely ended, it is a symbol of the New Year, and the revival of nature. Because of this and other associations, the plum tree and plum blossom are often used in metaphors relating to women and female beauty. A slender waist is compared to the twig of a plum tree, a beautiful woman is called a plum blossom, a rose-and-white face is called a plum-blossom complexion. In Chinese literature one often reads stories of plum blossoms that took the shape of beautiful girls. Well known is the charming story told in the *Lung-ch'êng-lu*.[47] During the K'ai-huang period (581–603) a certain Chao Shih-hsiung fell asleep when resting in a grove. He saw a beautiful girl in simple white attire, but surrounded by a subtle fragrance. Her attendant was a little boy clad in green. Chao talked and laughed with this girl till dawn. When he awoke, he discovered that he had been sleeping under a plum tree. It was in full bloom, and small green birds were twittering on its branches. As in many other countries, in China also the plum has sexual associations. *Mei-tu*[48] (plum poison) in both China and Japan is a usual word for venereal disease, *lo-mei*[49] (falling of the plum blossoms) may be used as a metaphor for defloration, and the word *mei* itself frequently occurs, both in China and Japan, in the names of houses of ill repute. Next to its beauty, it is also this connection with the generative forces of nature, that assured the plum tree its established place among the constant companions of the scholar.

Just like the crane, the plum blossom is said to be sensitive to the beauty of lute music. The *Ch'ing-lien-fang-ch'in-ya*[50] tells the following story. 'Wang Tzû-liang obtained a lute of very antique appearance. Every time he played it, there would suddenly blow a gentle breeze that made the plum blossoms in his garden come down in a dancing movement. Tzû-liang said with a sigh: "These blossoms not only understand words, they also understand music." '[51]

---

47 龍城錄, ascribed to the T'ang poet Liu Tsung-yüan, 773–819, 7th heading.
48 梅毒 (Jap. *baidoku*).
49 落梅

50 Appendix II, 6.
51 王子良得一琴, 質色甚古, 每一鼓清風忽發, 庭中梅花飛動, 子良嘆曰, 此花不獨解語, 更能知音.

Therefore playing the lute before plum blossoms is especially recommended; as an old poem says: 'Take your lute with you and play before an old plum tree.'[52] In prose and poetry the plum tree and its blossoms are repeatedly mentioned in connection with the lute, and in the technical terminology of the lute the plum blossom often appears: a certain touch of the finger technique is compared to

♯17: Playing the lute in the shadow of pine trees.
The man on the left is tuning a four-stringed guitar. Same source as ♯16.

52　携琴合向古梅彈.

plum blossoms floating on the waves, and a type of crack in the varnish of antique lutes is called 'plum-blossom crack' (*Mei-hua-tuan-wên*).[53]

As to the pine tree as an old symbol of longevity, its associations are so well known that after the remarks made above,[54] there is no need to add much more. Also the pine tree is credited with a great amount of vital energy; it remains green through winter, and old, gnarled pines suggest a vigorous advanced age. That nearly all its parts figure largely in the Chinese *materia medica*, must chiefly be explained by sympathetic magic. In the foregoing pages we have seen that the pine tree is constantly mentioned in connection with the lute; if the lute player is not represented as sitting in a plum grove, he will be seated on a moss-covered stone under a couple of spreading pines.

§3 LUTE AND SWORD

THE sword, symbol of military valour, was not much in favour with the literati, who, as a rule, considered all warlike pursuits as unbecoming to their dignity. Beginning with about the early years of the Ming period, literary sources have not much to say in praise of this weapon. Yet a sword belongs to the outfit of a scholar, and it will be seen in his library, hanging on the wall side by side with the lute. This seeming contradiction is explained when the older associations of the sword are taken into consideration.

Despite its warlike character, the sword maintained its place among the attributes of the scholar because of magical considerations: the sword is a powerful defense against the forces of darkness. The belief that cutting instruments scare away ghosts and demons, is, of course, spread over the whole world. In China we find that in olden times the sword belonged to the outfit of the Taoist devil-banner. Already in the writings of the Taoist writer T'ao Hung-ching[55] we find the statement: 'All who wish to study Taoist magic must possess a good sword, which should never leave their sides.'[56] Old treatises on the sword, such as the *Tao-chien-lu*[57] and the *Chien-chi*,[58] abound in stories about the magical properties of the sword: swords change into dragons, hidden swords betray their presence by super-

---

53 梅花斷文
54 p. 58.
55 陶弘景, 452–536.
56 凡學道術者皆須有好劍隨身.

57 刀劍錄, by T'ao Hung-ching, mentioned above.
58 劍記, by Kuo Tzû-chang 郭子章, 16th century.

natural phenomena, old swords may foretell the future, etc. Popular religion shows many traces of these beliefs in the magic power of the sword. Two swords buried under the threshold shall keep away robbers;[59] swords made of cash strung together will keep evil forces away, etc. An interesting survival is the Chinese custom of placing a big knife on the dead body in a coffin.[60] Nowadays it is explained as a means of preventing the ghost of the deceased from haunting the house. But it seems probable that this custom originated in the old rite of burying swords with the dead. For the sword also is considered as a container of Yang power, and as such the sword as burial gift must have had the same significance as the jade had as burial gift, i.e. to preserve the corpse from decay.

The traditional attitude of the later scholar to the sword as belonging to the library of the literatus is shown in the following passage from the *Tsun-shêng-pa-chien*.[61] It is the second half of a section entitled *Ch'in-chien*[62] (Sword and Lute). 'Since olden times the methods for making all sorts of things have been transmitted; only the art of casting swords is not recorded in literary sources. That is why nowadays there are no more knights-errant, and few famous swords exist; this is because the tradition of swordsmanship has been broken off. Moreover it is easier to handle a dagger than a sword, therefore though people now know how to carry daggers, they do not know how to carry a sword. As for me, although I do not use the sword for guarding against the violent and opposing the strong, I yet employ it for fortifying my mind and strengthening my spirit. If one can not obtain an old sword, then a good modern sword, like those manufactured in Yünnan, will do for being hung in the library.'[63] The author winds up by praising in a wealth of literary allusions the brilliant lustre of the sword, which outshines the stars.

The cultured scholar will prefer for his library a beautiful, antique sword, with a finely decorated scabbard, and covered with old inscriptions. But often an ordinary sword or dagger is used.

Of the copious references in literature to lute and sword together, I quote only one, the first couplet of the introductory poem to the famous '*roman de moeurs*', *Chin-p'ing-mei*,[64] which says: 'Opulence

---

59 See H. Doré, *Manuel des superstitions chinoises*, Shanghai 1926, p. 91.
60 *Ibid.*, p. 51.
61 Appendix II, 4.
62 琴劍
63 自古各物之製莫不有法傳流，獨鑄劍之

術，不載典籍，故今無劍客，而世少名劍，以劍術無傳，且刀便於劍，所以人知佩刀而不知佩劍也，吾輩設此，總不能用以禦暴敵強，亦可壯懷志勇，不得古劍，即今之寶劍如雲南製者，懸之高齋.
64 金瓶梅

and glamour have gone, and the guests have stopped coming. Flutes and cither are silent. Song and chant are no more heard. The heroic sword has lost its grimness, its beautiful shine has become dull. The precious lute has fallen asunder, and its brilliant studs are lost.'[65]

§4 SOME FAMOUS STORIES AND MUCH-QUOTED PASSAGES RELATING TO THE LUTE

THE 22 stories and passages translated below are all taken from the *Ch'ing-lien-fang-ch'in-ya*[66] and the *T'ien-wên-ko-ch'in-pu-chi-ch'êng*.[67] In many cases it would have been possible to trace the story to its original source, where often the text is more complete. But for our purpose it seemed better to give them in the form in which they occur in books on the lute, for then it will appear which particular points especially appealed to the lute masters. The stories need no commentary; they speak for themselves. And each of them may serve, in its own way, as illustration of some of the aspects of *ch'in* ideology discussed in the foregoing chapters.

1 Ou-yang Hsiu [the famous Sung literatus][68] used to say: 'I have assembled one thousand rolls with old records; of books I have collected ten thousand volumes; further I possess one lute, one set of chess, and usually thereto is added one pot of wine. Amidst these things I grow old, being as it were one of a company of six.' On account of this he chose as his literary name: the Retired Scholar One-of-six:

He also said: 'I used to suffer from fits of melancholy, and a leisurely life could not cure them. Then I studied the lute under the guidance of my friend Sun Tao-tzû, who taught me a couple of tunes in the Kung mode. I found enjoyment in these during a long time, and did not know that I harboured such a thing as melancholy.'[69]

2 Ch'ao Pi [T'ang period] used to play a five-stringed lute. When people asked the reason for this, he replied: 'First

65 豪華去後行人絕, 簫箏不響歌喉咽, 雄劍無威光彩沉, 寶琴零落金星滅, *Chin-hsing* is a literary expression for *hui* 徽; neither F. Kuhn nor O. Kibat in their translations of the novel has realized this, and they both render *chin-hsing* wrongly as 'Brilliant star'.

66 Appendix II, 6.

67 Appendix II, 18.

68 1007–72.

69 歐陽修言, 吾集古錄一千卷, 藏書一萬卷, 有琴一張, 棋一局, 而嘗置酒一壺, 吾老於其間, 是爲六一, 遂號六一居士.
又曰, 吾嘗有幽憂之疾, 而間居不能治也, 既而學琴于友人孫道滋, 受宮聲數引, 久而樂之, 不知疾之在其體也.

I strove to understand the meaning of these five strings with my mind; the second stage was that my soul sensed their significance. Finally I played them quite naturally, not knowing whether the five strings were I, or I the five strings.'[70]

3 Chang Hung-ching had an old lute. The shine of its varnish was entirely gone, and its colour was jet black. He had given it the name of 'Falling Flowers and Flowing Water'. One night he heard a rat make a loud noise. Fearing that it might gnaw his lute or his books, he ordered a maid servant to put on a light. Then he saw that one string of his lute had broken [and was hanging down], having strangled a rat. Chang Hung-ching was amazed at this, and changed the name of his lute to: 'Terror of the Rats'.[71]

4 Chang Chi, style Chung-ching, a man from Nan-yang, was skilled in healing illness. One day he entered a cedar wood, looking for medicinal herbs. There he met a sick man, who asked for a consultation. [Having examined him,] Chang Chi said: 'How is it that you have the pulse of an animal?' Then the man told him the truth, that in reality he was an old monkey living in a cave on Mount I. Chang Chi took from his bag some pills, and gave him one. Having taken this, the monkey was cured immediately. The next day this monkey came again in his human form, bearing on his shoulder an enormous log. He said: 'This is a cedar ten thousand years old. I offer it as a slight requital.' From this beam Chang Chi made two lutes. One he called Old Monkey, the other Ten Thousand Years.[72]

5 Silk worms are very clever; when they spin themselves into cocoons, they often take the shape of the things they come in contact with.

Once there was a young widow. Spending the night alone, resting on her pillow, she could not sleep. In the wall near her there was a hole, and through this she looked at the silk-

---

70 趙璧彈五絃琴，人問其故，曰，吾之五絃也，始則心驅之，中則神遇之，終則天隨之，不知五絃之爲璧，璧之爲五絃也．

71 張弘靜有古琴，漆光盡退，色如墨石，銘曰，落花流水，一夕聞鼠聲甚急，懼齧琴書，命婢以火燭之，見有斷絃，繫得一鼠，弘靜異之，改名曰鼠畏．

72 張機，字仲景，南陽人，精於治療，一日入桐栢，覓藥草，遇一病人求診，仲景曰，子之腕有獸脈，何也，其人以實告，乃嶧山穴中老猿也，仲景出嚢中丸藥界之一，服輒愈，明日其人肩一巨木至，曰，此萬年桐也，聊以相報，仲景斲爲二琴，一曰古猿，一曰萬年．

worms of her neighbour; they were just leaving their frames. Next day the cocoons all showed a resemblance with her face. Although one could not clearly distinguish eyebrows and eyes, still when seen from some distance they closely resembled the face of a sad girl. Ts'ai Yung, the famous scholar, saw these cocoons, and bought them for a high price. He reeled off the silk threads, and from it made strings for his lute. When he played, however, their sound appeared to be sad and melancholy. When he asked his daughter Yen about it, she said: 'This is widow's silk. When listening to its sounds one cannot but weep.'[73]

6 During the Chou dynasty Master Ching served in the State of Wei. He excelled in playing the lute. Prince Wên[74] was enthusiastic about it, and began to dance. Ching became angry, and struck the Prince with his lute. Then the Prince got angry, and ordered Ching to be dragged out of the Palace and killed. Ching said: 'I beg leave to say one thing before I die.' The Prince said: 'What is it?' Ching said: 'I have struck a prince like the tyrants Chieh and Chou, and not a wise ruler like Yao and Shun.' Prince Wên said 'I have been wrong,' and let him go free. But the lute he suspended on the wall, as a reminder.[75]

7 Wei Yeh, style: Chung-hsien[76] [well-known poet of the Sung period],[77] naturally loved songs and chants and did not strive after worldly fame. He lived in the eastern suburb of the town, where with his own hands he planted bamboos and trees. His abode was surrounded by a flowing water, and breathed an atmosphere of great profundity. There he dug out a cave of one fathom square, and called it 'Cave where harmony with Heaven is enjoyed'. In front of this he made a hut of grass, and there played his lute. When people visited him there, irrespective of whether they were of high or low standing, he would receive them in white clothes and a cap of black gauze. He took the literary name of 'Retired Scholar

73 蠶最巧, 作繭往往遇物成形, 有寡女獨宿, 倚枕不寐, 私傍壁孔中, 視鄰蠶離箔, 明日繭都類之, 雖眉目不甚悉, 而望去隱然似愁女, 蔡邕見之, 厚價市歸, 繰絲製琴絃, 彈之有憂愁哀慟之聲, 問女琰, 琰曰, 此寡女絲也, 聞者莫不墮淚.

74 426–387 B.C.

75 周師經仕魏, 善鼓琴, 文侯耽之, 起舞, 經

怒, 以琴撞文侯, 文侯怒, 使人曳下股, 將殺之, 經曰, 乞申一言而死, 文侯曰, 何, 經曰, 臣撞桀紂之君, 不撞堯舜之主, 文侯曰, 寡人過矣, 乃捨之, 懸琴於壁以爲戒.

76 960–1019.

77 His collected works, the Ts'ao-t'ang-chi 草堂集, are still preserved.

of the Grass Hut'. He played the lute and composed poetry, and therein found full satisfaction. When the Emperor T'ai-tsung of the Sung dynasty sacrificed at Fên-yin, he summoned Wei Yeh, but Wei Yeh did not go, giving illness as an excuse. One day, when he was busy teaching cranes to dance, he was informed that Imperial messengers had arrived. Then he took his lute in his arms, leapt over the fence and fled.[78]

8 In the time of the Emperor Hsiao-wên[79] there was found a musician of Prince Wên of Wei,[80] called Pao-kung, who was 180 years old. He used to say about himself that at the age of 12 he became blind, and that his parents then taught him the lute. He excelled in playing accomplished music, and did not lose his great skill, in spite of his great age. Thus Pao-kung since his youth played the lute for more than 160 years, and during all that time he never once knew what a lute looked like.[81]

9 Sun Fêng had a lute, which was called 'Turkey-cock'. When played, its tones were not very beautiful. Only when some-one sang would the strings of their own accord then ac-company it. So Sun changed its name to 'Singing by Itself'. On its bottom board there was a hole the shape of which resembled that of a moth. One day there came along a Taoist monk, begging for food. On seeing this lute, he said: 'Inside there is a moth. If it is not driven away, the lute will soon be worm-eaten.' Thereupon he took from his sleeve a small bamboo tube, and from it poured out a black medicine near the hole. No sooner had he done so than a green insect came running out. On its back it had a pattern of fine golden threads. The Taoist monk caught it and put it in the bamboo tube, then went his way. Thereafter, when a song was sung, the lute did not respond to it any more. Sun Fêng was amazed at this. When he told a sage of wide knowledge of this occurrence, the wise man said with a sigh: 'This [insect] was a rare treasure, called Chü-t'ung. When

---

78 魏野字仲先，性嗜吟咏，不求聞達，居州之東郊，手植竹木，流泉環繞，境趣幽絕，鑿土袤丈，曰，樂天洞，前爲草堂，彈琴其中，人訪之者，無貴賤皆白衣紗帽見之，號草堂居士，彈琴賦詩以自適，宋太宗祀汾陰，召之，辭疾不至，一日方敎鶴舞，報中使至，抱琴踰垣而走.

79 250 B.C.

80 426–387 B.C.

81 孝文時，得魏文侯樂工竇公，年一百八十矣．自言十三歲失明．父母敎之琴，能爲雅聲，能老不廢忘，然則竇公自少，鼓琴一百六十餘年，而平生未嘗識琴之形也.

it is put next to the ear of a deaf man, he will be immediately cured. It likes to eat cedar wood, but it likes especially old ink.' Only then did Sun Fêng realize that the black medicine which the monk kept in the bamboo tube was nothing but dregs of old ink.[82]

10 Ch'ên Chih loved the lute, and would play on it day and night without stopping. When he had done so for twenty-eight years, suddenly a purple flower blossomed forth from the lute. He ate it, and disappeared as an Immortal.[83]

11 Wang Ching-po was a man from Kuei-chi. His lute was called 'Influencing Ghosts'. Once he passed the night in a pavilion, on an islet near his town. That night there was a brilliant moon, and a light dew was settling down. By playing his lute he compelled the ghost of the dead daughter of Liu Hui-ming to come to him. She looked just as if she were alive, and two maids accompanied her.[84]

12 Hsi K'ang [famous lute player],[85] one evening was playing his lute, when suddenly a ghost appeared, wearing chains and sighing deeply. Lifting up his hands in supplication, the ghost said: 'Let me play a tune for you.' Hsi K'ang then gave him his lute, and he played; the tones were clear but uncanny. When questioned, the ghost did not answer. Hsi K'ang thought it might have been the ghost of Ts'ai Yung [the famous musician and statesman],[86] for he had died in fetters.[87]

13 Another evening when Hsi K'ang was playing the lute, there suddenly appeared a man more than ten feet tall, clad in black cloth and leather belt. When Hsi K'ang had given him a good look, he extinguished his lamp, saying: 'I would not venture to emulate the light of a goblin.'[88]

14 In the beginning of the Shao-hsing period [1131–62] Shêng

82 孫鳳有一琴, 名吐綬. 彈之不甚佳, 獨有人唱曲, 則琴絃自相屬和, 因改名曰自鳴. 但琴背有一孔若蛀者, 一日有一道人乞食, 因見曰, 此中有蛀, 不除之, 則將速朽, 袖中出一小竹筒, 倒黑藥少許孔側, 即有綠色蟲走出, 背上隱隱有金線文, 道人納蟲竹筒中, 竟去, 自後唱曲, 絃不復鳴矣, 鳳怪之, 有博物君子說及此事, 歎曰, 此異寶也, 謂之鞠通, 有耳龍人置耳邊少時, 即愈, 喜食梧桐, 尤愛古墨, 鳳始悟道人竹筒中藥, 蓋古墨屑也.

83 陳植好鼓琴, 晝夜不輟, 凡二十八年, 忽見琴生紫花, 食之卽仙去.

84 王敬伯會稽之人, 琴曰, 感靈, 一日洲渚中昇亭而宿, 是夜月華露輕, 敬伯鼓琴, 感劉惠明亡女之靈告敬伯, 就體如平生, 從婢二人.

85 223–62.

86 133–92.

87 嵇中散夜彈琴, 忽見一鬼, 械而長嘆, 舉其手袂曰, 爲君一調, 中散與琴彈之, 聲清冷遙, 問不對, 疑是蔡邕, 邕死之日, 身着桎梏.

88 嵇康燈下鼓琴, 忽有一人長丈餘, 着黑單衣革帶, 康熟視之, 乃滅燈曰, 恥與魑魅爭光.

Hsün was prefect of Hsiang-yang. He made himself a pavilion built over a stream, and there daily played his lute. One day a stormwind arose, and rain poured down. His lute changed into a huge red carp, and riding on it Shêng Hsün disappeared into the sky.[89]

15 Ch'ên Ch'iu-yang fell ill and died. His father thought much of him, and placed his son's lute before his soul-tablet. Always after that in the middle of the night the tones of this lute would be heard; they could be heard even outside the house.[90]

16 Chuang An-hsiang was once playing the lute when it was dark. At once close by the fingers of her right hand there appeared a golden flower, which filled the whole room with its shine. In remembrance of this occurrence, she composed the tune called 'Golden Flower'.[91]

17 In the beginning of the T'ien-pao period [550–9] Li Chia-yin was a great lover of the lute; he would never stop playing, whether it was summer or winter. By the side of his seat there grew up five-coloured agarics [symbol of longevity], all showing the shapes of Immortals.[92]

18 Tai K'uei [literatus of the Chin period],[93] in his youth already excelled in all arts, and was good at playing the lute. His lute was called 'Black Crane'. The Prime Minister, Prince Hsi of Wu-ling, despatched some people to invite him to come to his court. Tai K'uei then broke his lute to pieces before the eyes of the messengers, saying: 'Tai K'uei can not become a payed comedian at a prince's court.'[94]

(The same story is quoted in the *Ku-ch'in-shu*;[95] there the behaviour of Tai K'uei is contrasted with that of another famous lute player of the same period, Yüan Chan:[96] 'Yüan Chan was an expert on the lute. People heard of his fame, and came in great numbers, asking him to play for them. He played for all, noble and low, young and old. I

---

[89] 紹興初盛勛知襄陽，自造水閣，日鼓琴于此，一日風雨大作，琴化爲巨赤鯉，勛跨之騰空而去.

[90] 陳秋陽以病卒，其父思之，以琴置靈几，每夜半必聞琴聲，且達戶外.

[91] 莊暗香暗中彈琴，右手指有金花，照爛九案，因自作金花之曲.

[92] 天保初，李嘉胤素好鼓琴，冬夏不輟，所居座中生五色芝草，皆狀如神仙.

[93] Died 396; besides being a famous lute player, he was also known as a fine calligraphist and painter.

[94] 戴逵少有文藝，善鼓琴，琴名黑鶴，太宰武陵王晞使人召焉，逵對使者前引破琴曰，戴安道不能爲王門伶人.

[95] 古琴疏, ascribed to Yü Ju-ming 虞汝明; see the *Shuo-fu* 說郛.

[96] 阮瞻, style Ch'ien-li 千里.

consider the understanding shown by Yüan Chan superior to the persistency of Tai Kʻuei.')[97]

19 During the Chên-yüan period [785–804] Tsʻui Hui, having lost his way, fell into a dry well. At the bottom he found a cave. Having penetrated into this cave for several miles, he struck a stone door, and having entered it he found a room measuring more than a hundred feet. The walls were beset with jewels, the glamour of which illuminated the whole room. A lute was lying on a table. Tsʻui Hui observed all this, without understanding where he was. After some delay he started playing on the lute. Then suddenly a door in the back wall opened, and in came two girls, saying: 'How is it that Master Tsʻui makes bold to enter the palace of the Emperor?' Tsʻui Hui asked: 'Where is the Emperor?' They answered: 'He has gone to the banquet of Chu Yung [a personage of the mythical age, later revered as Fire God; the implication is that Tsʻui Hui had entered the palace of one of the mythical Emperors]. Thereupon the girls told him to be seated before the table, and play on the lute for them. Tsʻui Hui played the tune *Hu-chia* [see above, page 94: 'The significance of the tunes', under heading 2, where the origin of the tune is differently explained]. The girls asked: 'What tune is this?' He answered: 'It is called *Hu-chia*.' They asked further: 'Why is it called *Hu-chia*?' He said: 'The daughter of Tsʻai Yung of the Han dynasty was carried off by the barbarians as a prisoner. While in their midst she was moved, remembering her former life, and taking her lute she composed this tune, representing the mournful sounds of the barbarians blowing their reed pipe.' The girls were overjoyed, and exclaimed: 'What a beautiful new tune this is!' Thereupon they made him drink toasts with them.[98]

20 On a moonlit night Su Shih [the famous Sung literatus][99] heard outside his window a song. It ran: 'Tones, tones . . .

---

97 阮千里善彈琴, 人聞其名往來求聽, 不問貴賤長幼, 皆爲彈之, 余以爲安道之介, 不如千里之達.

98 貞元中, 崔煒因迷道失足, 墜一枯井中, 井中空洞, 傍行數里, 觸一石門, 入門一室, 可百餘步, 壁綴明珠, 光亮一室, 几上設琴, 煒細視莫測, 良久取琴試彈, 室後一戶, 忽啓有二女, 出曰, 何崔生擅入皇帝玄宮耶, 煒問, 皇帝何在, 曰, 暫赴祝融晏耳, 因命煒就榻鼓琴, 煒彈胡笳, 二女曰, 何曲也, 曰, 胡笳也, 曰, 何以爲胡笳, 煒曰, 漢蔡邕女, 被虜入胡中, 及歸感胡中故事, 因撫琴而成斯弄, 象胡中吹笳哀咽之聲, 女皆恬然, 曰, 大是新曲, 遂命酌而傳觴.

99 1036–1101.

You are ungrateful, truly you are ungrateful! You have treated me badly, up to this day. I remember that formerly I used to sing softly, softly, drinking small cups. One tune of mine was then deemed worth a thousand pieces of gold. Now I am thrown away at the base of an old wall . . . The autumnal breeze blows over the dry grass, the white clouds are high . . . The bridge is broken, the water flows on, and my lover is nowhere to be seen. Sadness, sadness, melancholy . . . ' Opening the window to trace this sound, Su Shih saw a slender young woman, who vanished under the wall. The next day he dug there, and found an old lute.[100, 101]

21 Wang Yen-po was playing his lute in a houseboat that was lying ashore for the night. Then he saw a girl, who drew aside the door curtain, and entered. She took the lute and started to tune it; the tones were very sad. When Wang asked her what tune she was going to play, she answered: 'It is called *Ch'u-ming-kuang*; only Hsi K'ang[102] can play it.' Wang asked her to teach it to him, but she said: 'This is not a tune that may be played at a lover's meeting. It is intended only for the enjoyment of recluses living on high rocks or in hidden vales.' Then she played the lute and sang thereto. She shared his couch with him, and disappeared at daybreak.[103]

22 Yüan Hsien [disciple of Confucius] lived in a little hut, his doorposts were mulberry trees, his clothes were made of coarse wool. The hut was leaking from above and damp underneath, but he sat there correctly, and played on an old lute. [In the meantime] Tzû-kung [another disciple of Confucius] had become a minister in the state of Wei, and he came to visit Yüan with a four-in-hand team and a suite of cavalry. When he saw Yüan Hsien he said: 'Alas! In what distress you are!' Yüan Hsien answered: 'I have heard that a

100 蘇東坡於月夜聞窗外歌曰,昔昔昔,你負心,眞負心,辜負我,到於今,記得當時低低唱,淺淺斟,一曲值千金,如今拋我古墻陰,秋風荒草白雲深,斷橋流水無故人,凄凄切切,冷冷清清,推窗卽之,見一女子冉冉沒於墻下,明日掘之,得古琴一張.

101 To the words of the girl's song, there was made a minor lute tune, entitled *Ku-ch'in-yin* 古琴吟 'Lament of the old lute'; G. Soulié (Appendix I, 3), has given on

p. 116 a transcription of this tune in Western notation. His translation of the words on p. 115 is full of mistakes, and should be disregarded.

102 See p. 55.

103 王彥伯維舟理琴,見一女子披幃而進,取琴調之,聲甚哀,彥伯問何曲,答曰,此楚明光也,唯嵇叔夜能之,彥伯請受,女曰,此非艷俗所宜,唯岩棲谷隱者可以自娛耳,鼓琴且歌,止於東楊,遲明辭去.

man who has no riches is said to be poor, and a man who has
studied the Way but can not practise it, is said to be in distress. Now I for one am poor, but I am not in distress. In
truth, doing things always looking for approval from the
bystanders, being partial in choosing friends, loving a display of benevolence and righteousness, and showing off
chariots and horses, these are things which I could not bear
to do.' Tzû-kung hastily went away, and looked sour for the
rest of his life.[104]

104 原憲居環堵之室，桑以爲樞，褐以爲裳，上漏下溼，匡坐而彈古琴，子貢相衞，結駟連騎而來，見憲曰，嘻，先生何病也，憲應之曰，憲聞之無財謂之貧，學道而不能行，謂之病，若憲貧也，非病也，夫希而行，比周而友，仁義之慝，車馬之飾，憲不忍爲也，子貢逡巡而退，終身猶有慚色. (Taken from the *K'ung-tzû-chia-yü* 孔子家語; the same story is to be found in a slightly different version in *Chuang-tzû*, book *Jang-wang* 讓王.

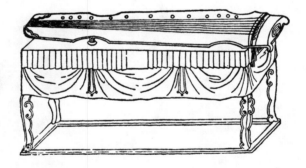

CHAPTER SEVEN

Conclusions

THE lute, the cither (*sê*), the reed-organ (*shêng*), and the quaint ocarina (*hsüan*), these are the instruments by which the ancient music of China can be studied. These instruments preserve tones that accompanied solemn sacrifices, notes that delighted the ears of ancient princes, more than three thousand years ago.

To revive this music, however, is no easy task. For the succeeding centuries have dimmed the tradition regarding the music of *sê*, *shêng* and *hsüan*: age has sealed their secrets. At present we find only some faint echos in their score for the ceremonial orchestra, stray fragments of what once must have been impressive solo music. It is only the lute that has an unbroken tradition. It was on the lute that many generations of scholars concentrated their musical efforts, inspired by reverent love for this instrument of the ancient sages. And so it was the lute that became a symbol of literary life and elegant refinement. At the same time it has retained its character of musical instrument, while *shêng*, *sê* and *hsüan* are more and more regarded as mere curiosities.

In the foregoing pages I have tried to describe one aspect of this unique Chinese musical instrument; I have tried to give the reader some idea of the place occupied by the lute in Chinese culture. I have tried to show how various, often originally conflicting elements, melted together and came to form a more or less unified ideology, the lore of the Chinese lute. And at the same time I have endeavoured to outline some historical perspectives. On rereading the above, my historical observations especially appear to me rather haphazard, and too much scattered over different chapters. As the material treated is almost entirely new, these defects were often unavoidable. Too often I was obliged to abandon the course of an argument, and branch off on some side track, in order to substantiate my theories. For the reader's convenience I here sum up in a concise form the conclusions that may be drawn from the foregoing chapters.

The origin of the lute lies hidden in China's past. There is evidence, however, that at some remote time, lute and cither were one and the same instrument: a stringed instrument, about the form and sound of which we can only make conjectures. This primordial lute must have borne an exclusively sacral character.

During the later part of the Chou dynasty, and until roughly the beginning of our era, we find lute and cither as separate, though still cognate, instruments, both used in the ceremonial orchestra. At the same time both were also used as solo instruments, for executing music of lighter genre. Yet it appears that it was especially to the lute that clung faint echoes of those ancient magical beliefs that were connected with old ceremonial music. This appears clearly from the story related in the *Shih-chi*, and given in section 1 of the preceding chapter: the lute is played at a banquet to amuse the guests, but unexpectedly it becomes the instrument through which hidden powers, originating in magic ceremonies of the dim past, manifest themselves in sinister omens. Thus gradually the lute is set more or less apart as a kind of sacred instrument. And when during the later Han dynasty the Confucianist literati are established as a mighty official caste, they declare the lute their special instrument. Here the ways of lute and cither part. The ancient magical notions that formerly were connected with music in general, are henceforth applied to one instrument in particular, the lute. Many of these notions are cast in Taoist formulae, these being by nature more suitable for that purpose than Confucianist terminology. Buddhism also makes its influence felt, and thus we find in the fourth and fifth centuries A.D. that something like a special *ch'in* ideology has been founded. The ceremonial orchestra, too, under literary influence, has become an expression of politico-philosophical conceptions. But it is in the lute ideology that the ancient magic conceptions survive: playing the lute is described as a means for prolonging life, and as an aid to meditation.

During the Sui and T'ang periods an intense artistic impulse inspired Chinese culture. Mainly through Central-Asiatic influence, the Chinese were obsessed by a hunger for bright and gorgeous colours, for highly melodious, light and entrancing music. New instruments were imported from foreign countries, and old Chinese instruments were put to a new use. The lute, with its rich acoustic possibilities, is tuned to less severe melodies, and is incorporated in the orchestra for entertainment music, to enliven literary gatherings and festive banquets. But on the other hand, as a reaction, some conservative scholars now start to define more sharply the principles of the special ideology of the lute, to guard their beloved instrument against the vulgarity of the crowd.

The Sung dynasty then shows both the profane and the sacred aspects of the lute, and between these two aspects its music is almost evenly balanced. It is a period of gestation, a slow preparation for the great climax. This process of maturation goes on for some time, until, at length, during the Ming period lute and lute music reach full fruition. The great importance of this period for the lute justifies a slightly more detailed treatment.

It is much to be regretted that it has become a habit of Western writers, when describing the history of China, to pass over the Ming dynasty in a few words, or at best, with a few pages. They dwell on the political decay that set in with the predominance of the eunuchs in Palace circles and, speaking of the cultural aspect of the period, they say that no new artistic impulses of importance are noticeable, that in all branches of art and literature nothing was accomplished beyond copying old models. And with regard to scientific pursuits, they repeat the judgement given by the scholars of the Ch'ing dynasty, pronouncing Ming scholarship shallow and uncritical.

Now, that Ch'ing scholars did little to show the glory of the Ming dynasty is quite understandable. The hand of the Manchu conqueror rested heavily on the Chinese intellect, and to grow enthusiastic over the merits of the former dynasty was courting disaster. Less excusable is the negligent attitude of Western scholars. For they have free access to the vast mass of original Ming materials that is preserved. That they did not use this opportunity, shows that until very recently there existed among Western sinologues a strong tendency to study only the approved sections of Chinese literature, books that were found in the Ch'ing catalogues. But in order to see the culture of the Ming period as it really was, we must entirely ignore Ch'ing materials; they can only blur our view. We must turn to the original Ming materials, which, fortunately, still exist in abundance. Ming editions of the works of almost every Ming literatus of any importance have been preserved.[1] Ming porcelain still tells its own tale, and genuine Ming paintings are by no means rare.

---

[1] During the Ch'ing dynasty the censor often took entire chapters out of these Ming prints; it is in Japan that one must look for unmutilated copies. For a great number of Ming editions were brought over to Japan shortly after their publication, and were carefully preserved. Such Ming editions are especially found in the collections of old feudal families. These books are called in the Japanese book trade *kowatari* 古渡り, and are*

Surveying these materials I come to the conclusion that from a cultural point of view, the Ming period was one of the most glorious epochs in Chinese history. It was the period that saw a culmination of pure Chinese culture, the period that shows the most complete expression of Chinese ideals. The foreign influences that entered China during the T'ang and subsequent dynasties had been digested; in the Ming period a complete amalgamation is effected. During this period the Chinese spirit blossomed most luxuriantly; it was during the Ch'ing dynasty that the withering set in. When a tree is in full blossom, its gorgeous beauty amazes the observer; little does he care what the branches and the trunk look like. With the coming of autumn, the blossoms fall down, then the leaves, and the observer sees the tree in a more realistic way; he sees that here branches are broken, there a stem ends in an abrupt gnarl. The observer will know more, but enjoy less. This image may give an idea of the fundamental differences between the general spirit of Ming and Ch'ing cultures. Ming scholars wrote enthusiastic eulogies on a passage in the Classics that struck them as eminently wise; Ch'ing scholars pointed out that the punctuation of one sentence was erroneous. Ming literati reprinted the poetry of the T'ang and preceding periods in magnificent editions, with graceful characters on large-sized paper. Ch'ing scholars reprinted this same poetry in cheap-looking editions, with small, angular characters, but with the text really improved.

During the Ming period the daily life of the scholar–official neared something like perfection. The literati of that time, mostly of an eclectic turn of mind, understood the secret of life, which consists of judiciously mixing beauty with comfort, and high ideals with purely practical views. This way of living is mirrored in the literature of the period. Numerous books are written on the refined pleasures of the cultured scholar. They describe in minute detail the art of tea drinking, the art of flower arrangement, of laying out gardens, of building rockeries, of playing chess and complicated wine games, of practising arrow throwing, ball games, and a multitude of other subjects that later were neglected, or fell entirely into oblivion.

---

*greatly valued. Japan generally furnishes important materials for our knowledge of Ming culture. In the turbulent years that marked the end of the Ming dynasty, Chinese priests, scholars and artists fled to Japan in great numbers, and were patronized by Japanese nobles and scholars. So great was their influence, that for obtaining a right understanding of, say Tokugawa culture, a study of the Ming dynasty is imperative; and, conversely, when studying the Ming period one cannot afford to disregard the mass of Ming material preserved in Japan.

It is only natural, therefore, that it was during the Ming period, too, that the lute and lute music displayed their full and most sublime unfolding. In cultural centers all over the country great lute masters arose, and numerous handbooks were published. Their composers did not aim at retracing the old music. Although they loved to dwell on the beauty of bygone days, this was a sentiment, a mood, but little conducive to intensive study. They composed very original and most attractive new tunes, to which they assigned the old approved titles. This music is new, but how rich in tone, what subtle effects, what fullness of musical expression! Granted that the Ming lute players were mediocre students of musical history (with some brilliant exceptions like the Prince Tsai-yü), it cannot be denied that they were gifted musicians.

In the circles of the literati, cultivating leisurely enjoyment and abstract contemplation, the various conceptions connected with the lute were more or less systematized and pressed into formulae. Since many of the literati engaged in Taoist disciplines for prolonging life, and interested themselves in the search for the elixir of life and similar pursuits, the magical character of the lute was stressed more and more. Now the system of *ch'in* ideology reaches its full development, and the significance of the lute is definitely fixed.

During the Ch'ing dynasty the life of the literati loses much of its glamour. Especially in the earlier part of the Ch'ing period, literary pursuits are postponed to military prowess: the most skilful brush is powerless when confronted with the swords and bows of the Manchu bannermen. Later, it is true, literary ideals reasserted themselves; but the vigour and *élan* of the Ming period were never regained. South China was less affected. Up to the present it is still in South China that remnants of Ming culture must be looked for. Also it was the southern provinces that produced most of the great lute masters of the Ch'ing period.

When the Manchu supremacy had become more firmly established, the rulers could devote more attention to literary matters. Then Ch'ing scholarship develops, and acquires its many distinguishing features: a sharp critical spirit, extensive antiquarian research, the compiling of enormous works of literary reference, etc. Now serious attempts are made to reconstruct the old music. Old musical scores are collected, various systems of notation investigated, and musical theory is re-examined.

Many useful books about the lute and its music are written, but important additions to the repertoire are few. For the most part, lute masters confine themselves to publishing the tunes of the Ming and preceding dynasties in revised forms. The system of *ch'in* ideology is not worked out further, often even completely disregarded. At best, the statements scattered over the various Ming handbooks are reprinted. In most handbooks the teachings on the significance of the lute are left out, and replaced by lengthy discussions on musical theory. A good example of such a dry handbook is the *Tzŭ-yüan-t'ang* handbook (cf. Appendix ii, no. 16). During the Ch'ing period, also, the social standard of the lute experts dropped considerably. While during the Ming and preceding periods famous lute performers were as a rule great literati or high officials, in the Ch'ing period they were mostly more or less professional musicians, who taught the lute for a living. One shall look in vain in biographical works of the period for the names of the publishers of the best handbooks.

The twentieth century brings the establishment of the Republic, and a revaluation of all values. Here we must break off our discussion of the history of *ch'in* ideology. Instead I may end with some remarks about the present state of lute music, and its future.

In the turbulent first decennia of this century the lute very nearly suffered the same fate as so many other Chinese old musical instruments, namely, to see its tradition broken off and its music forgotten. Fortunately a few old masters, scattered over the country, faithfully preserved their cherished art, and transmitted its secrets to a few pupils. They acted as guardians of the lute and its music, while the ranks of scholars who understood it grew thinner every day, and while younger Chinese musicians were entirely absorbed in studies of Western music.

Now, in recent years, the persistency of those few elder masters is bearing fruit. For gradually in China there has come into existence a class of younger musicians, who combine a sound Western musicological training with a deep interest in their own national music. Many of these have taken up the study of the lute; first they patiently learn the art from the few elderly masters that are left, then they investigate the materials thus obtained in the light of modern musicological science. From these researches we may expect important results.[2]

---

[2] How necessary the work of these scholars is, is all too apparent; for the ignorance of many present-day Chinese with regard to their own music is appalling. In 1937 I read in a Chinese-managed periodical, which as a rule maintains a high literary and scientific standard (*The T'ien-hsia Monthly*, iv, p. 54; Music Chronicle), strange statements like the following: 'Most of them [the Chinese musical instruments] are still quite crude*

The atmosphere that in former days surrounded the lute player will soon belong definitely to the past—together with so much that was charming in the old Chinese life. But lute music in itself has a bright future.

The present writer is one of those who—naive and overconfident, maybe—believe in the existence of eternal values. He believes that what is really good or beautiful will last for ever; that such things can be ignored, neglected or suppressed, but that they shall never vanish entirely.

It is for this reason that he ventures to publish the preceding pages on the lore of the Chinese lute, desultory and incomplete as they are. For the intrinsic beauty of the lute and its music are such as to justify his confidence that others will continue where he left off.

---

*and simple: they do not admit of the development of highly finished techniques Moreover, the tone qualities of the musical instruments are none too pleasing. The seven-chord ch'in (七絃琴) has hardly any sound at all.' Then the author of the article in question goes on to say that all Chinese instruments must be 'corrected', so as to make them reproduce the Western tempered scale. Such a proposal, involving as it does the perversion or wanton destruction of precious musical data, could only be made in a time like the present, where every day there is more music but less musicality, and where various sound-producing instruments throw the greatest masterpieces of Western music to the crowd to be scrambled for.

APPENDIX I

Occidental Literature on the Lute

1 J. J. M. Amiot, *Mémoires sur la musique des Chinois tant anciens que modernes* (Mémoires concernant les Chinois, vol. VI), Paris 1780.

This comprehensive work is the first detailed description of Chinese music published in Europe. Its learned author discusses Chinese musical theory in general, the twelve sonorous tubes, and some of the more important instruments used in the cere-monial orchestra. His sources are personal observation and such authoritative Chinese works as the *Lü-lü-ching-i*[1] by the Ming prince Chu Tsai-yü,[2] and the *Lü-lü-chêng-i*,[3] an official publica-tion dated 1713. This book shows the same merits and the same defects as other works by 18th-century missionaries on China. These learned priests made an excellent use of their daily contact with the flower of the Chinese literati; they carefully noted down the information supplied by the latter, and followed their advice regarding the books to be selected for further reference. On the other hand, the missionaries believed implicitly what their informants told them, and thought that their opinions on Chinese antiquity were unquestionable truth. Thus, for in-stance, with regard to music, the Chinese informants of our author gave him nothing but the traditional Chinese views on music, as explained in some officially sanctioned standard works of later date. Yet this book by Father Amiot is a remarkable effort; when read critically, it will supply even the present-day student of Chinese music with much useful material.

The author gives considerable attention to both *ch'in* and *sê*. In the first chapter of this essay I already quoted one of his re-marks on the importance of the lute in Chinese cultural life (cf. above, Chapter I, page 3). Interesting is a list of books relat-ing to the lute, which the author gives on p. 24. Unfortunately the titles are given in transcription only, without author or date; therefore some of the items I could not identify. As the list shows

---

[1] 律呂精義   [2] 朱載堉   [3] 律呂正義

which books on the lute were studied by Court circles in the 18th century, I reproduce it here, with my identifications added between brackets.

> (49) *Kou tchouen kin pou.*
>
> (50) *Chen ki mi pou* (*Shên-chi-pi-pu*,[4] by the Ming prince Chu Ch'üan; cf. Appendix ii, no. 11).
>
> (51) *Tay kou y yn* (*T'ai-ku-i-yin*,[5] same author).
>
> (52) *Kin jouan ki mong* (*Ch'in-juan-ch'i-meng*,[6] same author).
>
> (53) *Sien ko yao tché* (*Hsien-ko-yao-chih*.[7] The *Lü-lü-ching-i* mentions a *Hsien-ko-yao-lu*[8] by an unknown author).
>
> (54) *Tchoung ho fa jen* (*Chung-ho-fa-jên*,[9] a Ming treatise by an unknown author, mentioned in the *Lü-lü-ching-i*).
>
> (55) *Y fa kin pou* (*I-fa-ch'in-pu*).[10]
>
> (56) *Tchan tchou kin pou* (*Chang-chu-ch'in-pu*,[11] a Ming handbook mentioned in the *Lü-lü-ching-i*).
>
> (57) *Hoang sien kin pou* (*Huang-hsien-ch'in-pu*,[12] a Ming handbook mentioned in the *Lü-lü-ching-i*, better known as the *Wu-kang-ch'in-pu*,[13] pub. 1546; Huang Hsien occupied an official position during 1488–1505).
>
> (58) *Siao loan kin pou* (*Hsiao-luan-ch'in-pu*,[14] a Ming handbook mentioned in the *Lü-lü-ching-i*).

2 J. A. van Aalst, *Chinese music* (Imperial Maritime Customs, special series, No. 6), Shanghai 1884 (re-issued at Peking in 1933).

For many years this book was for occidental students the standard work for information regarding Chinese music. Though it contains not a few misstatements, and although most of its general observations are antiquated, it still is a usable book. It has a wider scope than Amiot's work, as here popular Chinese music is also included. There are many illustrations, but they are very poorly done.

The *ch'in* is treated on pages 59–62. The description found there is generally correct; only it should be remembered that the author's observations on lute music are based on the lute of the ceremonial orchestra, and that therefore the tuning, for

---

4　神奇秘譜
5　太古遺音
6　琴阮啓蒙
7　絃歌要指
8　絃歌要錄
9　中和發軔

10　遺法琴譜
11　張助琴譜
12　黃獻琴譜
13　梧岡琴譜
14　蕭鸞琴譜

instance, does not apply to the lute as solo instrument. On p. 60, the explanation of the finger technique of the right hand, the last sign (abbreviation of *ch'uan-fu*)[15] is wrongly explained; cf. the same sign in the list given by me above, p. 127, no. 10.

3 G. Soulié, *La Musique en Chine* (Extrait du Bulletin de l'Association franco-chinoise), Paris 1911.

When compared with the preceding item, this book shows considerable progress. It is far more scientific than van Aalst's, and the illustrations are more accurate and better executed. On the basis of its quality this work should long ago have superseded van Aalst's in sinological circles. For some reason or other, however, it has remained comparatively unknown, and until recent years van Aalst's book continued to appear in catalogues at a prohibitive price; that in 1933 it was reprinted, unrevised, tends to show how few are the serious students of music among present-day orientalists.

On p. 30 the author gives a fairly detailed description of the *ch'in*. He gives a list of 44 abbreviated signs used in *ch'in* notation, which means an improvement on the meagre list given by van Aalst, though it contains many inaccuracies; these will appear on comparing this list with the one given by me above, p. 124. On p. 36 a page from a *ch'in* handbook is reproduced, and explained in detail. On p. 115 a short lute composition (*Ku-ch'in-yin*)[16] is given in Western notation.

4 A. C. MOULE, *A list of musical and other sound-producing instruments of the Chinese* (Royal Asiatic Society), Shanghai 1908.

This paper contains accurate descriptions of a great variety of Chinese musical instruments. The author adopted the method followed by V. C. Mahillon in his excellent *Catalogue descriptif et analytique du musée instrumental du Conservatoire Royal de Bruxelles* (1893); he tries to be as detailed as possible with regard to measurements and transcription of the scales. Next to the instruments used in ceremonial music, we also find descriptions of very popular instruments, used in the streets of Chinese towns. These data are important, for street music undergoes many changes, and generally leaves no written records.

Pages 106–9 treat of the *ch'in;* the material is taken from Amiot, van Aalst, etc., and no new data are added.

---

[15] 全扶   [16] 古琴吟

5 L. LALOY, *La Musique chinoise* (part of the series: Les Musiciens célèbres), Paris, no date.

This small book, although of necessity rather popular, still is a very sound and useful survey of Chinese music, with the cultural and ideological aspects especially stressed. The illustrations are well chosen and of excellent execution. Contents:

 1 Les sources.
 2 La doctrine.
 3 Les destins.
 4 Le système.
 5 La gamme.
 6 Les gammes nouvelles.
 7 Les instruments.
 8 La notation.
 9 Musique religieuse.
10 Musique de chambre.
11 Musique populaire.
12 Musique de théatre.
13 Espoir.
14 Mélodies notées.

Pages 68–76 and 91–5 treat of the *ch'in*. The author duly stresses the importance of lute ideology, the deep significance of this instrument and its music. Historical and cultural background are briefly, but very aptly, sketched. This book I recommend as the best introduction to the subject of Chinese music in general.

6 M. COURANT, *Essai historique sur la musique classique des Chinois, avec un appendice relatif à la musique coréenne* (in: Encyclopédie de la musique et dictionnaire du Conservatoire, part I, pp. 77–241), Paris 1924.

M. Courant, the well-known French sinologue, to whom the orientalistic world is already heavily indebted for his magnificent Korean bibliography (*Bibliographie coréenne*, Paris 1894), has put us under a further obligation by this most detailed study on Chinese classical music. This essay is the most scientific and accurate account of Chinese music I know. Here for the first time the subject in its entirety has been investigated and reviewed by a competent scholar, who could consult all sources in the original, and in addition to that was—if my information is correct—himself a musician of no mean ability. Chinese musical theory is analyzed in detail, and its often obscure expressions are translated into Western terminology. Historical problems are discussed in detail, and in groping for their solution the author shows much discretion. First reading through the preceding item by Laloy, and then working through this essay by Courant, will in my opinion be the best preparation for anyone who proposes to do some research in Chinese music. Courant's essay is divided into four parts:

1 Théorie musicale.
2 Instruments.
3 Orchestres et choeurs.
4 Les Idées cosmologiques et philosophiques.

The *ch'in* is treated on pp. 163–75. After a careful description of the instrument itself, the author goes on to an investigation of its theoretical side, and discusses its tunings in detail. Then he gives about a dozen *ch'in* melodies in Western transcription, all taken from the *T'ien-wên-ko-ch'in-pu-chi-ch'êng* (cf. App. II, no. 18). He admits that these versions are arbitrary, as they must be because of the fundamental differences existing between the Chinese scale and ours; or, as the author puts it: 'Ce serait sans doute fausser l'essence des systèmes harmoniques chinois que de les vouloir réduire à nos formules' (p. 169). Yet his transcriptions are useful to give the student at least a general idea of what *ch'in* music looks like. I may add that execution on the cello comes nearest to the tone of the Chinese original. The essay ends with an extensive bibliography of Western and Chinese sources consulted, and a useful index where the reader finds the Chinese characters for every name and term occurring in the essay.

I may add in passing that the few pages treating of Korean music (pp. 211–20) are less satisfactory. To supplement what is given here, one should consult A. Eckardt, *Koreanische Musik*, Tokyo 1930. Sinologues I would refer to the *Ak-hak-kwe-pôm*.[17] This is the great Korean standard work on Chinese and Korean music, written in Chinese, and profusely illustrated. It was written in 1493 by the scholar Syông Kyôn 成俔. The Korean original is now extremely rare; fortunately in 1933 a good photographic reprint was published at Keijō, by the Koten-kankō-kai.[18]

[17] 樂學軌範   [18] 古典刊行會

APPENDIX II

Chinese Literature on the Lute

A GENERAL

1 *Ch'in-tsao,*[1] a collection of about fifty motifs of ancient melodies. This book contains no musical notation; only the title of each tune is given, with a few words about its composer, the circumstances that inspired him, the significance of the music, etc. As the oldest list of lute melodies extant, this book has great documentary value. Opinions differ as to whether its authorship must be ascribed to the famous literatus and musician Ts'ai Yung,[2] (133–92), or to the equally famous man of letters K'ung Yen.[3] The text is to be found in the *Tu-hua-chai-ts'ung-shu,*[4] a collection of reprints of classical works published in 1799 by Ku Hsiu[5] and the *P'ing-ts'in-kuan-ts'ung-shu,*[6] a collection of texts published by the great authority on the classics Sun Hsing-yen.[7] I have used the excellent Japanese official edition (*kampan*),[8] pub. in 1832 in one vol., where the text as established by Sun Hsing-yen is reprinted, together with the preface by the scholar Ma Jui-chên,[9] dated 1805.

2 *Ch'in-shih,*[10] 'History of the Lute', in 6 chs.; cf. *Imperial Catalogue,* ch. 113, leaf 8 verso. The author of this treatise is the great scholar of the Sung period, Chu Ch'ang-wên[11] (style: Po-yüan,[12] 1041–1100). Chs. 1–5 contain biographies of more than 150 famous lute players, chronologically arranged; the 6th ch. treats of the lute itself, and is divided into eleven parts. These discuss:

    1 Sonorous tubes.[13]

    2 Strings.[14]

---

1 琴操
2 蔡邕
3 孔衍
4 讀畫齋叢書
5 顧修
6 平津館叢書
7 孫星衍

8 官板
9 馬瑞辰
10 琴史
11 朱長文
12 伯原
13 瑩律
14 釋絃

3 Dimensions.[15]
4 Form.[16]
5 Tones.[17]
6 Modes.[18]
7 Songs.[19]
8 Manufacture.[20]
9 Beauty.[21]
10 Significance.[22]
11 History.[23]

The preface to this book is dated 1084. The author, prevented through illness from taking part in the literary examinations, devoted the greater part of his life to literary pursuits. He was especially interested in those objects that are dear to the literatus; his researches in this field are collected in his *Mo-ch'ih-p'ien*,[24] preface dated 1066. The author's grandfather, Chu I,[25] was an expert on the lute, and Chu Ch'ang-wên continued his tradition. The *Ch'in-shih* is written in excellent, highly polished prose. Unfortunately, historical details and precise information are sacrificed to the style; it is further to be regretted that the author never mentions his sources. Still the book contains much useful material. I used the edition as published in the *Lien-t'ing-shih-êrh-chung*,[26] a collection of reprints pub. at Shanghai in 1921; the originals were collected by Ts'ao Yin[27] (1658–1712).

3 *K'ao-p'an-yü-shih*,[28] 'Desultory Remarks on Furnishing the Abode of the Retired Scholar', in 4 chs.; cf. *Imperial Catalogue*, ch. 130, leaf 2 recto. The title of this book refers to an ode of the *Shih-ching* (Decade of Wei, 2),[29] which opens with the line: 'He built his hut near the stream in the vale.'[30] This book contains very detailed descriptions of all the objects belonging to the traditional outfit of a scholar of refined and cultured taste, e.g. old books and scrolls, incense, utensils for making tea, etc. To each of these objects a *chien*,[31] 'memorandum', is devoted; the *Ch'in-chien*[32] is to be found at the end of ch. 2. The compiler is the

---

15 明度
16 擬象
17 論音
18 審調
19 聲歌
20 廣制
21 盡美
22 志言
23 叙史

24 墨池篇
25 朱億
26 棟亭十二種
27 曹寅
28 考盤餘事
29 衛
30 考盤在澗
31 箋
32 琴箋

well-known Ming scholar T'u Lung.[33] In China this book was extremely popular; it was published in various editions, and may be found in several *ts'ung-shu*.[34] A nicely edited Japanese reprint appeared in 1803, with a preface by the Japanese sinologue Hayashi Jussai[35] (1768–1841).

4 *Tsun-shêng-pa-chien*,[36] 'Eight Treatises on Living in Accordance with Nature' (the title page of the original Ming edition, dated 1591, reads *tsun* 尊 instead of *tsun* 遵, which could be rendered as: 'venerating, valuing' life), 8 chs.; cf. *Imperial Catalogue*, ch. 123, leaf 2 recto. Compiled by Kao Lien,[37] a poet and playwright of the later part of the Ming dynasty. About his life and career little is known; a short biographical note may be found in the *Ming-tz'ŭ-tsung*,[38] ch. 4. His *Tsun-shêng-pa-chien* is an extensive encyclopedical collection, chiefly bearing a medical character; it indicates how, by following Taoist rules, one may live in good health and attain to a high age. But besides these, a great variety of other subjects are treated, special attention being given to dress, food etc. Thus this book is an important document for our knowledge of daily life and customs during the Ming period. As the title indicates, the work is divided into 8 sections. For our present subject the 6th section is the most important. It bears the title *Yen-hsien-ch'ing-shang*:[39] 'Refined enjoyment of elegant leisure'. This section discusses all subjects dear to the scholar: paintings and how to collect and preserve them; inkstones and ink, paper, brushes, brush stands, ornamental rocks, seals, etc. It is in this section that we also find a discussion of the lute, entitled *Lun-ch'in*[40] (pp. 70 ff.). Here the author gives a concise, but fairly accurate survey of the study of the lute. Thereafter we find some pages on cranes and how to rear them.

5 *Ch'in-ching*,[41] 'Classical Book of the Lute', in 14 chs., by the lute master Chang Ta-ming,[42] called Yu-kun. First preface by the Ming scholar Yeh Hsiang-kao[43] (cf. *Ming-shih*, ch. 240), dated 1609; second preface by Liu Ta-jên;[44] author's preface dated 1609. Undated colophon by Ch'ên Wu-ch'ang.[45] The original, finely executed Ming edition of this valuable book is extremely

---

33 屠隆, style: Ch'ang-ching 長卿, *Chin-shih* in 1577.
34 叢書
35 林述齋
36 遵生八牋
37 高濂
38 明詞綜

39 燕閒清賞
40 論琴
41 琴經
42 張大命, 右袞
43 葉向高
44 劉大任
45 陳五昌

rare; but occasionally Chinese or Japanese manuscript copies may be found. About Chang Ta-ming, who later also published a collection of tunes in notation, the *Yang-ch'un-t'ang-ch'in-pu*,[46] little is known except that he was a man from Fukien. The *Ch'in-ching* is remarkable in that it does not contain a single lute tune in notation. The work is concerned with musical theory, rules for the lute player, how to read the *ch'in-pu*, notes on famous old tunes and instruments, hints for appraising antique lutes, how to build lutes, how to select the correct surroundings for playing the lute, and finally an extensive collection of quotations from older literature.

6 *Ch'ing-lien-fang-ch'in-ya*,[47] 'Elegance of the Lute, from the Blue-Lotus Boat', in 4 chs.; cf. *Imperial Catalogue*, ch. 114, leaf 7 verso. A comprehensive collection of literary data concerning the lute, compiled by Lin Yu-lin[48]; author's preface dated 1641. Also, there are two prefaces by Ming painters, the first by Li Shao-chi,[49] the second by Chou Yü-tu[50] (for biographical notes cf. *Ming-hua-lu*,[51] chs. 6 and 4). The author says that he wrote this book while traveling by boat through Kiangsu Province, hence the title. The book contains valuable material though collected without much discrimination; many of the original sources quoted from are either lost now or difficult to obtain.

7 *Ch'in-hsüeh-ts'ung-shu*[52] (Collected Writings on the Study of the Lute); first edition (1911) in 32 chs., second enlarged edition in 43 chs. (1925). The collected writings of the contemporary lute expert Yang Tsung-chi.[53] In my essay I have repeatedly quoted from this work. It is, as far as I know, the only really original and thorough study by a modern Chinese on the lute and all questions relating to it. The author was a teacher of music in a school at Peking. This book is the result of the study of a lifetime, by a man who not only was a well-known lute player himself, but also had excellent opportunities for consulting literary and actual materials. Though one may not always agree with the author's conclusions, still it is a work that no serious student of the lute can afford to ignore. It is especially important to scholars not

---

46 陽春堂琴譜
47 青蓮舫琴雅
48 林有麟, style: Jên-fu 仁甫.
49 李紹箕
50 周裕度

51 明畫錄
52 琴學叢書
53 楊宗稷, style: Shih-po 時百 lit. name Chiu-i-shan-jên 九疑山人.

living in China or Japan, for here they will find data that are unobtainable outside the Orient: the author relates his discussions with great living lute masters, his experiences with curio dealers when buying antique lutes, his own attempts at constructing lutes, etc. A list of the various items this collection contains will show its rich contents.

A   *Ch'in-ts'ui*,[54] various studies on lute music, especially on the tunes; the fourth section deals with old instruments.

B   *Ch'in-hua*,[55] miscellaneous notes on the lute.

C   *Ch'in-pu*,[56] a special study on the oldest *ch'in* tune preserved, the Yu-lan[56] manuscript; further, a study on the tune *Liu-shui*.[57]

D   *Ch'in-hsüeh-sui-pi*,[58] stray notes of the author on various subjects connected with the lute.

E   *Ch'in-yü-man-lu*,[59] same as the preceding.

F   *Ch'in-ching*,[60] 'Mirror of the Lute', a collection of well-known tunes, transcribed in the special notation invented by the author: the *chien-tzû* are given both in their original and their unabbreviated forms; pitch and measure are accurately indicated. These notations should be a great help to everyone who tries to learn how to play the lute without a teacher.

G   *Ch'in-sê-ho-pu*,[61] tunes for lute and *sê* together, with special discussion of the tuning of the *sê*.

H   *Ch'in-hsüeh-wên-ta*,[62] all kinds of problems regarding the lute, discussed in dialogue form.

I   *Ts'ang-ch'in-lu*,[63] a most detailed description of the lutes in the author's collection.

J   *Ch'in-sê-hsin-pu*,[64] tunes for lute and *sê* together.

K   *Ch'in-ching-hsü*,[65] sequence to item F.

L   *Yu-lan-ho-shêng*,[66] a reaction upon the author's discussion of the *Yu-lan* tune, by Li Chi,[67] another contemporary scholar. Besides the items enumerated above, the collection contains several minor essays on musical theory, the sonorous tubes, etc.

54   琴粹
55   琴話
56   琴譜, 幽蘭
57   流水
58   琴學隨筆
59   琴餘漫錄
60   琴鏡

61   琴瑟合譜
62   琴學問答
63   藏琴錄
64   琴瑟新譜
65   琴鏡續
66   幽蘭和聲
67   李濟

8 *Ch'in-shu-ts'un-mu*,[68] a *catalogue raisonné* of practically all books on the lute that have been preserved, either in their entirety, or in title only, in 6 chs. Published by Chou Ch'ing-yün,[69] a great collector of books and manuscripts, and a friend of Yang Tsung-chi, the author of the preceding item. First preface by the famous bibliophile Miao Ch'üan-sun,[70] dated 1915,[71] second preface by the author, dated 1914. Two additional chs., entitled *Pieh-lu*,[72] list books about music in general. The items are arranged chronologically, and details about the authors and the editions are added; often the prefaces are reprinted in their entirety. See my remarks above, Ch. III, section 1.

9 *Ch'in-shih*,[73] biographies of famous lute players, in 8 chapters, compiled by Chou Ch'ing-yün. First preface by Yang Tsung-chi, undated. Author's preface dated 1919. The author intended this book as a supplement to the *Ch'in-shih* of Chu Ch'ang-wên (see above, no. 2). It is a useful source book, containing a tremendous number of biographical notes on people who in some way or other were connected with lute music: we find famous lute masters, well-known lute makers, editors of lute handbooks, etc. All items are arranged chronologically, and the sources indicated. The last chapter (*kuei-hsiu*)[74] is devoted specially to lady lute players.

10 *Chin-yü*,[75] subtitle: 'Special Publication on the Study of the Lute'.[76] Published by the 'Chin-yü Lute Association',[77] Shanghai 1940; one vol., 338 pages text, 16 pages photographs, one in colour.

This is a collection of 10 special articles on the lute, written by members of the Chin-yü Lute Association, all of them prominent experts on this instrument and its lore. The association was founded in 1939, sponsored by such well-known lute players as Messrs Ch'a Chên-hu,[78] Hsü Yuan-po,[79] P'êng Ch'ing-shou[80] and Wu Ching-lüeh.[81] Most of the members belong to the Yü-shan branch of the Kiangsu School. This branch was established by the Ming musician Yen Chêng.[82] In 1614 this master published his handbook, *Sung-hsüan-kuan-ch'in-pu* (see below, page

---

68 琴書存目
69 周慶雲
70 繆荃孫, 1844–1919.
71 旃蒙單閼 i.e., 乙卯.
72 別錄
73 琴史
74 閨秀
75 今虞

76 研究古琴之專刊
77 今虞琴社
78 查鎮湖
79 徐元白
80 彭慶壽
81 吳景略
82 嚴澂, style, Tao-chêng 道澂, literary name T'ien-ch'ih 天池, 1547–1625.

226). Next to a wealth of information on Yen Chêng and his school, this publication contains authoritative essays on all the more important aspects of the study of the lute, and gives several lute melodies, both in the traditional and the modern Chinese notation.

Also, this book contains four lists that will be of interest to the student of the present condition of lute studies in China. The first is a list of 223 present-day lute players, giving their full name, age, native place, occupation and address. The second lists 95 of the more prominent lute players; each item gives name, style and literary name of the person concerned, the school of lute playing to which he belongs, the lutes and lute handbooks in his collection, his favourite melodies, his publications and his hobbies. The third is a list of 75 antique lutes that are well known to connoisseurs. Each item is headed by the particular name of the instrument (examples above, pp. 104–5), and its model. Then follow its material (i.e. the kind of wood used for upper and lower board of the sound box), the colour and crack-marks of the lacquer, the quality of its tones, the material used for the tuning pegs, its date and the inscriptions inside the sound box and on the outside, the name of its builder, and the name of the present owner of the instrument. Finally, the fourth list gives particulars about 40 new lutes, built by present-day lute experts.

B SPECIAL

1 *Shên-chi-pi-pu*,[83] handbook for the lute, in 3 chs., by the Prince of Ning.[84] The author's literary name was Ch'ü-hsien[85] ('Emaciated Immortal'), therefore this handbook is also referred to as *Ch'ü-hsien-ch'in-pu*. Author's preface dated 1425. For details about the author, see below, pp. 214–15, where a list is also given of the books published by him. This is the oldest printed *ch'in-pu* preserved, but unfortunately extremely rare. The only Chinese catalogue in which it is mentioned is that of the famous Ming library, T'ien-i-ko; but various kinds of disasters have ravaged this library, and a recent study on the books that are left does not mention this valuable item (see *T'ien-i-ko-ts'ang-shu-k'ao*,[86] by the modern bibliographer Ch'ên Têng-yûan,[87]

---

83 神奇秘譜   84 寧王, personal name Chü Ch'üan (朱權, died 1448).
        85 臞仙   86 天一閣藏書考   87 陳登原

Shanghai 1932). The Library of the Cabinet (Naikaku-bunko)[88] in Tokyo has a fine first edition, and I possess a beautifully executed manuscript copy. This handbook is a magnificent example of Ming printing: three large-sized volumes, printed in big characters on good paper. It was already famous during the Ming period. Kao Lien (*op. cit., Yen-hsien-ch'ing-shang*, p. 78) says: 'The people of our day think the handbook *Shên-chi-pi-pu* by the Prince of Ning the best. But one should try to obtain the first, large-sized edition. The author had the text carefully collated and revised, so that every dot and every stroke is correct. This is a good handbook, which should be treasured. The later editions are not worth being looked at.'[89] The only objection to this handbook is that the author has not been consistent in his system of notation, and that the *chien-tzŭ* therefore have become unnecessarily complicated. One gets the impression that the compiler purposely made the notation obscure, so that only expert players could use it. He was very particular about a strict observation of the rules for the lute player: in his preface he says that, properly, only high officials should be allowed to occupy themselves with the lute.

12 *Pu-hsü-t'ang-ch'in-pu*,[90] another early Ming handbook, in 9 chs.; compiled by Ku I-chiang.[91] First preface by Sun Ch'êng-ên (cf. *Ming-shih-tsung*,[92] ch. 74), dated 1551; second preface by Wang T'ing,[93] undated; third preface by Ch'ên Chung-chou[94], dated 1559. Ch'ên Chung-chou did not sign his preface; he only added the imprint of a seal with his literary name Kang-i-tzû.[95] There is a colophon by Wang Ying-chên[96] (cf. *Ming-shih-tsung*, ch. 51), dated 1559. This handbook, too, is a fine specimen of Ming printing. Though rare, it is sometimes found in Chinese catalogues. Its contents are remarkable because of their originality: a great number of well-known tunes are given, but all were revised by the compiler, who considerably improved their musical value. The book bears an outspoken Taoist character.

---

88 內閣文庫
89 近世以寧藩神奇秘譜爲最，然須得初刻大本，臞仙命工校訂點畫不訛，是爲善譜可寶，若翻刻本不足觀.
90 步虛堂琴譜
91 顧挹江

92 孫承恩，明詩綜
93 王挺
94 陳中州
95 亢楊子
96 王應辰

13 *Ch'in-pu-ho-pi-ta-ch'üan*,[97] not divided into chs., compiler Yang
Piao-chêng;[98] first preface anonymous, and undated; second
preface by Liu Yü,[99] dated 1503. *Imperial Catalogue*, ch. 114,
leaf 7 verso. The two preceding items were examples of handbooks edited by scholars of high culture; this one was published
by a literatus of very low scholarly standing. The tunes are
given in a kind of simplified version, and all—as indicated by
ho-pi in the title—are accompanied by words. This text of the
songs must be of the editor's own making, for it is written in
a queer mixture of literary language and colloquial. The text
is interspersed with refrains like *ya-ya*, *ai-ya*, such as are used
only in Chinese popular music. Yet this handbook seems to
have been very popular; it was printed in an extraordinarily
great number of copies, so that even now it can easily be bought.
It saw a second edition, which can be distinguished from the
first by the fact that in the second one the picture after the
prefaces (representing the author playing the lute) is missing.

14 *T'ai-ku-i-yin*,[100] in chs., compiled by Yang Lun,[101] lit. name
Tung-an;[102] cf. *Imperial Catalogue*, ch. 114, leaf 8 recto.
Preface by Li Wên-fang,[103] colophon by Lü Lan-ku,[104] both
undated. A good Ming handbook, much better edited than the
preceding item. The *Imperial Catalogue* is much incensed at
the fact that on the picture in the first volume the author is
shown together with Chung Tzû-ch'i,[105] the famous lute player
of antiquity.[106] The arrogance of this picture seems to have
been recognized even at an early date, for most copies which
I have seen were printed from a revised block, where the image
of Chung Tzû-ch'i has been deleted from the unorthodox picture. To this handbook there is usually added a supplement
by the same author, entitled *Po-ya-hsin-fa*;[107] to this Yü Yen[108]
added a preface, dated 1609.

15 *Wu-chih-chai-ch'in-pu*,[109] in 8 chs., by the famous lute master Hsü
Ch'i.[110] First preface dated 1724, second, by Huang Chên,[111]
dated 1722; third, by Hsü Chün,[112] undated; fourth, by Chou

97 琴譜合璧大全
98 楊表正
99 劉御
100 太古遺音
101 楊倫
102 桐庵
103 李文芳
104 呂蘭谷
105 鍾子期
106 繪鍾子期像而以已像厠其後尤爲妄誕
107 伯牙心法
108 俞彥
109 五知齋琴譜
110 徐祺
111 黃鎭
112 徐俊

Lu-fêng,[113] dated 1721. This may be said to be the most popular handbook in existence. Printed in a large number of copies, it is nowadays easily obtainable at bookshops in China and Japan. The introductory chapters are very rich in contents, giving general information on the lute and its history, and an outline of *ch'in* ideology. It contains no new tunes, but all have been revised by Master Hsü Ch'i, and the tunes are recorded by his son (Hsü Chün, the writer of the third preface) and two of his pupils (the writers of the second and fourth prefaces), in the way the master used to play them. The tunes are recorded very carefully, with many additional indications regarding tempo, expression, etc. The scholarly standard of the book is not high: the style of the introductory parts is not very polished, and shows many misprints. But this does not detract form the musical value of the tunes. From a musical point of view, this handbook is the best of those published during the Ch'ing period.

16 *Tzŭ-yüan-t'ang-ch'in-pu*,[114] in 12 chs., by Wu Hung.[115] First preface by Li T'ing-ching,[116] second by Chang Tun-jên,[117] third by Ch'iao Chung-wu,[118] all dated 1802. Wu Hung continued the tradition of Hsü Ch'i (see the preceding item). The three people who wrote the prefaces were his pupils, who published the tunes as played by Master Wu Hung. This handbook is typical for the *ch'in-pu* of the Ch'ing period: in the introductory chapters not a word is said about the ideology of the lute. Instead we find lengthy discussions on musical theory; for these, as the preface says, Chang Tun-jên, who was a great mathematician, was responsible. Ch. 12 gives a number of tunes with the words added to the notation; this part was edited by Li T'ing-ching. A curious feature is that the title page bears the date 1801, while the prefaces are dated one year later.

17 *Ch'un-ts'ao-t'ang-ch'in-pu*,[119] in 6 chs., by Ts'ao Shang-chiung.[120] First preface by Yen P'ei-nien,[121] undated; author's preface dated 1744. Co-editors were Su Ching[122] and Tai Yüan.[123] This book gives various well-known tunes in comparatively

---

113 周魯封
114 自遠堂琴譜
115 吳灯, style: Shih-po 仕柏.
116 李廷敬
117 張敦仁
118 喬鍾吳

119 春草堂琴譜
120 曹尚絅, style: Ping-wên 炳文.
121 閻沛年
122 蘇璟
123 戴源

simple versions. The editing is very carefully done. With the *Wu-chih-chai* handbook, this *ch'in-pu* is much recommended by present-day lute masters. In 1864 it was republished by the lute master Chu T'ung-chün.[124]

18 *T'ien-wên-ko-ch'in-pu-chi-ch'êng*,[125] in 16 chs., published by T'ang I-ming,[126] in 1876. Author's preface, with the same date. This handbook, as indicated by the title, is a collection of reprints from other handbooks. Well-known tunes are often given in as many as five or six different versions. Many of the good *ch'in-pu* being very rare, it was the compiler's intention to put their contents at the disposal of lute students in a convenient form. The introductory chapters (which fill 4 volumes) are also compiled from other handbooks. This collection is very handy for quick reference. It is to be regretted, however, that the publisher confined himself to simply reprinting the various tunes, in exactly the same form as he found them (the sources being indicated in the lower part of the outer margin); thus there is no unity in the notation of the tunes. This inconsistency in the use of various *chien-tzû* will confuse the beginner. It would have been much better, if the publisher had transcribed all tunes in a uniform system. Some of his own compositions are inserted among the others; these are distinguished by the literary name of the compiler, *Sung-hsien*,[127] being printed in the lower outer margin. Still it is a useful book because of its varied contents. It is particularly recommended to such students as do not have a large collection of handbooks at their disposal.

19 *Ch'in-hsüeh-ju-mên*,[128] in 2 chs., by the lute master Chang Ho;[129] author's preface dated 1864. Reprinted several times, in various forms. This is the most elementary handbook for the lute player, recommended by present-day lute masters as the best introduction to the subject. The finger technique is explained clearly, the tunes are few, but each is fully annotated, and accompanied by a simpler score (*kung-ch'ih*[130] system). Anyone desiring to study the lute would do well to start by working through this handbook.

124 祝桐君
125 天聞閣琴譜集成
126 唐彝銘
127 松仙

128 琴學入門
129 張鶴
130 工尺

APPENDIX III

The Lute as an Antique

THE greater part of the articles which surround the Chinese scholar in his library not only serve as decorations, but are also at the same time objects of appreciative study.

A bronze sacrificial vessel of the Han dynasty placed on a carved ebony stand, enhances by its delicate outlines and intriguing patina the antique atmosphere of the library, while the archaic inscriptions inside its cover also furnish the happy owner with material for writing a learned treatise discussing its date and provenance; a coiled dragon of transparent jade lying on the desk serves the double purpose of holding a wet writing brush, and of providing the scholar and his friends with a topic for discussion on the use jade was put to by the ancients.

It is this tendency to appreciate antiques not only as works of art, but at the same time as objects for discussion and investigation, that confers upon the old-fashioned Chinese scholar a distinctly humanistic touch. The type of the Chinese literatus curiously resembles that of the classical scholar of medieval Europe. Just as the old humanist of Europe loved to surround himself with marble busts and bronze statues, caressing their exquisite shapes while at the same time attempting to decide their date and determine their style; or, of a quiet evening, enjoyed unrolling on his heavy desk old palimpsests, while appreciating the powerful writing penned on the greenish parchment, simultaneously trying to detect errors made by the copyists and looking for variant readings: so a Chinese scholar, while lovingly handling his treasures, will ponder over the correct interpretation of their inscriptions, and, dwelling in thought on bygone times, grope for an understanding of the significance the object had at the time when it was made.

To appreciate beauty in a scholarly way is termed in Chinese *wan*.[1] This verb pressuposes as its subject a man of scholarly tastes. 'Enjoying the moon' (*wan-yüeh*),[2] is but a very unsatisfactory transla-

---

[1] 玩   [2] 玩月

tion. Any ordinary person with an innate feeling for beauty may derive enjoyment from gazing at the full autumn moon. But it is only the cultured scholar who is able, when seeing this same moon, to remember some lines by a celebrated poet, to revisualize a painting by some famous artist, and by thus testing his own sensations by those of kindred spirits, experience that exalted joy that comes only from a full intellectual realization of the emotions of the heart. Nothing less than this, and probably more, is implied in the term *wan*.

This somewhat lengthy digression was necessary; without this preliminary understanding it would be difficult to interpret correctly one of the many aspects of that most accomplished of all Chinese musical instruments: the lute. For the lute, next to being a musical instrument, is also a favourite object for antiquarian appreciation.

As I have already pointed out above, the lute, though it is one of the regular paraphernalia of the Chinese scholar, is rarely played. Not because its music is irrelevant; on the contrary, it represents in the opinion of many the apex of Chinese music, quite unsurpassed in China's long history. But to play the lute expertly presupposes a study of years, and a competent master; but few scholars have the leisure and inclination to devote so much time to this art, and good teachers are comparatively rare. Therefore, while the enjoyment of playing the lute is reserved for a small circle of the happy few, appreciation of the lute as an antique lies within the reach of every scholar. It is this aspect of the lute that I propose to treat here.

*   *   *

When a scholar is lucky enough to obtain an ancient lute bearing inscriptions by the hand of some famous literatus of old, it is an event in his life, and often he will change the name of his library to commemorate the auspicious day. Thus Hsiang Yüan-pien,[3] one of the greatest connoisseurs and bibliophiles of the end of the Ming period, changed the name of his studio into T'ien-lai Hall[4] after he had acquired a lute called *T'ien-lai* ('Harmony of the Sphere').[5] This instrument had belonged to Sun Têng,[6] a famous lute master of the third century A.D. (Cf. the rubbing of the bottom board of this lute, reproduced in fig. 18.)

The predilection of the Chinese scholar for the romantic and the fanciful also found expression in the lute. From time to time iron,[7]

[3] 項元汴
[4] 天籟閣
[5] 天籟

[6] 孫登, style Kung-ho 公和.
[7] See fig. 19.

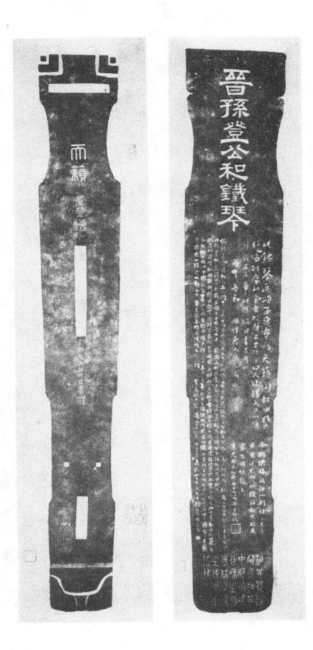

‡18: Rubbing of the lute *T'ien-lai,* that belonged to the Ming scholar Hsiang Yüan-pien.
On top the name of the lute, then the name Sun Têng, and his style Kung-ho in
a square seal. Under the Dragon Pond the inscription: 明項元汴珍藏 'Treasured
and preserved by Hsiang Yüan-pien, of the Ming dynasty'. Underneath two
square seals, reading Mo-lin 墨林, a literary name of Hsiang. Finally another square
seal, reading 子京甫印, Tzû-ching being Hsiang's style. (Author's collection)

‡19: (right) Rubbing of an iron lute of the Chin period. (Author's collection)

earthenware,[8] and jade[9] lutes make their appearance. Such lutes are useless as musical instruments, but they are highly valued as antiques. Scholars covered them with appreciative essays, lauding the inner significance of the lute and expanding themselves upon the principles of lute ideology. Figure 19 shows a rubbing taken from an iron lute said to have been made by Sun Têng.[10] It came originally from the collection of Hsiang Yüan-pien, but during the Ch'ing period eminent scholars like Juan Yüan,[11] Liang Chang-chü[12] and Chang Ting-chi[13] added appreciative inscriptions.

Such lutes, however, are exceptions. As a rule the antique lutes are made of wood; if they are still in fit condition to be played, this enhances their value. An antique lute should not be a mere curiosity; its strings should be sounded, to revive the forgotten melodies of olden times.

*   *   *

For judging an ancient lute there exist two main criteria: first, the condition of its lacquer, second, the inscriptions it bears.

Before discussing these points in more detail, a few words about the building of lutes are necessary.

The body of the lute, which functions as a sounding-box, consists of two wooden boards, superimposed one upon the other. The upper board, made of *t'ung* wood,[14] is concave, while the lower one, made of *tzŭ* wood,[15] is flat. On the inner side these boards are chiseled out, so that when fitted together they form a sort of oblong box. This box may have various models. Most common is the so-called *Chung-ni* model,[16] shown in figure 30; but many other models exist, varying from a simple straight box (*chêng-ho-shih*)[17] to models showing milled edges (*lo-hsia-shih*)[18] or the shape of a banana leaf (*chiao-yeh-shih*).[19] In the lower board two openings are cut out, which serve to transmit the sound; they may be compared with the two S-shaped sound holes of a violin, which also serve to increase the acoustic power of the instrument. It would seem that apart from minor differences the construction of the lute has remained the same since the Han period.

---

8 See *China Journal*, XI, 5: J. C. Ferguson, 'A Ceramic Lute of the Sung Dynasty'.

9 See numerous references in Chinese literature to *yü-ch'in* 玉琴.

10 See n. 6.

11 阮元, 1764–1849.

12 梁章鉅, 1775–1849.

13 張延濟, 1768–1848.

14 桐

15 梓

16 仲尼式

17 正合式

18 落霞式

19 蕉葉式

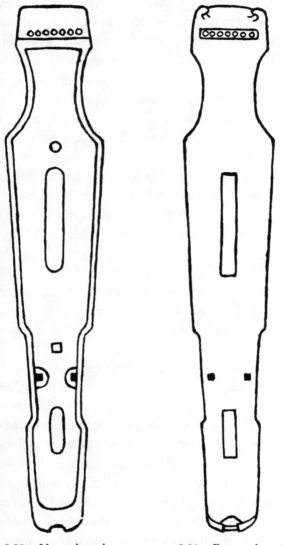

#20: Upper board.   #21: Bottom board.

There are special handbooks for the lute player, the so-called *ch'in-pu*,[20] which generally give more or less detailed instructions as to how lutes should be built. The most extensive of them is the *Yü-ku-chai-ch'in-pu*,[21] published in 1855 by a well-known lute master from Chekiang province, Chu Fêng-chieh.[22] This book does not contain any lute tunes, but is concerned solely with elaborate directions regarding the lute in general. The author not only gives his own opinions, but also often quotes from reliable older sources; for the

---

20 琴譜   21 與古齋琴譜   22 祝鳳喈, literary name T'ung-chün 桐君.

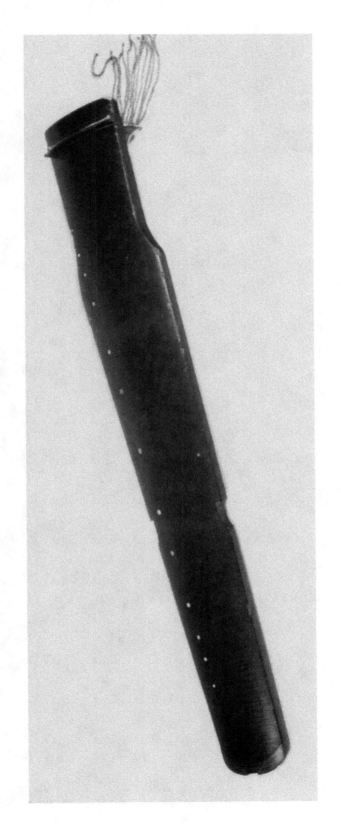

#21a : T'ang period lute from the Hōryūji Hōmotsukan in Ueno.
Courtesy of Tokyo National Museum and Kōdansha Ltd., Tokyo.

following observations I have therefore, unless stated otherwise, relied upon this source.

Just as with the masterpieces of Antonio Stradivari, so also with ancient lutes the sonorousness depends upon the quality of the wood used, and especially on that of the varnish with which it is covered. As regards the wood, *t'ung* and *tzŭ* are preferably chosen, but even other kinds of wood may be used; the most important thing is to see that the material used be old and entirely dry. Dry, decaying pillars from ruined temples, and even boards from excavated coffins are highly recommended. Fanciful associations also play a role; one should try to find a mouldering pine tree overhanging a bubbling mountain stream, or a weather-beaten cedar in a secluded vale.

The two boards having been hewn and chiseled into the proper shape (see figures 20 and 21), they are luted together with a special kind of glue, the main material of which is isinglass. The boards touch each other round the whole circumference, and they are further held together by two studs, one called the Heaven Pillar, *t'ien-chu*,[23] located right above the Dragon Pond, and the other called Earth Pillar, *ti-chu*,[24] to be found under the Dragon Pond. The former is round, the latter square, in accordance with the ancient Chinese belief that Heaven is round and Earth square.

Thereafter follows the most important phase of the building process: covering this sounding-box with a coat of varnish. As the word varnish suggests a rather thin coat, it is a misnomer in this connection; cement would be a more suitable term, as the thickness of this coat varies from 3 to 5 mm.[25] Its constitution resembles that of old Chinese lacquer in general; cf. the directions for making lacquer as given by T'ao Tsung-i[26] in his *Cho-kêng-lu*[27] (original preface dated 1366;[28] 汲古閣 edition, ch. 30, section Hsiu-ch'i),[29] and for a more detailed description, the Ming treatise *Hsiu-ch'ih-lu*,[30] by Huang

---

23 天柱

24 地柱

25 A curious parallel is found in the varnish used for covering old Arabian and Persian lutes, especially the *rubāb;* see H. G. Farmer, 'The Structure of the Arabian and Persian Lute in the Middle Ages', *Journal of the Royal Asiatic Society of Great Britain and Ireland,* Jan. 1939, p. 49. There the work *Kanz-al-tuhaf* is quoted: 'Some people powder glass and mix it with glue, which is then poured on the sound-chest in order that the tone of the instrument may be increased.' Farmer points out that in England in 1837 a similar device was discovered by J. F. Grosjean, a harp-maker of London; he said about his discovery: 'My improvement consists in applying vitrified or crystallized matters to sounding boards... Powdered glass ground very fine is sifted evenly over the sounding board, which has previously been warmed and coated with cement.'

26 陶宗儀

27 輟耕錄

28 汲古閣

29 髹器

30 髹飾錄

Ch'êng[31] (an old manuscript preserved in Japan, published in 1928 in Tokyo by the Tokyo-bijutsu-gakkō-kōyūkai;[32] original preface dated 1625, preface by the modern Chinese editor of the text, Chu Ch'i-ch'ien,[33] dated 1927. There also exists a Chinese reprint in folio of this edition by Chu Ch'i-ch'ien; the texts are exactly the same, except for the omission of the Japanese reading-marks, and a few marginal notes). There are, however, some important differences, as for instance that while applying the lute cement no layer of cloth is added. The *Ch'in-ching*,[34] a handbook for the study of the lute written by a famous lute connoisseur of the Ming period (cf. Appendix ii, no. 5), and published in 1609, gives the following directions as to how this cement should be made: 'Ashes from deer horns are the best material, but ashes from cow horns may also be used. One obtains the best results when these ashes are mixed with copper filings [other sources recommend gold or silver filings, and also powdered earthenware shards. Trans.]. When applied for the first time [it is implied that the mixture is diluted with thin glue. Trans.], the mixture is thin, and shows a rough surface. When it has dried, it should be polished with a rough stone. Applied as second coating, the mixture is thicker and more even; after it has become dry, it is polished with water. Polish two times with water, and three times with oil. When applied for the third coating, the mixture should be of fine consistency.'[35] This process is repeated until a perfectly smooth and even surface is obtained. When this is well dried, one proceeds to apply the last coat of lacquer, called, just as in the ordinary lacquer process, *tsao-ch'i*,[36] consisting of several layers of varnish. The colour of this varnish differs considerably: a deep black is most common, but red, greenish, spotted or marbled varieties are also used.

In course of time this coat develops tiny cracks, the so-called *tuan-wên*,[37] 'burst patterns'. It is by observing the shape of these cracks that connoisseurs determine the age of a lute.

On this the *Ch'in-ching* quoted above has the following to say: 'The age of a lute is proved by the *tuan-wên*. If a lute is less than 500 years old, it will not show cracks; the older it is, the more cracks it shows. There are many varieties of *tuan-wên*; the so-called serpent-

---

31 黃成
32 東京美術學校校友會
33 朱啓鈐
34 琴經
35 鹿角灰爲上，牛角灰次之，或雜以銅鑢屑

尤妙，第一次灰粗而簿，候乾用粗石略磨，第二次中灰勻而厚，候乾用水磨，二次水磨，三次油磨，次用細灰.
36 糙漆
37 斷文

belly cracks [*shê-fu*],[38] run transversely over the upper board of the
lute, one or two inches apart from each other, in even segments, giving the lute the appearance of the belly of a serpent. There are also
very fine cracks, called "cow hairs" [*niu-mao*],[39] resembling hundreds
and thousands of hairs; they generally appear on both sides of the
lute, but they do not show near the *yo-shan* [i.e. the high bridge on
right]; sometimes they may also be found on the upper side of the
instrument and on the bottom board. Further, there are plum-blossom
cracks [*mei-hua*];[40] these show a pattern resembling the petals of a
plum blossom. Cracks of this shape will not appear if the lute is not
over a thousand years old. Of all lacquered implements, only the lute
shows *tuan-wên*.[41] The reason is that in most cases of lacquer work
as a rule cloth is first applied, while with the lute this is omitted.
Another reason is that other lacquer implements are left standing or
lying about freely, while the lute day and night bears the strain of the
strings. Further, after many years the wood of a lute shrinks, and
becomes loosened from the coat of cement, which then cracks. When
one tries to polish away these cracks, or even when one tries to cover
them with a new coat of shining varnish, this only serves to make them
appear more clearly. The genuine *tuan-wên* are clear-cut, like the edge
of a sword, and can be distinguished thereby from the false ones.'
(ch. 6)[42] Next to the three kinds of *tuan-wên* mentioned above, some

38 蛇腹 also written 蛇蚹
39 牛毛
40 梅花
41 This statement is found in most Chinese
books, old and new, on the study of the lute,
although a Ming treatise on lacquer in
general (the *Hsiu-ch'ih-lu; see* n. 30) states
specifically that all lacquered objects are
liable in the course of time to develop *tuan-
wên* (*op. cit.*, page 20). I have come to the
conclusion that the lute experts are wrong
and that the *Hsiu-ch'ih-lu* is right. I found
tuan-wên of various types on the following
dated lacquered objects of the Ming period:
table tops (in the four corners and along the
edges, in one case parallel cracks over the
entire surface), boxes of various size and
shape (along the edges, and all over the
bottom), the undecorated bottoms of plates
and trays of carved red lacquer (*t'i-hung*
剔紅), and folding screens (mostly in the
four corners of a panel, but often also covering the entire surface in irregular pattern).
It is worth noting that I did *not* find *tuan-wên*
on lacquered baskets.

The conclusion is that all Chinese lacquer,

if applied on a ground of cement, will develop
tuan-wên, probably because the cement and
the lacquer itself have a different shrinking
coefficient. I do not feel competent to analyze
the physical properties in question, but
would suggest this as an interesting subject
of research for the technical experts connected
with musea of Far Eastern art.

42 古琴以斷紋爲證，琴不歷五百歲不斷，愈
久則斷愈多，斷有數等，有蛇腹斷，其紋橫截琴
面相去或寸或二寸，節相似，如蛇腹下紋，又有
細斷紋，即牛毛斷，如髮千百條，亦停勻，多在
琴之兩旁而進岳處則無之，又有面與底皆斷者，
又有梅花斷，其紋如梅花片，此非千餘載不能
有也，一應漆器無斷紋而琴獨有之者，盖器多用
布漆，琴則不用，皆器安閑而琴日夜爲絃所激，
又歲久桐腐而漆相離破斷紋隱處，雖經磨礪，至
再重加光漆，其紋愈見，然眞斷紋，如劍峰，僞
則否。

The *Ch'in-ching* quotes this passage ver-
batim from a Sung source, the *Tung-t'ien-
ch'ing-lu-chi* 洞天清祿集, a small book on
various antiques, compiled by Chao Hsi-ku
趙希鵠, member of the Imperial Clan who
flourished about 1230. This book, which
devotes a special section to antique lutes,*

sources mention also 'cracked-ice bursts' (*ping-lieh-wên*),[43] which seem to appear about at the same time as the plum-blossom cracks.

Observations in other handbooks are identical with the above. It should be noted, however, that opinions differ as to the exact number of years necessary to produce the various kinds of *tuan-wên*. The *Yü-ku-chai-ch'in-pu* quoted above gives considerably lower figures than the *Ch'in-chin*: 70 to 80 years for the 'cow hairs', 100 for the 'serpent belly', and 200 to 3000 for the 'plum blossoms'. The truth appears to be nearer to the first of these two estimates.

The handbooks warn especially against false *tuan-wên*: they may be made artificially by alternately exposing the instrument to cold and heat, and by other tricks. But their genuineness or lack of the same can be immediately detected: genuine *tuan-wên* do not break the smoothness of the surface of the lute. If so they would interfere with the music, for while playing the lute the fingers of the left hand often press a string down on the board, and rub it softly to produce

*escaped my notice while I was working on this monograph. Although it gives many interesting details about antique lutes, its contents do not, however, affect the main arguments brought forward by me in my work.

The *Tung-t'ien-ch'ing-lu-chi* proves that, during the Sung dynasty, various types of *tuan-wên* were already recognized, and their ages computed. Generally *mei-hua tuan-wên* 梅花斷文, cracks resembling the shape of a plum blossom, are taken to be the oldest; they are said to appear only if an implement is from 800 to 1000 years old. Next come the *p'ing-lieh tuan-wên* 冰裂斷文, cracks resembling burst ice, and thereafter the *shê-fu tuan-wên* 蛇腹斷文, which resemble the even segments on the belly of a serpent; the age of these two varieties is given as from 600 to 800 years. *Niu-mao tuan-wên* 牛毛斷文, cracks resembling fine, evenly distributed cow hair, and *liu-shui tuan-wên* 流水斷文, fine cracks unevenly distributed in a pattern that resembles the conventional Chinese way of representing waves, are generally considered as the 'youngest'; some sources contend that these two types of crack-marks will make their appearance after 70 or 80 years.

Before analyzing these data one must first discard the theory developed by some Ming writers that all these various types of *tuan-wên* will, in course of time, appear in succession on one and the same lacquered object. In other words, that for instance a certain

lute that was made in the tenth century, will in the eleventh century have developed cow-hair cracks, which after four or five centuries changed into serpent-belly cracks, which in their turn changed to the plum-blossom type. This, of course, is physically impossible. One could imagine that the serpent-belly type, for instance, if the process of bursting continues, develops into the burst-ice type; but it seems quite impossible that cow-hair cracks would change into burst-ice *tuan-wên*. It seems far more probable that once a lacquered surface has developed bursts, it remains that way; and that the pattern shown by the cracks is determined not by the age of the object in question, but by various other factors such as the nature of the surface on which the lacquer was applied, the constitution of the lacquer, climatic influences, etc. I know of no antique lute preserved to the present day which shows a type of *tuan-wên* different from that recorded by collectors who saw that instrument in the fifteenth or sixteenth century.

Therefore my conclusion is that *tuan-wên* are not to be considered as a criterion for dating a lacquered object; the presence of *tuan-wên* of any kind only proves that an object is at least not newly made. Thus the theories of Chinese lute experts on the value of *tuan-wên* constitutes one of those rare exceptions where a Chinese statement on a peculiarly Chinese object is definitely wrong.

43 冰裂文

#22: Impression of a seal, engraved in the bottom board: Han-chang-t'ang-chi 含章堂記 (from a lute in the author's collection)

#23: Shōsōin lute: the upper board. After the photo in Harada's Catalogue.

#24: Shōsōin lute: the bottom board. After the photo in Harada's Catalogue.

#25: Shōsōin lute: the enclosure on the upper board. After the photo in Harada's Catalogue.

#26: Shōsōin lute: side aspects. After the photo in Harada's Catalogue.

various kinds of vibrato. If the surface is not perfectly smooth, the string will rattle. Or, in the words of the Ming connoisseur Kao Lien:[44] 'If one runs one's fingers over artificial *tuan-wên*, they will be felt; but genuine cracks, although they are clearly seen, can never be felt.' (*Tsun-shêng-pa-chien*, chapter xv, p. 75)[45]

As regards the inscriptions of a lute, these may be divided into two categories: those inside the sounding-box (*ch'ih-nei*), and those on the bottom board (*ti-ming*).[46]

Those inside the lute are written or engraved on the inner side of the upper board, at a time when the two boards have not yet been fitted together. The characters are written in two columns, opposite the Dragon Pond, but well to the right and left, so that when the lute is finished, they are barely visible when looking obliquely through the Dragon Pond. Thus these inscriptions can only be written either when the lute is made, or when it has been taken apart for a second time, and entirely rebuilt. They therefore furnish the observer with dependable material for fixing the date of the instrument. These inscriptions mostly state the date, and the name of the builder or rebuilder. A well-known lute preserved at Peking bears, for instance, the following inscriptions: opposite the Dragon Pond, on the right, 'Rebuilt in 1636, by Chang Jung-hsiu from Kiangsu'; and on the left, 'Rehewn by the recluse of the Chiu-i mountain'.[47] According to connoisseurs this instrument dates from the Sung period (960–1279). In the Ming period (1368–1644) its cement was so damaged, that Chang Jung-hsiu found it necessary to take it apart and rebuild it. Then, in recent times ('Recluse of the Chiu-i mountain' is one of the literary names of a contemporary lute master, Yang Tsung-chi) it was again rebuilt, and this fact duly recorded.

While inscriptions inside a lute are usually written in ordinary characters, for the outside elegant and tasteful effects are aimed at. Here the scholar has every opportunity for displaying his refined taste and cultured penmanship. As a rule only the bottom board of a lute is used for inscriptions, it being considered bad taste for the inscriptions to show when the lute is lying on the table while being played.

First the inscriptions are written on the board with an ordinary writing brush, with very thick ink, usually red. When dried, the

---

44 高濂

45 僞者以手摩之裂紋有痕，眞者有紋可而拂之則無.

46 池內，底銘

47 明崇禎丙子古吳張睿修重修，九疑山人再斷.

characters are cut out in the lacquer with a set of fine chisels, the
same as used for engraving seals. The depth of the characters is left
to individual taste: some like to engrave them deeply, going right
through the coat till the wood is reached (*shên-k'o*),[48] others prefer
to cut away only the uppermost layers of the coat (*ch'ien-k'o*).[49] The
carving should be done with considerable care, as the varnish easily
chips off, and the cement underneath is very brittle and has a tendency to come off in irregular lumps. Clever engravers, however,
often utilize these peculiarities of the material for obtaining original
effects; they choose archaic styles of writing, in which rough and
irregular outlines are inherent. When the varnish crumbles off, the
irregular contours obtained will lend the inscription an appearance of
'antique rusticity' (*ku-cho*),[50] an effect much appreciated by connoisseurs (cf. fig. 22).

When the characters have been cut out, they are filled up with

48 深刻   49 淺刻   50 古拙

white, red, or green paint, sometimes also with gold lacquer. But the latter process is considered too ostentatious to be in good taste.

The simplest type of lute inscription is merely the name of the instrument, usually engraved above the Dragon Pond. Handbooks of the lute give lists of various special names of lutes, mostly borrowed from lute ideology; I refer to pp. 104–5 above.

Further, the whole bottom board of the lute is at the disposition of the amateur for engraving further inscriptions: lines of poetry, appreciative essays, classical quotations, impressions of seals, etc. Even the bottom of the two knobs for fastening the strings may be engraved with a seal or a few characters.

It goes without saying that these inscriptions furnish the connoisseur with abundant materials for exercising his discriminative powers; he must decide whether the dates tally, whether the contents of an inscription conform to the scholarly standards of the alleged writer, whether the style of the writing corresponds with that of other calligraphic specimens of the man who is asserted to have written the inscription, etc. But the appreciation of old lutes necessitates much discretion and experience; numerous snares and pitfalls await the unwary outsider. If the cement of an antique lute has been damaged badly, its owner will peel off the old coat, except those patches where the inscriptions are engraved; thereafter he covers the lute with a new coating, of the same colour as the old one. Then the bewildered observer sees a lute with all the marks of a genuine antique specimen, but with a brand new coat of lacquer. Again, a lute amateur, having obtained a fine old specimen bearing no inscriptions, will decide that it resembles a lute celebrated by some famous old writer. To enhance its beauty he composes an inscription for this lute; then, glancing through rubbings of autographs of the said famous man of old till he has collected from various passages all the characters he needs for his inscription, he copies them out on the lute. This method, known as *chi-tzǔ*,[51] though admittedly running counter to artistic principles, when expertly applied often produces remarkable results. Yang Tsung-chi in his *T'sang-ch'in-lu* openly states several times that he added in this way inscriptions to some lutes in his collection. The owner only means to make in this way an instrument more interesting for himself, but if the lute changes hands, the danger exists that some unscrupulous dealer will try to pass off such an instrument as genuine.

[51] 集字

A scholar without any real lutes at his disposal may still make studies in this field, for there exist numerous rubbings (*t'a-pên*)[52] taken from ancient instruments, which clearly show their shapes and inscriptions. Generally these rubbings show only the bottom board, but sometimes also copies of the other sides are added. Such rubbings may be traced again, and then a so-called *shuang-kou-pên*[53] is obtained.

After these preliminary remarks I shall discuss three antique lutes; the first and the last on the basis of photos of the originals, the second on the basis of a traced copy of the bottom board.

Those interested in further discussions of antique lutes I may refer to the *Ts'ang-ch'in-lu*,[54] where Yang Tsung-chi,[55] a lute master of Peking, gives detailed descriptions of 53 lutes in his collection. The book is to be found in the *Ch'in-hsüeh-ts'ung-shu*, which are Yang Tsung-chi's complete works; cf. Appendix II, no. 7.

*   *   *

The first lute to be discussed here, which is probably the oldest in the world, is preserved in Japan, in the Imperial Repository at Nara. This repository, the Shōsōin[56] was built in 752, as the chief treasure house of the Tōdaiji, the famous old temple. A great number of objects used in the Imperial Family were in 756 deposited here, as votive gifts to the chief deity of the temple, the Buddha Vairocana. A propitious fate has spared this repository from the calamities of nature and other vicissitudes, so that up to this day the collection may be seen in practically the same condition as it was more than 1200 years ago. Among these treasures this lute is to be found.

Notwithstanding its considerable age, this instrument has been preserved in excellent condition. Although the strings are gone, its body is still intact, and when newly strung it can doubtless still be played. It was placed in the collection in 817 (the 8th year of Kō-nin;[57] cf. *Shōsōin-gyobutsu tanabetsu-mokuroku*,[58] No. 99). Having been left undisturbed for such a long period, this lute constitutes a unique object for the study of the lute in general. Japanese scholars have carefully described the Shōsōin collection, and this lute has received due attention.[59] But as the investigators were not sufficiently con-

---

52 拓本
53 雙鉤本. See T. F. Carter, *The Invention of Printing in China*, New York 1931, p. 12, and my book: *Mi Fu on Inkstones*, Peking 1938, pp. 6 ff.
54 藏琴錄
55 楊宗稷
56 正倉院

57 弘仁
58 正倉院御物棚別目錄
59 See the magnificent *Catalogue of the Imperial Treasures in the Shōsōin*, edited by J. Harada, vol. II; also, *A Glimpse of Japanese Ideals*, Tokyo 1937, by the same author, pp. 120 ff.

versant with the study of the lute to be in a position to recognize all the remarkable features of this instrument, and to settle satisfactorily the various problems it calls forth, I may be allowed here to discuss this lute at some length.

This lute is in the first place remarkable because of its decoration, which is entirely different from all antique lutes which I had occasion to examine.

While antique lutes, as a rule, show no other decoration than their inscriptions, this instrument is covered on all sides with intricate designs in inlaid gold and silver.

The upper board (see figure 23) shows at the top a picture, enclosed by a lozenge-pattern border, all of inlaid gold (see figure 25). In its center a man is sitting beneath a blossoming tree; leisurely reclining against an elbow-rest, he is playing a mandolin-like instrument, which by its round body with the broad band over it, may be identified as a *ch'in-p'i-p'a*,[60] a forerunner of the Japanese *biwa*. Before this figure a repast is laid out on a mat, while on his right an ewer is standing. In front of this central figure one sees two others, sitting on panther hides; the left plays the lute on his knees, while on his left side a low table with some book-rolls on it may be discerned. The figure on the right leans with his left arm on a wine jar, while with his right hand he lifts a horn-shaped wine cup to his lips. In front of these three figures a peacock is dancing, the remaining space being filled with trees, plants, rocks and birds. On the right and left upper corner there is depicted an immortal, riding on a phoenix and bearing a standard, surrounded with a stylized cloud. Two similar genii are to be seen above the enclosure.

Under this enclosure a similar scene appears; here the center is again occupied by a blossoming tree, round which a creeper twines; a bird is perched on its top. To the left one sees a man playing the lute on his knees, a wine jar with a spoon in it standing on his left. The figure on the right is lifting a cup to his lips, and a wine jar of different shape is standing by his side. In front of these two figures a pond is seen, with crabs, snakes and other water animals appearing in its waves. The waters of this pond cover the whole surface of the lute, running downwards right to the end. Its banks run along the two sides of the lute, and show six human figures similar to those described above, three on either side; they are sitting among flowering bushes and flying and resting birds. The two figures, the wave designs and the thirteen studs are of inlaid gold, the other designs are of silver.

Turning now to the bottom board (see figure 24) again we find at the top an enclosure, containing a poem of eight lines, four characters each, and arranged in four columns. This inscription, like the rest of the decoration of the bottom board, is in inlaid silver. It runs: 'The significance of the lute is to purify evil thoughts by its tones. Even if one's nature is good, it shall still be deeply influenced [by the music of the lute]. It preserves the accomplished music, and drives away the lewd songs of Chêng,[61] restraining flightiness and extravagance. Its music is elevating, harmonious and correct. It brings enjoyment without being licentious.'[62] This is a poem composed to be engraved on a lute (a *ch'in-ming*)[63] by Li Yu,[64] a noted poet of the second century A.D. The inscription is quoted in full in a handbook for the lute of the Ming period (*Ch'ing-lien-fang-ch'in-ya*),[65] and in part in the huge collection of poetic reference, the *P'ei-wên-yün-fu.*[66]

As further decoration the Dragon Pond is flanked on each side by a running dragon, which is intended as a reference to the name of this aperture. Similarly the Phoenix Pool is flanked by two phoenixes, sitting on a flowering plant. Above and below the two holes there appears a flower motif, and above the inscription on top stylized rocks are seen. I would especially draw attention to the *tuan-wên* of the type called in lute terminology *ping-lieh*, 'cracked ice' (see p. 196), which appear round the inscription, and round the Phoenix Pool.

The sides of the lute are decorated with motifs of fabulous animals and flowers (see figure 26).

Inside the Dragon Pond there is an inscription, unfortunately only partly legible, which runs: 清琴作兮□日月，幽人間兮□□□. The missing character in the first line is easily supplemented; it could hardly be anything else than 光, giving the meaning: 'The lute of clear tones has been made, oh!, brilliant like sun and moon.' As for the second part of the other line, however, I would not venture to reconstruct it. Inside the Phoenix Pool is written: 'Made in the third month of the year *i-hai.*'[67] As no definite period is indicated, it is

---

61 The odes of Chêng and Wei 衞, bks. VIII and IX of the *Shih-ching* 詩經, were ancient love songs, and in Chinese literature are constantly used to denote lewd and vulgar music.

62 琴之在音，盪滌耶 (i.e. 邪) 心，雖有正性，其感亦深，存雅却鄭，浮侈是禁，條暢和正，樂而不滛 (i.e. 淫).

63 琴銘

64 李尤

65 青蓮舫琴雅, preface dated 1614, ch. 4.

66 佩文韻府, under *chêng-hsing* 正性.

67 乙亥之年季春造

impossible to say with absolute certainty for which year these two characters of the sexagenary cycle stand. J. Harada[68] proposes 795 A.D., this being the nearest year *i-hai* preceding that in which the instrument is recorded as having been put in the collection (817). Thus this date is quite arbitrarily chosen. Below I shall try to establish the probable date of this lute on sounder evidence.

For appreciating this lute the first question which must be considered—a question which has been passed over in silence by Harada and other students—is whether this instrument was made in China or in Japan. I have come to the conclusion that it was made in China, for the following reasons. In the first place the study of the Chinese lute was introduced into Japan at a fairly late date, i.e. in the middle of the 17th century, with the coming of the Chinese priest Hsin-yüeh.[69] This lute in the Shōsōin, and some other old specimens dating from the T'ang period preserved in Japan, were doubtless brought over from China not to be actually played, but as curiosities, carefully preserved because the Japanese envoys noticed that in China this instrument was a revered symbol of culture.[70] That there lived at the Japanese Court someone who was so deeply initiated in the study of the lute that he could build an instrument like this is highly improbable.

Secondly, I would point out that the lacquer of Japanese-made lutes —such as those which were built later by the Japanese disciples of Hsin-yüeh—is of an entirely different constitution from that of Chinese lutes; doubtless with a view to different climatic conditions, other substances were used in making this lacquer, which produces no *tuan-wên*. None of the many old Japanese-made lutes which I had occasion to examine show these typical cracks. Now the lute under discussion does show *tuan-wên*, and, as observed above, *tuan-wên* of a clearly pronounced Chinese type.

Thirdly, the technique of inlaid work used in the decoration is in the eighth-century inventory of the Shōsōin called *hyōmon*,[71] 'flat pattern'. According to Harada this instrument is the sole example of this peculiar technique.[72] In China however, this technique was applied for decorating lutes as early as the Han period, when it was

---

68 *Catalogue*, English notes on plates in vol. II.

69 心越, Jap. Shin'etsu; for more details about his personality and the role he played in Japanese cultural life, see pp. 225–8 below.

70 For a more detailed argument regarding this question, see pp. 217–24.

71 平文

72 *A Glimpse of Japanese Ideals*, p. 120.

called *yin-chi*,[73] so that this fact also tends to show that this lute was made in China, for else we could hardly expect that for the lacquer a technique would have been used which was unknown in Japan.

Having shown that this lute was made in China, I shall next try to arrive at an opinion regarding its age.

In the first part of this article I said that since the beginning of our era the lute has undergone practically no changes. But allowance must be made for the fact that literary evidence points to lutes prior to the T'ang period having been adorned with various kinds of inlaid work; later they were left severely undecorated, their charm consisting in the tone of the lacquer, the *tuan-wên*, and the inscriptions engraved on it. This change must in my opinion be ascribed to two reasons, first, the technique of playing, and second, artistic considerations. The finger technique of the lute in course of time grew more and more involved. To execute the delicate movements of the left hand, a perfectly smooth and even surface is necessary. Richly inlaid lutes, no matter of how good the workmanship, are liable in the course of time to show slight depressions and protuberances, which entirely spoil the tone of a string pressed down on those spots. As to artistic considerations, I may observe that during the T'ang dynasty, when the gorgeous art of India and Central Asia was flourishing in China, there is noticeable a tendency to return to more austere styles, an inclination to return to purely Chinese classical models. This tendency implies a preference for simple and natural beauty rather than artificial effects, for the invisible rather than the obvious. Later, during the Sung period (960–1279), this artistic current reached its summit in the paintings of the so-called Southern School.

Thus all lutes of the T'ang dynasty that have been preserved show no decorations. And when a scholar of the Sung dynasty, Ho Yüan,[74] embodied in his *Ch'un-chu-chi-wên*[75] a discussion of old lutes, he found it necessary to draw attention to old texts referring to decorated lutes, implying that in his time such lutes were no longer to be seen.

During the Han dynasty, however, it appears the lutes were occasionally lavishly decorated. The *Hsi-ching-tsa-chi*[76] written by Liu Hsin[77] says: 'The Empress Chao possessed a valuable lute, which bore the name *Fêng-huang*; it was entirely covered with figures of

---

[73] 隱起; see below, the quotation from the *Hsi-ching-tsa-chi*.

[74] 何薳, 11th century.

[75] 春渚紀聞, paragraph *Ku-ch'in-p'in-shih*

古琴品飾, 汲古閣 edition ch. 8, p. 2.

[76] 西京雜記

[77] 劉歆, died A.D. 23.

dragons and phoenixes, sages of antiquity and famous women, in a flat relief of inlaid gold and jade.'[78] Further we read in the famous poetical essay on the lute, *Ch'in-fu*,[79] written by Hsi K'ang:[80] '[The lute] is painted with the five colours, decorated with chased work, covered with designs and various patterns, inlaid with rhinoceros horn and ivory, marked with blue and green; its strings are made of Yüan K'o silk, its studs of jade of the Chung mountain, it shows figures of dragons and phoenixes, and of famous men of antiquity.'[81]

Now the Shōsōin lute serves as an illustration of such descriptions: it is decorated with flat inlaid work, showing dragons and phoenixes, and the figures of ancient worthies. Therefore I am inclined to consider this lute as being anterior to the T'ang period, and ascribe it to, perhaps, the latter part of the Six Dynasties (220–588 A.D.). In China even in former dynasties old lutes were preferred to new ones; therefore it is unlikely that the Japanese envoys brought from China a brand-new specimen, and far more reasonable that they procured a specimen that was already antique in the T'ang period. A study of the design of the upper board, however, enables us to narrow down the date further.

This design has not been sufficiently analyzed by Japanese scholars. J. Harada confined himself to a summary description.[82] A. Matsuoka[83] tries to identify the figures in the enclosure, and claims that they represent the old story of the great lute player Po Tzû-ya.[84] Po Tzû-ya found in his friend Chung Tzû-ch'i[85] the only kindred soul that could understand his music; when the latter died, Po Tzû-ya broke his lute, and never touched the strings again, because no one else in the world could understand his playing.[86] Of course this identification is entirely mistaken: firstly, three persons are seen and not two,

---

[78] Ch. v. 3rd heading: 趙后有寶琴曰鳳凰, 皆以金玉隱起爲龍鳳古賢列女之象.

[79] 琴賦; see *Wên-hsüan* 文選, ch. 18.

[80] 嵇康, 223–62.

[81] 華繪彫琢, 布藻垂文, 錯以犀象, 籍以翠絲, 絃以園容人絲, 徽以鍾山之玉, 爰有龍鳳之象, 古人之形

[82] See *Catalogue*, English notes to the plates of vol. II.

[83] *Sacred Treasures of Nara*, Tokyo 1935, p. 17.

[84] The authoress refers to them as Hakuga and Shōshiki, the Japanese pronunciation of the Chinese names. In this connection I would protest against this distressing habit that many Japanese and also foreign authors have of giving purely Chinese names only in the Japanese pronunciation, when writing in a Western language. (See the very pertinent remarks by L. Giles, in: *Sun Tzu on the Art of War*, London 1910, p. VIII.) This method is highly objectionable, because it confuses the unwary reader by giving him the impression that Japanese persons or objects are meant. It is to be hoped that this indiscriminate use of Japanese readings will be abandoned.

[85] 鍾子期

[86] See above, p. 73; also, *Lieh-tzû* 列子, ch. *T'ang-wên* 湯問, and various other Chinese sources mentioned above.

and moreover the third, who occupies the place of honour, plays the *p'i-p'a*, an instrument definitely belonging to popular music, and incompatible with one of the most revered lute masters of antiquity. And secondly we can hardly imagine Po Tzû-ya playing his beloved instrument while one of his hearers thrums a sort of guitar, and the other drinks deeply from a capacious goblet.

None of the previous students of this matter has realized that the upper board must be viewed as one single picture, lengthened to suit the shape of the lute. There is a pond, or maybe a rivulet, located in a beautiful scene of nature, on the banks of which are assembled a literary company, engaged in cultural pastimes: playing various musical instruments, wine games, composing poetry or appreciating calligraphies (see the book-rolls mentioned above), etc. Such representations of literary gatherings by the waterside abound in Chinese art. Especially famous are pictures representing the literary gathering at the Lan Pavilion. This occasion was immortalized by the *Lan-t'ing-hsü*,[87] an essay by Wang Hsi-chih,[87] the paragon of Chinese calligraphers. In the spring of the year 353 several men of letters met at the Lan Pavilion in order to celebrate the performance of the Vernal Purification ceremony (*hsiu-hsi.*)[88] They seated themselves along the water's edge, and played the literary game of the 'floating cups' (*liu-shang*):[89] cups were placed on lotus leaves floating on the water, and when such a drifting leaf touched the bank on the spot where one of the guests was sitting, he had to empty the cup and to compose a poem. Wang Hsi-chih collected the compositions made by his friends on this occasion, and added a prefatory essay, the *Lan-t'ing-hsü*. It is this essay that became a celebrated model both for literary composition and for calligraphy. Though some scholars doubt its authenticity, it has been copied and carved in stone numerous times, together with a picture of the gathering. This essay and its accompanying picture became so famous indeed, that already in early times it was a much-used motif for the decoration of objects connected with literary life: one finds it carved on the top of an antique writing desk, engraved on the reverse of an inkstone. So wide was its use, that in the 19th century it was even used to form the background of a receipt blank of a bank in Peking![90] Reproductions of

---

[87] 蘭亭序, to be found in nearly all *ku-wên* 古文 collections; translated in various languages, lately by Lin Yu-t'ang, in: *The Importance of Living*, New York 1937, p. 156. 王羲之.

[88] 修禊

[89] 流觴

[90] See Britton, on a horn stamp for receipt blanks, in: *Harvard Journal of Asiatic Studies*. III, No. 2.

good rubbings representing the text and the picture are to be found in the special Lan-t'ing number of the Japanese periodical *Shoen*.[91] Though greatly varying in detail, in their main lines these pictorial representations are always the same: one sees the pavilion by the waterside, surrounded by an ideal scenery. A brook is winding itself among gnarled trees, quaintly shaped rocks, and flowering shrubbery. Under rustling bamboos the guests are seated on mats and panther hides alongside the water, while attendants are running to and fro with wine jars and writing implements.

The resemblance with the scene depicted on the lute is obvious. There can be no doubt that the designer had in mind a representation of the Lan-t'ing Gathering when he made this decoration. Some details, as the floating wine cups, were left out, but others, like the panther hides on which the guests are sitting, scrolls, wine jars etc., are faithfully reproduced. The Lan-t'ing motif being a favourite decoration for all things connected with literary life, it is only natural that it was chosen also for the decoration of a lute. The musical element was stressed by adding the lutes and the *p'i-p'a*; at a literary gathering old tunes are played on the lute, while the *p'i-p'a* is used for lighter music.

But this motif of the literary gathering does not explain why three figures are set apart in the enclosure, nor does it explain the dominant position of the tree, and the genii floating in the air. These elements, and especially the arrangement of the picture, suggest an entirely different, un-Chinese subject, viz. a Buddhist representation of the Enlightened One, or of one of the deities of the Mahayanic Pantheon. As in such Buddhist representations, here also we find in the foreground a pond, only the lotus flowers are missing to make the resemblance complete. Then on a second plane some minor figures, and finally on the highest plane the chief figure, set apart on a throne —here indicated by the enclosure—the whole placed in paradisaical surroundings. Viewed in this light, all seeming incongruities fall automatically in their right places. The blossoming tree which figures so prominently is the Wish-granting Tree, the Kalpadruma of Indian mythology, which constitutes a regular feature of Buddhist representations, it being identified with the Bodhi tree, under which Buddha received enlightenment. The phoenix perched on top is the fabulous bird Garuda, closely connected with the Kalpadruma. The two genii in the upper corner are the indispensable attendants of

#27: Inscription on Shōsōin lute.

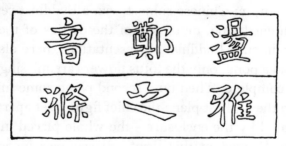

#28: Characters from Wei inscriptions.

every Mahayanic deity. The dancing peacock (Chinese lute ideology presupposes a dancing crane, *wu-ho*,[92] constantly mentioned in connection with the lute player) concludes the Indian element of this representation.

Thus it appears that the artist wavered between two different concepts, a purely Chinese one, that of the Literary Gathering, and

92 舞鶴. See above, pp. 145–6.

a foreign one, that of a Buddhist picture. Setting to work, he resolved to combine both.

When we now ask ourselves which period in Chinese history could be expected to produce such a dual representation, we immediately think of the Northern Wei period.[93] Under the rulers of this outlandish dynasty, who were fervent Buddhists, Buddhist art reigned supreme, and talented artists, combining Greco-Indian elements with Chinese styles, created works of art the magnificence of which is attested by such archeological sites as Yün-kang and Lung-men.

The style of the calligraphy, as shown in the inscription on the bottom board (see figure 27) confirms this date; when compared with the style of writing as seen on monuments of the Wei period (see figure 28)[94] the similarity is obvious.

On the basis of the above considerations I think we may assume with some confidence that the cyclic characters *i-hai* stand for a year of the Wei period, say 435 or 495. Thus this lute was in the T'ang period already a rare treasure, a suitable object to be offered to the Japanese Imperial Court.

To all appearances this rare instrument is the oldest lute still extant, a unique document both for the study of Chinese art, and for the study of the lute.

*   *   *

K'un-shan-yü, the second lute to be discussed here, is, according to authoritative Chinese opinion, one of the finest old instruments in existence. Notwithstanding its early date (T'ang period), it has been preserved in perfect condition, and has a remarkably fine tone.

I regret that I can only show here a traced copy of a rubbing of the bottom of this lute (see figures 29 and 30). As it is doubtful, however, whether at the time when I am writing this essay this rare lute is still extant, and as moreover it is connected with one of the most remarkable lute masters of present-day China, I may be allowed to include it in this essay.

This lute was the favourite instrument of Yeh Ho-fu, since the beginning of this century the greatest lute-master in Peking.

Yeh Ho-fu[95] was born in 1863 as the third son of a high Manchu

---

93 Pei-wei 北魏, 386–535.
94 The characters are traced after reproductions in *Shodō zenshū* 書道全集, vol. VII.
95 葉鶴伏, named Ch'ien 潛.

official, Grand Secretary Jui Lin.[96] Jui Lin is well known in history because in 1860 he was the commander of the Manchu forces that fought the British and the French in the battle of Pa-li-chiao. Yeh Ho-fu's elder brother Huai Ta-pu was an ultra-reactionary, and he played an important role during the Boxer troubles.[97] It would seem, however, that Yeh Ho-fu did not sympathize with the political attitude of his near relatives, and sided more with the reform party; he was keenly interested in Western science, and would talk with animation of the time when he was in charge of installing an electric plant in the Palace grounds. Up to the establishment of the Chinese Republic he occupied several administrative functions, and was well known for his scholarly tastes. His mansion in Peking, where he had collected many choice antiques and a fine library, was frequented by prominent literati and statesmen of the time, as for instance the two leaders of the progressive southern party at the Court, Wêng T'ung-ho[98] and P'an Tsu-yin.[99] Up to the end of the 19th century his house flourished; it was only with the Boxer uprising of 1900 that the decline started: during the troubles the greater part of his property was destroyed, and his political position weakened. In 1910 he lost his official position, and was reduced to utter poverty. It was then that he could convert a hobby into a means of support. Since his early youth he had been a lover of music; already as a boy, when his father was an official in South China, Yeh Ho-fu commenced studying the lute under the well-known master Liu Jung-chai[100] from Chekiang. He assiduously kept up this study, and in later years was taught by other lute masters of established fame, as for instance Chu Fêng-chieh (author of *Yü-ku-chai-ch'in-pu* described on p. 192), the Taoist Chang Ho,[101] author of the standard introductory handbook for the lute player, the *Ch'in-hsüeh-ju-mên*,[102] the Ch'an priest K'ung Ch'ên,[103] author of the lute handbook *K'u-mu-ch'an-ch'in-pu*,[104] Li Hsiang-shih[105] from Chekiang, and others. When the political changes had deprived him of his official income and his private means had dwindled to nothing, he moved to a small house near Lung-fu-szû, and earned his living by teaching the lute.

In the autumn of 1936, one year before his death, I had the privilege

96 瑞麟; see his biography in *Ch'ing-shih-lieh-chuan* 清史列傳, ch. 46.

97 See Bland & Backhouse, *China under the Empress Dowager*, pp. 130, 137, 141.

98 翁同龢, 1830–1904.

99 潘祖陰, 1830–90.

100 劉容齋

101 張鶴, style Ching-hsing 靜薌.

102 App. II, 18.

103 空塵

104 枯木禪琴譜, published in 1893.

105 李湘石

of studying the lute under his guidance. Yeh Ho-fu was a personification of the noblest traditions of the old-fashioned Chinese literatus; never rebelling against the fate which had deprived him of nearly everything, he lived quietly on in an enviable equanimity, enjoying playing the lute and composing poetry. His personality may be characterized by a quotation from Mencius: ' . . . not extravagant when rich and honoured, not forsaking his principles when poor and in a mean condition . . . that constitutes the great man.'[106]

Often I heard Yeh Ho-fu play on the *K'un-shan-yü*, his favourite lute, and on more than one occasion I heard him praise its superior qualities. At that time, however, I had no opportunity to copy its inscriptions. And when in 1937 I again visited Peking, the master had died—just one month before my arrival. As he left no sons, his scanty belongings were scattered, and among them also his lutes. No one could inform me as to the whereabouts of the *K'un-shan-yü*. So I gave up all hope for studying this unique instrument more closely, and only retained the memory of its exquisite tones, its interesting *tuan-wên* (of the type 'serpent belly'),[107] and its beautiful greenish patina. But a lucky accident came to my aid; when I got back to Tokyo, I found in the collection of R. Taki,[108] a Japanese musicologist who had visited Peking some years previously, a rubbing of the bottom board of this lute. The rubbing being badly done, the inscriptions were hardly legible (see figure 29); having studied it carefully during many evenings, I finally succeeded in deciphering all of it except the legend of one seal. Then I made a tracing after this rubbing, which is reproduced here (see figures 30 and 31).

The name *K'un-shan-yü*[109] appears at the top, three characters in chancery script (*li-shu*)[110]: 'Jade from the K'un-lun mountains'. The best jade coming reputedly from the K'un-lun slopes, long associated with Taoist lore, this name indicates value and rarity.

Underneath, on either side of the Dragon Pond, two lines of poetry are engraved. They extol the rare qualities of this lute: 'Its accomplished tones of clear profundity sing like tinkling girdle ornaments of jade; excellent material of high purity comes from the K'un-lun mountains.'[111]

These lines of poetry, together with the three characters at the top, formed the original inscription of this lute, as attested by the lowest

---

106 Book III, part II, 2: 富貴不能淫，貧賤不能移 . . . . 此之謂大丈夫.
107 See p. 138.
108 瀧遼一

109 崑山玉
110 隸書
111 雅韻清幽鳴玉珮，良材高潔發崑岡.

inscription. They were perhaps written by the great literatus Li Yung.[112] I have compared their style with specimens of Li Yung's handwriting as reproduced in vol. x of the Japanese collection *Shodō zenshū*, and find them indeed very similar.

The inscription in cursive script (*ts'ao-shu*)[113] was written by one of the most famous lute players of the early Ch'ing period, Chou Lu-fêng,[114] co-editor of one of the standard Chinese handbooks of the lute, the *Wu-chih-chai-ch'in-pu*.[115] It does not say where Chou Lu-fêng obtained this lute, but only praises its high qualities. The inscription might be translated: 'The material of this lute was reared on the southern slopes of I Mountain; it obtained its fragrance by the side of the Hsien Pond. Vague and vagrant, its tones are remote like high mountains and flowing streams.'[116]

This text consists entirely of allusions to the tenets of *ch'in* ideology. As regards the I-shan (a mountain in Shantung province), according to tradition the mythical Emperor Fu Hsi gathered there the wood for building the first lute. *Hsien-ch'ih* (lit. Hsien Pond), is the name of the music attributed to the mythical Emperor Yao. *Kao-shan-liu-shui* (high mountains and flowing streams), is the name of a famous lute tune, ascribed to the ancient lute player Po Tzû-ya.[117]

At the end of this inscription there is engraved an impression of a seal with the style of Chou Lu-fêng: *Tzû-an-fu*.[118] In the middle there is a fine large seal, reading: *Chou-lu-fêng-chia-ts'ang*[119] (Preserved in the family of Chou Lu-fêng).

The smaller seal to the left of this large seal is unfortunately illegible: apparently it is the seal of another owner of this lute, for I have succeeded in deciphering the penultimate character *chên*;[120] presumably the last two characters read *chên-ts'ang*,[121] 'treasured and stored away by . . .' The small square seal to the right reads: *Hsi-shih-chih-pao*,[122] 'A treasure rarely found in this world.'

The two white spots under these three seals indicate the holes for the two knobs to which the strings are fastened.

The lowest inscription (see figure 31), which is engraved in small regular style (*hsiao-kai*)[123] on either side of the Phoenix Pool,

---

112 李邕, style T'ai-ho 泰和, literary name Pei-hai 北海, 678–747.

113 草書

114 周魯封, style: Tzû-an 子安.

115 五知齋琴譜, preface dated 1721.

116 毓質于嶧山之陽，尋芳于咸池之側，蓬然與高山流水俱兮.

117 See p. 205.

118 子安父; *fu* 父 in this case is the same as *fu* 甫, meaning 'styled'.

119 周魯封家藏

120 珍

121 珍藏

122 希世之寶

123 小楷

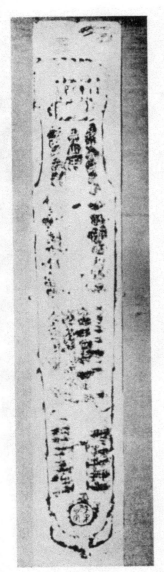

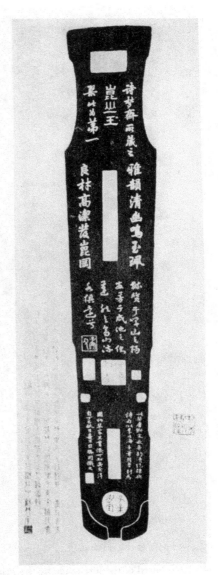

#29: Rubbing of the bottom board of the lute of Yeh Ho-fu.

#30: Tracing after the rubbing reproduced in #29.

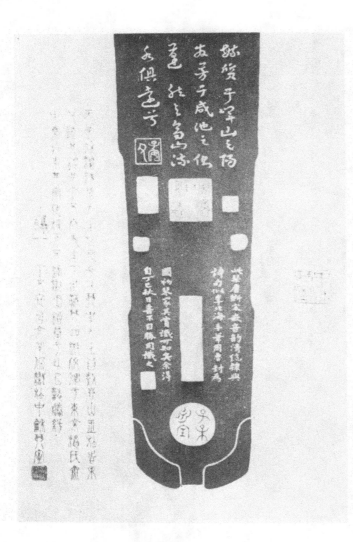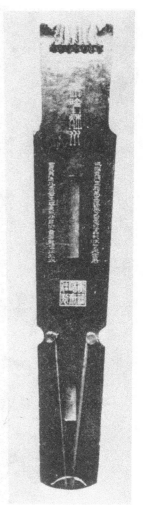

#31: Lower part of the tracing.

#32: Bottom board of the lute made by the Prince of Hêng. (Collection of *Cheng Ying-
sun*, Peking)

#33: Bottom board of a lute made by the Prince of I, preserved in Japan. Name: *Shuang-t'ien-ling-to* 霜天鈴鐸 'Bells on a frosty day'. The round seal reads: *I-fan-ya-chih* 益藩雅制 'Elegant product of the I fief'; the large square seal has the legend *yu-ch'êng-yang-tê* 游誠養德 'rejoicing in sincerity, nurturing virtue'. The grass-characters on either side of the Dragon Pond read 脆滑輕鬆搖霜天之鈴鐸, 翕純淑繹詠盛世之唐虞 'Crisp, gliding, light and loose, its tones tinkle like bells on a frosty day; harmonious and pure, it sings the golden age of Yao and Shun.' This lute was brought to Japan by the Ming refugee Chu Shun-shui, and later presented by him to his faithful Japanese disciple, the Sinologue Andō Seian (page 247). This instrument is still preserved in the Andō family, and in 1949 I had an opportunity to examine the inscriptions inside the sound box, facing the upper aperture in the bottom board.

On right:

'Upper and lower board joined together on an auspicious day of the 8th moon of the year 1579. Elegant product made by the Taoist Huang-nan, Prince of I, having obtained an old block of *t'ung* wood.'

萬曆己卯歲仲秋月吉旦合
益國潢南道人獲古桐雅製

On left:

'T'u Kuei, literary name Ssŭ-t'ung, a lute player of Nan-ch'ang, supervised the building of this instrument in ancient style, on the high command (of the Prince of I).'

南昌琴士思桐涂桂
奉命按古式監劉

I-wang, the Prince of I, named Hou-hsüan 厚炫, was a famous lute player; he succeeded to the fief in 1557. The *Ch'in-shih* states in ch. II, page 3 *verso* that most of his lutes were built by T'u Kuei.

It must be noted that although this lute was brought to Japan by so eminent a scholar as Chu Shun-shui, there are some doubts regarding its authenticity. The famous lute expert Yang Tsung-chi (see page 180, under no. 7) had an instrument with the same inscriptions, which he considered as genuine (cf. his treatise *Ch'in-hua* 琴話, page 15 *recto*).

is signed with the seal of the Ch'ing literatus Ching Chi-chün;[124] it says: 'This lute was hewn during the T'ang dynasty, and in the Sung period its left and right bridges [*lung-yin* and *yo-shan*, see p. 101] were renewed. Its tones are extremely clear. The *li* inscription, and the two lines of poetry thereunder, resemble the handwriting of Li Yung. The appreciative commentary to be seen above was written by Chou Lu-fêng, a lute player of the beginning of our dynasty. When in the autumn of the year 1857 I obtained this lute, I could hardly control myself for joy, and wrote the foregoing to commemorate the occasion.'[125] The word *ch'ien*[126] in the first line of this inscription generally means 'to inlay, to inchase'; but in handbooks of the lute it is used as a technical term, and indicates the process of adding the two bridges to either end of the body of the lute. For these bridges a specially hard kind of wood, like ebony or red sandalwood, is used.[127]

The round seal in archaic script underneath imitates the well-worn legend on ancient sacrificial vessels: *tzû-sun-yung-pao*,[128] 'May my children and grandchildren treasure it for ever.'

When Yeh Ho-fu obtained this lute, he added on either side of the three characters *K'un-shan-yü* an inscription of his own, saying: 'This is the best of all the lutes preserved in the Shih-mêng Library.'[129] *Shih-mêng-chai* was the name of Yeh Ho-fu's studio.

On my tracing, reproduced here, I added in the upper right corner an impression of Yeh Ho-fu's library seal, reading: *Shih-mêng-chai*.[130] The seal in the lower right corner is that of my own library, reading *Chung-ho-ch'in-shih*,[131] cut in imitation of the seal of the Ming Prince Chu Ch'üan (Ning). I also added on the left a colophon, relating the history of this tracing.

*   *   *

The third lute brings us to the Ming dynasty.

After China had been dominated for the greater part of a century by foreign rulers, with the coming of the House of Ming the country again enjoyed a Chinese dynasty. During this period (1368–1644) the fine arts flourished, protected and encouraged by Imperial favour. Next to the Emperors themselves, there were also several Imperial Princes who were ardent patrons of art and learning. Not less than fifteen Princes are enumerated as having patronized book printing,

---

124 景其濬
125 此琴唐斲宋嵌，音韻清絕，隸與詩句似李北海手筆，周魯封爲國朝初琴家，其賞識可知矣，余得自丁巳秋日喜不自勝，因識之·
126 嵌

127 See *Yü-ku-chai-ch'in-pu*, ch. II, p. 37.
128 子孫永寶
129 詩夢齋所藏之琴此爲第一
130 詩夢齋
131 中和琴室

and some of the superior editions which they had made are still preserved.[132] There was a great activity in artistic studies also. Endeavours were made to bring about a renaissance of the old classical music: here also the most outstanding name is that of a member of the Imperial Family, Prince Chu Tsai-yü,[133] whose works on music, as for example the *Yüeh-lü-ch'üan-shu*,[134] are still considered authoritative. And it was also Court circles that gave the impetus to the florescence of lute studies and lute music which was witnessed in the Ming period.

Four Princes are known as having been especially interested in the lute: the Princes of Ning,[135] of Lu,[136] of I,[137] and of Hêng.[138] Cf. the *Ts'ang-ch'in-lu*.

Prince Ning[139] was typical for his class and his time: deeply interested in artistic and abstruse subjects, not caring much for worldly things, he preferred to pass his days in cultivated leisure. He published books on history,[140] on Taoism,[141] agriculture,[142] geography,[143] medicine,[144] the calendar,[145] on literary games, etc.

Under his literary name Ch'ü-hsien,[146] 'Emaciated Immortal' i.e. crane), he was famous as a lute master; he is credited with having composed two well-known tunes, 'Autumn Geese' (*Ch'iu-hung*),[147] and 'Geese on the Sandbank' (*P'ing-sha-lo-yen*),[148] which are still played to this day. A collection of lute tunes compiled by him, the *Shên-chi-pi-pu*,[149] is still preserved. Other works on the lute written by the Prince, like the *T'ai-ku-i-yin*[150] and the *Ch'in-yüan-ch'i-mêng*,[151] seem to have been lost; some fragments are to be found in the *Tsun-shêng-pa-chien*.[152] Besides being an expert performer, the Prince was also well known as a builder of lutes; unfortunately specimens of his work are extremely rare. When accused of practising black

---

[132] See *Shu-lin-ch'ing-hua* 書林清話, ed. 1920, ch. 5.

[133] 朱載堉

[134] 樂律全書; see *Imperial Catalogue*, ch. 38, p. 5.

[135] Ning-wang 寧王

[136] Lu-wang 潞王

[137] I-wang 益王

[138] Hêng-wang 衡王. See *Ts'ung-ch'in-lu*, quoted above.

[139] Personal name, Chu Ch'üan 朱權 (died 1448).

[140] *Han-t'ang-pi-shih* 漢唐秘史; see *Imperial Catalogue*, ch. 52, p. 9.

[141] *Kêng-shin-yü-ts'e* 庚辛玉册; see bibliographical section of the *Ming-shih* 明史.

[142] *Shên-yin-shu* 神隱書; *ibid.*

[143] *I-yü-chih* 異域志; *ibid.*, ch. II.

[144] *P'ing-chi-ch'i-i-pao-ming-chi* 病機氣宜保命集; see the catalogue *T'ieh-ch'in-t'ung-chien-lou-ts'ang-shu-mu-lu* 鐵琴銅劍樓藏書目錄, pub. 1897, ch. 14, p. 24.

[145] *Chou-hou-shên-ching* 肘後神經; see *Imperial Catalogue*, ch. 111, p. 11; the *Ming-shih* gives *shu* 樞 instead of *ching* 經.

[146] 臞仙

[147] 秋鴻

[148] 平沙落雁

[149] App. II, 10.

[150] 太古遺音

[151] 琴阮啓蒙; see bibliographical section, ch. III.

[152] App. II, 4.

magic *(wu-ku)*,[153] the Prince retired to a mountain top, and passed his remaining days composing poetry and playing the lute.[154]

I could find less details about the other three princes who are constantly quoted in connection with the study of the lute; but we shall not be far amiss when we assume that they were personalities not unlike the Prince of Ning.

The Prince of Lu is especially known as a builder of lutes. Specimens of instruments built at Hangchow by him or under his direct supervision are often met with in Chinese collections; most bear dates of the Ch'ung-chên period.[155]

Further, lutes made by the Prince of I still exist in a fair number; one dated 1564 is recorded,[156] and one good specimen has been preserved in Japan, brought over from China by the Chinese refugee Chu Shun-shui;[157] the bottom board is reproduced in fig. 33.

The Prince of Hêng, next to being a great bibliophile,[158] was a famous lute amateur. As far as I know, he did not compose new melodies, but instruments built by him are counted among the finest specimens produced during the Ming period. While instruments built by the Princes of Lu and I may occasionally be seen, lutes built by the Princes of Ning and Hêng are very rare, and highly valued by connoisseurs. It is an instrument made by the Prince of Hêng that is reproduced here (see fig. 32).

The name of this lute is *Lung-yin-ch'iu-shui*,[159] 'Dragon Crying in the Autumnal Water'; the four characters in archaic style are to be seen at the top.

On the right and left of the Dragon Pond there appears a poetical essay in chancery script, praising the qualities of the instrument, and explaining its name: 'With one leap the dragon reaches the gates of Heaven; as a stormwind he compasses ten thousand miles in his flight. When he shakes his bristles, thunder and lightning roll and rattle; when he spurts his foam, a rainstorm gathers. Trying to express in an image the tones produced by the supreme Reason of the movement of the atmosphere, and by music and dance in their various manifestations, I at last lit upon a dragon crying in the autumnal waters.'[160] The first part of these lines is descriptive:

153 巫蠱

154 See *Ming-shih*, ch. 117; *Ming-shih-tsung* 明詩綜, ch. 1.

155 崇禎, 1628–44.

156 See *T'ien-wên-ko-ch'in-pu-chi-ch'êng*, App. II, no. 18, vol. I, sub *Shou-lu* 手錄.

157 See p. 247.

158 See *Ts'ang-shu-chi-shih-shih* 藏書紀事詩, pub. 1891, ch. 2, p. 18.

159 龍吟秋水

160 一躍天門，罡颷萬里，振鬣兮雷電鑑 (better: 鏗) 轟, 歕沫兮風雲際會, 鼓舞造化, 橐籥至理, 爰取物以喻音, 若龍吟於秋水.

since ancient times the dragon has been connected with storms and rain.[161] The second part explains why such a seemingly incongruous image as a dragon was chosen in connection with the tones of this lute: the maker meant to express in this name the impressive, super-human harmony of the universe. The term *t'o-yüeh*,[162] which I have translated as movement of the atmosphere, literally means a bellows: it is a quotation from the *Tao-tê-ching*, ch. v:[163] '[The space] be-tween heaven and earth is like a bellows.' The term *tsao-hua*[164] is also difficult to translate: it means natural evolution, as produced by the agency of the eternal cosmic forces.

Directly under the Dragon Pond one sees the beautiful square seal that marks all instruments of the Prince. It reads: *Hêng-fan-ho-chai-chia-chih*[165] ('Superior product of the Ho Studio, in the Hêng fief').

*   *   *

The above may suffice to give an idea of what antique lutes mean to the Chinese connoisseur, and what methods are followed for appreciating them.

It must be stressed again, however, that the lute should not be considered as a mere relic of bygone times. It does not primarily belong to the scholar's library, but to the pavilion in his garden, to the rivulets in secluded valleys, to the gnarled pines on the rocks. The lute is one of the many bonds that keep the literatus, notwith-standing his book learning, united with the cosmic forces of living nature.

---

[161] See M. W. de Visser, *The Dragon in China and Japan*, Amsterdam 1913, ch. v.
[162] 橐籥

[163] 道德經, ch. v.
[164] 造化
[165] 衡藩和齋佳製

APPENDIX IV

The Chinese Lute in Japan

ACCORDING to most Japanese sources the flourishing of the study of the Chinese lute in Japan (*kingaku*)[1] in the 17th, 18th and 19th centuries is due to the arrival in Japan, in 1677, of the Chinese Zen priest Hsin-yüeh (Jap. Shin'etsu).[2] This Chinese priest, who came to Japan as a refugee fleeing the troubles that marked the later years of the Ming dynasty, was a great lover of the lute; when he came to Japan he brought several Chinese lutes with him, and propagated the study of the lute in that country.

The problem is whether or not the Chinese lute was played in Japan even before the arrival of Shin'etsu. Both old and new Japanese authors disagree in their attitude to this question.

Music since olden times occupied an important place in Japanese cultural life. Old Japanese literature abounds in references to several kinds of musical instruments that were played in Court circles, and by all those who claimed to have elegant and refined interests. Among these several stringed instruments are mentioned; some of them are Japanese, others are of foreign origin. One reads about the *wagon* or *yamatogoto*[3] (a six-stringed cither, each string supported by a strut, *ji*),[4] the *sō*[5] (a 13-stringed cither, a Japanese adaptation of the Chinese *chêng*),[6] the *Shiragigoto*[7] (a cither, as the name implies, of Korean origin), etc. On the other hand most often we find simply the character 琴, read in Sino-Japanese: *kin*, and in Japanese: *koto*, without further indication of what instrument is meant. The pronunciation added in Japanese *kana*[8] to this character in the texts is *kin* or *koto*; sometimes the Chinese character is not used, and we find *kin* or *koto* in *kana* only; and sometimes we find expressions like *kin no koto*, etc. The problem is whether there are passages where the context shows that with one of these terms the seven-stringed Chinese lute is meant.

1 琴學
2 心越
3 和琴
4 柱
5 箏
6 筝
7 新羅琴
8 假名

I may start with giving a few examples, taken at random from the vast field of Japanese literature.

The *Montoku jitsuroku*, historical notes written in Chinese and covering the period 850–8,[9] mentions under the year 853 that a courtier called Sekio excelled in playing the *kin* : 'Sekio especially loved to play the *kin*, and the Emperor presented him with a secret handbook [for this instrument].'[10] Similar references are to be found in the *Shoku Nihon kōki*[11] (chronicle written in Chinese, covering the period 833–50), the *Gyoyūshō*,[12] etc. But especially old novels, written entirely in Japanese, like the *Utsubo monogatari*[13] (10th century), and the famous *Genji monogatari*[14] (11th century) abound in references to instruments called *kin* or *koto*.

Now some older Japanese writers maintain that in the passages referred to above *kin* is the only correct reading, and that the seven-stringed Chinese lute is meant. This is stated, for instance, by the learned physician and musicologist Suzuki Ryū.[15] In his book *Kingaku keimō*[16] (a handbook for the Chinese lute, written in Japanese), he devotes the 39th chapter, entitled, *Hompō kinkōhai*,[17] to the history of the Chinese lute in Japan. There he claims that wherever in ancient Japanese texts we find the character 琴 (he refers to the sources mentioned above), it means the Chinese lute. His argument is that although the Chinese lute was very popular in old Japan, it gradually fell into abeyance, till Shin'etsu's arrival in the 17th century brought about a renaissance. This argument he reiterates in the preface to his edition of the *Tōkō kimpu*.[18] He says: 'In ancient times in our country rites and music flourished; of the eight kinds of musical instruments (i.e. those made of wood, silk, bamboo, clay, metal, stone, leather, and gourd) none was missing. Most popular was the Chinese lute; it was an instrument constantly used by the nobility and high-minded people. This is proved by passages in historical works and other chronicles. But in medieval times, the study of the lute gradually fell into abeyance, and coming to the present time, its tradition was lost, and there was no one who understood this study. In the Kambun period, however, there came the naturalized priest Tōkō Zenji, named Shin'etsu. . . . Then gradually every-

---

9 文德實錄, completed in 878.
10 關雄尤好皷琴, 天皇賜其秘譜.
11 續日本後記
12 御遊抄
13 宇津保物語
14 源氏物語

15 鈴木龍, 1741–90; for details, see below, p. 235.
16 琴學啓蒙
17 本邦琴興廢
18 東皋琴譜; details below.

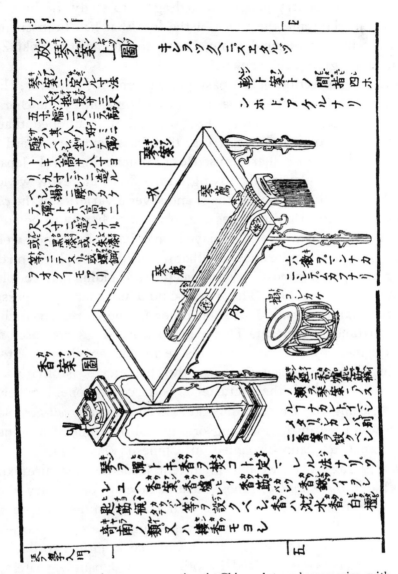

#34: Japanese picture, representing the Chinese lute and accessories, with
explanations in Japanese. From the *Kingaku nyūmon zukai* 琴學入門圖解,
a simplified handbook for the lute player, written in Japanese;
published in one volume at Kyoto, in 1828.

where in our country people started again to study the lute. That now in this late age the tones of the lute that had been silent for several centuries resound again, is due to the merit of Tōkō Zenji. Is this not a great achievement?'[19]

A closer inspection of the passages referred to, however, clearly shows that it is not the Chinese lute that is meant by the character 琴 in old Japanese literature. For we find it mentioned that the instrument in question has struts, that its sounds are heard at a considerable distance, that it is used for accompanying purely Japanese songs, that it is played when lying on the floor, etc. Now we know that the Chinese lute, unlike the *sê* and several varieties of the *chêng*, never has struts; that its tones are so weak as hardly to be audible outside the room where it is played, that its scale cannot well be adapted to the Japanese ones, and that it is made to be played on one's lap or on a special stand—its very structure precluding that it be played when lying on the floor. There can be no doubt that in the passages referred to, the *wagon*, *sō*, or some other Japanese or Chinese cither-like instrument is meant. That yet the word *kin* 琴 was used must be explained by the fact that this term had an elegant, literary flavour. Even at present in Japan the character 琴 is often used to write *koto*, although the character 箏 is the correct one. Further, the *ch'in* 琴, being the Chinese musical instrument *par excellence*, also in China was used in the meaning of 'musical instrument' in general; notice that a piano is called in Chinese *yang-ch'in*,[20] a violin *t'i-ch'in*,[21] etc. When we find in ancient Japanese literature expressions like *kokin*,[22] *dankin*,[23] these must be taken to be literary idioms, taken over from the Chinese. The character *kin* in these expressions does not indicate the Chinese seven-stringed lute, no more than *ken*[24] in Japanese texts indicates the Chinese straight sword.

These facts were realized by other older Japanese writers, for instance the well-known Japanese expert on the Chinese lute, Kodama Kūkū.[25] In a colophon to a manuscript copy of the Chinese lute handbook *Li-hsing-yüan-ya*,[26] he quotes some Japanese writers who aver that the *kin* mentioned, e.g. in the *Genji monogatari*, is the Chinese

---

[19] 蓋我古昔，禮樂之隆，八音之器，諸般皆備，而琴最盛行，爲士君子常御之器，乃諸史傳所載，可以徵矣，中世已後，漸廢不行，及至近代，竟失其傳，無復有道之者矣，寬文中，有歸化僧東皐禪師名心越…於是乎，四方稍復有道琴事者矣，嗚呼，使數百年已絶之徽音再振其響晚世者，東皐師之功，豈不亦偉哉.

[20] 洋琴

[21] 提琴

[22] 鼓琴

[23] 彈琴

[24] 劍

[25] 兒玉空空，1734–1811；details below.

[26] 理性元雅，by the Ming author Chang Ting-yü 張廷玉；see *Imperial Catalogue*, ch. 114, p. 7 verso.

lute. Then he goes on to say: 'I do not agree with this. Why? The *Genji monogatari* was written about 700 years ago. If the above statement were true, then in old families and famous monasteries there would certainly have been preserved many of these ancient Chinese lutes. Why is it that on the contrary only very occasionally one hears about such a thing? . . . In my opinion, our Empire Japan knew the Chinese lute for the first time after the day that Master Shin'etsu came from the west.'[27]

The modern Japanese musicologist Sanjō Shōtarō[28] comes to about the same conclusion.[29]

Some other modern Japanese scholars, however, still keep to Suzuki Ryū's argument, and maintain that it was the Chinese seven-stringed lute that was played on a great scale in ancient Japan. Prof. Tanabe Hisao[30] (well-known Japanese musicologist), for instance, sets forth this view in his *Nihon ongaku kōwa*[31] (Tokyo 1921), on pages 364 ff. To bear out this statement he quotes the following passage from the *Gempei seisuiki*[32] (historical notes covering the period 1161–81): 'She also is a sensitive lady, a great expert on the *kin* [or *koto*]. In former days Po Chü-i of China, calling lute, poetry, and wine his three friends,[33] nurtured his feelings by playing the lute . . . This lady, continually singing Po Chü-i's poems and playing the *kin* [or *koto*], purified her heart.'[34] After quoting this passage Prof. Tanabe remarks that it is clear that here the Chinese lute is meant, because of the reference to Po Chü-i and his lute. Now this argument of course does not hold; for the mere fact that Po Chü-i is mentioned does not constitute any proof. Po Chü-i and his lute are often referred to in Japanese novels when *Japanese* music is discussed. I mention, for instance, a passage in the *Genji monogatari*, in the chapter *Suetsumu hana*. The Princess after which this chapter is named is a famous performer on the Japanese *koto*; that here *koto* is meant is evident

---

27 予未以爲然，何則，源語之作，距今纔七百餘年，果如其言，則古家名刹，尙可存其器，而何其寥寥聞耶 . . . 以予臆見，則皇和之有琴也，刱于越公西來之日。

28 三條商太郎

29 See his *Nihon jōko ongakushi* 日本上古音樂史, Tokyo 1935, p. 137.

30 田邊尙雄

31 日本音樂講和, Tokyo 1921, on pp. 364 ff.

32 源平盛衰記

33 The quotation is from a poem by Po Chü-i, entitled *Pei-ch'uang-san-yu* 北窓三友; see the excellent study *Hakurakuten to Nihon bungaku* 白樂天と日本文學, Tokyo 1930, by Mizuno Heiji 水野平次, p. 378. For other references to cither-like instruments in the *Genji monogatari*, see *Genji monogatari no ongaku* 源氏物語の音樂, by Yamada Takao 山田孝雄, Tokyo 1934, pp. 80–108.

34 *Kore mata nasake aru nyōbō nite kin (koto) no jōzu to zo kikoetamaishi. Mukashi Kara no Hakkyoi wa kinshishu (koto, shi, sake) no mitsu wo tomo toshite tsune ni kin (koto) wo hiite kokoro wo yashinai tamaikeri. . . shi wo kono kita no kata tsune ni eijite kokoro wo sumashi koto wo danji tamaerikeri.*

from the context. Now a lady called Myōbu says of this eccentric Princess to Prince Genji[35]: 'Her only lover is her *kin*.' Prince Genji answers: 'Then of the "Three Friends" she at least has one . . . Let me hear her play.'[36] Thus here also Po Chü-i is mentioned, and here definitely a Japanese *koto* is meant.

This fact is not at all astonishing. The Japanese of olden times, though fairly well versed in Chinese literature, were often amazingly ignorant of what we would call 'things Chinese'. Thus it is very doubtful whether they realized that the *kin* mentioned in their favourite T'ang poetry was entirely different from cither-like instruments in use in Japan. Their knowledge of Chinese ways of living was as limited as that of our European medieval poets concerning daily life in ancient Greece and Italy. During the Heian period several Japanese missions were sent to China; the writings by the members of these missions, who knew daily Chinese life from their own observation, contain excellent accounts of religious and political conditions prevalent in China. But they write little about things Chinese; in this respect they conformed to Chinese literary tradition, which condemned the things of daily life as unworthy to write about. Thus we find in Japanese history that with regular intervals the Japanese deemed it necessary to work up arrears in their knowledge of Chinese reality. They found that they had been associating with terms in daily use in China, things quite different in shape and style from those really used by contemporary Chinese. Therefore, especially during the Tokugawa period, when the seclusion policy of the *bakufu* had limited the intercourse with China to the port of Nagasaki, the Chinese there were eagerly questioned by Japanese scholars: what dresses they wear, what utensils they use, and what Chinese houses and temples look like.[37] Such knowledge was especially important to

---

35 Kaneko ed., Tokyo 1938, p. 207.

36 *kin wo zo natsukashiki kataraibito to omoeru to kikoyureba, mitsu no tomo nite ima hitokusa ya utate aran. Ware ni kikase yo.*

37 The most remarkable example of the results of such an inquiry is the book *Shinzoku kibun* 清俗紀聞, 13 chs. in 6 vols., published in 1799 by Nakagawa Chūei 中川忠英, who served as a *bakufu* official (*bugyō* 奉行) at Nagasaki; this book contains the results of minute inquiries, patiently made with the Chinese at Nagasaki, especially Chinese and Japanese interpreters attached to the government office there. The book gives a detailed account of Chinese customs and Chinese

daily life, profusely illustrated with finely executed drawings. The famous Director of the Academy at Edo (the Seidō 聖堂), Hayashi Jussai (林述齋, 1768–1841) added the first preface. Even Chinese refugees were questioned. An interesting example is the *Shunsui shushi danki* 舜水朱氏譚綺, printed in 1708 in 4 vols., and compiled by the Japanese sinologue Hitomi Bōsai (人見懋齋, 1638–96); preface by the scholar Asaka Kaku (安積覺, 1656–1737), dated 1707. This book contains the material regarding 'things Chinese' obtained by Hitomi from the famous Chinese refugee at the Court of Mito, Chu Shun-shui (朱舜水 1600–82). Here we find* those Japanese who wanted to read Chinese novels : in such texts there occur many terms not to be found in Chinese dictionaries and other ordinary works of reference. Thus in the Tokugawa period we find special Japanese vocabularies of the Chinese vulgar language, where common household words, like spoon, table, comb, etc. are explained by drawings of the Chinese objects.[38]

The pre-Tokugawa Japanese missions to China had as their primary object the study of Chinese religious and political questions, and of Court and ceremonial music. It is quite understandable that the members of those missions were not in a position to study lute music, an art that was confined to intimate literary gatherings and the library of the scholar. Moreover, as we have seen above,[39] in China strict rules prohibited the teaching of the lute to unqualified persons, and, among them, foreigners are especially mentioned. While during the T'ang dynasty it was comparatively easy to obtain lutes, on the other hand teachers were few, and may be supposed to have kept to the rules limiting the transmission of the study of the lute to members of the privileged and highly exclusive class of the literati.

Yet Chinese lutes occasionally ended up in Japan. In Appendix III above I described the remarkable old Chinese lute preserved in the Nara Repository; the famous old temple, the Hōryūji,[40] also has in its collection a Chinese lute, dating from the T'ang period. But these lutes were not actually played. They were regarded merely as curiosities, relics from the 'Land beyond the Seas'.

Finally we must remember that in olden times Japanese knowledge of Chinese music was mainly secondhand, being chiefly obtained through the intermediary of Korea. Now in that country the Chinese lute as a solo instrument never became popular.[41] Although the Chinese lute was taken over together with the ceremonial orchestra, as a solo instrument its place was taken by a special Korean instru-

---

*drawings of Chinese clothing, furniture, temples, envelopes and letters, bills of fare, etc., with the dimensions added, and colour and material recorded with painstaking care.

Paul Carus based his publication *Chinese Life and Customs* (Chicago, Open Court Publ. Co., 1907) on this book, and reproduced a selection from its fine illustrations; see the author's statement on page 1.

38 For instance the *Shōsetsu jii* 小說字彙, published in one volume in 1791. First undated preface by the Japanese sinologue Takayasu Rooku 高安蘆屋, author's preface dated, 1784. The author gives only his literary name,

Shūsuien shujin 秋水園主人.

39 pp. 61 ff.

40 法隆寺

41 It should be mentioned, however, that during the Ch'ing period, when many Korean scholars used to visit Peking, a few of them made a study of the Chinese lute. During a visit to Seoul in 1949 I learned that the Korean poet and statesman Shin Ui (申緯, style Han-so 漢叟, literary name Cha-ha 紫霞, 1769–1847) was a great lute player, while in recent years Yun Hae-kwan 尹海觀, is also said to have been quite a creditable performer.

ment, the so-called *hyôn-kêm*.[42] This instrument is still very popular in Korea. It has six strings, of which the three middle ones are strung over sixteen bridges of varying height. It is played with a short rattan stick that serves as a plectrum. According to the *Ryang-kêm-sin-po*,[43] the Chinese lute was introduced into Korea about A.D. 600; the Minister Wang San-ak[44] recommended to use in its place the *hyôn-kêm*, invented by him. This instrument has its own notation, and its music is quite different from that of the Chinese lute.

Therefore we must assume that the character *kin*[45] in old Japanese texts stands for cither-like instruments, either of Japanese, Korean or Chinese origin. Both in China and Korea a great many varieties of the cither called *chêng*[46] were used. Since these instruments were widely used in both countries in both sacrificial and popular music, it is only natural that at an early date they found their way to Japan. And many Japanese thought these cither-like instruments were the Chinese lute so often mentioned in Chinese literature.

It is on the basis of the above considerations that I think we are justified in assuming that it was only with the arrival of Shin'etsu that the Chinese seven-stringed lute became really known in Japan. A few exceptions do not invalidate this argument; they were isolated cases that had no real influence on Japanese cultural life.[47] It was only with the arrival of Shin'etsu that the Chinese lute was really played in Japan, and found enthusiasts in broader circles of artists and scholars.

* * *

42 玄琴

43 梁琴新譜. (See M. Courant, *Bibliographie coréenne*, Paris 1896, part III, p. 133.)

44 王山岳; passed official examination in 552.

45 琴

46 箏

47 I mention, for instance, Fujiwara Sadatoshi (藤原貞敏, 807–67), the father of Japanese *biwa* music. He was a member of a Japanese mission to China that arrived there in 838, and made great efforts to study Chinese music. He married the daughter of his Chinese *biwa* teacher, and this girl is said to have been able to play both the *chêng* and the Chinese seven-stringed lute.

Much later the great Japanese sinologue Ogyū Sorai (荻生徂徠, 1666–1728) made a study of the Chinese lute, and wrote a book called *Kingaku taiishō* (琴學太意抄, dated 1722; preserved only in manuscript copies).

This, however, is an entirely theoretical essay, the materials for which have been gathered from various Chinese books on the subject. There is no indication that he really became a lute player.

The same may be said of Ishikawa Jōzan (石川丈山, 1583–1672). He was a great lover of Chinese poetry, who for the greater part of his life lived in retirement on a beautiful spot in the outskirts of Kyoto. His retreat was called Shisendō 詩仙堂; on the walls of his study he hung the images of 36 famous Chinese poets, and there he passed his days. He possessed a Chinese lute that had belonged to the famous Chinese scholar Ch'ên Chi-ju (陳繼儒, 1558–1639), which he greatly valued; but there is no indication that he actually played it. At present the Shisendō may still be seen in its original state, and the lute has also been preserved; nowadays the place is a nunnery.

#35: A banquet at the house of a Chinese merchant in Nagasaki. The diners on the right are playing *morra* with geisha girls. On the left a Chinese is playing the lute, accompanied on the *samisen* (three-stringed Japanese guitar) by a geisha. The picture of the lute is not very clear; it might also be a small *chêng*. From *Nagasakishi-shi* 長崎市史, *Fūzoku-hen* 風俗編, pub. 1925 by the Municipal Office of Nagasaki.

#36: A musical seance in the Chinese Factory at Nagasaki. One Chinese is playing the lute, while his friends accompany him on guitar, mouth-organ and flute. Part of a Japanese picture scroll, now in the library of the Imperial University at Kyoto.

The priest Shin'etsu was a highly interesting personality. In China he is practically unknown; but in Japan abundant materials[48] about him and his work have been preserved. For in Japan he became famous, and had considerable influence on the cultural life of the time.

Shin'etsu's lay-name was Chiang Hsing-t'ao,[49] and he was born in 1639. Having entered priesthood, he was enrolled in the Yung-fu monastery[50] at Hangchow. When the Manchus invaded China, in 1676 he left Hangchow and set out for Japan. In the first month of the year 1677 he arrived at Nagasaki in a Chinese ship, and there settled down in the Kōfukuji,[51] one of the famous local Chinese monasteries. Shin'etsu then was 38 years old. It appears from his writings that he was a priest of high culture, being at the same time a clever painter, poet, seal-engraver and player on the lute. At that time the great Tokugawa Maecenas, Mitsukuni, Lord of Mito,[52] had established in his fief in Eastern Japan near Edo, a center of learning where he had assembled the flower of Japanese scholarship. Mitsukuni was also greatly interested in Chinese studies, and had, in 1665, summoned to his court another learned Chinese refugee, Chu Shun-shui,[53] and made him his Chinese adviser. When Mitsukuni heard about the arrival of Shin'etsu at Nagasaki, he sent in 1678 a messenger, Imai Koshirō,[54] to invite Shin'etsu to come to Mito. At the time, however, the Tokugawa government did not allow Chinese to travel freely in Japan; they were allowed to stay only at Nagasaki, and for a limited time. Therefore a special permission had to be obtained. This took several years, and only in 1683 could Shin'etsu set out for Eastern Japan. It seems, however, that during the intervening years he could do some traveling in West Japan; for we read that he visited several centers of Buddhist learning, especially monasteries of the Obaku sect,[55] which were traditionally headed by a naturalized Chinese priest. Thus he came into contact with some of the famous Chinese abbots of this sect, notably the priest Mokuan.[56]

Arrived at Mito, Shin'etsu, encouraged by Mitsukuni, started manifold religious and artistic activities. He made a thorough study

48 Most informative are Shin'etsu's complete works, the *Tōkō zenshū* 東皐全集 in two volumes, compiled by Asano Fuzan 浅野斧山, and published in 1911. This edition also contains a complete biography, and reproductions of Shin'etsu's paintings, his calligraphy, and imprints of some of the seals carved by him. His grave is still to be seen near Mito. Also see E. W. Clement, 'The Tokugawa Princes of Mito', in *Transactions of the Asiatic Society of Japan*, XVIII (1890).

49 蔣興儔
50 永福寺
51 興福寺
52 德川光圀, 1628–1700.
53 See note 37 above, and p. 247 below.
54 今井小四郎
55 黄檗宗
56 木菴, 1611–84.

of the Japanese language, and was in regular intercourse with well-known Japanese scholars of the time. He founded the Gion temple[57] at Mito, and greatly influenced religious life. At his death in 1695 he was buried with great honour. It lies outside the scope of this essay to give a more detailed survey of Shin'etsu's cultural activities; here we shall concern ourselves only with his teaching of the Chinese lute.

If we were to believe the notes made by older Japanese lute enthusiasts, Shin'etsu had more than a hundred pupils who under his guidance studied the Chinese lute. Although this is an exaggeration, still the number of his lute disciples seems to have been considerable. Only a few of these, however, became really proficient on this instrument, and transmitted Shin'etsu's teachings along to their own pupils. Best known are the doctor of Chinese medicine, Hitomi Chikudō, and the Japanese sinologue Sugiura Kinsen.[58] Shin'etsu taught his pupils the finger technique and made them practise on simple lute melodies, for the greater part musical versions of famous Chinese poems. These tunes were eagerly noted down by his pupils, and it is on the basis of such manuscripts that afterwards the *Tōkō kimpu*[59] was published.

It is difficult to ascertain whether Shin'etsu as a lute player, judging by Chinese standards, ranked as an expert. At one time, basing my opinion upon the tunes preserved in the *Tōkō kimpu,* I was inclined to think that he was but a mediocre performer. For in this handbook only very simple and much abbreviated lute melodies are given; they lack all the grandeur of real lute music. On the other hand we have a letter of Hitomi Chikudō to Shin'etsu,[60] from which it appears that Shin'etsu advised him to use the well-known Ming handbook *Sung-hsüan-kuan-ch'in-pu;*[61] this would imply that Shin'etsu taught his advanced students on the basis of this handbook—which is by no means an easy one. Therefore it would seem that the handbook that bears Shin'etsu's name, the *Tōkō kimpu,* represents only the tunes that Shin'etsu taught to beginners. For advanced students did not need a special handbook; they could use the great Chinese *ch'in-pu.* Taking into consideration the meager evidence available, I now think we had better leave the question of Shin'etsu's abilities as a lute expert undecided. That he was not one of the great Chinese musicians,

---

57 祇園寺
58 See p. 232 below.
59 See p. 232 below.

60 *Tōkō zenshū,* ii, leaf 44.
61 松絃舘琴譜, preface dated 1614; see *Imperial Catalogue,* 113, leaf 8 verso.

however, appears from the fact that he left no important compositions of his own.

When he came to Japan, Shin'etsu brought three Chinese lutes with him. Best known is the instrument called *Yü-shun*[62] (Jap. Gushun), a fine Ming specimen, covered with red cement. This instrument was long preserved in the treasury of the Tokugawas of Mito. In 1834 the celebrated Mito scholar Fujita Tōko[63] was ordered to compose a Chinese essay, to be written inside the cover of the box this lute was kept in. This essay, entitled *Gushun kinki*,[64] is to be found reprinted in Fujita's complete works, the *Tōko ikō*,[65] and the original may still be seen on the box, now, together with the instrument itself, in the Imperial Museum, in Ueno Park, Tokyo. Secondly Shin'etsu had a lute called *Su-wang*,[66] (Jap. *So-ō*); this lute he presented to his pupil Hitomi Chikudō, and for some generations it was preserved in Hitomi's family. At present it seems to have been lost. Thirdly a lute called *Wan-ho-sung*,[67] (Jap. *Mankakushō*), preserved in the Gion temple in Mito.

In addition Shin'etsu taught his pupils how to make lutes themselves. These Japanese-made lutes are built from *kiri* wood, the same material as the Japanese *koto* is made of. Instead of the coat of cement of the Chinese lutes, the Japanese ones are covered with ordinary lacquer. This has the advantage of not being affected by the humidity of the Japanese climate; but on the other hand such a coat does not develop those tiny cracks (*tuan-wên*)[68] which give the sound-box of an antique Chinese lute its peculiar beauty. Of these Japanese-made Chinese lutes many are still preserved. I have in my collection seven specimens, which are in good condition and show interesting inscriptions. They are easily distinguishable from genuine Chinese specimens by the lacquer coating, and by the fact that the tuning pegs (*chên*),[69] are much shorter than those of the Chinese lutes. This is because the Japanese lute players rarely had a real lute table (which has a special cavity for the pegs), and usually played the lute either on an ordinary low table (see fig. 34), or on the floor.

Later Japanese lute players often could obtain real Chinese lutes from the Chinese in Nagasaki. Occasionally among the Chinese living there, or passing through, there were some who could play the

---

62 虞舜
63 藤田東湖, 1806–55.
64 虞舜琴記
65 東湖遺稿, edition of 1877, vol. 2, leaf 25.

66 素王
67 萬壑松
68 See above, pp. 194–7.
69 軫

lute. But probably they were not great virtuosi. Nagasaki pictures often show Chinese playing the lute, usually accompanied by other stringed instruments, and serving to enliven a dinner party (figs. 35 and 36). This fact alone already shows that those Chinese lute players were not real experts, for such would certainly not thus offend against the rules for the lute player.

Through Shin'etsu's teachings, and by studying Chinese books on the lute, Japanese players also became acquainted with lute ideology. It is not without interest to observe how in Japan there arose with regard to lute ideology controversies similar to those found in China.

In Chapter III, section 3 above, we have seen that lute players of the Confucianist school denied Buddhist priests the right to play the lute. Now in Japan about half of the lute players were Buddhist priests, and Japanese lute tradition is founded upon the teachings of Shin'-etsu, a Zen priest. The famous doctor of Chinese medicine, Murai Kinzan,[70] took exception to this. He learned the lute from a Chinese scholar who passed through Nagasaki, and claims to have the only real lute tradition. In the colophon to his *Kinzan kinroku*[71] he says: 'The lute is the great instrument of the Holy Sages, it includes all music. Of those things that the Superior Man has always with him, the lute is dearest to him, he does not suffer to be separated from it.[72] The Way of the Lute which in the Middle Age flourished in our country has now become lost. The methods of the lute as now practised in our country are all based upon the teachings of the two priests Shin'etsu and Mansō;[73] their methods for the greater part are those used by vulgar people of the Ming and Ch'ing periods. How could these two priests know the difference between elegant and vulgar? Therefore I did not relish the way these two priests play the lute, and for myself I have sighed over this for a long time. But traveling to Nagasaki, I met a Chinese called P'an Wei-ch'uan, and he taught me how to play the lute, and the finger technique.'[74]

Shin'etsu's pupils spread the study of the lute over the entire country. First the *kingaku* flourished among people of taste in Edo, roughly from 1770 till 1780. Its heyday falls in the subsequent

---

[70] See below, p. 248.

[71] *Ibid.*

[72] Quoted from *Fêng-su-t'ung-i*; see above, p. 72.

[73] See below, pp. 232–5, 247.

[74] 琴者聖人大器，而爲樂之統矣，君子所常御者，琴最親密，不離於身，我東方中古琴法已亡，今海內琴法，皆出于心越萬宗二僧氏之手，多是明清俗間之法也，二僧氏安知雅俗之分乎，余故不喜二僧氏之琴，竊歎嗟久矣，嘗游長崎，邂逅于清人潘渭川者，偶受琴法手勢．

Kansei and Bunka periods (1789–1817). During this period, playing the Chinese lute developed into a veritable craze: everyone who wanted to show his interest in elegant literary pursuits studied this instrument and wrote essays and odes in praise of its music. It was especially favoured by those in direct contact with Chinese studies, such as the *jukan*,[75] the Japanese sinologues in the service of the shogun, and by the so-called *tai-i*,[76] the doctors of Chinese medicine attached to the government. In addition, by all who were attracted by exciting novelties. Therefore we need not be astonished to find among these lute enthusiasts even some *rangakusha*,[77] students of Dutch learning. Many Japanese lute students soon dropped this subject, but there were also not a few more serious musicians, who carried their study through with great enthusiasm. Some even devoted their whole life to this music.

This sudden flourishing of the Chinese lute in Japan becomes quite understandable when one thinks of the fact that the Japanese scholars realized that now at last they had obtained the real Chinese lute, the name of which had been familiar to them for so long through their studies of Chinese literature. For as has been pointed out above, there can be no doubt that even as late as the Tokugawa period the greater part of Japanese lovers of Chinese studies fondly believed that the character *kin*[78] in Chinese texts stood for an instrument very much like the Japanese *koto*. This is proved by an inspection of Japanese illustrated editions of old Chinese books: there one regularly sees old Chinese poets playing upon the Japanese *koto*!

The seven-stringed lute however was too typically Chinese ever to become really a part of Japanese life. The music of the Chinese lute is based upon principles fundamentally different from those underlying Japanese music, and moreover its study presupposed a solid knowledge of the Chinese language, both written and spoken. As is well known, the Japanese have evolved a special way of reading Chinese texts, consisting of paraphrasing the Chinese in the Japanese vernacular; in this process the order of the words is drastically changed. As the text of the lute melodies could of course only be sung in the Chinese way, the Japanese lute player, when wishing to accompany his play by singing, had to learn how to read the text in the Chinese pronunciation. In Japanese handbooks for the Chinese lute, the Chinese pronunciation is added to the characters of the text

---

[75] 儒官   [76] 待醫
[77] 蘭學者   [78] 琴

in *kana*.[79] It goes without saying that thus the text became meaning-less to the average Japanese hearer. As a reaction to this, the Japanese lute player Uragami Gyokudō[80] composed purely Japanese texts for the lute melodies. It seems that shortly after the introduction of the Chinese lute into Japan by Shin'etsu, efforts were made to adapt the lute to Japanese music. The *Gyokudō zōsho kimpu*[81] says: 'Then it was asked: "Onoda Tōsen[82] used to play Japanese songs on the Chinese lute; but fearing that this was contrary to the principles of lute ideology, he did not show these attempts to others. Have you heard about this?" I answered: "In the Kambun period [1661–73], the naturalized priest Shin'etsu stayed at Mito; he excelled in playing the lute. Onoda Tōsen continued his teachings. The shogun ordered the official musician Tsuji Buzen-no-kami together with Onoda Tōsen to work out Chinese lute versions of Japanese songs. When these versions were ready, they were played in the palace of the shogun."'[83] These attempts, however, seem to have had but scant success. The majority of Japanese lute players aimed at singing the lute melodies in as purely Chinese a way as possible. Some even especially went to Nagasaki, there to learn from the resident Chinese the real Chinese pronunciation.

With the Tempō period (1830–44),[84] it seems that the interest in the Chinese lute decreased, and that its music ceased to be a subject of social importance. Henceforward experts on the lute must be sought for in some isolated monasteries, and in some exclusive circles of retired scholars. With the Meiji Restoration in 1868 a crave for Western things flooded the country, and later, in 1894, the Sino-Japanese war further decreased the interest in the Chinese lute. In the beginning of this century the Chinese lute had become a curiosity in Japan, and only very few people still knew how to play it. A final blow was the Great Earthquake in 1923, when numerous lutes in private collections and curio shops were destroyed. It is only in recent years that Japanese musicologists again are taking an interest in this charming instrument, which for two centuries was so intimately connected with the cultural life of the later Tokugawa period.

---

79 Thus the study of the Chinese lute stimulated, just as the Chinese reading of Buddhist texts introduced by the Obaku sect 黃檗宗 did, the study of the Chinese spoken language in Japan.

80 See pp. 237–9.

81 See p. 237.

82 See p. 236.

83 又問, 東川野廷賓, 嘗被國歌於七絃恐失琴意, 不示之人, 子聞其說乎, 曰, 寬文中, 歸化僧心越留錫水府, 善鼓琴, 廷賓傳心越彈法, 德廟命伶宮辻豐前守與廷賓, 謀被本邦之樂于七絃, 曲成也, 進奏於殿中.

84 天保

*   *   *

The materials regarding the transmission of the Chinese lute in Japan have never been assembled. Japanese sources occasionally give short lists of well-known teachers and their pupils, but none of these can make any claim at completeness. For more than four years I have been trying to supplement these lists. Some facts I discovered in prefaces or colophons to Japanese books and manuscripts on the Chinese lute, some on tombstones of lute players, some in the works of Tokugawa sinologues, and some in inscriptions on Japanese-made Chinese lutes. Finally I collected some minor data during a stay at Nagasaki. I have tried to assemble these scattered materials, and at last succeeded in piecing together a historical table to the transmission of the study of the Chinese lute in Japan, which is presented here. It is still far from complete, but yet it contains more materials than any of the Japanese tables I know of. Each of the persons tabulated is briefly discussed, and their activities with regard to the study of the Chinese lute are given in outline. A perusal of this list may give the reader a fairly correct idea of how, and by whom, the Chinese lute was studied in Japan, and what its cultural significance was.

The most important sources were the following:

a A manuscript entitled *Kingaku denju ryakkei*,[85] 'An outline of the tradition of *kingaku*', written by the Japanese lute expert Shinraku Kansō,[86] and dated 1813. The text of this manuscript, which was appended to a Japanese manuscript-extract from the well-known Chinese *ch'in-pu*, *Ch'in-hsüeh-hsin-shêng*,[87] by Chuang Chên-fêng,[88] I have published in my article 'Chinese Literary Music and its Introduction into Japan'.[89]

b An essay by the Japanese sinologue Nakane Shuku,[90] entitled *Shichigenkin no denrai*.[91] This essay is to be found in his posthumously edited works, the *Kōtei ibun*.[92]

c A list entitled *Kinkyoku sōden keifu*,[93] to be found in the *Tōkō zenshū*.[94]

d Two manuscript albums, now in the collection of the Japanese scholar Nakayama Kyūshirō.[95] In these albums several members of a Japanese association of lute lovers that in the eighties

85 琴學傳授略系
86 See pp. 240–2.
87 琴學心聲
88 莊臻鳳, author's preface dated 1664.
89 Commemoration volume for Professor Mutō, Nagasaki 1937.
90 中根淑, lit. name Kōtei 香亭, 1839–

1913.
91 七絃琴の傳來
92 香亭遺文, edited by Shimbo Iwaji 新保磐次, Tokyo 1916, pp. 442–56.
93 琴曲相傳系譜
94 東皋全集, II, leaf 61.
95 中山久四郎

gathered in a temple at Edo under guidance of the lute master Kodama Kūkū,[96] wrote down essays and poems on the lute, stray notes on the study of the lute, tunes in notation, etc. Each member wrote and attached his seals. Thus these two albums, though small and badly worm-eaten, contain valuable materials.

I have divided my list into two parts. The first I call *naiden*[97] ('inner tradition'); this is the line of Japanese lute players headed by the priest Shin'etsu. The second, which I call *geden*[98] ('outer tradition'), contains those Japanese lute players who learned the lute from Chinese laymen.

NAIDEN, THE INNER TRADITION

1 *Sugiura Kinsen*, named Masamoto,[99] a Confucianist scholar attached to the *bakufu*. He seems not to have published any literary works, and is chiefly known as an expert on the Chinese lute. He was first taught the lute by Hitomi Chikudō, then continued his studies under Shin'etsu himself. He carefully collected the various tunes taught by the master, and after ten years of study, published in the Hōei[100] period (1704–11) a handbook for the lute, called after the master *Tōkō kimpu*.[101] The first preface to this book is written by the famous Director of the Tokugawa Academy (the Seidō),[102] the sinologue Hayashi Hōkō (1644–1732);[103] further there is a preface by the Japanese lute player Hitomi Tōgen[104] and by the scholar Kō Gentai[105] (1649–1723). Kō Gentai was of Chinese descent, his grandfather being a Chinese from Fukien Province and interpreter at the Chinese office in Nagasaki; Gentai was known as an excellent calligrapher. The *Tōkō kimpu* gives a number of minor lute melodies in simple setting. As shall be seen below, this handbook was reprinted several times. I may mention here already, that the edition of 1827 is the easiest to obtain. This edition, in three volumes, contains about twenty tunes; all have the word added to the notation, and the Chinese pronuncia-

---

96 See p. 240.
97 內傳
98 外傳
99 杉浦琴川, 正職
100 寶永
101 東皐琴譜
102 聖堂 For details about this Academy,

known as the *Shōheizaka gakumonjo* 昌平坂學問所, see my article 'Kakkaron, a Japanese echo of the Opium War', in: *Monumenta Serica*, IV (1939), no. 2.
103 林鳳岡
104 See p. 235 below.
105 高玄岱

Historical table of the tradition of the Chinese lute in Japan

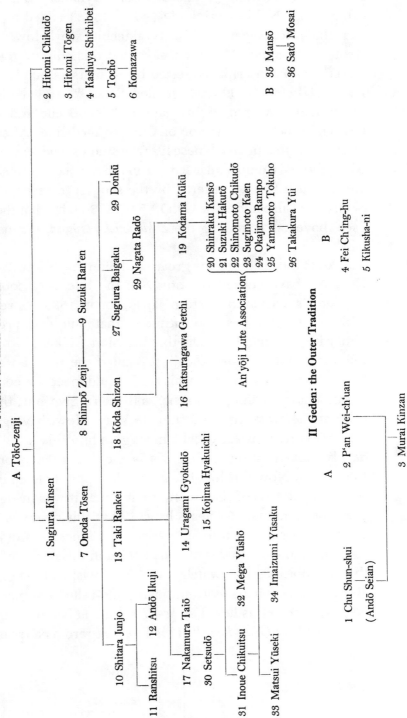

I Naiden: the Inner Tradition

A Tōkō-zenji

1 Sugiura Kinsen
7 Onoda Tōsen
8 Shimpō Zenji — 9 Suzuki Ran'en
2 Hitomi Chikudō
3 Hitomi Tōgen
4 Kashuya Shichibei
5 Tochō
6 Komazawa

13 Taki Rankei
18 Kōda Shizen
27 Sugiura Baigaku
29 Nagata Radō
29 Donkū

14 Uragami Gyokudō
15 Kojima Hyakuichi
16 Katsuragawa Getchi
19 Kodama Kūkū

An'yōji Lute Association
20 Shinraku Kansō
21 Suzuki Hakutō
22 Shinomoto Chikudō
23 Sugimoto Kaen
24 Okajima Rampo
25 Yamamoto Tokuho
26 Takakura Yūi

10 Shitara Junjo   12 Andō Ikuji
11 Ranshitsu
17 Nakamura Taiō
30 Setsudō
31 Inoue Chikuitsu   32 Mega Yūshō
33 Matsui Yūseki   34 Imaizumi Yūsaku

B
35 Mansō
36 Satō Mosai

II Geden: the Outer Tradition

A
1 Chu Shun-shui
(Andō Seian)
2 P'an Wei-ch'uan
3 Murai Kinzan

B
4 Fei Ch'ing-hu
5 Kikusha-ni

tion is indicated in the Japanese *katakana* syllabary. The famous calligrapher Nukina Kaioku[106] (1778–1863) added a preface, and the lute player Kojima Hyakuichi (see below no. 15) wrote a colophon. The latter says that this edition goes back directly to manuscripts collected by Shin'etsu's pupils.

2 *Hitomi Chikudō,*[107] 1628–96; named Setsu,[108] styled Gikei;[109] other name: Yūgen;[110] lit. names Chikudō and Kakuzan.[111] Originally he was a doctor of Chinese medicine. Afterwards he concentrated upon Chinese literary studies, and was appointed a *jukan,*[112] Confucianist scholar in the service of the shogunate. As such he was ordered by the shogun to assist Hayashi Shunsai[113] (also known as Gahō,[114] 1618–80), head of the Seidō (see above), in compiling the *Zoku honchō tsūgan,*[115] a historical work.

Chikudō is considered the greatest of Shin'etsu's lute disciples. He must have started the study of the lute very soon after Shin'etsu's arrival in Eastern Japan, for in 1685 his relations with the master were so intimate, that Shin'etsu presented him with a Ming lute. On this occasion Chikudō wrote the following note: 'Tōkō Zenji presented me with an antique lute, saying: "I wished to wait till I would meet someone with a true understanding of music, and then [give him this lute and] at the same time transmit its Way. Now, having met a man of elegant tastes, I feel I must give him this lute." I was deeply moved by these kind words and felt it was more than I deserved. Now this lute has inside the upper hole an inscription of some tens of characters, saying that it was made in the year 1564, that is, 121 years hence. That this object has lived through such a tumultuous period in Chinese history, and, escaping the vicissitudes of war, landed in this country, means that a propitious fate watched over it. I wished to engrave an elegant name on its bottom board, and asked the master for one. He named this lute *Yün-ho-t'ien-lai,* and below I engraved a seal reading *Hêng-hua.*[116] This lute I regard as a treasure of

---

106 貫名海屋
107 人見竹洞
108 節
109 宜卿
110 友元
111 鶴山
112 儒官

113 林春齋
114 鵞峰
115 續本朝通鑑
116 *Hêng-hua* 'Flower of the Hêng-fief'; apparently this lute was made by the Prince of Hêng, famous as a lute builder. See p. 215 above.

my house.'[117] In Chikudō's family the lute tradition was continued, his first pupil being his son, Hitomi Tōgen.

3 *Hitomi Tōgen*,[118] named Gin,[119] style Ronan.[120] He was taught
the lute by his father, and inherited from him Shin'etsu's lute
So-ō, and instruments for building lutes. He also was a Chinese
scholar, but little is known about his writings.

4 *Kashuya Shichibei*,[121] studied the lute under Hitomi Chikudō.
Little is known about him, except that he was a merchant of
Edo, a dealer in antiques, with a great interest in music. Some
sources say that he also studied the lute under Onoda Tōsen
(see below, no. 7).

5 *Tochō*,[122] styled Chōkō,[123] also Shishuku;[124] lit. names Shōka
Dōjin,[125] Goteki Sannin,[126] and Katei Dōjin.[127] Well-known
painter, poet and engraver of seals. During the Temmei period[128]
(1781–9) he published a book with imprints of seals carved by
him. He was a great lover of the Chinese lute, having been
taught by Kashuya, and also by Kodama Kūkū (see below, no.
19). There is preserved an interesting manuscript by his hand,
an essay written in Japanese and entitled *Kinden setsu*;[129] its
date is 1782.[130] Here he first gives an outline of *ch'in* ideology,
and then goes on to discuss the transmission of the lute in
Japan. He says that during a stay at Nagasaki, he was taught
the Chinese way of reading poetry by a Chinese there, Kung
Yün-jang,[131] lit. name Hsüan-chai.[132] Thus he could accompany
his playing on the lute with singing the Chinese poems. It is of
interest to note that he explains his lit. name *Goteki*,[133] 'The
Five Inclinations', as referring to his love for the lute, poetry,
calligraphy, painting, and cutting seals.[134]

6 A certain *Komazawa*.[135] Of him we know only that he was a

---

117 東皐禪師賜僕以一古琴，諭曰，欲待知
音者並傳其道，今欣遇雅尚，不得不己爲贈，僕
深感懇篤之言，且自愧之，其爲琴也，龍池之中
有數十字之題者，所謂嘉靖甲子製，及今百二
十一年也，經中朝亂離之際能免兵燹而到此，
可謂物之幸也，僕謂題佳名於琴腹，而請之師，
即題曰雲和天籟，而其下以衡華二字爲印，以
爲家寶．

118 人見桃源
119 沂
120 魯南
121 甲州屋七兵衞
122 杜澂
123 澂公
124 師叔

125 松窠道人
126 五適散人
127 華亭道人
128 天明
129 琴傳說
130 This essay was published by the
contemporary scholar Mimura Seisaburō 三村
清三郎 in the Japanese monthly *Shoen* 書苑,
vol. II, no. 1 (1938), under the title '*Goteki
Sensei kinden setsu*' 五適先生琴傳說.
131 龔允讓
132 遜齋
133 五適
134 琴詩書畫印
135 駒澤某

man from Susaka in Shinshu,[136] and that he studied the lute under Chikudō. Yet he must have played some role among players on the Chinese lute, for several sources mention his name.

7 *Onoda Tōsen*,[137] 1684–1763. Named Empō[138] (other sources give Teihin),[139] also Kunimitsu;[140] lit. name Tōsen. Chiefly famous as an expert on the Chinese lute. He studied the lute under Sugiura Kinsen, of whose family he was a hereditary follower. He is said to have had hundreds of pupils, who under his guidance made a study of the Chinese lute. Once the Tokugawa shogun Yoshimune[141] (1684–1751) summoned him to his court, and made him play for him the Chinese lute.

8 *Shimpō Zenji*,[142] no details known.

9 *Suzuki Ran'en*,[143] 1741–90; named Ryū;[144] style, Shiun.[145] Originally a doctor of Chinese medicine, a disciple of the famous doctor Asai Tonan[146] (1706–82). He was an eager student of Chinese literature, and made a special study of Chinese music. In 1816 there appeared at Osaka a book by him on musical theory, entitled *Ritsuryo bensetsu*.[147] He studied the Chinese lute under Shimpō Zenji (above, no. 8), and published in 1772 a small edition of the *Tōkō kimpu* in one volume. An advertisement on the last page of this book says that another study by him on the Chinese lute, entitled *Kingaku keimō*,[148] was also going to be published. I have, however, never come across printed editions of this book; but I obtained a finely calligraphed manuscript copy. Ran'en himself also built lutes. The *Kinzan kinroku* (see below, *geden*, no. 3) on leaf 8 mentions a lute called *Hsüan-hsiang*,[149] built by Ran'en after the model of the T'ang lute preserved in the Hōryūji. The inscription in the upper hole runs: 'Copy of a lute of the K'ai-yüan period [713–41], preserved in the Hōryūji in Yamato. Made by Minamoto (the original name of Ran'en) Ryū from Kyōto in the autumn of the year 1784.'[150]

---

136 須坂, 信州
137 小野田東川
138 延寶
139 廷賓
140 國光
141 吉宗
142 新豐禪師
143 鈴木蘭園

144 龍
145 子雲
146 淺井圖南
147 律呂辨說
148 琴學啓蒙
149 玄響
150 大和國法隆寺所藏開元琴之製天明四年甲辰之秋平安源龍造之

10 *Shitara Junjo*,[151] a man from Edo. With the four lute players described hereafter (nos. 13, 18, 27 and 29), he belonged to the most famous lute disciples of Onoda Tōsen. Unfortunately I could find no further details about him.

11 *Ranshitsu*,[152] the best-known lute pupil of Shitara Junjo. He was abbot of the Shinryūji,[153] a temple in Asakusa,[154] at Edo. In his later years he fell ill, and became blind; but this did not prevent him from continuing to teach the lute. This he only stopped when his end drew near and he lost the power of speech.

12 *Andō Ikuji*,[155] of whom nothing is known, except that Shitara Junjo considered him one of his best pupils.

13 *Taki Rankei*,[156] 1732–1801, named Motonori,[157] also Yasumoto,[158] styled Chūmei;[159] lit. name Rankei, also Eijuin.[160] Famous doctor of Chinese medicine, attached to the shogunate. Well known as a student of Chinese literature, and especially well read in old Chinese books on medicine. He studied the lute under Onoda Tōsen, and himself had many pupils who became well known as experts on the Chinese lute.

14 *Uragami Gyokudō*,[161] 1745–1820, style Kumpo,[162] lit. names Gyokudō and Bokusai.[163] A famous painter in the Chinese style from Kyoto. He was an enthusiastic performer on the Chinese lute, and was taught by a direct disciple of Taki Rankei. He published a handbook for the lute, entitled *Gyokudō zōsho kimpu*,[164] in one vol., published at Kyoto in 1791. This contains fifteen tunes, with the Japanese text of the melodies written out in *manyōgana*,[165] a more elaborae style of the Japanese syllabary *hiragana*. From these tunes it appears that Gyokudō made conscious efforts to give the Chinese lute a more Japanese character, for all of the tunes are purely Japanese; I cite titles such as *Aoyagi*,[166] *Sakurabito*,[167] *Ise-no-umi*,[168] *Umegae*,[169] etc. Some of these tunes are meant to be played by a duo of the Chinese lute and the Japanese *koto*.[170] After the prefaces this

151 設樂純如
152 蘭室
153 眞龍寺
154 淺草
155 安藤幾次
156 多紀藍溪
157 元德
158 安元
159 仲明
160 永壽院

161 浦上玉堂
162 君輔
163 穆齋
164 玉堂藏書琴譜
165 萬葉假名
166 青柳
167 櫻人
168 伊勢海
169 梅枝
170 與箏合奏

book gives some stray notes on the history of the Chinese lute in Japan; they are in dialogue form, and bear the title *Tōmon hassoku*.[171] On leaf 7 of this section Gyokudō explains why he tried to adapt the Chinese lute to Japanese music. He says: 'Master Rankei [see no. 13 above] studied the lute under Teihin [i.e. Onoda Tōsen, no. 7]. Visiting Edo on an official mission, I met Master Rankei and asked him to teach me the lute. Later, however, I thought to myself: the words of the tunes taught by him are all pronounced in the Chinese way, so that people who hear these songs cannot understand them. Not understanding them they are not influenced by them. Not influencing the hearers, this music cannot be used for teaching them.'[172] From an introductory note to this book, *Gyokudō kinki*,[173] it appears that the author obtained an old Chinese lute that was made by the Ming scholar Ku T'ien-su[174] in the Kambun[175] period (1661–73); this lute was brought to Nagasaki, where it came into the hands of the Chinese interpreter Liu I-hsien.[176] When Uragami finally obtained this instrument, which was called *Reiwa*[177] and further bore the seal Gyokudō-seiun,[178] he called his study after this lute, i.e. Gyokudō. Gyokudō was buried in the Honnōji[179] at Kyoto. When this temple burned down, his grave was replaced by a simple stone monument that is still to be seen today. On the two pillars the characters *reiwa* are engraved. Further, there still exists a stone tablet, erected in his honour on the place where he used to live, now the grounds of the Hōrinji,[180] in the outskirts of Kyoto. I visited this place in 1937, and made a rubbing of this inscription, written out by the famous Japanese scholar Rai San'yō (1780–1832).[181] The contemporary painter Hashimoto Kansetsu[182] published in 1924 a magnificent volume with reproductions of Gyokudō's paintings, entitled *Gyokudō kinshi iboku shū*.[183] It opens with a painting by Gyokudō's son, which represents the master with his beloved lute on his knees. To this book there is added a treatise called *Uragami Gyokudō*

171　答問八則
172　藍溪先生者，學琴於廷賓，余往祇役東
都時見先生，請彈法，退而竊謂，其歌曲華音，
而人聞之不解，不解則不感，不感則不足爲教.
173　玉堂琴記
174　顧天宿, style: Yüan-chao 元昭.
175　寬文
176　劉益賢

177　靈和
178　玉堂清韵
179　本能寺
180　法輪寺
181　賴山陽
182　橋本關雪
183　玉堂琴士遺墨集

jikō,[184] where one will find full details about his life and his lute.

Cf. also the publication *Uragami Gyokudō*, by Yano Kyōson,[185] one vol., Tokyo 1926. Among the illustrations there occurs a photograph of a lute made by Gyokudō himself in 1786, in imitation of a Chinese lute of the T'ang dynasty made by a member of the Lei[186] family, famous as lute builders. The brocade cover of this lute bears a lengthy inscription written by the well-known Japanese painter and sinologue Tomioka Tessai (1836–1924).[187]

15 *Kojima Hyakuichi*,[188] 1778–1835; named Ki;[189] lit. names, Hōrin[190] and Teiseki.[191] He is the best known of Uragami Gyokudō's pupils of the Chinese lute. He is described as a man of elegant tastes, learned in Chinese literature and a great calligrapher. His colophon to the *Tōkō kimpu*[192] is written in excellent *li-shu*, the so-called chancery script.

16 *Katsuragawa Getchi*,[193] 1751–1809; named Hoshū.[194] A doctor of Chinese medicine, physician to the shogunate. Getchi was a *rangakusha*,[195] a student cf Dutch learning, and one of the great pioneers of the introduction of Western medical science into Japan. As a lute player he belonged to the school of the other famous doctor, Taki Rankei.

17 *Nakamura Taiō*,[196] named Teiko,[197] style Shiken.[198] He also belonged to the lute school of Taki Rankei, and seemed to have enjoyed considerable fame as a lute expert. Unfortunately little is known about him.

18 *Kōda Shisen*,[199] died 1758; named Chikamitsu.[200] A famous mathematician in the service of the shogunate. He studied mathematics under the famous Nakane Hakuzan[201] (1662–1733), and was an excellent performer both on the Chinese lute, which he learned from Onoda Tōsen, and on the Japanese *koto*. He is said to have published a book on the Chinese lute in 8 chapters, containing 48 tunes; this, however, I have never been able to discover. In his family there were preserved all

184 浦上玉堂事考
185 矢野橋村
186 雷
187 富岡鐵齋
188 兒島百一
189 祺
190 鳳林
191 貞石
192 See p. 232 above.
193 桂川月池
194 甫周
195 蘭學者
196 中村太翁
197 貞固
198 子軒
199 幸田子泉
200 親盈
201 中根白山

the instruments for building lutes and for making the silk lute strings, copied after originals that had belonged to Shin'etsu.

19 *Kodama Kūkū*,[202] 1734–1811; named Shin,[203] style Mokuho.[204] (Not to be confused with the Chinese scholar Kodama Kizan,[205] who was also called Shin, but whose dates are 1801–35). A scholar known for his refined tastes, he published many books between 1750–70. He studied the Chinese lute under Kōda Shisen. He lived in Ushigome-ku,[206] a quarter in Edo. There he organized in a temple called An'yōji,[207] in Teramachi,[208] regular meetings of Japanese lovers of the lute. These meetings were attended by a great number of people, over a hundred in all. Most famous among these was Shinraku Kansō (see below, no. 20), who drew up a document regulating these meetings. Later Kūkū changed his family name from Kodama to Shukutani.[209] Kūkū also diligently studied Chinese *ch'in-pu*. I possess a manuscript, copied after the original manuscript by Kodama, which contains extracts from the *Ch'in-ching*,[210] by Chang Ta-ming.[211] In Kodama's preface he says that he compiled this manuscript because he found many discrepancies in the explanations of the finger technique in various Chinese *ch'in-pu*.

20 *Shinraku Kansō*,[212] called Tei,[213] style Shiko,[214] lit. name Aikendō.[215] Originally he was a samurai in the service of the *bakufu*, but later turned to literary and musical studies. He learned the lute from Kodama Kūkū, and seems to have been one of the prominent persons in the lute meetings at the An'yōji. It was he who drew up the rules for these meetings. This document is reproduced in the *Shichigenkin no denrai* by Nakane Kōtei (see p. 231); I translate it below, as it gives a good impression of the atmosphere surrounding the Chinese lute in Japan.

'In former days Ssû-ma Kuang[216] [the great Sung scholar, 1019–86] and his friends organized the *Chên-shuo-hui*,[217]

---

202 兒玉空空
203 愼
204 默甫
205 兒玉旗山
206 牛籠區; nowadays written 牛込.
207 安養寺
208 寺町
209 宿谷
210 See p. 179, n. 41.
211 *Ibid.*, n. 42.

212 新樂間叟
213 定
114 士固
215 愛閑堂
216 司馬光
217 *Chên-shuo-hui*, originally the name of an official banquet during the Eastern Chin period. Ssû-ma Kuang thus referred to his literary gatherings, where elegant taste was preferred to lavish entertainment.

"True Simplicity Gathering": those attending were served only a couple of times coarse rice and unstrained wine. From this may be gathered the mental attitude of the former sages: although they were honoured and wealthy, they were frugal and restrained themselves; they did not indulge in common habits and prodigality. Now we have concluded a pact among ourselves, following this example. We are poor, and we cannot afford luxury, and by nature we are averse to affectation and pomposity. So by necessity we conform ourselves to the spirit of true simplicity. Accordingly we have drawn up the following articles:

A *Members*: These are the regular members of our community. But also casual members are welcome, provided they are not vulgar. However, those who presume upon their dignity and boast of their wealth and those without learning shall not be admitted.

B *Time*: Every month there shall be one or two meetings, but only on holidays. Wind or rain shall make no difference. We shall gather between 9 and 11 in the forenoon, and separate between 5 and 7 in the afternoon; the meetings shall not be protracted into the night. Those who are late or fail to attend shall not be punished.

C *Place*: The An'yō temple in Ushigome. If necessary this place may be changed, but only for a Buddhist temple or a country retreat, far from the noise of the multitude.

D *Implements*: Tea and cakes, two lutes and two lute tables. If on a certain day there is present someone with much money, wine, fruit and some light dishes shall be allowed in addition.

E *Business*: Besides playing the lute: compose poetry and read books, write characters or paint, sing songs or play on other stringed instruments and flutes, according to each member's individual taste. But when many people meet, the conversation is liable to become noisy. When the talk is about the Chinese Classics, or when literary compositions are discussed, this of course is always elegant. Also it will be allowed to talk about abstruse things, and to criticize vulgar customs. However, talk about official matters and on commercial affairs, shall be strictly prohibited.

When this pact had been drawn up, I reported it to the master, and the master approved of it. But we consisted only of guests, and there was no host; thus, although we aspire at great simplicity, yet there must be someone who sees to the tea and cakes. A member said: "What about each time two members serving in turn?" The master said this was all right. Then I drew up the following list[218] of members regularly attending our meetings.

Drawn up by Shinraku Tei, in 1789.'[219]

This pact is evidently made after the model of Chinese 'Covenants for the Spiritual Community of the Lute' (see p. 69).

The meetings in the An'yōji lasted for about twenty years. About 1825 most of its members had died or were dispersed, and only a few remained.[220]

It was also Shinraku Kansō who, in 1813, wrote the *Kingaku denju ryakkei*, mentioned on p. 231).

He traveled about widely in Japan in search for old lutes, and he saw the relics of Shin'etsu in the Gion temple at Mito. In 1797 he visited the old Chinese school, the Ashikaga Gakkō,[221] and there copied out a manuscript on the lute by Hitomi Chikudō. Later he traveled to Hokkaidō, the extreme north of Japan. At Hakodate he obtained an old beam from a government building; from this he made the upper board of a lute. Then, at Matsumae,[222] he obtained a beam of wood called in the Matsumae dialect *ramani*,[223] said to mean *onkoto*,[224] 'honourable lute'. Using this wood for the

---

218 Nakane Kōtei, when he copied out this pact, unfortunately left out the list, which must have contained valuable materials for our knowledge of the Japanese lute players of that time.

219 琴會約

昔日司馬溫公輩爲眞率會，脫粟飯濁酒數行而已，可見先賢用心，雖在貴富節儉自守，不趨習俗奢侈也，今同社相約，倣而行之，蓋我輩貧而不能豐盛，又性質不能矯飾也，然則出于不得已而暗合眞率意者也，仍設條例如左.

一會之人，同社人也，若不速客不甚俗者弗妨，但挾貴誇富不解字等人俱不許.

一會之期，一月一擧或二擧，惟以暇日，風雨不更期，已集酉散，不卜其夜，失期者不到者並不罰.

一會之地，牛門外安養精舍也，若有故則換之必以佛院若別業，蓋避人家雜沓也.

一會之具，一茶一菓，琴二張几二坐，若當日頗有力者別供酒核點心等不復妨.

一會之事，彈琴之餘，賦詩誦書，作字描畫，或唱詞曲弄絲竹，從各所好，但衆人相會，語言易譁，或談經史論文章，固自佳，說鬼毀俗，又無不可，特不許說雲路談市井耳.

約成以告先生，先生曰善，而帷有賓無主，雖眞率誰能辨茶菓，同者曰，每會二人輪次以執其事，可乎，先生曰善，於是擧常會者名. 別列左.

己酉花期　　新樂定誌

220 See the charming essay by Sugimoto Kaen, translated below on pp. 243–4.

221 足利學校

222 松前

223 蘭馬尼

224 御琴

bottom board, he built a lute, which he took with him to the island Etoro.[225] That was in 1807, just when the Russian commander Khvostov made raids on Sakhalin, Naiho and Shana;[226] in the general confusion this lute got lost. In 1811, however, Shinraku again found it in the house of a Japanese gentleman in West Japan; a Japanese ship that was in the north during the Russian raids had brought the instrument back! On this occasion Shinraku wrote an enthusiastic note, stressing that the instrument of the Holy Sages is protected by Heaven against barbarian invasions and the vicissitudes of the ocean.[227]

21 *Suzuki Hakutō*,[228] another prominent member of the lute association of the An'yō temple.

22 *Shinomoto Chikudō*,[229] also a pupil of Kodama Kūkū. His name was Ren,[230] his style Shion.[231] He was known as a sinologue, and flourished in the beginning of the Meiwa period[232] (1764–72). Shinomoto was no mean Chinese stylist: Prof. Nakayama's manuscript album[233] contains an essay by him, entitled *Hanshu yayūki*,[234] which is written in excellent Chinese.

23 *Sugimoto Kaen*,[235] named Chūon,[236] style Ryōzai,[237] a physician attached to the shogunate. He was a prominent figure in the lute association of the An'yōji. In 1828 he wrote a preface to a manuscript lute handbook compiled by Yamamoto Tokuho. There he refers to the meetings in the An'yōji, which by then had well nigh come to naught. As this preface gives a good insight into the spirit in which those meetings of lute lovers were held, I translate it below.

'In my younger years I studied the lute under Kodama Kūkū and the priest Ranshitsu.[238] Among the pupils of Kodama there

225 擇捉島
226 See Sakamaki, 'Japan and the United States, 1790–1853', in: *Transactions of the Asiatic Society of Japan*, XVII (1939), page 178.
227 In 1949 I purchased in Tokyo a Japanese manuscript entitled *Kanso kinwa* 間叟琴話, which gives detailed information on the study of the Chinese lute in Japan in the later part of the Tokugawa period. In my Chinese publication *Tung-kao-chan-shih-chi-k'an* (東皐禪師集刊, The Commercial Press, Ltd., Chungking 1944, page 119) I gave a more elaborate version of the 'Historical Table of the Tradition of the Chinese Lute in Japan' above, (facing page 212);

when I have had time to work out the data contained in the *Kanso kinwa* I hope to publish a new historical table, incorporating this additional material.
228 鈴木白藤
229 篠本竹堂
230 廉
231 子溫
232 明和
233 See above, pp. 231–2.
234 泛舟夜遊記
235 杉本樗園
236 忠溫
237 良齋
238 See no. 11 above.

were Shinomoto Chikudō,[239] Shinraku Kansō,[240] Okajima Rampo,[241] and Yamamoto Tokuho,[242] all members of our lute association. But Tokuho since his youth was most keen, and excelled all others in playing the lute. Tokuho is named Rin, his literary name is Kakoku; he is a man from Ushigome, in Musashi [i.e. Edo].

Now I am a physician, I have to run hither and thither, and I cannot follow my inclinations. Tokuho however has clearly written out the transmitted lute tunes, and having made them into a handbook, asked me to add a few words by way of a preface.

The lute stands for the music bequeathed by high antiquity. One must have hills and mountains in one's breast, and one's belly must be full of ink [i.e. one must be a cultured literatus], before one may touch the lute. For its elegant tones cannot enter the ears of a vulgar person. Now Tokuho's work is violent, his occupation is vulgar in the extreme, he being a so-called unmounted police officer.[243] In the presence of others his conversation is tasteless, and his features are unattractive. But when Tokuho has one moment of spare time, he reads books and plays the lute, happily giving himself over to this music. He would not exchange his lot for that of the greatest men in the realm. How could it be otherwise? His refined disposition and his aloofness from earthly things can be judged hereby.

Now I for one am old and stupid; thirty years I have toiled in official life. Going back in my thoughts to past times, I realize that the trees on the graves of Kūkū and Ranshitsu have grown, while all the members of our lute association, one after the other, have passed away. Only I and Tokuho are still hale and hearty. Alas, human life is transitory, like a dream or like an illusion. Union and separation follow no fixed rules, sadness and mirth alternate with each other. Therefore I am glad that I and Tokuho are still in full health. This by way of a preface.

Written by Sugimoto Ryō, called Chūon, in the autumn of 1828.'[244]

---

239 See no. 22.
240 See no. 20.
241 See no. 24.
242 See no. 25.
243 徒監察 *kachi-yoriki*. The *yoriki* were police officers in the service of the *bakufu*. Constantly mixed up in brawls of unruly

samurai, and implacable persecutors of all partisans of the opposition to the Tokugawa government, they formed a much feared but greatly despised class.

244 余少時學琴兒玉空空及釋蘭室，其從空空學也，篠本竹堂，新樂閑叟，岡島蘭甫，山本德甫，皆同社，而德甫少年銳往最善鼓云，德甫*

24 *Okajima Rampo,*[245] another prominent member of the An'yōji lute association.

25 *Yamamoto Tokuho,*[246] one of the leaders of the An'yōji gatherings. The character of this police officer with elegant tastes has already been described. The manuscript albums of Prof. Nakayama give many examples of his literary activities. I quote one of his poems:

ALONE ON A DAY IN WINTER

'My humble door is securely fastened, seldom visitors come near it. I tend the dwarf plum tree that keeps me company in the twilight; the wind shakes its fragrant petals, and scatters them over the stone table.

And I see with astonishment that the blossoms form brilliant studs on my lute.'[247]

26 *Takakura Yūi,*[248] a pupil of Yamamoto Tokuho, who collected the tunes taught by him.

27 *Sugiura Baigaku,*[249] 1734–92; named Kai,[250] style Shiyō;[251] lit. names Baigaku and Gengai.[252] A man of scholarly interests from West Japan. Having come to Edo, he learnt the lute from Onoda Tōsen.[253] After he returned to West Japan, he there continued the tradition of the lute.

28 *Nagata Radō,*[254] named Ikei,[255] style Shiran.[256] Originally a merchant, he later devoted himself entirely to the study of the Chinese lute. He traveled extensively in Japan, everywhere searching for old lutes, and teaching the art of playing it to a great number of scholars and noblemen. He started his studies of the lute under Sugiura Baigaku, and continued them until his death, at the venerable age of 70.

名鄰，號蝸殼，武州牛門人也，既而余爲刀圭，
東西奔走，不能遂其好也，一日德甫，淨寫所傳
琴曲，以爲譜，乞余言，夫琴者太古遺音也，其
人胷有丘嶽，腹貯墨汁，然後始可彈，何者，雅
音不入俗耳也，德甫之職劇矣，其爲務也俗極
矣，所謂徒監察者也，在他人，言語無味，面目
可憎，而德甫乃得片時半日之閑，讀書彈琴，陶
陶乎樂，即南面百城，不能以代焉，此豈無得而
然乎哉，其胸襟之洒落不汙塵土，亦以是可知
耳，余也暮鈍，勞々宦海三十年矣，追思往事空
空蘭室墓木已拱，同社諸子亦相繼而下世矣，
獨余與德甫安健耳，嗚呼，人生茫々，如夢如
幻，聚散無常，悲觀頓異，而喜余之與德甫無恙
也，於是乎言.
文政戊子仲秋杉本良忠溫撰

245 岡島蘭甫
246 山本德甫
247 冬日獨坐
柴門深鎖屐踪稀，培養盆梅伴落暉，
風散香葩零石案，訝看琴面點清微.
248 高倉雄偉
249 杉浦梅岳
250 恢
251 土容
252 元愷
253 See no. 7.
254 永田蘿堂
255 維馨
256 子蘭

29 *Donkū*,[257] abbot of the Shōrinji,[258] in Fukagawa,[259] at Edo. Another pupil of Onoda Tōsen.

30 *Setsudō*,[260] 1783–1852; named Chizan,[261] lit. name Chōkai.[262] Chief priest of the Gansenji,[263] a temple in Dewa,[264] north of Tokyo. He started his studies of the Chinese lute in Nagasaki, and afterwards was taught by Radō[265] and by Nakamura Taiō.[266] Round 1828 he settled down in Osaka, and assembled many pupils, teaching them the Chinese lute and calligraphy.

31 *Inoue Chikuitsu*,[267] 1814–86; called Genzō,[268] foremost pupil of Setsudō. He must have been a musician of importance, for he is mentioned in many sources. Unfortunately I could discover no further details about him.

32 *Mega Yūshō*,[269] 1826–96; lit. names Teizai[270] and San'yū-zōro.[271] A doctor of Chinese medicine, born at Osaka in a wealthy family, in which many old Chinese books and manuscripts had been preserved. He himself being a voracious reader, he greatly augmented this collection, which he left to the Sumiyoshi Shrine at Osaka (later this shrine presented the books to the Osaka Library). He studied the Chinese lute under Setsudō, and collected seven antique lutes. He is further known as a painter and poet.

33 *Matsui Yūseki*,[272] named Ren.[273] A distinguished lute player of Edo, pupil of Inoue Chikuitsu. He possessed a dress of a Ming official, and used to play the lute clad in this garb.

34 *Imaizumi Yūsaku*,[274] 1848–1931; lit. name Mugai.[275] The last great Japanese performer on the Chinese lute, a well-known scholar and connoisseur. In 1877 he went to France, and worked in Paris under the great art-historian Guimet, in the Museum for Far Eastern Arts. After a stay of six years, he returned to Japan, and was employed in the Ministry of Education at Tokyo. He occupied various posts in the Japanese museum world, e.g. Director of the Fine Arts Department of the Im-

257 曇空
258 象林寺
259 深川
260 雪堂, Real name: Tōzaka Bun'yō
261 痴山
262 鳥海
263 願專寺
264 出羽
265 See no. 28 above.
266 See no. 17 above.

267 井上竹逸
268 玄藏
269 妻鹿友樵
270 貞齋
271 三友草廬
272 松井友石
273 廉
274 今泉雄作
275 無礙

perial Museum at Tokyo, thereafter Director of the Ookura Museum(Ookura-shūko-kan).[276] He learned the lute from Inoue Chikuitsu, and eagerly collected materials for the history of the Chinese lute in Japan. I have several manuscripts about the Chinese lute by him in my collection, and most of the books and manuscripts in Prof. Nakayama's collection bear his seal.

35 *Mansō*,[277] other name Chikuan,[278] a Chinese priest who played the lute; no further details known.

36 *Satō Mosai*,[279] named Itchō,[280] a sinologue who learned the lute from the priest Mansō. No source gives his name, but there is preserved a book on the Chinese lute published by him, the *Kokin seigi*.[281] To this book Mansō added a preface, which is printed in facsimile. This book gives a survey of the study of the lute, illustrated with finely executed pictures. The greater part of these pictures are copied after those in the *Yang-ch'un-t'ang-ch'in-pu*.[282]

GEDEN, THE OUTER TRADITION

1 *Chu Shun-shui*,[283] Jap. Shu-shunsui, 1600–82; name Tzû-yü,[284] style Lu-hsü,[285] lit. name Shun-shui. Famous Chinese refugee at the Court of Mito; he died just before Shin'etsu arrived there.[286] When he came to Japan, he brought some Chinese lutes with him. He himself apparently was not a lute player, but, as all Chinese scholars (and especially those of the Ming period), he had made a study of the lute, and knew how it was played. Chu Shun-shui gave one of his lutes, a Ming specimen made by the Prince of I,[287] to his Japanese pupil Andō Seian[288] (1620–

276 大倉集古館
277 萬宗
278 竺菴
279 佐藤茂齋
280 一張
281 古琴精義, in 2 vols., published in Kyoto.
282 See above, p. 121.
283 朱舜水
284 之瑜
285 魯嶼
286 For Chu Shun-shui, see E.W. Clement, 'Chinese Refugees of the Seventeenth Century in Mito', in: *Transactions of the Asiatic Society of Japan*, XXIII. His complete works, under the title of *Shu-shunsui sensei bunshū* 朱舜水先生文集 were published between 1711–15, at Edo, by the Mito clan. This

beautiful block print, in 28 chs. and 1 appendix, now is scarce. Further, there has been preserved a manuscript in 10 chs., entitled *Min-shuchōkun-shū* 明朱徵君集, compiled on the command of the Lord of Kaga 加賀. 1912, Inaba Iwakichi 稻葉岩吉, on the basis of these two collections, published the *Shu-shunsui zenshū* 朱舜水全集 in one stout volume. This is the most complete collection of materials regarding this interesting personality. In 1913 the Chinese scholar T'ang Shou-ch'ien 湯壽潛 published a Chinese edition of Chu Shun-shui's works, under the title of *Shun-shui-i-shu* 舜水遺書; this book is based upon Inaba's edition.
287 I-wang 益王; see picture of this lute, fig. 33.
288 安東省庵, 1620–1701.

1701), and he also presented him with some Chinese handbooks.
These materials were preserved in Andō's family, and later they
were studied by Murai Kinzan (see below).

2 *P'an Wei-ch'uan*,[289] a Chinese scholar who passed through
   Nagasaki, and taught the lute to Murai Kinzan.

3 *Murai Kinzan*,[290] 1733–1815; named Shun,[291] style Tanen;[292]
   lit. names Rokusei Dōjin[293] and Seifuku Dōjin.[294] A doctor
   attached to the shogunate, notorious for his ugly face. He was a
   great Chinese scholar, and an eager book-collector. Author of
   numerous books on medical subjects. Full materials about his
   activities as a student of the Chinese lute are to be found in his
   book *Kinzan kinroku*,[295] in one vol., published in 1806 by the
   Kenkakuzam-bō.[296] This nicely edited book opens with an
   autograph preface by the well-known Japanese scholar of Korean
   descent, Rijun,[297] Japanese name Takamoto[298] (1738–1813).
   Then follows a section called *Kindenki*,[299] where the author
   relates how he studied the Chinese lute. He was not satisfied
   with the tradition established by Shin'etsu, whom, being a priest,
   Kinzan deemed unworthy to touch the lute. In 1785 in Nagasaki
   he met the Chinese scholar P'an Wei-ch'uan, and from him
   learned the lute. Therefore Kinzan considers himself the only
   Japanese who possesses the real Chinese lute tradition. Then
   the author goes on to relate in great detail the history of the
   six Chinese lutes in his collection; they were called *Hsü-
   wei*,[300] *Chiao-hsüeh*,[301] *Lan-ssû*,[302] *Hsüan-hsiang*,[303] *Ku-yen*[304] and
   Hsiao-ssû.[305] He says that later he continued his studies of the
   Chinese lute on the basis of the materials of Chu Shun-shui,
   preserved in the family of Andō Seian. In addition, the book
   contains a number of lute melodies in notation. It closes with
   a colophon by the author, and an autograph colophon by the
   doctor of Chinese medicine, Ooki Kojō[306] (1741–1811).

4 *Fei Ch'ing-hu*,[307] a Chinese at Nagasaki.

289 潘渭川
290 村井琴山
291 杺
292 大年
293 六清道人
294 清福道人
295 琴山琴錄
296 劍閣山房
297 李順
298 高本
299 琴傳記
300 續尾
201 蕉雪
302 蘭思
303 玄響
304 古雁
305 孝思
306 大城壹城
307 費晴湖

5 *Kikusha-ni*,[308] the Nun Kikusha, 1753–1826; lay name Tagami
Michi.[309] Her husband having died young, she became a nun
and devoted her whole life to writing poetry and practising the
tea ceremony. She left a collection of Japanese and Chinese
poetry, entitled *Taori-giku*,[310] to be found in the *Keishū haika
zenshū*,[311] pub. in 1922 by Katsumine Shimpū.[312] This nun was
famous as a musician, and played the Chinese lute. It is not clear
where she first learned to play this instrument. But during a
stay at Nagasaki, in 1796, she was taught by the Chinese Fei
Ch'ing-hu, who also taught her how to read Chinese poetry
in the Chinese way. The *Taori-giku* contains a poem presented
to her by Fei Ch'ing-hu, together with a note in which
Fei Ch'ing-hu praises her talents (*Keishū haika zenshū*, page
360).

308 菊舎(車)尼
309 田上ミチ
310 手折菊

311 閨秀俳家全集
312 勝峰晋風

INDEX

ABOUT THE AUTHOR

ROBERT HANS VAN GULIK (1910–1967), demonstrated an early gift for languages, achieving fluency in Malay during elementary studies at the Dutch school in Java, where his father was posted in the colonial administration. By the time of his completion of a doctorate at the University of Utrecht, he had added Chinese, Japanese, Tibetan and Sanskrit, in addition to another half dozen Western languages, to his linguistic repertoire. His exceptional language skills served as a foundation for one of the most unconventional, and accomplished, careers in Asian scholarship in the twentieth century.

Dr van Gulik was a man of insatiable intellectual energy and curiosity. Personally an accomplished calligrapher, poet and musician, his academic interests were focussed on a wide range of esoteric, and previously neglected, topics of Sinology. His scholarly writings included monographs on Tang jurisprudence, Chinese classical music, Chinese connoisseurship, Daoist magic, Sanskrit studies in China and ancient Chinese sexual mores, among other subjects.

Van Gulik's accomplishments in these diverse areas of Sinology were all the more impressive considering that they were achieved while he pursued an active diplomatic career—holding posts up to ambassadorial level in China, Japan, Korea, India and Malaya among other locations—and simultaneously became a successful popular novelist. His 16 mystery novels, featuring the semi-historical figure Judge Dee Goong An, were eventually published in several Western and Asian languages, and remain popular reading to the present day.

OTHER TITLES BY AND ABOUT
ROBERT VAN GULIK
PUBLISHED BY ORCHID PRESS

Hayagriva: Horse-Cult in Asia; 2005. viii, 104 pp., 1 colour and 9 b&w plates, 3 line drawings, 245 x 175, hb. ISBN 9789745240742.

Mi Fu on Ink-Stones; 2006. xii, 71 pp., The original Chinese text of Mi Fu's Yen Shih is also reproduced, alongside the English translation. 2 colour, 11 b&w illustrations, map, index, 245 x 175, hb. ISBN 9789745240834.

Scrapbook for Chinese Collectors; 2006. 100 pp. incl. 84 pp. translation and notes and 16 pp. reproducing the original Chinese text; 3 b&w illustrations, 215 x 152, pb. ISBN 9789745240810.

Crime and Punishment in Ancient China: Tang-Yin-Pi-Shih; 2007. 212 pp., 4 b&w woodcuts, index, 245 x 175, hb. ISBN 9789745240919.

The Three Lives of Robert van Gulik: Diplomat, Author, Scholar. First English translation of the definitive biography by C. D. Barkman and H. de Vries-van der Hoeven. 324 pp., 42 b&w illustrations, bibliography, index. ISBN 9789745241329.

9 789745 242364

Whose Country Music?

In a period in which racism and gender inequity are at the fore of public, political, and scholarly discourse, this collection challenges systems of gatekeeping that have dictated who gets to participate in twenty-first-century country music culture. Building on established scholarship, this book examines contemporary issues in country music through feminist, intersectional, and postcolonialist theories, as well as other intertextual and cultural lenses. The authors pose questions about diversity, representation, and identity as they relate to larger concepts of artist and fan communities, stylistic considerations of the genre, and modes of production from a twenty-first-century perspective. Addressing and challenging the received narrative about country music culture, this collection delves into the gaps that are inherent in existing approaches that privileged biography and historiography, and expands new areas of inquiry relating to contemporary country music identity and culture.

PAULA J. BISHOP teaches in the Music Department at Bridgewater State University. She earned her PhD from Boston University with a dissertation on the Everly Brothers and has presented and published on the Everly Brothers, the Nashville songwriters Felice and Boudleaux Bryant, and feminism and country music.

JADA WATSON is an Assistant Professor of Digital Humanities in the School of Information Studies at the University of Ottawa. Principal Investigator of SongData, her research uses market data to address representation in country music. This work was cited in a brief submitted to the US Federal Communications Commission opposing radio deregulation, and the Recording Academy's Report on Inclusion and Diversity.

Whose Country Music?

Genre, Identity, and Belonging in Twenty-First-Century Country Music Culture

——

Edited by PAULA J. BISHOP
Bridgewater State University

JADA WATSON
University of Ottawa

CAMBRIDGE
UNIVERSITY PRESS

Shaftesbury Road, Cambridge CB2 8EA, United Kingdom

One Liberty Plaza, 20th Floor, New York, NY 10006, USA

477 Williamstown Road, Port Melbourne, VIC 3207, Australia

314–321, 3rd Floor, Plot 3, Splendor Forum, Jasola District Centre, New Delhi – 110025, India

103 Penang Road, #05–06/07, Visioncrest Commercial, Singapore 238467

Cambridge University Press is part of Cambridge University Press & Assessment, a department of the University of Cambridge.

We share the University's mission to contribute to society through the pursuit of education, learning and research at the highest international levels of excellence.

www.cambridge.org
Information on this title: www.cambridge.org/9781108837125

DOI: 10.1017/9781108937443

First published 2023

A catalogue record for this publication is available from the British Library.

Library of Congress Cataloging-in-Publication Data
NAMES: Bishop, Paula J., editor. | Watson, Jada, editor.
TITLE: Whose country music? : genre, identity, and belonging in twenty-first-century country music culture / edited by Paula J. Bishop, Jada Watson.
DESCRIPTION: [First edition.] | Cambridge, United Kingdom ; New York : Cambridge University Press, 2022. | Includes bibliographical references and index.
IDENTIFIERS: LCCN 2022025705 (print) | LCCN 2022025706 (ebook) | ISBN 9781108837125 (hardback) | ISBN 9781108927680 (paperback) | ISBN 9781108937443 (epub)
SUBJECTS: LCSH: Country music–History and criticism. | Country music–Social aspects.
CLASSIFICATION: LCC ML3524 .W46 2022 (print) | LCC ML3524 (ebook) | DDC 781.642--dc23/eng/20220531
LC record available at https://lccn.loc.gov/2022025705
LC ebook record available at https://lccn.loc.gov/2022025706

ISBN 978-1-108-83712-5 Hardback

Contents

Figures

Tables

Contributors

JANET ASPLEY read history at Sidney Sussex College, Cambridge, then studied fashion and textiles at De Montfort University. In the mid-1980s, she developed a passion for country music and, as a long-time contributor to *Country Music People* magazine, has carried out countless interviews and written even more reviews. Returning to study, she graduated in 2011 from the University of Brighton with an MA in history of design and material culture. Her doctoral thesis, "Hillbilly Deluxe: Male Performance Dress and Authenticity 1947–1992," brings together her interests in clothes and country music. Alongside her academic work, she runs a business, Dandy & Rose, making bespoke western shirts.

PAULA J. BISHOP is on the faculty in the Music Department at Bridgewater State University in Massachusetts, where she teaches a variety of courses on American vernacular music, as well as piano, music theory, and aural skills. She earned her PhD from Boston University with a dissertation on the Everly Brothers. She has presented and published on the Everly Brothers, duet practices, country music, Hawaiian music, and other aspects of American vernacular music. Her current research focuses on the country music songwriting couple, Felice and Boudleaux Bryant.

LEIGH H. EDWARDS is Professor of English at Florida State University and author of *Dolly Parton, Gender, and Country Music* (Indiana University Press, 2018, Foreword Book of the Year Award), *Johnny Cash and the Paradox of American Identity* (Indiana University Press, 2009), and *The Triumph of Reality TV: The Revolution in American Television* (Praeger, 2013). She researches intersections of gender and race in popular music, television, and new media. Her work appears in *Feminist Media Studies*, *The Journal of Popular Culture*, *Journal of Popular Television*, *Film & History*, *Narrative*, *FLOW*, *Journal of Popular Music Studies*, *Global Media Journal*, *Journal of American Studies*, and *Southern Cultures*. She is on the Institute for Bob Dylan Studies advisory board and the editorial boards of *Journal of Popular Television*, *The Popular Culture Studies Journal*, and *Pop Culture Universe*.

SOPHIA ENRIQUEZ (she/her) is Assistant Professor of Music at Duke University, where she also teaches in the program for Latinx Studies in the Global South. Her work investigates Latinx music, migration, and belonging in the Appalachian region of the United States. Other interests include the Mexican American heritage of Mississippi, the intersection of music and agriculture, and public ethnomusicology. She earned her PhD in ethnomusicology at Ohio State University as well as graduate certificates in folklore and women's, gender, and sexuality studies, and is an active performer of Appalachian and Mexican folk music.

NADINE HUBBS is the author of many essays and two award-winning books, *The Queer Composition of America's Sound* (University of California Press, 2004) and *Rednecks, Queers, and Country Music* (University of California Press, 2014). She coedited with Francesca Royster an award-winning JPMS special issue, *Uncharted Country: New Voices and Perspectives in Country Music Studies* (2020), and is currently writing *Country Mexicans: Sounding Mexican American Life, Love, and Belonging in Country Music*. Her publicly engaged scholarship has appeared with *The Guardian, Los Angeles Times, New York Times*, BBC, NPR, and other outlets. Hubbs is Professor of Women's and Gender Studies and Music, Faculty Affiliate in American Culture, and Director of the Lesbian-Gay-Queer Research Initiative at the University of Michigan.

PHOEBE E. HUGHES holds a PhD in musicology from Ohio State University. Her research interests include gender, sexuality, identity, and genre in country and other popular musics. Her dissertation project investigated race, gender, and genre in country music, focusing specifically on female crossover artists from the 1960s to the present day. Hughes also holds degrees in music and history from Northern Arizona University and an MA in musicology from West Virginia University.

REBEKAH HUTTEN is a PhD candidate in musicology and feminist studies at McGill University and editor for Reed & Quill and *MUSICultures*. Her research explores genre and gender in popular music communities, focusing on women's musical labor in the Annapolis Valley, Nova Scotia. You can find her writing in *Beyoncé in the World: Making Meaning with Queen Bey in Troubled Times* (Wesleyan University Press, 2021) and the *Society for American Music: The Bulletin*. She holds an MA in musicology from the University of Ottawa and bachelor's degrees from Acadia University.

KRISTINA JACOBSEN lives, works, and teaches in the bordertown of Albuquerque, New Mexico, which sits on unceded Sandia Pueblo and

Navajo Nation land. She is a cultural anthropologist, ethnographer, and Associate Professor of Music and Anthropology (Ethnology) at the University of New Mexico. A touring singer-songwriter, she is the author of *The Sound of Navajo Country: Music, Language and Diné Belonging* (University of North Carolina Press, 2017), which won the 2018 Woody Guthrie Award for the most outstanding book on popular music (IASPM-US). At the University of New Mexico, Jacobsen founded and cofacilitates the Honky Tonk Ensemble and coordinates the Songwriting in Community program. Her current ethnographic project focuses on ethnographic songwriting and language reclamation on the Italian island of Sardinia, where she was a Fulbright Scholar from 2019–2020.

TRACEY E. W. LAIRD serves as Harry L., Corinne Bryant, and Cottie Beverly Slade Professor of Humanities and Professor of Music at Agnes Scott College in Atlanta, GA, where her teaching and research address intersections of US music, regional and racial identity, and media. She is an author or editor of five books, including *Louisiana Hayride: Radio and Roots Music Along the Red River* (Oxford University Press, 2004; 2015); *Shreveport Sounds in Black and White*, edited with Kip Lornell (University Press of Mississippi, 2006); *Austin City Limits: A History* (Oxford University Press, 2014); *Austin City Limits: A Monument to Music* (Insight Editions, 2015), coauthored with Brandon Laird; and, most recently, the 50th Anniversary edition of Bill Malone's groundbreaking *Country Music, USA* (University of Texas Press, 2018).

KRISTINE M. MCCUSKER holds a PhD in history, folklore, and ethnomusicology from Indiana University and is Professor of History at Middle Tennessee State University. She's the author of *Lonesome Cowgirls and Honky-Tonk Angels* (University of Illinois Press, 2008) and the coeditor of *A Boy Named Sue* (University Press of Mississippi, 2004) and *Country Boys and Redneck Women* (University Press of Mississippi, 2016). Her articles have appeared in *American Music, American Studies,* and *The Oxford Handbook of Country Music*. She is writing a National Institutes of Health-funded study of southern death rituals. She is the coexecutive director of the Oral History Association.

JOCELYN R. NEAL is the Bowman and Gordon Gray Distinguished Term Professor of Music at the University of North Carolina at Chapel Hill. She holds a PhD in music theory from the Eastman School of Music. Her research addresses analysis of country music, music and dance, and songwriting. Her publications include *Country Music: A Cultural and Stylistic*

History (Oxford University Press, 2012; second edition 2018); *The Songs of Jimmie Rodgers* (Indiana University Press, 2008), and, coauthored with Bill C. Malone, *Country Music, USA* (Texas Press, second revised edition, 2010), along with numerous journal articles and book chapters. Neal directs the UNC Bluegrass Initiative.

RISSI PALMER, who describes her musical style as "Southern Soul," has received widespread media attention in national publications, including *Ebony, Billboard, People, Newsweek, Huffington Post, Rolling Stone*, and *The Wall Street Journal*. She has performed on the CBS Morning Show, CNN, Oprah & Friends, at the White House, Lincoln Center, and the Grand Ole Opry. Palmer made music history in 2007 with the release of her top-forty debut single, "Country Girl," becoming the first African American female to appear on *Billboard*'s Hot Country Songs chart since 1987. She is now the host of the Apple Music Country show, Color Me Country Radio w/Rissi Palmer, and administers the Color Me Country Artist Grant Fund to provide grants for artists of color pursuing careers in Country and Americana Music.

ALICE RANDALL is the most successful Black female country songwriter in history. She has worked in Nashville across four decades serving in a variety of overlapping and award-winning roles, including songwriter, publisher, screenwriter, and scholar. Trisha Yearwood, Reba McIntire, Garth Brooks, Glen Campbell, The Nitty Gritty Dirt Band, Lil Hardin, and DeFord Bailey are some of the acts with whom she is most closely associated. Currently Professor, Writer-in-Residence, and Andrew W. Mellon Chair in the Humanities at Vanderbilt University, she teaches *Black Country*. Her memoir and a history of Black people in country music, *My Black Country*, is forthcoming.

NANCY P. RILEY is Lecturer at Belmont University in Nashville, TN. She completed a PhD in musicology and ethnomusicology at the University of Georgia in Athens, with a graduate certificate in women's studies. She has contributed articles related to country and alt.country music in *The SAGE International Encyclopedia of Music and Culture* and *The Grove Dictionary of American Music*, and also published in the *International Journal for the Scholarship of Teaching and Learning*. She has also collaborated with PBS Learning Media to produce education curriculum to support documentary projects of Ken Burns.

RACHEL SKAGGS is the Lawrence and Isabel Barnett Assistant Professor of Arts Management in the Department of Arts Administration, Education, and Policy at The Ohio State University. She completed her PhD in sociology at Vanderbilt University as the American Studies Fellow at the Robert Penn Warren Center for the Humanities. Her research focuses on social networks in music industry careers, arts entrepreneurship, rejection and failure in the arts, and public perceptions of artists.

STEPHANIE VANDER WEL is Associate Professor of Historical Musicology at the University at Buffalo (State University of New York). She has published on Gene Autry and Patsy Montana in the *Musical Quarterly*, Loretta Lynn and the singing voice in *The Oxford Handbook of Country Music*, and Webb Pierce in the essay collection *Honky Tonk on the Left: Progressive Thought in Country Music*. Her book *Hillbilly Maidens, Okies, and Singing Cowgirls: Women's Country Music, 1930–1960* was published in March 2020 by the University of Illinois Press.

JADA WATSON is a white researcher living and working on unceded territory of the Algonquin Anishinaabe Nation. She is an Assistant Professor of Digital Humanities in the School of Information Studies at the University of Ottawa. Watson leads the SSHRC-funded SongData project (www.SongData.ca), which focuses on the role of market data in the formation and evolution of genre categories. This work has been published in *Popular Music & Society, Popular Music History*, and *American Music Perspectives*. She has released a series of public reports addressing representation on country music radio, including three prepared in consultation with Woman of Music Action Network and another in partnership with CMT's EqualPlay campaign. This work has been cited in a legal brief submitted to the US Federal Communications Commission, as well as in the Grammy Recording Academy's Report on Inclusion and Diversity.

∾ "She went to Nashville to sing country music"

Gatekeeping and the Country Music Industry

PAULA J. BISHOP AND JADA WATSON

In the Spring of 2021, Marquia Thompson, the granddaughter of country artist Linda Martell, started a GoFundMe campaign to raise funds to produce a documentary on the singer's career. Martell went to Nashville in the late 1960s to sing country music, signed a recording contract with Shelby Singleton on Plantation Records, and became the first Black female country artist to chart on *Billboard*'s Hot Country Singles in 1969. For the last fifty years, Martell has been absent from the received historical narrative of country music and, as Thompson reflects, "never exactly got her due in terms of business in Nashville" (Moore 2022) – with questions about unpaid royalties emerging as work on the documentary began in 2020. The stories of artists like Martell, who participated in the creative work of the country music industry yet were forced to the margins, have recently begun to surface through recovery work of artists, journalists, and researchers, complicating the genre's historical narrative, raising the question: "whose country music is this, anyway?"

This recovery work was due in large part to the efforts of Rissi Palmer. In 2019, as the country music industry grappled with the presence of Lil Nas X's release "Old Town Road," Palmer was frustrated. Media noted the same five Black artists – Charley Pride, Darius Rucker, Jimmie Allen, Kane Brown, and Mickey Guyton – as if these were the only artists of color to participate in the country music industry. She took to Twitter (@RissiPalmer May 23, 2019) to set the record straight on the presence of Black artists in the industry, correcting a misconception about the number of Black women who had charted (often reported as zero) by naming Linda Martell (1969), the Pointer Sisters (1974), Dona Mason (1987), herself (2007/2008), and Mickey Guyton (2015). Followers immediately chimed in listing dozens of Black women in country music. The magnitude of the response inspired her to create a podcast, *Color Me Country*, named after Martell's 1970 album of the same name (*All Things Considered* 2020). Palmer sought to give space to Black, Indigenous, and artists of color (hereafter as BIPOC) who have contributed to country music, "who for too long have lived outside the spotlight and off mainstream airwaves" (*Color Me Country*). Before she launched the podcast,

1

Apple Music Country Radio invited her to be part of their radio initiative, giving her access to resources to produce the show and a large audience. In addition to introducing new artists, Palmer educates listeners on the artists like Martell who laid foundations for later generations of BIPOC artists. Following the launch of *Color Me Country*, *Rolling Stone* (Browne 2020) published the first in-depth interview with Martell in over fifteen years and CMT honored her with the EqualPlay Award in June 2021, both initiatives finally bringing her work into the story of country music. Palmer's show is part of broader restorative work by artists, journalists, and researchers who are recovering the stories of BIPOC artists erased by the industry's restrictive and exclusionary practices. What emerges through this work is a picture of the industry as a vigorously controlled system that has constructed a very narrow view of what constitutes country music and who is eligible to participate.

How We Got Here

The country music industry has historically been defined through a "Southern thesis," which suggests that the music emerged from the countryside and mountain hollows of the rural US South, linking the artists and music to agrarian economy, social conservatism, and rural lifestyle. This thesis consciously constructs rigid binaries that define the music and its musicians in terms of geographic ("south" vs. "north" / "rural" vs. "urban") or stylistic affiliations. Perhaps more critically, this paradigm is linked to Jim Crow Era racial constructs that have privileged the work of white artists and marginalized the contributions of Black, Indigenous, and artists of color. Black and white musicians played and listened to the same music, but it was the work of record executives – who segregated their music along a color line to market music to white ("hillbilly music") and Black ("race music") communities – that established arbitrary genre categories that structured the music industry. Though "hillbilly" and "race" are no longer used today, the racial segregation established by the industry in the 1920s was institutionalized through the development of the systems of production, distribution, and recognition in the 1950s; maintained throughout the second half of the twentieth century; and remain firmly embedded within the popular music industry's structures today. As a result, Black and of color artists have remained at the margins of the country music industry; although a handful of artists have been successful, the majority have been ignored, silenced, or excluded by the establishment.

Country music scholarship has until recently served to reinforce this industrial narrative construct. The first published history, Bill C. Malone's *Country Music, USA,* has played a significant role in perpetuating the industry's white, southern racial framing of country music history. Although updated and revised four times since 1968 with an expanded time-line, the book continues to present a constricted view of the genre's history, creating a metanarrative of the history of country music that has constrained scholarship and created a narrow view of the genre, its creators, and its consumers. A cursory glance at the literature that followed Malone's text shows the terms used to capture the evolving musical sound and reveals a pendulum swinging between two constant poles of "traditional" and "country pop." Richard Peterson (1997) uses "hard core" and "soft shell," Joli Jensen (1998) "down home" and "uptown," and Barbara Ching (2003) "hard coun-try" and "mainstream." These are loaded stylistic definitions that are used to define its associated artists with "authentic" and "artificial" practices, with "low" and "high" class culture, with "rural" and "urban" values. This binary narrative echoes the marketing constructs created by the industry in the 1920s, effectively putting music and musicians in boxes, separating them into cat-egories, and then using those categories to elevate some and disregard all others. More critically, these practices serve as a powerful exclusionary tool that obscures and even erases the contributions of artists born outside of the US South, persons of color, women, and LGBTQIA+ artists.

Theories of social remembering offer a critical framework for conceptual-izing the impact of this narrative paradigm on the development of country music scholarship. Barbara Misztal's (2003) work encourages us to consider more fully the role that these dominant narratives play in shaping cultural memory, evaluating the ways in which privileged voices are canonized and "remembered," while others are cast away and "forgotten" (Watson 2020a). Already culturally disadvantaged by discriminatory practices within the industry, certain artists – notably women, artists of color, and LGBTQIA+ artists – are further marginalized in the kind of historical narrative created by the industry and reinforced through Malone's Southern thesis, perpetu-ating a practice of favoring artists that fit into his white, Southern, male, working-class model. Over the course of the first two decades of the new millennium, scholars have actively contested the "Southern thesis," pointing to the significant role that urban musical communities (Huber 2008, 2014, 2017; Tyler 2014), African American musicians (Huber 2013; Hughes 2015; Miller 2010; Pecknold 2013a), and women (McCusker and Pecknold 2004, 2016; McCusker 2017) have played in shaping commercial country music. Other studies have chronicled the industry-imposed segregation of southern music in the mid-1920s, when OkeH records reduced the once-fluid network of musical styles into distinct genres tied to specific racial identities. As both Karl Hagstrom Miller (2010) and David Brackett (2016) have observed, the blues became the music of African Americans (released in OkeH's "race" records series) and folk/country became the music of rural white southerners (in OkeH's "hillbilly" records series). Pecknold (2013b) argues that this fictive construct has been perpetuated by the industry and embedded in the broader country music discourse. The work of these scholars represents some of the recovery of lost and hidden voices within the prevailing meta-narrative, showing that they are not the exceptions. The *Oxford Handbook of Country Music,* published in 2017, synthesizes this foundational work and offers a state of the field for key themes and issues within country scholarship. The collection's authors grapple with the challenges of viewing country music through a narrow lens, suggesting a path forward for future scholarship.

Despite this recovery work, Malone's tome continues to pervade country music culture. Documentarian Ken Burns turned to *Country Music, USA* as the main source for his eight-part, sixteen-hour documentary of the genre for PBS. Burns's *Country Music* further advances the closely circumscribed historical narrative of the genre into the multicultural, globalist twenty-first-century pop culture memory, making it even more urgent that other scholarly voices enter the discourse around the genre. As *New York Times* writer Jon Caramanica (2019) quipped in his review of the documentary, "Tell a lie long enough and it begins to smell like the truth. Tell it even longer and it becomes part of history."

In a period in which racism and gender inequity are at the fore of public, political, and scholarly discourse, the chapters in this collection address issues of gender, race, class, and geography as they are shaped by and relate to contemporary country music identity and culture. Building on the recovery work of the authors noted above, we examine contemporary issues in country music through feminist, postcolonialist, and critical race theories, as well as other cultural lenses. The authors pose questions about diversity, representation, and identity as an act of cultural remediation and as they relate to larger concepts of artist and fan communities, stylistic considerations of the genre, and modes of production from a twenty-first-century perspective.

Whose Country Music?

Who is permitted to participate in the genre and how they participate are critical issues within the cultural/social context of country music. On the surface, the issue appears to be driven by the economics of record production – industry players study their markets and choose product strategies that meet the demands and needs of the consumer at a cost that maintains an acceptable profit margin for everyone involved. But as our collection demonstrates, what Pierre Bourdieu (1984) would call the "field" of cultural production encompasses more than the physical production and distribution of the "product." It includes radio stations, streaming services, tour operators, talent managers, lawyers, and accountants. So, too, does it include artists, songwriters, session players, touring band members, roadies, sound engineers, postproduction personnel, and all the other creative and support personnel required to make a live or recorded performance. Outside of the business of music, fans, critics, and scholars participate in cultural production.

Every one of these individuals or institutions acts as gatekeeper of the sound and identity of country music. Social psychologist Kurt Lewin (1947) theorized gatekeeping as a set of channels where products and processes exist and flow, with forces that determine what can and cannot pass through a gate into another channel. The gatekeeper chooses from the available input based on organizational rules and expectations, as well as personal ones (White 1950). In the field of country music, an "item" might not pass through the gate if it does not fit the preferred model of authenticity or sound. Gatekeepers in this space, then, are cultural mediators in the Bourdieusien sense. The term "mediator," though, suggests neutrality, but, as Lewin (1947) and particularly David Manning White (1950) have demonstrated, gatekeepers invariably insert personal choices into the process.

Gatekeeping, as generally described in media and mass communications studies (Shoemaker and Vos, 2009), does not specifically account for the bidirectional nature or the multiplicity of the gates in the entertainment industry. In communications channels, information flows to the gate where the gatekeeper culls it based on organizational and/or personal rules and expectations. In the music industry, though, gatekeepers also control access to the channel and therefore access to the product and the processes that create and control the product (here "product" means physical or digital performances, as well as all other tangible and intangible elements associated with the performance). Celebrated songwriter Alice Randall opens the collection with a memoir of her experience navigating the gates in the country music industry. The first Black female songwriter to write a No. 1 charting record, Randall shares her story of pursuing "mailbox money" – from her decision to move to Nashville to become a songwriter and publisher, to the early conversations she had with the white men signing and working with songwriters (i.e., the gatekeepers to the publishing world), to the work that she did to learn what makes a "hit" and how to navigate the industry's structures. At the same time, she honors Black artists whose stories are often ignored by the industry and highlights the contributions of numerous women whose work behind the scenes helped to shape the development of the industry.

Kristine M. McCusker and Rachel Skaggs further illustrate how multiple players can act in concert to restrict access to the resources (broadly conceived). McCusker describes how a record label limited the ability of The Chicks to receive fair compensation. Radio station programmers reduced their access to airplay and therefore to consumers (fans) by contextualizing Natalie Maines' remarks in 2003 about George W. Bush as a political act that defied the norms of country music. Skaggs explains how publishers, labels, and artist representatives have created publishing deals for songwriters that have worked to define the sonic boundaries of country music as well as define who is assigned the label of songwriter and can financially benefit from the publishing revenue. Jada Watson similarly argues that data – presumed to be neutral – does in fact control access to the systems of production and consumption, effectively erasing voices that cannot achieve a measurable data presence.

Most studies of gatekeeping in the music industry have focused on the means of production and consumption (e.g., radio stations [Rossman 2012], local scenes [Balaji 2012], streaming services [Bonini and Gandini 2019]), with little attention afforded to consumers (fans) or surrogate consumers (critics, scholars).[1] The digital revolution and the prevalence of social media have redistributed power in ways that elevate the consumer's role as gatekeeper and have resulted in scholarly attention. For instance, Kimery S. Lynch (2020) argues that digital gatekeepers on Reddit can control the social reality and understanding of a popular Korean band, BTS, along a transcultural axis. Rebekah Hutten's chapter draws attention to the surveillant nature of social media platforms and demonstrates how the fans attempted to define the terms by which Beyoncé and The Chicks could or could not participate in country music. Sophia Enriquez centers scholarship as a form of cultural gatekeeping that controls access and therefore perceptions of the field of inquiry, asking us to consider how citational practices define the scholarship and limit participation.

---

[1] Paul M. Hirsch (1972) differentiates the surrogate consumer from the consumer in his gatekeeping model, though he depicts these surrogates as an extension of the cultural distributors rather than the consumers.

Pamela J. Shoemaker and Tim P. Vos (2009) assert that gatekeeping determines social reality. In media studies, this means that the information (news) received by individuals through gatekeepers (news organizations) informs their world. In the entertainment industry, the actions and decisions of cultural actors define the "reality" of the product for the artists, fans, critics, and all the production entities. Though scholarship tends to focus on "industry" agents, these other individuals and entities act as gatekeepers that operate in the country music ecosystem to mark out belonging through codes of conduct or behavioral expectations. Stephanie Vander Wel historicizes comedy as performed by women in country music and offers a close reading of how female artists have used humor as a resistive force in the industry. Through a close analysis of lyrics, vocal performance, and musical style, she demonstrates how these carefully controlled boundaries can be subverted, creating new spaces for female performers. Conversely, Jocelyn R. Neal depicts the boundaries around male performativity, working-class identity, and geographical imagery. While the scene may have changed – from the rugged ranches of the Southwest to the lush tropical beaches of the Caribbean – the expectations of male identity have simply moved to the new location with little change. Phoebe E. Hughes describes heteronormative relationship expectations. Drawing on the archetype of the "gentleman," she lays the foundation for the concept of a gentleman in country music and shows us the complicated nature of romantic interactions in song narratives. Within the lyrical framework, women do not have agency, which Hughes locates in the lack of consent asked for or granted. What we see in the work of these three authors is a combination of actors – artists, industry, fans, journalists – mediating the behavioral expectations.

This relationship between these cultural mediators creates a feedback loop, constantly reinscribing particular values and worldviews on the music, musicians, and audiences. The feedback loop extends to what Hirsch (1972, 647) called the "surrogate consumers," which, in our model, includes scholars. Sophia Enriquez illustrates the feedback loop between the industry and scholarship, noting how readings of Latina subjects in lyrics are ignored, a direct result of the exclusion of BIPOC artists from radio airwaves, the popularity charts, and the historical narrative (Watson 2021). Her analysis of several songs reveals the objectification of Latinas by white male artists. At the same time, she demonstrates how contemporary Latina artists are reclaiming their agency and sexuality. In Enriquez's work, we are asked to disrupt the feedback loop by considering the other voices who contribute to the music and the environment and read these words through additional lenses. She goes further, cautioning that to do so is the only sustainable and equitable direction forward for the field of country music studies.

Central to this conversation is authenticity and identity in the country music field. Authenticity is a negotiation with the past, as Paula J. Bishop details in her exploration of the rhetorical use of nostalgia. She offers a framework for understanding nostalgia, incorporating psychological and sociological conceptions of the concept. She examines the historical arc of nostalgia in country music, noting the ways in which country artists refer musically and lyrically to other artists as a means of establishing the lineage within the historical narrative of the genre. Connecting with the past and demonstrating one's place in the genre is integral to country music authenticity. Janet Aspley looks at fashion, in the form of the Nudie suit, as a central component of authenticity in the twenty-first century. Aspley historicizes Nudie's style, pointing to its Ukrainian and Mexican origins in spite of its perception as a quintessentially American country music style. The Nudie suit, as Aspley shows, was central to male country music identity in the 1960s. When it returns into fashion in the twenty-first century, the Nudie suit and its successors (e.g., Manuel, Atwood) are worn by artists who are working at the margins of the mainstream – women and queer artists, as well as noncountry artists. No longer a signifier of mainstream country, artists such as Orville Peck, Lil Nas X, and the Highwomen have turned to this style as a way of forging their own unique country music identity. Nancy P. Riley takes us even closer to the edges of the country music ecosystem in her analysis of Chicago-based Bloodshot Records and the emergence and reconfiguring of so-called Americana music in the twenty-first century. Through an intertextual reading of the label's first and twenty-first anniversary albums, Riley explores how Bloodshot positions itself in opposition to the mainstream – as a community of musicians drawing on small-scale practices to forge more intimate relationships with fans. But the distinction between mainstream and indie labels is no longer – and has never truly been – clear, and Riley's chapter considers how the Covid-19 pandemic has brought these spaces closer together. Leigh H. Edwards brings us an example of one of the most authentic mainstream country music artists, Dolly Parton, who paradoxically built her authenticity on her terms, and has continued to redefine it, most recently turning to twenty-first-century media tools to update her authenticity narrative. Focusing on her Netflix series *Dolly Parton's Heartstrings* (2019), Edwards considers how the singer-songwriter revises/rewrites narratives to classic songs from her catalog in a way that allowed her to reframe her cultural politics, challenging the conservative reactions to her support for the LGBTQIA+ community, while at the same time critiquing gender stereotypes. Perhaps more critically, in an industry that has continually buried/ignored its multiracial and ethnic roots, the series afforded Parton a platform to express her support for the Black Lives Matter movement (Newman 2020). Edwards challenges us to consider the role that media plays in Parton's twenty-first-century reimagining, showing us how "Jolene" offers the singer the opportunity to reject white, middle-class gender codes of respectability and domesticity. Parton's attempts to rebrand her authenticity and cultural politics come at an interesting time in the history of the industry and of the United States, as it coincides with her financial contribution to vaccine research during Covid-19 and to public debate over the perception of her as a hero, a debate that is fueled by the very same media tools that Parton herself uses (Cottom 2021a; Martinez 2021b).

What emerges from conversations about the industry, codes of conduct, and authenticity is a porousness and fragility of the perceived boundaries of country music culture, identity, and style. This is particularly striking when we examine country music within geographic and racial boundaries, which are equally as arbitrary as those of musical genres. Both Kristina Jacobsen and Nadine Hubbs deal directly with national boundaries, drawing out the idea of country music as a border culture. Jacobsen describes country musicians who are negotiating identity as they move across boundaries, crossing the border from the Navajo reservation to border towns that surround it to perform for audiences that are largely white. For the musicians with which Jacobsen works, musical performance disrupts Colorado's settler-colonial history. Hubbs describes communities of Mexican Americans living in Texas and California, whose engagement with country music similarly disrupts perceptions about country music audiences. Jacobsen and Hubbs refer to boundaries that can be drawn on paper, but Tracey E. W. Laird deals with arbitrary boundaries of musical style – those demarcations of genre that were institutionally defined by the industry in the 1920s. She describes the work of Rhiannon Giddens, whose research has been integral to the recovery of Black American musicians and musical traditions. Through conversation with the singer-songwriter and analysis of her first two solo albums, Laird illustrates how Giddens actively dismantles these genre structures, revealing the sonic and spiritual connections between a range of musical styles.

Throughout the chapters in this book, the authors deal with a variety of boundaries – genre, institutional, performativity, identity, geographical, racial – and question who is permitted to participate within the mainstream. This becomes particularly evident in Rebekah Hutten's analysis of Beyoncé and The Chicks' performance of "Daddy Lessons" at the fiftieth anniversary of the Country Music Association Awards ceremony in November 2016, which provoked a range of impassioned responses from the industry, fellow artists, and country music fans. As Hutten argues, these boundaries don't exist unless someone is watching and policing them. Drawing on theories of surveillance, her analysis of audience and social media responses to the performance exposes and destabilizes the power structures that have attempted to control the industrial narrative. In this chapter, we see that fans play a critical role in gatekeeping, dictating who gets to perform on country stages and how.

This collection challenges the paradigm in which scholarship unquestioningly remains in lockstep with the industry's white heteropatriarchal narrative, drawing on new theories and methodologies to critique the institution of country music (both scholarship *and* industry), and we are not alone in this work. Artists, journalists, and researchers have been actively pushing back at this received narrative that follows from Malone's early work. Palmer's work with "Color Me Country Radio" is but one example. And she expands on this action-driven work in the epilogue to the collection. Palmer's experience, as revealed in the collection's closing chapter, is reminiscent of Randall's in the book's opening. She reveals to us how little has changed for Black women in this industry. Like Palmer, Mickey Guyton, Cam, Maren Morris, Amanda Shires, and Jennifer Nettles use their social media platforms and access to national media to advocate for change in the industry. Karen Pittelman, Country Soul Songbook, Holly G. and the Black Opry, Rainbow Rodeo, and others are working to build new spaces for artists that have been shut out of the industry, while Jason Isbell and Tyler Childers use their musical platform to model what allyship can look like – even publicly learning from their mistakes. Andrea Williams, Jewly Hight, Marissa Moss, and Lorie Liebig are actively documenting and exposing different forms of oppression through their reporting on the industry. The work presented in this book coincides with the public conversations initiated by these artists and journalists and has implications for the future of country music scholarship. And yet, as Rhiannon Giddens says (quoted in Laird's chapter here), "we have a lot of work to do."

PART I

Industry

1 | Mailbox Money

Novel Liberation Strategies of a Black Female Country Songwriter

ALICE RANDALL

"XXX's and OOO's" is a song about female money anxiety, about the need to "try to keep the balance up, between love and money." It suggests that the balance may be impossible to achieve, leaving women to seek shelter in "God" and "good wine" from economic and emotional distress. I cowrote "XXX's and OOO's" in 1994 with Matraca Berg, with each of us drawing on our own "cash cow" experience.

The first verse spotlights work done outside the home, emphasizing the need to "go to work" and worries about the impact of appearance (through direct reference to "TV diet guru lies" and "makeup") on a woman's ability to earn.

The second verse spotlights the second shift many women work each day, the return home to housekeeping tasks, "fix the sink, mow the yard." The specific duties cited, tasks stereotypically gendered masculine and often outsourced to *paid* male contractors, plumbers, and gardeners, are here claimed as *unpaid* female labor.

This introduces yet another source of money and work disquiet, "it really isn't all that hard, *if* you get paid." There's a lot of pressure, a freight of fear, on that little word "if." "How hard is it to work if you don't get paid?"

Aretha Franklin, who makes a cameo appearance in the bridge, knew something about female money anxiety and the money anxieties of artists. She famously demanded her performance fee in cash prior to taking the stage and kept the satchel containing her pay near her feet throughout her performances.

Name checking Aretha does more than give an iconic face to female money anxiety. By putting the names "Aretha Franklin and Patsy Cline" in Trisha Yearwood's mouth, and in that order, country is no longer a space where whiteness always comes first, and Blackness is invisible. And it is no longer a space in which females get written about but don't write. Aretha was an accomplished songwriter; Patsy, a prolific letter writer. The song describes literal black marks (ink) on white paper, "She signs her letters with XXX's and OOO's" to emphasize the truth girls write. By embedding Franklin and Cline, one Black, one white, in the text, we created surrogates for ourselves and establish – on multiple levels – that writing is an elemental aspect of "American Girl" identity.

"XXX's and OOO's (An American Girl)" is a song that earned me twentieth- and twenty-first-century mailbox money.

"Mailbox money" is Music Row slang for money earned by successful songwriters from songs that get recorded and get played out in the world.

In the twentieth century, mailbox money was typically a combination of monies earned from mechanicals (royalties based on physical singles, albums, cassettes, and CDs) and monies earned from performance rights (license fees by radio stations, television stations, live music venues, bars, restaurants, and more) paid to the big three performing rights organizations, ASCAP, BMI, and SESAC. Old-timers boiled all that down to "records and radio."

In the twenty-first century, mailbox money is typically a combination of monies earned from legacy sources, "records and radio," collected by old and new PROs (performing rights organizations) and old and new MROs (mechanical rights organizations), and monies earned from digital music providers and online music videos, some of which is collected by the Mechanical License Collective. Twenty-first-century mailbox money boils down to radio and streams.

What follows is a mailbox money memoir written by a Black and female country songwriter who did not get to twenty-first-century mailbox money without navigating the external obstacles and internal anxieties addressed in her biggest hit.

The "XXX's and OOO's" money story starts in 1993 at a country music celebrity bowling event hosted by BMI's legendary Frances Preston to raise funds for cancer research.

Between frames, I met a Hollywood agent who knew that Brandon Tartikoff, the former president of NBC and Paramount pictures, was looking for a writer to develop a TV series about the ex-wives of country stars that he wanted to call "XXX's and OOO's."

I got the job. Tartikoff set a deal at CBS and soon in addition to cowriting the script and coproducing the pilot, I was writing the theme song. My publisher, Donna Hilley at Sony/ATV, was thrilled. I invited Matraca Berg to cowrite. We worked hard and got nothing. Eventually, I made the call to my publisher to break the bad news. I would not have the theme song in the new CBS pilot. They would use a country classic.

The next day, demoralized, I slapped a smile on my face, clipped a bow in my daughter's hair, and drove her to school. I was jumping into the shower when my bedroom phone started ringing. A permission slip that my first grader "had to have" wasn't in her backpack. I stepped into the shower cussing at myself for being a failure as a mother and a money-maker. Hot water was spraying on my head, when these words came to me, "You got a picture of your Mama in heels and pearls, and you're trying to make it in your daddy's world."

I rushed to my daughter's school with the permission slip, then over to Matraca's. When she opened her door, I spat out new lines, before saying hello. She waved me in. The lines to the second verse came to Matraca almost as fast as the lines to the first verse had come to me. We told the truth we were living, how hard it was to make money, make love, and care for family all in the same day. The whole song was written in less than ninety minutes.

Fast forward. Wynonna Judd recorded the song but doesn't show up for overdubs. We're back to using a country classic. Except I knew a singer, a woman who had years before sung demos for me, who had the vocal control and voice required to sing on Wy's tracks and eclipse Wy's performance, and she was at a nearby studio working on her own album. I raced to where Trisha Yearwood was recording. I blasted past the receptionist and into Trisha's session. I blurted out the truth starting with, "We have known each other since our first marriages . . ." I entreated her to help me save my last best chance to have a big hit. Trisha said, "Yes." That generous woman left her own session to save mine.

On the July 9, 1994, *Billboard* Hot Country Songs chart, "XXX's and OOO's" was listed as the No. 1 country single. The single would spend two weeks at No. 1.

We were on our way to "XXX's and OOO's" mailbox money. We didn't know that the mailbox money earned would provide some of the funding I needed to write *The Wind Done Gone* (2001), *Pushkin and the Queen of Spades* (2004), *Rebel Yell* (2009), *Ada's Rules* (2012), and *Black Bottom Saints* (2021), all of which reference Black presence in country music. We didn't know a radical plan I started hatching in 1980 would come to full fruition in the twenty-first century.

***

In no small part, my move to Nashville, Tennessee, a city where I had no friends, family, or set job, in the winter of 1983 was a conscious effort to acquire the economic wherewithal required to thrive as a fiction writer.

The plan had first begun to take shape in the fall of 1980, my senior year at Harvard University. I was fresh out of a two-century, multi-language survey of "Women's Writing," and completing an undergraduate thesis on Jane Austen, when I realized that I, too, wanted to be a novelist.

Recognizing that the strategies and resources available to Austen were not available to me, and aware that Zora Neal Hurston had late in life worked as a maid to support herself and her writing, I determined I would support my fiction writing by becoming a country music songwriter and publisher.

For a young Black woman born in Detroit, Michigan in 1959, my plan wasn't as audacious or original as it may seem. I knew Anna and Gwen Gordy were successful songwriters who had founded a record company, Anna Records, a year before their brother Berry Gordy founded Motown Records in 1959. I also knew Loucye Gordy, until her death, ran the two primary Motown publishing companies, Jobete and Stone Diamond. The first hit single on the Anna label was "M-O-N-E-Y" recorded by Barrett Strong. Motown, the city, the record label, and that song taught me to take my own entrepreneurial ambitions seriously.

Before Motown taught me, my family taught me more. I am a third-generation entrepreneur. My grandfather moved from Selma, Alabama, to Detroit, Michigan, where he established a dry-cleaning business, Ran's Cleaners, on the city's lower East Side in Black Bottom. My father, who ran coin-operated laundries and dry-cleaners, reinforced the lesson. When I asked my father what his favorite color was, he said green because it was the color of money – his idea of child's play was allowing me to sort change from the laundries. Daddy regaled me with stories of a coffee shop not far from the original offices of Motown, where "sharks" would sit waiting for despondent songwriters, exiting "Hitsville" to pop in for a consoling cup of java. The sharks would buy the songs rejected by Motown outright and cheap, for fast cash, then carve them up for parts, lines, phrases, and titles.

My father's money tales felt foreign and faraway at Harvard – except when I was talking to my freshman roommate Emily's mother Gloria Messinger. Gloria also told money tales. One that made a vivid impression? Graduating from Yale Law School in 1954, she was offered jobs at top law firms – as a secretary. Only ASCAP offered her a job as a lawyer. She took it.

Our paths crossed several times during my undergraduate years. She fueled my ambition to become a country songwriter by sharing the information that revenues from ASCAP's Nashville office were steadily increasing. By the time graduation rolled around, she was ASCAP's managing director, and arguably the single most powerful woman in the music business.

Some months after graduation, I reached out to say I was ready to launch my career in country music. Gloria arranged a songwriting audition for me in New York with Hal David, one of the great lyricists of the twentieth century and President of ASCAP.

Hal offered his judgment that my song ideas were "country," my phrasing was "country," and my storytelling was "country" – but country like he had never heard. He flattered me by stating that the only thing wrong with my best lines was he hadn't written them. And yet, he wasn't sanguine about my prospects of "making it" in Nashville.

Music Row, I was warned, was exceptionally close-knit and insular. It had its own distinct business culture, language, style, and campus. They suggested an "Award Season" "scouting trip" to test the waters.

Award season in Music City is a seven-day extravaganza of breakfast parties, luncheons, cocktail parties, dinners, after-hours bashes, high-stake business meetings, annual meetings, romantic assignations, and shopping sprees, all scheduled around four major events, the Country Music Association Awards and the ASCAP, BMI, and SESAC awards banquets. Awards season usually falls in October.

Every meeting Gloria set for me was with a white man, specifically, Buddy Killen, Ralph Murphy, Archie Jordan, Waylon Holyfield, Bob Morrison, and Ronnie Gant, the men who would play a significant role in Gloria being able to announce a year later during Awards season that ASCAP had collected 202,582,000 million dollars.

I showed up to the building where Hank Williams, Sr. had picked up his publishing checks, the Acuff-Rose office, wearing a light gray skirt suit. Ronnie Gant, who ran Acuff-Rose publishing, was wearing jeans and a button-down shirt. He had his feet up on the desk and started peppering me with questions the moment I settled into the chair opposite him, ending with, "Where *are* you from?" When I answered, he shook his head like it hurt. He had arrived at a conclusion, "I don't see it. I just don't see it. You need to go back to wherever it is you came from." Then, perhaps remembering who had gotten me into the room, he walked back the complete dismissal. He said he would show my lyrics to two of his younger writers who were more familiar with "raw" material.

A few weeks after I returned to Nashville, I got a letter from Ronnie Gant saying he had shared my lyrics with Mark D. Sanders and Randy Albright. All three men had come to the same conclusion: "You have no talent whatsoever." That was the day I decided to move to Nashville.

Ronnie's tone was the catalyst. And that word "see." He looked at Black, female, suit-wearing me, and he didn't "see" anyone he thought could possibly ever earn mailbox money. And this was a man whose salary was paid for by songs written by Hank Williams, Sr., who learned to pick poetry from a Black street musician called Tee-Tot. He was acting like Lil Hardin hadn't played on Jimmie Rodgers's iconic single "Blue Yodel #9"; like Elvis Presley hadn't learned to sing "Hound Dog" from Big Mama Thornton; like Black Ellen Snowden didn't fiddle and give birth to the sons Ben and Lew Snowden, who taught the song "Dixie" to white Dan Emmett; like country wasn't an Afro-Celtic genre with Black presence and influence all up in it, no matter what lies Bill C. Malone told in *Country Music, USA*.

I was moving my Black and female body from Washington, DC, to Music City, and I was going to find a way or ways to make this truth known: Black women helped birth country.

It was time to secure funding and make a tighter plan for getting to mailbox money. I called on another Harvard connection, Edith Gelfand. Edith grew up in Brooklyn and started listening to country music while skiing in Vail. A childless lawyer, married to a doctor, she was willing to take on risky investments. She offered me $100,000 for twenty percent of the publishing company we would form, Midsummer Music.

On February 18, 1983, I hit the road with three friends, one woman and two men, in a rented car pointed South. On the twelve-hour drive, we sang along loud to the radio. The song that had me mesmerized? "Faking Love . . . only temporary lovers as we lie here to each other. . .faking love." Buddy Killen, one of the people I met on my scouting trip, had produced "Faking Love" and told me all about its cowriters, the legendary Bobby Braddock who wrote "D-I-V-O-R-C-E" and my all-time favorite country song, "He Stopped Loving Her Today," and an eighteen-year-old songwriter phenom Matraca Berg.

My weeks quickly took on a particular structure. The newspaper arrived on Sunday, including a local entertainment magazine listing all the song-writer's nights. Every Sunday I would choose the shows I would attend. One a night minimum. Sometimes I hit three in a single night. Then I slept with the radio on. I had a notebook that I was determined to fill with potential collaborators, song titles, business advice, and the lyrics to every song on the Hot 100 on the radio. In the front covers, I created an evolving map/chart of the connections/power structure of the country music indus-try as I encountered it. The head of the ASCAP office, Connie Bradley, for example, was married to Jerry Bradley, who was the head of RCA for over a decade. Her father-in-law Owen Bradley was a legendary producer. Her brother-in-law Harold Bradley was a noted session musician. Together and separately, the Bradleys owned multiple recording studios and publishing companies. During the week I would work my way through, one song at a time, the *Billboard* Hot Country Songs chart. The goal was to have heard, and outlined, every single song. I reached that goal. After I'd been at it a few months, each week only brought one or two new songs. That gave me time to go to the basement of the Country Music Hall of Fame and start looking at the sheet music of country classics.

I paid particular attention to songs that were not about love. I knew the country song genre drew: 1) from a ballad tradition that privileged the sung narration of history and current events ("Dear Uncle Sam" and "Galveston"); 2) from worksong, folksong, and blues traditions, which centered on the challenges of poverty ("Don't Forget the Coffee Billy Jo" or "Sixteen Tons"); and 3) from both white evangelical Christianity and Black gospel traditions, which appreciated songs that explicitly addressed God (such as "Drop Kick Me Jesus Through the Goal Post of Life" or "Why Me Lord?"). My chief strategy to becoming a successful songwriter and publisher was to write and publish songs in these categories.

I referred to this as "getting out of the traffic." In the post-*Urban Cowboy* boom of country song success in the 1980s, many writers and publishers were hyper-focused on achieving their own "Looking for Love (in all the Wrong Places)" major mailbox money by exploring the new sexual freedoms in the context of country romance and making it rhyme. Although there were non-love songs on the *Urban Cowboy* soundtrack, including "Hello, Texas" (performed by Jimmy Buffett), written by Robby Campbell and Brian Collins, and Michael Martin Murphy's brilliant "Cherokee Fiddle" (sung by Johnny Lee), the three biggest songs to emerge from the film were love songs. My new acquaintance Bob Morrison and his cowriters Wanda Mallette and Patti Ryan had spent three weeks at No.1 with "Lookin' for Love."

In search of inspiration for my non-love songs, I started exploring the oldest sections of the city and ended up on the banks of the Cumberland River on 2nd Avenue at a dress shop owned by Barbara Kurland, which is a very good thing because, as Michael Martin Murphy explains in "Cherokee Fiddle," "if you wanna make a living you got to put on a good show." I needed work clothes that worked.

Barbara Kurland had them. Her dress shop was in a nineteenth-century brick building across from a feed store. She sold cow-punk couture.

Clothing is an aspect of the construction of country music "performance identity" and (as I had discovered in Gant's Acuff-Rose office) "work identity." In the twentieth century, Manuel and Nudie were the most visible architects of the performance style, and they had an impact on the work style. As a person attempting to work in the industry, my clothes were work tools that marked or unmarked me as a viable member of the community.

Costuming is one reason that Lil Hardin and Ray Charles are not recognized for their seminal contributions to country: they didn't "dress country." Lil Hardin's costumes reference leisure and luxury. Racism and sexism are the primary reasons Lil gets erased, but costume and image play a role: she sings in elegant debutante-type gowns. Image was also, I believe, a delaying obstacle to the long overdue induction of Ray Charles into the Country Music Hall of Fame in 2021. Those who worked in the twenty-first century to see the placement of a plaque honoring Charles on the wall of the hallowed Rotunda among the other – and many lesser – greats had to overcome the visual impact of his seminal album. The cover of his master-piece *Modern Sounds in Country and Western Music* is a striking red, white, and black cover that features Charles in a black tuxedo jacket, white shirt with studs, and what appears to be a cross between a black tie and an ascot, with his signature dark sunglasses. Charles looks the picture of urban and urbane-understated wealth and cool. There is not one iota of country bumpkin in the picture – though there are bars and bars of beloved-by-country-bumpkin-strings, and all his gut-bucket-rugged-cross-Black coun-try vocals on the iconic album.

I purchased most of the clothes I worked the Row in from Barbara. She curated an inventory that helped to define a new, but distinctly recogniz-able, Music Row insider work uniform. I can still remember some of those one-of-a-kind, artsy, and affordable pieces: I chose dresses from her collec-tion that slyly referenced Black banjo playing women, Black fiddling women, Black blues shouting women, and Black gospel singing women *might wear*; dresses my grandmother *did wear*. Those dresses allowed me to walk in and announce without a word that I was connected. There was something liberating about walking the Row and knowing I did not need to be a breastless, hipless woman in a suit, to be a significant power. Barbara Kurland helped me get to that.

And she provided me with insider information about songwriters and recording sessions. Barbara's daughter Amy Kurland had just opened the Bluebird Café, which was fast becoming the gathering spot for working songwriters. Her husband Shelly Kurland was one of the most in-demand session players and string arrangers in the city. Nashville was a very small town.

Dressed for a new brand of success, and with a head full of the hottest songs on the country charts from studying *Billboard* and the weirdest country songs through immersing myself in that old sheet music and decades of demo reels (through a Barbara Kurland connection), I checked in with ASCAP's Bob Doyle. He had someone he wanted me to meet, Diana Reid Haig.

Diana was working at House of David as a studio manager and occasionally as recording engineer. The Sarah Lawrence graduate arrived in Nashville in 1981 and has been called the first female sound recording engineer on the Row. Diana and I started writing.

Everything about Diana was fifties. That's how she aesthetically negotiated a place for herself on the scene. She drove a two-tone 1956 four-door Chevy Bel Air, which was dark gray and cream. Her front room boasted an extraordinary collection of fifties-era television sets that were never turned on. A vintage record player with vintage singles was always going.

When our first song "Dangerous Curves," a cow-punk version of a fifties doo-wop was completed to our satisfaction, armed with the knowledge, probably from Barbara, that Steve Earle was cutting soon, it made sense to us to call Bob Doyle, talk him out of Steve Earle's phone number, then cold call Steve at his home to pitch the song.

It did not make sense to Steve. He started cussing. He called me everything but a child of God. A week later he called me on my rotary home phone at the number I had scribbled on the label. "You're going to be a hit songwriter one day and I'm going to help you." Steve and I set up standing writing appointments. The songs "You Tear Me Up," "Half-Way Home," and "You Can't Break My Heart" were my cowriting 101 class. In my father's terms, I was learning to "print money." I was still looking for a "gold mine," a writer I could publish.

I found one at the Weenie Roast.

The Weenie Roast was an annual Music Row summer ritual. Everyone, literally everyone was invited; anyone could just show up, and most folks doing any kind of work on Music Row came. It was hosted by a bank that liked being known as the "musician's friend." I attended my first Weenie Roast wearing one of my Barbara Kurland purchases. A tall man with dark eyes struck up a conversation. He was an extremely well-read surfer from California and seemingly high as a kite on ambition to be a hit songwriter. When he told me he wrote for Acuff-Rose, I asked him what his last name was. He said, "Sanders." When he discovered I was a songwriter, he invited me to write. I told him he didn't want to write with me because I had "[n]o talent whatsoever." When he realized that I was quoting his own words back to him, half-embarrassed, half-amused, he repeated the invitation to cowrite. This time I accepted. I was eager to prove Mark and his boss wrong.

Our first cowrite produced the cringeable, "I Don't Want to Be Your No. 1 (I Want to Be Your One and Only One)." Mark had seen and rejected my best ideas. His publisher wanted love songs. I had veered from my established strategy. The next time we sat down to write, I worked my plan. I suggested we write a song about religious hypocrisy and unwed mothers. He liked the idea. I pitched a title, "Reckless Night" and lines from a rough draft he had previously seen and dismissed. This time he was intrigued.

By the time we completed "Reckless Night," a song that would get recorded, I knew I had found a radically under-utilized and radically underfunded asset. Mark was substitute teaching five days a week to pay his bills. I suspected we could lure him away from Acuff-Rose if we offered a big enough draw. And I believed if we encouraged him to start writing something other than the love songs Ronnie was hankering for, he might be the Midsummer gold mine.

Mark wasn't ready to sign with Midsummer yet. We didn't have a plugger other than me. He believed I could write. He wasn't sure I could plug.

I found my song plugger looking for a writer who would let me pitch. Karen Conrad approached me between sets at one of the bars on 8th Avenue, Douglas Corner, or the Sutler. She came straight to the point, "I see you all the time. We should know each other. Come see me." Then she gave me her card. The way she went back to working the room, I knew I would take her up on the invitation.

One conversation convinced both of us that our interests were aligned. My business partner Edith and I contracted with Karen to pitch the Midsummer catalog. The woman who had pitched Jimmy Buffett and Jim Croce and had stepped out to form her own publishing company was now pitching me. Karen was thrilled to be, as she described it, "No longer hanging on by my fake fingernails" and to be able to use some of the money we were paying her to pitch to fund signing her own writers. At that time no bank in Nashville would loan a female independent publisher money for the purpose of running her business. It was a big win-win.

It was time to have another conversation with Mark Sanders. He had moved from Acuff-Rose to Maypop, a publisher owned by the band Alabama. We offered a big draw, I think I remember it was $37,500, with the stipulation he couldn't keep substitute teaching – he had to write full time. And we strongly encouraged him to write songs about something other than love.

Soon enough Mark was writing for Midsummer Music, Karen was pitching our songs, and we had an office in the cool Audio Media Building on 19th Avenue South. All we were missing was that first cut – for me as a songwriter and for Midsummer Music as a publisher.

Steve Earle helped get that done. One afternoon, he invited me and a visiting out-of-town friend of mine to hang out with him at the publishing company where he was, Silverline-Goldline. His publisher, Pat Halper, joined the conversation. Before I knew it, my friend was mansplaining to Pat Halper, one of the first women to be hired by a major publisher, why she needed to listen to "Reckless Night" and get it recorded.

Ever gracious, and often amused, Pat listened to the cassette demo of the song. Then she opined the song could be perfect for the Forester Sisters – and she was pitching at Warner Brothers for the Forester Sisters the very next week. Though she had nothing to gain financially, Pat pitched the song to her friend Paige Levy, the A+R (Artist and Repertory) executive at Warner Bros. working with the Foresters. I was on my way to having a song on their most successful album and the B-side of a No. 1 single. The album *The Forester Sisters* reached No. 4 on *Billboard*'s Country Albums chart. And in time they would prove to be one of the most successful all-female country groups with fourteen Top 10 singles.

The same week Pat got "Reckless Night" "on hold," I got engaged to be married to my daughter's father. Mark sang "Reckless Night" at my wedding reception in Washington, DC. Shortly after the wedding and honeymoon, my new husband joined the State Department and we shipped out to the Philippines, where the country standard, "Baby I Lied," performed by my friend Deborah Allen and written by Deborah and her then-husband Rafe Van Hoy, would become the theme song for the People Power Revolution. For my first anniversary, my husband got me a Shih Tzu puppy; we named him Reckless. I was based in Manila but commuting to Nashville.

My first long summer writing trip I got invited to attend Farm Aid, which in 1986 was still being held on Willie Nelson's ranch outside of Austin, Texas. Bonnie Raitt's mesmerizing performance of "Angel from Montgomery" would have been the highlight of that trip, but that got eclipsed. An acquaintance tried to pressure me into joining in the illicit druggy fun. I declined but ended up coaxing them into trying a jolt of sobriety. In the Austin airport, flying back to Nashville, the lines to "Girls Ride Horses, Too" began to take shape. It was a story song about a drug-running man who tries to intimidate a girl and ends up getting robbed and educated by the girl.

As I remember it, Mark Sanders and I took about three days to get that song written right. Then Karen got it cut almost as quick. Her old friend Tommy West was producing an album for Judy Rodman, newly signed to MTM Records, a country label founded by television star Mary Tyler Moore. Soon enough Mark and I had our first Top 10 Hit – and the mailbox money was rolling in.

Edith remembers that I came to her one day and said, I no longer want to be management, I just want to be an artist, by which I meant songwriter and novelist. And I remember that, too. It was exhausting trying to be an artist and management. And we weren't making big bucks yet. I had an idea. Bob Doyle was leaving ASCAP to start his own management and publishing company based on a new writer–performer he had discovered, Garth Brooks. I suggested we join forces in publishing. We did. It was a most excellent business decision.

I remember I sold a part of the company to Edith when my daughter was born, in 1987, decreasing my share to fifty percent. By 1990 I had sold Midsummer completely to Edith and signed with SonyATV, the company that Buddy Killen had built, which by the time I arrived was led by a financial force of nature that was Donna Hilley – a big, blonde, and brilliant, shark.

Donna rose from being a secretary at Tree to being the head of the conglomerate Tree, which became Sony/ATV. She was ready to conquer Hollywood and thought I "might-could-be" her ways and means. She knew I had written Reba McEntire's video of the year, "Is There Life Out There," and had some spec screenplays that were music driven. She gave me a hefty advance. And she got me invited to that celebrity bowling event, where I met the Hollywood agent.

I was signed to Donna at Sony/ATV publishing when I cowrote "The Ballad of Sally Ann," a song about a Black wife who seeks justice for her Black husband who is lynched between their wedding and their reception. It was recorded by Mark O'Connor and the New Nashville Cats in 1990. It didn't connect with a large audience then or bring me much mailbox money in the twentieth century.

It's doing a lot better in the twenty-first. The American Music Shop video of the song featuring John Cowan on lead vocal was posted to YouTube on January 4, 2013, by Mark O'Connor's account. As of this writing that video has 93,766 views on that platform. Some consider it a modern bluegrass classic. Songs I wrote, published, and got recorded; songs in the twentieth century about the homeless, about small towns being smaller for girls, about environmental justice, about Black Cowboys, about slut shaming, about gender-based religious hypocrisy, about suicide and drug addiction among prostitutes on the American frontier that languished as album cuts in the twentieth century, earning little and having less social impact than I dreamed, than I wished, than I worked for, are connecting to audiences in the twenty-first.

"Went for a Ride," a song about a Black cowboy, which I cowrote with Radney Foster, has over 300,000 streams on Spotify alone. "Who's Minding the Garden" has 10,000 streams and was discovered on a streaming platform by a church that has now worked it up as a hymn for their in-person services that are also available virtually. In the twenty-first century, including "XXX's and OOO's," my songs have now racked up more than twenty-three million streams on Spotify.

Midsummer Music is still in business to this day. And Mark? He proved to be a gold mine for Midsummer and after Midsummer. He's had fourteen No. 1 hits, fifty singles, and over 200 cuts. His biggest song? "I Hope You Dance," recorded by Lee Ann Womack, which he wrote with my daughter's Saturday night babysitter – Tia Sillers – after I introduced them.

In 2022, Midsummer Music came back to me. Things are looking up. I am trusting that the Mechanical Licensing Collective is going to provide me with a whole new source of twenty-first-century mailbox money. And of course, I no longer step out onto my porch to pick up a check. I log into my email.

Sometimes when I go to my online email mailbox to see how much money I've made, I think of a Black woman born in Nashville in 1945 known on Music Row by a single name, Shirley. She came to work each day in a variation of the same crisp uniform, bright-colored tailored shirt and trousers. Shirley Washington found a room for me to write when I hadn't reserved a room. Sometimes she elevated me to the boardroom. Washington wasn't an "official" writer's rep, but she always had a seat, a cold Co-Cola, and advice for me. Shirley knew people would make an appointment to write and not bring their best lines, their best hooks, or their best melodies. She knew who was too racist or too sexist to write hits with me. She knew which of my outfits worked and which didn't work. She knew better than anyone else in the ASCAP building. And she wasn't afraid to tell me.

Shirley Washington began at ASCAP in 1982. She retired in 2010. For twenty-eight years, she played a role in connecting writers to other writers, to their official performing rights reps, and in getting the daily business of ASCAP done.

Every time I pick up my twenty-first-century mailbox money, I am benefitting from a woman who in the twentieth century worked on the Row in her version of a nineteenth-century maid's uniform.

I still "work the Row" and I work it in a uniform. There are many versions, but they are all head-to-toe black and drapey. That's what I wore when I joined the Vanderbilt University faculty in 2004, to teach Country Lyric in American Culture; it's what I wear when I teach Black Country, including the day Mickey Guyton visited class. It's what I wore consulting for and appearing in the documentary series, *Country Music* (2019) by Ken Burns, and the PBS documentary film on Charley Pride, *I'm Just Me* (2019). My uniform is my tribute, hiding in plain sight, to the only Black woman working Music Row when I arrived, a woman who contributed collaborative insight, administrative acumen, and elbow grease to the business of country music and yet got written out of too many histories of the business because of the uniform she wore. Whose country? Shirley's country. My country, too.

2 | "Dixie Chicked"

Sony versus The Chicks and the Regendering of Country Music in the Early Twenty-First Century

KRISTINE M. MCCUSKER

At a March 10, 2003, concert in London, England, The Chicks' lead singer Natalie Maines criticized President of the United States of America George W. Bush for his desire to invade Iraq. From the stage she said, "We don't want this war, this violence, and we're ashamed that the President of the United States is from Texas" (Sisario 2020). *The Guardian* quoted Maines' words in its concert review on March 12, 2003. Within days, the words had been repeated across the world, infuriating conservative country music fans, radio broadcasters, and radio conglomerates alike (Clarke 2003). Within months, The Chicks' music disappeared from country music radio. This action made political sense for a genre that has long been described as conservative (whether this is true is debatable). But it made little economic or cultural sense because of the trio's status as the most successful all-female country music group of all time (Dansby 2001a). Why, then, did radio stations shoot themselves in their own economic and cultural foot?

If you dig deeper into the history of turn-of-the-century country music, canceling The Chicks made perfect economic sense. More importantly, it made cultural sense to those invested in nostalgic images of country music's past, its rural roots, and its longing for a time when women supposedly knew their place. Coming some eleven months after the trio filed a major counter lawsuit against their publisher, Sony Records, and after they joined other artists in organizing against the big recording companies, The Chicks attempted to transform the recording industry's economies as well as country music's culture. Their lawsuit reflected that stance, particularly through their use of Racketeer Influenced and Corrupt Organizations (RICO) precedents, used by the United States Department of Justice to pursue and dismantle criminal syndicates.

Given that The Chicks recently dropped "Dixie" from their stage name in light of the Black Lives Matter movement, this article reflects that change except in those instances where the language is historically accurate, for example, to be "Dixie Chicked" is to be summarily excluded from the country music industry, language formed in 2003 (Sisario 2020). The term thus remains in the title to reflect this history.

27

They also exemplified a profound cultural threat to the genre as country music came to a reckoning in 2003 and 2004, when a clash between public performances and country music's longtime business practices caught The Chicks in its web as country radio decided to reimagine a genre that had strayed too far from country music's roots. It was too Adult Contemporary, there were too many women on stage and in the audience, and there were too many challenges against norms, both business and musical. It was time to move back to the ways of George Strait and George Jones, albeit modernized, for the twenty-first century. The political conservatism that emerged after the September 11, 2001, attacks did not hurt, given that it valued men's voices, deemed patriotic and military. Toby Keith and Darryl Worley, with their whiskered faces and aggressive stances, modeled the new masculinity that accompanied this new country music.

The outcome was immediate as programmers erased women from country music stages, even though The Judds, Shania Twain, The Chicks, and dozens of other female musicians had dominated the airwaves and record charts in the 1980s and 1990s. Indeed, Jada Watson (2019b, 548) demonstrated that "[w]ith the exception of 1997, women occupy the top of the chart for 38.3% of each year between 1996 and 2000 . . . this period of activity is notable for the number of women charting, and the number of female-led songs debuting, peaking, and remaining at the top of the chart." Radio programmers (mostly white and male) relegated women to a more passive role: as the main consumers of country music who only wanted to see men performing on stage, a sort of male fantasy play, where women were cast as desiring sexy male stars and jealous of other women who performed. This chapter examines the broader cultural, economic, and political shifts that undergirded the meaningful changes in country music performances and players from the 1990s to the early 2000s, which had profound implications for who and how an artist might claim to be a "country" performer.

The ultimate exclusion of white women (Black women were rarely welcomed on stage from the genre's beginnings) from radio in the early twenty-first century went entirely against country music radio's roots when it formed in the 1920s and 1930s. As I have argued in my book, *Lonesome Cowgirls and Honky-Tonk Angels*, performing women were critical to taming the new, unruly, and dangerous medium (McCusker 2008). Radio, beamed directly into the nation's living rooms deemed private and sacred, could disrupt that sacred space with immoral content unfit for a wholesome atmosphere. Female performers cast as southern mothers and cowgirls assured audiences that radio would first do no harm. Women were also essential in defining which content might work for that same audience. Barn dance radio programs, variety music programs that featured music, comedy acts, and sponsors' ads, promoted southern mothers and western cowgirls, who personally guaranteed programs would meet their own civilizing standards. While women never outnumbered men on stage, their presence had a significant cultural effect beyond mere numbers. The vast success of early country radio is apparent in the numbers. There were some 500 barn dance programs by 1939 in the United States, and WLS Chicago's program, the *National Barn Dance*, was regularly ranked in the top ten programs nationally. Its star, Lulu Belle Wiseman, was also named Radio Queen in 1936, beating out other luminaries like Helen Hayes (McCusker 2008). From the first, the genre's main audiences were never farmers or rural folk, at least exclusively, but lonely, nostalgic migrants to the big city who wanted to hear music that sounded like home. That ability to cater to multiple audiences affirmed the genre's economic and cultural power and made it a music that could bend and morph according to broader national trends.

The Great Depression helped radio's popularity by killing the recording market from about 1930 until after World War II ended. When the recording industry reemerged, barn dance radio eventually died out, eclipsed by television shows by 1949, which fostered dramatic changes in radio programming. Instead of variety shows, now the disc jockey format featured the latest country music recordings. The new format forced country artists to focus on record sales rather than selling a sponsor's product, and the vaunted No. 1 seller became a way to define success, even participation, in the industry, by both artists and industry executives. Scholars followed suit, focusing their scholarship on extant records, rather than radio programs, because recordings were easier to come by (McCusker 2008, 2017). Female musicians including iconic musicians Kitty Wells and Patsy Cline in the 1950s and Tammy Wynette, Loretta Lynn, and Dolly Parton in the 1960s paved the way for lesser-known female musicians to follow them onto the charts (Neely 2004; Keel 2004). Female audiences adored them, seeing their own lives on stage, and eagerly purchasing records like Lynn's "The Pill" (1975) because the song featured women's frustrations with pregnancy, hard work, and men's sexual freedom. Building on the success of Lynn and others in the 1960s and 1970s, in the 1980s, a subtle "feminist movement," according to journalist Beverly Keel (2004), presaged a generational, cultural, and economic shift in country music that exploded in the 1990s. The changes were incipient in the 1980s, with K.T. Oslin's *80s Ladies* selling a million copies in 1987, but required a shift in sound and business practice to come to fruition.

Garth Brooks' career was that shift as his marketing model, business acumen, and song catalog emphasizing a modern country aesthetic created new audiences beyond strictly traditional country music ones (Craig Campbell, conversation with author, April 12, 2021). In fact, Brooks' music catered to a generation raised on the rock bands Journey and Boston (Stimeling 2014). His third No. 1 hit, "Friends in Low Places," reworked older honky-tonk themes from the 1950s into a contemporary vision of a working-class man upbraiding his elitist ex, preferring beer and his friends over champagne and an ivory tower. Brooks emphasized strategic fan engagement, famously signing autographs for twenty-three hours straight at the Country Music Association Music Fest (previously known as Fan Fair) (Lindquist 2017; Dukes 2018). Former Sony marketing executive Craig Campbell (2021) recalled, "He was brilliant about starting fires all over the place. Every new artist should spend two hours with Garth Brooks and see how he treats fans . . . [and] the people around him."

Brooks' commercial success motivated a new generation of country music singers who catered to this new audience, wanting to hear country music's good storytelling and harmonies. Female musicians especially reflected the dreams, desires, and anxieties of that audience, who now pursued college degrees and lived in the suburbs. Previous iterations of country music that revolved around barns and hay bales were uninteresting. Music critics like Bruce Feiler (1996) argued that country music audiences had "become younger and better educated," making it the music of "white flight" – that trend of white Americans leaving cities for racially homogenous suburbs. The songs focused on white middle-class anxieties associated with those suburbs like unpaid bills, men making more money than women, and heartbreak, all the while longing for a time, according to The Judds, where a tractor (according to their 1984 hit song, "John Deere Tractor") could make the world seem right. The genre's nostalgia was a comforting reminder that, in the face of suburban anxieties, an easier, simpler time existed; one could take a break from contemporary insecurities and wallow in the past, if only for a moment.

Female performers catered to these anxieties, using older musical themes rendered in modern country sounds. Mary Chapin Carpenter's hit song, "He Thinks He'll Keep Her," from a Geritol ad from the 1970s (Geritol was a vitamin marketed to adults), hit No. 2 on the *Billboard* Hot Country Songs chart in 1993, and was reminiscent of the feminist overtones of "The Pill" ("The Women of Country Music Sing 'He Thinks He'll Keep Her'" 2004). Shania Twain's vast economic success encouraged frustrated women, who wanted to be economically independent, that other women were doing just fine and that they could, too (Keel 2004). Dozens of female performances brought new audiences to the genre who did not want to listen to icons Jones and Hank Williams, Jr., but to Reba McEntire, Twain, Faith Hill, Martina McBride, Kathy Mattea, Carpenter, LeAnn Rimes, Patty Loveless, Trisha Yearwood, and more, creating a steam-rolling effect, where one woman's music led to purchases of other women's music (Wells 2001). Twain also began filling arena-sized stadiums, beginning in 1996, and Carpenter performed during Super Bowl XXXI's pre-game show in 1997 (Hudak 2020).

Mainstream television recognized the importance – and economic impact – of these stars. For example, CBS filmed a special country concert called *Women of Country* in 1993, a show where some female stars performed their current hits, including a rousing rendition of "He Thinks He'll Keep Her" by Carpenter, backed by stars Emmylou Harris, Loveless, Pam Tillis, Yearwood, Mattea, and Suzy Bogguss. Later, contemporary country artists remember this era fondly, with Lauren Alaina's 2019 single "Ladies in the '90s," namechecking McEntire, Hill, The Chicks, Twain, and Deana Carter.

The 1990s musical successes also capitalized on the genre's gendered roots from the 1920s and 1930s. Lee Ann Womack's "I Hope You Dance" (2000), with a video showcasing her daughters, mimicked Lulu Belle Wiseman's motherly image from the 1930s. The Chicks' "Cowboy, Take Me Away" (from *Fly* [1999]) was inspired by Patsy Montana's million-seller "I Want to Be a Cowboy's Sweetheart" (1935), a song The Chicks covered before they were famous. Carpenter's "He Thinks He'll Keep Her" may have come from a Geritol ad, but its laments about a married woman's lot in life could have come straight from Mother Maybelle and Sara Carter's "Single Girl, Married Girl" (1927), another song that rued married women's experiences, cooking, cleaning, and raising babies. In many ways, one could argue that country music in the 1990s really harkened back to its pre-1950s roots, at least lyrically and thematically if not musically, to the days when southern mothers and cowgirls affirmed to their radio children that, in the midst of vast changes, the world was going to be alright (McCusker 2008).

Country music's commercial success in the 1990s eclipses any other decade of sales, with much of the success coming from female performers. While Brooks may have crashed multiple sales records, including having the top seven best-selling country albums of all time, only one other man, Kenny Rogers, broke into the list of the top fifteen best-selling country albums list, according to the Recording Industry Association of America.

The Chicks, Twain, Taylor Swift, and Cline round out the top fifteen (Casey 2018). Generally, these sales were the result of appealing to listeners outside the traditional country music audience who were under the age of thirty-five (Weisbard 2017, 240). Programmers responded to this success by saying, "[N]ow they're [women] driving the bus" (qtd. in Weisbard 2017, 241). In fact, some asked whether male country listeners were being left behind (Weisbard 2017, 241) because these women sang to and about other women's experiences. Pushback, then, was inevitable from programmers, who were (and are) mostly white and male (Deborah Wagnon, conversation with author, April 6, 2021). They refused to play McBride's "Independence Day" in 1994, for example, because the song was about murdering an abuser (Keel 2004).

Into this moment stepped sisters Martie and Emily Erwin (now Martie Maguire and Emily Strayer), who formed a band called the Dixie Chickens in 1989. The group, however, did not achieve commercial success until they added Natalie Maines as their lead singer and changed their name to Dixie Chicks, just after signing a memorandum agreement with Sony's Monument Records in mid-1995 (Hess 2020; Wagnon 2021). With Maines' addition, their sound shifted to a fused country-pop music sound, different enough for some to accuse the band of "selling out," but interesting enough to make noncountry fans tune in (Friskics-Warren 2002). Sony and The Chicks then signed a long-form contract in 1997, the standard contract that was structured "to allow labels to extract much of their earnings from the handful of blockbuster albums each year" (Philips 2001). Recording contracts always favored the label because they were written in a trickle-down format. This meant the record company and all contributors (e.g., the producers, costumers, video producers) were paid first before the artists saw a dime (John Dougan, conversation with author, 2019; Wagnon 2021; Beverly Keel, conversation with author, April 5, 2021). The rarity of a blockbuster success, moreover, meant that one success paid for all the investments into other acts that never "broke" or became financially successful.

The initial marketing plan for The Chicks' emphasized a broader audience than just country radio (Campbell 2021). Craig Campbell, who was on The Chicks' marketing team at Monument Records, recalled that he and others devised both a textbook strategy for the first single, "I Can Love You Better," as well as an untraditional one that focused on them as a novelty act. Thus, in typical form, The Chicks visited as many radio programmers as possible, and in atypical form, performed on "B-level" television shows (meaning fewer viewers) like the *Sally Jessy Raphael Show* and the *RuPaul*

Show. The strategy worked: *Wide Open Spaces*, released in 1997, sold over fourteen million records. The band followed up with *Fly* in 1999, which sold ten million records (Casey 2018). Audiences, many of them female, flocked to the arenas The Chicks then began selling out. Campbell remembers seeing them perform in Clarksville, Tennessee, at Riverfest and described the audience he saw there:

The first probably ten people deep were little girls who wanted to be Dixie Chicks. Then the next ten or twenty deep were women who identified with the music. And then the guys who were in the back wanted to be with the Dixie Chicks. That's the best way I can describe how that crowd looked because it was like different sections all the way back. (Campbell 2021)

Journalist Chris Willman (2005, xiii) simply (and dismissively) described their audience as "gaggles of girls."

Quickly, The Chicks ran up against the Nashville music industry's implied rules and restrictions that had been forged by the men who held the real power in the business: radio programmers and producers. Nashville insiders describe it this way. It's a:

[C]ult, you're either in or you're out. Membership matters . . . [there are] unwritten rules of Nashville you learn by being in it. It's not broadcast. Premier one: be nice to radio because without it you will make it or not make it. At the same time, if you are a country music artist, profess your joy and gratitude for being able to be in country music and never suggest that you might want to cross over and become a pop artist because you will go into the ether. (Wagnon 2021)

That cult, however, required relatively warm relationships that symbolized the genre's claims of authentic, meaningful music that connected emotionally with listeners, at least superficially, setting up a music system that was ironic and insular (Campbell 2021). Dan Daley (1998), whose book, *Nashville's Unwritten Rules*, documented the industry in this era, described these ironies, claiming it was "rigid, familial, and benignly feudal."

That feudal society was transformed, thanks to the Telecommunications Act of 1996, which allowed companies to own multiple radio stations simultaneously, for example, emergent radio conglomerates like Cumulus (445 radio stations) and Clear Channel (now iHeartRadio, 1,200+ radio stations). They became new players in policing country radio musicians and playlists. After September 11, 2001, for example, Clear Channel sent a memo to its stations, telling them to pull all hip-hop, metal, and hard rock songs off its lists (Dougan 2019). One of the consolidation's outcomes was how performers became famous. The Chicks' manager, Simon Renshaw

(2003), testifying before the US Senate Commerce Committee, documented the vast effect the Act had on country musicians specifically:

Before the 1996 Telecommunications Act, artists and record labels worked well with the radio industry. Each side needed the other, and while each exerted as much influence and leverage over the other in the daily give and take between them, a delicate balance emerged. This system, while imperfect, still worked. All of that has now changed. The mad rush to consolidate dramatically tipped the balance in favor of the radio industry. They now have unprecedented influence and control over the artists and record labels . . . Without radio airplay a new act has very little chance to succeed. Access to radio is absolutely essential.

Renshaw (2003) argued that centralized programming created significant "cultural damage," too, because conglomerates favored centralized programming with more homogenized playlists with relatively similar sounds. What was different from the early days of radio was that now one company owned multiple radio stations from multiple genres and strove to conduct its business cross-genre without regard to local- or genre-based practices or sounds.

The Chicks made radio-friendly music that the radio conglomerates liked but refused to adhere to Nashville's strict etiquette. Maines, according to one journalist (Shaffer 2019), was "a point of contention amongst critics even before *Wide Open Spaces* hit shelves," with one critic referring to Maines as a "chubby loudmouth" (Crain 2000). Their antiauthoritarianism was part of their persona that their audiences loved, and Nashville executives tolerated. *Time*'s Josh Tyrangiel (2002) wrote, "Until recently, their [The Chicks'] breaches of country etiquette had the harmless air of cheerleaders caught smoking under the bleachers; they were rascals but loveable rascals." The skeptical eye came in part from The Chicks' stage attire and demeanor, which were not the traditional ladylike personas, but raucous events where one had fun rather than good manners. Bill Friskics-Warren (2002) called their stage dress country "post punk, neo hippie" ensembles, a refreshing change to other more conventionally dressed stars. Their musical skill reinforced their brash stage presence: they were eclectic, stellar musicians, heavily influenced by bluegrass and rock n' roll as well as Texas music. They used what were by then nontraditional instruments for women like the banjo and fiddle and channeled an "Outlaw" vibe not unlike Merle Haggard and Willie Nelson in the 1970s (Friskics-Warren 2002). Lyrically, they merged pop music sounds with standard country instrumentation and themes. The song "Goodbye Earl" from *Fly*, where the song's protagonists murder wife-beater Earl by dousing his black-eyed peas with poison, brought on claims of feminist aggressiveness, and twenty radio stations banned the song outright (Friskics-Warren 2002; Keel 2004). Some pointed out the ironies that in a genre known for its "murder girl ballads" like "Pretty Polly," which featured women's murders, Brooks' "Papa Loved Mama," which described a husband murdering his wife, had no problem finding airplay (Hamessley 2005).

Country music radio did not think it had a choice as to whether it played The Chicks' music if it wanted to remain economically viable (Friskics-Warren 2002). Darren Davis, a program director for the now-defunct Infinity Broadcasting network, said in 2002, "Sure, we have a choice [in whether to play The Chicks' music], but one also has a choice to cut off one's nose to spite their face. The Dixie Chicks are the biggest of the big right now. We play their music as often as we can get it on the air." In other words, The Chicks might have ruffled feathers, but as long as they were generally acquiescent and sold a lot of records, no one was in a hurry to muffle them.

That blind eye changed to a scrutinizing one with The Chicks' decision to challenge the industry's business practices. Insiders blame journalist Dan Rather for planting the initial seed when he suggested, in an interview with The Chicks in October 2000, that Sony Records was making a lot of money from them ("60 Minutes II [60 Minutes Wednesday] Stories with Dan Rather" n.d.). No clip of the interview remains, but insiders describe Rather calculating that a CD cost approximately $17 and then multiplying that number by the number of albums The Chicks had sold (Campbell 2021; Keel 2021; McKay 2000). Insiders called it "irresponsible journalism," in that Rather did not know that Sony did not make that amount of money per CD, in fact much less (Campbell 2021; Keel 2021). The Chicks were caught off guard by the amount, however, and the moment seems to have catalyzed them to review their contract.

The Chicks first joined with other musical artists who were also challenging their record labels, for example, Don Henley, Rimes, Courtney Love, and others who wanted to make structural changes to the industry (Friskics-Warren 2002; Renshaw 2003). At the time (2000–2), five recording companies – Time Warner, EMI, BMG, Universal Music Group, and BMG Entertainment – owned 90 percent of the recording business, bringing in $40 billion per year and giving them a sense that they could act with impunity (Chang 2002). There were particularly egregious examples of record company misconduct with older artists whose works were re-released on CDs without any royalties paid to them, for example. The Drifters, the Coasters, the Chambers Brothers, and Main

Ingredient all sued, with appellate courts siding with them (*Tony Sylvester, et. al., vs. Time Warner, 2004*).

Contemporary stars thought bigger than royalties, however (Philips 2002). Artists started an organization called Artists Versus Piracy to fight for control of their digital copyrights. Love then brought a lawsuit against Vivendi Universal, calling her recording contract a kind of "indentured servitude" (Chang 2002). Claiming record companies constituted a "cartel" and were "archaic," musicians then lobbied the California State Legislature with the intention of "radically rewrit[ing] the economics of the music business" and to make sure "the industry as we know it would cease to exist" (Philips 2001). The California hearing had global potential because the music business was centered there and could affect music practices globally (Chang 2002).

Musicians wanted to negate one particular portion of California's labor code called the seven-year rule, which made most labor contracts (like a recording contract) null and void after seven years. The seven-year rule had emerged when Olivia de Havilland took the Hollywood studio system and its exploitative long-term contracts to court in 1943 and won in a California State Supreme Court in December 1944. This decision had far-reaching consequences for other movie stars – and their contracts – who were now only beholden to a labor contract for seven years, not for a lifetime (Chang 2002; Berkvist 2020). But in 1989, the state legislature exempted musicians from the seven-year rule, giving record companies long-term hold over them. Think of it this way: if a band was required to supply the record company with seven albums, it did not matter whether it took seven years or twenty years to produce them. The number of albums dictated the length of time with a record company, not years of service (Chang 2002). Hoping to motivate California authorities to pass new legislation, musicians such as Rimes, Henley, and R&B singer Patti Austin publicly testified on September 5, 2001. The Chicks did not testify but sat in the audience as the testimonies were given (Philips 2001, 2002; *The Lompoc Record* 2001; Holson 2002). The momentum, however, withered quickly with the September 11, 2001 attacks just six days after the meetings.

The Chicks tried other tactics as well, moving them from "rascals to rebels," according to Tyrangiel (2002), when they created "the ugliest financial squabble in recent country history," just before their appearance in the California State Legislature. On July 13, 2001, The Chicks notified Sony they would not be delivering their next release *Home*, the group's third album per the long-form agreement signed in 1997. The Chicks, by their own accounting, claimed Sony had defrauded them of $200 million – "systematic thievery" in their words – and they would do no more work until they renegotiated their contract (Philips 2002). In part, The Chicks were responding to the facile calculations Rather had made in their interview: he suggested that Sony was making approximately $17 per CD and yet The Chicks were seeing very little of that money (Campbell 2021). Rather, of course, did not take into account the costs of producing CDs and other inherent production costs, but the point was made. *Time* magazine quoted Maines as saying, "Every new act signs a bad deal. But we never dreamed that the s_____ [sic] contract we signed wouldn't even be honored" (qtd. in Tyrangiel 2002). Campbell recalled, "It was a huge deal the minute it came out," and other unnamed musicians told The Chicks to "keep their mouths shut" since many viewed the lawsuit as a significant breach of Nashville etiquette (Campbell 2021; Tyrangiel 2002). In response, on July 17, 2001, Sony filed a breach of contract lawsuit against The Chicks, and on August 28, 2001, The Chicks countersued (Dansby 2001a, 2001b).

The Chicks hired lawyer Donald S. Engel, later called a "Persistent Contract Lawyer to the Stars," who helped musicians such as Donna Summer, Olivia Newton-John, and Frank Sinatra renegotiate unfair entertainment contracts (Webber 2014). Under his guidance, The Chicks cited five specific issues with their Sony contract in the Southern District of New York:

- There was a breach of contract, meaning the terms, particularly royalties, set out in the long-form contract had yet to be paid in full. This was a key issue, in that The Chicks asserted that Sony had failed to pay them the money that was owed to them.
- This constituted fraud for the same reason.
- This led to a breach of fiduciary duty, meaning Sony had not fulfilled its responsibilities in paying The Chicks correctly.
- Sony also "misrepresented and failed to disclose material facts regarding a producer's [Nashville producer, Paul Worley, who produced *Wide Open Spaces* and *Fly*] royalty rate." Indeed, The Chicks alleged, at a minimum, Sony had overcharged them $150,000 for Worley's services.
- Sony had behaved as a corrupt organization as defined by the Racketeer Influenced and Corrupt Organizations Act (RICO).

It was this fifth claim that likely frightened Sony the most. RICO statutes had been passed in 1970 to dismantle the Mafia, as part of the Organized Crime Control Act, and were later used against other multiple, potentially corrupt organizations (Ashley Carter, conversation with author March 26, 2021; *Sony Music Entertainment Inc. v. Emily Burns Erwin Robison, et. al.* 2002; Staff of the Organized Crime and Gang Section 2016). RICO statutes made illegal those business networks that controlled the pricing, distribution, and profits of a certain market (the Mafia's control of various vice rackets, for example) across state lines, comprising an elimination of the free market (Carter 2021). RICO claims disparaged the company charged, given the "almost inevitable stigmatizing effect on those named as defendants, ... courts should strive to flush out frivolous RICO allegations at an early stage of the litigation" (*Katzman v. Victoria's Secret Catalogue* 1996). A RICO claim also allowed for three times the damages asked for, if proven (Carter 2021). It was thus this charge that made the recording companies take notice because its implications went far beyond The Chicks' contract, becoming a bargaining chip for them to sign a new contract (*Sony Music Entertainment Inc. v. Emily Burns Erwin Robison, et. al.* 2002).

The court upheld one of The Chicks' claims, denied several others, and allowed them to refile on some of the more damaging claims. The outright win was on the fourth issue: the court found that The Chicks had sufficiently proven that they had been overcharged for Worley's services (*Sony Music Entertainment Inc. v. Emily Burns Erwin Robison, et. al.* 2002). The key financial relationship – that of Sony's lack of a fiduciary responsibility to The Chicks, the first, second, and third claims – was upheld. Sony argued the company merely collected money owed to The Chicks, passing it on after subtracting what the women owed Sony. Because it did not actually gather money from customers directly, these practices did not constitute a fiduciary relationship, according to the court and affirmed by case law and multiple precedents. The first through third claims were thus dismissed with prejudice, meaning there was no chance to refile (Chang 2002).

The RICO claims still had real potential to make systemic changes, however. According to court documents, The Chicks argued that Sony had engaged in a "pattern of racketeering activity sufficient to survive a motion to dismiss, based on their allegations that the predicate acts were related, had similar purposes, participants, victims and methods, and that the acts extended over a substantial amount of time" (*Sony Music Entertainment Inc. v. Emily Burns Erwin Robison, et. al.* 2002, 5). In other words, the company was similar to the Mafia in its business practices, in that when it formed agreements with record clubs and foreign distributors, it created relationships – not unlike the Mafia's – that crossed state and national boundaries. Therefore, it had become a criminal enterprise that used its power to defraud The Chicks. While The Chicks did not provide enough specific data to uphold this claim, the court gave them leave to replead once they had it.

While the lawsuits were working their way through the courts, The Chicks finished their new album, *Home*, and then actively shopped it to other record companies. However, once the court handed down its mixed decision on April 11, 2002, negotiations reopened with Sony. In return for a $20 million payment and a higher (20%) residual rate, The Chicks agreed to fulfill their original contract for seven albums. The Chicks would release their albums through their own label, Wide Open Records, but the albums would be marketed and distributed by Sony (Tyrangiel 2002; Philips 2002). Once the settlement was announced, tensions seemed to go on mute, with *Home* selling albums in numbers similar to *Fly* and *Wide Open Spaces*, until Maines spoke her infamous words from a London stage and radio programmers and others decided to "cancel" them (Willman 2005; Rossman 2012).

The resulting expulsion from country radio has been cast as a political act, with Republican-leaning programmers and conglomerates deciding anyone who disagreed with the Republican president had to be muzzled. But the reasons were far broader than just a perceived verbal gaffe. Radio programmers used Maines' words as an excuse to shift the genre away from female acts, willingly accepting the economic cost. That shift came before Maines' statement, with *Billboard* magazine reporting by July 2003 that "female [country] artists have become a fading presence" (Stark 2003). Programmers blamed a "sameness" of sound. The journalist Phyllis Stark cited "radio's well-documented objections to what some programmers perceived as the pop direction of the latest albums from superstars Faith Hill and Shania Twain. More telling, programmers also cite a lack of substantive songs being recorded by women and more interesting music coming from male acts" (Stark 2003, 73). Retrospectively, looking back on the era, radio programmers affirmed this, saying "pop crossover artists like Shania Twain and Faith Hill [took] the format in a different direction than it ultimately ended up being." Nate Deaton, a radio general manager, said, "I think there was a big move in this format in the late '90s to an AC [Adult Contemporary] radio format ... It wasn't necessarily just the female artists ... (But) it really didn't separate us enough from the AC stations" (Willman 2020). One could add that not only was the music not interesting in programmers' eyes, but it came with a healthy legal challenge no one wanted to consider.

To make these changes, programmers used a variety of tactics. They first constructed a myth that, because country music audiences were (and are) primarily female, they wanted to hear men (Keel 2015b). This became the cultural justification to eliminate women from country radio in favor of an almost exclusively male lineup that was willing to follow the Nashville cult's rules (Willman 2020). Programming quotas also helped. Beginning in the mid-1970s, programmers put in mechanisms to limit the number of artists who were played on the air. Where once 60–70 records were in rotation, now only thirty-five records were played by the mid-1970s (Watson 2019b; Weisbard 2017). Scholar Eric Weisbard argues that country radio, as "gatekeepers" to the genre, gained "an unusual power to introduce new performers and preserve older ones" (Weisbard 2017, 229). Record labels upheld the practice out of fear that programmers would eliminate all of their artists, affecting women as well as older male artists like Jones, who complained loudly that their music was no longer played (Trigger 2015). Thus, as Watson (2019a/b) found in her statistical analysis of country music, 40 percent of the No. 1 country songs came from women in the late 1990s; from 2002 onward, only 13 percent did. The exclusion later became naturalized. As one radio consultant, Keith Hill, said, "Trust me, I play great female records and we've got some right now; they're just not the lettuce in our salad. The lettuce is Luke Bryan and Blake Shelton, Keith Urban and artists like that. The tomatoes of our salad are the females" (qtd. in Keel 2015a).

The narrow focus on The Chicks' elimination from the country music genre as the outcome of a political opinion rather than as part of a broader context does not adequately explain The Chicks' ultimate exclusion from country music charts. That broader context allows us to see the multiple factors that went into the remaking of the country music genre and charts at the turn of the twenty-first century, a cultural shift that led to the exclusion of most women from country radio and then, country charts. Whether it was shifts in radio formats, testimony in front of legislative bodies, lawsuits, or poorly phrased statements from international stages, this constellation of factors led to the most successful group in country music history being expelled from radio, and in lockstep went other women who represented a version of country music male programmers no longer wanted to play.

3 | How 360° Deals Homogenized Country Music

RACHEL SKAGGS

Released on November 4, 2014, on YouTube, Sir Mashalot, the username of country music songwriter Greg Todd, released a video titled "Mind-Blowing SIX Song Country Mashup." The three minutes and fifty-five seconds of the video is comprised of a synthesis of six country songs: "Sure Be Cool if You Did" by Blake Shelton, "Close Your Eyes" by Parmalee, "This Is How We Roll" by Florida Georgia Line, "Ready Set Let's Roll" by Chase Rice, "Chillin' It" by Cole Swindell, and "Drunk on You" by Luke Bryan. The songs were released between February 2012 and February 2014, and they each performed well according to measures of commercial success. Four peaked at No. 1 on the *Billboard* Hot Country Songs chart ("This Is How We Roll," "Chillin' It," "Drunk on You," "Sure Be Cool if You Did"),[1] "Ready Set Let's Roll" peaked at No. 5, and "Close Your Eyes" peaked at No. 11.

This video's interspersed mix of song clips convincingly makes the case that much of the music that was popular during this time was homogenous, rather than just cohesive or emblematic of a particular moment in music. Todd changed the key for some of the songs to ensure that they would not be dissonant when played as one unified mashup, but even beyond this change, the tracks share a number of other similarities. In particular, the lyrical themes contained in the songs are remarkably alike, referencing the Fourth of July, being outdoors at night, trucks, drinking beer or liquor, listening to loud music on speakers, and a general evocation of chill, cool, or otherwise relaxed feelings.

Despite convincing explanations of the songs' similarity based on country's genre conventions and the limitations of the chromatic scale (Parton 2015), underlying the ways that the songs sound and the themes put forth in the lyrics is the social arrangement of the creation of country music, including their temporal position as singles in a particular social and economic moment. They were meant to fit in – their purpose was to ensure an economic return in a turbulent time when the record industry was

---

[1] Peak dates in order of appearance in this chapter: March 29, 2014; March 1, 2014; July 7, 2012; March 9, 2013; November 1, 2014; December 20, 2014.

hemorrhaging money and seeing low returns on capital investments into artists. During this period, roughly beginning in 1999, the transition from record-breaking album sales and high earnings across the recorded music industry to a digital music economy, where songs were often illegally downloaded and sales plummeted, caused a number of ricocheting changes. The economic sum of these changes accounted for substantial losses in the US record industry, with RIAA (2020) reporting a 66.2 percent revenue loss (in 2019 dollars) from the total 2000 revenue of $21.3 billion to 2015's total revenue of $7.2 billion. Economic downturns, however, have implications that reach much further than quantifiable losses alone. These losses had far-reaching effects, including changes to recording contracts, called "360° deals," on which this chapter is focused. I argue that these economic and bureaucratic changes ultimately altered collaborative patterns between songwriters and recording artists, which, in turn, facilitated the creation of a set of more homogenous songs.

To understand the downstream effects of the industry's economic challenges and the resulting contractual changes, I draw on interviews with country music songwriters who wrote successful songs, defined by a song's appearance on the *Billboard* Year-End Hot Country Songs chart, Nashville Songwriters Association International's List of "Songs I Wish I Had Written," the *Nashville Scene*'s list of "Year-End Critics' Picks," or the Grammy Nominees for Country Song of the Year from 2000 to 2015. The individuals who participated are given pseudonyms for privacy, in accordance with my IRB ethics agreement. Though the interviews focused on a variety of topics over the course of an hour or more, the responses in this chapter detail their experiences of writing songs during the era when 360° deals were implemented and how this affected their careers and their songs. Through these interviews, I show how the larger industry conditions in the early twenty-first century led to the institution of the 360° deal, how that construct shaped the cowriting sessions where songwriters create music, and how the resulting songs emerged as a more homogenous set.

Art worlds are social, and the conventions that characterize art are socially constructed and arranged by the people who make up the social group (Becker 1982). The similarities between songs of a certain era are not limited to country music; indeed it is important for songs to be optimally differentiated from peer songs to be successful (Askin and Mauskapf 2017). Songs meant for popular, widespread success have to sound similar enough while still maintaining originality. Even the case of the YouTube mashup suggests the importance of the social patterns that led to the songs' similarity. NPR interviewed Greg Todd on a segment of *All Things*

Considered, where he voices his frustration: "Todd says it's hard to break past the gatekeepers of popular country music. But he's considering writing a 'seventh song that fits right into this mold. At the very least, they can't tell me it doesn't sound like a hit'" (*All Things Considered* 2015).

Cultural products are a reflection of the society to which they belong. This truism extends beyond aesthetic and topical trends to the social and political economic construction of the conditions in which music is created. The unique matrix of technology, law and regulations, industry structure, organizational structure, occupational careers, and markets shapes the kind of cultural product that can emerge in a given time and social context (Peterson and Anand 2004). Sociological thought implores us to consider musical genres as communities (Lena 2012). The people whose collective action, affiliation, and work creates music genres are bound together by more than only the common ties of aesthetic taste and historical genre conventions. Regardless of whether or not Todd's song would fit into the mold of the other songs in his mashup, it is unlikely that his song would be recorded and released on a major artist's album without the right social connectedness between Todd and others in the Nashville music industry. It is not only aesthetic conventions that are being performed, recorded, and marketed as singles but also the enactment and perpetuation of the structure of power that is encoded in the collaborations that make country music.

A Bro-Country Backlash

Tyler Mahan Coe is the host of the podcast *Cocaine and Rhinestones*, which focuses on narratives around country music in the twentieth century. In response to complaints about country music in the twenty-first century "ruining" the genre, Coe illustrates the lineage of trends in country music eras after declaring, "The story of country music radio from its beginning until now is a story of homogenization" (Coe 2017). He says:

I'm sure many of you remember in the '90s, older country artists talked a lot of trash about what was being played on the radio. Waylon Jennings may never have really used that extremely vulgar simile to describe Garth Brooks' music, but he did say very critical things about Garth Brooks. Now, you go listen to the trash Luke Bryan puts out and tell me that doesn't make Garth Brooks sound like Buck Owens. Well, that's not what a lot of fans of "real country" thought in the '90s when Garth Brooks "ruined country radio." Or, in the '80s, when Urban Cowboy "ruined country radio." Or, in the '70s when Olivia Newton-John won a CMA award for Most Promising Female Vocalist of the Year, and a bunch of traditional country acts, like Porter Wagoner and Conway Twitty, all got together at George Jones' and Tammy Wynette's house to form the Association of Country Entertainers to protest smooth pop "ruining country radio." But, in the '60s, the Nashville Sound had already "ruined country radio." And that started in the '50s because Elvis Presley "ruined country radio." When drums started showing up on more country records in the '40s, well, it flat out "ruined country radio." And that only happened because in the 1930s people like Bob Wills couldn't settle the hell down and play some nice, pure country music, like Jimmie Rodgers or The Carter Family.

The songs during the period of my study are homogenous too; they cohere around the bro-country style, which Coe (2017) references as the "trash Luke Bryan puts out." As a sociologist I am not a country music critic and do not make aesthetic judgments about the quality of music during this or any period. Rather, my concerns are in the structural underpinnings of the production of songs, and my approach to understanding homogeneity in music is based on underlying patterns of collaboration in the creation of songs.

Sociologist Richard Peterson identified this same problem as a characteristic of the fabricated authenticity that proliferates the country music industry. Peterson (1997) argues that it is a seemingly impossible combination of authenticity and originality that make country songs and their artists carve out and perform their credible personas. Peterson (1997, 230) goes on to note that while there can be innovation and style changes that exist within authenticity, "some interests in the field as well as some outside are always working to change the structure of the field to their own advantage, while those who identify their interests with the current system staunchly defend the status quo." Both Coe and Peterson are concerned with country music in the twentieth century, but the twenty-first century brought changes to the genre that are not purely stylistic. The drastic downturn in the sale of albums and songs contributed to an alteration in the social conditions that led to these six homogenous songs and the countless others that dominated the genre beginning in the mid-2000s. The search for stability and economic return in a down market shaped the social arrangement behind the creation of homogenous songs, forcing people to write in a narrow groove in hopes of album cuts, radio spins, and digital streams.

The 360° Deal in Country Music

The recorded music industry was shaken and economically destabilized at the turn of the millennium because of the digitization of music (Stahl and

Meier 2012). The technological innovation that allowed music to be stored, sold, and distributed on the Internet was slow to be adopted by record labels. The shift to digital music distribution was not stopped by the lack of legitimate places to purchase music online as digital music piracy came into vogue, enabling fans to illegally download music from sites like Napster, Limewire, and Kazaa (Bender and Wang 2009). Even the sales patterns for legal digital music downloads shifted the landscape of music (Stahl and Meier 2012); sites like iTunes allowed for the album to be "unbundled," allowing consumers to easily pick and choose which single tracks to purchase individually (Zhu and MacQuarrie 2003). Later in the decade, digital streaming platforms like Spotify, Pandora, and YouTube solidified the digital music economy, further shifting the economic structure under which music is created.

The loss from declining sales was initially felt by record labels. In turn, they became increasingly financially conservative and risk averse. This is visible in the number of acquisitions and mergers that record labels underwent during this time period, shrinking from six to three major record labels from 2000 to 2007 (Hiatt and Serpick 2007). One way that record labels contended with the precipitous drop in revenue was a new contractual arrangement known as the 360° deal. These contracts were introduced as a way for record labels to recoup some of the revenue lost with the decline of recorded music sales and limit labels' uncertainty about returns to the career-building work they do for artists, thus shifting the power balance in the music industry (Marshall 2013). Rather than typical recording contracts wherein record labels earn revenue from signed artists' recorded music, 360° deals entitle record labels to revenue from artists' other money-making activities, including recorded music, publishing, mer-chandising, licensing and branding opportunities, and touring income (Marshall 2013; Stahl and Meier 2012). Though these contracts are legal agreements between artists and their labels, they have had wide-ranging outcomes on others in the country music business and on the music itself after their introduction in 2002 (Marshall 2013). By 2008, all of Warner's new acts were signed on 360° deals, with other labels shortly following suit (Stahl and Meier 2012).

What is it about 360° deals that contributed to increased homogeneity among songs in the bro-country era? Publishing, one piece of the 360° deal for artists, is seen as a dependable revenue source even during bad economic times (Marshall 2013), so copyright is a strategic piece of the contracts that labels sought to bring under their domain. Under 360° deals, song creation (i.e., publishing rights) becomes part of the recording artist's contractual obligations in addition to recording, touring, and selling merchandise. Compared to genres like rock, where self-contained bands who write their own songs are the norm, and pop, where the artist is included in the large cowriting groups that fashion top forty hits, country music at the beginning of the 2000s was a genre that still relied heavily on an occupational division between the recording artists who interpreted and performed songs written by a mostly separate group of professional songwriters.

How a Contract Can Change the Songs People Write

The songwriters interviewed for this research laid out the impact that the 360° deal contracts have had in their careers on who they write with and on the music that they write. There has long been a "slot" process that governs what kinds of songs get cut and released on a recording artist's album. Given the turn from physical album sales, the material constraints that limited songs to a finite number per album disappeared. If an artist wanted to release 100 songs as an album, there is no physical or technological constraint standing in their way. Despite the lack of physical limits in the number of songs that are released as an album, industry norms still dictate how many songs will be included on a record. Songwriter Danny Barker talks about how slots apply to curation of an album. He says:

It seems like everybody's trying to fit everything into that one little window, you know. Well, let's say like back in the day, Alan Jackson was cutting a record. He's probably gonna put like twelve songs in a record and you start to think, "Okay, well, the A&R people are probably gonna come up with five songs, Alan was probably gonna write three or four." Yeah, and then so that leaves maybe two slots over, you know. How am I gonna get in that little window?

The "little window" that Danny identifies is the space for outside cuts on an artist's album. The changes to collaborative norms mean that the chances of a professional songwriter having an outside cut on a record have shrunk. In the past, to get into that "little window" of opportunity, the quality of the song was key. Logan Ellis describes this system, saying,

If you didn't write a great song, you didn't have a snowball's chance in hell of getting on a record. I mean, as a whole – I mean there were a few artist writes going on back then, like an album cut or something like that – but man if you were making a record and gonna be a hit on a radio, that song was pretty well written.

As Logan reveals, country artists did cowrite some of their music in past decades, but for the most part, songwriters were focused on writing an excellent song so that it would be selected and included on an album.

Before the turn to a digital music economy detailed in this chapter, having a cut on an album meant that many songwriters would earn royalty income whether or not their song was a single. The structure of mechanical royalties in the United States pays 9.1 cents per song sold, to be divided by the song's writers and the songwriters' publishers (US Copyright Office 2018). This meant that for a song on a platinum album that was written by two staff songwriters, each writer could expect to make approximately $20,000. Getting a few album cuts each year would be enough for writers to make a decent living even without having a chart-topping single or having their song play on the radio even once. That too has changed in the time since sales have dropped and streaming has prevailed because of the unbundling of albums.

The economic downturn experienced by labels that induced them to create the 360° deal has also impacted songwriters' careers and earnings. One of the songwriters I interviewed, Dylan Robertson, comments on his experience with compensation from streaming services:

From a new artist standpoint, streaming is great. You know look at all this, the exposure that it gives to the music, but I think for songwriters, it's robbery. And, it's absolute robbery. I mean, for example, I had a song that was a top twenty hit on the radio, and it did great and everything. That same song, and this pales in comparison to other numbers, this is an example. My song had almost, like almost, over half a million streams and it paid like $180. You know there's just, there's something really, really wrong with that.

The story that Dylan tells is not unique, and both recording artists and songwriters have come forward to show the public how little they are compensated by streaming platforms for their music. The current royalty rate is fractions of a penny per stream. Since copyright law is the purview of the federal government, songwriters, recording artists, and record labels must directly lobby the US Congress if they want to change the payout rate. There is no avenue for an individual songwriter to request more money from any entity that licenses their work other than joining in the industry-wide struggle for copyright reform. Songwriter Michael Lewis passionately described to me one such lobbying trip to Washington, DC:

I took this to Congress one time to show them. And, for a quarter, which is a three-month period, [my song] gets played around 17,000,000 times, okay. So either people have requested or they played 17,000,000 times, my song. My part for that was $103 for 17,000,000 plays, and that's what I'm talking about that it has to catch up . . . We're not trying to make a huge amount of money. We just want it to be fair.

This was a big moment for Michael, but he told me that he was readily dismissed so that congressional voting could continue, with little recognition of his presentation by his representatives. It was a tough crowd.

When album sales were high, more songwriters made a living writing a more diverse set of songs. While constraining, the system of "slots" on an album allowed for a more varied array of music to be profitable for Nashville songwriters (see Peterson and Berger 1996). Perhaps a song would not be fit for radio but could still merit a slot on a recording artist's album as a quiet ballad or quirky novelty song. In light of changes in contracts and organizational structures, songwriters now face a more competitive market for getting songs cut and feel that there has been a closing of opportunity, particularly to get outside cuts, that is, having a song recorded by an artist that is not cowritten by the recording artist. Writing a good song is no longer enough to make a living or a career as a songwriter. As the industry has changed to meet the new era, songwriters too have had to change the way they do business.

In the Room

Since songwriters have no tools through which to directly alter their economic stake in the music they write, they cannot command more value from the songs they create. Instead, they have had to find ways to shift their strategic orientation toward cowriting in order to continue getting cuts and to exploit their copyrights. This is an entrepreneurial shift from the past occupational role of a professional songwriter. The response that songwriters have taken toward the goal of getting their songs cut in the era of 360° deals is to write as much as possible with recording artists – both established artists and potential up-and-comers.

Songwriters must now strategically consider who is "in the room" for cowriting sessions (Skaggs 2019). Dan Stone indicates the degree to which his personal schedule of cowriting appointments has changed on a day-to-day basis.

In the '80s and '90s, and even the early 2000s, four days out of five, I would write with other professional writers or one other professional writer to try to get an outside song cut. Maybe one of those days, I'd write with an artist or a band. And I'd say that's reversed, that it is more like three days out of five, I'd write with an artist or a band, and two I might write with another professional writer.

This shift has changed who Dan works with each week, but cowriting songs with recording artists is a strategic choice guided by the perception that collaborating with artists will lead to more cuts and a more successful songwriting career.

Cultivating a relationship with emerging artists is a strategy that many songwriters employ. There is more to the strategy than simply writing with established artists who are more likely to guarantee spins, sales, and streams on the songs they release. It is more of a gamble in terms of opportunity cost to write with a new artist who does not yet have a record deal, but the dividends are higher for songwriters who establish themselves as a new artist's close collaborator early on. Logan Ellis says:

Any writer in town will tell you right now, we're all hashing it out with every young artist that comes through town. I mean if they think they're going to get a record deal, you know you wanna hit it off with them and you wanna write that song that's their first single. Or you wanna write that song that you know they love and cut, and then hopefully the next record deal you get to write something else that they love and cut, and hopefully you get to latch on to somebody that you'll have that run with.

The actual job and role remain the same for songwriters whether they are writing with other professional writers or working with recording artists in the room: spend three hours writing the music and lyrics of a song that should both inspire and move people as well as be a commercial, thus financial, success. Though the goal remains the same, the ways collaboration works when writing a song have at times had to change. Jack Fraser calls the strategy of having a writer in the room, "a game" when he refers to the change in approach that he and his peer songwriters had to make in order to continue getting songs cut. He says that playing this game means that, "we couldn't just write songs by ourselves or with our buddies that we respected anymore. We had to have an active role. That's a tough thing when somebody's twenty years old with a record deal, and they don't have the craft but they're calling the shots. It's a little backwards." Recording artists have a set of pressures and expectations for their work and music that differs from what songwriters have to consider in the writing room.

The majority of a recording artist's income comes from live performances and touring, so the nature of live performance is part of their consideration when writing songs. Whereas a songwriter might be concerned about writing the best song, period, a recording artist is likely trying to write the best song that will be well-received in a multi-thousand-person arena show populated by the fanbase he or she has worked to cultivate. Dan Stone, though not a recording artist, identifies the goals that artists have in mind when they write:

One big difference now is that songwriters, because artists are so involved in the songwriting process, some artists are very aware of the live audience, the concert audience. Why are they at the concerts? What do they want to hear? Where do they want to see you? When before, radio was way more of a driving force. And it still is an important force, but it's the live audience, the live show song is a huge part of what we consider.

Concerts have changed, too, further pushing songs toward those party anthems that, as Jack Fraser puts it, can work "energy wise" for a crowd of 30,000 people. Logan Ellis comments on the reduction in diversity even in a single concert setlist:

It used to be a show you go to and they kick it off and they'd rock you for a couple songs, and then they'd sing a ballad. And then they might, you know, [sing] a couple more songs and they'd sing another ballad. And it was that ebb and flow, ebb and flow, and now it's just straight across. I mean it's just like, "Oh my gosh don't sing a ballad."

The requisite up-tempo party atmosphere that keeps the energy high in arena concerts and contributes to the lack of a good "ebb and flow" between ballads and up-tempo songs further pushes music toward a homogenous musical style.

Though continuing to write songs for the stage in order to financially maintain a career in songwriting, some writers express displeasure in sacrificing diversity in songs to achieve the recording artist's goals. Lucas Lane says:

Artists only really make money now through touring. So, they play these huge vacuous spaces, you know, of at least 18,000 to sometimes, you know, 60,000, 100,000. So, you know, "He Stopped Loving Her Today" would not, is not, gonna work really in a huge space like that. You've gotta have simpler songs and simpler lyrics, with faster tempos to fill these huge vacuous spaces. I mean it's just a compounding problem. But, you know, if you and I or the manager or an artist, we'd be like, "Okay. I get that you wanna hear, you know, 'Fire and Rain.' I get that you love 'Fire and Rain.' 'Fire and Rain' is not going to work today. So, don't pitch us 'Fire and Rain' when you go to the publishers."

Lucas ends the thought emphatically with a final reference to James Taylor's ballad: "Don't write 'Fire and Rain'." Jack Fraser agrees with the sentiment Lucas expressed, saying, "I don't know that country was ever meant to be arena-sized. I should say that I wish there was a little more room for everything." The belief and assumption that underlie Jack's statement is that there is no room in country music for songs that do not fit into the narrow window of up-tempo songs that are written with a mind toward live performance.

Bro-country, the most characteristic style of country music during the period of this study, relies on the kind of songs with "hooks that lean toward pop and hefty guitars that tilt toward rock" (Rosen 2013). The sub-genre takes from hip-hop iconography and musicality as the notion of "country" is changed in an increasingly neoliberal period (Cottom 2018). Bro-country's characteristic hip-hop rhythms, rock sounds, and pop lyrical hooks were made for artists by artists through their collaborations with professional songwriters with the express purpose of being played live in front of a large audience. Further, if the artist and his or her record label get a portion of the revenue from beer sales, which is not uncommon, it is likely that they write songs that make people want to party and buy the brand of beer with the best revenue kickback. Much of the cliché branding, thematic tropes, and sounds of the bro-country era are hence a direct result of the structures that created them and are targeted to make the most revenue possible within the new system (Marshall 2013; Skaggs 2019).

There is a shrinking opportunity to make money on album cuts because of the shift to a singles-driven and streaming music model and the pressure to write with recording artists to increase the chances to get a cut at all. The result of this is that songwriters are all writing toward the same small target, both lyrically and musically, according to their artist cowriter's goals. The uncertainty of markets for songs induces people to attempt to repeat what was successful in the past, which results in the landscape of commercial music being more lyrically and musically homogenous. Songwriters recognize this tendency. Sam Clark says that because of this, "you get A&R people just chasing something in their safety zone as whoever has written the most hits lately. So, well, we had a [hit song-writer's] song. We had a [prominent female recording artist-style] song. We had a, whatever. It should've worked. We did our part." There is a sort of fatalism that I heard in my interviews, with many hit songwriters saying that all they could do was wait until the styles changed to write other kinds of country music. This too is indicative that the conventions and homo-geneity of the bro-country era were structural and woven into the fabric of the mid-2000s rather than being simply a product of the preferred style of song creators.

Out of the Room

At this point in the narrative, it has probably become apparent that the commentary from songwriters about the impact of the 360° deal on co-writing and on homogeneity has come from only men. Homogeneity extends past aesthetic features into a proscriptive profile of who the writers of these homogenous songs are. While songwriters like those profiled in this chapter find that the structural constraints of new contracts lead to their waning ability to make a living and create good music, the women who I interviewed for this project did not focus on these same concerns. Just as there is a structural explanation that I provided for why country music from 2000 to 2015 became more homogenous and coalesced into the bro-country style, there is a structural explanation for why women did not talk about 360° deals with nearly the level of salience or derision as the men I interviewed.

From 2000 to 2015, forty-eight percent of successful country songs, as defined in the sampling frame above, were written by a cowriting group that contained the song's recording artist. This pattern is gendered, with women's songs accounting for only twenty-nine percent of successful songs. However, female artists are more likely than is statistically expected to be the cowriter of their own songs compared to their male peers.[2] What can we make of this? At first glance, it might be interpreted as women having a proportionally higher stake in the more powerful occupational role of this time period, since artists who cowrite the songs they record and perform are more able than professional songwriters to ensure that their songs make it onto an album. However, another reading of these findings tells a story about how women are primarily accepted into the occupation of songwriter by virtue of their role as a recording artist and are less likely to be able to make a living as a professional songwriter without being a recording artist. For this reason, women in my sample were more likely to benefit from 360° deals than my male interviewees, who were primarily professional songwriters, since a higher proportion of women in the sample were also their songs' recording artists. However, their experiences are only a few in an industry that has historically denied equal opportunity to women.

Conclusion: Why Hit the Same Notes?

The unpredictability around what will be successful in culture industries means that people in that industry will try a variety of tactics to recreate success. The difference that we see in the interviews with Nashville song-writers who were successful in this time period is the change in their

---

[2] N = 1197 songs; CHISQ 4.351, p = .037.

relationships with recording artists. Rather than individuals in distinct occupations working to create and recreate successful songs, the industry's declining revenues resulted in contractual changes for recording artists that inherently changed the opportunity structure for professional songwriters. The resulting shift in creative power from the songwriter to the recording artist means that the content of country songs has also shifted toward major label artists' goals and needs.

The effect of these changes has entirely restructured the careers of professional songwriters and the music that they create. Since 360° deals require that artists write a portion of their own songs, regardless of their songwriting aspirations or talent, the incentives of cowriting have been restructured toward privileging having an artist "in the room." The shift reoriented the songwriting process toward the artist's personal brand and contributed to the genre's perceived homogeneity. The homogenous, archetypal artists signed by labels are now also writing songs, further entrenching a more homogenous set of people, in terms of their race, gender, gender identity, sexual orientation, and social class, into the collaborative web of country music creators. Understanding the dominant structuring forces of an industry allows us to more clearly see the opportunity structure for that industry. In short, taking this kind of macro, industry-level perspective illuminates who and what are valued within the dominant structure of contemporary country music. As Tressie McMillan Cottom (2021) writes, "Country music – especially mainstream country music – is all about being white." Collective action structures the industry to be racialized as white and gendered as male (Watson 2019a, 2019b, 2021). To deviate in one's identity is a mark against the requisite position-ing for inclusion, which is again reflected in the set of songs that emerges from those who are included.

In recent years, scholarly discourse, music criticism, and backroom industry conversations have centered on country music's lack of inclusion of artists who don't fit the gender, racial, or cultural mold of the artists who performed each of the six songs mashed up in Sir Mashalot's YouTube video. To be sure, explicit discrimination exists, and it is important to identify and understand the structures that contribute to insidious homogeneity in the conventions that shape the aesthetic features and opportunity structure for creating music. Homogeneity, in both lyrical tropes and musical styles, is a consolidating force that limits the possibility of expression and the inclusion of individuals who are able to participate in expression. Music that sounds the same and represents a consistent monolithic theme is likely being created by people who come from similar viewpoints. If this is what the mainstream center looks like, it is difficult to believe that diverse viewpoints will make it into the writing room, let alone onto an album.

As a sociologist, my methodological approach privileges generalizability and systematic analysis of empirical data in order to comment on structures of power and inequality. Through the process of inquiry around the emergence of 360° deals and their implications for songwriting, I collected interviews with individuals representative of successful songwriters from 2000 to 2015. In so doing, the voices that make up my corpus of empirical data likewise reflect the entrenched power structures that existed among successful songwriters of the period. Hence, it is important to emphasize what I have mentioned throughout this chapter: there is deeply structured inequity in the country music industry. In addition to the concerns of mainstream commercial songwriters and the artists' with and for whom they write songs, there are deeper patterns of exclusion that limit who can participate in commercial, so-called major label, country music. In particular, Black country music artists and songwriters, other artists and writers of color, and white women find that despite talent, creativity, and putting in the work, they are structurally barred from entry into the kinds of contracts, collaborative creative partnerships, and access that allow full participation in the genre.

4 A Double-Edged Sword

Industry Data and the Construction of Country Music Narratives

JADA WATSON

In September 2007, Rissi Palmer's debut single "Country Girl" entered *Billboard*'s Hot Country Song (HCS) chart. Radio was reportedly "slow to embrace" the single (Associated Press 2007), which peaked at No. 54 and exited the chart after just seven weeks. With "Country Girl," Palmer became the first Black female solo artist to chart in twenty years – since Dona Mason's "Green Eyes (Cryin' Those Blue Tears)" and Nisha Jackson's "Alive and Well" charted in 1987. Before them, nine songs by Ruby Falls, one by the Pointer Sisters, and three by Linda Martell charted in the 1970s. Palmer charted two more songs in 2008, and only Mickey Guyton's "Why Baby Why" (2016) charted on HCS afterward.[1] Songs by these women had short life cycles on the longest-running *Billboard* country chart, leaving behind a faint data trail marking their time in the industry's mainstream. Except for Martell, Palmer, and Guyton – whose careers have received increasing media and scholarly attention,[2] the stories of these other women have been left out of discourse about Black artists in the country music industry and they remain unknown to country music fans. Without chart-topping hits, their careers received limited attention (if any) from the press, their music was not widely distributed, and, as a result, their contributions have not been recognized by the industry's institutions – they don't even have entries in the Country Music Hall of Fame and Museum's *Encyclopedia of Country Music* (in its second edition [2012]). In an industry tightly centered around documenting, preserving, and promoting its heritage, these women, rendered invisible by the industrial system, have been largely expunged from country music's institutional memory.

Billboard chart data plays a critical role in capturing institutional memory, but they should also be seen as a tool for *directing* and *shaping* it. As I have argued elsewhere (Watson 2020a), *Billboard* charts function as

---

[1] Guyton's debut single "Better Than You Left Me" charted on *Billboard*'s Country Airplay chart, peaking at No. 30 in 2015.

[2] See Pecknold (2018) and Browne (2020) for research on Martell; King and Foster (2018) for writing on Palmer; and Mack (2020) and Watson (2022) for discussions of the career and music of Guyton.

curatorial instruments that systematically "remember" some artists, while "casting away" (or "forgetting") others. My previous work (Watson 2019b, 2020a), focusing on the HCS chart between 1996 and 2016, considered how changes in chart methodology contributed to the declining presence of female artists in country music's commercial culture. But disappearance can only be traced if artists *appear* in the chart data in the first place. What happens if they never *really* chart in a manner that is detectable, traceable, or reproducible within the industry's business model? What if they never chart at all? How does the absence of a group (or groups) of artists influence industry decision-making? Treating chart data as a part of the industrial system – as a tool that instructs, directs, and (by extension) restricts artists – allows us to understand how weak data trails (trails that are short, trails that peak in the bottom of the chart, trails that are few) are used to justify excluding Black and of color artists (in general) and women (specifically) from participation. In this way, chart data becomes an integral part of the process that secures the industry's white racial narrative, dictating who "belongs" in country music.

This chapter engages in a data-driven analysis of *Billboard*'s HCS chart to consider the ways in which chart data has served to dictate or reinforce industry practices. I take as my starting point 1958 – a point that aligns with the regularization of *Billboard*'s weekly charts, the establishment of the Nashville industrial system, and the formation of the Country Music Association, and includes every song that charted until 2016, covering a near sixty-year period of the industry's history. This data was augmented to include the biographic details of the artists responsible for these songs to facilitate intersectional analysis of the artists that have contributed to the development of country music culture. To consider the impact of chart data on country music's cultural identity, I am also bringing into this discussion datasets that capture the award history of the Country Music Association (CMA) and the Academy of Country Music (ACM), as well as inductions to the Country Music Hall of Fame. These recognition systems (charts, awards, inductions) are deeply interconnected: charts may provide an indicator of industry trends, but awards and inductions (both of which rely to varying degrees on charts as a marker for contention) codify the past and direct the future. I am interested in tracing data through recognition systems in the industry, considering how their repetition constantly reaffirms racialized and gendered boundaries inscribed within the industry's structures. Taken together, these four datasets offer the opportunity to reflect on how data dictates industry practices, obscuring and erasing the contributions of Black and of color artists.

To engage in this critical evaluation of the industry's cultural system, I draw on Patricia Hill Collins' (1990, 21) concept of the "matrix of domination." Developed as a framework for describing institutional discrimination, Collins' matrix consists of four interlocking domains that explain how social or industrial systems are configured, are administered, and become engrained in organizational practice and are ultimately experienced by individuals. These structural, disciplinary, and interpersonal domains (each themselves oppressive systems) are connected through media and culture, which circulates ideas and ideologies, normalizing rhetoric by perpetuating established narratives and undermining the seriousness of discrimination embedded in their structures. Reconfiguring our conception of the country music industry through Collins' matrix frames business decisions in relationship to its structural configuration, allowing for a deeper understanding of how structural decisions made in the 1920s have been upheld and maintained through everyday practices in the industry (labels, radio, charts), are reinforced through discourse and recognition systems, and impact artists in the industry.

One of the ways in which we can begin to understand how an industry matrix works is through data, a regime deeply embedded in each of the matrix domains. The country music industry relies on various forms of data to make business decisions – from artist development to eligibility for opportunities and awards, and to evaluate risk and return on investment before signing new artists. In this way, data (in the form of sales, radio airplay, charts, streams, and even social media engagement) could be viewed as a component of the matrix, repeated within and between each domain, becoming part of practice, discourse, and culture. The concept of "repetition" is integral to understanding how the data regime operates in the industrial matrix. Sara Ahmed (2014) defines the relationality of repetitive practices through the example of academic citation. Through the development of a scholarly body of literature, she writes, white men cite and teach the works of other white men, a form of repetition that legitimizes and solidifies a patriarchal system. As these repetitive practices build up and legitimize white men, they also marginalize, delegitimize, and reject others. More critically, this repetition normalizes oppressive behaviors and ideas about who belongs to an institution, serving to further cement them (white men *and* the behaviors) within institutional structures. Within the country music industry, we can trace repetition through industry data – through the HCS chart and other recognition systems. We can learn through this data how repetition reaffirms structures, reinforcing the sound and image of the white male prototype.

Non-prototypical artists within this system – those not prioritized in the system – experience varying degrees of what Valerie Purdie-Vaughns and Richard Eibach (2008) term *intersectional invisibility*, defined as the systemic failure of individuals with intersecting identities to be recognized as members of a community. Because race has historically been associated with Black men and gender with white women (Crenshaw 1989), Black women are relegated to a position of acute social invisibility in most social and cultural systems (Purdie-Vaughns and Eibach 2008, 381) – an issue that pervades the country music industry. Bringing these concepts together offers a framework for examining how the codes and conventions embedded within the industry's structures are repeated through the industrial matrix, impacting charts, awards, and inductions, and ultimately contributing to the reinforcement of whiteness and erasure of Black and of color artists from country music culture.

Configuring the Industry's Structural Domain

The popular music industry developed in the 1920s along a "musical color line" that echoed Jim Crow segregation. Even though Black and white musicians played and listened to the same music, when record executives developed marketing strategies for records in the 1920s, they created two categories – "hillbilly music" and "race music" – through which they would record white and Black musicians and then market to white and Black communities, respectively (Miller 2010). While these specific marketing categories are no longer used today (replaced with "country" and "R&B"/ "soul" by the 1950s), the racial segregation established in the 1920s was "enshrined in institutional practices" and "ha[s] had a profound effect on the circulation of music" (Brackett 2016, 25) – deeply embedded in systems of production (labels and publishers), distribution (radio formats, media/ magazines, digital service providers),[3] recognition (popularity charts, awards), and canonization (halls of fame, museums, encyclopedias). These labels have also been have also been encoded in the metadata structures used to physically separate albums in record stores, to categorize

---

[3] Radio, the industry's primary means of distribution throughout the twentieth century, developed in parallel to the industry in the 1920s and within the same socially segregated context (Barlow 1999; Smulyan 2004; Weisbard 2014). As a result, Black entertainers faced barriers and limitations both on air and behind-the-scenes (many of which persist in the twenty-first century).

music in mail-order record club pamphlets and in music magazines (as in *Billboard*), and to even define the algorithms that underpin the recommender systems of digital service providers, each reinforcing the musical color line inscribed in the industry in the 1920s. These systems are deeply interconnected, networked around a business model that responds not to audience interest but to *data* (sales, radio airplay, streams, and social media engagement) generated from the very systems. The data resulting from their actions then influence how labels sign, promote, and support artists, feeding back into the system from which they emerged.

The country music industry grew out of these racially segregated structures that formed in the 1920s (Miller 2010), centralizing in Nashville, Tennessee, in the 1950s through the development of a network of recording studios, record labels, and publishing houses, and deeply connected to commercial radio. As Travis D. Stimeling (2020, 43) reveals through first-person accounts in *Nashville Cats*, labels in Nashville reinforced segregation of the broader industry's racialized marketing strategies by recording Black artists on gospel and R&B records but refusing to record their country offerings. Although Black, Hispanic, and Latinx artists often resisted the industry's exclusionary practices, Charles Hughes (2015, 2017) and Amanda Marie Martinez (2019, 2020, 2021a) have shown the various ways in which the industry disregarded country music's multiracial and multiethnic roots and instead promoted a white racial narrative. These early actions played a critical role in maintaining the white racial framing that pervades public discourse about the country music industry.

Deeply connected to these structural issues are other forms of oppression – sexism, heterosexism, transphobia, ableism – that have likewise been embedded within the industry's structures since the early days of the recording industry. The country music industry has long-perpetuated a form of gender-based programming that has relegated white women to a secondary position within the industry, while excluding Black and of color women. As Kristine M. McCusker (2017) has observed, since the earliest days of the genre, white men have been associated with "public work" and commercial success, with white women tucked away in domestic, administrative, and musically supporting roles. With strong ties to social conservatism and religion, country's first female artists – Maybelle and Sara Carter, Moonshine Kate, and Rose Maddox (to name a few) – often appeared on stage with their husbands or male family members, a constant reassurance for record-buyers that the social order in which women performed familial roles endured in the genre ("Women of Country" 1993). Behind the scenes, the country music industry has historically employed a quota system that has limited the space available to white women on label and publishing rosters, and on radio playlists (Watson 2019a, 2019b). Although female artists captured 33 percent of the industry market by 1999, changes in radio programming in the late 1990s resulted in a drastic decline in the number of songs by women on radio playlists, resulting in fewer songs on charts, and nominations for awards (Watson 2019b, 2020a). Within this oppressive system, LGBTQIA+ artists are strikingly absent and have historically been forced to hide their gender identity and sexuality to participate in the industry (Hubbs 2014; Beyer 2021; Watson 2021). These interlocking forms of oppression have impacted both the lives and careers of artists, while at the same time reinforcing and perpetuating the white supremacist and heteropatriarchal structures on which the industry was built well into the twenty-first century.

Sixty Years of (White) Country Songs

Charts provide what Will Straw (2015, 129) calls a "physical representation of that intangible phenomenon of popularity," ranking popularity based on sales, radio airplay or streams, or some combination of these materials processes. While on the surface, charts appear to be benign and equitable (tallying radio airplay/sales to produce a weekly list ranking the most consumed records), both the categorization system and methodologies underpinning the charts have reinforced the industry's structure.[4] *Billboard* launched the Country & Western (now HCS) and Rhythm & Blues charts in 1958, an action that reinforced racial segregation at a pivotal movement in the development of the industry. Over the course of the sixty years that followed (the years of this study period), HCS changed in name and size, as well as in the data source used to calculate chart positions (Whitburn 2018), from the hybrid tabulation of radio airplay and retail sales (1958–1990), to the digital tracking of radio airplay via Nielsen Broadcast Data Systems (1990–2012), and finally back to a hybrid method calculating popularity via the blending of sales, radio airplay from *all* formats, and streaming activity, each tracked by Nielsen BDS (2012–present). While these changes in tabulations coincided with developments in technology, the industry's underlying structures remained unchanged. As a result, each methodology has perpetuated and indeed exacerbated inequities deeply embedded in the industry's structures.

---

[4] My previous work (Watson 2019b, 2020a) offers detailed discussion of the chart methodologies that *Billboard* used for this chart between 1996 and 2016.

Examining representation through an intersectional lens brings to light the dynamics of power and oppression based on the overlapping identities of artists permitted to participate in the industry's mainstream. The chart dataset used for this study consists of the 18,654 songs that debuted on the *Billboard* HCS chart between January 1, 1958, and December 31, 2016, and includes each song's debut and peak position and date. Each entry was coded with attributes describing the ensemble type (solo, duo, trio, and group/collaboration), race and ethnicity (white, Black, artist of color, or multiracial/ethnic ensemble), and gender (male, female, or male–female ensemble/collaboration). To prepare the dataset, I referred to previous studies examining race and gender on *Billboard* charts to develop this coding system (Lafrance et al. 2011, 2018; Watson 2019b, 2021). Like Lafrance et al.'s study (2018, 4), using one label to draw together artists of several ethnicities (as "artists of color") might be read as an attempt to reinforce the hierarchy of racial importance that positions white and Black artists as a standard and Biracial, Indigenous, Hispanic/Latinx, and Asian American artists as an exception. Rather, this decision was taken to ensure coherent and consistent analysis of the data, while also establishing continuity with other data-driven studies examining representation on both country and popular music charts.

Representation on Billboard's Hot Country Songs Chart

Over the course of the sixty-year study period, regardless of how the data are examined, the number of songs by white male artists exceeds the number of songs by all other artists and collaborations. As summarized in Table 4.1a, 94.1 percent of the unique artists that have had songs debut on the chart between 1958 and 2016 have been white artists – 57.9 percent were male artists, 20.7 percent were female artists, and 15.5 percent by male–female ensembles or collaborations. This means that just 5.9 percent of the unique artists with songs debuting on the chart were Black (0.9%), Biracial, Indigenous, Hispanic/Latinx or Asian American (1.5%), and multiracial/ethnic ensembles or collaborations (3.5%). While indeed all Black and of color artists are underrepresented, Black and of color women represent just 0.5 percent of the charting artists (combined) over this sixty-year period.

These figures remain consistent when shifting to focus on representation of artists responsible for all 18,576 songs that charted over this period, summarized in Table 4.1b. The percentage of songs by white artists (94.4%) is similar here, and the overall distribution remains relatively unchanged

Table 4.1a. Percentage of unique artists with songs debuting on Hot Country Songs Chart (1958–2016)

	Male artists (%)	Female artists (%)	Male–female ens./collabs. (%)	Total (by cultural identity) (%)
White artists	57.9	20.7	15.5	**94.1**
Black artists	0.6	0.2	0.1	**0.9**
Artists of color	1.2	0.3	0.0	**1.5**
Multiracial/ethnic ens.	1.9	0.1	1.5	**3.5**
Total (by gender identity)	**61.6**	**21.3**	**17.1**	

Table 4.1b. Percentage of songs charting on Hot Country Songs Chart (1958–2016)

	Male artists (%)	Female artists (%)	Male–female ens./collabs. (%)	Total (by cultural identity) (%)
White artists	66.8	21.7	5.9	**94.4**
Black artists	0.9	0.1	0.1	**1.1**
Artists of color	3.1	0.5	0.0	**3.6**
Multiracial/ethnic ens.	0.6	0.0	0.3	**0.9**
Total (by gender identity)	**71.4**	**22.3**	**6.3**	

for Black and of color artists (with a marginal increase for men and decrease for women). The most notable change occurs between white male artists and white male–female ensembles: white male artists are responsible for 66.8 percent of the charting songs, with just 5.9 percent by white male–female ensembles/collaborations. While this might seem like a significant change from the representation of unique artists noted in Table 4.1a, most of the unique male–female ensembles (82.7%) were special collaborative recordings between solo artists that resulted in just one or a small number of charting songs. These statistics, then, confirm the white male dominance on the industry's longest-running chart and reveal the subordinate position of white female artists and male–female ensembles and collaborations. More critically, they confirm that Black and of color artists occupy limited space within the industry; with just 0.6 percent of the charting songs over six decades, Black and of color women are rendered nearly invisible within country music culture.

Figure 4.1 maps the distribution of the 18,576 charting songs by both race/ethnicity and gender, separated into three graphs. While the data was separated for legibility of the data, the data trails for Black and of color artists (especially women) are not, in fact, legible. Their data are so faint

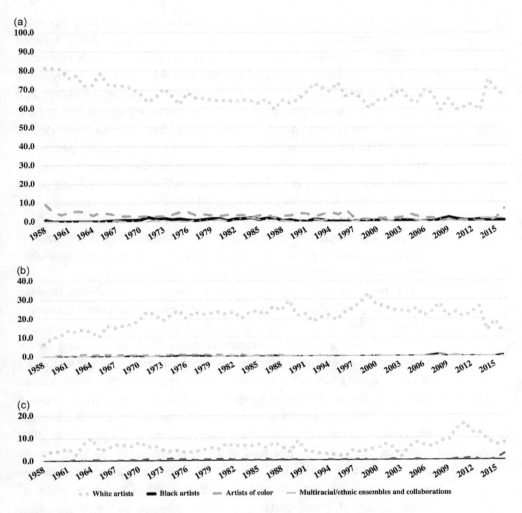

Figure 4.1. Distribution of songs by race and ethnicity and gender on Hot Country
Songs Chart (1958–2016)
(a) Distribution of songs by male artists (average 72.0%)
(b) Distribution of songs by female artists (average 21.5%)
(c) Distribution of songs by male–female ensembles (average 6.5%)

that it is difficult to distinguish because the trails comprise a devastatingly
small percentage – even in peak years. These Figures capture the magnitude of their underrepresentation and visualize the systemic erasure of their
data trails from historic record.

Songs by white male artists maintain an average of 67.7 percent – clearly
dominating the charts. Despite a 26.3 percent decline between 1958 and

1999, there is not a single year in this period in which songs by any other group of artists overtake theirs on the charts. As their songs declined through to 1999, songs by white women and white male–female ensembles and collaborations increased, filling the available space. Songs by white women come in second to white men over this period, averaging 21.0 percent of the charting songs. White female artists are shown here to have their strongest showing in the late 1990s, rising from 6.5 percent in 1958 to a peak of 33.1 percent in 1999, then declining slowly to 12.8 percent by 2016. Songs by white male–female ensembles also increase, from 2.4 percent in 1958 to a peak of 16.4 percent in 2011, then declining to 7.8 percent by the period's end. Averaging 94.8 percent of the charting songs, this figure reveals the rate at which white artists dominate the charts, as well as the privileging of white *male* artists, outlining a gendered hierarchy within these clearly racialized structures that have historically cast white women in a subordinate role to white men.

The remaining 5.2 percent average of songs are distributed between Black (0.8%) and of color artists (3.4%), and multiracial/ethnic ensembles (1.0%). As with white artists, songs by Black and of color men and multiracial male ensembles outnumber those by women – and by an average of 88.8 percent. While there is no discernible trend (or semblance of racial equity) between 1958 and 2016, it is notable that there was an increase in the percentage of songs by Black and of color artists between 1969 and 1989. Drilling in deeper in this period shows that Black artists averaged 1.4 percent of the charting songs, peaking at 2.3 percent in 1987. However, this should not be read as a sign of change in the industry: the majority (74.8%) of the 147 songs by Black artists that charted in this period were by just four male artists – 45.0 percent by Charley Pride alone.[5] While artists of color chart consistently (though in small numbers) throughout this entire period, the same trend is true for their presence on the chart. Between 1969 and 1989, artists of color average 3.9 percent of the charting songs, peaking at 6.2 percent in 1975. Here, too, 49.2 percent of the songs are by just four white-passing artists with Indigenous heritage. Despite the increase between 1969 and 1989, then, drilling into the data shows that just a handful of Black and of color men dominate, exposing a form of tokenism that gave the appearance of change within the industry.

---

[5] In this period (1969–1989), Big Al Downing and Stoney Edwards each charted fifteen songs (10.2% each), O.B. McClinton charted fourteen (9.5%). The remaining thirty-seven songs were released by fifteen artists, including all but four of the songs by Black women named at the start of the chapter.

Following this two-decade period with increased representation of Black and of color artists, the chart became increasingly whiter. By 1998, 98.2 percent of the songs that charted were by white artists – averaging 97.0 percent until 2015. This is a particularly critical observation to draw forward because it follows the passage of the 1996 Telecommunications Act. The Act significantly altered commercial radio, deregulating ownership by loosening ownership caps, ultimately permitting a single company to purchase multiple stations in a market.[6] As smaller companies were swallowed up by larger conglomerates, programming centralized; not only did this reduce the number of station playlists (and the number of slots for new songs), but it placed the control over programming decisions in the hands of just a few actors within the radio industry (Moss 2019). Radio programmers had over the course of the twentieth century already gained a lot of control over which artists could be heard on radio (Peterson 1978; Weisbard 2014; Watson 2019b); following the Telecommunications Act, they gained considerable power over the development of the industry. The HCS chart was generated by radio airplay alone during this period (1990–2012). These findings suggest that changes in radio ownership and programming resulting from the Act significantly altered the country music ecosystem: not only do songs by white women decline following the Act's 1996 passage, but songs by Black and of color artists nearly disappear.

The final methodological change in October 2012 – a return to a hybrid method that blended audience consumption metrics of digital sales and streams alongside radio airplay – resulted in an increase in songs by Black and of color artists. This increase began slowly in 2008 when Darius Rucker, Rissi Palmer, Crystal Shawanda, and Star De Azlan launched their careers but continued largely on the activity of songs by Rucker. By the final year of this study period, songs by white artists dropped to 87.2 percent. While this means that there was an increase in songs by Black and of color artists, all but one were by men and only two of the fourteen songs charted for more than two weeks. Thus, although there was an increase in songs by Black and of color artists in the final years of this period, the short period of time on the chart suggests that these songs were not heard in high rotation on the radio, and had limited impact via streaming and sales.[7]

---

[6] For example, Clear Channel (rebranded as iHeartMedia in 2014) grew rapidly from 40 stations to 1,240 by 2002 – thirty times more than allowed prior to 1996 (DiCola and Thomson 2002).

[7] At the time an independent artist, Kane Brown had five single-week charting records, while *The Voice* contestant Sundance Head had four single-week charting records. See Watson 2020a for more on songs with short life cycles.

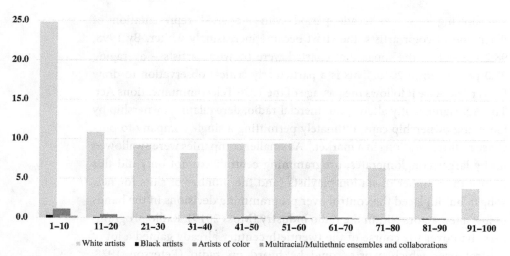

Figure 4.2. Distribution of charting songs by their peak position (in percentages) on Hot Country Songs Chart

Examining the frequency of songs by their peak position puts into stark relief the racial inequities within the industry, revealing where songs by Black and of color artists, and multiethnic ensembles peak. The histogram in Figure 4.2 tracks songs by their peak position revealing the rate at which white artists dominate not just the coveted top twenty positions of the chart, but the bottom positions as well. More than 60 percent of the songs by Black and of color artists peak outside of the Top 10. Nearly 70.0 percent of the songs by Black and of color artists that peak within the Top 10 are by just five artists – 25.2 percent of which were by Charley Pride. More critically, a Black female artist has yet to crack the Top 10 of the industry charts: Linda Martell's "Color Him Father" remains the highest-charting song by a Black female artist, reaching No. 22 in 1969. If all artists were treated equitably within the industry ecosystem, one group of artists would not dominate to this extent.

Discussion: Redlining in the Country Music Industry

Billboard charts relay critical information about the shape and evolving identity of a musical genre. But they also, as I have stated elsewhere (Watson 2020a), tell us something about how the industry functions – how groups of artists are privileged or disadvantaged within a genre's institutional practices. The results of country music's longest-running industry chart reveal a racial and gendered hierarchy within the country

Table 4.2. CMA and ACM nominations and Country Music Hall of Fame inductions (up to 2016)

	White artists (%)	Black artists (%)	Artists of color (%)	Multiracial or Multiethnic ens. (%)
CMA: Single of the Year	92.8	1.6	3.6	2.0
CMA: Album of the Year	91.3	2.0	2.8	4.0
CMA: Artist-centered awards	94.0	1.5	4.5	0.0
ACM: Single of the Year	94.4	0.4	5.2	0.0
ACM: Album of the Year	92.2	1.6	5.7	0.4
ACM: Artist-centered awards	96.7	0.9	2.4	0.0
Hall of Fame Inductions	94.6	2.0	3.4	0.0

music industry. While the results are not altogether surprising, the depth to which they persist in the twenty-first century is a sign of the deep embeddedness of white supremacy within the industry's structures, suggesting significant barriers to entry on the chart for Black and of color artists.

But just as there are barriers to entry on the charts, the chart itself becomes a barrier to opportunity and access to resources within the industry. Not only has HCS chart data historically been referred to when making decisions about signing new artists, marketing and promotions, touring and festivals, red carpet appearances, and more (Watson 2019b), but this data is also used to determine eligibility for nomination to awards within the industry. Rooted in the concept of "excellence," industry awards are bound within a framework that promotes a set of criteria designed with "merit" in mind. The CMA and the ACM began awarding prizes in the late 1960s, using chart positions to determine the pool of songs eligible for nomination. In the fifty awarding years that align with this study period, white artists average 95.0 percent of the nominations for artist-centered awards with both organizations and 92.7 percent of the Single and Album categories (see Table 4.2).[8] The nominations echo the findings of the chart, revealing that 75.0 percent of the nominations for Black artists are by Charley Pride and that white-passing artists with Indigenous heritage have the most nominations for artists of color. Mickey Guyton

---

[8] For this study, artist-centered awards include New Artist categories, Male and Female Vocalist, and Entertainer of the Year. Although Single and Album categories are also awarded to engineers and producers, this study considers only the nominated artists.

became the first Black female artist to receive a nomination for the ACM's New Female Artist of the Year category in 2016.[9] The historic exclusion of Black and of color artists within the industry has meant that their careers cannot be weighted in comparison to the white men and women whose data trails are long, deep, and thick, resulting in limited access to opportunities within the industry. Although in the twenty-first century, eligibility has expanded to include other metrics such as digital media, ticket sales, television and film appearances, songwriting credentials, and contributions to the industry, charts still play an indirect role because they govern access and exposure. Even when charts do not directly determine eligibility, then, artists that are not charting do not have the same footprint on radio, on digital media, or on tours and festivals, rendering them unlikely to be considered. Given the results of the longest-running country chart outlined here, songs by Black and of color women are unlikely to meet the basic terms of entry for eligibility. These issues ultimately dictate the induction processes for the Country Music Hall of Fame. While charts are a revolving archive of contemporary talent, the Hall of Fame not only codifies the past but also provides continuity to the industry's narrative of whiteness. Of the 149 artists inducted up to 2022, just three are Black men (inducted in 2000, 2005, and 2021), and four are white-passing artists with Indigenous heritage.

The HCS chart plays a critical role in promoting a deficit narrative for Black and of color within the industry that serves white racial interests. Rather than seeing their absence on the charts as indicative of a systemic problem, the industry (labels, radio, publishers) uses the lack of data to justify and maintain institutional practices that reject Black and of color artists. Only a few Black and of color artists have succeeded against these restrictive practices. Not only has their success not reduced the overall racial gap, but the industry continues to blame inequities on the Black and of color artists who have not succeeded on this uneven playing field – an argument that is *still being made* by white industry professionals in the 2020s (Cusic 2022). Echoing law scholar Dorothy A. Brown (2021, 197), white industry professionals argue that if one Black or of color artist can make it, they all can. For them, she writes (197), "failure lies not in the system but in the individual." Industry policy and collective prejudice, then, have worked together to maintain what George Lipsitz (2018, vii) terms a "possessive investment in whiteness" that is responsible for the

---

[9] Guyton was nominated for ACM's New Female Artist award again in 2021 - five years following her first nomination.

racialized hierarchies that persist within country music. For the industry, whiteness has a "cash value," accounting for the perceived quality of whiteness - and *proximity to* whiteness – and the advantages that come to businesses that profit from discriminatory practices. The industry benefits from inherited criteria that "pass on the spoils of discrimination to succeeding generations" (2018, vii). The business model thus becomes a self-fulfilling prophecy: it encourages investment in whiteness, because whiteness has historically provided financial advantages.

What emerges through this industry data, is a deep form of cultural redlining that relegates the music of Black and of color artists – especially women – to the margins of the industry. While the concept of "redlining" has historically been used to understand how customers have been denied policies based on race and ethnicity, SafiyaUmoja Noble (2018) draws on this concept to explain how technology and algorithms directly or indirectly use criteria like race, ethnicity, and gender to make decisions, assessments, and recommendations. Her writing on technological redlining and algorithmic/data discrimination resonates in cultural spheres, where contemporary decisions are based on historic – and discriminatory – data. What is critical to understand is that the data underlying the chart, awards, and induction processes are *human-made,* they are the results of practices in the industry – not of an audience or market response to music. Redlining is most visible in the country music industry in ranking of songs by their peak positions (Figure 4.2), a kind of "geography" of the chart that draws a deep line around the space that Black and of color artists occupy: residing largely within the bottom positions of the chart – charting for an average of eight weeks. Having a weak data trail, then, means not just that the artists responsible for these songs were more likely to be passed over for industry opportunities or dropped by labels for inactivity but that their failure to succeed will be used to deny access to future artists – blaming artists, not the white supremacist system.

Reproducing Inheritance

> Data is a double-edged sword. In a very real sense, data have been used as a weapon by those in power to consolidate their control – over places and things, as well as people.
> Catherine D'Ignazio and Lauren F. Klein (2020, 14)

Repetition is integral to the inner workings of the country industry's model: the data generated within and by each domain of the matrix of industrial domination is then used to make business decisions. In short, data is repeated from one domain in the industry matrix to the next, becoming a regime through which decisions are made, practices are regulated, and cultures are defined. The white patriarchal industry has, to borrow from Ahmed (2014), "inherit[ed] decisions that mark exclusions for them, without them, decisions that mark edges, marking out where they do not have to go."

But just as the system depends on repetition, it also relies on erasure – on forgetting. If songs by white artists are played more on radio (Watson 2021), they have greater access to the charts – entering in greater numbers, climbing higher, and accumulating more value (both financial and cultural capital), positioning them in contention for awards and (over time) inductions to the Hall of Fame. But their domination of chart and industry culture is secured by the removal of traces of the Black and of color artists who were there before. Removal, as Ahmed (2019, 167) states, can be inherited. Nowhere is this inheritance more visible than in the stories of the Black women – of Linda Martell, The Pointer Sisters, Ruby Falls, Nisha Jackson, Dona Mason, Rissi Palmer, and Mickey Guyton – whose songs have left faint data trails on the HCS chart. Or of the numerous Black women whose songs did not make it to the charts. Through the double processes of accumulation and removal embedded in the industrial matrix, the industry maintains and upholds a white supremacist and heteropatriarchal narrative, cementing, as Ahmed says (2014), "mechanisms that ensure the persistence of that structure," holding onto, investing in, and reproducing its inheritance.

PART II

Codes of Conduct

5 | Why Country Music Needs Latina Feminism

SOPHIA ENRIQUEZ

> There is a pretense to a homogeneity of experience covered by the word *sisterhood* that does not in fact exist.
>
> Audre Lorde (1984, 116)

Audre Lorde's words from 1984 have circulated in recent years as writers call attention to how mainstream feminism has historically produced false notions of a shared woman struggle that is only exacerbated by feminist media representations (Shiva and Kharazmi 2019). What many women of color have named as "white feminism," mainstream feminism falls short in its attention to intersectional analyses of women's diverse lived experiences and the systems that shape them (Moon and Holling 2020; Ortega 2006). Cate Young (2014) describes white feminism as "any expression of feminist thought or action that is anti-intersectional. It is a set of beliefs that allows for the exclusion of issues that specifically affect women of color." This chapter considers how narratives of country music – as both a popular music industry and subject of scholarly study – have been shaped by deep investments in white feminism and require tools from women of color feminisms for the telling of more complete narratives about who creates and listens to country music. I argue that the investments in white feminism on the part of country music practitioners and scholars alike have supported the widespread objectification, sexualization, and exclusion of women of color in country music.

This chapter focuses on Latina women's place in country music and investigates the potential of Latina feminist frameworks in country music studies. According to a 2016 study by the Country Music Association, Latinx country music consumers in the United States had increased 25 percent since 2010. The growth of Latinx country music is important for the aim of this chapter – and moreover of this collection – in two notable ways. On the one hand, Latinx country artists and listeners often remain underrepresented in conversations about who listens to and creates country music. On the other hand, recent conversations around race and representation in country music offer progress toward a future of country music in which women of color are central. As such, the analysis in this chapter is twofold. I use lyric analyses to demonstrate the extent to which country lyric conventions of white male country artists have commodified Latina women. Lyric analyses of contemporary Latina country artists, however, also show how the frameworks of Latina feminism work against the exclusionary grain of mainstream feminism. Ultimately, this chapter contributes perspectives from Latina and Chicana feminism to these transformative conversations as ways through which country music studies might deepen its understanding of Latina women and be better equipped to engage intersectional feminist thought as country music continues to expand its reach.

Whiteness in Country Music Studies

Whiteness has been central to country music scholarship since its emergence. Though Bill C. Malone's 1968 *Country Music, USA* is often hailed as the first important historical account of country music, it also served to establish a white male scholarly gaze, focusing on white male country musicians and paying little-to-no attention to race and representation in country music. The scholarly attention to country music and other popular musics, such as rock and jazz, was a progressive turn for music studies as a whole, but this early homogenizing approach to country music studies also perpetuated the myths that women and communities of color did not participate in country music as listeners or practitioners and that the work of scholars of color was not relevant for country music studies. In the 1990s and early 2000s, women writers began to feature more prominently in country music studies, as did women as topics of country music scholarship. Mary A. Bufwack and Robert K. Oermann's 1993 book *Finding Her Voice* laid out a social history and biography of women in country music. Women writers began to contribute to broader edited volumes on country music and in 2004, Diane Pecknold and Kristine M. McCusker published one such edited volume that featured a majority female authorship. As evidenced in *A Boy Named Sue,* these contributions to country music scholarship about women by women began to assess how women as a social category have been marginalized from the industry through discriminatory practices and toxic masculinities. More recent contributions, too, such as *Country Boys and Redneck Women* (also edited by Pecknold and McCusker 2016), offer a more substantive look at gendered and class-based struggles in country music, as well as a detailed understanding of women's contributions to country music. In all of these instances, however, conversations about gender and sexuality in country music often fail to incorporate an intersectional feminist lens and, at a minimum, cite women of color widely. Consider, for example, the 2017 study titled "Girl in a Country Song," in which the authors discuss the various patterns of women's objectification in popular country songs from 1990 to 2014 with no mention of how conditions of race establish women's objectification in the first place (Rasmussen and Densley 2017). It is concerning that although country music scholarship focused on women and gender emerged well after the proliferation of women of color feminism by writers such as scholarship by women of color writers such as bell hooks, Angela Davis, Audre Lorde, Gloria Anzaldúa, and Cherrie Moraga in the 1960s–80s, it has generally failed to make substantial efforts to include such perspectives. Put differently, conversations about "women" in country music are often decidedly – and implicitly – conversations about white women and don't include the experiences or perspectives of women of color.

Recent strides have been taken toward a more complete and expansive country music studies that include the perspectives of women of color – both in actual authorship and citational practice. In July 2020, scholars Nadine Hubbs and Francesca Royster coedited a special issue of the *Journal for Popular Music Studies* titled "Uncharted Country." The special issue was the first collection of country music studies essays edited by and including contributions of LGBTQIA+ and of color scholars. This issue comes seven years after the similarly interventional collection *Hidden in the Mix: The African American Presence in Country Music* edited by Diane Pecknold (2013a), which shows how country music is heavily racialized as white and how Black artists have nevertheless asserted their presence in racialized spaces. "Uncharted Country" provides further historical grounding for country music's racialization and offers other diverse per-spectives about Jewish, LGBTQIA+, Latinx, and indigenous relationships to country music and stands to disrupt the reputation country music studies has held as a majority white academic space.

Country Music Studies and Loving, Knowing Ignorance

The previously mentioned growth of country music's Latinx consumer base generates a more detailed discussion about Latinx representation. In an editorial for *The Medium*, Rosario Moreno offered her perceptions as a Latina country music listener. Moreno narrates her experience attending a concert as part of country artist Luke Bryan's "What Makes You Country" tour in 2018 and contextualizes the dominant narrative of country music that centers on whiteness. Moreno writes, "Among my Latinx friends who don't like country music, there's the running joke about its racial undertones. Though country music lyrics tend to lean towards personal experiences instead of politics, the lifestyle a [sic] country song has typically been synonymous with conservative, Republican values." Moreno identifies the tension between young Latinx country listeners and these stereotypes:

I've come to believe that this discord in country music speaks to the greater growing pains the United States is experiencing. Latinxs and other minorities are changing the image of what a "traditional" American looks like and though it may be hard for a portion of this nation to handle, we aren't going anywhere. (Sorry, not sorry.) Country music, like other institutions, is going to have to ask itself how it chooses to position itself in a future where Latinxs have a substantial buying power and only grow as a demographic with each generation. Country music may not be ready to make a Nike/Kaepernick sized shift, but making more appeals to the Latinx demographic, especially through common values like family and love would be a step in the right direction.

Moreno continues that the "right direction" she envisions is one that will include her experiences in the context of immigration and citizenship, stating that "I'm always going to love the fun and romantic songs country music produces, but when my personal experiences as a Latina from a community of immigrants, are acknowledged and even defended, that's a gamechanger." In the context of these sentiments from Latina listeners such as Moreno and the moment of consciousness about race and representation in country music, I turn now to what Latina feminist scholar Mariana Ortega (2006) has identified as a "loving, knowing ignorance" to better understand the obstacles of white feminism within the country music industry and scholarship that prevent the changes Moreno calls for.

At the crux of white feminism is its dependence on ways of knowing and understanding the world based on the lived experiences of whiteness. As Dreama Moon and Michelle Holling (2020, 253) discuss, white feminism "ideologically grounds itself in a gendered victimology that masks its participation and functionality in white supremacy." By virtue of its prioritization of white lived experiences, white feminism does the damage of erasing the knowledge and perspectives of the world that come from the experiences of women of color. Mariana Ortega (2006) explains that the success of white feminism in evading this epistemic violence against women of color comes from the breeding of a "loving, knowing ignorance." According to Ortega (2006, 57), loving, knowing ignorance is "ignorance of the thought and experience of women of color that is accompanied by both alleged love for and alleged knowledge about them." For Ortega (61), loving, knowing ignorance is thorough and complete:

this loving, knowing perceiver may be engaged in knowledge production about women of color in various ways: by citing the work of women of color, by including women of color in her political and practical agenda, by making claims about the lives of women of color, by classifying the experience of women of color, or by systematizing her findings about the experience of women of color.

Ortega warns, however, that loving, knowing ignorance actually has the potential to be quite superficial when claims about women of color on the part of white women are inaccurate, incomplete, or inadequately represented. Of course, Ortega's warning calls attention to the diversity of lived experiences of women of color. I emphasize that a consciousness about and study of Ortega's notion of loving, knowing ignorance holds white women accountable to the reasons for and context with which they engage the voices of women of color. In accepting the presence of and taking accountability for a loving, knowing ignorance, white women are able to relax fears of being named a failed feminist and direct the energies of their privilege toward systemic changes. In the ongoing response of the US academic community to institutional violence against people of color, white women in particular are increasingly encouraged to exhibit a feminist sensibility that wields their positions of power to bolster visibility of educational resources, community initiatives, and solidarity networks for people of color. Of course, these responses are necessary and important. But, as Ortega argues, white women traverse a "dangerous terrain" when there is a widespread claim for concern about women of color yet a passive participation in the habits/acts that perpetuate ignorance about them. Put differently, white feminist solidarity – when claimed as such – also does the work of re-centering the feelings, efforts, and concerns of white women in conversations about race.

Ortega warns that the loving, knowing white feminist, if not held accountable, wields the power to construct the very realities she may claim to abhor – a reality in which

the voices of women of color are still taken seriously only if well-known white feminists quote them, in which white feminists who read the work of one woman of color think they understand the experience of all women of color, in which the words of women of color are quoted briefly rather than analyzed in depth, in which the experience of women of color are homogenized, in which women of color are seen as half-subjects who need to be "given a voice". (62)

The potential harm, then, is not in white women scholars writing about white women in country music. Rather, the harm is in scholarship that is not intersectional – that does not consider the voices, experiences, or perspectives of women of color alongside issues such as gender and class. If the work of white scholars in country music studies is to focus on white women in the country music industry, the only way in which it can avoid loving, knowing ignorance of white feminism is by close engagement with Black, Indigenous, Latina, and women of color feminisms. Following Maria Lugone's (1987) notion of "world-traveling," the loving, knowing, un-ignorant white woman feminist holds space for women of color in a way that doesn't indulge the sense of satisfaction she might feel in that holding but that allows women of color to enter and exit at their own will, on their own terms, in their own way. Taking to heart Ortega's loving, knowing ignorance among other frameworks of women of color feminism is crucial if future country music scholarship is to tend to these oversights.

The "Sexy Latina" in Country Music

This loving, knowing ignorance in country music studies has manifested in scholarship's neglect of the overt objectification and sexualization of women of color, particularly Latina women, in country music lyrics. Latinx scholars have shown how media-based representations of Latinas as the sexy, curvaceous, ethnic other form potent scripts of femininity and Latinidad in the context of the US Latina experience (Beltran 2002; Molinary 2007; Molina-Guzman 2010). Here, I locate the trope of the "sexy Latina" in mainstream country music examples from the early 1990s to present the way in which the sexy Latina falls into a colonialist system of heteronormativity, sexuality, and femininity that re-centers the white woman while hyper-sexualizing and objectifying Latina women. The sexy Latina maps onto tropes of what Isabel Molina Guzmán and Angharad N. Valdivia (2004, 211) have referred to as "tropicalism." Within tropicalism, they write, "attributes such as bright colors, rhythmic music, and brown or olive skin comprise some of the most enduring stereotypes about Latina/os." In country music, the sexy Latina is often signaled by the artists' use of Spanish language words and catchphrases, as demonstrated in the examples below, and demonstrate excessive attention on the part of male country artists and songwriters to physical characteristics Molina Guzmán and Valdivia identify.

Along with American white male country singers such as Jake Owen and Luke Bryan, Tim McGraw has profited widely off the trope of the sexy

Latina. McGraw's fifth studio album, *A Place in the Sun,* was released in 1999 and featured the chart-topping singles "Please Remember Me," "Something Like That," and "My Next Thirty Years." Among these more well-known titles, even the album's less popular tracks rose on the country charts. One of those tracks titled "Señorita Margarita" narrates a man's loneliness and longing for an ex-lover, which he seeks to relieve with the company of "Señorita Margarita." The narrator laments his loneliness and how he "still loves her, still needs her," in reference to his ex-lover. A proposition follows in which the narrator addresses Señorita Margarita, saying "I'm just hopin' you can comfort me." The song continues "I hope you realize this is a one-night stand / I'm gonna get her back I know I can / So let's keep this between you, me, the salt and the lime." In this case, the sexy Latina is one dimensional – she is flattened as a placeholder of sexual desire, unnamed, and assumedly consenting. The narrator fully acknowledges her temporary use as well as his control over the conditions in which she is used. The sexy Latina is fleeting – she is present just long enough to become the object of men's sexual desire but not long enough to be rendered fully human or substantive enough for meaningful partnership.

McGraw later released another hit that features the unnamed sexy Latina. "Felt Good on My Lips" reached No. 1 on *Billboard*'s Hot Country Songs chart in 2012. The song narrates an encounter between a man and a Spanish-speaking woman. Although the sexy Latina is still unnamed, her origins are briefly alluded to. The narrator explains that her name "was a hand me down name / from the side of a family that long ago / came over here on a boat from somewhere in Spain." Of course, the sexy Latina's Spanish origins could signal a vast range of migratory and colonial histories. In this sense, there can be no sure claim about her ethnic or racial makeup. And yet regardless of her racial background, the sexy Latina is positioned as a temporary and fleeting character. As she "tipped the DJ to play her favorite song / a Spanish little number that was rocking on strong," the listener understands that she is an active speaker in the scenario, navigating both Spanish and English. The title phrase "it felt good on my lips" recurs to map the progression of the dynamic between the man and the sexy Latina, moving from the mystery of her origins and name to the satisfaction and pleasure of the physical encounter.

For many male artists, the sexy Latina only appears briefly in contexts such as these – a scene at the bar, a one-night stand, or a distraction from the stressors of a working-class lifestyle. The sexy Latina is not only a temporary love affair that starts over a drink at the bar as is the case for

McGraw but often also a conquest or achievement of desire in a foreign place. In most cases, the sexy Latina is located in Mexico – her sex appeal is emphasized by her sun-kissed skin and "tropical" aesthetic in the context of her alleged homeland. Just as the portrayal of Mexico in country music as nothing more than a tropical vacation destination is a farce in its nonrecognition of anti-migrant racial violence and inhumane conditions for Latinx migrants at the US–Mexico border, so too is the sexy Latina's ties to Mexico, the Spanish language, and heteronormative relationships an inaccurate and incomplete picture of Latina women. Blake Shelton's 2003 single "Playboys of the Southwestern World" exemplifies this mentality that binds the sexy Latina to this narrative and reproduces a colonial conquest of Latina women. Shelton's song tells of a friendship between two men in which they set out to "go down to Mexico / chase señoritas, drink ourselves silly / show them Mexican girls a couple of real hillbillies." Here, the conquest over Mexican women is not only a fantasy but a fully developed plan predicated on the assumption that "all those little brown-eyed girls / want playboys of the southwestern world." Zac Brown Band's 2009 hit "Toes" similarly locates the sexy Latina in Mexico. The sexy Latina plays the role of the bartender whose "body's been kissed by the sun." She serves rum to the narrator as he dips his toes in the sand, wishes away worries, and bolsters his sex appeal to other local "*muchachas*" by "throwing *pesos* their way."

Ironically, well-known white male country artists have recently been involved in efforts to expand country music's listening audience to Spanish-speaking Latinx communities in the United States. For example, Billy Ray Cyrus recently recorded a Spanish version of Don Von Tress's "Achy Breaky Heart" which he popularized in 1992. Featuring Cuban-American Latin pop star Jencarlos Canela, the latinized version of the well-loved country song featured new verses translated into Spanish and Caribbean musical references such as the conga drums. McGraw's "Humble and Kind," topped country and pop music charts in 2018. A year later, McGraw released a version of the song in Spanish, titled "Nunca Te Olvides de Amar," and loosely translated by Argentine singer/songwriter Claudia Brant. In an interview with *Billboard*, McGraw commented on the impetus behind the release of "Nunca Te Olvides de Amar," stating that "My Spanish may not be perfect, my accent may not be perfect, but if I can reach out and touch someone in a language that's not my own – that's a good enough reason to try." Yet these recent efforts on the part of white, male country artists to expand country music's listening audience by the translation of well-known country songs to Spanish are easily obscured by their long-time participation in the exploitation of Latina women.

Even in attempts to care for the communities in which Latina women belong, examples from white male country artists repeatedly arrive at the same conclusion about Latina women: they are sexy, foreign, and disposable, happily making US vacationers more comfortable in Mexico and filling sexual desire after a night out drinking at the bar. This trope of the sexy Latina in country music is dangerous for a multitude of reasons. First, it works to minimize and homogenize Latina lived experiences. These examples depict Latinas in stereotypical ways that emphasize physical features such as dark skin, dark hair, and a sex appeal on the dance floor that, because they speak Spanish and embody the markers of tropicalism, renders them exotic. This stereotype does not account for the diversity of Latina racial identities, erasing in particular Black and Indigenous Latinas, and also erases the experience of queer or differently abled Latinas, reinforcing stereotypes of sexiness and heteronormativity to Latina listeners. The trope of the sexy Latina also homogenizes the experience of Latina women by connecting Latina identity with a knowledge of the Spanish language, disregarding the experiences of the many thousands of US Latinas who don't speak Spanish. Second, the trope of the sexy Latina positions her femininity as something which she can neither fully relinquish nor realize. The feminine-presenting Latina listener who wishes to embrace sexiness or sensuality is met with the notion that her sexiness is, in the context of country music audiences, to be interpreted as invitation and consent. The Latina woman in the country song is voiceless and communicates instead with her body. This commodification of Latina bodies as also portrayed in popular media has the potential to spread the harmful message to young Latina listeners in particular that their bodies must not only conform to a hyper-sexualized prototype but that their sexuality is not negotiated on their own terms. Third, and most disturbingly, the trope of the sexy Latina in country music reproduces a centuries-long history of violence against Latin American women. Scenarios and situations that portray the sexy Latina as an object of conquest for the white male country artist, in this case, acts as a lyrical re-creation of the acts of sexual violence, rape, and conquest that many male country artists' ancestors likely participated in. Through this interpretation, country music's obsession with the sexy Latina carries the weight of generational colonial trauma and only serves to deepen the wounds of such histories without even acknowledging them.

The blame of these longstanding lyric conventions that explicitly objectify Latina women need not be placed on white women practitioners or scholars of country music. Rather, understanding that these harmful conventions have been long overlooked as a function of their embeddedness in a white supremacist and patriarchal system – even one in which white women are active in conversations about race and representation – brings previously silenced Latina perspectives to the fore. Since country music scholars have noted the ways in which white women are sexually objectified in mainstream country music, it is likely that they will agree about the egregiousness and danger of the trope of the sexy Latina in mainstream country music and the potential to alienate Latina listeners. However, the un-checkedness of mainstream country's exploitation and typification of Latina women until now is symptomatic of a loving, knowing ignorance that directs energies and attentions away from a women of color-centered approach and toward the concerns of white women.

The Latina Present and Future of Country Music

Despite these enduring conventions that objectify and sexualize Latina women, Latina artists are finding ways to navigate the country music industry. The recent shifts in country music scholarship I drew attention to earlier in this chapter are parallel to conversations and efforts in the country music industry that are working toward a more inclusive praxis, and which are led by Black women. For example, Mickey Guyton has highlighted the experiences of Black artists in country music with her 2020 single "Black Like Me," which then earned her a Grammy nomination in 2021, making history as the first Black solo female artist to be nominated in a country category. In recognition of Guyton's work building networks for women of color country artists, breakthrough Latina country artist Valerie Ponzio (whose work I discuss later in this chapter) tweeted:

I had recently moved to Nashville w/naive hopes of bringing my Latina voice to music city. Mickey Guyton was performing a writers round . . . The second Mickey saw me she said "are you an artist? I want to connect you w/a show they might do for artists of color. Message me!" She has been advocating for BIPOC even when the industry kept passing her up.

A growing network of women of color country artists speaks to the emergence and success of other Black female artists such as Reyna Roberts, Yola, Miko Marks, Kären McKormick, and Brittney Spencer, who continue to prompt conversations about representation in country music and whose efforts are foundational for the success of Latina women who have yet to feature prominently in the country music industry.

A Spotify curated playlist titled "Country Latino" launched in early 2021 and features Latina country artist Valerie Ponzio who narrates romantic and sexual experiences in a way that reclaims the trope of the sexy Latina and positions her from the Latina voice/perspective. This repositioning resonates with the Latina and Chicana feminisms I've illuminated thus far and situates Latina country artists as working against the grain of white feminism and its loving, knowing ignorance.

Ponzio first gained attention as a contestant on season twelve of *The Voice* in which she impressed a four-judge panel with a rendition of June Carter Cash and Merle Kilgore's "Ring of Fire" in a blind audition. Ponzio's 2019 single titled "*Órale*," Spanish for "right on!" or "hell yeah!" is influenced by her childhood, where she frequented Mexican block parties in the borderland city of El Paso, Texas. Ponzio's lyrics weave through images of a crowded dance floor in a driveway and "*tecates* and *tequila*," popular alcoholic beverages among Mexican consumers, as she encourages her dance partner with "*órale!* I want you to dance with me" and "Don't be shy, come on, just say *órale!*" Ponzio's use of a widely recognized Mexican Spanish colloquialism like *órale* speaks to cultural components of Mexican American communities like those Moreno (2019) calls for. It also positions her as a Latina Spanish-speaker country artist who speaks both Spanish and English to audiences. Ponzio's 2018 EP featured her song "Timeless" in both English and Spanish, with the Spanish version offering a close translation of the original English lyrics. In "Timeless," Ponzio evokes the imagery of the sexy Latina I discuss above. She sings "Looking in the mirror, dark red lipstick / Your hands sneak up on my hips as you zip me up / Tight little black dress I know you like / Turn around, stare into your eyes as I fix your tie." Unlike the trope of the sexy Latina as portrayed by male country artists, Ponzio narrates an encounter of attraction from the perspective of a Latina woman herself. In other words, she turns the sexy Latina trope on its head – the Latina singer, Ponzio, not only has agency over her own body and the way it is described, but the presumably male counterpart in this scene from "Timeless" is unnamed and ambiguous. In this sense, Ponzio's owning of the imagery of the sexy Latina reveals a framework of Latina feminism in country music songwriting that prioritizes the vice of the Latina narrator, allowing her to, recalling Ortega, "enter and exit" at her own will.

Similarly, Mexican American country artist Leah Turner reclaims the trope of the sexy Latina in her 2020 single "Once Upon a Time in Mexico," which tells of a woman's summer love affair with a Mexican cowboy. In this instance, the scenes that McGraw and others have exploited (drinks on the beach and sensual dancing, for example) are told from the experience of the narrator/Latina herself. In an interview with CMT, Turner shared "I want women to feel it's OK to feel sexy" (qtd. in Shelburne 2020). Turner and Ponzio's positioning of sexuality and agency in these contexts renders a Latina feminist listening framework that redirects listeners to an autonomous Latina body, voice, and experience.

According to Spotify, the Spanish version of Ponzio's "Timeless" received significantly more streams than the English version. Similarly, Turner's "Once Upon a Time in Mexico" has quickly become her most frequently streamed single. This data suggests Ponzio and Turner's success in appealing to a largely untapped Latinx country listening demographic. Ponzio and Turner are joined by other young Latina artists who are emerging in country music such as Hayley Orrantia, former member of country-pop girl group Lakoda Rayne, and Kat Luna of the country duo Kat and Alex, who recently released a Spanglish rendition of their successful single "How Many Times."

Other Latinas are finding ways to reimagine well-known country songs in English and traditional Spanish language songs alike. Canadian Mexican country artist Lindi Ortega connects to Latinx audiences with an instrumental version of Chilean *nueva canción* leader Violetta Parra's "Gracias a La Vida" on her 2018 album *Liberty*. Four-time Tejano Music Award nominee Veronique Medrano is also featured on Spotify's "Country Latino" playlist for her 2021 rendition of Roy Orbison's 1962 country ballad "Crying." In Medrano's bilingual version, themes of love, loss, and despair are told from the perspective of a woman who sings "crying," *llorando,* in Spanish, in an emphatic, emotive way consistent with that of traditional Mexican *rancheras*, or country songs. Medrano's Mexican American stylistic interpretation of "Crying" builds bridges among Spanish and English-speaking country music listeners, in that it registers the traditional ranchera singing of female artists such as Lucha Villa, Lydia Mendoza, and Chavela Vargas, while also appealing to early rockabilly and country music listeners who are more familiar with Orbison's version. Artists such as Medrano present white country music audiences with a traditional Mexican style in the framework of a familiar country song in English.

Together, these artists speak to the growth of Latina representation in country music, which requires much closer attention on the part of country music scholars. Let us turn to invitations from Latina and Chicana feminists to imagine and to practice vulnerability when thinking about what a more careful approach to women of color in country music entails. During a keynote lecture at the Indiana University/Ohio State University Graduate Student Folklore and ethnomusicology Conference in 2020, scholar Rachel González-Martin presented "magical thinking" as a mechanism of decentering white, hegemonic discourse in folklore studies. González-Martin (2020) asserted that magical thinking "ought to not only be understood as an acceptance of knowledge and control of knowing that comes from magic as science, but also the ways in which entextualizing forms of folklore work to constitute community imaginaries." Music as an entextualized form, and the vernacular role country music often assumes through its connections to local communities, place, and tradition, makes for similar conditions by which magical thinking is also a deconstructive, generative practice. Magical thinking here is not to be confused as an imagination *about* the experiences of Latinas and women of color – rather, it is an expansive framework for the new perspectives that emerge when the Latina and other women of color feminisms are active and disruptive in a space where they have previously been ignored – in the case of this chapter, country music studies. González-Martin ultimately argued that magical thinking as a tool of Latina feminism acts as a departure point for a vulnerable, reconfigured, inclusive model of folklore studies in the United States, asserting that with the "efficacy of magical thinking and healing comes complex cultural collisions much of which is rooted in memory and necessary forgetting. What can we keep from the institutional memory and what must be 'killed' before we are able to imagine who we might become?" González-Martin echoes Chicana feminist calls to air out the dirty laundry of academia's investments in whiteness. She invites us to imagine a folklore studies, or country music studies, in the case of this collection, that embraces and looks forward to the future, leans into the difficulty of the unlearning that lies ahead, and humbly relinquishes knowing.

More widespread knowledge about Latina women in country music provokes the magical thinking of the future of a country music studies and industry. Magical thinking is also the work of imagination, and imagination is radical knowing. The women of color feminisms I've referenced throughout this chapter locate the body in social and political systems – imagination, in turn, locates the body in alternative situations, futures, and dreams. The act of imagining, as practiced by women of color thinkers, allows for the simultaneous contraction and expansion of oneself and sets of knowledge. Country music studies, and other music studies with their roots in white supremacist ideologies, are long overdue for an active practice of radical, magical thinking that is rooted in the work of perspectives of women of color. What would a country music studies – or popular music studies, more broadly – that fully acknowledges its loving, knowing ignorance and seeks to unlearn itself look like? What new directions, formulations, or creative ideas might emerge from a country music studies that is rooted in Black, Indigenous, Latinx, and women of color feminisms and is designed to create a more equitable share for women of color scholars? How will more Latinas like Ponzio, Ortega, and Turner show up in country music if the country music industry and scholarship alike take seriously the frameworks of Latina feminism and apply them to inclusive practices of love and care? I have attempted to demonstrate how the tools of women of color, Latina and Chicana feminism, clear space for more honest conversations and prompt actions that respond to these questions. One obvious answer lies in the call for scholars who engage country music as an object of study to seriously center women of color feminisms in their work. Yet, white scholars should not rely on the intellectual labor of women of color thinkers as the sole means by which their work is legible in contemporary discourses of race. As such, country music studies must be unafraid to maintain a critical stance of its history with and participation in white supremacy and white feminism. If writers who are engaged in white, patriarchal lineages like that of country music do not acknowledge them as such – and are not concerned about them as such – they participate in the erasure of the voices of color upon which the fundamental success and knowledge of the music they study is built.

These practices I draw attention to and call for are not new or revolutionary, however slow they may be to arrive in country music studies. They are the minimum of what is necessary for country music studies to remain relevant in critical conversations of race, representation, and a more equitable academic praxis in a fourth-wave feminist paradigm. The Latina futures of country music are part of a broader sustainable future of country music which requires the welcoming of new voices and epistemologies – a new scholarly space in which the amity of loving ignorance about Latina women and women of color is instead a relationship of accountability and vulnerability forged by careful listening and constant reconfigurations of knowing.

6 | Pistol Annies

Country Rebels with Humor

STEPHANIE VANDER WEL

Humor has been a prevalent performative strategy in country music since the commercial genre was first produced and marketed via radio and recording in the 1920s. With network radio stations broadcasting barn dance programs during the Depression-era, country music flooded the airwaves by extending the entertainment and amusement of the popular stage to radio. Specifically, early barn dance radio incorporated the theatrical traditions of blackface minstrelsy and vaudeville in a range of comedic characters that highlighted the buffoonery and grotesque mimicry of race, ethnicity, and region, purposefully clashing with the decorum and pretensions of white middle-class society (Green 1976, 68–72; Cusic 1993, 45; Jones 2008, 3–12). Considering country music's roots in comedy, I am interested in how female country musicians have incorporated the theatrics of humor and the politics of laughter in their stage acts and musical performances. As Constance Rourke's (2004, 86) foundational study on American humor exclaimed, "[L]aughter produced the illusion of leveling obstacles in a world which was full of unaccustomed obstacles." This chapter connects the comedic practices of female country artists of the past to the tactics of women in twenty-first-century country music located in a context of vocal production, song narrative, musical style, and stage and video performance. For female country artists, humor has proven to be an effective approach in confronting the pressures and scrutinizing gaze of hegemonic society, as well as the gendered restrictions of the country music industry itself.

Though country music historians have explored the cultural work of male country humor, few scholars have examined the use of comedy in women's performances, apart from those of Minnie Pearl, whose illustrious career was intertwined with the commercial rise of WSM's barn dance program, the *Grand Ole Opry*, and Nashville's country music industry, making it difficult to overlook her legacy (Fredriksson 2000; Malone 2002, 176; Fox 2009; Ellis 2010, 162). The historical record, however, points to a number of important country comediennes and the significance of humor in women's country music. In my book *Hillbilly Maidens, Cowgirls, and Okies: Women's Country Music, 1930–1960,* I illuminate the centrality of the theatrical in the performances of female artists whose musical parodies, often conveyed by means of vocal style and production, erupted in transgressive moments of laughter. Lulu Belle, who emerged as one of the stars of the *National Barn Dance* in the 1930s, cultivated a vocal approach that satirized the nasal twang techniques associated with country singing in her songs about courtship and marriage ("Wish I Was a Single Girl," 1939) and slapstick routines that called into question gender norms. Rose Maddox, whose career developed in the 1940s and 1950s dance halls of California, incorporated similar theatrical and vocal devices.

In addition to these figures in my book, June Carter, who developed her comedic routines with the original Carter Family and later with Maybelle Carter and the Carter Sisters, appeared on the *Opry* alongside Minnie Pearl in the 1950s. Similar to the performances of Lulu Belle and Maddox, Carter exaggerated her nasal twang approach to underline the comedic and subversive qualities of the white rustic southern woman in songs such as "Country Girl" (1949). What these examples point to are the ways female country artists have embodied the theatrical elements of the "unruly woman," which has been defined by media feminist scholar Kathleen Rowe (1995, 10) as "an ambivalent figure of female outrageousness and transgression with roots in the narrative form of comedy and the social practices of carnival," the home of inversion and fantasy. For Rowe, the unruly woman has continued to pervade various forms of culture and media in which she appears as a "rule-breaker, joke-maker, and public, bodily spectacle" (1995, 12), disrupting the usual fate of women under patriarchy.

Extending Rowe's understanding of female unruliness to country music, this chapter explores the comedic effects of female country acts that have turned the transgressive behavior of the unruly woman into signifiers of white rustic working-class womanhood, which often and purposefully stand in stark contrast to the control and rigidity of dominant society. The humor spills forth from the clashing of expectations, of the rustic unruly woman purposely disregarding the social values of patriarchy. As philosophers and thinkers of humor have demonstrated, we commonly laugh at those moments of incongruity when expectations are subverted, and paradoxes emerge. The Danish philosopher Søren Kierkegaard (1987, 83), for example, argued that the "primary element in the comical is contradiction." I point to those performative moments of contradiction in early and mid-century country music and extend my analysis to the contemporary ensemble "the Pistol Annies," comprised of Miranda Lambert, Angaleena Presley, and Ashley Monroe. The Pistol Annies, performing the cultural defiance of the unruly woman in their songs "Bad Example" (2011) and "Got My Name Changed Back" (2018), wield the rhetorical devices of incongruity in their comical performances of recalcitrance, of gleefully disregarding white middle-class propriety and patriarchal expectations.

I begin with Lulu Belle in the context of 1930s barn dance radio to support my claims about the larger themes of comedy in women's acts. Lulu Belle, following in the theatrical footsteps of vaudevillian Elviry Weaver, adopted an aggressive comic manner while clothed in exaggerated feminized and rustic attire in her performances on WLS's the *National Barn Dance* (Fox 2009; Vander Wel 2020). Her mix of masculine and feminine codes was part of a tradition of comediennes who reconfigured male-defined comic roles developed in blackface minstrelsy and ethnic humor. As historian Alison Kibler and others have shown, women who took over the gender-bending theatrics of cross-dressed male performers enacting the nagging blackface wench or the coarse Irish maid did so by means of exaggeration and grotesque comedy (1999, 62; Lavitt 1999, 261). Yet these performances of unruly women still represented a contradiction in terms of gendered expectations as vaudevillian female performers continued to define these comic roles as purposefully standing apart from the ideals of the domestic feminine. Lulu Belle transferred the physical, verbal, and sexual excesses associated with working-class, Black, and immigrant women to her impersonation of the female white Southern rustic in her comedic routines. Her early performances on radio, for example, were often juxtaposed against a more genteel image of Southern white femininity, as enacted by another WLS star, Linda Parker, billed as the "Little Sunbonnet Girl." Whereas Parker appeared as the young genteel mountain maiden who had learned her folk songs from her mother, Lulu Belle played the unruly hillbilly clown, often stealing the show from Parker with her kinetic humor and caricatures of white Southern womanhood. Indeed, her clowning on the stage of the *National Barn Dance* drew the ire of the announcer of the program, Hal O'Halloran, who would chastise Lulu Belle on the air and in front of the live audience. She, however, soon learned that by verbally outwitting the announcer and hence challenging the male authority of the barn dance program, the audience laughed even louder at the gendered inversion of power (Vander Wel 2020).

The music of the Maddox Brothers and Rose also translated the theatrics of barn dance radio, including performances of female unruliness, to country music. As a raucous, entertaining live spectacle in California's 1940s and 1950s dance halls and roadhouse, the family ensemble recorded well-known songs, turning them into musical parodies and models of humor (Vander Wel 2020). In their 1951 recording "Alimony (Pay Me)," for example, the ensemble remakes Bill Cox's 1934 song "Alimony Woman," an advice song to unsuspecting men whose wives had apparently become wretched shrews demanding divorce and alimony. The humor lies in the way Rose Maddox's performance transforms the wench-like song into an anthem of independence for women during the post–World War II period of heightened domesticity. Maddox beckons her audience of "single girls" to listen to her story about the conflicts of marriage, offering a solution for those who should ever find themselves unhappily married: sue for alimony. Maddox's loud brassy chest timbre, especially when she belts the opening lines of the chorus ("to pay me alimony, I had him up in every court in town to pay me alimony") combined with the song's instrumental arrangement of swing rhythms and riff-based guitar solos, contributes to the assertive and exuberant image of the protagonist being awarded court-sanctioned alimony. Maddox's divorced woman, thus, emerges not only unscathed from the dire effects often associated with divorce but also triumphant in her gleeful disregard of the increased social pressure of 1950s domesticity.

Along with these musical moments of meeting and overcoming cultural expressions of misogyny, the comedic theatrics of incongruity, epitomized by Lulu Belle, has helped give shape to wider expressions of gender variance in women's country music. June Carter's performance history is a case in point. Appearing first with the original Carter Family, June Carter started her slapstick routines of kinetic humor on border radio in 1939. Initially, as a tweenager, she invented the comedic role of Aunt Polly, an old maid character straight from vaudeville. Carter's young age and perceived innocence starkly contrasted with her performance of a character type known for aggression and vigor and linked to female impersonation. After the original Carter Family dissolved in 1943, Maybelle and the Carter Sisters continued the family act on a number of barn dance radio programs, including the *Louisiana Hayride*, before they became part of the *Opry* in the 1950s. During this time, Carter changed costumes, so to speak, and cultivated the persona of a young country woman in "Country Girl," a song that had been part of her country girl act with the Carter Sisters while traveling with the comedy team Homer and Jethro, who provided the instrumental accompaniment to Carter's recorded performance. "Country Girl," a cover of Little Jimmie Dickens's 1949 hit song "Country Boy" (written by Felice and Boudleaux Bryant), transfers the comedic tropes associated with white masculinized rustic pride to a depiction of the white

Southern rural woman. Yet Carter makes the song her own through her use of parody. She exaggerates her Southern accent and nasal twang approaches in her singing and speaking voice while extending the lyrical setting of country authenticity to this model of Southern womanhood, pitting it against those "folks who think that they're so dagburn highfalutin." In the chorus, Carter then belts out her melodies and further paints the country girl in tones of comedic rebellion. She raises "cain" on Saturday night, presumably at the local honky-tonk, redeems herself Sunday in church, and is back behind the plow on Monday. Her dynamic and chest-dominant vocal techniques combined with vocal growls highlight the edginess of this white country protagonist. In this cover of Dickens's "Country Boy," Carter embodies the "masculinized" practices of rural labor and Southern culture characterized by the dualistic lifestyle of Saturday night hedonism and Sunday morning piety (Cash 1941, vii; Malone 2002, ix). Her audience, thus, laughs at the ways the country girl, realized by means of grotesque comedy, collides with the class prescriptions of gender norms.

Country music's theatrical traditions allude to the ways class formation, emerging in the nineteenth century, coded working-class women "as inherently healthy, hardy, and robust – often masculinized," as sociologist Beverley Skeggs notes (2001, 297). Carter's enactment of the country girl toiling away behind a plow pointed to these perceptions of working-class women's proximity to laboring male bodies. The physicality and by extension sexuality associated with the bodies of working-class women aligned them more with depictions of male laborers or with nineteenth-century sexologists' perceptions of female inverts than with the passivity and domestic ideals of femininity as a white middle-class identity. As Nadine Hubbs (2014, 122) has noted, working-class constructions of womanhood have given rise to elements of gender variance that have much in common with the look and manner of queer women. Consider k.d. lang's 1989 song "Big Boned Gal" (1989) about a country woman who gets dressed up to go to the local dance as an incarnation of the mannish hillbilly. The song's gender variance, couched in the theatrical and comedic tropes of country music, contributed to lang's androgynous image and queer presence in country music before she came out in the 1990s. Dolly Parton's famous campy images of white Southern working-class womanhood is another well-known example of country humor and theatrics. Combining the image of the naive but sexualized country girl that proliferated throughout barn dance radio with the campy sophistication of Mae West, Parton has provided, as Leigh H. Edwards (2018, 2) notes, "an exaggerated performance of country womanhood." Parton's "poor white trash" look serves not only as a means to slam middle-class norms but also to underscore the cultural and commercial power of female spectacle making in country music. Parton herself referred to her look as a "gimmick" designed to attract commercial attention in a male-dominated country music industry that had habitually downplayed female artists (111).

Comedy, especially in the form of camp and parody, has proven to be a powerful rhetorical device for women in country music. The performances of the unruly white Southern woman who meets and conquers the abuses of patriarchal culture can be seen in a recent and salient example, such as The Chicks' song and music video "Goodbye Earl" (1999). The trio sets the Southern dark humor of a Flannery O'Connor short story or a Flannie Flagg novel to a music video about domestic violence. The revenge fantasy depicts two female friends, Mary Ann and Wanda, triumphing over domestic violence by murdering Wanda's husband Earl, the perpetrator. In the closing chorus, lead singer Natalie Maines sings an upbeat vocal melody, accompanied by Martie Maguire's and Emily Strayer's joyful sounding vocables, "na, na, na," with the entire small-town community, including the dead and decomposing Earl, joining Mary and Wanda in a celebratory dance. Yet during the midst of their commercial success in country music, The Chicks were banned from country radio when Maines bluntly and humorlessly spoke against the United States' imminent invasion of Iraq in 2003.

More recently, the 2015 controversy known as "TomatoGate" serves as another reminder of how women in contemporary country music still face the misogynistic barriers of the country music industry. As Beverly Keel (2015a) and others (Hodak 2016; Watson 2019b) have reported, radio consultant Keith Hill advised radio stations to play fewer songs recorded by female country artists largely because he believed that 70 to 75 percent of country radio listeners were women who preferred to listen to male performers. With this logic, Hill explains that female country singers are the tomatoes of the salad, the garnishes, while the lettuce, the actual substance of the salad, is made up of male stars. Without the support of radio airplay in a genre where that has been a major component for success, as musicologist Jada Watson (2019b) has exemplified, it has been increasingly difficult for female artists to acquire the commercial exposure needed for their recordings to hit the charts. Even the award-winning country star Miranda Lambert recently asserted, "I had to sing with someone with a penis to get a number one" (Yahr 2018).

Lambert, well aware of the gendered disparity in country music, has made a point to work with and promote women performers and songwriters, resulting in her collaborative work with Ashely Monroe and Angaleena Presley as a member of the Pistol Annies. The ensemble first started to appear in 2010 with Lambert working in unannounced perform-ance sets of the trio in her live tours until her audiences started to expect and cheer the presence of all three singers on stage (Hight 2018a). Since then, they have released four commercially successful albums with *Hell on Heels* (2011) and *Annie Up* (2013) hitting the Top 10 on *Billboard* 200, the third album *Interstate Highway* (2018) receiving a Grammy nomination for Best Country Album, and the Christmas album *Hell of a Holiday* (2021) reaching No. 7 on *Billboard* Americana Folk Albums. At a time when female country songs account for only 13 percent of radio airplay (Watson 2019b; Yahr 2020) and bro-country songs about masculine bravura have dominated not just radio but also the country music charts, the members of the Pistol Annies have banded together to sing about female subjects whose humor and laughter expresses "resistance, solidarity, and joy" (Rowe 1995, 5).

If the figure of the unruly woman manifested in the gender-bending comedic theatrics of the popular stage, which had a direct bearing on country music, then the Pistol Annies inhabit a performative space of exaggeration, parody, and spectacle, the basis of camp (Bergman 1993, 12). Their very name, the Pistol Annies, encapsulates the historical theat-rics of the unruly rustic woman by gesturing to the legendary status and staged displays of the sharpshooter Annie Oakley, featured in the nineteenth-century traveling show Buffalo Bill's Wild West. Indeed, each member has adopted a particular persona: Lambert as "Lone Star Annie" referring to her Texas roots, Presley as "Holler Annie" invoking the terrain of her home state Kentucky, and Monroe as "Hippie Annie," adding a countercultural element of the cosmic cowgirl to the trio's outlaw image. The Pistol Annies, with a mix of glitzy glamour and independent fierceness, encapsulate the panache of the wild West spectacle that extended to barn dance radio and country music.

In addition to their theatrical flair, the trio writes songs that purposefully connect to the lives of women. Monroe, for instance, has stated that she "takes pride in fans telling her they can relate to songs not delivered from the point of view of a dude in a beat-up ball cap" (Wood 2018). Appreciators continually comment on the Pistol Annies' cultural and musical expressions of empowerment. The fan Tammy Winn, for example, has stated "It's girl power, it's real life, it's heartache, it's victories, it's all that wrapped up in one" (Edgers 2018). In understanding how their sense of fun and humor translates to their songwriting, music critic Jewly Hight

(2018a) quotes country artist Patty Loveless, who explains that the Pistol Annies' frank musical messages resemble those of Loretta Lynn, in that they give the impression of "friends getting together and talking about issues." Some of the issues that the trio addresses are divorce, as in "Got My Name Changed Back," where they turn a tragic experience into a moment of triumph for their audience of women, and the class biases of gender, as in "Bad Example," where they celebrate female working-class subject positions. Their music thus transforms the everyday pressures of conforming to gender ideals and the tragedies of heartache and loss, stemming from real life, into comedic tales, insider jokes for an audience of women in the know.

As songwriters and performers, however, they move fluidly from comedic performances of histrionic unruliness to poignant sonic portraits of female subjectivity and class identity grounded in themes of sexual and romantic desire, familial relations, the Southern home, and the struggles of addiction. The efficacy of their songwriting lies in a savvy command of a variety of musical idioms, including the blues ("Hell on Heels"), old-time music ("Damn Thing," "Bad Example," "Lemon Drop"), honky-tonk ("Blues, You're a Buzzkill," "Dear Sobriety"), rockabilly ("Hush Hush"), and riff-based southern rock ("Unhappily Married," "Loved By a Working Man," "Got My Name Changed Back") while showcasing their vocal harmonies typical of country music and even 1960s girl groups. Their varied song themes point to the permeable relationship between comedy and tragedy, a topic that philosophers and critics have long expounded upon. In the words of philosopher Martin Donougho (2016, 204) summarizing Hegel's main ideas on comedy, "the action of comedy begins where tragedy leaves off." Unlike the tragic figure, the comic protagonist masters the plot and situation, making it clear he or she is not the victim but rather the victor. For Kierkegaard (1987, 83), the tragic and the comic are both based in contradiction, "but the tragic is the suffering contradiction, the comical, the painless contradiction." Comedy, thus, enables a way out of the dilemma while tragedy only envisions despair and emotional pain.

Bearing comparison with The Chicks' approach to the topic of domestic violence in "Goodbye Earl," the Pistol Annies highlight themes of seriousness in their songs that erupt in delight and humor as they triumph over obstacles rooted in patriarchy and class-based prejudice. Just as Rose Maddox turned the litigious process of divorce, which can be a source of emotional and monetary loss, into a feminist protest, the Pistol Annies approach the same topic in a similar vein while magnifying with humor the sexual and economic autonomy of the newly divorced woman in "Got My

Name Changed Back." Their performances of subversiveness unravel the tragic and are often rooted in heightened displays of sexuality and/or the masculinized codes of working-class womanhood, colliding with the social expectations linked to gender and class norms.

In this sense, the Pistol Annies make use of social incongruities, positioning their musical narratives against what is considered conventional modes of gendered comportment. This is exemplified in "Bad Example," in which the humor arises from a narrative based in negation. The trio performs a "bad example" of femininity that points to the comedic lineage of the unruly country woman. In the opening chorus, they explain, "Somebody had to set a bad example, teach all the prim and propers what not to do." While underscoring they are the "bad example," they elaborate that nobody wants to deviate from middle-class behavior apart from them. They happily defy the rigidity of conformity in their declaration that they are "born" to "ramble," enacting the masculinized role of the rambler free from social constraints.

Adding another layer of signification to this narrative about class and gender is the musical setting that recalls the vernacular roots of country music, specifically the string band tradition of old-time music and vocal harmony approaches. "Bad Example" is a quick-tempoed song of boom-chuck rhythms and straightforward harmonic progressions that opens to a syncopated diatonic arched-shaped melodic line finger picked on the acoustic guitar. Contributing to the invocation of traditionalism, the vocal arrangement features Lambert singing the melody in her characteristic nasal twang vocal manner, Presley sings the lower harmony part, and Monroe the higher harmony part. Whereas old-time music has been seen as a folk tradition from which commercial country music emerged, the popular music industry stigmatized it as musically uncultured, marketing it as "hillbilly" music (Pecknold 2007; Brackett 2016; Vander Wel 2020). The Pistol Annies play up the dual reception of old-time music by taking pride in their country roots as insiders of Southern vernacular tradition while also utilizing these idioms to underscore the ways their performance of white working-class Southern womanhood clashes with the taste, and hence, pretentiousness of the upper classes.

In the first verse, Presley elaborates upon her subject position by means of a class system of taste. She prefers to live in a trailer instead of one of "those swanky big brick houses" so that she can afford to show off her Cadillac, a flashy commodity of conspicuous consumption. The automobile has also been a sign of masculine mobility with carmakers designing and selling their vehicles as markers of male virility (McCarthy 2007, 127).

Inverting the codes of gender and sexuality associated with the automobile, Presley flashes her own showy materialism and sexuality with the "honk if you're horny sticker" plastered on the back of her Cadillac. In live performances at the Brandt Center in Saskatchewan (September 2012) and Aaron's Amphitheatre at Lakewood Atlanta (October 2012), Presley elaborates upon this lyrical narrative in a performance schtick of slapping Lambert on the backside as if she were the Cadillac (the object of desire), humorously playing with themes of female desire and feminized objects in her performative appropriation of masculine bravado.

In her solo verse, Monroe denounces the socio-economic privileges of young women whose "rich daddies" can buy "them a degree," pointing to the prevalence of wealthy families paying exorbitant amounts of money to prestigious American universities for their children's admittance, a phenomenon that recently made national news. In contrast, Monroe proclaims her family's working-class legacy as she emphasizes her identity as a "third-generation bartender" by means of vocal slides and embellishments. Bartending, traditionally a male vocation, was seen as an example of specialized knowledge of mixology and part of the male-dominated sphere of the tavern. Yet Monroe's declaration that she is a "third-generation bartender" points to the historical conditions that led to the feminization, beginning in the 1980s, of this once male-dominated vocation (Cobble 1991, 167–170). Throughout, the Pistol Annies perform a class subject that represents working-class women's historical links to masculinized forms of leisure and work that extend to bodily displays of sexuality (especially in Presley's solo verse).

The humorous effect of pitting a musical representation of working-class womanhood against the taste and behavior of the upper classes is a common strategy in the music of female country artists. Just as Lulu Belle purposely worked to defy gendered expectations by playing to the stereotypes of the Southern rustic Other, Carter's "Country Girl" wielded the tropes of the mannish female rustic to present an authentic country identity, one that isn't too highfalutin. Even more recent songs, such as Gretchen Wilson's 2005 "Redneck Woman" incorporates a masculinized identity, in this case, the redneck, in a performance of a working-class woman whose consumer practices (buying lingerie at Walmart instead of Victoria's Secret) and behavior (keeping the Christmas lights up all year) clash with the habitus of white middle-class femininity (Hubbs 2014). Following this tradition of humor and defiance, the Pistol Annies' performance of white Southern working-class womanhood combines a sense of fun with dignity that stands apart from their portrayal of the upper classes as uptight, boring, and morally corrupt. Their "bad example" of femininity creates the effect of thumbing their noses at these class antagonisms, of not caring about dominant society's ideas of economic and material success while flaunting their working-class pursuits of pleasure and vocation. What's more, their incorporation of southern vernacular traditions in a narrative about negating white feminine codes of propriety and economic privilege simultaneously indicates a sense of southern working-class pride and magnifies popular culture's class-based perceptions of "hillbilly" music.

While the Pistol Annies confront the biases of class, in "Got My Name Changed Back," they take on serious themes that have been standard fare in country music. Yet, instead of emphasizing the despondency associated with divorce in countless honky-tonk ballads or the volatile anger of the scorned woman as in Lambert's solo recording "Crazy Ex-Girlfriend," (2007), the ensemble reconfigures the emotional response to one of elation. In this process, "Got My Name Changed Back" elaborates not necessarily on matters of the heart but upon the patriarchal legal and linguistic procedures of divorce for heterosexual women who change their surnames upon marriage and back to their birth names after divorce. Even with feminist challenges to a custom that beckons to a historical period of patrilineal property rights and inheritances, this feminized linguistic ritual of heterosexual women remains prevalent in US society (Stoiko and Strough 2017, 297). The Pistol Annies thus depict and address a shared experience among heterosexual women while also encouraging divorced women to reclaim their linguistic identity and socio-economic autonomy, similar in theme and tone to Maddox's "Alimony." With a lyrical narrative that transforms the tragic as well as the rigidity of patriarchal law into a comedic and liberatory narrative, the music video focuses on the campy swagger of the trio in a musical setting of contrasting stylistic idioms, offering a clever and witty commentary about the divorce process from a woman's perspective.

Specifically, the music video underscores the humor of the trio reimagining a divorce hearing and the bureaucratic aftermath into exaggerated displays of heightened sexuality and celebration. The opening sequence, for example, features each member dressed in a glitzy fashion of form-fitting, sequined attire, accessorized with stilettos, feather boas, sunglasses, and brightly colored eye shadow. Presley, pregnant at the time, wears a form-fitting dress that accentuates her pregnant body and recasts a maternal image into a sexualized one. The flashy dress of the three members gives the impression that they are about to embark on an evening out to a glamorous nightclub. Instead, they sashay into the courthouse, where Lambert's divorce hearing takes place, then to a Tennessee Department of Motor Vehicles to legally change their surnames on their driver's licenses, and finally to the bank to withdraw funds from a marital joint account.

Each scene is further marked by a community of participants who celebrate the newly acquired divorced status of the members of the Pistol Annies. While Lambert frankly explains in the beginning of the song, "It takes a judge to get married, it takes a judge to get divorced," the Pistol Annies are greeted by a knowing Black female judge, who officiates marriages and grants divorces, and a white female stenographer, undermining the white patriarchal culture of the legal system. Lambert proceeds to explain the reason for the divorce, her "ex" who she "adored . . . got along with a couple of road whores," raising the eyebrows of the judge and stenographer and blurring this fictional account with her recent 2015 divorce from country music artist Blake Shelton. Lambert then flirts with the male bailiff by giving him a coy smile as she sings, "I don't want to be a missus no more," embracing her newfound status as a divorced woman, sexually free from the constraints of marriage. Once the divorce is granted, the male bailiff pops open a bottle of champagne, labeled "Free Dom," and all in attendance join in celebration.

The following scenes continue to depict the revelry of the Pistol Annies as they reclaim their linguistic identities and financial security after divorce. From the courthouse, they go to the DMV and submit paperwork to change their last names on their individual driver's licenses. After Monroe's photo is taken for her new Tennessee state driver's license, confetti flies through the air to mark this exultant occasion. At the local "New Freedom Bank," Presley withdraws money from and terminates her joint bank account with her former husband. The bank personnel hands her a bouquet of flowers to mark this important occasion. Another bank teller wheels in an elaborately decorated cake of toy army men surrounding the figure of the bride and aiming their guns at the groom, emphasizing the fact that Presley is the clear victor of this battle over the accrued assets of the marriage. The humor emerges from the ironic bestowing of flowers and cake upon Presley. These gifts are typically intended for the commemoration of a wedding anniversary, not for cleaning out the joint bank account.

Contributing to the impression of elation in these individual scenes of the music video is the musical setting, specifically the Southern rock arrangement of the song. From the beginning, the drum's syncopated pattern, lead electric guitar's riffs, and the banjo's twangy brightness dominate the instrumental texture and provide a driving beat that accompanies the Pistol Annies' strutting entrance to the courthouse, the DMV, and the bank. Moreover, the electric guitar plays extended take-out solos to the images of the court bailiff popping open the champagne bottle, confetti flying through the air at the DMV, and Presley, Lambert, and Monroe celebrating at the bank. The campy fun presented in the music video, combined with the driving rhythms of Southern rock, underlines their rebellious performance that confronts a misogynistic stereotype, the heartless greedy female divorcee, a figure that appears in countless male country songs, including Cox's 1934 "Alimony Woman," Ernest Tubb's 1953 "Divorce Granted," Jerry Reed's 1982 "She Got the Goldmine (I Got the Shaft)," and Montgomery Gentry's 2011 "I'll Keep the Kids." The Pistol Annies throw this image of womanhood into comedic relief as they all belt out the line, "I broke his heart and I took his money," thereby playing upon and making fun of the misogynistic fears and anxieties expressed in patriarchal society.

While the song thematically invokes the unruly woman, the Pistol Annies musically include contrasting vocal approaches in a musical setting of Southern rock. If "incongruity is often seen as being the most important cause of humour" (Brøvig-Hanssen and Harkins 2012, 92), then the trio's distinct use of musical pastiche lends comedic weight. Lambert approaches the lead vocal part in a declamatory manner that erupts momentarily into a belting tone from pushing the chest voice above the vocal break. Her vocal line is built of repeated pitches in three distinct vocal ranges, which Lambert sings first in a clipped conversational tone in the mid-chest range, leaps a fifth to belt the pitches that fall in the higher chest range, and then drops an octave to the lower chest voice. In effect, Lambert gives the impression of addressing her female audience in a frank tone that momentarily becomes louder and more determined. In the hook ("I got my name changed back") for example, Lambert emphasizes the importance of linguistic identity by vocally approaching the lyric "my name" with a belting chest timbre before descending to her lower range to sing "changed back" in a more relaxed manner. Lambert's crisp and, at times, belting vocal sound is met by the stylized harmonies, "yeah, yeah," of Presley and Monroe, giving the impression of the call and response vocal arrangement in the style of 1960s girl group songs. With Presley and Monroe adding their vocal and metaphorical support to Lambert's narrative, the vocal arrangement creates a sonic atmosphere of empathy and identification among women (Warwick 2007).

In the closing section, the Pistol Annies switch vocal roles from a 1960s girl group to the 1940s trio, the Andrews Sisters, as they repeat the hook of the song, "I got my name changed back," with smooth sounding harmonies and open rounded tones. They conclude by substituting the lyrics with nonsense syllables that they scat in harmony reminiscent of the Andrews Sisters, who imitated the vocal techniques of the well-known jazz vocalist Ella Fitzgerald. The juxtaposition of incongruous musical styles contributes to the song's campy sonic display about the feminized experience of divorce. Yet, at the same time, by including musical styles from distinct historical periods, the narrative suggests that these linguistic processes associated with the legality of marriage and divorce have been a constant in US women's history, forging a connection with their female audience.

Though humor has been an integral part of the Pistol Annies' act, a number of female country artists have incorporated the comedic elements of incongruity, parody, and exaggeration, inhabiting a performative space of female unruliness, contributing to their commercial and cultural visibility. The comedic edge of spectacle making can be seen in Maren Morris's "Rich" (2016), in which she includes elements of male hip-hop in her performance of female swagger, especially as she raps the line, "Me and Diddy drippin' diamonds like Marilyn." Similar to the Pistol Annies' campy displays of triumph in "Got My Name Changed Back," Morris's boastings act as metaphor for women in maintaining the upper hand in heterosexual romantic relationships. In addition, Maddie and Tae's "A Girl in a Country Song" (2014) operates in the realm of parody to offer an explicit critique of the objectification of women in male country music videos. Steeped in gendered inversion, the duo's music video features rustic-looking men attempting but failing to fit their various body types into the tight-fitting attire designed for women's idealized bodies. As an audience, we laugh at the duo's ability to lay bare the absurdity of the country music industry's gendered contradictions.

Just as the Pistol Annies have used comedic approaches in their music to connect with a female fanbase the all-female Black family trio Chapel Hart has used humor as a form of engagement with some of the main themes of country music in songs such as "Jesus and Alcohol" (2020) and "You Can Have Him Jolene" (2021), laying claim to a genre that has been coded white and male. Bringing to the fore a common paradox in southern culture – Saturday night revelry and Sunday morning piety – "Jesus and Alcohol" suggests that the antidote for a broken heart lies in the healing powers of Protestant faith and the consumption of alcohol. With a comedic music video in which lead singer Dania Hart plays the jilted bride left at the church's altar and ZZ Top's Billy F. Gibbons acts as the minister, Chapel

Hart's hyperbolic performance tears down the boundaries of the profane and sacred, demonstrating the trio's southern roots. Moreover, Kacey Musgraves's verbal humor and campy performances are particularly striking for the ways she has challenged the narrowmindedness of small-town life while still connecting to a broad listening fanbase despite the sexist practices of country radio. In "Biscuits" (2016), for example, she encourages her listeners to be less judgmental and more accepting of cultural differences with a homespun metaphor, "mind your own biscuits and life will be gravy." The music video purposefully draws upon the history of comedy in country music by placing Musgraves, costumed in a short gingham dress, at the center of what appears to be a barn dance program. In this playful display of country camp, the music video and Musgraves's performance critique the conservatism associated with not only small-town life but also country music culture. The subversive qualities of female humor persist in the music of contemporary female country performers for a reason. Women's comedy enables critique, connection, and community in commercial settings that defy and supersede the white patriarchal frame of country music.

7 | From Bros to Gentlemen

The Problem of Consent in Contemporary Country Music

PHOEBE E. HUGHES

Country singer Michael Ray croons "so why even bother / lookin' at the reasons not to / maybe we ought to," the opening lines to his hit single "Think a Little Less." Released in 2015, this ballad tells the story of a sexual encounter of two (presumably) consenting adults after a night out at a bar, where both parties are trying to keep their romantic rendezvous private. Though this song appears harmless enough, Ray's words "kiss a little more / think a little less" are heard over a dozen times throughout the song and beg the question: if this interaction is consensual, why does the subject of the song need to "think a little less?" Ray's song illuminates the deeply contextual and gendered nature of consent in heterosexual relationships, a troubling aspect of the predominantly white, male artists who have pushed country music's men closer to what *New York Times* pop music critic Jon Caramanica (2017a) describes as the "gentlemen" of country music. According to Caramanica (2017a), the country gentlemen "focus on uncomplicated, deeply dedicated love or, alternately, being hopeless on the receiving end of heartbreak . . . [oozing] respect, charm, and, occasionally, dullness." In the September 22, 2017, episode of the *Times's Popcast*, Caramanica (2017b) extended his analysis, pointing to a gender "crisis" within country music that has created the need for the development of a "gentler man," a persona best exemplified by such artists as Thomas Rhett, Sam Hunt, Brett Young, Michael Ray, Brett Eldredge, and Chris Young.

This analysis of male behaviors and masculinities has been widened more recently in the journalistic realm, described as "boyfriend country," a quaint term coined by journalist Tom Roland (2019) meant to describe a type of "male sensitivity" embodied by artists who are often married and engaged, their partners also in the public eye (Yahr 2021). "Country gentlemen" and the "boyfriends" of country music have been positioned against "bro-country" men – Luke Bryan and duo Florida Georgia Line, among others – a phenomenon that arose during the 2010s with party songs promoting hook-up culture (a commonly used term for casual sexual encounters) like Luke Bryan's "Country Girl (Shake It For Me)" (2011) or Kip Moore's "Somethin' 'Bout a Truck" (2011), which flooded the airwaves during the 2010s (Bernstein et al. 2019; Rosen 2013). The phrase "country gentlemen" offers an alternative to the bro-country phenomena. These terms – "bro-country," "country gentlemen," "boyfriend country," coined by journalists, offer an opportunity to nuance the scholarly discussion of twenty-first-century country music.

Recent country music, often referenced as "contemporary" country music or "radio" country music, from the late 2000s and 2010s has received little scholarly attention, and existing scholarship focuses on the effects and sounds of the "bro-country" phenomena (Leap 2020; Orosz 2019; Densley and Rasmussen 2018). A study of country music lyrics from the 1990s and early 2010s found that there has been an increase in references to women associated with sex and alcohol, directly linking to "negative attitudes toward women [creating] an environment optimal for sexual assault of women" made possible by continued media exposure, of which music is a key component (Densley and Rasmussen 2018, 116–17). This corresponds with the well-documented increase in reference to alcohol and sex in popular music over the past several decades (Christenson et al. 2012, 121–9; Andsager and Roe 2003, 79–97). The music of the boyfriends and gentlemen of country music identified by music journalists has not received the same critical attention as songs about alcohol consumption, sex, and female objectification because those topics are not explicitly present in boyfriend/gentlemen songs. Songs of Caramanica's "gentleman" type do not raise the same red flags as songs that more overtly perpetuate negative attitudes and potential violence against women.

The music of the country gentlemen and boyfriends has been marked as "good" with little question by music critics because they are a stark departure from the themes of bro-country (casual sex, partying, support of male promiscuity, objectification of female subjects in songs). These discussions often focus on changes in thematic content between the bros and gentlemen/boyfriends in contemporary country music. As music theorist Jeremy Orosz (2019, 3) has argued, songs like Florida Georgia Line's "Cruise" remix featuring Nelly from 2013 or Luke Bryan's "My Kind of Night" from the same year contain a combination of "dance-friendly beat [s] and auto-tuned vocals" that were the dominant sonic force on the US *Billboard* Hot Country Songs chart in 2013 and beyond. These production elements, borrowing heavily from Top-40 pop and hip-hop, are present on nearly all radio country of the 2010s, regardless of the thematic content of the song. Song theme and lyric content form the basis of this chapter because the vast majority of country music heard on the radio over the past decade is sonically consistent regardless of theme. This musical consistancy reinforces the narrative evolution of consent in contemporary country music.

Beyond sonic elements, the "gentleman" in country music has a long-standing history. Early country singer Chet Atkins was known as the "Country Gentleman" because of his dapper dress and association with the development of the pop-influenced Nashville Sound in the late 1950s (Jensen 1998, 4). The term has also long been attached to the moral guidelines of a Southern gentleman: "a man of chivalric manners and good breeding; a man of good social position; a man of wealth and leisure" (Gross 2010, 1). "Country gentleman" and "country boyfriends" of the 2010s reflect the same basic ideas of the Southern gentleman but are best situated within a white, rural masculinity sociologist Braden Leap (2020, 166) connects to white heterosexuality "celebrated in mainstream country" that has continued to uphold a "hegemonic masculinity that facilitates the reproduction of inequalities between and among men and women." This understanding of a white masculinity is even more important when looking at songs that are outside of the alcohol and hook-up infused music so often discussed in scholarship about country music of the 2010s. I offer here a more critical reading of songs about romantic love and relationships. Using case studies from the music of Thomas Rhett and Sam Hunt, I move past the journalistic terms of "bro-country" and "country gentlemen" or "boyfriends." I use the term "consent song" to center the narrative evolution that exists within contemporary country music as the thematic content of songs has moved beyond explicit sexual content and overt female objectification. Instead, consent songs focus on romantic love and relationships, perpetuating interactions between partners where consent is assumed but never explicitly (or even vaguely) indicated.

Consent, though an ambiguous concept, is typically defined as "freely given verbal or nonverbal communication of a feeling of willingness to engage in sexual activity" (Hickman and Muehlenhard 1999, 259). It is marked by a set of complex issues surrounding forms of communication and includes a range of sexual activities, often informed by the context of a relationship (Humphreys 2007, 307). The duration of a relationship regularly dictates how consent is identified. In a longer relationship – one lasting more than two dates – consent is more passively established as previous sexual activities are assumed to be consensual but are not explicitly articulated (309). Gender is also an important factor in establishing consent. In heterosexual relationships, women are the partners who most often set boundaries, and most frequently "interpret explicit sexual consent as more necessary during sexual encounters, regardless" of the relationship's length or status (313).

Songs that music journalists have described as the country gentlemen or boyfriend type, like Ray's "Think a Little Less," are not meant to serve as guidelines for how to behave in real life. Yet, as sociologist Richard Peterson (1997, 3) describes, country musicians piece together musical features like instrument choice, vocal qualities, and songwriting traits with lyrical content and themes to create a "fabricated authenticity." This carefully crafted sensibility allows audiences to assume that country music offers them reality or truth – a set of values, traditions, or norms – even though this reality is not apparent within the music or outside it. Considering that country music is meant to offer pieces of the truth to listeners, this realism represents the identification, explanation, and depiction of boundaries within relationships: consent, typically interpreted by women who are conspicuously absent from these songs. In a genre both dominated by men and meant to represent or interpret listeners' everyday experiences, close investigation of contemporary country music and the predominantly white, male artists who sing it allows us to identify unspoken issues at stake in this music. Including how and when in these songs women's voices may be heard, silenced, or made irrelevant by harmful representations of relationships and sexual intimacy.

This chapter presents an analysis of music and lyrics, demonstrating how "consent" songs promote idealized romance and assumed consensual heteronormative narratives. Although the bulk of this analysis will focus on lyric qualities, sonic markers also help define the contemporary country music landscape in which "consent" songs (and hook-up songs) have flourished. Songs that have hip-hop, trap, and pop stylings are nearly omnipresent in the general landscape of contemporary country music, and most music on radio comes from the white, male artists who dominate the format (Watson 2019a). The stylistic qualities of hook-up and "consent" songs are similar, so the difference between them comes primarily from lyric content. I will focus here on songs by two solo male artists (Thomas Rhett and Sam Hunt) because "consent" song narratives seem to come only from male artists, and these male, majority-white artists dominate the industry, regardless of country music's diverse audience and history (Watson 2020a, 7; Pittelman 2018).

Framing "Consent" Songs

I divide "consent" songs into two different categories: real-life consent songs and hypothetical consent songs. Real-life consent songs present clear connections to the artist's life through verbal or visual references in interviews, music videos, and live performances often literally describing or representing the artist's personal life. They can also be spoken in the present tense without flashbacks or narrative leaps. Often songs of this type include specific details of a present tense idealized version of the relationship, the romantic partner, and of sexual intimacy. Examples of real-life "consent" songs included Thomas Rhett's "Die a Happy Man" (2015), discussed below; Chase Rice's "Eyes on You" from *Lambs & Lions* (2017); Kane Brown's "Homesick" from *Experimental* (2019); and Morgan Evans's single "Diamonds" (2019). All four of these tracks are about the singers' relationships and families and provide details about their relationships as corroborated through interviews and magazine articles (Reuter 2018; Whitaker 2019; Roland 2020). A consenting relationship within the song is contextualized through the artists' public personas, which include these details about their personal lives.

Hypothetical "consent" songs present a narrative or story in which the authenticity of the characters can be questioned through lyric ambiguity, often exacerbated through timeline and narrative leaps that disrupt a sense of temporal reality within the song's storyline. Jocelyn R. Neal (2007, 42) describes this phenomenon in country music generally as a "time-shift narrative," which includes a "combination of poetic devices, formal structures, and stylistic harmonic elements that together project the segmentation and passage of time." Hypothetical "consent" songs feature adjusted timelines that show an idealized or fantasized situation. Examples of hypothetical "consent" songs include Brett Eldredge's "The Long Way" from his self-titled album (2017) or the Eli Young Band's "Love Ain't" (2018). Both songs recount tales of potential relationships, where the male narrator is describing romantic possibilities without the relationship coming to fruition within the song or having an attachment to the singer's life outside of the song's boundaries. They include details like what the female subject is missing out on by either being with another person or just not having met the narrator yet. Hypothetical "consent" songs also problematize country music's moral authority as constructed through tropes of authenticity. Assumed authenticity and the constructed reality of country music allow listeners to ascribe song narratives to their own lives. With "consent" songs, assumptions of an authentic reality create dangerous real-world blurring of how a consenting relationship could or should look. This is especially troubling, considering the already fraught and complex nature of consent in the real world, which so often relies on nonverbal social cues and preexisting relationships. I argue here that both types of "consent" songs, hypothetical and real-life, trade on country music's long history of perceived authenticity, where country music culture affords assumptions about artistic authenticity and the constructed reality of country music (Peterson 1997). This allows listeners to ascribe song narratives, be they real or hypothetical, to their own lives perhaps even seeing these songs as guides for social interactions.

Case Studies: Real-Life and Hypothetical Consent Songs

The beginning of the "country gentlemen" trend was marked with the release of Thomas Rhett's second studio album, *Tangled Up* (2015), which featured Rhett's hit single "Die a Happy Man," a "straightforward" love song about Rhett's relationship with his wife (Caramanica 2017b). "Die a Happy Man" is a typical representation of monogamous love that is popular in country music. The song feels deeply personal but still offers listeners enough space to attach the narrative to their own lives. Rhett's personal authenticity, an image of sameness and relatability, is shaped in part by his crafted image on social media. Rhett and his wife Lauren Akins's social media presence creates an impression that their relationship is grounded in positivity, love, and mutual respect. A central element of this presence is the addition and visibility of their children and the candid appearance of many photos and videos. Lauren Akins frequently posts images of herself on Instagram, shifting between photos without makeup and giving insight into her less-than-glamorous "mom life" alongside crafted images of her and Rhett's home and family life, and images of their red-carpet-ready outfits (@laur_akins, Instagram photo, November 24, 2019, and May 9, 2020). Their love story has been rehashed in various popular magazines, such as a *Good Housekeeping* feature story ahead of Rhett's appearance as host of CMA Fest (Country Music Association Festival) in Nashville (Finn 2020).

Despite appearing to be a "straightforward" love song, "Die a Happy Man" is a critical example of how the duration of a relationship impacts the presence of consent. Typically, the longer a sexual relationship's duration, the clearer sexual intent is perceived and deemed acceptable, or consensual (Humphreys 2007, 313). This assumption of consent can be seen in "Die a Happy Man" because of how the song is contextualized as a reflection of Rhett's relationship. Without this contextualization, "Die a Happy Man" could be read as a proclamation of love, with reassurances and explanations of why the narrator loves the subject of the song. The song gives no apparent timeline for the relationship, simply presenting it as a happy, consensual, long-term relationship without any sort of backstory. This leaves the listener wondering how much time the pair spent together before they reached the level of intimacy described in the song. Answers to these questions can be learned from what is publicly known about Rhett and Akins, but not from the song (Carter 2017). If the song was not contextualized within Rhett's marriage, it would seem far creepier because questions about who and what the narrator is talking about would remain unanswered. This could also be understood as another instance of assumed consent because of the long-term nature of the relationship described but only within the context of Rhett's marriage.

That "Die a Happy Man" seems to give listeners an intimate view into Rhett and Akins's relationship is not inherently problematic – relationships and interpersonal intimacy are a typical trait in most country music, which prides itself on telling the truth about relationships. This song makes benign activities such as dancing in the living room seem like magic – making normal, relatable experiences appear as the height of romance. Rhett's lyrics contrast these benign activities with a bucket list of travels and adventures, all of which are made to seem less important than the maintenance of the relationship at home. His list includes building a mansion in Georgia, driving a sports car along the California coast, and seeing the Northern Lights and the Eiffel Tower. His list is qualified, and the relationship normalized by Rhett's acknowledgment of just needing to hold his partner's hand to feel their romantic connection he frames as love. Rhett goes on to explain parts of his affection for the subject, contextualized as true and real because Rhett is the narrator and his wife is the subject. Rhett and "Die a Happy Man" seem to do everything right: references to alcohol and sex within the boundaries of a presumably consenting relationship.

Where Rhett's "Die a Happy Man" shows how consent is contextual, the examples of Sam Hunt's music reveal a different set of dangers when the lack of consent is more expressly represented within a song. Sam Hunt's 2014 release of *Montevallo* sent ripples throughout the country music industry. The album included hip-hop and trap production elements, all cues to much of the contemporary country music of the 2010s. Many of the songs achieved immense crossover success on Top-40 radio and popularity charts. Hunt's vocal approach involves a noticeable speak-singing, with a limited melodic range that creates catchy hummable tunes often described as "Drake-esque" – referencing rapper/singer Drake (McKenna 2017). These features make Hunt's music appealing for airplay on country radio and as a crossover song to the mainstream. Although it is hard to mark Hunt's debut album as beginning this turn to hip-hop production for country music outside of bro-country, it is not a far stretch to understand the album and its reliance on the "consent" song tropes as having laid the groundwork for the continuation of both the sonic and lyrical elements of Hunt's music into much of what is produced today. I will present two case studies here from Hunt's music, the first being "Take Your Time," from *Montevallo* (2014), and then "Body Like a Back Road," Hunt's 2018 smash hit later released on *Southside* (2020).

"Take Your Time" begins with a slow guitar melody, followed by Hunt's speak-singing voice describing interrupting the female subject of the song in a bar: "I don't mean to bother you but . . ." This opening line is bashful and unassuming, giving listeners a first glimpse at the narrator's interaction with the woman he is both talking to and about. Hunt makes the interaction seem appropriate through the bashful nature of the opening line and a repeated statement of concern about taking the subject's time (a line which forms the title of the song, "Take Your Time"). These qualifications set Hunt and the song apart from its hook-up song counterparts, becoming a nod or acknowledgment of the fact that his approaching a person, a woman, in a bar, could have specific and often negative connotations. To counterbalance these issues, Hunt fully sings the next phrase attempting to justify the interruption before going back to speak-singing as in the opening verse. He speak-sings quickly while he is being potentially inappropriate and slows down to actually sing when his words rationalize or apologize for his actions. The speed differences of Hunt's vocal shifts between speech and singing dictate when he is behaving in a way that appears predatory to women or is simply cajoling the subject to get what he wants. It is a subtle nuance within the song but occurs with regularity, often masked by flashy pop production and Hunt's smooth but unremarkable voice.

Important to this ambiguous interaction revolving around "taking time" is the narrator in the first verse noting that the female subject is not looking for any sort of relationship. Hunt speak-sings rapidly about what he knows about the subject, her name and that she does not want a relationship, before reverting to slower vocalization as he works to paint himself as a "good guy" not wanting to be misunderstood. The effect of the rapid speak-singing serves to coax and manipulate the subject of the song. This phenomenon is even more apparent when the lines Hunt fully sings, "I couldn't just walk by," attempt to placate the woman's hesitations (perhaps fears) identified in lines like "I don't wanna wreck your Friday." If the listener takes his self-presentation at face value, the remainder of the song might be read as quiet, unassuming persuading: the narrator wants the subject's attention, and he aims to get it by reassuring the female subject of his good intentions, setting up the possibility of future interactions in a casual, nonthreatening way. The pattern of speak-singing versus fully singing the story continues as Hunt works to emphasize his qualifications as a "good guy" that the female subject should not fear. It is only in the first chorus that the listener gets to hear Hunt sing for more than a few moments. Using a simple vocal melody marked by short declarative statements, Hunt convinces the woman in the song to spend time with him.

It is in the second verse that the listener gets a lyrical glimpse of the female character. Hunt speak-sings about how one of the subject's friends is going to save her from Hunt, who has approached the subject unsolicited in a bar. Mutual agreement to prolonging the encounter is emphasized through subsequent lyrics detailing everything the subject *could* have done to escape the narrator but did not. The lyrical description captured in this interaction functions in two ways, first indicating that the narrator knows his behavior is inappropriate or threatening, and second, implying that (in his view) the female character feels okay about the interaction and does not want to be saved by her friends. This verse gives the impression that the subject both did not take any verbal or physical action (like walking away) or tell Hunt to leave her alone. What is more important, however, is that the subject is not given the space or opportunity within the song to express displeasure during the encounter because the narration comes from the man's perspective as he presses for attention. That the female character does not walk away is taken as consent, even though she might feel trapped. This aspect of the interaction is reflected lyrically, but Hunt's melodic line is expanded toward the end of this phrase with sustained vocals on the word "here" twice before an elided transition into the chorus. These more clearly sung lines create a calmer and more intimate sonic environment, inviting the listener in as the narrator gets what he wants: the girl's "time." The musical invitation frames this predatory encounter as a desirable interaction, and the constructed authenticity of country music invites listeners to apply it to their own lives.

One important feature of "Take Your Time" is the chorus, which offers continuous reassurances of the narrator's intentions. Taking the subject's "time" does not mean wanting to have just a casual sexual relationship with her, nor does it imply "going home" with her. The first half of the chorus begins with more generic reassurances about the immediate future, not changing the subject's present or future plans. But the second part of the chorus begins with a line that both suggests and puts off what might imply a long-term relationship, like meeting each other's family. This denial is, however, balanced between an interaction that is outlined as outside of the boundaries of a casual hook-up. The next few lines emphasize the purity of the narrator's intentions, as Hunt gives reassurances that he does not want a casual sexual encounter and just wants to spend time with the subject. The idea of time here pushes beyond the immediate bar meeting context, confirmed in the bridge through continued reassurances, followed by a reiteration of the chorus with melodic embellishments reassuring the subject of Hunt's "good guy" qualifications. These last few vocal moments of the song hit at the crux of conflict within the story of "Take Your Time."

The narrator's desire to be perceived as "good" is presented vividly in the choruses, even though the setup in the first verse implies that the female subject did not want an interaction or relationship. Yet, just as quickly as the woman's wishes are presented in the first verse, they are dismissed. The listener does not learn of or hear about consent from the silent partner as the pattern of speak-singing and melodic singing progresses through the song. The woman does not get her time as Hunt's speak-singing lurks between personal intimacy and a violation of personal space. Perhaps most importantly for listeners mapping this interaction onto their own lives, Hunt's presentation of his "good guy" qualifications is never directly contradicted: his testimony indicates that he believes himself to be a gentleman, allowing listeners to hear the song as romantic rather than uncomfortable. The self-assuredness of Hunt's "good guy" qualifications ultimately allows "Take Your Time" to represent the type of heterosexual masculinity that criticizes bro-country men (Leap 2020, 183) but does not engage with consent beyond the male narrator's interpretive lens of the situation; the female's voice and autonomy are not present.

The content of "Body Like a Back Road" is remarkably similar to "Take Your Time," with descriptions of meeting a girl in a bar and representing the beginning elements of a relationship from only one perspective. "Body Like a Back Road" sets up a far more casual image through its musical arrangement. The song opens with a loosely arranged but appealing opening tag marked by sharply plucked acoustic guitar notes layered with electric finger-snap sounds. Together, these elements serve to give a solid backbeat that is neither fully acoustic or electronic. In fact, no solid drum-set groove is heard until the start of the second verse, after the first complete chorus. To add to the curated informality of the introduction and the first verse, there are voices talking in the background, giving the impression of the recording occurring in a live bar setting. This sonic environment sets the tone for the location in which the characters of the story in "Body Like a Back Road" first meet. Indeed, the first truly audible human sounds are a cat-calling whistle and a murmur of male objectification before the singer (our narrator in this story, and the male half of the heterosexual relationship) begins speak-singing about the first time he met this girl.

The nameless female object in the song is described from the start based on where the narrator knows she is from and a description of her hair. Her entrance to the bar is described as so breathtaking the male almost falls out of his chair. In a manner both dramatic and humorous, the song continues describing the first meeting with the girl, and how it took a longer period of time to get her number. But once our narrator finally gets to know this girl, their relationship is described as having a longer history. This longer history is described within the context of a sexual encounter in a vehicle and leads into the chorus. Although it would be easy to brush off the introduction of this song as a means to get to the more enticing and provocative descriptors – sexual and bodily objectifications – of this girl, I would submit that the song dangerously assumes but never explains her consent by using the quick elision between the first verse and chorus to gloss over important details of a relationship's progression. Lyric interplay between verse and chorus constructs a larger picture of the unfolding relationship within "Body Like a Back Road." Loaded with sexual innuendo, the second verse begins with a description of the girl's physical attributes. Paired with the timeline and geographical place descriptions within the chorus, the listener gets the distinct impression that the relationship has progressed to a point where the pair have spent enough time together, in a variety of locations, to know each other well. Descriptors of the subject's body are used in conjunction with place descriptions of the backroad – it makes it seem like a real, relatable place with real, relatable characters by drawing on tropes of small-town living that are well represented in country music.

"Body Like a Back Road," like a lot of Sam Hunt's music, bridges the gap between the love songs of Thomas Rhett and the often-criticized hook-up culture promoting music of bro-country artists like Luke Bryan or Florida Georgia Line. The physical objectification of the woman and the spaces she occupies allows this song to inhabit the middle ground between clear hook-up culture and established romantic consent, working back and forth across that boundary. This combination of traits makes it difficult for a listener to find fault: after all, the song promotes heterosexual, consensual romance that is full of desire (at least for one partner), even though it also references blatant sexual innuendo and a questionable first encounter. One example of this complicated contrast within the song was manifested by Hunt's performance of "Body Like a Back Road" at the Academy of Country Music Awards in May 2017. He began the performance on stage, then went into the audience, approached his wife, Hannah Lee Fowler, and sat on the arm of her chair. This performance overtly contextualizes the song as being about Hunt's relationship with Fowler, though the writing process involved a deliberate construction of multiple verses layered together to create a "feeling" rather than tell a specific story (Associated Press 2017; Paulson 2018). Hunt's performance also positioned him as one of the country gentlemen, serenading his wife and reinforcing the lyric ambiguity between casual hook-up and long-term romance that "Body Like a Back Road" trades on. This ambiguity is portrayed both through the words and vocal presentation of the song and how the song and singer are mediated through publicity and performance. "Consent" song's broad appeal as romance carefully framed through video and social media is precisely why they are a problem. Narratives within these presumably romantic songs, whether they are framed as real by the artist or not, represent an appealing version of reality to listeners that could be easily misconstrued resulting in inappropriate and potentially illegal sexual encounters.

Conclusions: "Consent" Songs Are Not Leaving Us

Since the release of Hunt's *Montevallo* and "Body Like a Back Road" and Rhett's hit songs about his wife, there have been countless tracks released by male country artists attempting to represent consenting, monogamous heterosexual relationships as ideal. Indeed, representations of this kind have become so common one is almost hard-pressed to find a hook-up song on the radio airwaves in 2021. Most recently, this turn of country music has been dubbed "Boyfriend Country," with its relationship-touting narratives that seem like charming odes to the singers' girlfriends or wives, continuing to promote heterosexual monogamy by erasing the female participant's voice and autonomy (Roland 2019). Although I have only given a few detailed examples of "consent" songs, this style of song and the types of relationship narratives they contain are nearly omnipresent within country music today. Like Sam Hunt's *Montevallo* (2014), his more recent release, *Southside* (2020), represents romance and relationships in the same way. Chris Lane, Chase Rice, Kane Brown, Brett Young, Keith Urban,

Jimmie Allen, Luke Combs, and the duos Dan + Shay and Florida Georgia Line are just a few artists who have written and released songs that have been praised for their emphasis on relationships and commitment over the last five years (Roland 2019).

As the case studies show, contemporary country music presents a kind of moral ambiguity moving beyond good and bad, "gentlemen" or "bros." The mixture of consensual and coercive elements of heteronormative relationships in the music of Sam Hunt along with other artists releasing similar sounding music creates a troubling paradigm for listeners' identification with songs, and their potential expectation of their own relationships. In a heterosexual context, this could take the form of female audience members identifying with the songs or a male listener assuming a female partner's comfort levels based on "consent" song narratives. The role of country music in American popular culture is defined by the authentic moral authority it claims, and this genre of music is formatively represented by white, male artists. These contemporary bros-turned-gentlemen are the face of the contemporary country music industry. They put forward a heterosexual, monogamous relationship narrative, while also normalizing a variety of coercive behaviors on the part of romantic men.

In today's polarizing and personal socio-political landscape, sexual assault and misconduct are being openly questioned within the country music industry (Yahr 2017; Moss 2018). It is through the #MeToo movement and country music radio tours that consent has turned into a buzzword that should make everyone question their behavior and interactions (Watson 2019b, 2020b; Yahr 2017; Pittelman 2018). The country music industry, rooted in white supremacist systems that generate inequalities based on race and gender, is in need of deconstructive work to create a more equitable environment for artistic production (Williams 2020). Focusing on musical and lyrical content that helps uphold these systems of inequity, such as "consent" songs, is essential in the effort to move country music, and the popular music industry more broadly, toward a mode of existence that does not cause harm to practitioners or fans (Williams 2020; Pittelman 2018). It is essential that the stories told within mainstream country music offer points of entry for listeners and artists who are not white men. Journalistic support of artists like Hunt and Rhett seen through their framing as "gentleman" and "boyfriends" in country music by Caramanica and Roland is one way that these standards of harm, in this case questions of sexual assault and abuse, are allowed to continue because the songs are not explicitly bad, they are just better than what there was before. "Consent" songs uphold this imbalance through their popularity – Sam Hunt's "Body Like a Back Road" and Thomas Rhett's "Die a Happy Man" were chart-topping hits with crossover success – and this popularity is upheld by industry practices favoring white men (Watson 2019a; Associated Press 2017; Carter 2017). An artist's reality or the hypothetical possibilities of "consent" songs are very tantalizing. Their tropes allow for the imaginative and relatable possibilities of a country song to dictate expectations for the listener's reality and potentially inform listener's behaviors in the real world. As I have shown, "consent" songs are problematic because they create unrealistic expectations for the listener's life through framing an idealized romance as a possible and desirable reality. Taking a critical eye to the content of these popular songs pushes against the narrative of the "good white men" of country music.

8 | Cowboys on a Beach

Summer Country and the Loss of Working-Class Identity

JOCELYN R. NEAL

The waves crash onto a rocky shoreline next to California's coastal State Route 1; vast expanses of sandy beaches are dotted with surfboards; a few lone palm trees cast long shadows; the sun sets in red-gold fire over the ocean. Occupying these scenes is a ubiquitous lone figure: a male cowboy – wearing boots and jeans, a blue denim shirt, and a white cowboy hat tipped low over his eyes – asleep on the sand or strumming his guitar. Since about 2000, this vignette has been appearing with increasing frequency in country music videos, a medium known for conventional deployment of setting, scene, and reference. While the cowboy figure is at home in both the country music genre and its video manifestations, the seaside settings appear to contradict the well-established conventions of place and space in country music, outside the norms of the urban–rural tension, and idyllic depiction of farms, fields, and Southern small towns that have long been cultivated in the genre.

This shift in setting, specifically the migration of country music to the beach, invites contemplation of larger shifts in meaning within country music. In some ways, the songs and music videos that have brought about this change continue a long tradition in country recordings. But where that beach imagery had previously been a marginal counterpoint to the more dominant narratives of place, it shifted in the 1990s to become an increasingly prominent theme and slid into a central position in the 2000s. As the beach setting took root, it subtly displaced and replaced some of the conventional associations of meaning in country music. Where the rural farms and ranches evoked codes of white, male working-class sustenance, physical labor, and pride in forging a symbiotic relationship with the land, the new beach imagery offered a different catalog of associative meaning: leisure, escape, travel away from one's home and roots, a sense of unbounded freedom, and a new destination or goal for the road-trip narrative already embedded in country music.

This chapter traces the rise of beach imagery as a setting and reference point in country music, both in song narratives and music videos, since the 1990s. That trajectory follows country music's sounds and stories through Latinx and African-diasporic musical borrowings, the geography of southern border crossings, Mexico as place, and a tropical escapism that manifests in instrumentation, rhythms, and references to Caribbean Island traditions. The prevalence of beach references by the early 2010s offered new, multivalent potential to artists, who could draw on that setting to deploy extra-narrative and conflicting-narrative videos for a new audience. These beach references also provided opportunities for intertextuality across genre lines. Finally, this chapter suggests that, in spite of their ubiquity, these beach settings in country music are only comprehensible to their audience because the underlying cultural meaning of country music has fundamentally changed.

Down Mexico Way

The trend toward beach videos in the late 2010s was a confluence of two distinct yet interrelated themes in country music's past. One of those themes was the incorporation of musical styles and images collectively referred to as "island sounds": elements from Jamaican Reggae and its predecessors, from Calypso, and from a range of Latinx folk and dance music (including cha cha), rendered as a referential sonic stew. The second theme was references to places south of the US border, most frequently Mexico, as a destination and site offering escapism, freedom, and exoticism. Together, these two historical threads in country music wove together an amalgamation that was substantively different in meaning than their individual historical predecessors.

Mexican musical styles have long had an audible presence in country music, while the physical places and imagined cultural spaces have been featured in the songs' stories and corresponding visual representations. British journalist Adrian Peel (2014) and other writers have documented much of this history. Essentially, the geographic origins of western swing, honky tonk, and Bakersfield music, each shaped by the demographics of the regions where those musics developed, ensured that the instruments, melodic and harmonic figures, and rhythmic patterns from Mexican traditions were formative ingredients in country music. We hear those elements in the twin trumpet lines in Bob Wills's "San Antonio Rose" (1940) or in guitarist Grady Martin's licks in Marty Robbins's "El Paso" (1959) (Neal 2019, 76–7, 190–1).

On top of the musical references, the plot lines of old western movies became the fodder for song lyrics: head south to Mexico for libations and love interests, and to escape the reaches of American law. The original touchpoint for this theme is Gene Autry singing "South of the Border (Down Mexico Way)." The song, which appeared as the title song in a Republic Pictures 1939 movie, featured habanera rhythms, an accordion solo, and the "ay ay ay ay" lyrics best known from the nineteenth-century Mexican song "Cielito Lindo." In subsequent decades, country artists tapped Mexico and its lore for countless song narratives, including Jim Reeves's, "Mexican Joe" (1953), a large swath of Hank Snow's work such as "When Mexican Joe Met Jole Blon" (1953) and "Nuevo Laredo" (1967), and many others.

The modern presence of this theme traces its most direct origins, however, to "The Seashores of Old Mexico," written by Merle Haggard and first recorded by Hank Snow in 1971. The song's narrator is an older man recalling his past. In his tale, he high-tails it out of Tucson, Arizona, with the law on his heels; travels through Mexico, where he loses his money and resorts to hitchhiking; and eventually winds up in a beach town, where he meets his love interest and settles down. Other songs in the 1980s and 1990s employed this general narrative (notably Eddy Raven's "I Got Mexico" [1984]), but "Seashores" remained one of the best known through a string of cover versions.

Those cover versions rode a surge of popularity for Mexico-themed narratives in the late 1990s into the early 2000s (Table 8.1). This attention to Mexico was partly the result of The North American Free Trade Agreement (NAFTA; 1994), which prompted a significant bump in tourist travel – tourist arrivals nearly doubled from around 600,000 in 1992 to nearly 1.2 million in 1996 (Trading Economics n.d.). The boom was also the result of a twenty-year effort by the Mexican government and private industry to build Cancun into a premier tourist destination – an effort that crested in the 1990s (*Yucatan Magazine* 2019). And for the subsequent decade, public conversations – both positive and negative, sometimes idealistic, politically charged, and racist – about immigration and a widening Mexican diaspora in the United States helped keep the region in the public conscience.

It was within this overall context that George Strait's cover of "The Seashores of Old Mexico" (2006) appeared, bringing to fans not only a new version of an old country song but also an instantiation of a new cowboy persona, where the term persona refers to a representation of a person that includes aspects of their performed and sometimes fictionalized identity, layered onto a real identity (the concept of persona is borrowed here from Auslander 2019, drawing on Frith 1996). Over the course of the video, four distinct personas are presented to the viewer: the living individual (George

Table 8.1. Representative 1990s–2000s mainstream country songs with narrative themes centered on Mexico

Song	Artist *Billboard* Hot Country Songs peak position / Top Country Albums peak position of the album that included this track
"Gulf of Mexico"	Clint Black (1990) -- / No. 1
"O Mexico"	Trisha Yearwood (1995) -- / No. 3
"Refried Dreams"	Tim McGraw (1995) No. 5 / No. 1
"Rodeo or Mexico"	Garth Brooks (2001) -- / No. 1
"Good to Go to Mexico"	Toby Keith (2002) -- / No. 1
"That's Why God Made Mexico"	Tim McGraw (2002) -- / No. 2
"Playboys of the Southwestern World"	Blake Shelton (2003) No. 24 / No. 2
"Stays in Mexico"	Toby Keith (2004) No. 2 / No. 3
"Not Enough Tequila"	Terri Clark (2005) -- / No. 4
"Beer in Mexico"	Kenny Chesney (2005 album, 2007 single) No. 1 / No. 1
"The Seashores of Old Mexico"	George Strait (2006) No. 11 / No. 1

Strait, an actual person from Texas), George Strait (country star, singer, public celebrity, and the actor in the video), the protagonist in the song (the narrator, voiced as first-person "I" in the lyrics), and the protagonist's younger self in the video (described in the lyrics and present in the video, portrayed on screen by actor Jason Gerhardt).

The video explicitly fuses those personas into a single entity: an incarnation of the iconic country music cowboy. Particularly in country music, genre-specific conventions have primed fans to make that leap: Richard Peterson laid out a sociological explanation of how and why country fans so readily fuse singer and protagonist into a single persona; Peterson's (1997) prototype is Hank Williams, Sr., who established "singing of his own life in song as the model for the would-be authentic country music entertainer" (see also Neal 2019, 133–4 and 446–7). And by 2006, George Strait's quarter-century career had already cultivated a loyal fanbase that was deeply invested in the idea that Strait's songs – and the characters in them – were very much an extension of him as person and as singer. Such an unchallenged fusion of personas, however, glosses over the rich analytic potential of recognizing their individual roles in performing the video's cultural work, as music scholar Brad Osborn has articulated (2021, 52–4; Osborn's exposition is heavily informed by Auslander 2019). Similarly, Carol Vernallis (2004, 56–7) points out that a performance in a video foregrounds "candor, self-disclosure, and direct address," while also frequently breaking the "fourth wall" or stepping out of character. The following analysis teases apart the personas and examines how the "Seashores" video explicitly fuses them, ultimately re-situating the iconic country cowboy on a beach and enabling a much larger shift in cultural meaning.

The "Seashores" video begins with a young man in a western-yoked shirt and cowboy hat, in a 1970s phone booth, calling his friend in Mexico ("Hola!") and declaring he is in trouble. A brief, two-second cut away from those characters establishes George Strait, barefoot, in jeans, blue denim shirt, and white cowboy hat, stationary in a chair on a sandy beach, a pale blue ocean bay stretching out behind him. The stasis of Strait in his chair, singing the song, contrasts sharply with the fast-paced actions of the young cowboy. At the beginning of the video, the readily apparent age difference between Strait and the young cowboy marks them as different people. Furthermore, the contrast in their pace of action suggests that the video is employing the common convention of singer-as-bystander, while the characters reside in the plot without interacting with the singer.

The video unfolds in what Matthew Ferrandino and Brad Osborn (2019) call an explicit-narrative plot, in which the visual narrative is a detailed realization of the song's lyrics. We watch the young cowboy play poker, get robbed, and hitch a ride in a truck filled with chickens and goats. Clips of the truck moving across the screen and out of the shot convey a strong sense of a long-distance journey as the young cowboy travels across Mexico. These shots are interspersed with cuts to Strait, still in the same chair, planted and unmoving on the beach.

A few details in the video complicate any simple assumptions about the relationship between Strait (the singer) and the young cowboy. For starters, the young cowboy's appearance resembles a younger incarnation of Strait; enthusiastic fans even speculated that the actor playing the young cowboy was actually George Strait's son, Bubba (Fanjoy 2006). That resemblance foreshadows a fusion of their personas. However, the lyrics offer one jarring moment of doubt regarding any connection between the song's protagonist, the character depicted in the lyrics, and the young cowboy on screen: "She loved a gringo, my red hair and lingo," sings Strait, yet neither actor Jason Gerhardt nor George Strait has red hair. For that brief second, the listener is reminded that the song's lyrics are, in fact, neither an autobiographical reminiscence of Strait-the-singer nor of the young cowboy at all, but that moment passes quickly, overshadowed by the many ways in which the video invites fusion of the personas and an autobiographical interpretation of the song.

Meanwhile the musical setting, a lilting triple-meter classic arrangement with country strings and plenty of steel guitar, conveys the passage of time through a series of "pump-up" harmonic modulations – an arranging technique that was wildly popular in the 1970s, the same era when Merle Haggard wrote the song (Ricci 2017; Neal 2016, 261–2). At time 2:34 and again at 3:13, the song "shifts gears" by modulating up a half-step to a new key. Each of those modulations to a new tonal center functions as a musical metaphor for the passage of time: a new key signifies a new chapter in the plot or a new scene in the unfolding narrative.

With the passage of time and distance established in the narrative, through the videography itself, and in the musical setting, video director Trey Fanjoy sets up the viewer for some video sleight-of-hand: one camera shot starts out pointing at Strait in his chair, then begins to circle around him. As it moves around the circumference of its circular trajectory, the camera passes around a palm tree that momentarily blocks the view of Strait from the camera (timing 3:40–45). As the camera continues past the palm tree, he comes back into view, but instead of George Strait in the chair from which he has not moved since the beginning of the video, the audience sees the young cowboy, having changed costumes and now wearing the same clothes that Strait had on – blue denim shirt, white cowboy hat. The message to the viewer is that the young cowboy – whose adventurous journey has been depicted in both lyrics and video – is, in fact, Strait, both the narrator in the lyrics and the singer. One cut later, the camera returns to Strait, back in his chair. But in that one brief yet very significant shot, the video tells the viewer quite explicitly that the singer/performer in the video, the song's narrator, and the young cowboy/protagonist are one single, out-of-time, multifaceted, and multigenerational persona: a cowboy (with a back-story) sitting on a beach.

At the end of the video, Strait finishes singing and drops out of his "performer" persona, joking with the other actor on screen that he might head back to Tucson. To the viewer, it is unclear whether Strait has slipped into character as the cowboy in the story or has slipped entirely out of character and is just George Strait, the person, breaking the fourth wall and chatting after singing a song. That ambiguity is basically the point: in the absence of other information, the viewer allows those personas to encompass Strait (the country star) too. That cowboy persona now has a back-story (the travels shown in the video), a lifespan (we see him age from young to old), an iconic wardrobe (the costume that both individuals in the video end up wearing, which will later become ubiquitous in cowboy/beach videos), and a celebrity identity (as Strait).

"The Seashores of Old Mexico" video elevates the beach setting into a significant setting within country music's geography and also inscribes the beach with referential meaning as the ultimate destination for a cowboy's escape. Settings have always mattered as markers of genre, and they work with specific codes of meaning in those genres (Vernallis 2004, 75). And while the beach settings were not all that novel in country music, Strait's video made the beach a more cogent setting within the genre, specifically a contrasting option to the conventional country narrative along an urban-rural axis (Watson 2019c) that had been particularly prominent in the 1990s. The beach narrative offered a flexible and useful alternative: one could leave a rural small town and escape to somewhere desirable; one could also leave a city and escape to somewhere desirable but not hampered by the cultural limitations of the farm-town imagery. And that travel-and-escape narrative offered vast potential as a new entry within the genre's tropes.

"The Seashores of Old Mexico" helped inscribe that particular narrative on the country genre through its memorable visual palette. The color saturation of the video, the green of the palm tree, the contrasting shades of blue between ocean and sky, the single splash of red in the Mexican-striped blanket on Strait's chair, and the repetition of the same basic camera shot sear imprint on the viewer's mind like a postcard. Fanjoy (2006) explained the efforts to which the crew went to create that picture, even dredging the lagoon near the beach to remove some dark-colored algae. And the repetition of the shot reinforces that single, iconic image, easy to recall and easy to catalog, for the viewer, similar to the way that the matching costumes created the iconic cowboy persona in the viewer's experience.

Sounds of the Islands

The second relevant reference point from country music history that took on a substantive presence around 2010 is what fans and critics alike casually identify as "island sounds," an amalgamation of reggae and calypso that collectively references the Caribbean region and cultures. The musical ingredients that evoke this theme range from steel drums, or steel pan, to the off-beat guitar rhythms of reggae (known by different terms including after-beat and upstroke), bossa nova bass patterns, and melodic fills that evoke a broad range of regional styles from Puerto Rico down to Trinidad and Tobago. The visual corollary includes white sand beaches with crystal blue water, palm trees, and colorful drinks with elaborate garnishes. Ask even a casual country fan who is at the heart of this trend, and they will likely answer: Kenny Chesney.

Long before Chesney made "island sounds" a mainstream part of country music, however, Jimmy Buffett and the Coral Reefers Band had handed country music fans an imagined country music fantasy island located in the Caribbean. While Buffett's role in country music had been largely forgotten by many listeners in the 2010s, in the late 1970s, his music was intertwined with the genre. Buffett's self-penned hit most associated with the island sound was "Margaritaville" (1977), which rose to No. 13 on *Billboard*'s Hot Country Songs. Three years later, Buffett recorded "Hello, Texas" as the opening song for *Urban Cowboy*, a movie that came to define an entire era of country music. And along the way, Buffett offered country fans a collection of music that drew on Caribbean influences while remaining loosely tethered to country music through overlapping fanbases and Buffett's own musical biography.

Just a few years after "Margaritaville," Howard and David Bellamy picked up the thread and carried it even more centrally into country music. The brothers grew up in Darby, Florida, just north of Tampa, and interviews with them frequently describe them absorbing Caribbean styles, rhythms, and instrumentation from local migrant Jamaican farm workers (Shelburne 2005; Bellamy et al. 2018, 159). After some modest success for about a half decade, the Bellamy Brothers landed their first No. 1 country hit in 1979 with what they refer to as their Groucho Marx line, "If I Said You Had a Beautiful Body, Would You Hold It Against Me?" accompanied by Latin-infused guitar lines of descending parallel thirds. The next year, "Dancin' Cowboys" took the sound even further in the genre-blending approach: they layered cowboy lyrics over syncopated infusions of reggae. The Bellamy Brothers held to this formula and earned mainstream hits with "Redneck Girl" (1982) and "Get Into Reggae, Cowboy" (1982). The timing of those particular tracks was ideal for their careers: those songs were released just as the line dance scene of the mid-80s ramped up in country music, and their Latin-infused beats fit the line dance patterns in ways that the neotraditionalist fare of George Strait and friends never did. As a result, their Caribbean country sound took on a disproportionately large role in country music.

Sliding forward into the 1990s, the historical line of "island sounds" in country music generally runs through Garth Brooks's "Two Piña Coladas" (1997) and then catches Alan Jackson covering "Margaritaville" (1999), followed by Jackson's duet with Jimmy Buffett on "It's Five O'Clock Somewhere" (2003). "It's Five O'Clock Somewhere's" video, also directed by Trey Fanjoy, provides another significant point of reference for this developing travel/escape/beach narrative in country music: in addition to the themes of escapism and leisure, in "Five O'Clock," Jackson and his band are seen traveling across the ocean – visually moving to a remote place, just as the protagonist did by truck in Strait's video. Jackson's protagonist escapes his working-class job ("paid by the hour," close over-sight by the "boss") and arrives at a lively Caribbean-styled bar for his "lunch break," accompanied by the island-sounds vibe of the recording. At the end of the song and video, Jackson welcomes a guest appearance by Buffett, who sings the chorus and then, in conversational patter during the song's outro, discusses what time it is with Jackson, and concludes, "It's always on '5' in Margaritaville, come to think of it!," transporting fans back to the imagined island escape he had conjured two decades earlier (see Bowen 1997 for a discussion of the geography of "Margaritaville").

Jackson's song amplified another aspect of country music's traditions: line dancing to Latin rhythms, just as country fans a generation earlier had done to the Bellamy Brothers hits. These songs' rhythmic grooves invited dancers to do a "Cowboy Cha Cha," one of several cha-cha-style-choreographed line dances usually done with a dance partner that borrowed from the 1950s Latin cha-cha craze; these country cha chas were extremely popular coast to coast in the late 1990s (Neal 1998, 328; Pittman et al. 2005, 134). Jackson's song joined such hits as "Neon Moon" (Brooks & Dunn), "My Maria" (Brooks & Dunn), and the aforementioned "Two Piña Coladas" in heavy rotation for dancers in country bars. For the fans, the combined meaning of the song "It's Five O'Clock Somewhere" fused the visual images (bars filled with Jimmy Buffett fans wearing Hawaiian leis, a luxury yacht on the open ocean) with a sonic experience of music that let them escape to their imagined Margaritaville and the physical embodiment of the song through a Latin-styled dance, swaying, spinning, and triple-stepping ("cha-cha-cha"). The multisensory experience – which fans often encountered in a country bar and in the company of other country fans – wove the beach and island sounds into the core identity of the genre. Following on Jackson's heels, by the time Chesney released the album *When the Sun Goes Down* (2004), the injection of Caribbean sounds, including steel drums and off-beat guitar strums, was simply accepted in country music, coexisting with the cowboy identity (in which Chesney occasionally indulged) and other long-established personas.

Continuing that musical lineage was the Zac Brown Band. Several of their recordings, notably "Toes" (2009) and then "Jump Right In" (2012), were saturated with musical elements borrowed from Caribbean musical styles, and the videos for those tracks added one additional element (along with beaches and tiki bars) to the expanding narrative: the songs' videos introduced an awkward American tourist named Flody Boatwood, loud, shameless, uncool, and entirely out of place in the tropical paradise settings. In spite of his garish behavior, he is nonetheless embraced by the locals: attractive women flirt with him; local musicians let him jam with them; and he injects himself into the scene and place evoked by the island-styled music. And these songs and associated cultural references did not require any cowboy connections to grant them access as mainstream country. The island sounds, visuals, and narratives had simply become part of the country genre's catalog of scenes and themes.

Conflicting Narratives

When two or more media streams combine, the potential exists for each to convey its own narrative and meaning in ways that can be congruent, complementary, or contrasting with the other streams' narratives. Such principles have underpinned academic approaches to analyzing music videos for years, expressed with varying vocabulary such as "conformance," "complementation," and "contest" (Cook 1998, 98). Osborn's (2021, 68–9) terminology for describing the relationship between a song's narrative and a video's is explicit, extra, complementary, or conflicting, namely those that adhere to the details of the lyrics, those that enhance the lyrics, those that run parallel to them, and those that offer a contrasting narrative entirely. The ubiquity of these new south-of-the-border places and images offered the potential for country artists to explore both complementary and conflicting narratives in their music videos.

One such instance of a complementary narrative is Frankie Ballard's "Sunshine and Whiskey" (2014). The song's lyrics ground it in Georgia, but its music video conveyed a road trip to a dusty, dry town, ambiguously located somewhere between Southern California and Mexico. Referring to one line in the song, "Chillin' on a beach with my sweet Georgia peach," Ballard explained: "The obvious thing [for that song's video] was to go to the beach, and I didn't want to do the obvious thing. I wanted to have the emotion of the song, but in a different way. So the desert, the Southwest, that little Mexico vibe, it fit with the song, but wasn't so obvious" (Hudak 2014; see Neal 2016 for another example of a conflicting narrative).

With that kind of flexibility in place, country artists are free to create multivalent song/video pairings. One of the pair can reside in the urban/rural axis of farms-and-fields, nostalgia for small towns, and the value of a day's hard work, or in other words, long-established country music tropes; the other can adopt these now-established settings of beaches, Mexico, or tropical islands. Deana Carter's song "We Danced Anyway" (1996) lacked any specificity of place, but her music video set the narrative in Puerto Rico, Carter barefoot on a sandy beach, palm trees in a sunset, and the Puerto Rican flag and name visible in one shot. Another of many such examples is Dustin Lynch's "Small Town Boy" (2017), which includes lyrics about dirt roads and John Deere, while its video places him in his cowboy hat on a beach.

With these conflicting-narrative videos, country artists effected a change in the cultural meaning of their music: they explicitly connected the genre to associations of escapism in the form of beaches, Mexico, warm weather, sunshine, and summertime. The conflicting-narrative videos allowed the more traditional country lyrics about John Deere tractors or wage labor for an unreasonable boss-man to connect with listeners through the beach images. In short, a listener might empathize with the metaphoric struggles of the song's protagonist but imagine the idyllic resolution to the conflict at a seaside beach resort rather than in an actual, rural small town in the middle of a dusty field. Sociologist Tressie McMillan Cottom placed her finger on the pulse of country music's new underlying narrative with this pithy summation: "I'm going to flip my boss off today and ride off to the coast" (qtd. in Berlatsky 2014). The second half of that phrase, namely the escape to the coast, was a fundamental change from country music of the past and the specific element that gave country music new meaning and new means to connect to fans for whom the old themes did not resonate.

Salt on Their Boots

By 2019, cowboy boots on the beach were a cliché in the genre's music videos. Perhaps the most striking adoption of this image was Jon Pardi's

"Heartache on the Dance Floor" (2019), whose video left a heartbroken Pardi sleeping on the beach in his boots and hat, and Pardi and Thomas Rhett's duet, "Beer Can't Fix" (2020). Pardi, originally from Dixon, California, crafted the image of a cowboy on a beach into a personal signature and part of his musical brand. When Rhett and Pardi met up to film "Beer Can't Fix" (2020), video director Shaun Silva explained the concept: "Basically, the concept is that there really isn't a concept!" Filmed in Key West, the resultant video opens with two brief scenes showing a fast-moving speedboat zipping across wide expanses of open water – the "travel" and "escape" tropes. The cowboy persona is fully present with Pardi in jeans, blue button-down, and white cowboy hat. Pardi and Rhett strum their acoustic guitars on the back of a traveling boat, and they line dance on the beach. Meanwhile, the song's lyrics recount watching sports, hanging out at a lake, and stressing about work. In sum, this purportedly unscripted visualization of the song defaulted to the cowboy-on-a-beach trope, using a sun-drenched summer escape to the beach as a complementary narrative to the lyrics' assertion that a beer can fix any problem.

Boundaries

Time and again, these cowboy-on-the-beach songs exploit not only the settings and themes discussed herein but also the specific gendered roles present in that narrative. The cowboy lying in the sand is cast as male (and white, young, and with an athletic physique). None of these characteristics surprises a country listener, who is aware of the extremely imbalanced presence of male and female artists in mainstream country radio or the well-researched and documented structural sexism that pervades almost every aspect of the country music industry (see, for instance, Watson 2019b). But the gendered nature of this particular narrative goes beyond the gender bias in songwriters and performers: the cowboy-on-the-beach plays into the larger trends, whereby the genre of country music itself adopts a masculine persona within pop culture. In many of these metanarratives, country music represents itself metaphorically as a male character, while aspects of the noncountry world – pop music, global travel, cosmopolitan experiences, urban identity, etc. – is cast as a female character (Neal 2016, 4–6). And within these beach narratives, the male cowboy character becomes a personification of country music. This analysis in no way excuses the rampant sexism or justifies the rigid gender norms that pervade country music but rather interrogates the gendered discourse as it appears in the music and videos within the mainstream country music scene.

The few female country singers who have worked within these tropes of travel to Mexico and beaches reveal just how deeply ingrained the gendered nature of the trope is. Crystal Gayle recorded "This Is My Year for Mexico" (1975) around the same time as Haggard's "Seashores of Old Mexico," yet in Gayle's song, the female protagonist only imagines going to Mexico to escape the drudgery of her life rather than actually taking the journey. Three decades later, as George Strait's "Seashores" was shaping country music's themes, Terri Clark recorded "Not Enough Tequila in Mexico" (2005). Clark's female protagonist heads to Mexico to escape the memories of a heartbreak, but unlike the dominant narrative in the male country artists' songs, Clark's attempt at chasing away her heartbreak with a trip south of the border is unsuccessful: Mexico cannot work its magic on her.

Leah Turner's entry into this discourse comes with the added cultural perspective of her identity as a Latina singer. In "Once Upon a Time in Mexico" (2020), Turner adopts the beach narrative and brings it to visual life in a cinematic video showing Turner and her cowboy-lover. Turner has explained that the song and video are a tribute to and re-telling of her parents' romance: her father is an American rodeo star; her mother is a Mexican American dancer and jewelry designer. What is notable about the video's narrative, which is entirely congruent with both the lyrics and the story of her parents, is that the cast of characters and the narrative align with the typical deployment of this trend: The cowboy is the white outsider coming to Mexico; the female character is Turner herself; the beach is where he finds his love interest. In sum, where women have engaged with these cowboy-on-the-beach narratives, they have frequently ended up reinforcing the gendered aspects of the trope: male cowboys are the ones who successfully escape to the beach and tropical climes.

One final video analysis illustrates the boundaries, limitations, and shortcomings of the beach setting and travel-and-escape tropes in country music's cultural conversation: Luke Bryan's "One Margarita" (2020) adopts the beach imagery and island sounds that had taken up residence in country music and embraces the outsider-tourist persona that Zac Brown had introduced. Unlike the previous examples that exploited contrasting-narrative videos and complementary-narrative videos to expand the meaning of those songs, however, Bryan reverts to a single stream of interpretation: the opening sequence shows an ostentatious, fast-moving yacht traveling across an open ocean toward its destination: a beach resort party. Tokens of Mexican culture – a Mariachi band, Day of the Dead Calacas, and oversized sombreros – circulate through a crowd, who are dressed as tourists. Bryan clowns in front of the Mariachi band and tries on their hats. The Mariachi band appears incongruous with the recording; the song is grounded in a calypso beat, and the listener never hears the sounds of the Mariachis even as they appear several times on screen. Filmed at Bryan's country festival, "Crash My Playa" in Cancun, Mexico, the entire music video and song in combination suggest that their primary narrative is a marketing blitz for the festival.

"When you think of summertime, what comes to mind? For me, it's sunny, daytime drives in the car with the sunroof open and the windows rolled down with country music blaring. To be completely honest, *I'm not even a country music fan*," declared a popular lifestyle and travel blog (vacationsmadeeasy.com). Bryan's song and music video make sense to country listeners who proudly announce that they are not country fans. Without the cowboy persona, without the grounding of lineage through George Strait's narrative or Alan Jackson's connections to Jimmy Buffett, Luke Bryan's video floats on its own. To borrow Cottom's summation, this song and video capture the sentiment of "rid[ing] off to the coast," but carry none of the working-class, historically grounded narrative from country's traditions that used to come before the beach vacation.

The case study of "One Margarita" suggests that the beach settings and island sounds that showed up in country music in the 2000s relied on multivalent readings for their grounding in country music. In those instances, the cowboy/working-class persona did significant rhetorical work, as did the lyrics in songs with a conflicting or complementary narrative. And the Caribbean references to island sounds wove both tradition and dance in their present usages. In other words, country music's backstories and journeys need a starting point every bit as much as a destination.

PART III

Authenticity

9 | Dolly Parton's Netflix Reimagining

How Her Twenty-First Century "Jolene" Revises Country Music's Authenticity Narrative

LEIGH H. EDWARDS

In her Netflix series, *Dolly Parton's Heartstrings* (2019), Parton turns eight of her classic songs into television episodes, expanding the lyrics into fictional stories and reframing songs like "Jolene" (1973) to speak to contemporary socio-historical concerns as she updates her authenticity narrative. By using this innovative Netflix narrative format, where her songs "come to life" as television stories, Parton banks on new media trends to appeal to new audiences. Comprised of eight episodes, the series expands her songs into fictional stories "based on the stories and songs of Dolly Parton," like "Two Doors Down" and "Sugar Hill." Appearing as a character in some episodes, executive producer Parton also introduces each, explaining how she wrote each song and its original context, and how she drew on the lyrics and aspects of her life story to expand into dramatic TV stories. Parton's Netflix series exemplifies "transmedia storytelling," Henry Jenkins's (2006, 3) term for the increasingly common media industry technique of telling stories in a coordinated way across multiple media platforms, such as from albums to television to films, serving corporate synergy. Long before the more recent popularity of that trend, Parton used that kind of technique, taking songs and stories about her life and reimagining them on a mass scale in forms such as films, musicals, Dollywood theme park attractions, websites, smartphone apps, and television series on streaming platforms. The Netflix series illustrates how Parton updates her authenticity narrative in a new media context and amplifies her gender critique of country music's authenticity narratives.

The "Jolene" episode is especially important because it epitomizes how Parton reframes her projection of authenticity and her star image. The original song "Jolene" is about a woman (an unnamed speaker) who is worried that her unfaithful male partner will leave her for Jolene, and she begs the other woman not to "take her man." In the television episode, the woman, now named Emily, befriends Jolene, who is a young, struggling country singer and waitress at a honky-tonk bar owned by Parton's character, Babe. Emily later accuses Jolene of having an affair with her husband and ostracizes her, but they reconcile when Emily finds out Jolene is not involved with her husband. Jolene, who had been involved with another married man, decries a double standard of scapegoating women, argues that the men should be held responsible for their own infidelities, and defends her sexual freedom, although she decides to stop dating married men out of female solidarity. Jolene goes on to become a successful country singer. Reversing the gender politics of the original song, the episode depends on complex intertextual references to earlier Parton songs in order to critique gender stereotypes.

I argue that in this episode, Parton essentially delivers an "answer song" to herself intertextually. Parton introduces the episode by warning us to forget everything we think we know about Jolene: "After five decades, you might think you know her, but you are in for some big surprises" (Fleming 2019). Reimaging the classic song a half century later, Parton creates a new "twenty-first-century" Jolene. In the original song, when the speaker begs Jolene not to "take" her man, the lyrics have often been interpreted as blaming the "other woman" for male infidelity. This episode lets the previously voiceless Jolene "talk back" against double standards. The surprise twist is that the episode voices Jolene's viewpoint, as she calls herself a "twenty-first-century feminist."

As I will detail below, the episode also makes a gender critique by having Jolene sing Parton's classic autobiographical song, "Just Because I'm a Woman" (1968), which slams double standards and women being judged for sexual relationships outside of marriage. Parton based it on frustration that her husband was upset over her previous relationships (Parton and Oermann 2020, 73). The episode provides a new twist on the country "answer song" genre, where female singers lyrically "talk back" to male singers whose songs stereotypically blame the "other woman" for male infidelity. Parton, in effect, makes an answer song to herself, and to "Jolene's" reception history. Here, the character Jolene, a struggling country singer, composes and performs "Just Because I'm a Woman" onstage. She rejects responsibility for male infidelity and false accusations that she had an affair with the married man in question, and she resists being judged for waitressing at a honky-tonk bar or for affairs with other married men. New Jolene instead calls for female agency and sexual freedom and rejects moral judgment of female performers. Reinforcing that critique, Parton sings in the episode in character as Babe, who is also a country singer; she defends Jolene and defies being judged as a bar owner and singer.

Through this "twenty-first-century" "Jolene," the episode critiques gender stereotypes in country music performance history, particularly as they intersect with those of class and race. A white, working-class character, new Jolene rejects white, middle-class gender codes of respectability and domesticity. More broadly, the episode condemns how western culture has historically denigrated female performers by associating them with prostitution and promiscuity and reinforcing a virgin–whore dichotomy.

The series underscores how Parton's gender performance itself challenges country music's gender stereotypes. This reframing of her work also revises larger narratives about country music history. As critics such as Diane Pecknold and Kristine M. McCusker (2016) and Jada Watson (2019b) have argued, we must continue to account for more nuanced readings of gender in the genre. My argument is not about Parton's authorial intention but rather about how her work and media image function as "texts." Through historicized textual analysis and discussions of gender and media theory, I demonstrate how Parton's texts revise older country music authenticity narratives and speak to the range of gender expression and critiques in the genre, particularly as they intersect with race and class.

Her work also raises issues of mass mediation and how the genre utilizes changing media history, including the dominance of transmedia storytelling in our current digital era. Here, Parton deploys her media image and stage persona in new contexts. Because recent media trends focus on self-branding and on creating a celebrity persona that can be marketed as "authentic" across multiple different media platforms, Parton can easily benefit, since she has long engaged in that kind of self-branding. The Netflix context is significant. Amanda Lotz (2017) has shown how streaming platforms like Netflix target broader global audiences and encourage more direct relationships with consumers. I would argue that consequently, they are ideal spaces for self-branding – Parton's fans follow her there.

In my book, *Dolly Parton, Gender, and Country Music* (2018), I called for the establishment of Dolly studies as a field because she is a key case study for such issues in country music studies and a flashpoint for larger cultural discussions. It is vital for scholars to continue to do more intersectional analyses of country music, accounting for the ways in which gender, race, and class categories have shaped institutions like the country music-industry and have impacted artists, audiences, and larger cultural reception. In Parton's case, what fascinates me is how her authenticity rhetoric can accommodate critiques of her, as in some disappointed reactions to her "5 to 9" Super Bowl ad (2021), which was viewed as reversing the original "9 to 5" (1980) song's pro-labor themes. Yet most critics are quick to say that they still love her anyway, as I will discuss below. I argue that in part, that deep affective investment in her reflects the ongoing appeal of her gender critique, her use of emotional realism, and how her transmedia storytelling remains so powerful.

While critics have decried structural inequities in the country music industry, intersectional critiques remain important, particularly since you can now see a trend of some segments of the industry undertaking a neoliberal appropriation of diversity, equity, and inclusion language for the purposes of public relations but without making meaningful structural changes, as in industry rhetoric promoting awards show appearances involving BIPOC artists, such as cohosting performances by Kane Brown, Darius Rucker, and Mickey Guyton, or for LGBTQIA+ artists such as Brandi Carlile or for white, cisgender heterosexual female artists. For example, the CMAs in 2019, cohosted by Parton, Reba McEntire, and Carrie Underwood, trumpeted Parton as the first solo host of the CMAs (1988), the second woman after Loretta Lynn to win Entertainer of the Year, and featured numerous female performers in a "women in country" segment. However, that segment could also be read as the industry trying to use female singers like Parton as symbols for inclusivity while not yet making enough structural changes to address gender and other inequities. As a meaningful artist, Parton herself is more than just a symbol, of course.

Parton's oeuvre also speaks to how scholars might use transmedia storytelling in the twenty-first century as one framework to analyze country music. Likewise, her work suggests the importance of addressing intertextuality in country star images, such as how the Netflix episodes reference Parton's earlier songs and film roles. In addition, her use of emotional realism could be a primer for affect studies applied to country music.

Transmedia Storytelling and Branded Authenticity

Parton's transmedia storytelling profits from media convergence, a digital-era development in which formerly separate media have come together on the same platforms, combining old media (broadcast, analog, print) and new media (interactive digital media). Drawing on these techno-cultural changes, multi-platform storytelling is not a new technique but has become a dominant model in contemporary media, partly driven by 1980s media deregulation and corporate synergy. It benefits from what Jenkins (2006, 3) terms "participatory culture," where fans seek content across digital platforms, particularly since the early 2000s rise of Web 2.0, which focused on social media and user-generated content. With over 31 million social media followers, Parton collaborates with content creators and companies and employs an "image manager" yet controls her own media image, content, and brand (Edwards 2018, 186).

Parton's careful use of transmedia storytelling also illuminates evolving models of stardom. Rooted in her autobiographical authenticity narrative, her star image perfectly suits recent models of stardom, where the self is fluid and performative, the media representation branded and commodified. In my book, I detailed how Parton uses a rhetoric of real and fake to create a knowingly commodified star image; she conveys a knowingness about the fakeness of media images but nevertheless insists on the underlying sincerity of her life story and personality communicated through songwriting. In "Backwoods Barbie" (2008), she sings "I might look artificial / but where it counts I'm real." She calls her "look" – exaggerated makeup, big wigs, plastic nails, elaborate costuming including five-inch heels – "fake," a gimmick to gain attention and then capture audiences with her songs, but simultaneously asserts her underlying genuineness and "realness."

The trend Parton epitomizes, of musicians using transmedia storytelling to frame themselves as a brand, is part of a broader dynamic under a neoliberal economic model, which promotes the idea of the entrepreneurial self as a brand, whether musicians branding their work or social-media users monetizing digital content. As Eric Harvey (2017, 118) has shown, the popular music "star-as-commodity" is now marketed as a "one-person brand," just as brands project an image of authenticity to engage loyal consumers, what Sarah Banet-Weiser (2012) calls "branded authenticity." Richard Dyer's (1979) "star image" refers to a film star's cultural meanings; he argued stars function symbolically as attempts to assuage capitalism's contradictions via a meritocracy discourse, of fame for some special talent. Of course, star images do not resolve inequity but instead reveal the changing concerns of different socio-historical moments. Here, Parton's star image illuminates how neoliberal rhetoric is shaping popular music trends.

Parton is a powerful case study for how popular music functions as a both/and space – site for affective expression and audience identification but also obviously mass culture commodity shaped by the music industry's political economy. In knowingly manufactured authenticity, Parton lives and thrives. Again, some critics objected when she reframed "9 to 5" (1980), her pro-labor rights song, as "5 to 9" (2021), a rewritten version used in a Super Bowl ad for a webhosting company that profits from a neoliberal gig economy that undermines stable jobs. Yet those critics were quick to say they still love Parton (Bennett 2021; Sexton 2021). This affective investment in Parton, one that can accommodate criticisms, indicates, on one level, her use of what Jenkins calls "affective economics" (2006, 3) – marketing designed to engage consumers' emotions, or neoliberalism's commodification of aesthetic and emotional labor (McRobbie 2002, 100). However, on another level, it also speaks to Parton's projection of sincerity and her authenticity narrative's ongoing affective power. Indeed, Parton's songwriting has always drawn heavily on what Stuart Hall and Paddy Whannel term "emotional realism." Hall and Whannel (1964, 269) famously theorized popular music as a contradictory mixture of both art and commodity, both "the authentic and the manufactured," an "area of self-expression" and "a lush grazing pasture for the commercial providers." Within popular music's status as commodified mass culture, audiences still make meaning in unpredictable, multilayered ways. As George Lipsitz (1990, 22) has argued, popular music serves as "a repository of collective memory" and exposes "the tension between music as a commodity and music as an expression of lived experience." Part of what drives this contradictory dynamic in Parton's reception is her careful construction of her authenticity narrative, evident in how she retells songs in new contexts.

Parton's Authenticity Narrative, Country Music's Authenticity Debate

Before exploring the "Jolene" episode more fully, it is necessary to establish how Parton constructs authenticity in her stage persona and star image, and how she intervenes in country music's authenticity debate. In her songs, autobiography, and interviews, Parton frequently tells a version of her life story of growing up impoverished in the Smoky Mountains in East Tennessee, overcoming hardship to succeed in country music. Important to analyze for the cultural impact of her over sixty-year career, Parton has written over 3,000 songs, sold over 100 million records, won 11 Grammy Awards, starred on film and television, is recognized for her literacy program, Dolly Parton's Imagination Library, donating over 100 million books, and for philanthropy like her million-dollar donation for Covid-19 vaccine research (Lordi 2020).

In a career navigating a still male-dominated industry, Parton demonstrates how some female performers facing structural inequity undertake complex gender performances. Recent scholarship reveals more complex gender dynamics in the genre than once thought, not just a strictly policed binary (Pecknold and McCusker 2016, vii; McCusker and Pecknold 2004, xix; Stimeling 2017, 3; Watson 2019b, 538–60). Thwarting gender stereotypes and claiming female agency, Parton famously left producer Porter Wagoner to control her own career; she owns her song publishing rights and started her own record labels. Recent female performers like Brandi Carlile, the Highwomen, Rhiannon Giddens, Kacey Musgraves, and Mickey Guyton cite her inspiration as they still face inequity like lack of access to country radio (Lordi 2020). Country music has been symbolically associated with a rural, white, southern, working-class culture, even though the genre's origins and audiences have always been broader (Malone 2003, 68; Jackson 2018, 4). Parton's explicit advocacy for LGBTQIA+ rights speaks to a long-running, marginalized, progressive strain. As scholars such as Nadine Hubbs (2014, 7–8) have shown, country artists and audiences are more varied than the conservative stereotype and include a progressive strain with cross-racial class alliances, working-class advocacy, and LGBTQIA+ advocacy (see also Hubbs and Royster 2020, 1–10; Pecknold 2013b, 1–15; Jackson 2018, 4). Hubbs traces the stigmatization of country as an example of middle-class stereotyping of working-class audiences. Because of her diverse fanbase Parton illustrates the broader audiences and political complexity in working-class audiences. However, country music authenticity rhetoric remains gendered and racialized; supposedly authentic "hard country" is framed as masculinized, closer to "folk culture" roots, while purportedly "sell-out" country pop is framed as feminized "mass culture" (Peterson 1997; Stimeling 2017). The problematic race and gender valence of these symbols of folk authenticity becomes even more evident, given the ongoing struggle for Black, Indigenous, and artists of color, LGBTQIA+ artists, and women artists to gain access to country radio in the face of structural discrimination (Hubbs and Royster 2020; Watson 2019b, 2021).

The Netflix series makes Parton's cultural politics a central theme, framing her as anti-racist, pro-gender equity and LGBTQIA+ rights, a figure who can unite a divided nation, reflecting recent press coverage. Parton has long been seen by scholars as part of a common country dynamic wherein stars like Johnny Cash appeal to both sides of the aisle (Edwards 2009, 6–7), what journalist Chris Willman calls "omnipoliticians" (2005, 248). Recent journalists have picked up on this dynamic, framing Parton as a uniting presence in a politically divided nation, tagging her "The United States of Dolly," an almost universally beloved cultural icon, an "actual angel" for vaccine funding and empathetic pandemic songs like "When Life Is Good Again" (Zoladz 2019; Lordi 2020; Smarsh 2020).[1] While Parton does not publicly take a stance on party politics, she is asked often if she is a feminist. Customarily, she replies she does not identify with that label but does not mind if others frame her that way, although in her autobiography, she calls her responses to childhood gender inequity "early Appalachian feminist tactics" (Parton 1994, 56–7). Calling the feminist query a "tricky question," she recently elaborated: "I suppose I am a feminist if I believe that women should be able to do anything they want"; she is "not ashamed" of that label but does not "really go for titles," and "there's a group of people that kind of fit into that category more than me." She clarified: "And when I say a feminist, I just mean I don't have to, for myself, get out and carry signs. I just really feel I can live my femininity and actually show that you can be a woman and you can still do whatever you want to do" (Carlisle 2020). Her response is in keeping with her generation's white, working-class singers, who did not identify with a perceived middle-class women's movement but could be seen as part of popular feminism. Parton has previously responded to social critiques of attractions at Dollywood by apologizing for and changing content or policies seen as discriminatory.[2] The Netflix series much more explicitly articulates Parton's current framing of her cultural politics, implicitly pushing back against an earlier conservative backlash she faced due to her LGBTQIA+ advocacy and coinciding with her publicly expressed support for the Black Lives Matter Movement (Newman 2020).[3]

Parton's star image is complex, with multiple layers to unpack, just as star images more generally are polysemic texts that can be analyzed for their range of meanings. My longer argument in my book, to summarize and build on it here, is that Parton's star image and oeuvre intervene in the country genre's authenticity debates through her "fake and real" rhetoric in her authenticity narrative, combining her knowingly artificial image with sincerity in her personality, life story, and lyrics. Her sincerity claim fits what Jimmie N. Rogers (1989, 17–18) terms country music's "sincerity contract," wherein performers promise to remain true to their roots and not "sell out." I argue Parton uses two specific gender tropes from country

---

[1] Smarsh's book (2020), from *No Depression* articles, was the basis for the NPR podcast, "Dolly Parton's America" (2019).

[2] Scholar Jessica Wilkerson (2018) has critiqued labor conditions at Dollywood, which is managed by Herschend Entertainment.

[3] Scholar Tressie McMillan Cottom (2021b) argues that the cultural reception of Parton in terms of country music as a genre reflects structural racism.

music history in her media image and stage persona: the innocent mountain girl and the scandalous "backwoods Barbie" tramp. She jokingly explains her inspiration: "I kinda patterned my look after Cinderella and Mother Goose – and the local hooker" (Bufwack and Oermann 2003, 363). By stitching together and exaggerating the two, the trope of the innocent mountain girl and what she dubs her "poor white trash hillbilly hooker," Parton critiques them both as limiting stereotypes, iterations of the virgin–whore dichotomy in western culture.

In her oeuvre, Parton's "mountain girl" image is a critique of the idealized Appalachian girl as a problematic white, working-class stereotype in country music history. Meanwhile, her tramp image decries another limiting white, working-class stereotype in the genre, the "hillbilly" framed as "low Other." Parton's exaggerated parody of the tramp creates ironic distance from the stereotype. In my book, I detail how Parton deploys camp as a style and performance mode of over-the-top theatrical artifice that grew out of twentieth-century gay subculture (Edwards 2018, 31). She critiques and transgresses these gender codes through her camp performance of them. Significantly, Parton is the only country star who cites a prostitute as the inspiration for her look, basing it on a prostitute from her hometown because she thought the woman's look was beautiful (Bufwack and Oermann 2003, 363), what she calls in "Backwoods Barbie" a "country girl's idea of glam" (2008).

Parton's authenticity narrative intervenes in the genre's foundational debate about what counts as "true" country music versus what is "fake" or manufactured, a tension between folk culture and mass culture. The genre insists on rural, folk culture origin stories as opposed to commercial, fallen, tainted mass culture – a rhetoric of purity versus the market (Stimeling 2017). Gendered and racialized, the genre's authenticity rhetoric reflects the history of popular music genres as racialized marketing categories. Diane Pecknold (2007) has detailed the historical discourses that obscured country music's multiracial history and its origins as a syncretization of Anglo-European and African musics; the industry created marketing categories when it was commercializing in the 1920s that attempted to segregate white and Black artists, and the ongoing impact of those categories is evident in how the industry professionalized beginning in the mid-twentieth century. Pecknold and other scholars have continued to trace the histories of artists and audiences that have pushed back against these genre, gender, and racial boundaries (2013a; Hubbs and Royster 2020).

In my book, I show how Parton's gender performance critiques country's authenticity rhetoric that favors an idealized, masculinized folk culture over a supposedly corrupting, feminized mass culture, and how it criticizes the genre's stereotypes of southern white, working-class femininity. The stereotype of mass culture as feminizing and corrupting is a broader one in US culture, framing mass culture as a "fallen," commercialized force (Lipsitz 1990, 22), which is a reaction to modernity, defined as the conditions of social life after the rise of industrialization and capitalism. As Lipsitz (1990, 22) has noted, modern mass culture expresses nostalgia for earlier folk culture it has commodified or marginalized. Likewise, the industrial-era categories "folk culture" and "mass culture" are arbitrary and permeable; folk music always mixed commercial and folk, as did country and earlier old-time music, hence country's folk versus the market rhetoric is a fantasy projection (Malone 2003, 68). It was when academics in the early twentieth century began cataloging folk music that they created the tension between "folk" purity versus "mass" culture (Filene 2000).

As Parton's media image combines the "real" and the "fake," I argue that it implicitly references folk culture and mass culture, and it offers one solution to the genre's broader authenticity debate by bridging those categories. Parton's star image claims both sides of the binary at once, both folk culture and mass culture, country's folk roots as well as its mass culture commodity status. Both real and fake, folk and mass, Parton's work questions the lines between those categories, questioning genre "purity" and what gets to count as "real" country music (Edwards 2018, 7). Parton's songwriting mixes folk culture and mass culture elements. Parton calls some of her music "blue mountain," meaning her mixture of Appalachian folk and traditional music as well as bluegrass. More broadly, her songwriting uses features of old-time Appalachian ballads. Meanwhile, she was also a pioneer in country pop (and was criticized for it), positioned as a crossover genre that symbolizes highly commercialized mass culture. The song "Jolene" uses Appalachian folk elements updated to modern country. Kate Heidemann (2016) notes metaphorical lyrics similar to Appalachian ballads and modernized old-time elements like keening fiddles mixed with modern honky-tonk pedal steel guitar, plus Parton's guitar riff with fingerpicking reminiscent of earlier picking and banjo roll patterns; Lydia Hamessley (2020, 121) details links to Appalachian ballads.

One Netflix episode introduction perfectly encapsulates the gender performance dynamic I detailed above. Introducing the "Cracker Jack" episode, from her song about her childhood dog, Parton speaks from a Dollywood theater stage set, in front of a small wooden shack, hay bale, and apple cartons, with a visual projection of fields and mountains on a screen in the background. Wearing a campy yellow gingham low-cut dress, flowers in her hair, exaggerated makeup, wig, and five-inch heels, Parton carries a sequined guitar. On cue, a dog made up to look like Cracker Jack runs onstage. Parton exclaims: "Ain't you the cutest thing?" (Tommy 2019). The scene evokes mountain girl symbolism: her yellow gingham dress, flowers in her hair, and the mountain field. She combines that image with her "Backwoods Barbie" tramp symbolism, with exaggerated makeup, wig, and low-cut dress. She combines folk culture symbolism, including her acoustic guitar, with mass culture, as this image of pastoral folk culture nostalgia is commodified on a mass culture stage. It is knowingly "real" and "fake," the conscious exaggeration a campy joke the audience is in on, and it references numerous country music performance tropes – from the country bumpkin female rube comedian to Parton's signature caricature of Daisy Mae (the cartoon character from Al Capp's *L'il Abner* comic strip, a stereotype of an oversexed "hillbilly"). The episode updates the song by following the dog's owner into adulthood as she and her female friends advocate for LGBTQIA+ rights, redeploying Parton's star image.

Netflix's Version of Dolly

The series depends on Parton's authenticity narrative, particularly her use of autobiography as the basis for genuineness. In the "Jolene" episode, Parton claims: "[T]he songs that withstand the test of time are the ones that are written from the heart" (Fleming 2019), invoking an idea of sincerity based on her familiar heartfelt persona. In her appearances, the series references Parton's star image, including intertextual references to past performances.

The series illuminates how Parton's authenticity narrative intervenes in the country genre's larger authenticity debates, adding new layers to her narrative. While Parton has long made social critiques, this series amplifies them; in her appearances as herself, she explicitly critiques gender stereotypes, advocates for LGBTQIA+ rights, and supports anti-racism. The plotlines further these critiques. For example, "Down from Dover" decries racism, portraying a Vietnam-era interracial heterosexual couple facing discrimination. "These Old Bones" condemns mountain-top removal, environmental degradation, and classism as a mountain woman stops a logging company from seizing land for coal mining in 1940s Appalachia. "Two Doors Down" denunciates homophobia as a gay man comes out to his disapproving mother at his sister's heterosexual wedding. Parton introduces the episode, calling for LGBTQIA+ rights and inclusivity; in the episode, she sings as herself at the wedding reception and unites her diverse audience, from conservative grandmothers to gender nonbinary teens, in their shared love of Dolly. Parton's concert performance is pedagogical, educating the mother out of discriminatory views.

Twenty-First-Century Jolene and Gender Stereotypes

The "Jolene" episode epitomizes how the series updates Parton's star image. Parton's fictional character is the bar's star, often singing onstage, but she is stigmatized by white, middle-class "polite" society; the episode critiques the moral put-down of female performers, linking to Jolene's story and Parton's star image. Parton introduces the episode via autobiography: she wrote the song from jealousy over a "red-headed woman" bank worker who flirted with her husband, the name was a fan's she met at an autograph session.

The plot follows Jolene (Julianne Hough) as she fights gender discrimination. Fired as a bank teller for flirting with a male customer, she is judged for working at the bar. Jolene befriends Emily (Kimberly Williams-Paisley), a white, upper-middle-class woman (the original song's speaker), who helps Jolene gain singing opportunities. However, when Emily later mistakenly thinks Jolene is having an affair with her husband, Jolene is ostracized by Emily's Women's League friends – white, upper-middle-class characters who decree the bar immoral. Jolene says she had affairs with other married men, but not Emily's husband. She argues the married men are cheating, not her, and defends her own sexual freedom, calling herself a sex-positive "twenty-first-century feminist," implicitly a third-wave feminist. When Parton's character, Babe the bar owner, jokes, "Oh good Lord, you'd flirt with a napkin," asking why she is "running around with all these no-good men," Jolene replies: "I'm just a healthy twenty-first century self-defined feminist who does what she wants, who she wants, when she wants." However, she decides to stop having affairs with married men in consideration of other women's feelings. In a recurring series dynamic, an intervention by Parton (here as Babe) restores harmony between characters; she is the salvatory character, like the "Dolly the Uniter" press coverage of her. Babe convinces Emily that Jolene "might have made mistakes" but "doesn't deserve" public shaming. The episode concludes with Jolene performing "Just Because I'm a Woman" onstage in Nashville two years later, with Emily and her husband in the audience, emphasizing restored female friendship and a denunciation of scapegoating.

Making Parton's star image part of the story, the episode accentuates her stage persona's "tramp" elements and gender critique. It intertextually references her earlier film role as the madam in *The Best Little Whorehouse in Texas* (1982), Parton's campy Mae West homage. Similarly, her exaggerated makeup and clothing reference stereotypical tropes of prostitution, with fishnet stockings and lingerie-based outfits, including a sequined lace-up dress and halter top with a polka-dotted shirt (referencing Parton's Daisy Mae caricature). When Babe and Jolene sing a duet onstage, their performance registers how female singers are commodified and objectified. After a man catcalls her, Parton deploys her oft-repeated stage-patter quip: "I told you to wait in the truck! They don't ever listen, do they?" Invoking her comic stage persona, she also makes a "boob joke" as ironic commentary. Parton often uses such humor to defuse misogyny, yet she also invokes a theatrical burlesque tradition to recuperate class and gender abjection – she uses irony and camp to reclaim the fallen woman image and defiantly imbue it with positive meanings (Edwards 2018, 91). Deploying a both/and rhetoric of sincerity and irony together, Parton uses parody and camp to critique how female singers are commodified.

While many possible interpretations exist, the original "Jolene" lyrics can be seen to conform to traditional gender role stereotypes by holding the other woman responsible, not the cheating man. A theme of invisible male privilege is at the song's core. The lyrics omit his culpability since the speaker will not leave him (the lyrics do not specify if they are married). They do not question the male prerogative to pick the object of his desire. Addressing Jolene in the second person, as "you," the speaker positions herself as supplicant deferring to Jolene's power to possess the man and cause her heartbreak. Like a literary blazon, the lyrics catalog Jolene's perceived beauty and feminine virtues: "flaming locks of auburn hair," her "eyes of emerald green," her soft voice "like summer rain," and her pleasing smile "like a breath of spring." The lyrics suggest Jolene might choose to accept the man's advances "just because" she "can," as if to prove her power in a patriarchal system.

In contrast, the speaker imagines herself powerless in a female competition for male affection; her "happiness" depends on whether Jolene decides to "take" her man, because the speaker "cannot compete" with her. Abdicating her own choice, the speaker articulates a self-sacrificing femininity; powerless even to "keep from crying," she could "never love again" because "he's the only one" for her. She tells Jolene: "I had to have this talk with you," although we do not know if that talk is actual or one the speaker imagines having. She gives Jolene the power to interpret her – to judge and act on her message, to make sense of her pain, to frame it ideologically. If that conversation is merely imagined, the speaker is already performing that act of interpretation by imagining Jolene like an "ideal reader" or "ideal listener" that she herself brings to life in the text, by imagining someone with the power to solve her suffering.[4] The speaker also offers her suffering to the audience as a text to interpret.

However, Jolene's power is contingent and limited, based on the man desiring her as a sexualized object who fits traditional feminine gender codes of pleasing behavior; her only power is granted by a patriarchal hierarchy, she does not have full agency within that system. Framing her through the male gaze, the lyrics look at her traditionally defined beauty (unless one reads the song as a homoerotic female gaze, as Hubbs [2015] has argued). While Jolene has the power to choose and is not wholly passive, she cannot speak or respond to the male gaze framing her as a sexualized object. The speaker will submit to Jolene's decision, but the real power is the unquestioned male prerogative.

"Jolene" is a "problem song" in Parton's catalog because it upholds gender stereotypes most Parton songs critique. The episode proffers a fantasy resolution, letting Jolene "talk back" and advocate male account-ability, rewriting the song's cultural politics. The original song is context-ualized via white, working-class Appalachian femininity; not leaving the unfaithful man, the speaker upholds a broken domesticity. Heidemann (2016) argues the song aspires to normative white, middle-class femininity lyrically and musically. Netflix Jolene is different; she rejects white, middle-class domesticity but also revises its power dynamic. Here, middle-class Emily is willing to leave her husband and demand male accountability; supporting Jolene's viewpoint, she rejects gender stereotypes and white, middle-class respectability.

By prioritizing female solidarity and agency, the episode generates new gender critiques, removing power hierarchies caused by male prerogative. It aligns Jolene with Parton, whereas the original song aligns Parton with the speaker because Parton framed the song paratextually[5] as partially based on her life. It underscores how much her oeuvre draws on autobiography and the importance of intertextuality and paratextuality to her star image.

---

[4] In psychological pain but speaking out, the speaker is not exactly the "body in pain" from Elaine Scarry's (1987) theory of the world-destroying effects of physical pain, but her suffering similarly threatens to "unmake" her world; in speaking out, she seizes power to "make" her world.

[5] See Gérard Genette's (1997) theory of paratexts.

As Jolene speaks Parton's own words, the episode reimagines the song "Jolene," infusing it with the gender politics of "Just Because I'm a Woman," updating the country answer song for a new media, twenty-first-century context. It comments on country authenticity. When Jolene tries to write a trite hit song, saying "I just need a song that will sell," Parton's character responds with the earlier-cited quotation: "The songs that withstand the test of time are the ones that are written from the heart." Implicitly, heartfelt songs are "better" because sincere. They are also the ones that sell, underlining how country packages projections of authenticity as mass culture commodities.

More broadly, the episode strengthens Parton's gender critique, adapted to new contexts and media, targeting Netflix's broader global audience, just as the series uses Parton's star image to critique double standards. Likewise, *Dolly Parton's Heartstrings* critiques homophobia and advocates for LGBTQIA+ rights and pictures with Parton hailing and uniting a diverse audience. While layering in these social critiques, the series illuminates how Parton's media image combines "real" and "fake," folk culture and mass culture, in her authenticity narrative, and how it bridges those categories in country music's broader authenticity debate. The series epitomizes her use of transmedia storytelling and branded authenticity, even as it underscores her use of emotional realism and the ongoing power of her autobiographical authenticity narrative. As it engages these larger issues, it shows how Parton's gender critique can help reframe country music history.

10 | "When Britney [Spears] Ruled the World"

Expanding the Stylistic Boundaries of Nostalgia in Country Music

PAULA J. BISHOP

In October 2018, Lauren Alaina released her single "Ladies in the '90s" cowritten with Amy Wadge and Jesse Frasure. The opening of the song suggests a nostalgic look at childhood when Lauren Alaina learned to sing while riding in the backseat of her parent's car listening to songs on the radio. The chorus of the song references artists through cleverly chosen lyrics from chart-topping songs of the 1990s. For instance, she sings, "I just wanna feel like ladies in the '90s / Turn the dial and find me some Strawberry Wine," a nod to Deana Carter's 1996 hit "Strawberry Wine." Walker Hayes takes a similar approach in "'90s Country," released a few months before "Ladies in the '90s." Acknowledging artists of the past in song lyrics is not new in country music, but Lauren Alaina's song – unlike Hayes – refers *only* to women, and specifically ones who, to quote the lyrics, "dominated" radio and "weren't afraid to make a statement" in the 1990s, or, as one writer exclaimed, "when Britney [Spears] ruled the world" (Despres 2018). Her list extends beyond country music to include seven artists from pop, rock, and R&B. While the song establishes her broad musical lineage and evokes nostalgia for a previous decade, it also comments on the nature and porousness of genre boundaries, both musical and rhetorical. A close reading of her song in its contemporary, historical, and genre contexts reveals some of the ways that the generation of country artists coming of age in the second decade of the twenty-first century are redefining and expanding the stylistic boundaries of the genre, as well as the nostalgic tropes that have been used for decades in country music.

This chapter first defines nostalgia and explores its affective and performative use in country music, particularly references to other artists in the lyrics. The remainder of the chapter considers why the 1990s serve as a nostalgic touchstone. This examination reveals how female artists in the twenty-first century are constructing their lineage in country music, using nostalgia as a modernizing gesture rather than one that seeks to establish narrow country music credentials. Referencing other artists reinforces the traditional country music gesture of honoring your past, but choosing outside of the "canon" of artists emphasizes the new generation's desire to cross or eliminate the genre (and even racial) boundaries that have dominated the recording industry since the 1920s. Their choices reflect the broader changes taking place in the industry, one in which women are carving out new musical and narrative spaces.

Nostalgia, Broadly Examined

Nostalgia was first defined in 1688 by Swiss medical student Johannes Hofer as a neurological medical condition caused by homesickness, particularly among soldiers fighting far from home. At the beginning of the twentieth century, the medicalized definition shifted to refer to a psychiatric condition that included anxiety and melancholy yet was still centered on a yearning for home. By the middle of the century, nostalgia came to be understood outside of the medical arenas as more than just homesickness and focused more on a longing for something or sometime in the past. This yearning for the past is usually driven by some discontent with or anxiety about the present and is often triggered in the wider culture by social upheaval, after significant events like wars and terrorist attacks, or during periods of economic troubles like the Depression of the 1930s. By the late twentieth century, though, postmodern critiques pointed out that nostalgia served to misremember or deny the past, to construct something that never was (Jameson 1991). Others look beyond the misremembering and reframe nostalgia as a way to understand how people perceive, remember, and incorporate the past into their current narrative (Scanlan 2004; Hutcheon 2000). This latter understanding proves the most useful for the analysis here because we can see the ways that nostalgia has been and is being used to construct and reconstruct the narrative of country music history.

Psychologists theorize two components to nostalgia: autobiographical memories and emotion (Sedikides, Wildschut, and Baden 2004). The memories could be of an event, situation, place, or cultural artifact (e.g., a song) to which one feels an emotional connection. While psychological studies focus on the nostalgic memories of a real or lived experience, the central nostalgic memories can also be of an imagined (happier) past, in other words, "the good old days." Anthropologist Arjun Appadurai (1996, 76–8) calls nostalgia without reference to a lived experience "armchair nostalgia."[1] Whether real or imagined, though, the memories central to

---

[1] Appadurai (1996, 76–8) connects armchair nostalgia to commerce, citing the ways that historical references are used to market products by creating a longing for something the consumer may

nostalgia are encoded with an emotional component that improves and accompanies later recall. For example, Lauren Alaina associates positive emotions with the memory of riding in the car and listening to the radio. Remembering the car rides is not simply the remembrance of the facts but of the feelings that accompanied that moment. When music accompanies the original moment in time – for instance, songs heard on the car radio – it, too, is encoded with the memory, therefore, hearing the music can trigger the retrieval of the memory and the accompanying nostalgia (Baumgartner 1992; Juslin et al. 2008; Zentner et al. 2008).

Researchers have shown that the memories created in youth and the music encoded with those experiences form a strong basis for nostalgic recall (Davis 1977; Barrett et al. 2010; Ryynänen and Heinonen 2018; Krumhansl and Zupnick 2013). In fact, recent studies (Ford et al. 2016; Krumhansl and Zupnick 2013) connect familiarity with songs and the age of the listeners when they first heard a particular song to the probability of generating nostalgic feelings. The songs themselves become triggers, creating what music and memory researcher Lauren Istvandity (2018; Istvandity and Cantillon 2019) calls the "lifetime soundtrack," defined as the metaphorical list of canonical songs that accompany autobiographical memories. It is personally constructed but highly influenced by outside forces such as caregivers, peers, and the medium through which music is consumed. As Kenny Chesney sang, "We all have a song that somehow stamped our lives / Takes us to another place and time" ("I Go Back," 2004).

Lauren Alaina was born in 1994 so her nostalgia for that decade is probably a construct. She likely heard the songs from the 1990s well into the first decade of the twenty-first century, which would have provided material for her constructed (armchair) nostalgia. In contrast, Walker Hayes invokes a lived rather than imagined past in his song "'90s Country," released a few months before "Ladies in the '90s." Like Lauren Alaina, Hayes quotes the lyrics of twenty-two songs released in the 1990s by both male and female country artists. Hayes was born in 1979, therefore his teen years coincided with the 1990s, making that decade a distinct point of reference for him. He told CMT, "I feel like, when we are young especially, while we are experiencing so many 'firsts,' when songs move us, we recall exactly where we were when we heard them. Also, the experience of hearing a song for the first time has so much to do with the emotions it will evoke in us for the rest of our lives" (Stecker 2018). Data

never have had or experienced. This notion deserves further consideration in the context of the recording industry broadly and country music more specifically.

scientist Seth Stephens-Davidowitz (2018) confirmed Hayes's self-reflection about the youthful development of musical taste in his study of data from Spotify. He analyzed the number of plays of songs that were hits between 1960 and 2000 against the age of the listeners in his study and discovered that men develop their tastes between the ages of thirteen and sixteen, and women between eleven and fourteen. Cognitive and behavioral studies confirm that exposure during the formative teen years is a strong predictor of nostalgic recall (Barrett et al. 2010; Holbrook 1993; Ryynänen and Heinonen 2018). Whatever decade our teen years predominantly fall in, then, becomes a touchpoint in our lived experience, a time of presumed happiness to which we can return in our minds.

Performative Nostalgia

Most studies of nostalgia and music focus on the affective nature of nostalgia, in other words, what listeners experience emotionally and how they connect the music to their lives. Nostalgia can also be performative, primarily through the images in the lyrics. Lyrical nostalgia in country music typically involves references to pastoral scenes, sometimes of what seems to be a premodern world, meant to comfort and alleviate the stress of the modern world by invoking an imagined past when things were supposedly better. The log cabin, in particular, became a nostalgic symbol that helped reconstruct and reinterpret the past, propelled by Fiddlin' John Carson's 1923 recording of "Little Old Log Cabin in the Lane," a minstrel show tune written in 1871 by Will S. Hays. Told from the perspective of an elderly (presumably freed) slave, the song fondly recalls the times when the slaves sang in the sugarcane fields, then gathered at night to sing and dance as he played the banjo. Despite the cabin's current decrepit condition, it serves as a nostalgic reminder of the "good times." Carson's recording adheres largely to Hays's original, though Carson drops the plantation dialect that might have marked him as Black, thus changing the subjectivity of the song and reconfiguring the nostalgia. The log cabin as a nostalgic symbol of better times has permeated the genre since Carson's recording because nostalgia for an imagined past sells well (Olenski 2016), particularly in difficult times. Performers today continue to invoke nostalgic images such as dirt roads, barns, creeks, hound dogs, and small towns to signal another time, as well as to demonstrate the performer's understanding of the lyrical tropes of the genre and therefore her artistic authenticity.

Nostalgia is also "performed" by country music artists by referencing past artists in a song, usually by naming the artist in the song lyrics, quoting a song title or lyrics as Lauren Alaina did, or borrowing a musical gesture such as a recognizable melodic line. It is a way of paying tribute, particularly to those who have died. For instance, there are at least sixty songs that honor the memory of Hank Williams, Sr. and recognize his importance to the genre, despite his relatively short career.[2] These began shortly after Williams's death (January 1, 1953) with Ernest Tubb's "Hank, It Will Never Be the Same Without You" (1953). The early 1950s was a period of consolidation and growth for country music and thus the death of Williams was shocking on both an individual and collective level. Shortly after Tubb's tribute to Williams, the husband-and-wife duo Wilma Lee and Stoney Cooper recorded "I Dreamed of Hillbilly Heaven" (1954), in which Stoney dreams of meeting Will Rogers and other country stars – including himself and Wilma Lee – at the pearly gates. The list is all male except for Wilma Lee. In 1956, Jimmy Martin recorded "Grand Ole Opry Song," which names some of the then-current members by name or by song (again, an all-male list, with the exception of Minnie Pearl). "Hillbilly Heaven" and "Grand Ole Opry Song" establish the canonical list of musical ancestors, as well as the practice of using songs to proclaim one's lineage and place in that lineage. These songs and others like them work, too, to establish the white male inheritance of the genre.

Paying tribute in song to the living and those who have died continued into later generations. For instance, George Jones's "Who's Gonna Fill Their Shoes?" (1985) enumerates the artists Jones considers the greatest in the genre, and Phil Baugh's song "Country Guitar" (1985) names the great country guitarists then imitates them musically. Country music hopeful Tom James Allison related to me that he named Dierks Bentley in his song "This One's for Nashville" because "he [Bentley] is the reason I got into country" (Twitter response to author, May 21, 2019). Malin Pettersen told me, "Willie [Nelson] is my hero so I might not have mentioned the song-writer in the song ['Sad Songs and Waltzes,' based on Nelson's song of the same name] if it had been someone else" (Twitter response to author, May 21, 2019). "Ladies in the '90s" serves as a way for Lauren Alaina to pay homage to the women who came before her, and she says as much in interviews: "I literally have my dream and believe in it because of Shania Twain, because of Faith Hill and because of Martina McBride, and because

---

[2] This figure is based on my database of over 300 songs that reference other artists by name, lyrics, or musical gesture.

these women did it" (Eicher and Kelly 2019). She, like others, continue the practice of paying tribute to the past through song lyrics.

In addition to paying tribute and establishing a lineage, the references to other artists can operate as signifiers for a concept. For instance, including "Johnny and June (Cash)" in the lyrics becomes a reference point for love; Willie Nelson for partying or being an outlaw; and Hank Williams, Sr. for a honky-tonk attitude or place, as well as for the price of fame. An artist or artist's song can act as a soundtrack to an event, as in Jason Aldean's "Johnny Cash," in which he escapes town with his sweetheart while Johnny Cash plays on the radio. Likewise, the sounds of George Strait, Brooks & Dunn, and Tim McGraw provide the background to typical Friday nights in Dylan Scott's "Nothing to Do Town." The names from the past can also signal a certain time, as is obvious in "Ladies in the '90s" and Walker Hayes's "'90s Country," but any reference to Shania Twain or Garth Brooks could stand in for that decade.

Songs like "I Dreamed of Hillbilly Heaven," "Grand Ole Opry Song," and "Ladies in the '90s" point out that naming past artists does more than just pay tribute. It also establishes a connection with those artists and authenticates the current singer's identity as an inheritor of the country music tradition. Generally, lineage refers to one's direct and distant ancestors, people with whom we share some amount of DNA and therefore some characteristics. With cultural products like music, the shared DNA is the music and the ideas about music. As in society, some musical family trees are perceived as more esteemed than others, and we are quick to seek connections to those.

Nostalgia and Genre Boundaries

Nostalgia in country music performs rhetorical work by invoking the imagined and real past for affective and performative reasons. The "past" is a narrative of country music's history co-constructed by the artists, the listeners, and industry players, resulting in a form of collective genre discourse. The discourse serves to manipulate and control the ideology by creating boundaries around the genre, particularly racial and gender ones (van Dijk 2006). The nostalgic references to artists of the past define the ideological narrative through the canonical list of individuals who have presumably mattered in the genre's history and have been elevated within the hierarchy of the past. Historically, that canonical list has been topped by Hank Williams, Sr., Merle Haggard, Johnny Cash, George Jones, Willie

Nelson, Waylon Jennings, Dolly Parton, George Strait, Loretta Lynn, and Hank Williams, Jr.[3] The canon of artists, as communicated through the lyrics of songs since at least the 1950s, acts persuasively to police the boundaries of the genre. Though George H. W. Bush (1991) proclaimed that country music was the "story of America set to music," the list demonstrates that the story is particularly white, mostly male, and bound by notions of traditional gender roles.

Lineage and pedigrees also function to police boundaries. Pedigrees are the record of the ancestry of a person, animal, or object, and are used to determine if the artifact belongs to a particular group. Pedigrees are constructed and controlled by those with institutional power and can be used as much to *include* as to *exclude*. An easy example to grasp is purebred dogs registered with the American Kennel Club: one ancestral misstep and your dog is no longer "pure." In country music, a combination of label executives, radio programmers, and chart makers – the majority of whom are white males – create boundaries around what is and is not country music (Smith et al. 2021). This delineation is sometimes explicitly called out by naming certain artists to point to what is *not* country; for instance, Brooks & Dunn name P. Diddy, a rap artist, in "Play Something Country," following it with "I didn't come here to hear something thumping from the city." Brooks & Dunn define the boundaries of their country music as white, rural, and not driven by the rhythmic elements of hip-hop.

Despite the overwhelmingly white male narrative of country music history as told through the references to artists in songs, women (in this case, all white) have appeared in songs, usually sung by women. Using those songs as a guide, a proper matrilineage would include Loretta Lynn, Dolly Parton, Patsy Cline, and Tammy Wynette. In "Ladies in the '90s," Lauren Alaina references female country artists Reba McEntire, Deana Carter, Shania Twain, Faith Hill, and the Chicks, all of whom would probably pass muster with the Nashville gatekeepers, but Lauren Alaina brings other foremothers into her ancestral claims by naming songs by some of the powerful women of pop, hip-hop, and R&B, including Madonna, Alanis Morissette, the Spice Girls, Britney Spears, Destiny's Child, TLC, and Christina Aguilera. By doing so, she broadens the

---

[3] To my knowledge, Charley Pride is the only Black artist to be referenced in the songs, though he makes only a handful of appearances: "You Can't Win, Stewart" by Stewart Wynn (1959), "Freightliner Fever" by Red Sovine (1969), "You Never Even Called Me By My Name" by David Allan Coe (1975), "She Took Charley's Pride and Freddy's Heart" by Virgil Fleming (c. 1975), "How to Be a Country Star" by the Statler Brothers (1979), and "That's Country Bro" by Toby Keith (2019).

rhetorical scope and meaning of her song. We can read her inclusion of noncountry artists as a work of resistance, a way of pushing back against the watchdogs and staking out a wider narrative space.[4] Rather than accepting the prescribed influences for an authentic country music origin, she takes control of her heritage, as well as her image. She illustrates this transition by explaining that when she wrote "Barefoot and Buckwild," released as a single in 2013, she was in a "phase where I was really trying to chase what the men were saying. I love that song, very proud of it, but I wrote that song at a time when bro-country was very heavy, and I was like almost trying to chase that a little bit" (Eicher and Kelly 2019). In the song, the (female) singer seems to be unable to resist the temptation of being with a man she describes as "trouble," and yet she looks forward to riding in the pickup truck with her feet up on the dash and arm hanging out the window, cruising along dirt backroads – typical bro-country lyrical images. By the time she released *The Road Less Traveled* in 2017, though, she reclaimed her authorial voice, telling an interviewer, "I fully embrace that I will not say what Luke Bryan is going to say. I'm going to say what a woman is going to say" (Eicher and Kelly 2019). With "Ladies in the '90s," she explicitly breaks out of the confines of country music and expresses independence and autonomy.

The inclusion of pop, hip-hop, and R&B also indicates the influence of those genres on country music in recent years. Country music has always absorbed and reflected a multitude of styles, but as Jewly Hight (2018b) wrote, even though "most mainstream country artists are still expected to pledge their fealty to the format and court radio's long-term support," which typically means adhering to the strict sound template approved by the labels and radio programmers, the sonic signature of country music is changing. To some, though, it seems the sounds from other genres must be muted on entry into country music. Kelefah Sanneh (2015) of *The New Yorker* described Sam Hunt's borrowings from hip-hop as "softer and sneakier" than what other singers do. *New York Times* critic Jon Caramanica (2016) refers to those who would bend the genre's profile as "dissenters" who have been "sneaking in rhythmic vocal tics learned from rappers." But some country music artists are boldly acknowledging and claiming those influences rather than rejecting them or suppressing them in their artistic work. They are staking out the gesture of incorporating "outside" influences as a stylistic principle and aesthetic intention. For this

---

[4] We should note, though, that the only Black artists named are noncountry, and thus Lauren Alaina reinforces the racial segregation of country.

generation, genre boundaries are permeable if indeed they exist. Whether it's an evolution in the sound or a passing fad (as Caramanica called it), the inclusion of other musical styles and/or the implicit or explicit musical namechecking reveals a significant difference in the current generation of artists, one that suggests that the sound will continue to change.

Rather than this being a reactionary position, it is more likely the result of this generation growing up in the age of digital downloads and streaming music services. As has been widely noted (Spilker 2017), digital music delivery has changed the method of consumption of recorded music. Listeners have expanded their sonic palette in a cross-genre fashion and have become cultural omnivores, sampling from a giant international buffet. As *New York Times* jazz and pop critic Ben Ratliff (2016) writes, "There is a possibility that hearing so much music without specifically asking for it develops in the listener a fresh kind of aural perception, an ability to size up a song and contextualize it in a new or personal way, rather than immediately rejecting it based on an external idea of genre or style." Ratliff's point about developing your musical taste independent of the cultural authorities is important to consider when examining the country music being produced today because some of these omnivorous listeners have become performers. "Ladies in the '90s" is just one example of this, as are the recordings of Maren Morris, Kacey Musgraves, Kalie Shorr, and others. Kacey Musgrave summarized it when she posted this on her Facebook page the day after winning Album of the Year at the Country Music Association Awards: "I am forever proud for my perspective and my version of Country music to be recognized. I revere the roots of this beautifully historic genre to my core. It's been embedded in me since childhood, singing traditional country and western music since I was 8. Preserving those elements while having the courage and freedom to infuse other influences is everything to me."

Nostalgia for the 1990s

Since Lauren Alaina and her contemporaries were not in their formative teen years in the 1990s, what is it about that decade that triggers nostalgia for it? It was the time before the Y2K scare when we thought our entire infrastructure would crash because of a pervasive (but fixable) software error in storing the year portion of the date. The '90s were before the dot.com and housing bubbles burst, causing recessions; before 9/11 and heightened security; and before the widespread use of the Internet in most public and private spaces. People purchased their music mainly on CDs because long-playing records, 45s, and cassette tapes had largely gone away, and Apple had yet to introduce the iPod and iTunes.

As Rob Sheffield (2018) wrote in *Rolling Stone*, 2018 was the year for 1990s nostalgia across multiple genres. He suggests that the 2000s and 2010s were a disappointment because they lacked a dominant musical identity in the way that previous decades have, as far as white America is concerned. Using his logic, we look back at the 1920s as the era of the flapper, the '50s as the decade that brought us rock 'n' roll and teenagers, the '60s as the time of social protest and the counterculture, and the '70s, of course, is forever associated with the rise (and fall) of disco. The '90s saw an explosion of musical sounds and styles, including mainstream hip-hop and gangsta rap, grunge, so-called "alternative" genres like alt.rock and alt.country, and "bubble gum" pop. The expansion of the sonic landscape was aided by a number of factors, among them the introduction of compact disc technology and digital music formats.

Sales for CDs began in 1984 and made 0.9 percent of the total volume of recorded music sales in the United States that year. By 1999 – the peak year for CD sales – they comprised 80.9 percent of the total sales and their volume (938.9 million) exceeded the total volume of sales of all formats in 1984 (673.9 million) ("US Sales Database" n.d.). A good portion of those music sales resulted from consumers purchasing older titles in order to upgrade their collection from vinyl to CD. Artists gained new fans because of the availability of both their older and newer material in retail outlets. With low production costs and the artificially expanded catalog, the 1990s proved to be an exceptionally profitable decade. As *WIRED* magazine's then chief editor Chris Anderson (2004; see also 2008) noted, availability of back catalog items widened consumer tastes:

People are going deep into the catalog, down the long, long list of available titles, far past what's available at Blockbuster Video, Tower Records, and Barnes & Noble. And the more they find, the more they like. As they wander further from the beaten path, they discover their taste is not as mainstream as they thought (or as they had been led to believe by marketing, a lack of alternatives, and a hit-driven culture).

Researchers have reported (Brynjolfsson et al. 2003; Waldfogel 2017) that an increase in consumer supply (for instance, a bigger back catalog of CDs) leads to an increase in consumption. Furthermore, digitization has created space for more entries from independent labels (Handke 2012). Listeners can re-experience favorites from their own past, as well as discover newer and older music from outside their typical listening patterns. Their sonic palettes and understanding of genre boundaries necessarily expanded from this exposure.

The introduction in the 1990s of the MP3 file format, an efficient and compact method of digitizing analog audio, led some labels like Sub Pop to experiment with distributing digital files, but they gained ground when people extracted music from CDs into MP3 files and shared them across networks (Napster being the primary peer-to-peer music sharing platform). Legal battles over copyright infringement brought on the demise of Napster, but at nearly the same moment, Apple released its MP3 player, the iPod, and a download service, the iTunes Music Store, that allowed consumers to legally and cheaply purchase digital music (Witt 2015; Fairchild 2015; Smith and Telang 2016; Waldfogel 2017). Streaming – perhaps more than any other technological innovation in the recording industry – disrupted the economics of record production and consumption, as well as the concept of style and genre boundaries. Unbundling the album allowed consumers to purchase tracks à la carte and curate their own understanding of artists, styles, genres, and historical periods. Personal and social discovery mechanisms (i.e., how to find new music) shifted from a reliance on radio to the use of recommendation algorithms on delivery and streaming services like iTunes and Spotify, respectively, as well as various mobile applications, social media platforms, and reality TV. The result has been further destabilizing of genre boundaries – at least in the consumer's mind – and the opportunity to construct nostalgia in new ways.

Maybe more importantly for Lauren Alaina and other female artists, the 1990s was a decade when "the ladies dominated" (her words) the radio waves. In country music, many of the top slots on the *Billboard* charts were occupied by women such as Shania Twain, Reba McEntire, Faith Hill, LeAnn Rimes, Martina McBride, Trisha Yearwood, and the Chicks. The pop charts, too, included female megastars such as Madonna, Christina Aguilera, Britney Spears, Céline Dion, Whitney Houston, Alanis Morissette, and the Spice Girls. Missy Elliott, Lauryn Hill, Mary J. Blige, TLC, and Destiny's Child even made some inroads in hip-hop, a notoriously rigidly male-dominated segment of the recording industry.[5] The 1990s was a lucrative period for women artists across the board. As one blogger wrote, "These women were powerhouses. Top 10 hits, awards galore. And SO.MUCH.FEROCITY." (Shabazz 2017). The impression that women were

---

[5] See Lafrance et al. (2011, 2018) for additional details concerning gender representation on the pop charts.

gaining power in the industry was bolstered by the success of the Lilith Fair, a concert tour featuring all women that ran from 1997 to 1999.

It was also, as Beverly Keel (2004) has described, the critical moment when the narrative for women in country music shifted. That decade saw an uptick in women singing songs that expressed a desire for equality, agency, and autonomy in relationships and the world, though this was tempered by an awareness that the edges had to be softened to be accepted by label executives and radio programmers. Lauren Alaina acknowledged the rising self-awareness and rhetorical strength of these songs in an interview, saying "I grew up in a time where Trisha Yearwood, Reba McEntire, Dolly Parton, Shania Twain … women on the radio, just … talking about shaving their legs [a reference to Deana Carter's 1997 hit 'Did I Shave My Legs for This?'] and whatever they wanted to talk about … And the songs even, were like, hey, we're girls, and we're proud of it" (Eicher and Kelly 2019). Keel's prediction that the women of the '90s would inspire "a younger generation to build on the foundation [they] established and push it to the next level" would seem to have finally panned out, if perhaps a generation later than anticipated (Keel 2004, 177).

Why the gap? As Jada Watson (2019b) has pointed out, between 1996 and 1999, women artists managed to have a significant showing on the charts. Someone like Lauren Alaina, born in 1994, just as women are gaining ground, reached her formative teen years around 2007–2012, a period when women's presence on the charts receded. For instance, in 1999, the gap between women and men in the No. 1 position of the *Billboard* Hot Country Songs chart was only four songs, but the following year it widened to fourteen and was twenty-two by 2009. All other metrics explored by Watson (2019b) further underscore the declining presence of women on the charts and the radio in the post-2000 years, so that by 2018, only about 11 percent of the year-end top country songs were recorded by women, as compared to 2000 when they recorded a third of them. Lauren Alaina and her contemporaries come of age when fewer women are present in country music, and those that do seem to hold less power than their predecessors. The decade of the '90s is therefore more attractive as a point of reference for an aspiring female country artist than the 2000s or 2010s.

The loss of women on the radio has not gone unnoticed by artists such as Lauren Alaina. In an interview on the podcast *All Our Favorite People*, she reveals that she often gets asked why there are so few women on country radio (Eicher and Kelly 2019). Her concern is as much about this situation as the message implied by the question, that somehow women *can't* be successful or fulfill their dreams because of industry or cultural gatekeepers. She tells her interviewers, "I don't know how to flip that conversation into, 'hey, this is what I *can* do because I'm a woman. I may have to work harder and I'm willing to do that. And when I win, I'm gonna win big because I worked twice as hard.'" As a songwriter who absorbs, reacts to, and incorporates what is going on around her, she wrote "Ladies in the '90s" as a response. By referencing some of the top names of the decade, Lauren Alaina says that she is offering proof that women have been on the radio and can be again. But her song also works to highlight the lack of powerful women on today's charts, and therefore, enters the extramusical discourse on the structural issues facing women in country music known as "Change the Conversation," initiated by Keel, Leslie Fram, and Tracy Gershon, and amplified through the work of others such as the Song Suffragettes, the Women of Music Action Network, and podcasts like *Women Want to Hear Women*, hosted by Elaina Smith.

Curating Nostalgia

Linda Hutcheon (2000, 196) notes that "nostalgia requires the availability of evidence of the past." She suggests that, thanks to the Internet, the availability of information about the past creates the potential for endless nostalgia. In the music world, this nostalgia is fed through re-releases/re-issues, covers, download and streaming services, movies, television shows, and videos on YouTube, including archival performance footage, official artist videos, fan-created videos, remixes, and covers by amateurs and professionals. We now have a bottomless well of evidence of the past. But the past has long been present in music – isn't the mere act of Brahms playing Chopin on the piano a form of evidence and an enactment of nostalgia? – but, the explosion of the Internet and digital media since the 1990s has created a deeper well from which artists like Lauren Alaina, Walker Hayes, and others draw when imagining and re-imagining the past.

Svetlana Boym (2001) categorizes nostalgic tendencies as restorative and reflective. Reflective nostalgia focuses on longing and loss, and the feelings invoked by (imperfect) remembrance becomes the point of the nostalgia, not the actual return or the object itself. With restorative nostalgia, however, there is an urge, desire, or imperative to reconstruct the past and build monuments to it (think of all those statues and monuments to the Confederacy). Traditions are a way of connecting to the past in an uncertain future, but they can become overly formalized in ways that the original was not. In fact Boym (2001, 41) notes that the more that change induces anxiety, the stricter those traditions can be. She further theorizes that as feelings of insecurity caused by modernization, progressive social change, economic frailty, and so on grow, the need to assign blame increases. One must protect against whoever or whatever is perceived as causing the distress in order to restore an imagined community. Invented nostalgic traditions are a salve for the affliction but also the litmus test for belonging.

Artists covering a song or referencing an artist in their own song operates as a form of restorative nostalgia. Invocations of nostalgia in song (the log cabin, the dirt road, the revered artist of the past) also point to claims of authenticity. If you know of these things (or know how to reference them properly), you stake your claim. By demonstrating your belonging, you guard against the social, cultural, and industrial changes that threaten the present.

Restorative nostalgia also works to draw distinct boundaries around the past, to say who or what is authentic in that reconstructed past and to exclude those who do not fit. Boundaries around that past can be drawn and redrawn as needed to preserve its constructed purity. The nostalgic references to a (white) rural past serve to inscribe racial boundaries. The references to certain canonical (mostly male, nearly all-white, cisgendered, and heterosexual) artists reinforce those boundaries. Songs like "Ladies in the '90s" and the musical borrowings from hip-hop and pop evidenced in country recordings in the early twenty-first century (e.g., Kane Brown, Sam Hunt, Maren Morris) signal a kind of defiance of boundaries in the younger generation of artists. As they expand the sound and point to a wider lineage for their understanding of country music, they redraw the nostalgic boundaries of country music and consequently begin to reframe our understanding of the past.

11 | Rhinestone Revivals

Repurposing the Nudie Suit for The Twenty-first Century

JANET ASPLEY

On the homepage of his official website, Joshua Hedley is pictured dressed in a striking green western-style suit. It is embellished with chainstitch embroidery, the pictures outlined in rhinestones. The design celebrates Hedley's home state of Florida; the curve of the smile pockets is mirrored by the back and tail of a large panther. Stately herons stand on his sleeves, and on the unseen back of his jacket is a large alligator in an Everglades setting; snakes coil up a tree on the leg of his trousers. Although the suit was made for the promotion of Hedley's debut album *Mr. Jukebox* (2018) by Indiana-based designer/maker Jerry Atwood of Union Western Clothing, it continues a tradition originated by Nudie Cohn, proprietor of Nudie's Rodeo Tailors of North Hollywood, for the male stars of country music's post–War commercial boom. The western-styled "Nudie suit" featured jewel colors, pictorial embroidery, and sparkling rhinestones, incongruously juxtaposing them with the materials and construction values of traditional bespoke men's tailoring. The resulting "Nudie suit" was the defining "look" for male country stars throughout the 1950s and although its presence diminished after the mid-1960s, it has survived and developed as the focus of several revivals, including one that has gathered pace over the past decade.

Below the photograph of Hedley is a quote in which he reflects on the hard country values of his music: "Classic country is like a suit. Nothing about a men's suit has changed in like 100 years. Classic never goes out of style." Although Hedley's musical argument can be substantiated, his sartorial one is more problematic, though pertinent. The design of men's suits has not remained static over the last century; rather, it has changed as changes in its wearers' lives have subtly, and sometimes radically, altered its use. The Nudie suit has also materially changed over its seventy-year history, as has its meaning within country music culture. In partnership with the "classic country" with which Hedley himself identifies, embellished western-style tailoring has developed into an important signifier of authenticity, a concept whose own meaning is subject to shifts.

In this chapter, I focus on the revival of the Nudie style in which Hedley is a participant, alongside fellow country music purists; male and female

Americana artists; artists who push at and expand the boundaries of country, including queer and Black musicians; and musicians from outside the genre. I contextualize the revival in the seven-decade history of the Nudie suit, and its changing uses within country music. Although the importance of other designer/makers such as Rodeo Ben and Nathan Turk[1] is acknowledged, in considering the historical perspective I will focus on my account of the style's history on Nudie Cohn and Manuel Cuevas, who was Nudie's head designer in the 1960s and 1970s and is now a respected maker in his own right. As the leading influences on embellished western wear within country music, their work is most frequently referenced in the twenty-first-century revival.

Although the Nudie style is often referred to as country music "costume" (La Chapelle 2001) and sometimes "fashion" (Gnagy 2017), in my own work, I have avoided both descriptions. "Costume" implies the portrayal of a theatrical character (Isaac 2014, 555). By contrast, the close and still developing association of the Nudie suit with narratives of authenticity, which in the twenty-first century remains the essential framework for understanding its role in country music, means that country singers wear a Nudie style suit in order to express their "true selves" and their claim to be "real country." This argument is the driver for my research (Aspley 2020). "Fashion," although "bound up with our sense of self both as individuals and as groups" (Craik 2009, 2) is closely associated with the industrial and consumer practices that perpetuate it. Patrik Aspers and Frédéric Godart (2013) draw a useful distinction between "fashion" and "style" that goes some way toward providing a lexicon of reference for the Nudie suit. Building on Aspers's (2006, 75) definition of a "style" as a collection of material characteristics involving fabric, embellishment, cut, and construction, which persists and forms a "multidimensional aesthetic system that is produced and extended over time," Aspers and Godart (2013, 174) argue that such styles "constitute a lasting cultural reference that is subject to fashions but is not a fashion in itself." As both performance dress and subcultural clothing worn by fans of country and Americana, embellished western wear shows exactly this characteristic: it constitutes a coherent scheme of clothing defined by its history and cultural

---

[1] "Rodeo Ben" Lichtenstein (1893–1985) was based in Philadelphia and worked with both Hollywood and music clients, including Gene Autry and Roy Rogers. With a similar clientele, Nathan Turk, who was based in Los Angeles, is perhaps best known for creating the outfits for The Maddox Brothers and Rose, who were marketed as "The Most Colorful Hillbilly Band in America."

meaning, which nevertheless retains the ability to change in response to fashion. In this chapter, I will use the terms "style," or the generic "dress," setting aside space to discuss the Nudie suit revival's relationship with commercial fashion's recurring interest in the history of western wear.

Nudie Cohn, Myth Maker

When Nudie Cohn set up Nudie's Rodeo Tailors in North Hollywood, California, in 1947, business in western wear was booming almost as fiercely as that of country music, which had recently adopted cowboy clothing as its signature look (George-Warren and Freedman 2006, 147).[2] As the most important subordinate of the sound of country, its look has formed a vital, active component of the music's culture. Western wear, while not the only look associated with country, is its "most iconic" motif (Gnagy 2017, 419). Post–World War II country music was eager to distance itself from the poverty and drabness of the "hillbilly" label that had dictated its pre–War image by appropriating some of the glamour generated by Hollywood western movies (Malone and Laird 2018, 160; Lange 2004, 63). Singing cowboys like Roy Rogers and Gene Autry augmented the powerful mythology that had surrounded the American West since the creation of nineteenth-century Wild West shows, in whose "kaleidoscope of color" (Reddin 1999, 55) cowboy bands were an important element. Other elements of western mythology also chimed with that of country music. The fearlessly pioneering cowboy, like the Post–World War II country singer, was presented as white, an identity that, both for commercial and cultural reasons, screened out historical evidence of racial diversity (Glasrud and Searles 2016). Movie cowboys were anchored to a past that never was – in the same way, country music was anchored to a mythology of the South and of Southern music that was homely, rustic, and entirely white. When it adopted western wear as its signature style, hillbilly music married two powerful mythologies – that of the South and that of the West – to create a third mythological space called "country."

Nudie also built a mythology around himself, maintaining an air of mystery around his origins for most of his career until, in an unpublished autobiography written with Petrine Mitchum toward the end of his life, he disclosed that he had been born Nuta Kotlyrenko in 1902 in Kiev, now in

---

[2] George-Warren and Freedman (2006) describe how western wear became "nationally popular" in post–World War II America, spawning countless outfits, both mass produced and homemade.

Ukraine, and arrived in the United States at the age of eleven, a survivor of and refugee from the region's pogroms (Cohn and Mitchum 1979).

Until his collaboration with Mitchum, Nudie declined to explain why his hand-tooled boots, made in his own workshop, were mismatched, hinting darkly at painful memories. The emergent tale is one of the first pair of boots he owned during his impoverished New York childhood – a similarly mismatched pair given to him by a charitable teacher. This emphasis on his life as a "rags to riches" fulfillment of the "American Dream" echoes the similar biographies of his country music customers. The tale tells of the transformative power of clothing, through which an individual can express a changed self: no longer the poor immigrant from Brooklyn, Nudie is transformed into Hollywood's clothier to the stars, a successful business-man whose boots are unmistakably fancy, and handmade. The mismatch-ing of the boots, however, conveys the notion that the "real" Nudie remains within, relaying a cryptic message about his pride in the changes he has made. An outsider who held the romance of the Hollywood West in his crowded shop and created a mystique around himself, Nudie, the self-creator whose roots as a Middle European Jew were unacknowledged until near the end of his life, was paradoxically a fitting architect of the trans-formative process through which farm boys became Opry stars.

In the fiercely commercial environment of 1950s country, Nudie under-stood that his work had two functions: to entertain and to sell. He collabor-ated with his customers to produce a style of stage dress that projected a visual narrative of their career, aimed at making the wearer both memor-able and appealing. Through the embroidery on his suit, a star might present a carnivalesque alternative identity in whose playfulness the audi-ence could collude, often based on the singer's imaginary participation in a narrative of the West. A prominent example was Ray Price's "Cherokee Cowboy." Price's suits were embroidered with representations of the Hollywood "Indian," such as totem poles, shields, and even the head of a Native American man in a feathered warbonnet.[3] Other artists wore a logo that depicted their own name; Porter Wagoner's suits unfailingly included wagon wheels. Song title suits illustrated an artist's hit records, lodging

---

[3] Though Price claimed Cherokee ancestry, and his birthplace is often erroneously given as Cherokee County, Texas (rather than Wood County, Texas), it seems likely that his choice of name was in fact bound up with the merging of the Drifting Cowboys and The Western Cherokees to form his band in 1953 (Keinzle 1995).

The phrase "Hollywood 'Indian'" is used here to draw contrast between the mythologized, stereotypical figure created by Hollywood, reflected in Nudie's work, and the historical dress practices and artefacts of historical indigenous American peoples.

their titles and themes in the audience's consciousness, and cementing the wearer's status as a star. George Jones had both a "White Lightning" and a "Window Up Above" suit, for example, both made in the early 1960s.[4] An artist's home state was often represented: Mel Tillis, like Joshua Hedley a native of Florida, owned a suit embroidered with pictures of alligators. As soon as they take the stage in a Nudie suit, a musician tells their audience something about their identity, both personal and professional.

Nudie Suits and the Narrative of Authenticity in Country Music

The Nudie suit, with its distinctive brand of embellishment, has both reflected and been an active player in the construction of narratives of authenticity, helping to define and redefine notions of "real country." During the Nudie suit's heyday, from the 1940s to the mid-1960s, its iconic status was built on the contribution it made to the dualities that are core to country music performance and culture. The Nudie suit engages with the juxtaposition of the "real" and the fake, natural and artificial (Fox 1992), commercial and sincere, comedy and tragedy (McLaurin and Peterson 1992, 6). Barbara Ching (2003, 27) identifies a paradoxical performance of masculinity based on exaggerated failure, in which male country stars "manage to be at once rich, famous and abject failures." The tailored bespoke suit, whose understated marks of craftsmanship traditionally epitomize power, authority, and good taste and whose crisp uniformity conveys a conformity to group values, is subverted in Nudie's gloriously kitsch glitzy reinterpretation. The Nudie style also contributed to the construct of the male country star as a man who, though elevated by talent and hard work, remained in touch with his working-class origins. Its embellishment is a marker of proud working-class taste, signaling both the wearer's stardom and the continued existence of the "real" man, whose origins are in poverty. A Nudie suit both set a 1950s country star apart from his audience and signaled that he was just like them.

However, as the Nashville Sound era dawned, country music's audience gained in education and prosperity and the industry reconfigured itself accordingly (Pecknold 2004, 103). The chosen attire of the era aligned its male stars directly with their audience, in much the same way as the more recent

---

[4] Both suits can be seen on display in The George Jones Museum in Nashville, Tennessee.

commercial form "bro-country" did when it adopted the uniform of plaid shirt and well-worn jeans as stage attire. The polyester leisure suit, uniform of the salesman (Cunningham 2005, 198), was now often worn onstage.

Henceforth, the Nudie suit would be the look associated with the nostalgic sound of hard country, a tool for artists engaging actively in the hard-core/soft-shell dialectic identified by Richard Peterson (1997), in which country cyclically searches for a lost "authentic" past. In the twenty-first century, this has remained the most prominent use of the Nudie suit. On the cover of *Hold My Beer, Vol 2* (2020), for example, Wade Bowen and Randy Rogers are shown leaning against the vinyl-covered bar stools of a bar, both wearing suits by Manuel Cuevas. The album includes the track "Rhinestoned," in which the singers declare "Country music's got me rhinestoned," as a way of describing their long-time affiliation with the country music of the "Good Old Days."

The current resurgence event is one of a chain of revivals that have each contributed a story to a framework for authenticity to which musicians constructing their own claims can refer. Whereas Joshua Hedley looks to the "classic" era of the 1950s and early 1960s, many artists in the authenticity-based field of Americana align themselves to the founders of country rock who in the late 1960s and early 1970s themselves used the Nudie style to look backward and sideways at hard country, a form that they considered more "real" than that produced by the Nashville industry. California-based musicians, including The Flying Burrito Brothers, The Grateful Dead, and Michael Nesmith, celebrated country's emotional truth while rejecting its commerciality and conservative political and social attitudes, using irony as a mediator, a device which Pamela Fox and Barbara Ching (2008) have identified as foundational to the establishment of alt.country, and which continues into Americana. The Nudie style was an instrument of expression for this balance of reverence and irony.

A suit from this period, worn by Gram Parsons on the cover of The Flying Burrito Brothers' *The Gilded Palace of Sin* (1969), has been both pivotal in the development of the Nudie suit as a signifier of authenticity and an important catalyst for the twenty-first-century revival. Designed by Manuel Cuevas, then head designer at Nudie's, in collaboration with Parsons, its embroidery motifs, which include marijuana leaves, poppies,

---

[5] In a 2010 interview with the author, Manuel described the suit as a "beautiful collaboration." Original sketches for the suit, now in the collection of The Autry Museum of The American West, Los Angeles, show both his and Parsons's handwriting (identified by the author from the latter's notebook [No Depression 2012]).

and pills, celebrate the 1960s counterculture in which Parsons was so enthusiastic a participant.[5] In stark cultural contrast, the flames of Hell climb up its legs, and a sparkling cross of redemption shines on the jacket's back. The suit is a material expression of the liminality that Michael Grimshaw (2002, 97) has identified as being at the root of Parsons's "legacy as . . . both creator of and searcher for authenticity."

In both popular commentary and academic analysis, Parsons is regarded as having laid the groundwork that has allowed hybrid forms of country to blossom. He is a significant inspiration to musicians, in the field of Americana and beyond. In 2017, the Texas-based designer/maker Kathie Sever of Fort Lonesome embroidered one of many outfits inspired by Parsons's suit for the then-rising Americana star Margo Price. The outfit, which Price called her "Suit of Good and Evil," was unusual, in that it echoed both the spiritual and the hedonistic themes of Parsons's suit; it featured marijuana leaves alongside praying hands, a devil's head, and a snake coiled around a shining cross reminiscent of that on the back of Parsons's jacket.[6] This is but one among a myriad of examples of clothing inspired by Parsons's *Gilded Palace* suit worn by musicians in rock, pop, and Americana over the past two decades, all designed to celebrate Parsons and to align the wearer with his perceived authenticity (Mackenzie 2011, 127).

Ascriptions of authenticity are cumulative, and the impact on twenty-first-century wearers of a further rhinestone revival, led by the "neo-Traditionalist" artists of the late 1980s and early 1990s, is also evident. Nudie himself had died in 1984, so the designer of choice in this period was his erstwhile head designer and son-in-law, Manuel Cuevas. This revival was again both Los Angeles-based and oppositional to Nashville's perceived commercialism, centering around Dwight Yoakam, whose version of the Nudie style oozed an unmistakable California Cool. Manuel's innovation in the style rests on his expression of his Mexican heritage; he uses smooth satin stitch embroidery reminiscent of the Spanish shawls known as Manton de Manila, and often features Hispanic motifs, particularly roses and Day of the Dead imagery. For the cover of Yoakam's 1987 *Hillbilly Deluxe*, Manuel styled the singer with a look that was part vaqueros, part punk, and part Bakersfield; the waist-length Hispanic jacket, similarly cut to those worn in the 1960s by Yoakam's hero Buck Owens, was vibrant turquoise, embellished with silver and gold embroidery; Yoakam's

---

[6] MissMargoPrice. "My Suit of Good and Evil." *Instagram.com*, 29 June 2017.

trademark torn skintight jeans were customized with the addition of hand-engraved silver conchos (Manuel, interview with author, 2008).

This generation of musicians emerged from a South transformed by migration, prosperity, and education. Yoakam (1985, 6) himself was the son of Kentuckians who had migrated to Ohio. He staked his claim to be "hillbilly" on his family history. In this historicized version of the music, what one knew, had heard, and loved, preferably from a young age, was as important a claim to authenticity as an impoverished childhood had been in the 1950s. It was common for artists of this era to include a cover of a classic country hit on their albums or in their shows, as a demonstration of their allegiance to and knowledge of country music "tradition."[7] A Manuel jacket served the same function, and by the early 1990s had re-entered the mainstream, as major stars like Alan Jackson and Randy Travis became his customers.

For some wearers whose careers began in this era, including Yoakam himself, Marty Stuart (who is also a collector of the style), and Jim Lauderdale, Manuel's work has been an enduring element of their presentation. All three are now associated with and have been honored by the Americana format and are themselves beacons of authenticity to younger artists, helping to fuel the current rhinestone revival.[8] Their influence is evident in the suits that the Texas-based band Midland wear on the cover of their eponymous debut album (2018), which makes direct reference to a range of Nudie suits. Their embellishment includes poppies from Parsons's *Gilded Palace of Sin* suit and the lightning strikes of George Jones's early 1960s "White Lightning" suit, but their waist-length jackets recall those made popular by Yoakam. The suits are as clear an acknowledgment of influence, and a claim to a referential form of authenticity, as is the band's name, taken from Yoakam's song "Fair to Midland" (2003).

Nudie Revivals and Their Relationship to Fashion

From the drape suit of the late 1940s, evident in Nudie's work for his early clients, to the flared trousers worn by The Flying Burrito Brothers and the

---

[7] Yoakam's debut album *Guitars, Cadillacs, Etc, Etc* (1986) included "Heartaches by The Number" (recorded by Ray Price in 1959) and "Ring of Fire" (by Johnny Cash in 1963).

[8] All three of these artists are recipients of Awards from the Americana Music Association: Yoakam, Artist of the Year 2013; Stuart, Lifetime Achievement, 2005, Duo/Group of the year, 2017; Lauderdale, Artist of the Year 2002, Wagonmaster Award 2016. The house band for the Americana Music Association's Honors and Awards Show is dressed by Manuel, who loans garments for the occasion.

shrunken proportions of the suits worn on the red carpet in 2019–2020 by Lil Nas X, the Nudie suit has reflected the cut of fashionable menswear. It has also enjoyed its revivals at times when western wear has been a prominent trend in mainstream fashion.

The Nudie suit's original integration into country music culture took place at a time when cowboy clothing was a veritable craze, alongside western cinema. The countercultural revival reflected the importance of the cowboy look to hippy clothing, and the 1980s revival followed hard on the heels of the fashion for western wear generated by the movie *Urban Cowboy*. The current revival is also in part inspired by the interest of fashion brands in western wear. Tailored menswear embroidered with western and floral motifs has been shown by Dolce and Gabbana (A/W 2016 collection) and Gucci (Spring 2017 collection), perhaps in a direct reference to the Nudie style. In the ultimate endorsement of the style's current influence on fashion, Jerry Atwood's work was featured in *Vogue* United States' "American Edition" (Yotka 2021) alongside the observation that "few garments are quite as American as the Nudie Suit." Elvis Presley, whose association with Nudie, though highly publicized, was fleeting, is the only customer of Nudie's mentioned, and the word "country" does not appear in the short piece at all, suggesting that in the context of fashion, the role of the Nudie suit in country music is of little interest, or even incomprehensible.

Its location in a period of fashionability for western wear, and for country music itself, has typically propelled Nudie revivals beyond the genre, prompting Nudie, basking in recent visits from Twiggy and The Rolling Stones, to tell *The Sunday Times Magazine* in 1972, "They used to call my outfits corny. Now they call them mod." In the 2020s, the involvement of professional stylists has accelerated and broadened the style's revival. Within country, the design of a suit is traditionally a collaboration between artist and tailor, a relationship that cements the style's function as formative of performance identity. By contrast, the Los Angeles-based stylist Catherine Hahn has been the catalyst for a playful adoption of the Nudie style for rock and pop performers. Jerry Atwood's 2019 powder pink suit for Lily Allen, for example, is decidedly British in tone, featuring the London Tube map, the NHS rainbow symbol, a British Bulldog, and the left-wing politician Jeremy Corbyn (Tonks 2019). Hahn's highest-profile client is the rapper Post Malone, who has worn Atwood's work as occasion and stage wear, beginning with the 2018 American Music Awards (Luu 2018).

The current revival also reflects a long-established practice, where the Nudie style has been adopted to acknowledge the influence of country on a particular album or phase of their career.[9] On the promotional tour for her 2018 country album *Golden*, Kylie Minogue, her band and dancers performed against a desert landscape backdrop while dressed in western wear, a use of the style that endorses Malone and Laird's (2018, 560) observation of what they call "the *American Idol* proposition ... like a mask, musical style is a set of characteristics or codes the most gifted performers can put on or take off at will." Allen, Post Malone, and Minogue, all dressed for a particular moment in their career by a professional stylist, are unlikely to adopt rhinestone tailoring as a mark of long-term artistic identity in a way that artists within the country/Americana genre have, any more than Kylie has done more than play foster parent to its sound. The "Nudie Suit" look is one that can now be "put on or taken off" as a point of historical reference, a glancing signification of knowledge of the authentic, or simply a fun, cool look that few others would dare try.

The Nudie Style and Country Music Masculinities

With its color, sparkle, and floral embellishment, Nudie's style was surprisingly feminized, originating as it did within a music whose surrounding culture was that of the fiercely heteronormative white Southern patriarchy. It is tempting to build on this interpretation and to style the Nudie suit as an expression of what Pamela Fox (2009, 72) sees as a "feminization" of country music brought about by postwar challenges to gender roles and encapsulated by the music's emotionalism. Nudie himself recognized that his designs had a feminine quality, speculating to an unknown interviewer in 1974 that they were popular because "every man has an aspect of woman in his personality." The trope of the "Lavender Cowboy," whose effeminacy was suggested both by his flamboyant dress and his musical performance, was common currency in the western movies that Nudie and his tailoring contemporaries dressed (Vander Wel 2019, 229) and effeminacy, often expressed through dress, has long been "the most common and clichéd marker of homosexuality in men" (Geczy and Karaminas 2013, 50). In the field of music, however, there is also a swagger about the man who wears feminized dress, daring the audience to question his "manhood." Faced with Lefty Frizzell's initial reluctance to wear rhinestones for fear of "looking like a sissy" Nudie used "a little psychology," telling his customer,

[9] Historical examples include The Rolling Stones, Elton John, and k.d. lang.

"It takes guts for a man to dress up in flashy clothes. Only a tough guy can get away with it" (Cohn and Mitchum 1978). There are echoes here of Marjorie Garber's (2009) argument that the adoption by male stage performers of elements of the "masquerade" of femininity (for example, makeup, big hair, or colorful clothes) while presenting themselves as heterosexual create a space of "unmarked transvestism" that "can be read and double-read, like a dream, a fantasy, or a slip of the tongue," paradoxically to produce a form of "hyper masculinity." This she sees as the explanation of Andrew Ross's (1989, 164) more direct observation of the late 1980s rock scene that "the most masculine images are signified by miles of coiffured hair, layers of gaudy makeup and a complete range of fetishistic body accessories, while it is the clean-cut, close-cropped Fifties-style Europop crooners who are seen as lacking masculine legitimacy." If the Nudie suit's apparent femininity complemented the vulnerability expressed through country's lyrics of loss and humiliation, it also expressed a measure of masculine confidence. As the neo-Traditionalist wearer, Jim Lauderdale told me when I asked him in 2008 whether his magenta Manuel suit was a way of being in touch with his feminine side, "I'm secure enough to let that show, I guess."

Since its inception, this flamboyant form of dress has been both sanctioned by and confined to the stage. Mel Tillis told me in 2015 that wearing a Nudie suit "made you feel like you were a star, boy, and you wore them proudly!" nevertheless adding, "I wouldn't be caught dead in one of those other than the stage!" By subverting the accepted norms of manly attire in so celebratory a manner, the Nudie suit in its heyday not only affirmed a pride in working-class taste, it expressed male confidence. In the Post–World War II cultural environment, where Southern white working-class men were facing a seismic power shift, country music's loud, sparkly embroidered suits were a way of broadcasting a claim for their values and culture to remain dominant.

Women and the Nudie Style

Throughout its history, the Nudie suit has been predominantly associated with male performers. Its core dichotomy, which sets high taste artisanal tailoring skills alongside low taste aesthetics, is specific to the values of menswear; its color and embellishment are given meaning precisely because they are worn incongruously by men. A Nudie suit is simply not as noticeable, or meaningful, when worn by a woman.

The contrast between the Nudie suit and women's stage wear during its heyday is revealing. As I have argued, the swagger of rhinestone tailoring contained an implicit defense of the dominance of Southern white masculinity in the Post–World War II years. It also reinforced commonplace gender norms that characterized male performers as workers outside the home, and women as tied to it (McCusker 2017). Both Nudie and his contemporary Turk dressed women musicians, but they were an exception and, usually, like Rose Maddox or Pearl Butler, performed alongside similarly dressed men as part of a duo or group. Sometimes women performers wore cowgirl outfits but were often dressed in homely, rustic gingham. As the 1960s progressed, women's dress moved away from gingham and toward cocktail dresses (Jensen 1998, 101). However, under close examination, these more "sophisticated" garments are often revealed as home or dressmaker-made, relying on applied braid to add sparkle, rather than the labor-intensive individually set rhinestones of a Nudie suit. In a country music ensemble show, the status of the "girl singer" was clear, not only from her interaction with the star but also from the quality of her stage clothing.

By contrast, since the early 1990s, a time when, despite the limitations placed on their success by restrictive industry practices, they were the "artistic and commercial center" (Bufwack and Oermann 2003, 471) of the industry, women performers have used the Nudie style to carve out a space for themselves in the music, implicitly making their own claims, not only to authenticity but also to artistic parity with their male counterparts. Manuel's customers in this era included Pam Tillis, Trisha Yearwood, and Kathy Mattea, and reflected the image they conveyed of "bright, aware, take charge ladies" (Bufwack and Oermann 2003, 483).

In the past decade, women in the field of Americana have made a still more explicit claim to space, airtime, and recognition; their participation in the rhinestone revival is the visual representation of this claim. Atwood has made a series of Nudie-style outfits for Nikki Laine, and Margo Price has been dressed not only, as I noted above, by Fort Lonesome, but also by Nashville-based Ashlyn Evans. The Americana female "supergroup" the Highwomen were pictured at the launch of their career in 2020 first in outfits by Atwood, then, under the headline "Country Music Is a Man's World. The Highwomen Want to Change That," in Manuel (Weiner 2019). In wearing Manuel's distinctive rhinestone tailoring, they give notice of their claim to a share in the heritage and artistic respect long enjoyed as an entitlement by his male clients.

The Nudie Style and Queer Sexuality

As I argue above, the feminized aspects of the style, sanctioned by its use as performance wear and buried beneath heterosexual swagger, were largely unacknowledged during its heyday. In the countercultural era, they aligned with decorative male fashion of the era and androgynous standards of male beauty. Two decades later, Dwight Yoakam's skintight jeans and stage dancing, in which he often turned his back to the audience, wiggling his rear, allowed him to adapt his waist-length Manuel jacket to the aggressively tantalizing male display conventional to rock performance; if a male, as well as a female gaze, was invited, the call was covert.

In the twenty-first century, the camp aspects of the style are being spoken aloud and celebrated by two artists whose personae issue a direct challenge to the confinement of country music masculinity to straight, white men. In 2019 Lil Nas X's worldwide hit "Old Town Road" was removed from the *Billboard* Hot Country Songs chart for allegedly not containing "enough elements of today's country music," sparking speculation that it was the artist's identity as a Black man, rather than his music that created the barrier, and that his exclusion marked "the continued segregation of country music" (Laver 2019).

When Lil Nas X appeared in the mini-movie style video that accompanied a remix of the song with Billy Ray Cyrus ("Old Town Road (Official Movie)," 2019), he wore a suit by Jerry Atwood, whose embellishment included his name alongside horses, horseshoes, and floral motifs; the design was evocative of an outfit Nudie's might have made for Roy Rogers. If "Old Town Road" drew attention to the marginalization of the Black roots of country, his appearance in this video, and at subsequent award shows (Thomson 2019), in Nudie-style suits, once the preserve of the white faux-cowboy, staked a claim for the reinstatement of the historical figure of the Black cowboy in both country music and the popular consciousness.

Hodo Musa, who acts as stylist to Lil Nas X, has clearly chosen the Nudie style to reinforce his alignment to country music, however short-lived that identification proves to be. In 2020, she acknowledged his western wear as "costumey" and stated her intention to make his look "a little more fashion" (Krager 2020). The prominence of western wear in high fashion noted above has allowed a smooth transition. For the 2020 Grammy Award Ceremony, Lil Nas X, who came out as gay in 2019, wore a shocking pink suit by Versace, still with his trademark short jacket, accessorized with matching cowboy hat and boots, silk scarves at his wrists, and a mesh shirt (Tran 2020).

The outfit both merged the rhinestone cowboy look with hip-hop "bling" style and melded it with references to BDSM and the biker "leather-man," both archetypes of queer style that were enough established by the late 1970s to appear as part of The Village People's stage wear. As Adam Geczy and Vikki Karaminas (2013, 86) observe, while the "leatherman" look was overtly queer, the cowboy was among a range of gay "types" represented by the band that were drawn from heterosexual paradigms of masculinity. Writing specifically about queer style in the twenty-first century, Shaun Cole (2015, 197) adds another hypermasculine stereotype, particularly embraced by African American and Latino gay men, which he calls "hip-hop realism"; hip-hop style is referenced through the Versace outfit through its branded, bright gold buttons. As well as representing Lil Nas X's hybrid musical influences, the Versace outfit's playful amalgam-ation of these queer archetypes, and their rendering in shocking pink, perhaps reflect Cole's (2015, 205) observation that gay men in the twenty-first century no longer feel the need to ally with the binaries of "effeminate" or clone "butch" style, negotiating instead a wholly personal route between "visual expressions of masculinity and femininity." Lil Nas X's visual, as well as his musical, style issues a challenge to country music that is embedded in twenty-first-century concerns with identity in the fields of race, gender, and sexuality.

Orville Peck, who is styled by Catherine Hahn, has combined the language of BDSM style with the Nudie style to reinforce this challenge. He teams his suits, whose makers include Jerry Atwood, with a leatherette mask, customized by the addition of long fringe. Like the "Cherokee Cowboy" (Ray Price) and "Young Sherriff" (Faron Young) during the Nudie suit's zenith, Peck presents a carnivalesque cowboy identity. However, there is now no "regular guy" persona to accompany the fantasy cowboy. Peck's name and history are undisclosed, and his face is hidden behind the mask, so Peck appears as a "character," perhaps even as a parody of the stock figure, the Gay Cowboy.

This suggestion of parody has invited accusations of inauthenticity for Peck. In an interview with the magazine *Attitude*, he counters by arguing that the exclusion of gay people from country music is because of a "stigma that country music as an establishment has kind of pushed," claiming that gay people have a greater right to play the music than "well-adjusted, straight white men or whatever ... I think that it's meant to be for people who feel like freaks" (Joannou 2020, 39). Alongside this claim to entitle-ment for access to country music, Peck challenges its traditional binary gender constructs by performing material previously associated with women's voices and stories, such as Bobbie Gentry's 1969 song "Fancy."

This tale of an abused and trafficked woman and her eventual triumph through resilience pairs Peck's remodeled country music manhood with the women country performers, whose combination of vulnerability and strength have made them gay icons; to cement the association, in 2020, Peck released a video with one of these women, Shania Twain.

Peck's use of the Nudie style suit is an element in challenging long-established norms of binary gender and heteronormative sexuality in country. Hahn's and Atwood's collaborations for him make this challenge overt in their use of images that would have been considered transgressive in the style's history. While Nudie was happy to celebrate the drug culture through Gram Parsons's *Gilded Palace* suit, by his account to Mitchum, the only commission he ever rejected was one to embroider "some pornography" on a suit. By contrast, Atwood has rendered for Peck, on a powder blue suit, a version of the imagery (two cowboys facing one another, naked from the waist down, their penises almost touching) made famous by Vivienne Westwood's 1975 "Gay Cowboy" T-shirt, itself taken from the artist Jim French's 1969 homoerotic series "Cowpokes" (Kaufmann-Buhler et al. 2019). This use of punk-inspired shock tactics to subvert the style sits alongside Peck's softer, more emotive self-disclosures to produce a powerful challenge to constructs of masculinity in country and Americana.

Conclusion

The twenty-first-century rhinestone revival has taken place at a time when mainstream fashion is inspired both by western wear and more specifically by the work of Nudie Cohn. It has also coincided with an explosion of debate about what country music is, to whom it belongs, and where it comes from, which challenges established norms of gender, sexuality, and racial identity. What began, in the hands of traditionalists like Joshua Hedley and Americana artists like Margo Price, as an extension of the established role of the Nudie style in country and Americana's narrative of authenticity has now emerged with an aesthetic of its own, which is helping to carve out new identities in the music. There are signs that the purely referential stage of the style's revival has passed; Kathie Sever told me that requests for variations on the Parsons *Gilded Palace* suit are less frequent now, perhaps as the twenty-first-century Nudie style develops its own markers. In this creative environment, the Nudie style has become a vehicle not only for recalling and honoring the past but also for building a future.

12 | Country Music Doesn't Have to Suck

Intertextuality, Community, and Bloodshot Records

NANCY P. RILEY

Much remains to be written regarding music in the time of Covid-19, but during the height of the pandemic, Bloodshot Records responded in a predictable fashion. On July 3, 2020, as cases of Covid-19 continued to surge, Bloodshot released *Pandemophenia* (2020) as a digital-only compilation, featuring artwork by Markus Greiner depicting a stylized version of the now-familiar spiked coronavirus, with many of the active artists on the label's roster performing original songs, b-sides, alternate versions, and covers. Describing the project, the label notes the importance of community, a value emphasized with its very first album *For a Life of Sin: A Compilation of Insurgent Chicago Country* (1994), but also apt in the midst of a global pandemic: "Getting these artists together on one release, in a time when we can't all be together, is special in and of itself. It's a reminder of the simple, but profound, joys music brings to us, individually, and as members of a missed community" (Bloodshot Records 2020). Bloodshot Records, an independent Chicago-based record label, was formed in 1994 when Eric Babcock, Rob Miller, and Nan Warshaw released *For a Life of Sin*, featuring Chicago artists and bands playing various styles of country music.[1] The "insurgent country" noted in the album title highlighted the founders' and many Bloodshot artists' roots in the Chicago punk and underground rock scene while also separating the label and the album from mainstream country.

Bloodshot became a key contributor to alt.country in the 1990s. As Fox and Ching (2008) argued, alt.country was a social and cultural movement that was characterized by a rhetoric of taste and cultural capital, an ironic relationship to capitalism and commodification, and an adherence to ideas of authenticity and tradition. As for its sonic elements, alt.country favored older styles of country and hybrid styles featuring influences from rock or

---

[1] Babcock left the label in 1997. Warshaw publicly resigned on March 12, 2019, following a public statement by former Bloodshot artist Lydia Loveless on Instagram (@lydialovelesss, Instagram, February 16, 2019). Loveless recounted instances in which Warshaw's longtime domestic partner, Mark Panick, sexually harassed her (Bernstein 2019). A lawsuit between Miller and Warshaw regarding the future of the label is ongoing to date.

punk and also embraced aging country stars who were no longer commercially viable. The umbrella of "alternative" covered a wide-ranging and eclectic group of artists, musical styles, and fans, all in opposition to the mainstream (12–13). As the boundaries of alt.country were always porous (see trade magazine *No Depression*'s tagline regarding alternative country, "whatever that is"), perhaps its demise was inevitable. Whether alt.country's historical moment simply waned or followed the history of commercial country music with a movement toward the mainstream and institutional power and capital, as suggested by Pecknold (2008), the music formerly known as alt.country is now referred to as Americana or roots with an even wider stylistic range. Whether one views this music as a subgenre of country or rather an adjacent genre, given its embrace of traditional country musical styles and artists, it is relevant in a discussion of country, broadly defined.

Distinctions between alternative and mainstream or independent and major labels are not always clear. Scholarship has typically privileged small-scale or independent efforts associated with alternative styles and movements as "authentic" and of a higher aesthetic quality contra major labels, but this is certainly debatable regardless of style and genre.[2] Small-scale production and consumption practices are not a panacea for the music industry nor for country music in the twenty-first century. Clearly, major labels and mass-oriented practices are culturally significant and have much to offer in the realms of aesthetics, scope, and obviously, popularity and capital, and "indie" and "major" are not mutually exclusive categories and practices (Lee 1995). Major labels and artists have long employed practices associated with smaller endeavors, such as targeting niche audiences particularly through subsidiary entities, or as regularly practiced in country, placing artists and fans in close proximity at events like the Country Music Association's Fan Fair (later renamed CMA Fest) (Ellison 1995). Meanwhile, the institutionalization of Americana, as represented by the Nashville-based Americana Music Association, arguably follows models employed by mainstream country, such as general professionalization, a reliance on radio (terrestrial and streaming), and weekly charts.

---

[2] Mall (2018, 445) provides a thorough literature review, and warns against "indie prejudice," defined as "a dismissive approach to the study of major labels and musical mainstreams that impacts our ability, as a scholarly field, to speak with authority about the largest segments of the commercial record industries and thus the most popular of popular musics."

Regardless of genre, the benefits of independent and small-scale practices are worth exploring, including ideological, aesthetic, and practical concerns. Independent labels are typically characterized by greater flexibility, employ a small staff and are thus more expedient in decision-making, can be driven by aesthetics and ideology rather than exclusively profit-driven, lack executives or investors to please, and offer possibilities of increased creativity and diversity (Mall 2018, 260–1). Practically, independent labels are more accessible to artists and fans and can foster more intimate relationships and community. The existence of indie labels, like any small business, can be precarious, and conversely, success and growth may marginalize fans and communities, as business practices complicate the concept of "independence" altogether (Lee 1995). Nevertheless, the distinction between mainstream, major labels, and small(er) independent entities has been acknowledged and discussed in depth regarding pop and/or rock aesthetics and practices yet remains unexplored within the realm of country music, and Bloodshot Records provides a model of small-scale production and consumption aesthetics and practices within Americana and the country music industry.

For the remainder of this chapter, I consider the identity and core values of independent Chicago record label Bloodshot Records by examining two compilation albums, specifically *For a Life of Sin: A Compilation of Insurgent Chicago Country* (1994) and the label's twenty-fifth-anniversary compilation, *Too Late to Pray: Defiant Chicago Roots* (2019). Bloodshot Records' ongoing use of the compilation format has been commercial indeed but has also been strategic for establishing the label's brand and identity rooted in ideas of authenticity. This format maintains a connection to the label's roots in the Chicago punk and underground rock scene and an adherence to a DIY (do-it-yourself) aesthetic, highlighting the preference of small-scale production and consumption practices within a music community. *For a Life of Sin* established the label, laying the groundwork for its identity and branding based on conceptions of authenticity, and the twenty-fifth-anniversary compilation pays homage to the Chicago music scene that gave rise to Bloodshot Records and embraces the diversity of the musical community the label has supported and helped to sustain, demonstrating the broader shift from alt.country to Americana/roots. Examining these snapshots of Bloodshot Records' musical offerings and practices and their related intertextual meanings not only reveals a deeper understanding of the label and its history but also demonstrates the role and importance of independent record labels and nonmainstream musical practices within country music in the twenty-first century.

For a Life of Sin

For a Life of Sin was released as "a snapshot of a scene at that time, a subset of the Chicago indie rock scene that hadn't yet been identified," featuring artists or bands that "had some element of traditional country running through their music" (Warshaw 2009). Released in 1994, cofounder Rob Miller (in conversation with the author, June 16, 2011) notes that these bands weren't necessarily trying to be "country," but identifies the connections between the "punk mentality" of older forms of country music and famous country musicians, such as Hank Williams, Sr., or Bob Wills. Bloodshot specifically acknowledges the importance of the Knitters, one of the first bands to play and record country music despite a punk background, claiming that without the Knitters there would be no Bloodshot (Carmean 1999).[3] The Knitters are a version of Los Angeles punk band X, and closely associated with cowpunk in southern California in the 1980s. Miller (1999) recalls becoming a "convert": "I started seeking out the names on the songwriter credits – the Haggards, the Carters, the Ledbetters – and I haven't looked back since. Country music doesn't have to suck."

For a Life of Sin features several key artists who have contributed to the label's reputation and identity, most notably Jon Langford. A Welsh-born musician and visual artist, Langford has been heavily involved with Bloodshot since this album and makes more appearances on Bloodshot's compilations than any other artist. A part of numerous bands and musical projects, his longest affiliation has been with the Brit punk band, the Mekons, formed in the late 1970s. Upon relocating to Chicago, Langford eventually formed a side project called The Waco Brothers, an alternative country group whose debut album was Bloodshot's first non-compilation full-length release, *To the Last Dead Cowboy* (1995). "Over the Cliff" is the second track on *For a Life of Sin* and features an upbeat, honky-tonk style, with a twangy electric guitar hook and bouncing bass line. The oppositional lyric, "success on someone else's terms don't mean a fucking thing" characterizes the song's general antiestablishment sentiment.

Grammy-nominated Robbie Fulks, who eventually released many albums on Bloodshot, contributes the humorous and bluegrass-influenced "Cigarette State" to the compilation, and longtime Bloodshot band Bottle

---

[3] Bloodshot released the tribute album *Poor Little Knitter on the Road: A Tribute to the Knitters* in 1999, duplicating the Knitters' *Poor Little Critter on the Road* (Slash Records 1985) track for track with the addition of one previously unreleased track performed by the Knitters themselves, "Why Don't We Even Try Anymore."

Rockets add their everyman roots-rock track "Every Kinda Everything." The Handsome Family, longtime friends of the label, appear, and Chicago-based Freakwater also contribute a track. Freakwater was on Chicago label Thrill Jockey at the time but eventually released an album on Bloodshot in 2016. Freakwater is Catherine Irwin and Janet Bean, and typically bassist David Wayne Gay, with a rotating collection of side players playing acoustic instruments such as guitar, banjo, mandolin, and fiddle, although a pedal steel and drums appear on some tracks. The harmonies of Irwin and Bean are often compared to those of The Carter Family and their overall sound is generally referred to as "old-time" (Reece 2017). "My Old Drunk Friend" is typical of Freakwater with its sometimes dark and self-deprecating humor heard in lines like "Everytime you walk in, I should run the other way," and "I should have moved to New York City, but I never was that cool / I just languished in the Midwest like some old romantic fool." The song opens with an acoustic guitar and falls into a lilting three with Irwin and Bean's trademark unpolished harmonies.

Two tracks on the compilation are by the Sundowners, saluting the city's long tradition of live country music dating back to the *National Barn Dance*, the variety radio show that is often cited as a precursor to the *Grand Ole Opry* (Berry 2008). The Sundowners were a Chicago country music institution. Comprised of lead guitarist Don Walls, rhythm guitarist and lead vocalist Bob Boyd, and steel guitarist and bassist Curt Delaney, the band never had a hit but performed four nights a week weekly from 1959 to 1989 at a club called the Double R. Ranch in the Chicago loop, earning a loyal cult following (Hoekstra 1998, 30). Their two tracks "Rockin' Spot" and "You Don't Know What Lonesome Is" reference early rock 'n' roll and western swing, respectively.

Intertextuality was introduced in the 1960s by Julia Kristeva to analyze literary texts but has been applied to a wide array of musics by scholars and musicologists using varied and numerous approaches (Castonguay 2018, 61). Musical intertextuality, or what Serge Lacasse (2018) terms "transphonography," offers a framework to explore the connections and relationships between musical and nonmusical "texts." The particular musical styles featured on *For a Life of Sin* refer back to past iterations of country music history, suggesting alt.country's rhetoric of taste and authenticity while evoking specific musical traditions (Fox and Ching 2008, 8–9). Beyond the musical texts, the discourse surrounding this album proclaims the label's antiestablishment positionality and validates the contents of the album, as seen in the liner notes for the album with the acknowledgment that "we're all exiles trying to keep our feet out of the corporate dog shit." This statement critiques the mainstream and places it at a distance from this album, its artists, and the record label.

Bloodshot also asserted a localized authenticity due to its founders' work within the local music scene and its use of the compilation format (both recorded and in live events), evoking the practice of mixtaping. A mix tape is a noncommercial collection of songs compiled by a single individual, often specifically for another individual. The practice was made possible by technological advancements in recording equipment and the accessibility of cassette tapes. Flourishing in the 1980s, mixtaping typically involved careful curation, thought, time, and often unique and creative user-created artwork on the cassette cover (Drew 2005, 535).[4] As Lacasse and Bennett note (2018, 314), mixtaping constitutes a form of cultural capital, and as Paul (2003) argues, subcultural capital with DIY and alternate modes of music sharing and distribution as a way to bypass the larger commercial structures of the music industry. Bloodshot's founders curated the label's first album using the audio tracks submitted by individual artists and bands. Such curation, along with the juxtaposition of bands and artists, recalls the practice of mixtaping, and was based on the founders' experiences of regularly spinning records and DJing at local bars. Bloodshot's compilations followed a mix tape's format, and the record label appropriated the political and cultural meanings associated with mix tapes, including small-scale and DIY models of cultural production and distribution.

Bloodshot's reputation in Chicago was clearly established with its first compilation but gained a robust following due to its regular live events. Such events spoke to practices that defined the local punk scene, which has long privileged live music and performances, but these events also built community and provided publicity for the label (Faris 2004; Sanden 2013). Bloodshot's first public event was a pair of CD release shows for its first album, featuring live performances from bands on *For a Life of Sin*, and the label has consistently hosted numerous shows featuring multiple bands and artists from its roster, along with "friends" of the label who are not signed, but who the label might be interested in signing in the future, or those who are simply like-minded artists. Certainly, album release parties are standard fare for bands or record labels, but for a compilation of local acts, such an event was even more fitting. In addition to CD release shows, the record label has regularly appeared at music festivals such as CMJ (an annual music conference and new music showcase associated with the magazine

---

[4] The practice was mythologized in Nick Hornsby's 1995 book *High Fidelity* and the 2000 movie adaptation.

College Music Journal) in New York and South by Southwest in Austin, hosting both official and unofficial events, and more recently at AmericanaFest in Nashville. These events not only provide exposure to new audiences but also allow for collaboration among artists and facilitate relationships between bands and individuals who may or may not know one another. Cofounder Rob Miller recalls that when *For a Life of Sin* was released, country- and roots-influenced bands in Chicago were not necessarily aware of one another, and the first Bloodshot record served as a type of catalyst. He recalls (2010), "Two or three of these bands could start playing together, and then the crowds got bigger and bigger ... [T]hey were playing together, all of a sudden, people going 'there's this great scene in Chicago'."

According to scholar Jnan Blau (2009), "[A]ny act of performance ... generates new meanings, even as those meanings are shaped by the past." Bloodshot's live events were performances by multiple bands and artists but were also performative and intertextual for the record label. That is, these events and interactions served to construct the overall identity of the label, referencing its earliest album *For a Life of Sin*, the compilation format generally, and the record label's commitment to a live music scene. Further, the nature of such events included the individual live performance by artists on Bloodshot's roster, hearkening back to past performances, recordings, events, and experiences. Simultaneously, community and camaraderie was fostered among its artists and fans, past and present.[5] Thus, these literal and figurative networks reinforce ideas of tradition and authenticity that were valued within alt.country at the time, but the intertextual meanings of these albums and events also highlight the importance of community and shared music-making as a value and defining characteristic of Bloodshot Records.

Too Late to Pray

In November 2019, Bloodshot Records released *Too Late to Pray: Defiant Chicago Roots* (2019) to mark its twenty-fifth anniversary, described as a "redux" of the label's first release, *For a Life of Sin: A Compilation of Insurgent Chicago Country*. Much has changed in the past twenty-five

---

[5] This also follows Philip Auslander's (2006, 102) concept of a persona, extended broadly to a record label, in that "both the musical work and its execution serve the musician's performance of a persona."

years, and Bloodshot's position within the music industry has shifted from a "scrappy" upstart to an established entity, reflecting the shift from alt. country's historical moment to the rise of Americana and roots music, due in part to the creation and growth of the Americana Music Association. Throughout its history, Bloodshot maintained its adherence to the community, the compilation format, and live events but broadened its musical styles and lessened its oppositional stance regarding the mainstream.

This evolution can be seen in an examination of *Too Late to Pray*. The label's early proclamation of "hundreds of sonic variations" was both hyperbolic and aspirational at its founding, but twenty-six years later, such a claim is more accurate, as Bloodshot boasts hundreds of albums, dozens of artists, and an expanded generic scope. This diversity is acknowledged in the title of the album and the replacement of "insurgent country" with "defiant roots." The latter rings a similar tone yet presents a more fitting representation of this eclectic collection of songs, though many tracks still fall under the category of "country." The formats of these releases speak to their eras, as *For a Life of Sin* was released on CD, and *Too Late to Pray* is available via numerous streaming services, CD, and 12" LP, and limited-edition deluxe color LP, notably produced in Chicago at Smashed Plastic Record Press.

As a compilation, *Too Late to Pray* can stand alone as an album or a distinct listening experience. However, it cannot be fully understood as "Bloodshot Records' twenty-fifth-anniversary album" without context and considering what Lacasse (2000, 57) terms the "network of interaction" between the actual songs on the album (covers and originals) and extra-phonographic materials, including liner notes, illustrations, and reviews. Further, Richard Middleton (2000, 74) describes a "performance-event" (based on Mikhail Bakhtin's "utterance") and notes these are always structured dialogically and the "whole history of previous usages of its terms, themes and intonations ..." must be considered in order to be understood. A whole history is beyond our scope here, yet for this performance-event, or compilation album, earlier usages must be investigated, including any previous compilations and practices that have preceded *Too Late to Pray* and the specific compilation it references.

Too Late to Pray is described as a "redux" of the earlier album, but it is also in dialogue with a "previous usage," *For a Life of Sin*. Some of the "terms and themes" are obvious; others are multivalent, invoking numerous texts and meanings. *Too Late to Pray*, like *For a Life of Sin*, takes its title from the Hank Williams, Sr.s' song "Lost Highway," and both feature original artwork by Jon Langford. His cover art for *Too Late to Pray*

Figure 12.1. Album art for *Too Late to Pray: Defiant Chicago Roots* by Jon Langford

(Figure 12.1), titled "Backstage in Opry Heaven," includes references to "Deck of Cards," the original Langford artwork from *For a Life of Sin*, most notably a winged angel in the background of both pieces. "Deck of Cards" features primarily deceased country stars as "Backstage in Opry Heaven" includes a more eclectic group, conspicuously a dinosaur and a vampire.

The diversity seen in the artwork can be heard on the various tracks of the album, for example, Langford's track, "I am a Big Town" (featuring Steve Albini). An important figure in the Chicago music scene, musician and recording engineer Albini is a widely known producer of alternative and indie rock. Although famous for his work with bands such as Nirvana, the Pixies, and PJ Harvey, he has worked on hundreds, if not thousands of albums, including several Robbie Fulks projects on Bloodshot (Faris 2004, 431). "I am a Big Town" provides a description of Chicago, noting general impressions and critiques, "there are monsters on the prowl . . . there's trouble everywhere," and "it's always rush hour, always traffic . . . no one knows anybody here." Musically, the song is diverse, with hints of his upbeat twangy contribution on *For a Life of Sin*, "Over the Cliff," with its bouncing bass, but nearly halfway through the "I am a Big Town," the tempo and meter change. The song ends with an instrumental outro featuring guitar reverb and distortion, hinting at Albini's (and Langford's) punk backgrounds.

In addition to Langford, the compilation's twenty additional tracks feature artists from *For a Life of Sin*, including Freakwater, the Handsome Family, and Robbie Fulks. Kelly Hogan also appears, long associated with the record label as both a soloist and collaborator. However, Hogan's most notable connection to the label could be that she was its first paid employee in 1997. Besides these familiar names, the album highlights several local country acts, who can be found regularly playing any number of venues around Chicago. The Hoyle Brothers' track "A Little Bit of Buck" comes straight from their weekly honky-tonk happy hour performances catering to two-steppers at indie rock venue Empty Bottle (name checked in the opening track on the album, "The Last Honky Tonk in Chicago"), and you can hear the supergroup Western Elstons nearly every Wednesday at historic Simon's Tavern in the Andersonville neighborhood. The latter band is comprised of drummer Alex Hall, "local guitar icon" Joel Paterson, and Scott Ligon and Casey McDonough, both of NRBQ and The Flat Five. Their western swing-influenced track "Toast That Lie" was written by Scott's brother, Chicago songwriter Chris Ligon (Bloodshot Records 2019).

Although country is well-represented on this album, the cover songs present an eclectic collection of references, paying homage to various genres and historical eras. A cover song is a performance or recording of a song that is associated with another artist, and a discussion of covers involves several components, acknowledging not only the "star text" or star persona of the artists receiving tribute but also the featured artists, the "original songs," and the covers (McDonald 2000, 6; Lacasse 2018, 20). Artists may cover songs to satisfy audiences, to prove his or her abilities with reliable and familiar material, or to establish a particular musical lineage. While *For a Life of Sin* did not include any covers, many tracks on the album referenced historical musical styles, providing some amount of alt.country legitimation and "musical lineage" for Bloodshot. But the use of covers on "Too Late to Pray" seems to serve a larger purpose, such as highlighting individual artists' creativity and offering a broader and more diverse view of music history (Solis 2010, 300).

The first cover on the album is the second track, Tammi Savoy and the Chris Casello Combo's "If It's News to You," featuring Savoy on vocals, Casello on guitar, backed with bass and drums. The Tammi Savoy and the Chris Casello Combo typically perform original 1940s-, 50s-, and 60s-inspired music, along with covers from those eras, often in vintage attire and period-appropriate hairstyles. On her website (n.d.), Savoy notes her influences as Ruth Brown, Lavern Baker, Ella Fitzgerald, Sarah Vaughan, and others, including Esther Phillips.

"If It's News to You" was originally recorded by Little Esther in 1957. Esther Phillips (1935–1984) was a singer who recorded a variety of styles throughout her career and began singing as "Little Esther" with Johnny Otis and his rhythm-and-blues band in the 1950s. After that group disbanded, she dropped "Little" and began performing as Esther Phillips, and her version of the country song "Release Me" reached number one on the R&B chart (O'Neal and van Singel 2002, 769).[6] With recordings of various genres and hits into the early 1980s, Phillips was championed by Kenny Rogers and The Beatles, but her career was plagued by addiction, leading to her death at the age of forty-eight (756–7).

Given their general commitment to historical performance, Tammi Savoy and the Chris Casello Combo's take on the song follows Phillips's original closely. Both versions are in E-flat major and follow a 12-bar blues chord progression with lyrics in an AAB pattern throughout. The overall arrangement of both recordings is as follows: four-measure introduction, verse one, verse two, bridge, verse three, guitar solo, bridge, and repeat of verse three. The only notable difference is in instrumentation; Phillips is accompanied by horns, guitar, bass, and drums, and Savoy by guitar, bass, and drums. Such a cover not only demonstrates this duo's mastery of historical styles and practice but also highlights the work of a lesser-known star from another era.

A cover that veers from the original source material and represents a creative interpretation is Freakwater's minimalist take on The Rolling Stones' "Sway" from the 1971 album *Sticky Fingers*. The Rolling Stones tapped into "roots" music for their studio albums between 1968 and 1971, drawing extensively on blues, country, and gospel, and this cover evokes both these histories and the legacy of the Stones. The original recording of "Sway" is performed by a full band of rhythm and lead guitar, piano, strings, bass, drums, and lead and backing vocals. In contrast, Freakwater's version is Catherine Irwin and Janet Bean on vocals and Irwin on banjo. In addition to the scaled-back instrumentation, the track is half the length of the original, which is perhaps best known for the instrumental outro featuring an extended virtuosic guitar solo by Mick Taylor.

In addition to the difference in the gender of the performers, Freakwater alters the lyrics slightly throughout the song, such as in the refrain, resulting in a shift of the original song's persona (Lacasse 2018, 20). The original version begins, "It's just that demon life has got you in its sway," and in subsequent refrains "you" changes to "me." Freakwater maintains "you" throughout. This alteration is subtle but paired with the sparse performance style provides a new interpretation of the song. The narrative of The Rolling Stones' version implies the possibly detrimental rock 'n' roll

---

[6] Although artists such as Patti Page, Kitty Wells, and others had success with the song on country charts, Phillips's version did not chart in country. This was the same year that Ray Charles released *Modern Sounds in Country and Western Music* (1962).

lifestyle of sex and drugs with references to "that demon life" and "friends out on the burial ground." However, as the guitar solo extends and the instrumental overtakes the vocals, the narrative is not resolved but perhaps embraces a nihilist subjectivity or even transcendency as the track fades. Comparatively, Freakwater's sparse presentation reads as more exposed, even vulnerable, but kept at a distance with the objective "you." The song concludes with neither a transcendent nor nihilistic moment but rather one of resignation. In the final line, the vocals and banjo conclude with the final line "It's just that demon life."

The use of covers on this compilation provides a musical lineage to various historical eras and styles and also demonstrates the creative interpretations of the artists. This stylistic diversity represents an increased range for Bloodshot Records, reflecting both the local Chicago community and also trends within Americana. Indeed, in addition to those discussed previously, the album includes country covers of artists such as Loretta Lynn, Willie Nelson, and Floyd Tillman, while covers of Leonard Cohen and early David Bowie also appear. Other original tracks introduce new artists Wild Earp, Half Gringa, the duo Bethany Thomas and Tawny Newsome, and more. Taken together all the artists on the album represent not only the sound but also the community of Bloodshot Records. As the liner notes state, "Some of the artists you may have heard of; some are woven so tightly into the fabric of the city, it's hard to imagine a time without them; some we've claimed, whether they like it or not, as natives; some you might be hearing for the first time; and some you may never hear from again" (Bloodshot Records 2019). This inclusion of those "you may never hear from again" speaks to the label's commitment to its city and community of musicians of which it is a participant and, in many ways, has fostered over the past decades. This is also a direct commentary on *For a Life of Sin* and the artists who have come to define Bloodshot Records, juxtaposed with those we have not heard from since that album. Also, this community is not only the performers. The printed acknowledgments offer gratitude for contributions from all parts of the local scene, including musicians, performers, venues, door people, bartenders, sound engineers, and the list goes on.

Given the wide range of artists and songs on this album, the liner notes provide valuable information for even those insiders who are familiar with Bloodshot and its history. Many artists have not appeared on previous projects and have not been associated with the label before. Further, without the notes, it is likely most listeners would not recognize the covers mentioned above. The liner notes, and indeed the entire album, reference

Bloodshot Records' history with visual, aural, and even literary references that longtime fans and supporters will recognize, be it from past albums, events, or even conversations with Bloodshot artists and employees. Longtime Chicagoans might read about old venues and bars, long closed, and restaurants now shuttered, and bemoan the good ol' days, yet the label connects past and present, "[F]or everything that is gone, for every skeleton or ghost of what was, there are always new hustles and hustlers keeping the city as bustling and weird and wonderful as we found it" (Bloodshot Records 2019). Whether it is Langford's artwork, his voice or that of Kelly Hogan or Robbie Fulks, or the picture of the bar at Delilah's on the inside sleeve of the album, *Too Late to Pray* can be read as a multilayered inside joke or a love letter to the Chicago indie music scene, but it also speaks to Bloodshot Records' fans and community it has built over the past twenty-six years along with the changing landscape of alt.country and Americana music (Ferguson 2019).

Conclusion

In March 2020, the Covid-19 pandemic served as an equalizer for performing artists around the globe. Social networks and streaming platforms were inundated with livestreams, be it an unknown singer-songwriter or a superstar, broadcasting a performance from a living room, bedroom, or backyard, in light of the shutdown and its canceled tours, events, and loss of income. Yet as the pandemic wore on, responses became more varied, as some artists established a livestream schedule to perform regularly, others ceased the practice altogether to focus on other projects (musical or otherwise), and those with greater resources, perhaps via major labels or corporate sponsors, took on more ambitious projects.

Bloodshot Records did what it has always done and released a compilation album featuring many of its artists. The label described the project in the following way:

Pandemophenia is a thank you to all the fans who have been so supportive during this challenging time. It is something positive to enjoy and something for the artists to share with the world while they're grounded. And, of course, hopefully it'll put some cash in their alarmingly empty pockets. Getting these artists together on one release, in a time when we can't all be together, is special in and of itself. It's a reminder of the simple, but profound, joys music brings to us, individually, and as members of a missed community. (Bloodshot Records 2020)

The description acknowledges the general state of the music industry but also references any number of Bloodshot events that had to be canceled, including annual South by Southwest events in March 2020, where many of the artists on this compilation had been scheduled to perform. The emphasis on community and pressing economic concerns are also not surprising. Such a response was not unique to the label, as other entities released projects, streaming playlists, and video content throughout the pandemic. For example, in the early weeks of 2021, the album *The Next Waltz, Vol. 3* (2020), a compilation produced by Americana artist Bruce Robison, featuring numerous Americana artists, began moving up the Americana Radio Albums Chart, and soon reached the number one position for the week of February 9, 2021 (Irons 2020).

Although the distinction between the practices of mainstream, major labels and small(er) entities is becoming less clear, the role of independent labels must not be overlooked in the modern music industry, and in country specifically. Clearly, indie does not equate quality or success, yet small-scale production and consumption practices are just as important as those of major labels and mass-oriented practices, as demonstrated by the history and work of Bloodshot Records. From its origins and role within alt.country to its longevity and influence within Americana, the record label's emphasis on community, collaboration, history and tradition, and live events remains incredibly relevant.

Prior to the pandemic, the changing landscape of the music industry was evident with the rise of streaming services and inviting alternate and varied modes of production and consumption of music; Covid-19 further illuminated such practices and trends. Within this evolving landscape, artists of all statures work to control their careers and output, and collaborations, live performances, and music festivals are critical to artists' success. Of course, Bloodshot Records was not the first label or entity to rely on compilations and collaboration, yet for the majority of musicians and artists, access to resources and capital, rather than modes of practice, remains the stark dividing line between indies and majors. As such, the significance of small-scale production and consumption is apparent, and the contributions of independent record labels are critical to a thriving and diverse country music. Whether artists approach these as a stepping stone to mainstream country recognition and success, that is, major label deals and the like, grassroots music-making and musical community can be an important and valuable end unto itself. Regardless of the scope of production and consumption, we can all agree with Miller (1999) that "country music doesn't have to suck."

PART IV

Boundary Work

13 | Playing at the Border

Navajo (Diné) Country Music and Border Town Racism

KRISTINA JACOBSEN

May 1, 2009: I arrive early and by myself at the American Legion Hall, Unit 75,[1] in Cortez, Colorado, to set up my lap steel guitar and check into the local Motel 6 before my gig that evening with the band, Native Country. As I walk past the American flag by the entrance, I am greeted by a small group of aging Anglo Veterans, wearing WWII and Korean War baseball caps. "Are you with the band?" they ask curiously, querying if I am the band's manager when I respond affirmatively. I confirm the band name written on the marquee, adding that the band is from the nearby Navajo Nation, and that the bandleader and manager, Tommy Bia, is also Diné. There is a long pause, then; "I didn't know it was a skin band,"[2] a septuagenarian in red suspenders named Ron[3] says, disappointment registering on his face. Ron goes on to state that, for him, "Native" means being "native" to the state of Colorado, not "Native American," and so he assumed it was an "Anglo" (white)[4] country band.

In Navajo reservation "border towns" like Cortez – communities notorious for their histories of racial tension – how do Navajo country bands assert an Indigenous presence when playing in "Anglo" venues like the American Legion Hall? By contrast, what sort of erasure takes place in historically Indigenous territories and towns (such as Cortez) that border Indigenous nations, such that the word "Native," in a surreal turn of settler nativism, comes to signify not Indigenous but an Anglo, Coloradan identity, instead (Razack 2002)? Finally, how do "Native bands"[5] become

---

[1] American Legion Auxiliary, Unit 75, Ute Mountain Post, Cortez. www.facebook.com/pages/American-Legion-Cortez/1626875777551482.

[2] "Skin" is a pejorative term used to refer to Native peoples throughout the American west. Like many insider/outsider terms, "skin" can also be a term that is used affirmatively when used by individuals that identify as Native.

[3] "Ron" is a pseudonym.

[4] "Anglo" in its US southwestern usage is a term I use throughout this chapter and denotes a white person of European origin.

[5] "Native band" in this context typically refers to Navajo country bands. When Navajo musicians play other genres of music, the genre is usually specified, as in "Native punk bands" or "rez metal." Thus, the unmarked term "Native band" evidences country music's hegemony within this music scene.

perceived as both "matter out of place" and "sound out of place," when playing a genre of music perceived by many Americans as both "white" and originating from the American south (Douglas 1966, 44; Hammond 2011; Mann 2008)?

Drawing on two and a half years of ethnographic fieldwork[6] singing and playing with three Diné (Navajo) country bands both on and off the Navajo reservation (Jacobsen 2017), I explore how one Native band lives and responds to border town racism and settler nativism in towns bordering the Navajo Nation, the largest Indian reservation in the United States. I illustrate how country music, a genre that has been embraced by Diné people since the late 1930s, serves as a flashpoint for racialized forms of difference and belonging within the liminal space of the Navajo reservation border town. Settler nativism is defined as settler disavowal of Indigenous land, where "European settlers thus *become* the original inhabitants and the group most entitled to the fruits of citizenship" (Razack 2002, 1–2). I argue here that music performance becomes a condensed site for the enactment and negotiation of border town tensions, microaggressions, and more blatant forms of racism, providing key insights into the ways in which Indigenous country music unsettles Colorado's own settler-colonial history and the histories of the border town southwest.

Positionality and Fieldwork Methodologies

My own positionality performing with Diné country bands was complicated by my whiteness, my class privilege, and my gender. A Scandinavian-American woman from rural New England, I have lived as a guest for extended periods in various parts of the rural Navajo Nation, including Crownpoint, Rough Rock, Tsaile, Chinle, and Many Farms. I have also now lived and taught in two Navajo border towns – Flagstaff and Albuquerque – for much of my adult life. In the bands I played with, my Anglo identity often created assumptions based on skin-color privilege and social class in off-reservation spaces. For example, as recounted in the story

---

[6] Fieldwork took place from 2008–2011 and was made possible with funding from the Wenner-Gren Foundation, the Jacobs Research Funds (Whatcom Museum), and the Lynn Reyer Award in Tribal Community Development. Ethnographic research permits were granted by the Navajo Nation Historic Preservation Department and the Duke University Internal Review Board.

above, bar owners, bartenders, and managers often assumed that I, as the only Anglo and the only woman in the band, was either the band's manager, the PR person, or the bandleader of Native Country (I was not).[7]

In country music, women are more frequently featured as vocalists and less often as "lead" players, or instrumentalists that play the main licks and solos during the song. This also held true in the reservation bands in which I played. Although I play the lap steel guitar and was prepared to play in a lead player capacity at gigs, I was rarely afforded that opportunity. Rather, with most bands, I typically played short instrumental "fills" between the vocal lines for instrumental color on my steel behind the lead guitar player or played acoustic rhythm guitar.

Finally, in the anecdote recounted at the beginning of this chapter, there was an important element of assumed "white complicity" at play, in which Ron assumed that he and I, as people who both presented as "white," could assume a common viewpoint and therefore use racist terms in each other's company with a wink and a nod. When I voiced discomfort and did not agree to the terms of the conversation he proposed, I was also given a milder version of the treatment the rest of the band received when they arrived later that night and played a vibrant and largely successful show: that of being made to feel unwelcome, and out of place.

Native Country Band

Native Country is comprised of four Diné men and, during the time I played with them, one Anglo woman.[8] The band, pictured in Figure 13.1, was founded by band leader and lead singer Tommy Bia[9] of Many Farms, Arizona (Navajo Nation). The band consists of Tommy's son Arlondo on drums, Tommy's nephew LeAnder Bia on lead guitar, and Tommy's paternal grandfather by clan[10], Errison Littleben, on vocals and

---

[7] For a similar dynamic between Anglo and Indigenous musicians, see David Samuels' *Putting a Song on Top of It: Expression and Identity on the San Carlos Apache Reservation* (2004).

[8] I continue to sing and play with the band when I am invited to do so but am no longer a full-time band member.

[9] At the request of band members, I use musicians' real names throughout this chapter.

[10] A person with four Diné grandparents will have four Diné clans, typically introduced when people are first meeting one another to establish relationality and kinship between one another.

Figure 13.1. Native Country Band at Windy Mesa Bar in the Navajo border town of Page, Arizona.
Photo Credit: Doug Reilly, used with permission

rhythm guitar. During my tenure as a full-time band member with Native Country, I sang harmony and lead vocals and played guitar. Like the rural high desert from which the band members hail, the band's sound[11] is raw and gritty, with a strong bass drum and electrified country sound, replete with lots of vocal reverb. The Native Country setlist featured many of the songs in the larger "Native band" canon, including hard country, honky-tonk, and historical ballads from the 1960s, '70s, and '80s by Waylon Jennings, Johnny Horton, Merle Haggard, Ernest Tubb, Johnny Cash, and Gary Stewart.[12] Other songs in our set included hits by other Indigenous country groups, such as the well-known song "Sweet Navajo Love" by the White Mountain Apache band, Apache Spirit, and rock and surf-rock tunes from the 1960s and '70s. When I joined the band, we also

[11] A selection of recordings from Native Country can be heard at: https://soundcloud.com/kristinajacobsenmusic/thanks-a-lot?in=kristinajacobsenmusic/sets/native-country-band-songs
[12] Songs included "Tonight the Bottle Let Me Down" and "Silver Wings" (Merle Haggard), "Room at the Top of the Stairs" (Eddie Rabbitt), "Cindy" (The Beach Boys), "Whispering Pines" (Johnny Horton), "Thanks a lot" (Ernest Tubb), "She's Acting Single, I'm Drinking Doubles" (Gary Stewart), and "I Still Miss Someone" (Johnny Cash).

began to cover songs by female vocalists and songwriters such as Kitty Wells, Loretta Lynn, and Lucinda Williams.[13] Songs on the setlist also included duets between me and Tommy, such as Waylon Jennings and Anita Carter's "I've Got You," Freddy Fender's "Before the Next Teardrop Falls," and Kris Kristofferson and Lorrie Morgan's version of "Help Me Make It Through the Night." Most songs played in the Native band canon are cover songs,[14] and most songs are performed in English, with occasional Navajo loan words replacing pronouns and place names (Jacobsen 2009).

Native bands play primarily live dance music, as their performances are often accompanied by the two-step, a partner dance that moves in a counterclockwise direction. Sets, both on-reservation and off, feature little-to-no stage patter between songs (typically delivered in a mix of Navajo and English), and shows usually last for four hours, running from 9 p.m. to 1 a.m. with one brief break in the middle. Basic instrumentation for most reservation country bands is electric bass, electric lead guitar, electric or acoustic rhythm guitar, drums and a lead singer; fiddles, steel guitars, and three-part harmonies onstage are rare, and bands that feature them stand out in this very local scene. Most musicians are self-taught or learned the rudimentary skills of their instrument in school or at church and then continued to study on their own to achieve playing mastery.

Playing in a band can be grueling, thankless work, and bands often drive between one to four hours, one way, to play a gig. Pay from a gig rarely covers more than a musician's gas mileage and a few meals (typically $100/person or less), and, depending on how well known the band is and how widely a show was promoted, audiences of up to 300 people to sometimes only three to four people at a show. Clearly, bands do not play for the money they receive. Rather, during my ethnographic research, I learned that musicians play instead for the love of the music, the camaraderie it fosters among male musicians, in particular, and for the ability to get out of one's hometown and see new parts of the southwest (Jacobsen 2009, 2017). Many bands are all-Diné, but others are intertribal and interracial, featuring musicians from a broad swath of southwestern Indigenous communities along with Anglo and Hispanic musicians. Similarly, audiences at

---

[13] These songs included "It Wasn't God Who Made Honky Tonk Angels" (Kitty Wells), "You Ain't Woman Enough to Take My Man" and "Fist City" (Loretta Lynn), and "Crescent City" (Lucinda Williams).

[14] Although there are many talented Diné songwriters, original songs are less often featured in the Native band canon.

Native band "dances" are a mix of Native, Anglo, and Hispanic fans; for the gigs I participated in, our audiences were majority Diné. During our one and a half years of steady gigging in 2008–2009, most of our gigs were played in off-reservation border town bars (in Cortez, Gallup, Page, Winslow) or in other neighboring Native Nations (Hopi, Jicarilla Apache).

Diné Military Service and Country Music

The band members of Native Country belong to a higher status, landholding family[15] from the central part of the Navajo Nation (the Chinle Valley) with some family members historically holding visible posts in the Navajo Tribal Council, the Navajo Nation's primary governing body. Band members Tommy, Arlondo, Errison, and LeAnder work "day jobs" in facilities management, biomedical engineering, maintenance, and security, respectively, at Indian Health Services (IHS) clinics on the reservation. All band members speak fluent English and also speak and understand the Navajo language (Diné bizaad). Thus, and contradicting the narrative of country music as an exclusively working-class form of music, by reservation standards, Native Country band members are solidly economically middle class, and, in terms of social status and prestige, they are upper-middle class.

The band members also have strong ties to the US military, an entity in which Diné and US Native nations are disproportionately represented – over 10 percent of Navajo Nation serves in the US military (National Indian Council on Aging 2019). Many Diné citizens see military service as prestigious, where Diné veterans see their service as defending the US nation, but also, crucially, as defending their own nation, the Navajo Nation, as well (Jacobsen 2017; O'Connor and Brown 2013). As an example, bandleader Tommy Bia's three brothers, his niece, and his nephew have each served in branches of the Army, the Navy, and the Marines. Most significantly, Tommy's father, the late Andrew Bia Sr. (pictured in Figure 13.2), served as a Navajo code talker from 1944 to 1945, where he trained at California's Camp Pendleton, served in Hawai'i, Guam, and South Japan, and helped to create an unbreakable double code for the US Marines during World War II, definitively aiding the victory in the Pacific Theater (Durrett 2009). Today, Code Talkers hold an especially high status within Diné society and are considered to be modern-day

---

[15] Owning land and livestock and having a grazing permit are all markers of status, both past and present, in Diné communities.

Figure 13.2. Photo of the late Andrew Bia, in southern California, 1944, shortly after his release from the Marines.

Photo used with permission of Tommy and Arlondo Bia

warriors who fought not only for the protection of their people but also for the preservation of their heritage language, *Diné bizaad*.

Andrew Bia Sr. was a proud veteran, a Marine, a successful rancher, and a Navajo Nation tribal employee. He was also a lover of country music, and especially of Johnny Cash. Andrew was fully bilingual in Navajo and English at a time when, in the mid-1940s, few Diné people on the reservation were. He had a cosmopolitan view of the world, loved to travel, and imparted this passion and a love for music to his twelve children, including his son, Tommy Leroy, and his grandson, Arlondo.

Mapping the Navajo Nation and Its Borders

Located in the Four Corners region of the American Southwest, the Navajo Nation (Figure 13.3) has about 173,000 citizens living within its borders and a total enrolled citizenry of approximately 332,000 (Arizona Rural Policy Institute, n.d.). A sovereign nation with its own judicial, executive,

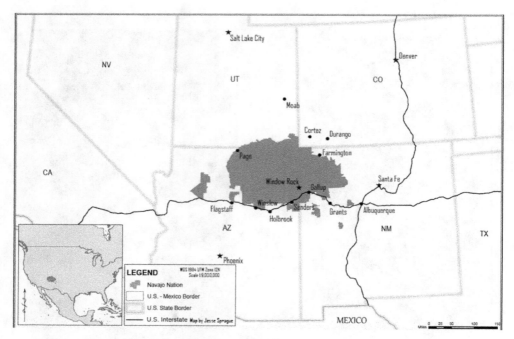

Figure 13.3. Map of the Navajo Nation.
Map created by Jesse T. Sprague, used with permission

and legislative bodies, Navajo Nation citizenry is as culturally, economic-ally, religiously, and racially diverse as the US nation that surrounds it. The Navajo Nation spans some 27,000 square miles – roughly the size of the US state of West Virginia – and includes one main reservation and three, separate "satellite" reservations. Close to one-third of Diné choose to live off the reservation, leaving *Diné Bikéyah* (the historical Navajo homeland) for employment, education, and military service (Arizona Rural Policy Institute, n.d.). In addition to living in almost every state in the Union as well as overseas, many Diné citizens also live in high numbers in the border towns directly surrounding the reservation, towns such as Albuquerque, Gallup, Farmington, and Grants in New Mexico; Winslow, Sanders, Flagstaff, and Page in Arizona; and Durango and Cortez in Colorado.

As per Navajo Nation Tribal Council Law, the Navajo reservation is also "dry," meaning that no alcohol can be sold or consumed on Navajo Nation land; thus, there are no bars.[16] This means that, for the fifty-plus country

---

[16] Exceptions to this rule are the bars in three of four Navajo-owned gaming enterprises: Fire Rock Casino, Northern Edge Casino, and Twin Arrows Casino Resort.

bands on the reservation, the majority of Native band gigs – typically in bars, casinos, or private clubs – take place off-reservation in border towns. The working gig economy for many Diné musicians depends on playing shows in border towns such as Cortez, however fraught these places may be.

However, playing in venues far from home also puts traveling musicians in a uniquely vulnerable situation and speaks to the larger structural inequalities undergirding both the need to travel for gigs and the social and economic precarity of Diné musicians in border town spaces. For example, bandmates told stories about aggressions and microaggressions in the space of the border town, where their families would get served last at a local diner, or didn't get served at all, or received poor table service because management has told the waitstaff that "Navajo people don't tip." At a local Walmart in Page, Arizona, Arlondo the drummer and I were followed around the store as we shopped for music gear by an Anglo woman who gave us visibly hostile stares as we stood in line to pay. Later that night, the owner renegotiates the door money, after the show, at the biker bar we're playing.

Cortez is a rural ranching town of a little under 9,000 residents, located in the "high desert" of the Colorado Plateau, about forty miles north of the northern boundary of the Navajo reservation and the Navajo town of Shiprock (*Tsé Bit'á'í*), New Mexico. Founded in 1886 as a labor camp for Anglo men[17] building water diversion channels for the lush Montezuma valley, Cortez is now a majority Anglo town (around 66%), with sizable Hispanic (15.6%), Ute and Navajo (14.1%, combined) communities. Named after the Spanish *conquistador*, Hernán Cortés, Cortez's economy depends on tourists en route to Mesa Verde National Park and to tribal parks on the Navajo Nation, including Four Corners National Monument and Monument Valley Tribal Park. As the name of the American Legion Hall, "Ute Mountain Post" implies, Cortez, and the neighboring towns of Mancos and Durango, have also been home to multiple trading posts since their inception; the Anglo man, Ron, from the opening story, was a trader and owned a trading post on the Ute Mountain Ute Reservation. The town's economy also depends on money spent by citizens from the Navajo Nation, Southern Ute, and Ute Mountain Ute reservations, who often do their weekly errands and grocery shopping in Cortez. Some Cortez

---

[17] According to Maureen Gerhold, local Anglo ranchers and white European immigrants provided the labor pool for this project; local Indigenous and Hispanic residents were not hired (in Kendrick 1981).

business owners suggest that around 80 percent of revenue spent in Cortez comes directly from the pockets of Native citizens (Navajo Nation Human Rights Commission 2010).

Despite these statistics, downtown Cortez itself, like so many southwestern border towns, feels very much like a white social space (Lee and LaDousa 2015), where business owners, city council members, and the people seen in local coffee shops and restaurants along Cortez's main street are primarily Anglo. As a "patriotic veterans' organizations devoted to mutual helpfulness" (American Legion Hall, n.d.), Legion Halls are also known by many as racially homogenous, hetero-normative white social spaces where borders and boundaries, particularly those of race, citizenship, and gender, are strictly policed (Fletcher 2017; Murphy 2018). In border towns, Anglo audiences are often the default demographic for Native bands. As Gilbert and Malcolm (2019, 1) note, "border towns depend upon the products, labor, and economic activity of Native Americans . . ., yet power and resources are disproportionately held by non-Native residents."

Cortez is located on unceded Indigenous land belonging to the Ute Mountain Ute Tribe, Southern Ute Tribe, and the Navajo Nation. It is an occupied and resettled place, and as such, in the logic of settler colonialism, its non-Native residents seek to erase that history and to tightly police boundaries to eliminate identities and sounds which threaten the clarity of the border town's reinvention as white social space. In these and other ways, "Border towns, then, practice colonization as a collective value" (Denetdale 2016, 125).

Like so many southwestern border towns, Cortez is also a town known for its racism and its violent enforcing of cultural boundaries and increased police surveillance of Indigenous bodies (Silversmith 2015; Quintero 2020). This is in keeping with the "long-standing legacy of violence experienced by Native Americans in majority-white urban spaces abutting tribal lands" (Gilbert and Malcolm 2019, 1). For example, Cortez is known for a vicious form of hate crime known as "Indian rolling," where non-Native teenagers sometimes "roll" – slang for various forms of bodily assault – Native men experiencing houselessness (Donaldson 2006). In Cortez, Farmington, Albuquerque, and elsewhere, these and other explicitly violent acts have resulted in severe injury and death to Indigenous people, many of them Diné men. As one unsheltered Diné man living in Cortez shared at a public hearing of the Navajo Nation Human Rights Commission: "These guys in Cortez, redneck kids practice their Tae Kwon Do on us drunks" (Denetdale 2016, 126).

Another example of the policing of perceived social boundaries in Cortez, in this case of both citizenship and gendered identity, is witnessed in the 2009 documentary film, *Two Spirits* (directed by Lydia Nibley). *Two Spirits* documents the life and brutal death of self-identified two-spirit, Cortez citizen and Diné high school student, F.C. Martinez, murdered due to their gender fluidity at the hands of an Anglo teenager behind the Cortez Fairgrounds. Other murders of Diné people, in Farmington, Albuquerque, and in Winslow, Arizona, at the hands of Anglo and Hispanic teenagers and police, attest to systemic violence inflicted on Diné bodies as a mechanism for differentiating "settler futures" from "Indian pasts" (Baker 2006; Keane 2014; Landry 2014; Paterson 2015; Denetdale 2016; Tuck and Yang 2016).

But there is also often great affection associated with these same border towns: "town" is the place you go with your family each week, traveling long distances in your "ride" to do errands, share a favorite meal, attend a livestock auction, sell your cattle, and purchase hay and ranching supplies; it's the place where you spend quality family time with loved ones. I recall traveling with Diné friends, for example, back from a livestock auction in Cortez, with a newly purchased sheep in a large wire dog crate in the back of my pickup truck. As we rolled through the Walmart parking lot in downtown Cortez, our sheep bleating loudly, a Diné woman unknown to us jokingly called out from the sidewalk: "mutton[18] time!" to uproarious response and shared laughter. Families I have known appreciate the quality of the alfalfa sold in Cortez and say Colorado alfalfa is richer and denser than its New Mexico or Arizona counterparts and also enjoy the beautiful drive through the now-lush Montezuma valley, the product of Cortez's irrigation history. Border towns, for Diné families and for Native bands, are a sort of economic and cultural catch-22, where it's difficult to live with them and even more difficult to live without them. In subtle and explicit ways, Diné people in border towns are often made to feel that they, rather than settler communities, are matter out of place.

"Matter *out* of Place"

Anthropologist Mary Douglas (1966), in her chapter "Pollution," gives the example of "dirt" as a type of matter out of place. She uses the concept of

---

[18] A Diné delicacy.

dirt to explain how human communities create categories of belonging and unbelonging based on perceptions of what they see as "clean" and what they see as dirty or "polluted." In particular, she shows how what is considered "dirt" or "dirty" is completely context-defined. Dirt in a garden is perceived differently than dirt on a kitchen countertop; "dirty" sneakers on the floor versus sneakers on a bedroom pillow changes the perception of cleanliness of those same sneakers. Dirt is not an absolute category. Transgression or breach of norms of cleanliness and pollution, she notes, "is punished by political decree, sometimes by attack on the transgressor, and sometimes by grave or trivial sanctions" (199). Crucially, Douglas traces the ways the concepts of cleanliness and pollution are translated to people, where marginalized communities who are seen as "matter out of place" are viewed by the dominant community as unclean, as vectors of contagion, and are consequently treated as sub-human.

In the case of the southwestern border town, these judgments are made primarily by non-Native, and most typically Anglo-identified, settler communities living in formerly Indigenous territories. Here, "marginal or ill-defined social states" (Douglas 1966, 200) such as people in transit, unsheltered individuals, people with ambiguous or fluid gender identities, or those perceived as racial, political, or cultural "outsiders," are seen as dangerous for the social boundaries that they subvert through the sheer fact of their existence. Crucially, this perception of subverted social boundaries sanctions non-Native border town residents to treat socially marginalized Indigenous community members, in turn, "like dirt."

In addition to social boundaries and social states, physical margins and geopolitical borders also play a part in Douglas's research. Matter out of place applies "not only [to] marginal social states, but [to] all margins, [where] the edges of all boundaries which are used in ordering the social experience, are treated as dangerous and polluting" (Douglas 1966, 200). As Estes (2015) and Yazzie (2014) note, jurisdictional borders between the reservation and adjacent state land become the explicit site of extreme police surveillance and dramatic partitioning of Native and non-Native social spaces (see also Estes et al. 2021).

We see such a partitioning in Ron's commentary on the band's identity, relayed at the beginning of this chapter, and in the discomfort he expressed in learning that we were a "Native" band.[19] Here, the idea of a Diné country band, playing a historically "white" genre of music on occupied Indigenous

---

[19] Speaking to the band about this incident, much later, they seemed in many respects less upset by it than I was. Ron's response, although disappointing, didn't surprise them.

land, is a disruption to a given and naturalized settler social order, one which associates whiteness with American country music. Furthermore, we can see how a gender-mixed Diné band called "Native Country," hired to play in the white social space that is the Cortez American Legion Hall, also threatened multiple and clear-cut categories of "us" versus "them," "settler" versus "native," and "man" versus "woman," fundamentally undermining the purity and "cleanliness" of that exclusionary space. Finally, the fact that the band itself was interracial, featuring four Diné men and one Anglo woman, could be further understood to unsettle a border town logic that discourages contact between "settlers" and "Natives" in general and, per-haps, between Native men and Anglo women, demarcating and partition-ing Anglo bodies from Indigenous bodies in the built environment of the American Legion Hall. As Diné historian Jennifer Denetdale notes, "We are still treated like we don't belong . . . like we're the invaders" (in Gilbert and Malcolm 2019, 1).

Sound as Matter Out of Place

But sound itself can also be perceived as a kind of matter out of place. In their analysis of "noise," and of what is deemed "noise" versus what gets called "music," Pickering and Rice (2017, 2) examine how definitions of noise and noisiness are essentially anything heard as "unwanted sound." "Noise" is something that disrupts a given social and sonic landscape, and thus is perceived as deviant sonic behavior (Pickering and Rice 2017, 1; Chávez 2017, 199). Similar to dirt, what is deemed noise is also highly subjective and is not an absolute category. Rather, it is a value judgment on the desirability and appropriateness of a sound within a given social context. As Douglas (1966, 10) noted, "what is clean in relation to one thing may be unclean in relation to another." In a similar way to how social transgressors are treated as "dirty" or contagious, sounds that are "anom-alous and ambiguous ... are often seen as disgusting, disruptive, and dangerous" (Pickering and Rice 2017, 7).

Noise as "sound out of place" helps us to contextualize the response of our red-suspendered septuagenarian. Indeed, Ron's response and dismissal of the band was a response not only of discomfort but also of mild disgust. Our music, even before we had begun playing it, was already noise to him. Native Country was heard, in this moment of intercultural encounter, not only as matter out of place but sound out of place. Consequently, Ron decided to hear our music as "noisy."

However, if Native bands are perceived by some as being matter out of place in border town spaces such as Cortez and in venues such as the American Legion, Native bands are perceived as being profoundly rooted *in* place when performing in reservation spaces. As I have documented elsewhere, Diné musicians have been publicly performing country music since at least the early 1950s and listening to country radio since the 1930s; performing country music in reservation spaces is now considered so Diné, and so commonplace, that country music for an older generation of Diné people now forms a part of what is considered Navajo "tradition" (Jacobsen 2009, 2017).[20] Following this, when Diné musicians play other genres of music, such as blues or metal, they sometimes run the risk of being told they "don't sound Navajo." This loaded charge is, in some ways, the Navajo version of calling someone a "hat act" in the country music world, implying that you "wear the hat" but don't "live the lifestyle" (Lewis 1997, 164; Peterson 2004, 98). From this angle, playing country music in reservation spaces is thus a sort of quintessential sounding-in-place and a sounded assertion of being matter-in-place within Indigenous territory and on Diné land.

Colorado NATIVES and The Unbearable Whiteness of Colorado

Within the American Southwest, Colorado is known for a certain kind of whiteness and wealth: it is often a privileged, wealthy, and cloistered whiteness, with clear tensions and distinctions between "native,"[21] more conservative-leaning (and often less wealthy) Coloradans in the rural part of the state, now comprising less than half of the state's population (47%), and more liberal-leaning transplants living in larger, metropolitan centers such as Denver, Boulder, and Colorado Springs. Colorado transplants in particular are also associated with skiing and the multimillion-dollar Colorado ski industry, where "ski culture" aggressively cultivates its own kind of white social space (Coleman 1996, 590). As Coleman (1996, 1) notes in "The Unbearable Whiteness of Skiing," "in the American West, a region noted for its racial and ethnic diversity, ski resorts have remained as white as snow."

---

[20] For younger Diné, punk, metal, and hip-hop are now also very popular and have large followings on-reservation and off.

[21] For clarity, non-Native Coloradans identifying as "native" to Colorado are denoted using a lower case "n."

In contrast to the neighboring states of New Mexico and Arizona, where Hispanic and Indigenous histories and presences are more palpably seen and felt,[22] Colorado has rewritten its settler history as the "other Alps," a rugged resort destination associated with Scandinavian histories of outdoor recreation and a Nordic, alpine experience (Coleman 1996). While Colorado is known for some of the most brutal massacres and labor suppressions in the American West, including the Sand Creek (1864) and Ludlow (1914) massacres, to the unwitting Coloradan moving to the state today, it is as if the brutality of these events has been excised from collective Colorado memory, replaced by the "purity" and whiteness of the powder snow its many ski resorts now make.

But another, more rural kind of whiteness is also cultivated in Colorado. In towns like Cortez, akin to the Bundy family's[23] identification as "rebel cowboys," we also see rural Anglo westerners bent on taking back what they perceive as "their" land, rewriting a history of settler nativism that places them front and center in Colorado's present and future (Levin 2016). In this narrative, Indigenous communities are framed as something of the past but not of the present or the future. Perhaps unsurprisingly, this same demographic also features numerous country music fans, represented by the aging country music fans I encountered at the Legion Hall on that May afternoon in Cortez.

Nowhere is this suppression of memory and strategic reinvention of the present more visible than in the popular Colorado bumper sticker juxtaposing the snow-capped peaks of the Colorado Rockies from the Colorado license plate with the word: "NATIVE" (Figure 13.4).

Created in 1979 by oil landman Eric Glade, this "pre-Internet meme" plays on Colorado nativist pride and anti-expansionist anger at the growing number of Colorado transplants and "ski bums" (Kenney 2018). Crucially, and to the confusion and surprise of many non-Coloradans, this bumper sticker does not indicate that the vehicle owner identifies as Native American; rather, it indicates that a person is "native" to the state of

---

[22] As per the 2019 Census, Colorado remains overwhelmingly white (67.1%), with Latino residents comprising 21.7 percent and Indigenous residents ca. 1.6 percent of the state population (United States Census Bureau). By contrast, New Mexico is 37.1 percent "white alone," 49.1 percent Latino, and 10.9 percent Native American (www.census.gov/quickfacts/NM) and Arizona is 54.4 percent "white alone," 31.6 percent Latino and 5.3 percent Native American (www.census.gov/quickfacts/AZ).

[23] The Bundy's are Nevada cattle ranchers, known for their years-long armed standoff with the Federal Bureau of Land Management opposing federal overreach and restrictions use of public lands for grazing purposes.

Figure 13.4. Image of NATIVE bumper sticker

Colorado since settlers arrived in Colorado. Thus, in a bizarre turn, Ron heard a band name like "Native Country" and, likely drawing on discourses of nativism as seen in the NATIVE bumper sticker, thought – or chose to believe – that the band members were Anglo Coloradans instead. Seen from this perspective, the bumper sticker implies that a "native" Coloradan, almost by definition, is *not* Native American: the meme is premised on a kind of implicit and naturalized whiteness built on the erasure of Indigenous presences.

Concluding Thoughts: On Belonging and Settler Nativism

What went into the making of this moment of racialized mis-encounter and boundary fortification in an Indigenous border town in the southwestern United States? Throughout this chapter, I have sought to contextualize and historicize some of the essential threads of our experience as an interracial group of traveling country musicians in Cortez, Colorado.

But there is another, perhaps more straightforward way to narrate the same story. A Diné country band shows up to play a show at the American Legion Hall in Cortez, Colorado, in May of 2009, in a town on sovereign Diné land, close to the northern Diné sacred mountain known as *Dibé Ntsaa* (Mount Hesparus or Big Sheep Mountain). The bandleader's father was a Navajo code talker, and our bandleader, Tommy, grew up in a military family speaking English, Navajo, and some Spanish. He grew up listening to and learning to love country music, from the days when he herded sheep with his brothers and cousins, listening to KOMA (AM 1520) out of Oklahoma City in the 1960s on a battery-powered, AM radio, on a mesa called Carson Mesa, named after the famous and hated American military commander, Kit Carson. Tommy is a successful rancher and farmer, branding his own calves each year, ear notching his sheep, selling his steer, and purchasing hay and ranching supplies in the border town of Cortez, Colorado each month. By any of these metrics – as the son of a lauded veteran, as a country musician, as a rancher, and as a Diné man on his own ancestral land – he belongs.

Acknowledgments

Thank you, first and foremost, to the band, Native Country, for generously allowing me to continue to write about them. Making music with you all has been one of the immense pleasures in my life. Thank you to Graduate Assistant Sasha Arteaga for assistance with copy edits and to colleagues Elspeth Iralu and Kerry F. Thompson for their insightful comments and feedback on this chapter: it is much the better, and I am much the richer, for the conversations we have had.

14 | Country-Loving Mexican Americans

Dual Patriotism and Inevitable Fandom among Mexican American Country Music Lovers[1]

NADINE HUBBS

To say that Mexican Americans are one of the fastest-growing fan groups in US country music is not to say they are new here. People of Mexican descent have been active as country listeners and creators for decades, and Mexican influences have shaped country music from its early days. In this chapter I draw on multidimensional evidence, including conversations and participant-observations with Mexican American country fans in Texas, California, and beyond, to argue that – in addition to being European American, African American, and Native American music (Malone and Laird [1968] 2018; Lewis 2001; Pecknold 2013a; Giddens 2017; Samuels 2004; Jacobsen 2017) – country is Mexican music and thus is "quintessentially American" in ways more profound than this frequent descriptor typically conveys.

I present instances from my fieldwork, including one in which Mexican American fans' *musical* country loving connected to country loving in realms of *national* identification and belonging. Listening to patriotic country songs, these fans' country music loving spurred expression of a distinctly Mexican American, bicultural love of country in the national sense. Here and elsewhere my interlocutors connected with what they regarded as country music's "Mexican values," and they emphasized the role of belonging, not as something Mexican American fans might acquire via country music but in terms of how country music *belongs to* its

[1] This research was generously funded by the University of Michigan Institute for Research on Women and Gender; College of Literature, Science, and the Arts; and Office of Research. It was further enabled by veteran empirical researchers who took time to share their experience and expertise with me, starting with Michele Demers and Emily Youatt. Jason De León shared his interview audio methods and lent me his recorders. Elizabeth F.S. Roberts helped in realms from research to grant writing to reading this chapter and offering valuable comments for improvement. I am grateful to Kate M. Rodriguez and Angelene Ku for their preliminary assistance and Sergio G. Barrera, M. Leslie Santana, and Kerry P. White for essential onsite research assistance. I owe thanks to the editors of this volume for their many astute comments and suggestions, to all the audiences who engaged with this work, and to Jacqueline Avila and Sofía Mosqueda for their input. Ultimate appreciations go to the country-loving Mexican Americans who generously shared their time, experiences, and analyses with me.

Mexican American fans. Underscoring the Mexican origins of cowboy and ranch culture and of the US Southwest itself, they made a powerful case.

The very existence of Mexican American country music lovers – or "Country Mexicans," to borrow a term that has entered the Urban Dictionary – comes as a surprise to some people, especially outside Latine circles.[2] I offer three possible reasons for this response. The first is a strong association between country music and whiteness that is as old as commercial country music itself. In the 1920s the dawning US record industry established "old-time music," later known as country, as a white counterpart to Black "Race records," later known as R&B. Record executives confected these categories to artificially segregate music of Black and white working-class southerners and thus to market racially branded music in the Jim Crow era (Tosches [1977] 1996; Lewis 2001; Miller 2010; Huber 2013; Pecknold 2013a; Hubbs and Royster 2020).[3] Since the moment of its racialized origins, country music has often been heard as white rural or working-class culture and, from there, stereotypically linked to bigotry – sexism, homo- and transphobia, and especially racism (Hubbs 2014). In his article "Why Does Country Music Sound White?" (2008), the geographer Geoff Mann starts from the presumption that country music sounds white and focuses on why (i.e., country lyrics' nostalgia themes and whitewashing of racist US history).

Second is a tendency to associate Mexican Americans primarily or exclusively with Mexico and Mexican culture and often Spanish-language music and entertainments. Most broadly this may bespeak a perspective on "Mexican American" emphasizing "Mexican" over "American."[4] Relatedly, fellow non-Latine colleagues have sometimes expressed surprise on hearing of my research on Mexican American country fandom, which often seems to reflect the academics' own distaste for country music and attributions here of retrograde politics, racist and perhaps anti-immigrant. Some are particularly dubious about the possibility of Mexican American listeners engaging with (read: stomaching) country music's patriotism, which,

---

[2] S.v. "Country Mexican": the 2012 entry defines Country Mexicans as Mexican Americans who love both "country" and Mexican culture and lists country music first among their characteristic love objects: www.urbandictionary.com/define.php?term=Country%20Mexican.

[3] A growing body of scholarship shows how the country music industry "laboriously enforced whiteness" (Pecknold 2013b, 4), actively maintaining country's racialization years after its birth as a commercial music. See Pecknold (2013b), Brady (2013), Burns (2020), Martinez (2020), and Neal (2020).

[4] In the United States, as in Mexico and at the border, the story is far more complex and has been analyzed in terms of transnational and postnational dynamics in musicological studies such as Simonett (2001), Madrid (2011), and Ramos-Kittrell (2020).

according to one recent academic commentator, presents "as a core American value[,] ... often in love it or leave it terms" (Meier 2018, 105). But in fact, my fieldwork with Country Mexicans revealed cherished deep engagements with patriotic US country songs among Mexican American country music fans.

A third likely reason for nonrecognition of Mexican American country music involvements is that some of the elements of country music widely perceived as most emblematically American are actually Mexican.

This chapter derives from field research I conducted in 2017–2019 to illuminate Mexican American involvements in country music, a remarkably potent popular-culture form for examining social, cultural, and political formations. My focus, notably, is not on working-class Spanish-language music of Northern Mexico or the US Southwest, not *norteño*, *ranchera*, or *tejano* music. Rather, it is on engagements and contributions of Mexican-descended people in mainstream US country, a music that has often been framed as "quintessentially American" – as it was, for example, in Ken Burns's 2019 PBS documentary series, *Country Music*.

If the image of a Mexican American country music fan is hard for some people to conjure, the Country Mexican is nevertheless real and, in some parts of the United States, an established presence. And that presence is increasing. In 2016, the Country Music Association (CMA) announced that Hispanics had become one of the fastest-growing fan groups in country music (Unknown 2016).[5] I see good reasons to believe that the majority of those Latine fans are Mexican American. For one thing, country music has long been prominent in Southwestern states that border Mexico and have large Mexican American populations – which suggests the need to study country music as border culture, as this chapter emphasizes. Another indicator is the fact that Mexican Americans make up nearly two-thirds of all Latines in the United States.[6]

Given the rapid and little-recognized growth in the ranks of Country Mexicans; the importance of race, ethnicity, and migration in current national dialogues; and the persistent underrepresentation of Latines in US media (Smith et al. 2015), Mexican Americans' popular-culture engagements merit attention – and surely no less when they involve a music often associated with white bigots. In light of the scarce data on Mexican

---

[5] Mexican Americans' presence was evident, too, among the survivors and victims of the 2017 mass shooting at the Route 91 Harvest country music festival in Las Vegas.

[6] The US Census American Community Survey estimates that people of Mexican descent comprised 63 percent of all Latines in the United States in 2018 https://data.census.gov/cedsci/table?q=latino%20population&tid=ACSDT5Y2017.B03001

American popular-culture engagements, I solicited first-hand accounts from Mexican American country music lovers. In addition to this empirical research, my work entails historical and musicological research. I examine the present and past of country music engagements among fans, artists, and influencers of Mexican descent and illuminate social and cultural life and belonging on this site. And I link my efforts to produce knowledge about Mexican American musical engagements to the larger stakes attaching to such knowledge. As David F. Garcia (2019) shows, long-standing ignorance about historical Latine musical contributions in the United States helps to perpetuate anti-Latine racism up to today.

Spending Time with Country Mexicans in the Southwest and Midwest

In 2017–2019, I carried out fieldwork with Country Mexicans in the Southwestern states of Texas and California and in the Midwest, using participant-observation in dance clubs, conducting one-on-one interviews, and leading focus groups. My eighteen interlocutors surely did not represent all Mexican Americans, but they ranged in age from twenty-one to seventy-four, varied by region, and included both LGBTQ- and cis/straight-identified men and women. They skewed strongly working class by background (of these, some remained in the working class, and some pursued upward mobility), and all identified as Mexican American country music fans.

Millennial Country Mexicans in South Texas

In the Texas borderlands I spent time at Hillbilly's, a popular country dance club in the McAllen metropolitan area, where communities' Latine population rates ranged from 92 percent to 100 percent. Even in late July the club filled up on a Wednesday, its weekly student night. A few hundred people, mostly twenty-something millennials and about 95 percent of Mexican descent, two-stepped, line-danced, and socialized into the wee hours. The club took its name from the Appalachian figure and pejorative label that represented commercial country music in its early decades, the 1920s–1950s. But the crowd inside – nearly all wearing boots in the triple-digit heat – bore greater resemblance to the Southwestern cowboy (and occasionally, cowgirl) figure that started to replace the "hillbilly" in the 1940s, when country music nationally took a turn into western swing (Ginell 1994; Cusic 2011).

I also traveled to the nearby university town of Edinburg and led two focus groups comprised of eight Mexican American millennial country fans, aged twenty-two to thirty-four.[7] Some were straight and some LGBTQ-identified, but all were Mexican-born and bilingual, came up working class, and earned college degrees in this town, at the University of Texas Rio Grande Valley. The alma mater of the eminent Chicanx, feminist, and queer studies scholar Gloria Anzaldúa, UTRGV is known for its strong Chicane studies programs.[8] In focus groups inside the university's Center for Mexican American Studies, I asked participants what they liked about country music. Within the context of our country music discussion, I asked, too, what Americanness meant.

Focus-group participants described country music as uniquely relatable to their lives, feelings, and (in their words) "Mexican values" of family, faith and morality, hard work ("without ever getting rich," one woman added), love, and patriotism. Notably, their claims and descriptions arose later, in virtually identical terms, among Mexican American country fans from other parts of the United States, suggesting widely shared perceptions, among these Mexican American country music lovers, of resonance between country music and Mexican American cultural values. Recently the Mexican American country artist Leah Turner likewise claimed that "Latino culture and country music culture 100% mirror one another" and illustrated by listing the same cultural values – though she replaced patriotism with drinking (Martinez 2021a). There is no universal agreement on what counts as Mexican American values, and the question is contested among scholars (Garcia 1995, 6). Different surveys and studies offer different accounts of such values, but family, faith, and patriotism typically rise to the top (see, e.g., Gebler et al. 1970; Garcia 1973; Knight et al. 2010). Less contested is the general notion that core cultural values are a "fundamental component of a group's culture" that unify, identify, and symbolize the group and its members (whatever the group). Rejecting them can lead to permanent exclusion from the group, and violating them can inspire social outrage and even political rebellion (García-Quijano and Lloréns 2019).

The country fans in my South Texas focus groups heard country music in terms of a working-class ethos and felt attached to this aspect of the music, even as some pursued middle- and upper-class careers and lives

---

[7] Millennials were born 1981–1996. Of the eight participants in my Edinburg focus groups, six were late millennials born between April 1992 and February 1995 (aged twenty-two to twenty-five at the time of our July 2017 meeting), and the other two were millennials born in 1983 and 1987, respectively (aged thirty-four and twenty-nine).

[8] I use the gender-inclusive terms *Latine*, *Chicane*, and *Tejane* throughout this chapter, except in cases where I know an individual's more specific self-identification. As Richard T. Rodríguez (2017) points out, the *Latinx* label was coined with queer-specific meaning by queer figures including Anzaldúa.

(one woman who strongly identified with what she heard as country's working-class ethos was in medical school). This jibes with sociologist Pierre Bourdieu's (1977) notion of *habitus* as a set of attitudes, tastes, and dispositions that are shared among people of similar backgrounds and endure beyond changes of circumstance and station. Some participants invoked a grassroots mantra, "Remember where you came from," to reconcile the potentially delicate issues of rising out of the social class of one's family and childhood. The phrase is a reminder not to lose respect for one's people or place of origins in the pursuit of upward mobility.[9] Just as country music has often served among Anglo-white fans as a marker of working-class status or identification, country fandom also marked working-class origins and identifications among these variously upwardly mobile Mexican American interlocutors.

But in Texas as in California and elsewhere, Mexican Americans' country engagements further signified in terms of bicultural identification. One serious country dancer and regular concertgoer described country serving as a "bridge between my two cultures." A fiftyish professor and health sciences researcher from Indiana, this Veracruz, Mexico, native also confirmed country music's alignment with her "Mexican Values" (specifying that, as an atheist, she related to country songs' morality, not faith). Separately, both she and another Mexican-born, Midwest-based Gen X (b. 1965–1980) academic offered that the themes of loss and sadness in some country songs reminded them of similar themes in *mariachi* songs, which the writer Brenda Salinas has termed "crazy tragic."[10]

Multigenerational Country Mexicans in Northern and Southern California

In addition to first-generation college-educated millennials in Texas, I spent time with Mexican American country fans in greater Los Angeles and up the coast in Santa Clara County, California. Ranging in age from twenty-one to seventy-four, they included students, tradesmen, a tattoo artist, a cook, and a schoolteacher. By comparison to the Texans I spoke

---

[9] The US historian Jessica Wilkerson (2018) unpacks this phrase, which her grandmother said to her when she left rural East Tennessee for college. Wilkerson hears multiple resonances here, a "call to home" but also "a way of disciplining," a warning against the ways education could change one so as to be "no longer recognizable" in one's place of origins. I would also compare the southern colloquialism "Don't get above your raisin'," which served as the title of a 1951 song by bluegrass legends Lester Flatt and Earl Scruggs and of Malone (2002): *Don't Get Above Your Raisin': Country Music and the Southern Working Class*.

[10] Salinas (2016) was discussing Vicente Fernández's iconic 1978 mariachi track "Volver, Volver."

with, these Californians demonstrated certain differences in their perspectives on country music and pathways to country involvement. For example, Leo, a twenty-four-year-old welder from East L.A., was a Chicano-identified music lover who came to country music through his primary engagements with punk and ska. These engagements included the Orange County punk band Social Distortion, which has many Mexican American followers and in its four-decade history has had two long-serving Mexican American drummers, Gonzalo "Charlie" Quintana and David Hidalgo, Jr., Leo came to country music, too, through the elders in his music-loving family, especially his "uncles" (as he calls his father's cousins).

I spoke with Leo and two of his thirty-something uncles – millennials all – in the Orange County shop where one worked as a highly regarded artist creating Chicane-themed tattoos and designs on paper. All three showed certain California leanings in their musical engagements, including a penchant for classic Bakersfield country stars Buck Owens and Merle Haggard. Without prompting, however, they also echoed the Texans' previous statements about country music's working-class "Mexican values." In every focus group, in California and elsewhere, we discussed the appeal of country music to Mexican American listeners. Participants expressed appreciation for country lyrics and instrumentals and some, when prompted by my questions, drew comparisons to Mexican music they knew – styles such as mariachi and genres such as *corrido*, a narrative ballad form originating in Northern Mexico in the late nineteenth century and still thriving today (Wald 2001). Corrido may have been one genre the Mexican American country artist Johnny Rodriguez had in mind when he emphasized, recalling his South Texas upbringing: "You have stories in Mexican music, and country music said almost the same thing, just in different languages" (Burns 2019). In my conversations with Mexican American country music lovers, no one ever said to me, "I like country music because it reminds me of *ranchera*" – or corrido, or any other form of Mexican music. These fans loved country music on its own terms.[11] Many of them did say, however – especially in Texas – that they loved country music because they were Mexican and that being Mexican made this inevitable.

---

[11] As I mention elsewhere in this chapter, some of my interlocutors drew links between certain aspects of country music and various styles of Mexican music. Some also spoke of (not themselves but) non-English-speaking family members relating to country music through parallels with, for example, corrido or banda.

The Mexican American fans I spent time with further indicated that song lyrics were a focal point of their country listening and pleasure, and some invoked knowledge of English as a determinant of becoming a country fan, or not. In Texas, fiddle arose often as a favorite instrument, and one man, a fan and a musician, likened the fiddle in country to the clarinet in *banda* (Mexican wind band) music – perhaps in connection with both instruments' sometime role of providing treble filigree over the ensemble texture.[12] The Texan fans also gave a shout-out to Texas country and emphasized that their favorite music included live sets from such artists as the Randy Rogers Band and the Josh Abbott Band, both stars of the Texas Red Dirt music scene.

Gender and Sexuality, and Love of Country

Elaborating country music's cultural compatibility with their "Mexican values," some female participants expressed a sense of comfort with country styles of gender, sexuality, and embodiment. They noted appreciatively that country's relatively chaste lyrics and dance styles allowed them to play songs for family members, to dance with their moms, and, by contrast to some other music they enjoyed, to dance in public without feeling physically vulnerable or uncomfortably sexualized.[13] In Gilroy, California, Ralphy, a twentyish firefighter trainee and fan of Luke Bryan, Jason Aldean, Keith Urban, Sam Hunt, Brad Paisley, and Florida Georgia Line, voiced his appreciation of country lyrics' use of language respectful toward women, by contrast to song lyrics in other styles whose language he perceived as disrespectful toward women. Roxy, a lesbian-identified millennial in South Texas, relished country music's use in Texas' gay male *Rey Vaquero* (Cowboy King) beauty and talent pageant. Following her tip, I attended Chicago and Las Vegas *reuniones vaqueras* (cowboy conventions), weekend-long events rich in performance and display on multiple interconnected fronts, including music, *mexicanidad*, cowboy culture, and LGBTQ culture and sociality (see Hubbs 2020).

Conventional framings of country music position it as quintessentially American – often patriotically and even jingoistically so – and as ultra-white.

---

[12] Traditional banda music developed in nineteenth-century rural Sinaloa, at the confluence of Indigenous streams of music making, a European military band craze, and German immigrant traditions. Contemporary banda thrives in dance clubs in Mexico and US cities including Chicago and Los Angeles, which is also a center of its production (Simonett 2001).

[13] In particular, they mentioned here rap and reggaeton.

But the Mexican American country fans I spoke with in Texas heard mainstream US country music differently. They, too, understood it as markedly American – and at the same time, as distinctly Mexican. One described country as an expression of "what it means to be Mexican" in America. And although some of my (noncountry-loving) academic colleagues expected country's patriotic American themes to elicit alienated or objecting responses from Mexican American listeners, my interlocutors evinced no such response. On the contrary, they expressed their enjoyment of country's patriotic songs. Most strikingly, Texas focus-group participants described how such songs stirred in them deep feelings about being American – and Mexican.

The songs inspired participants' pride and gratitude in being American. They spoke of their appreciation for the opportunities and the "good life" they were able to have in the United States, and for the efforts and sacrifices their families had made to give them these things.[14] Their reflections flowed seamlessly into expressions of pride and gratitude for their Mexican culture and heritage. The Texas-Mexican millennials embraced patriotic American country songs as reminders of blessings they did not take for granted and of pride in both their Americanness and their Mexicanness. Far from hearing country musical patriotism as excluding them, these listeners reveled in red, white, and blue appreciation and belonging. And they enjoyed the same feelings concurrently in shades of green, white, and red.[15]

In Northern California, another young, bilingual country fan, Denisse, expressed the same sense of "dual patriotism," a trait that has been noted in previous research with Mexican Americans (Garcia 1973, 48–9; 1995). A father–son pair of Mexican American country fans in Southern California registered related comments. Raymond, a forty-five-year-old UPS delivery driver, husband of country fan Carla, and parent of two-year-old Ramón, voiced his approval for country songs that convey acknowledgment to American troops. His seventy-four-year-old father, Reynaldo, a retired aircraft mechanic and long-time devotee of Patsy Cline and Freddy Fender, among other artists, agreed. Discussing their

---

[14] One survey indicates that most Mexicans (57%) see better life opportunities in the United States and see friends and relatives living there as having "achieved their goals" (Pew Global Attitudes Project 2009, 1).

[15] The South Texas focus groups took place in late July 2017, six months after the Trump inauguration, and the California focus groups – with Reynaldo, Raymond, and Carla in Orange County and Denisse and Ralphy in Gilroy – took place in late December 2017 and – with Leo and his uncles in Orange County – late November 2018.

feelings in this regard, both men cited their experience serving in the US Army. Country music outsiders and critics often read pro-troops expressions in country music as political statements. I see this, however, as a category error. With four-fifths of the all-volunteer US military coming from the working class, country artists and listeners with working-class ties are more likely than others to have family or friends serving in the military. In this context, the troop shout-outs cherished by Reynaldo and Raymond represent not any political stance, but rather a form of community and familial support (Hubbs 2014, 138, 141).[16]

Country Music as Mexican Music: Love and Theft

There was a point in the Texas focus groups when the discussion of Mexican American ties to country music took a different, less celebratory turn. Discussing the reasons for (what he described as) country music's familiarity to Mexican American fans, one participant, Isaías, cited histories of US imperialism and of cultural and territorial appropriation. Explaining country's familiarity and, by his account, *inevitable* appeal to Mexican Americans, Isaías and other interlocutors pointed to evident roots of country music in Mexican music; ranch life, work, clothing, and language; and US-seized lands (totaling 55 percent of Mexico's territory, according to the 1848 Treaty of Guadalupe Hidalgo). Many concurred with the perspective expressed by one interlocutor: I am *Mexican*; how would I not like country music? And country music's first Mexican American star, Johnny Rodriguez, would seem to agree. Two years after these borderlands focus groups met, PBS aired Ken Burns's *Country Music*, which included Rodriguez (b. 1951) discussing his upbringing in Sabinal, Texas, ninety miles' drive from Mexico, and recalling that country was "the music of *our people*" (2019; emphasis audible in original).[17]

The well-known phrase "We didn't cross the border; the border crossed us" invokes the history of US acquisitions and seizures of Mexican territories and its profound and enduring social, cultural, political, and demographic effects. Over the course of the group exchange with their

---

[16] Country fans do not all come from the working class. But the music itself often cultivates a working-class focus in its themes and preoccupations, including call-outs to the troops. Country music receives a lot of play, to racially and ethnically diverse audiences, on US military sites (Neal 2006).

[17] The Rodriguez clip twice quoted in this chapter is available at www.pbssocal.org/country-music/ken-burns-dayton-duncan/.

peers – many of whom, in this instance, had been college friends and cohorts – these Texan country fans suggested how country music might be part of this story. Here on the US–Mexico border, most focus-group participants seemed to have familiarity with ranch life, if not direct family connection to it. *Moda vaquera* (cowboy wear) and other signifiers – pickup trucks, livestock – arose frequently in the conversation. These fans were acutely aware and appreciative of country music's use of the markers of ranch life. They cited it as an aspect of country's relatability for fans like them, and they emphasized the Mexican origins of these pillar elements of country music. Indeed, the clues remain: "ranch" comes from *rancho*, *rodeo* is a Spanish word, and "buckaroo" (as in Buck Owens and His Buckaroos) is an anglicization of *vaquero*. And then there are the cowboy hats, boots, shirts, belts, and buckles, Mexican in origin and long ubiquitous in country music.

It seems ironic that some of the prime markers of country music's "realness" for these listeners – the cowboy and life on the farm, *el rancho* – have been cited in middle-class Anglo-white criticism as signs of its fakeness and phoniness.[18] More than ironic is the fact that US non-Latinos and people all around the world understand the cowboy as an original "American" folk hero ("no icon is more 'American' than the cowboy," a recent *Country Queer* article declares [Brothers 2020]). In fact, the cowboy, his techniques of horse- and bull-riding and lassoing, and the structures of US rodeo, including not only the competitive events but the food, music, and dancing, were introduced to the United States from Mexico only in the latter half of the nineteenth century, having already been cultivated by Mexican vaqueros for some 250 years (LeCompte 1985). The cowboy was popularized in the United States after 1885, through "Buffalo Bill" Cody's Wild West show and its many imitators. Contemporary Mexicans would readily recognize US country artists' hats and boots as Mexican and the fancy, sparkly "Nudie suits" worn by country artists as versions of *el traje de charro*, the regalia of competitive and show cowboys (*charros*) that became the Mexican national costume in the nineteenth century and remains that of the mariachi. The label *Nudie suit* itself obscures an important history of Mexican American influence on country music. It refers to Nudie Cohn (1902–1984), a Ukrainian immigrant tailor who designed rhinestone suits for the stars at Nudie's Rodeo Tailors in Los

---

[18] In Hubbs 2014 (39–41, 52), for example, I discuss charges of "phoniness" in country by the conservative journalist Mark Judge and of disingenuousness in country's themes by the indie musician and commentator Wil Forbis.

Angeles. But many of the most celebrated examples of the genre – including the iconic poppies, pills, and pot leaf suit worn by Gram Parsons in 1969 – were created by Cohn's assistant (and eventual son-in-law) Manuel Cuevas (b. 1933), a Mexican immigrant who did his earliest, youthful work designing and creating clothing in Mexico (La Chapelle 2001; Hubbs, conversation with Manuel Cuevas, December 14, 2018).

Country Music and Mexican American Belonging

In recent years, the notion of belonging has been often deployed, in migration studies and elsewhere, as a concept that attends to the social, cultural, and political, beyond the narrow legalistic confines of citizenship. To invoke the concept of belonging in the present study could suggest a certain common-sense reading of the 2016 CMA announcement on the growth of Latine country fandom, one whereby Latines are viewed as embracing country music, understood as a "quintessentially American" culture form, and thus becoming more "Americanized." But the discourses that unfolded in dialogue among the Mexican American participants in my South Texas focus groups point to a different sense, and directionality, of belonging, one in which, as these interlocutors suggested, American country music belongs to its Mexican American fans.

Of course, all popular music belongs to its fans; this has always been a vital fact of music fandom. But the borderlands country lovers, millennials well versed in Chicane and Tejane history, were suggesting more than that. The pair of maps in Figure 14.1 can help to illustrate the implications of their comments.

Both maps represent what is today the continental United States. They capture two different moments in time, separated by 172 years and innumerable social, demographic, and geopolitical changes. And yet the maps' shaded areas indicating Mexican presence are remarkably similar. Both maps mark out a region, stretching from the Gulf of Mexico west to the Pacific Coast, that sustained Indigenous and Mexican life for hundreds of years, including most recently 175 years under the US flag. What these paired maps highlight, in other words, is precisely *not* a diaspora – not a dispersion of Mexican émigrés into foreign lands. Indeed, viewed in comparison to the pre-1848 map, the shading in the 2019 map powerfully illustrates the phrase quoted above, "We didn't cross the border; the border crossed us," and can suggest why it has served as an activist chant for Chicane rights in the United States.

(a)

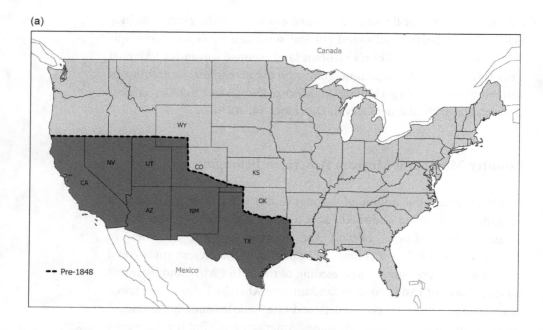

(b)

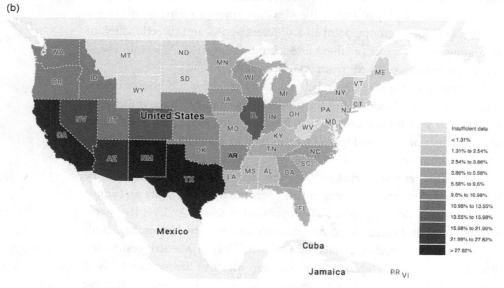

Figure 14.1. Not a diaspora: shading indicates territories claimed by Mexico before 1848 (top map) and Mexican-descended US population levels in 2019 (bottom map).

Top: Map created by René Duplain, GSG Centre, University of Ottawa, on April 26, 2022.

Bottom: *Source data*: "Hispanic or Latino: Mexican, 2019." Social Explorer (based on data from US Census Bureau).

These maps may also explain certain research challenges I have encountered in my project and, ultimately, help to illuminate the cultural context in which country music's Mexicanness might be understood. For example, I have encountered hints and claims of deep, foundational Mexican influences on country music, of which I will cite a pair of instances: First, some people have suggested that the origins of country's "yeehaw" shout of excitement or emotion lies in the *grito* (cry of emotion [Salinas 2016]) of the mariachi and of corrido ballads.[19] Second, the principal instrument in country and many other US popular music forms, the guitar, originated in Spain in the early 1500s and reached North America ca. the mid-1500s with Spanish colonizers who sailed to Mexico.

I have sought specific evidence on such points to flesh out the story of Mexican roots in country music, but my efforts have been mostly frustrated. Perhaps it will always be, as George H. Lewis (1991, 85, quoting Octavio Paz) put it in his examination of the influence of Mexican music on American rock and country, that Mexican influences present as a "vague atmosphere" and float above American popular music "as a 'ragged but beautiful ghost ... never quite existing, never quite vanishing.'" But more concretely, I understand the difficulty of tracing such influences as a telling indicator of the nature of cultural exchange, overlap, and mutual inextricability between two nations that share a 2,000-mile (3,145-kilometer) contact zone, or border, and a history of its vast movements and dislocations. Music cares nothing about political or geographic boundaries. Imitation and borrowing are the air that musicians breathe. Given these facts, precisely documenting country music's Mexican origins may be impossible. Still, I stake my work on the belief that further research can increase knowledge in this realm and expand existing definitions of country music and American culture in needed directions.

Thus, if the field of country music studies has not examined its object as an instance of border culture, it is nevertheless ripe for such treatment.[20] This may seem most obvious in connection with hillbilly music's Depression-era turn toward cowboy songs and western swing, a dazzling, danceable hybrid of blues, jazz, country, and Mexican music most famously associated with the smooth-bowing fiddler Bob Wills and His Texas

---

[19] Hurtado (2019) also cites "speculation" that the grito was the source of early country star Jimmie Rodgers's iconic "Blue Yodel" but offers no details.

[20] Vargas's (2019) article on twentieth-century border radio raises intriguing possibilities for country music studies investigating contact and influence across the US–Mexico border.

Playboys.[21] A half-century after the birth of western swing, Wills would be cited prominently by tejano pioneer Little Joe Hernández in "Redneck Meskin Boy" (1981, 1986).

Fifteen years of picking Texas cotton
Tequila 'n' Texas women bring me joy
Truth is, I grew up on Bob Wills's music
I'm just a good ol' redneck Meskin boy[22]

Little Joe's tejano music here is an offshoot of norteño, country, blues, and rock no less dynamic or eclectic than his idol's Western swing. His lyrics, meanwhile, celebrate Texas country music and culture and its defining role in his identity as a Texas-Mexican musician and person (see Texas Commission n.d.). Sounds and text converge in an account of the artist's country-music involvements and Tex-Mex lifestyle, sung over a norteño polka groove alternately punctuated by a gleaming horn line and Nashville chicken pickin' guitar fills from his band, La Familia. Like my millennial Texan interlocutors, nearly four decades later, who connected with country music's "Mexican values," Little Joe in "Redneck Meskin Boy" attested to a mutually constitutive relationship between country music and Mexican American self-construction, for the artist and fan alike. And like the maps in Figure 14.1, Little Joe's classic autobiographical track addresses a question implicit in the foregoing discourses of country-loving Mexican Americans: Why does country music sound Brown?

Conclusion

The notion of the Country Mexican clashes with country music's US-national and Anglo-white image. But a growing body of critical and historical scholarship decenters whiteness and details country music's origins and ongoing history in relation to interracial working-class culture. The founding of the US record industry in the 1920s, in the time of Jim Crow segregation, imposed racial division on southern working-class music and, in an era obsessed with eugenicist and folkloric differentiation, confected stylistic difference through the racialized marketing categories of

---

[21] See Phillips (2018) on Wills's fiddle playing. The jazz critic Norman Weinstein (2003) has written of what he hears as the improbability of western swing's combination of elements. Sure, Bob Wills was "a creator of [an] eccentric mutation of big band swing, but the steel guitar and fiddles?"

[22] Lyrics transcribed by the author.

race and old-time music (Miller 2010). Since then, country has seen changes in sound and aesthetics; musical, cultural, and geographic influences; and demographics, including an influx of middle-class suburban listeners since the 1990s. But in the public mind, country music has remained a white and working-class, hence retrograde, culture form.

Research shows that higher-status listeners reject country as music of less-educated, low-status whites and that this "anything but country" perspective has actually grown since the 1990s (Bryson 1996; Lizardo and Skiles 2015). But when Mexican American fans appear under country music's (putatively) Anglo-white working-class brand, it puts both class and race-ethnicity in relief and usefully unsettles the conventional wisdom on all sides. Race and class are mutually entangled in the American social fabric, though prevailing logic often casts them in an either/or binary.

By viewing country music and its constituency in ethnically and culturally inclusive terms, my research on Country Mexicans both registers the increasing diversity of country's present-day constituency and further reveals the music's multiracial, multiethnic, and multicultural history. Greater knowledge of Mexican American involvements can help to undo the historical erasures of a century's representation of country as whites-only music. And it can contest the socially and politically corrosive forces that fragment the US working class, past and present, by race and ethnicity. The fans and artists represented here challenge dominant perspectives on both country music and Mexican Americans. Their multilevel country-loving engagements are proof that country music is even more quintessentially American than we have imagined.

Hearing Racial Politics in Beyoncé's and The Chicks'
"Daddy Lessons"

REBEKAH HUTTEN

> Beyoncé is going to light up that stage with Daddy Lessons & dare
> someone to tell her it isn't country enough.
>
> Mikki Kendall (@karnythia, Twitter, November 2, 2016)

Beyoncé's and The Chicks' performance of "Daddy Lessons" at the fiftieth annual Country Music Association (CMA) Awards Show contradicted the widely held belief that country music is inextricable from white identity. "Daddy Lessons" was political from the beginning of their performance: the very presence of racially diverse female musicians working in collaboration on the CMA stage became a rallying cry against a music industry that has sought to maintain its hegemony since the 1920s (see Figure 15.1). The performance engendered multiple levels of cultural-political dissent: on one level, the performance recalled the interracial working histories of country music by displacing the dominant white-male-heterosexual identity typically associated with the genre. On another level, the performance sparked "genre surveillance" in the form of hostile social media reactions by a faction of fans in country music culture. These fans voiced disdain toward the performance on social media, bringing into sharp focus the mechanisms by which country music is heavily surveilled – not just by industry insiders, but also by fans. In December 2016, a month after the CMA performance, these forms of surveillance intensified when Beyoncé's application for "Daddy Lessons" to be considered in the Grammy Awards country music category was rejected (Associated Press 2016). The country committee's refusal of her song was certainly not without historical precedent: the mainstream country music industry has long excluded women, LGBTQIA+ people, and people of color from full participation. This refusal, and fan reactions intended to police the genre, both worked as tactics of surveillance within the well-documented lineage of enforced racial segregation in, and gendered exclusion from, the genre (Miller 2010; Hughes 2015; Mather 2017; Pecknold 2013a; Watson 2019b).

Figure 15.1. Beyoncé and The Chicks performing at the Country Music Association Awards show.
Beyoncé and the Dixie Chicks performing at the CMA Awards on November 2, 2016. © Walt Disney/ABC Television; Creative Commons Attribution-NoDerivs 2.0.

This chapter theorizes genre surveillance as a ramification of the century-long practice in the country music industry of gendered exclusion and racial segregation along, to use W.E.B. Du Bois' (1903, 1940) terminology, the color line. Defensive comments posted on social media before, during, and following the performance reveal that country music's boundaries are not fundamentally musical but racialized and gendered. As such, genre surveillance describes the nonmusical regulatory tactics imposed upon a musical style. "Daddy Lessons" demonstrates how these exclusions operate within the country music industry. While practices of genre surveillance have damaging effects, Beyoncé's and The Chicks' performance also operated as a form of "dark sousveillance" (Browne 2015) by making visible histories of racial politics present within the genre. Dark sousveillance flips surveillance on its head, inverting surveillance through acts of resistance as part of the broader effort toward racial equity (Browne 2015). In this way, Beyoncé's and The Chicks' performance of "Daddy Lessons" invites reflection on how surveillance is both enacted and opposed.

Structures of Surveillance

> Surveillance is nothing new to black folks. It is the fact of anti blackness.
> Simone Browne (2015, 8)

Policed sound is predicated on historic structures of segregation and surveillance, one of which is Bentham's panopticon (1791).[1] Jeremy Bentham, an English social reformer, fabricated his ideal prison layout as a circular building with cell windows facing inward to a central watch-tower. This model would allow a few guards to watch hundreds of inmates from their central vantage point. In Michel Foucault's (1980, 148) writings on discipline and power, he reads Bentham's "technology of power" as having conceptual ramifications for how subjects discipline both them-selves and others in surveillance societies more broadly. Though Foucault's account of Bentham's panopticon is ocular-centric, visuality is but one of many technologies of power. Sound studies scholars have relocated aural surveillance in Bentham's (1791, 78–9) original panopticon plan: inspectors aurally spied on inmates through a network of "conversation tubes" that linked cells to a central chamber. In this way, "the history of surveillance is as much a sound history as a history of vision" (Bull and Back 2003, 5).

In the context of musicology and sound studies, musical segregation is often theorized along what Du Bois' (1903, 1940) termed the "color line," conceived as an invisible barrier that separates white and Black people to maintain segregation. Karl Hagstrom Miller (2010, 2) theorizes a "musical color line" that led to the racial segregation of certain genres; for example, blues music became linked to Black people and country to white people. Similarly, Jennifer Stoever's (2016, 11) work on the "sonic color line" outlines a long history of aural surveillance in which musical sounds – tones, timbres, styles, and accents – are encoded with racialized signifiers. Race is thus not only seen but arguably *heard* in certain genres.

From a spectatorship perspective, Beyoncé's and The Chicks' CMA performance certainly complicates a tidy conceptualization of surveillance. First, there were, and are, multiple audiences: the live audience in the

---

[1] This chapter uses the term "surveillance" in reference to explicit acts of institutional monitoring and regulatory watching by individual citizens. Institutional surveillance takes a variety of forms, including data collection on social networking sites or security technologies like closed-circuit television (CCTV), a type of video surveillance used around the globe but most heavily in Britain, China, Russia, and the United States (Moody and Bischoff 2021).

Bridgestone Arena in Nashville, Tennessee; the virtual audience watching the live-streamed show; the fans and critics who took to social media to broadcast their reactions; and a "continual audience" who still have access to the performance online. Second, because of these multiple types of audiences, surveillance was enacted in various ways, notably on social networking sites (SNSs). Facebook and Twitter provided CMA audiences with a platform to voice their opinions on Beyoncé's and The Chicks' performance, thus playing a significant role in shaping country music discourse, particularly when considering how journalistic sources used SNS posts and comments to shape an overarching narrative about how Beyoncé's and The Chicks' performance sparked an angry backlash. Within the fields of surveillance studies and governmentality, SNSs have been described as panoptic (the few watching the many), synoptic (the many watching the few), and omnioptic (the many watching the many) (Rose-Redwood 2006; Chalkley 2012; Siapera 2012; Amiradakis 2016). As such, the CMA performance invited three types of surveillant watching:

1. a *panoptic* industrial surveillance – the mainstream country music industry – which regulates performance line-ups, radio broadcasting, awards shows, and playlist categorizations;
2. a *synoptic* audience who watched the live show, either in person or via broadcast, and who can still view the performance online; and
3. an *omnioptic* audience collectively watching one another react to the performance on SNSs.

Though surveillance is harmful, surveilled subjects do not simply accept their objectification. Dark sousveillance, in Simone Browne's words, describes mechanisms by which racialized people subvert surveillant procedures. Browne (2015, 21) roots dark sousveillance in acts of subversion that "[plot] imaginaries that are oppositional and that are hopeful for another way of being." The French prefix, "sous," meaning "under" or "beneath," indicates a critique from below, strategies that Browne positions as "necessarily ones of undersight" (21). Her term builds on Steve Mann's (2003, 333) theory of sousveillance as a means by which people "neutralize surveillance." The critique and cooptation of anti-Black surveillance technologies are acts of dark sousveillance. "Dark sousveillance," Browne writes (2015, 21), "is a site of critique, as it speaks to Black epistemologies of contending with anti-Black surveillance, where the tools of social control in plantation surveillance or lantern laws in city spaces and beyond were appropriated, co-opted, repurposed, and challenged in order to facilitate survival and escape." Browne's work nuances Foucault's idea that surveilled subjects necessarily self-regulate and self-discipline and highlights Black Americans' individual and creative tactics in the "flight to freedom" (21). For instance, Browne uncovers historical examples of dark sousveillance, such as African American spirituals and songs that contained life-saving information about escape routes or approaching slave patrols (21–2). While Beyoncé and The Chicks experienced panoptic, synoptic, and omnioptic surveillance, their performance can also be considered an act of dark sousveillance, given how Beyoncé counteracted anti-Black ideologies through the musical and visual reminder of country music's Black American roots.

Furthermore, "dark sousveillance" is a term that not only describes acts of resistance against surveillance but additionally is, "a reading praxis for examining surveillance that allows for a questioning of how certain surveillance technologies installed during slavery to monitor and track blackness as property ... anticipate the contemporary surveillance of racialized subjects, and it also provides a way to frame how the contemporary surveillance of the racial body might be contended with" (23–4). Black people have historically been kept under observation in surveillant societies, with contemporary musical participation proving no exception. As such, in this chapter, I engage dark sousveillance as a method for interpreting Beyoncé's and The Chicks' resistance against genre surveillance.

Interracial Histories of Country Music

Starting in the 1960s but increasingly since 2010, musicologists, cultural studies scholars, and country music historians have questioned the "Southern thesis" of country music proposed by influential country music historian Bill C. Malone. A teleological proposition, Malone's (1968, ix) southern thesis maintains that country music linearly evolved exclusively in the rural southern United States. A lasting effect that the southern thesis has had on country music historiography is the erasure of the participation of people of color from the genre (Huber 2017; Enriquez 2020). Here, I briefly trace significant inroads within country music scholarship on the interracial history of the genre and its subsequent whitewashing throughout the twentieth and twenty-first centuries.

Despite the musical color line that resulted from the Race and Hillbilly record label divide in the 1920s (Roy 2004), country music has a long interracial working history (Hughes 2015; Pecknold 2013a). Extant documentation of cross-cultural musical histories in the United States extends back to the late seventeenth century, arising from the proximity of African American slaves and poor white farmers and sharecroppers (Jamison 2015, 12; Mack 2020a, 151). Though country music is predicated on the participation of diverse peoples, there is a commonly held perception that country music "sounds white," prompting Geoff Mann (2008, 75) to "wonder what whiteness sounds like, and how it is heard ... whiteness can, and frequently does, sound like country music." Mann shows that country music has been used to produce whiteness through such channels as commercial radio chart categorizations, marketing strategies, cultural histories, and academic research. He writes (83), "it has taken a great deal of ideological work both to make country the sound of American whiteness, and, at least as importantly, to make it continue to 'call' to white people, in effect, recruiting white people into a particular understanding of white racial identity. The ideological work that goes into producing country music as white is bound up in the cultural practice of nostalgia, sonic "authenticity," and American nationalism (86).

Several scholars have recovered the work of Black musicians in country music recordings and narratives of working environments in the twentieth century. Some of these recuperated musicians include Linda Martell (Pecknold 2016), singers Arthur Alexander and Joe Tex (Hughes 2015), and pianist Lillian Armstrong (Huber 2013). Patrick Huber (2013, 20) rediscovered nearly fifty African American musicians featured on commercial hillbilly records recorded between 1924 and 1932. Latinx and Indigenous musicians have similarly been active in, but whitewashed out, of the genre (Enriquez 2020; Jacobsen 2017). However, even a cursory glance into the supposedly profuse whiteness of the genre reveals that the dominant story about country music's past is incomplete (see Royster 2022).

The legacy of interracial collaboration in country music history invites speculation surrounding genre and identity. Some musical genres are commonly thought to be attached to specific identities. David Brackett (2016, 27) identifies the phenomenon of "style-genre-audience associations" to argue that genre-identity homologies are deeply ideological, rather than true or false. Identification with genres on an identity basis may, in reality, extend beyond the perceived homology but as a lived experience can be felt as profoundly true by audiences and musicians alike, even when such homologies may have been fabricated by record labels, radio formats, and chart classifications. Country music was, and largely still is, believed to be attached to a white, southern, and rural identity: an ideologically driven conception that masks its own reality. Its identification as legibly homologous with this identity in the 1940s and continuing throughout the rest of the twentieth century renders musicians and audiences who are not white-southern-rural as illegible. And illegibility, in the case of country music, in particular, is bound up with the surveillance of both genre and race.

An oxymoron emerges: how can one be both invisible *and* surveilled? Jade Petermon (2014, 1) offers "hyper(in)visibility" to describe processes by which Black women are simultaneously hypervisible and invisible in the context of western neoliberalism; they are "looked at but not seen." Petermon draws from Audre Lorde (1984, 42) who states, "Within [America] where racial difference creates a constant, if unspoken, distortion of vision, black women have on one hand always been highly visible, and so, on the other hand, have been rendered invisible through the depersonalization of racism." Put differently, the white gaze effectively erases Black subject positions, forcing Black people into a state of objectification: a double bind. Petermon explains that while the media is saturated with representations of Black people (resulting in hypervisibility), there remains a poverty of specific, nuanced, and realistic Black subjectivities (resulting in invisibility). Petermon's hyper(in)visibility captures the paradox of Beyoncé's performance at the CMAs. She is hypervisible: her presence as a Black woman on the country music stage is always already marked. Yet, by this same logic, she is rendered illegible and invisible to many viewers and listeners. Because her presence resists the homology between country/white/male, her subjectivity (and the broader subjectivity of Black participation in country music, historically and presently) is subjected to erasure.

By contrast, white bodies in country music go unmarked; whiteness and masculinity are neutral and naturalized. Mann (2008, 92) explains how the "whiteness" of country music is an ideological production achieved through iterative actions and discourses: "Iteration is also normalization; and inevitably involves the creation of obviousnesses, a movement toward silence and generalization. Iteration marks, but it marks so much that the mark becomes unremarkable." Mann's explanation of iteration resonates with Sara Ahmed's (2019, 41) theorization of use; she writes, "The more a path is used, the more a path is used. How strange that this sentence makes sense. There is more to more; more creates more. However, much usedness is shaped by the past usedness points toward the future: used as being directed toward that which has become easier to follow." That which is repeated, re-iterated, and re-used can be bound up in issues of power and identity. Country-*iterated*-as-white leads to the perceived naturalness of whiteness; that "path" becomes easier to use (to follow, to tread) for other white men. When the supposed neutrality of whiteness is exposed, white defensiveness rears its head; in the case of the CMAs, tactics of genre surveillance are used to shield country music from Beyoncé's Blackness and The Chicks' anti-Republican-ness.

Black, Indigenous, Hispanic, Asian, and other people of color, urban, northern, queer, and women country musicians (in any interlocking union of these identities) are illegible to some white audiences and producers, but even further, are surveilled under the political system of what bell hooks (2004, 17) calls imperialist white-supremacist capitalist patriarchy. But of course, people who are not white, male, straight, rural, and Southern listen to and make music that falls into the grouping of country. As Pecknold (2013b, 12) explains, "racial crossover destabilizes the very concept of genre, reliant as it often is on homological conceptions of audience culture." Reactions to Beyoncé's and The Chicks' performance highlight the surveillance that characterizes country music as a white-male-heterosexual institution, one instance of the industry's panoptic eye – and fans' synoptic eye – over those who cross the musical color line. These genre "rules," however, are not steadfast but breakable, and perhaps even more so with the increased availability of user-generated platforms, like TikTok and Bandcamp, which provide alternative routes to producing music.

Disrupting the CMA

The Country Music Association was founded in 1958 to preserve and promote the genre of country music, initially through the mediums of commercial radio, *Close Up* magazine, and promotional brochure mail-outs (Pecknold 2007, 140–2). The CMA was integral to the development of the country radio format and in shifting public perceptions of the genre from one associated with "uneducated and uncouth" hillbillies to blue- and white-collar workers (Pecknold, 149–52).[2] Since 1967, the CMA has held an annual awards' show to showcase artists working in the genre. The

---

[2] This shift in associations was marked by *Billboard*'s move from using the label "hillbilly" to "country and western" in June 1949 (Brackett 2016, 227).

2016 CMA awards show was of particular import, marking the organization's fiftieth anniversary. Hosted by country musicians Brad Paisley and
Carrie Underwood, the show featured forty-five group and solo performers. Of these performers, seven were people of color. Of the fifty-four artists
nominated for an award, sixty-nine percent were white men, and thirty-
one percent were white women. The bulk of the performers were country
musicians, with a few exceptions: gospel group The McCrary Sisters (who
performed with Maren Morris), acapella group Pentatonix (who performed
a tribute to Dolly Parton with Jennifer Nettles), and R&B singer-songwriter
Beyoncé. However, the artists who performed at the CMAs draw from a
striking range of musical genres. Several of the white artists who performed
audibly pull from musical cultures with deep roots in Black traditions: rock,
gospel, R&B, blues, hip-hop, and rap (particularly the performances of
"May We All" by Florida Georgia Line and Tim McGraw, "My Church" by
Maren Morris and The McCrary Sisters, and Chris Stapleton's and Dwight
Yoakam's "Seven Spanish Angels"). Country music is not created or
performed in a vacuum; it is not "one thing." The musical fluidity of
country raises the question: who can "bend" genre rules? Who is permitted
to bring in musical styles from "outside" of country without facing reper-
cussions? The answer is almost always going to oscillate around the color
line. In fact, the very notion of a musical style being "outside" of country
music is destabilized by the reality of the genre's soundscape. "Daddy
Lessons" itself is a compendium of musical and cultural histories.

Combined with musical signifiers to New Orleans second-line style brass
ensembles, histories of banjo playing in African American communities
(Thomas 2013), politics of the Nashville music industry, and Texan home-
places, "Daddy Lessons" can be interpreted as both an autobiographical
statement of Beyoncé's multivalent roots and a broader reference to dia-
sporic Black musical traditions. Beyoncé and The Chicks introduced
"Daddy Lessons" by each intoning the word "Texas" in a low voice; a
New Orleans-style brass section filled out the song's harmonic texture; a
nod to African American country musician DeFord Bailey was encoded in
a harmonica solo, and the surprise inclusion of an excerpt from the song
"Long Time Gone" acted as an indictment of Nashville's country music
scene and reminded viewers of The Chicks' long exile from the country
music industry (Watson and Burns 2010). The lyrics of "Daddy Lessons"
outline a daughter's relationship to her father by reflecting on her youth
and the lessons he imparted. The father character in the song is a whiskey-
loving, motorcycle-driving, classic rock fan, gambler, and gun rights advocate. He advises his daughter to avoid men like him, and in the chorus, the

lyrics are sung partly from the father's perspective: "When trouble comes to town / and men like me come around / oh my daddy said shoot."

Such lyrical commentary on the right to bear arms carries with it a complicated racial history. As Francesca Royster (2019, 70) writes of the lyrics to "Daddy Lessons," throughout the 1960s and 1970s "the Black Panthers' embrace of the right to bear arms promised by the Second Amendment was a central aspect of their criminalization in the eyes of those who feared them." These references to bearing arms are further complicated by Beyoncé's Black Lives Matter messaging throughout her 2016 album *Lemonade* and her 2016 Super Bowl performance of "Formation," both of which protested police shootings of Black men and boys. "Daddy Lessons" thus presents a tension between the rights of all Americans and the often racist misapplication of the law. Beyoncé sings, "Daddy made me fight / it wasn't always right / but he said 'girl it's your second amendment,'" expressing a form of dark sousveillance by lyrically reappropriating a weapon often used by white men in power to threaten the lives of people of color; further, representations of women with guns do not often appear in media texts or mainstream cultural discourses.

Dark sousveillance was enacted with the surprise incorporation of the song "Long Time Gone" midway through the performance. "Long Time Gone," written by Darrell Scott (2000), critiques the Nashville music industry, particularly in the last verse, which structurally functioned as a bridge during the "Daddy Lessons" performance. Beyoncé and Maines sing in two-part harmony: "Now they sound tired but they don't sound Haggard / they've got money but they don't have Cash / they've got Junior but they don't have Hank," before leading back into the chorus of "Daddy Lessons" with the phrase "My daddy warned me about men like you" with "Long Time Gone" used as the bridge, the structure of the song thus *reframes* the lyrics of "Daddy Lessons" as a warning against men not just at large but within the Nashville country music industry. Including this particular excerpt from "Long Time Gone" was rather bold, considering that The Chicks had not been invited to perform at the CMAs since they were blacklisted from country music radio in 2003, after Maines publicly criticized former President Bush's choice to invade Iraq in March of that year (Watson and Burns 2010).

Of their performance, journalist Jewly Hight (2016) aptly points out, "From a historical angle, [Beyoncé's] country excursion represents something more like reclamation than invasion, since the genre's roots entwine with African American folk, blues, string band and pop contributions." Yet, many fans interpreted her reclamation as politically invasive.

Social Media Surveillance

Reactions to Beyoncé's and The Chicks' performance unfolded on social media platforms, presenting a juxtaposed mixture of angry critique from traditional country music fans and musicians, and joyful celebration from others. The polarization expressed on social media during and after the performance reveals the political and culturally constructed roots of country music that, when disturbed, cause white discomfort, anger, and hostility. Country musician Travis Tritt was notably vocal, posting a series of tweets lamenting country music's absorption of, and into, pop music. Tritt (@travistritt, November 5, 2016) tweeted: "I don't think there was anything 'country' about it. It was a pop song done by pop artists." In an interview with *Billboard*, an anonymous Nashville music manager spoke about the performance, telling the reporter: "I was sitting behind Alan Jackson, and he actually stood up from the front row and walked out in middle of the performance, so I think that spoke volumes for the *traditional, real* country acts" (qtd. in Willman 2016, my emphasis). This music manager positions country music as having a core of "traditional, real" musicians, a sentiment echoed by CMA viewers in the comment sections of various Facebook posts.[3]

Pop music is (and always has been) interpreted as posing a very real threat of infiltrating country music and making it less traditional, invoking a surveillant response in many commenters. One wrote, "As if this isn't TRUE country music as it is . . . you have to go and disgrace it even more with an artist that absolutely does not belong there . . . and as for The Chicks we won't even go there . . ." (CMT Facebook post 2016). This comment tips over into a xenophobic sentiment (*absolutely does not belong there*), an opinion shared by many others: "They had no business being on that stage while REAL country talent was sitting in those seats. This was an unbelievably disappointing and disrespectful decision" (*Country Living Magazine* Facebook post, November 2, 2016). Another person wrote, "Are you kidding me? I love country, but the pop stars need to stay where they are. It's ruining country" (CMT Facebook post, November 2, 2016). The thought of mixing any type of genre infuriates some CMA fans:

If we are watching the CMA's that's cause we want to watch country. If I wanted to watch Rock awards I would watch the rock awards if I wanted to watch Hip Hop Awards I would watch The Hip Hop Awards, etc . . . and I certainly don't want to

---

[3] These comments (anonymized in this chapter) were collected from two Facebook posts, one on the page for *Country Living* Magazine and the other on the page for CMT (Country Music Television). Original spelling and grammar have been retained while emojis have been omitted.

see Beyoncé. I can't believe that you guys actually invited her to come on this program especially over all the controversy that she has had surrounding her. She is racist, she is anti-law enforcement and she supports at least two terrorists groups that I know of. And let's bring back country music. Pop music is not country music. I don't mind mixing genres of music sometimes but sometimes I want to hear one specific kind of music. The country music stations on the radio are no longer country music those are pop stations #bringcountryback #dumpBeyoncé. (CMT 2016)

Beyond pop and country being viewed as morally incompatible, the above commenter describes Beyoncé as racist (meaning anti-white), anti-law enforcement (meaning anti-white), and a terrorist supporter due to her alignment with BLM and the Black Panther Party (meaning, again, anti-white). Beyoncé is seen as posing a threat to country music and, by extension, the identity of many white fans. The hashtag #bringcountryback is itself an echo of former US president Donald Trump's slogan "Make American Great Again," a statement that relies on antebellum nostalgia that appeals to white supremacist, xenophobic, anti-immigrant, and anti-Black ideologies. Another comment was explicitly rooted in xenophobic rhetoric, remarking, "Omg what's this crap about Beyoncé performing at the CMAs? Um no? Go away? Go back to your own genre?" (qtd. in Ali 2016). The sentiment expressed here is connected to anti-immigrant jingoism ("go back to your own country"), and the implication is that Beyoncé should not be permitted to perform music unassociated with Black identities.

The commenter quoted at length above was not alone. Another wrote, "This ruins the CMAs for me... she has no business there. Can't stand her racist cop hating ass. What a disgrace" (CMT). Others argue that pop music is morally decrepit due to its vulgarity, mobilizing sexist epithets to denigrate Beyoncé: "Wow @CMA Country Music Association, are you really going to risk losing your devoted country fans by putting this skank on??? She does not deserve the spotlight; she is a racist cop-hater who dresses/performs like a tramp on stage. I started listening to country music a few years ago to try to escape from the moral decline of pop music...this is really a let-down" (CMT). Others were less adept in hiding their racism, using racial stereotypes to belittle Beyoncé's husband, Jay-Z:

And that lost you a TON of viewers ... All that seems to come on the radio anymore is the pop country crap, now you've got a person who showed support for the black panthers at the super bowl and is married to an ex drug dealer rapper, on your stage ... And both are liberal Hillary supporters ... Good job Nashville ... As for my house, we will not be tuned in because of this. (CMT)

These three comments each bring up race, describing Beyoncé as "racist" (against white people) and connecting her usual genre, pop music, to an imagined anti-white (not to mention "skanky") leftism.

Liberal-and-country are irreconcilable to many of these writers, with country-as-conservative seen to be the only valid option. In the perspective of these commenters, Beyoncé and The Chicks are considered to be anti-American and therefore the "opposite" of country music values, which are, one would think from reading these comments, exclusively pro-military and pro-police. Beyond country music as pro-military/police, The Chicks are characterized as treasonous: "Hated it!! Beyoncé is NOT country!! She hates the BLUE and a disgrace to our law enforcement! As far as The Chicks...TRAITORS!! Should never of had either on the 50th Anniversary!! Way to much talent in the room that's way better than any of them put together!! You asked...I gave it to you!" (*Country Living*).

Such angry reactions to Black success are conceptualized by Carol Anderson (2016, 4–5) as systematic "white rage," a function of racist complexes triggered by the advancement of Black people. For instance, some commenters on Twitter mobilized colorblind ideologies to support their comments that Beyoncé "does not belong" at the Country Music Awards. One Twitter user wrote: "Beyoncé is not a country artist therefore she doesn't belong at the CMAs ... it has nothing to do with her skin color" (qtd. in Breezy 2016). Despite an insistence on the irrelevancy of skin color, the issue of cross-genre collaborations is indivisibly bound up in race. Justin Timberlake and Justin Bieber each performed at the CMAs to wide acclaim, certainly not facing the backlash directed toward Beyoncé. Because Timberlake and Bieber are ideologically compatible with mainstream country music's image, they were not subject to the level of genre surveillance imposed upon Beyoncé and The Chicks.

The overwhelming sentiment of these comments is that Beyoncé is "not country." In outlining what they do think that she is – anti-police, pro-Black, anti-military, unpatriotic, slutty, R&B, pop, terrorist – these commenters provide a template of what they believe country music to be: morally "traditional," pro-military, patriotic, pro-law enforcement, pro-white: in other words, only white. In an incident starkly similar to the sentiment of this comment, record producer Buddy Killen (1993, 159–160) recalls a story about an experience country singer Joe Tex had at a gig in the 1950s. Tex was kicked off stage by the white club owner, who yelled, "He ain't country, he ain't white, he can't be country. Get him off there." Both the musical color line (Miller 2010) and the sonic color line (Stoever 2016) were perceived as transgressed by Tex's presence on this honky-tonk stage in Texas in the mid-twentieth century, as well as by Beyoncé's presence at the CMAs, thus soliciting surveillant responses from synoptic viewers. Though many of these commenters brought up rhetoric around musical transgression as a reason for their critique, the real issue was not sonic but racial. These reactions indicate how genre surveillance does not necessarily rely on musical sounds in policing who can participate in some genres but rather on imagined connections between certain sounds and certain identities. The synoptic audience took to social media for the express purpose of surveilling the genre, voicing an inhospitable message to Beyoncé and her collaborators: Leave. This is our genre. Recall the epigraph to this chapter, a Tweet written by Mikki Kendall on the night of the performance: "Beyoncé is going to light up that stage with Daddy Lessons & dare someone to tell her it isn't country enough." In telling her she was not country enough, these commenters actually told her she was not white enough.[4]

Conclusion

Beyoncé's and The Chicks' performance of "Daddy Lessons" at the fiftieth annual Country Music Awards functioned as a moment wherein the perceived boundaries of country music as fundamentally wrapped up in white identity was challenged; white fans' digital dialogue surrounding the performance attempted to maintain country music's whiteness through surveillant rhetorical tactics. While this analysis of the digital dialogue on social media surrounding the performance is rather depressing, a hopeful effect of the performance persists. As a public intellectual, Beyoncé has consistently taught her audiences about Black American history through her performances, a lesson especially emblematized by a lyric from her song "Formation." She sings, "Come on ladies now let's get in formation," where getting "in formation" (through activism) and getting "information"

[4] Though this chapter theorizes it specifically in relation to country music, genre surveillance has the potential to be mapped on to other music-identity homologies. For example, genre surveillance could be applied to cultural critic Hanif Adurraqib's experience of racialized exclusion at punk shows, spaces deeply rooted in masculinity and whiteness (2017), or William Cheng's musicological investigation into the murder of Jordan Davis, wherein the perpetrator Michael Dunn felt threatened by the volume of rap music coming from Davis' vehicle. Cheng contextualizes this violent instance within racist listenings of "black sonic excess" (2018). Sonic respectability and its transgression – Black sonic excess – are also regulated by surveillance (Cheng 2018).

(through education) are posited as two sides of the same coin. Through "Daddy Lessons," Beyoncé taught her audiences about the history of country music, lessons consistent with her long lineage of pop culture pedagogy. Such instances include her 2015 Video Music Awards performance in which the word "Feminist" was projected on the screen behind her, and throughout her 2016 visual album *Lemonade*, in which Afrofuturist visual aesthetics and pointed references to slavery are seamlessly melded. A proven impact of *Lemonade* on its audiences was that it not only educated viewers on the oppressions Black women face but also inspired viewers to conduct research so that they could better understand the references embedded in the album (Edgar and Toone 2017, 9; Sheehan 2021, 172). Audiences used the album as a mechanism to "[imagine] what new spaces of justice might look, sound, and feel like in their own communities across the country and around the world" (12). With an influence as wide as Beyoncé's, it is possible that her performance of "Daddy Lessons" at the CMA's similarly inspired viewers to reconsider the perceived linkage between country music and white identity and to imagine such "new spaces of justice."

"Daddy Lessons" stimulated public conversations about race, gender, and country music by presenting an audible and visible challenge to the imagined homology between whiteness and the genre and brought onto the country music stage a lesson in its interracial past. As Lucy Caplan (2020, 310) writes on the perception that classical music is a white-only space, "Segregation was never tantamount to absence." The same holds true for country music. Not simply utopian in its imaginative scope, "Daddy Lessons" reckons with the history of the sonic color line at a time when diverse artists like Lil Nas X, Orville Peck, Mickey Guyton, Jade Mya, and Rissi Palmer came into the spotlight, collectively pressing against and shifting the supposedly rigid confines of country's identity-based signifiers. Genre surveillance is destructive, but such resistant tactics – acts of dark sousveillance – shift the borders of the genre, effectively expanding what it can mean to "be country."

16 | "We Have a Lot of Work To Do"

Rhiannon Giddens and Country Music's Mixed Roots

TRACEY E. W. LAIRD

On Tuesday, September 26, 2017, in Raleigh, North Carolina, Rhiannon Giddens addressed a crowd of bluegrass music lovers. She recalled her recent experience performing on the *Grand Ole Opry*, where she had appeared as a member of the Carolina Chocolate Drops. They were the first African American string band to play Nashville's iconic radio barn dance in all its ninety-plus years. In this keynote for the yearly International Bluegrass Music Association meeting, Giddens (2017) reflected on performing as a string band – one of country music's proto-typical ensembles – on country music's most celebrated stage: "people started calling it a Healing Moment. But I have to ask: a healing moment for whom? One or two Black groups or one or two Black country stars is not a substitution for recognizing the true multicultural history of this music. We have a lot of work to do."

In this moment Giddens threw down a challenge: to disentangle past and present knowledge about country music with race as it is understood and experienced in the United States. This is work she began as a founding member of the Drops, and work she continues via solo and collaborative projects since. I will explore some ways she does so in two albums, her solo debut *Tomorrow Is My Turn* (2015) and its follow-up *Freedom Highway* (2017), including Giddens's own perspective during a Fall 2020 interview. To do so, I first pick up Charles Carson's (2012) idea of "art as historiography." I draw on recent scholarship about the fluid and con-structed nature of genre from David Brackett (2016).[1] I also adapt insights from Nina Eidsheim (2012), who analyzes intersections between voice timbre, race, and perception. In the end, I unpack how a musical category like country gets wrapped up with social categories like race or gender – and not simply wrapped, but twisted, gnarled, and knotted. I contend that this has never been an honest way to structure musical knowledge and commerce, as it obscures the heterogeneity at the vital core of all US music, country included. Giddens's first two solo projects map more relevant and

---

[1] Brackett's work builds on that of Georgina Born (2000).

accurate frameworks for understanding the breadth and interconnected-ness of American music-making.[2]

Rhiannon Giddens is uniquely positioned to push forward the work of reframing American music: country, folk, blues, and all that follows. She is a biracial woman from the American South, educated at a conservatory-style institution to sing opera but also at the feet of Joe Thompson, one of the last of a generation of old-time Black string band musicians. The artistic clarity of her work is all her own, however, and it is timely. The year 2020 saw a global pandemic upend normal routines for people from every social sphere and occupation. Amid this, the Black Lives Matter movement mushroomed: video of unarmed George Floyd murdered on May 25, 2020, by a Minneapolis police officer made the statistics about violence against Black men too real to shrug off yet again. From at least five different time zones, quarantined against the Covid-19 outbreak, my undergraduate students and I met via computer and cellphone screen. We learned as well as we could about music history while protests against racial injustice spilled into streets from my own city of Atlanta, Georgia, to Kenosha, Wisconsin; from Portland, Oregon, to Brooklyn, New York. These scenes attest the need for a long-overdue reckoning of national identity in relation to a dark and broken racial past. Music is one place to start.

Pre-pandemic writers sometimes pondered country music developments as a microcosm for larger US culture. For example, the debut hit "Best Shot" by Black American country artist Jimmie Allen figured prominently in a 2019 *Huffington Post* piece titled "Why Is Country Music Considered So White?" (Himmelman). Two years prior, Amanda Petrusich (2017) questioned "the perplexing whiteness of country music" for *The New Yorker*. The stark parade of grief and tragedy in 2020 lends urgency to the question. They make Giddens's words echo louder: we have a lot of work to do.

The typical story of US popular music is, at its heart, framed by race. Its parallel tracks are well trod, lined with neat and familiar signposts for music history. To one side, there's British balladry, Appalachia, fiddling, and banjo, then country music and, to the other, the African slave trade, Deep South, work songs and field hollers, then blues. These tracks overlay a historically situated conception of race that misconstrues the true nature of both the music and the society that claims it. The tracks are simple, binary,

---

[2] Justin Davidson (2019) describes her winning the MacArthur Genius Award in 2017, and some creative directions her solo work has taken since then.

Black, and white. Early labels of race and hillbilly changed over time to R&B and country, but the "conceptual schemes" they denoted remained solidly in place (Lakoff 1987, 262).[3]

Handy metaphors for American music include streams running in parallel to feed a larger river, an image I myself have evoked in writing (Laird 2005, 2015). Another is a woven fabric, where the warp and weft of different threads form a larger whole.[4] The divisible components for both these analogies mirror surface, overdetermined views of race that are distinctly American. They fall short of deeper, underlying realities of the nation's cultural makeup. Through her music, Giddens directs our attention to a deeper level: not to the woven fabric but to the yarn itself. Country and other US musical genres are best grasped at the level of raw materials, not the final patterns. What sets US music apart are its fibers, gathered from the rovings and slivers of Indigenous, European, and African people, and formed into thread on a spinning wheel of history at least 400 years old. That is much older than the earliest recordings, which were shaped by the circumstances of their own time. Therein lies the rub.

Musicologist Charles Carson (2012, 111) coined a phrase "art as *historiography*" to characterize creations, both visual and musical, that question commonplace, generationally handed-down narratives about culture (italics in original). Carson's particularly interested in works by African American artists that complicate simplistic understandings of Black culture. For example, the artist Jefferson Pinder's part-visual, part-performance Missionary Project snips apart and recombines bits of recordings – "the industry's own products" – to contradict "commercialized representations of Black identity" (Carson 2012, 105). The work challenges inherited narratives of Black culture, which, I would add, inevitably alters stories of white culture as well.

Carson's examples include "Snowden's Jig," from the Drops' Grammy-winning 2010 album *Genuine Negro Jig*. This is a nineteenth-century tune, controversially attributed to the white minstrel Dan Emmett; its subtitle names the larger album. A plaintive fiddle dominates the recording, proceeding at a deliberative tempo that is at odds with the jauntiness implied by "jig." Beneath the fiddle rolls the steady stomping beat over eight counts

---

[3] Lakoff (1987) here contemplates epistemology and the illogic of external metaphysics versus internal metaphysics. The former presumes the existence of an external reality apart from perceiving beings; the latter agrees that reality exists but that its nature cannot be imagined apart from the perceptual apparatus of human beings.

[4] Kip Lornell and Anne Rasmussen (2016), for example, evoke weaving to describe the breadth of music-making outside mainstream US genres.

with emphasis on one, four, and five (x••xx•••), with a secondary handclap emphasis on seven. Above this floats the quick syncopated gestures of the "bones," a percussive sound linked to blackface minstrelsy. This performance invites a reconsideration of our neat genealogies of white music and Black music during the nineteenth century. Historians know that narratives about the past shape the present. What does it mean if the genealogies are not so tidy after all? Carson (2012, 103) asks the question this way: "How are our experiences of the present affected by the histories we have been given? Or, put more plainly: what would the present look like if the narratives of our past included things like *Black roots music*?"

Giddens's first two solo recordings glimpse some possible answers. By the time she made the IBMA speech, she had already completed both albums. They are "historiographical" in Carson's sense, pointing the way to a more complete narrative that restores that which has been "ignored, overlooked, written out, or silenced in favor of what seem to be more or less widely accepted teleological narratives" (Carson 2012, 96). They assert a distinctly American voice and, at the same time, challenge the distinctly American approach to sorting musical genres via race. They reframe the whole story in significant ways.

The 2015 solo debut *Tomorrow Is My Turn* consists mainly of covers. French popular song, jazz, Appalachian balladry, spirituals, folk songs, and traditional Irish singing get knit together so tightly, they form a unified pattern. From this pattern the artist fashions an inexorably American tapestry. Each track stands on its own technical and topical merit, worth diving into song-by-song, and each either written or memorably performed by women pioneers. Taken as a whole, this album works at a level the linguist George Lakoff (1987, 68) calls a gestalt, or "a complex, structured whole." As a musical gestalt, *Tomorrow* connects voices in US music history most often considered apart. In that way, it performs an act of recovery and re-membering. The hyphen inserted in "re-member" distinguishes its use from simple connotations of "recall" and points to the idea that identity is constructed via narrative – a concerted effort to put back together that which has been dismembered or fragmented.[5]

---

[5] Re-membered (with the hyphen) is associated with writer and cultural theorist Gloria Anzaldúa (2009), specifically her later thinking on what she termed the "Coyolxauhqui process." It also appears in the anthropological work of Barbara Myerhoff (1982) on social experiences of aging, as well as in therapy and organizational psychology contexts. All uses, including my own, converge on the assertion that our personal and collective narratives – the stories of past, present, and future – constitute our current lived realities and determine future ones.

The album's first three songs give a sense for the whole. Here and throughout, Giddens demonstrates vocal ability of striking range and nuance. She sings strong and clear on the album's opening "Last Kind Words." Her country chops shine in "Don't Let It Trouble Your Mind," where she leans into rising phrases and places an inflective "cry" in her voice at just the right moments. Then follows a strident *a cappella* call punctuated by instrumental chords, the opening and closing gestures of the work-song-inflected "Waterboy." These opening cuts link three women who dwell, at least according to conventional wisdom, in separate musical orbits: Geeshie Wiley, Dolly Parton, and Odetta. Of the three, the first is least known. Wiley recorded "Last Kind Words" for Paramount in the early 1930s at a session with another long-forgotten blueswoman Elvie (or L.V.) Thomas (Giddens 2015; Sullivan 2019). Giddens (in conversation via Zoom with the author, October 16, 2020) recalls it was a conscious decision "to open up the record with a completely obscure Black woman who represents such a huge army of such people who we've forgotten from the past, but that was a deliberate choice." She takes the tune at a plodding pace. Fuzzy-sounding electric guitar dances carefully around the mandolin, both support for the vocals and counterpart for the instrumental turns that follow every couple of stanzas.

The three songs range widely across moods and subjectivities. "Last Kind Words" typifies the personal and intimate musings of downhome or "country" blues. The somber phrases evoke, most specifically, the narrator's resignation facing possible death in "the German war." Other references are more opaque or evocative. There is poverty: "When you see me coming, look across the rich man's field / And if I don't bring you flour, I'll bring you bolted meal." There is death, faced by a mother who admonishes her daughter: "don't you be so wild." There is distance from a lover as "deep and wide" as the Mississippi River: "I can stand right here, see my babe from the other side." The Parton tune that follows is similarly framed as a person-to-person conversation but contrasts the former's grim sobriety with flip defiance at the end of a romance. "Waterboy," distinct from the intimacy of the first two, draws from that collective body of colloquial images bubbling over from the nineteenth century into early recordings. Floating phrases evoke luck and strength – the "Jack O'Diamonds" and a hammer that's "goin' to bust this rock, boy, from here to Macon" – carried by a voice that is by turns bluesy, jazzy, subtle, and ardent (Muir 2010). All the while the band behind Giddens, with producer T-Bone Burnett at the helm, kicks and struts its way through a New Orleans barrelhouse romp.

To follow "Last Kind Words" with Parton and Odetta is to delve beneath the surface of US music and its history. These tracks invite the listener to discover kinship between the songs while reckoning distinctions between the artists who first recorded them. Giddens (2020) said, "People always talk about the US as a melting pot but in terms of music it really is true." Yet, Wiley, Parton, and Odetta don't get put in the same pot; instead, they get sorted out on the counter as discrete dishes: downhome blues, classic country, and Civil Rights-era folksong, with all the extrasonic taste those genres evoke. *Tomorrow Is My Turn* mingles the flavors in one American pot. When I asked Giddens about the extent to which juxtaposing genres was intentional, she said, "I'm not blurring the genres, I'm just disregarding them because they're all false anyway. They're all fake, and they're all created, and they're all, you know, constructed for reasons that have nothing to do with the music" (Giddens 2020).

In song choice, style, and substance, the rest of the album keeps pace. Giddens follows "Waterboy" with a cover of "She's Got You," the Hank Cochran tune made famous by Patsy Cline. Harmonized background vocals and horn section give this classic country song an old-school R&B feel, as Giddens describes in the notes, with more restrained vocals over a slow, lilting duple compound beat. "Up Above My Head" comes next, kicking off like rockabilly before a singing and shouting choir of background singers injects old-time gospel feeling and a fiddle enters to turn the verse. From the vantage point of country music, the album *Tomorrow* sets Parton and Cline within a musical framework wide enough to include Nashville but also much, much more of the American musical picture. A spirit of artistic genealogy pervades the album, playing out like a pilgrimage to musically intrepid matriarchs right up to the wistful, banjo-driven coda "Angel City," its only newly composed song. There is no single genre label that describes this album.

Musicologist David Brackett (2016, 23) scrutinizes what he calls "homologous music-identity relationships – that is, identification in which a category of music corresponds to a preexisting demographic category of some kind." His ground-shifting book *Categorizing Sound* (2016) cuts a fresh path through familiar terrain of convenient labels for grouping musicians and recordings on one side and, on the other, fixations with race, class, and even region that these historically situated terms enshrine. Brackett explores the extent to which this equation, where one set of musical traits ascribe to Black musicians and others to white musicians, is inadequate to truly explain the reality of mixed-up American music-making from the beginning.

Genre is dynamic; not a static collection of characteristics, its parameters shift over time. Musical homologies arise from the interplay between commercial entities like record companies, music-makers, audiences, and media, against a background of social and political history, all of which change over time as well. One genre's associations, for example, with region, class, or race, can move and they can overlap. Yet, these associations can also become ossified, and when they do they create limitations or blindness with regard to the interconnected origins of musical traditions. Homologies conspire against artists and listeners the same way and can abridge the repertoire available to a musician or likewise narrow the musical expectations of audiences. Thus, when a singer or picker makes music that doesn't match their demographic, it can feel like a revelation, or a "healing moment."

Another force at play is the nature of commercial enterprise. The music industry and media tend to self-perpetuate the categories that attended their rise. This is not an issue for country music alone. It drives other types of music as well. In his memoir *How Music Works,* for example, musician David Byrne, who is white, recalls his experiences with the rock/pop band Talking Heads. Their song "Once in a Lifetime" failed to gain radio airplay despite its heavy rotation on MTV. Rock stations thought "it was too funky; not really rock. And the R&B stations wouldn't play the song either." As Byrne (2012, 54) reflects, though exceptional media outlets exist, "by and large the world of music in the United States is only slightly less segregated than other institutions. A lot of businesses might not be overtly racist, but by playing to their perceived demographic – which is a natural business decision – they reinforce existing divisions. Change does happen, but sometimes it's frustratingly slow."

Giddens described a similar experience during an interview for a 2019 *New Yorker* profile. She had released the recording *Songs of Our Native Daughters*, a project with three other musicians, all women of color who also play banjo. Channels of distribution and media coverage were shaped by homology. Because the recording came out on Smithsonian Folkways, "it won't be covered by any black press," Giddens said. "We took the [Smithsonian] platform that was offered" (Sullivan 2019). She goes on to describe being turned down to perform at the Apollo Theater, a historically African American venue. Though all four musicians on the *Songs of Our Native Daughters* project identify as Black, their presentation got in the way. The same tension Byrne notes between race, musical sound and, in their case, record label shaped access to audiences and venues. This paradigm has grown tiresome, and it's time to shake it loose.

The recording industry began during an era when belief in fundamental race-based distinctions between human beings – including assumptions of white superiority by the dominant population in power – justified Jim Crow laws to separate people and limit freedom and opportunity for those deemed less worthy. This stemmed from reductionist notions that significant differences in beliefs, abilities, values, and, ultimately, human worth exist among people of different races. Then and now, these assumptions hamper US society from fully realizing our own foundational ideals of equality and freedom. They also structured the ways musical sounds got sorted into categories as the popular recording industry took shape, beginning around 1920. Race records and, eventually, hillbilly records were labels to help potential consumers readily find music they wanted to hear (see Brackett 2016, 1–40), assumed meaningful and relevant to an imagined audience of record buying US public at the time.[6] That early twentieth-century audience existed in a US society deeply scarred by a Jim Crow point of view.

Because race so strongly marks it, country music makes a useful access point for identifying how inherited concepts of US music and the people who make it are overdue for revision. Racism infused the organization of the recording industry and its products at a structural level. With the exception of its most egregious expressions, this is how white supremacy works. It operates on the level of norms so deeply ingested as to flavor every human interaction across visible difference. In this way marketing categories made to sell records reinforced segregation and bolstered racist attitudes that perpetuated it for generations. These labels set patterns of thinking that shaped the industry, media representations, and scholarship in ways that prove hard to shake. They remain with us today.[7]

As African Americans gradually gained greater opportunities to live as full members of US society, a Jim Crow framework for popular genres (the kind fueling subsequent moral panics over ragtime, jazz, rock 'n' roll, then hip-hop) gave way to something more akin to *Plessy vs. Ferguson* (1896), the court case precedent for the defective concept of "separate but equal." All this is to say, collectively speaking, the typical way to think about US

[6] Brackett (2016, 31) writes of how "musical categories grew out of and contributed to a preoccupation with race, class, and geographical regions and how these might be articulated to technological developments and the imperatives of economics. Thus, knowledge about people and music participated in the process of finding an efficient model for the music industry that would coordinate production and consumption."

[7] See Jada Watson's chapter in this volume, which demonstrates with data the extent to which this white supremacist system has been reinforced and remains operative.

music is binary and racialized: separate-but-parallel streams that spring from dramatically different experiences of Black folks and white folks. The streams occasionally cross and occasionally flow together but otherwise can be mapped neatly according to demographics.

It is a convenient metaphor – two separate but equal streams of Black and white music – for those of us who teach, talk, think, or write about US popular music. It offers a useful structure for parsing music in a systematic way, cutting neat courses through complicated materials and, thus, allowing for cogent, organized discussion of music history. Furthermore, it mirrors the real-world categories of race and hillbilly. Yet, the metaphor also reinforces race-based divisions our society has outgrown. It is polluted with tired old notions of how demographics like race correlate to music (among other things). Were it not so, the Carolina Chocolate Drops' Opry performance wouldn't be noteworthy, much less someone's healing moment.

It should be noted that the Drops were not the first Black musicians to perform on the Opry. The noteworthiness of their moment had something to do with rattling the stale-but-convenient race-based paradigm. At this point, the research of musicologist Nina Eidsheim (2012) becomes helpful in pursuing this. Eidsheim examines commonplace stereotypes about what sounds Black or what sounds white at the level of vocal timbre. Knowledge of a singer's racial identity constitutes part of the "extrasonic information" that, as she demonstrates, bears on musical experience and meaning. Both singing and its perception are situated within a set of sociohistorical boundaries for performer and audience. An African American singer who "sounds Black" may be presumed to have polished and perfected innate qualities in his/her voice. But to what extent are they innate versus situated from the singer's very first utterance? Eidsheim posits that every person navigates circumstances and expectations throughout a lifetime. Speakers and singers intone, enunciate, and develop structures that produce their voice, always situated; that is, within that individual singer's historically circumscribed context.

Listeners, too, are situated beings for whom "extrasonic information" shapes the perception of sound. That would include conventions that country is a white genre, while R&B is Black. Categories that chart music and catalog it for sale affirm this as a kind of cultural law (see Brackett 2016, 28). In the case of country, elements of dress, vocal style, instrumentation, pronunciation, and subject matter are all part of what Brackett (26) names a "shared, tacit understanding about which differences are meaningful." Race – more specifically, whiteness – marks country music's identity more deeply than all other extrasonic elements. Its whiteness is propped by the conceptual weight of more than a century of the recording industry. No institution represents country music better than the *Grand Ole Opry*. The Drops' first Opry appearance could only be "healing" for audience members experiencing a breach in the internalized assumption that country music is white.

An exceptional musician like country superstar Charley Pride foiled racial expectations via his music at the Opry a half century earlier. Yet his success, understood to be a remarkable mastery of the white genre by a Black performer, confirmed the accepted "music homology," that the exception proves the rule. Pride framed his country music career with a sense of surprise – expressed when he referred to his "permanent tan" or to not sounding "like he was supposed to" (Malone and Laird 2018, 373). The Drops, by contrast, conveyed a sense of reclamation and recovery. They achieved their mission, in part, via the historical reach of their repertoire, extending way before for great calcification of early recording genres, back to the source in order to reveal the true complexity of American music and culture.[8]

In a 2020 interview (Figure 16.1), Giddens arrived at the notion of a mother tongue as one way to conceive US musical genres as they settled in a hundred years before. Italian, French, Spanish – all derive from Latin, and speakers of these languages can recognize elements of Latin although they do not speak it. Furthermore, these languages have offshoots. So, there are "dialects in Naples, dialects in Sicily," and so on, "and they're all quite different from each other but they're still quite related to the main language which is itself a direct descendent from the mother tongue of Latin. . . . And what happened with the recording industry is exactly what has happened with languages: you get it codified." Despite the standardization of a language, some speakers retain dialects, and, sometimes, someone recovers a forgotten connection between their speech patterns and the mother tongue. Here's where the metaphor stretches back to the Drops. Prerecording repertoire is like a "mother music" for all the twentieth-century genres and their offshoots post-1920. Thus, "it's not about getting diversity into this music; it's putting it back. Because it always was." Giddens (2020) said, "If that is the one thing that people get from what I say, that makes me happy."

---

[8] Foundational sources for prerecorded US music-making include Southern (1971) and Epstein (1977).

Figure 16.1. Screenshots taken during Zoom interview between the author and Rhiannon Giddens on October 16, 2020

Her second solo project continues this work of reconnecting – musical re-membering – but with more overt political significance. Released earlier the same year of her IBMA keynote, *Freedom Highway* is mostly originals. Its most unforgettable songs convey voices of enslaved women during the Civil War, mined from Giddens's study of nineteenth-century slave narratives. Songs that recover forgotten, erased voices of Black American women are also the ones with most prominent fiddle or banjo. These songs employ traditional string band instrumentation – the forms, styles, and timbres of country music – without quaintness or nostalgia. They wed these sounds to words giving voice to wounds of a nation's past that must be faced in order for them to be healed.

In "Julie," Giddens molds history into the simple strophes of a ballad, one of country's most typical musical forms, with lyrics that convey a scene or event. Topical songs about tragedy, sometimes narrative, sometimes dramatic, are core to country's musical origin stories. They remained vital into the mid-century, as recordings like "The Wreck of the Old 97" and "Death of Little Kathy Fiscus" attest. In ballad style, "Julie" gives voice to a Black woman silenced by the circumstances of slavery during the Civil War. The song lyrics unfold as dialogue, revealing a fraught relationship between master and slave, personal in the entwined daily living yet toxic to its core. Switching perspectives every other verse, the "mistress" fears the oncoming Union soldiers and their threat to her life and treasure; "Julie" makes clear that any affection for her mistress shrivels compared to her hunger for freedom and her bitterness in enforced servitude. As Julie puts it baldly in the lyrics, "In leaving here, I'm leaving hell."

"At the Purchaser's Option" likewise weds lyrics of a woman's suffering with a familiar verse-chorus form. Minus its words, the chorus rolls along in an anthem style – narrow in range, simple in musical phrase structure (essentially a-b-a-b') and repetitive in lyrics with three parallel lines that build to a final contrast. But then the words, their larger context, and the persistent anthemic delivery confront the human cost of slavery head on:

You can take my body,
You can take my bones,
You can take my blood,
But not my soul.

The verses adopt the anguished voice of a woman being advertised for sale in an August newspaper sometime during the 1830s. The advertisement, which Giddens ran across during her research, gives passing mention to a nine-month-old baby boy, who would be available "at the purchaser's option." This appalling scene from American history is underscored by the sparse musical setting of banjo, drums, and bass. Circular in structure, the song's opening returns at its close, a symbol of the dehumanizing cycle of chattel slavery. The song's video shows a simple still image of Giddens in a chair, middle of a dirt road, surrounded by tall sugarcane plants on either side; the newspaper clipping appears above her in the sky at the beginning and, as the song progresses, abstract drawings of a dark female figure holding a baby leap in and out of the frame.

"Come, Love, Come" sounds more bluesy than other cuts, but muted by way of its delivery. It foregrounds that same hollow-sounding nineteenth-century replica banjo played by Giddens throughout the project. Her instrument joins with bass, guitar, and percussion so dampened that it sounds more like cardboard or a piece of wood than a modern drum. The words again illuminate human experience, in this case that of an escaped slave during the Civil War who, following soldiers to Tennessee, now awaits the arrival of a loved one. The song conveys an agonized, uncertain state marked with potent use of silence, repetition, and an elaborated, extended final treatment of the chorus.

Other songs cover the same wide range of styles found in *Tomorrow*: from the sparse instrumental "Following the North Star" to the full, tightly composed tune "The Love We Almost Had." The verses of the latter song get punctuated by a bass-and-piano-driven strut, while a prominent muted trumpet adds both comment and harmony to the main vocals. The only two covers, "Birmingham Sunday" and the title cut "Freedom Highway," anchor the project in spirit and history to the 1960s. These songs seam centuries of mass race-based slavery with the decades of institutionalized oppression that separate Emancipation from advances made during the Civil Rights Movement.

Sonically they stand out for evoking 1960s–era Black music styles. "Birmingham Sunday" brings an organ-driven gospel feel. "Freedom Highway" recalls a 1970s soul anthem, fueled along by an electric guitar ostinato. At the same time, both covers speak to the present. "Birmingham Sunday" does so by altering its final refrain, changing past tense "and the choirs kept singing of freedom" to present. This small move shifts the affective emphasis, from the innocence and strength of conviction among victims of the Birmingham church bombings to ongoing determination to keep singing until hate- and race-based violence is categorically exposed and justly redressed. "Freedom Highway" sets horn riffs in dialogue with the female/male harmonized voices of Giddens and singer, songwriter, and producer Bhi Bhiman, ending with a strident trumpet solo that sounds more like a rally cry than a tribute. The song alternates verses that question the state of US society with simple repetitive lines of the kind crowds sing in a protest march.

The political potential of the two Civil Rights era covers stems not from their associations with social justice activism alone. It is once more the historiographic work they accomplish. Originally recorded by Joan Baez and the Staple Singers, respectively, "Birmingham Sunday" and "Freedom Highway," like other emblematic songs of the 1960s folk movement, have been compartmentalized based on race. Political implications in this case are direct: audiences who otherwise share common goals and visions for society get segregated. As musicologist Julia Cox (2018a, 7), writes regarding folk music: "due to the racialized nature of music marketing, artists across the color line and from different musical categories are rarely placed in conversation."[9] Returning to an earlier food metaphor, the two songs are dishes cooked with similar ingredients, yet presented as entirely distinct cuisines. "Freedom Highway", then, restores the full conversation, blending Baez and the Staples in the same pot as voices for Civil Rights justice. The gestalt whole has the potential to push against racialized boundaries still framing our media, our music classrooms, our paradigms for sorting and understanding American music history.

It bears repeating: the historical narratives we internalize shape lived reality for both good and ill. Scholars ask new questions and seek new insights into the past and the present. Musicians like Giddens are uniquely positioned to sing new questions and insights into being. Articles, books, and chapters in books reach a relatively small audience. A song is different. Giddens once suggested a song can achieve in short order the same as a whole stack of books, "for the ease with which it can touch emotion and create empathy with a subject that people didn't feel before" (qtd. in Kinder 2015, 33). Thus, Giddens realizes a reconception of music into being through her voice (Eidsheim 2012, esp. 19); she sings the reconception of country music and of Black music as American music. And it's worth listening as if the life of our nation depends upon it.

The philosopher Ludwig Wittgenstein (1968, 48), in the book *Philosophical Investigations,* wrote, "One thinks that one is tracing the outlines of the thing's nature over and over again, and one is merely tracing round the frame through which we look at it." Change the frame, and everything we know about "the thing" changes too. In 2020, it is clear that our structurally simple, racially binary narrative for American music cannot support the full, robust reality of US culture. It never could. As Giddens (2020) said, "[A]s soon as people's feet hit America, stuff was coming together ... the evidence is legion." Scholars like Shelly Fisher Fishkin (1995) and John Edward Philips (1990) were pointing out in the 1990s how its hybridized, adaptive nature – Blackness and whiteness in tension with one another – distinguishes US cultures from all others in the world. A more usefully accurate frame would have room for brownness as well. Jim Crow was wrong: musical miscegenation is that which makes American music American. Why is it so hard to stop talking about this music as though he was right?

---

[9] She talks of this effect in relation to Joan Baez's recording of "Birmingham Sunday" and Nina Simone's song "Mississippi Goddam," songs from the same era, directly responding to the same 1963 act of terror. Similar dynamics bear on versions of "Birmingham Sunday" by Baez and Giddens, analyzed in Cox (2018b).

When it comes to popular music in general, and country music in particular, different tasks each require a different tool. The first is a rear-view mirror, for recognizing the historical roots of genre categories like country. The second is a microscope, for examining ways this category shapes and limits music for both performers and audiences. Country and other US genres bear the weight of assumptions about people, music, and history that are overdetermined by race and oversimplified for convenience. To dissect how that is so is one way to answer Giddens's call, but it cannot stand alone. Scholars, listeners, writers, filmmakers, and musicians must find ways to dig more deeply into the dynamic, mixed-up roots of American music, and craft a more complicated, more accurate narrative.

Giddens's work is one starting point for reconceptualizing US music with knowledge that narratives of the past shape the present. When she sings a country song, Giddens is not demonstrating that a Black musician can convincingly perform white country music; she demonstrates that country music is not white in the way people have presupposed. Her musical embodiment of American identity is critical to embrace at this agitated moment in the nation's history: in the end, US culture's mixed-up roots constitute all that is special and unique about it, and therein lies the source of hope and healing. Americans – particularly white Americans – must face rather than look away from difficulties of the past in order for our society to move forward.[10] Her work demands exactly that. She cannot do it alone.

[10] Giddens discussed this with Emma John (2018).

∿ | Epilogue

Country Music Needs a Revolution

RISSI PALMER

Who knew that twenty-two years ago when I began this musical journey that I was making a political statement by just being myself, an eighteen-year-old Black girl from St. Louis, Missouri?

At the time, I didn't see it that way.

My story begins like so many others. I had a dream to sing on big stages and hear my music played on the radio. To see my name in lights. Country music was a big part of the soundtrack of my life. My family listened to Patsy Cline and Aretha Franklin with equal fervor. Encouraged by my first managers, also Black women, to pursue my dreams of country music stardom in spite of the fact that I didn't see myself reflected in the artists (I didn't yet know about the many Black women who came before me, like Linda Martell, Lenora Ross, and Ruby Falls).

My time in Nashville is best summed up with a quote from Charles Dickens: "It was the best of times, it was the worst of times . . ."

I signed my first publishing deal in Nashville at nineteen in 2000. I sang at Tootsies until the wee hours of the morning and played writer's rounds at the Bluebird Café. I endured LOTS of rejection, which made me appreciate the big yes moments even more.

All the work paid off in 2008, when I fulfilled a lifelong dream of playing the Grand Ole Opry and became the first Black woman in twenty years to appear on the *Billboard* Hot Country Songs chart with "Country Girl," "Hold on to Me," and "No Air." Unfortunately, disputes with my record label brought it all to a screeching halt and I left Nashville in 2010, feeling largely abandoned by the industry, like an experiment that failed.

Do I believe race is why I didn't reach the level of stardom I'd hoped for? No. Do I believe that I faced hardships that my peers didn't because of race? Yes, absolutely.

When I arrived in 2000, no one was talking about race openly. I was told to keep my head down, not talk about it, and let my work speak for itself, so I pretty much did that. That didn't keep it from coming up, however. I smiled and brushed off what we now called microaggressions on a pretty regular basis. There was a whole meeting about my hair being too much like an Afro. It ended with me taking pictures with a photographer who had no clue how to light Black skin in a wig made of silky Malaysian hair cascading down my back and a short, Jennifer Aniston-like bone straight wig. It was a MESS. Luckily, the publicist from the label, Dawnalisa, spoke up and set up a "test" shoot with a photographer who knew the right lighting, using my own clothes, and my own hair . . . Those shots ended up being the first pictures the world saw of me.

It was apparent that the "appearance" of me was an issue that needed to be figured out from the very beginning of my time in Nashville. My very first meetings with country record labels were sight unseen; a well-meaning insider would take my music, without a picture, and play it for the executives. If they loved it, THEN they would do the reveal. Once I came into the room, the questions would inevitably begin and they were always the same: "We need to figure out how to market someone like her. . . ." My accent was scrutinized, song choices were suddenly conundrums wrapped in enigmas because how would we ever find songs for "someone like me" . . . Someone like me. By the end of that first year, I had seen almost all the major labels and was offered a demo deal and lots of "come back when you've recorded/written more songs." None of them took a meeting with me ever again, and it would be seven years before I was offered a deal, from an independent record label called 1720 Entertainment.

Music videos were the next place where my outward appearance proved to be a field of landmines. In a meeting with video director Kristen Barlowe about the treatment for my single "Country Girl" my then manager (a powerful white man who, at the time, managed some of the biggest pop acts in the business) tried to convince us that we needed to confront the race thing head on because "everyone would be thinking it anyway." His suggestions to be "controversial" included me having a huge Black family sitting in a kitchen eating watermelon (yes . . . watermelon) while a "Big Mama" cooked for us, me walking into an all-white honky tonk, the natural "record scratch" and awkward silence that would cause but then being saved by a benevolent white cowboy, and finally, all of this action ending in an all-Black church with a Gospel choir . . . because, why not? Needless to say, you could hear a pin drop in the room. It was a resounding "Hell Naw" from me, the end of that management relationship, and the eventual creation of the beautiful and representative video (featuring my actual grandmother) that Kristin had originally proposed. The video received airplay on CMT, VH1, and was shown in Apple stores (a little foreshadowing right there . . .) and remains a fan favorite for its depiction of all shapes, sizes, and colors.

When planning the video for my second video for "No Air," the debate wasn't just *my* race this time, it was the race of my love interest. Because "No Air" is a song about heartbreak, it kind of begs for a lover. There was much meeting and conversation about who I should be singing to. Should he be Black or White? What wouldn't offend the country music fans? I remember vividly wanting a particular Black football player I had been crushing on to be the one I rolled around with in the sand. Though Kristen and I loved that idea, it was ultimately shot down, and I was left rolling and wandering around the beach on my own. It turned out to be a beautiful video, but I'm always reminded of all the back and forth and the mess that happened behind the scenes. This video also marked the beginning of the end of my relationship with 1720.

My radio promotions, marketing, and publicity teams worked so hard for me and my music and it showed. Here we were, this small independent label fighting for airplay along with all the majors. It was an absolute miracle they were able to get "Country Girl" and "No Air" to chart, let alone into the fifties and forties on *Billboard* (to THIS day, Linda Martell is still the highest-charting Black woman on the *Billboard* Hot Country Singles chart, making it to the twenties . . . in 1969). Radio tour brought its own set of obstacles for me. I remember hearing a member of my radio team speak with a certain program director, asking outright what it would take for them to play my music and them firmly responding that they wouldn't play my music simply because of the color of my skin. I went through what I call "authenticity tests," where I was asked questions about obscure country music to see if I knew it, or questions about the validity of my country roots, or if I was using country music to get to pop. I can remember asking a white peer if a certain station asked them the same questions and them laughing incredulously and saying no.

Even my relationship with the fandom was fraught at times, providing some really painful and really triumphant moments during this journey. For every "I'm so glad to see someone that looks like me in country music" comment or inbox message, I was called a "Nigger" or "Black bitch" online, in reviews of my first album, in direct messages, on pages dedicated to bashing me specifically, and hate mail. Letters that looked like fan mail would come to the record label and then be sent to me. I would excitedly open them, only to be confronted with someone's resentment of my Black presence in "their music." I remember being so anxious about it that my publicist Schatzi advised me never to google myself or read the comment section . . . I still don't to this day. There is the infamous "box incident" that my close friends and I recall from that time. I had received a package wrapped in a brown paper bag with very scribbled writing on it. My building super sat it right outside my door, which was unusual. The fact that I had been receiving such hateful mail and I wasn't expecting anything at the time left me unnerved by this box. I proceeded to call my friends, my manager at the time, and eventually my neighbor to try to figure out what to do. I poked at it with a broom handle, afraid to pick it up. I seriously thought that maybe someone sent a bomb or something. Eventually, my neighbor came over and helped me open it . . . it was DVDs I had ordered online and forgotten about. We used to tell that story and laugh. With time, that story has become less funny and more indicative of what was going on behind all the smiles and singing that the public saw from me. I was scared and weary. There are many more stories I could tell like this from that time, being kicked in a crowd while hosting an event, being prevented from walking on stage by a security guard, and so on, and so on.

Looking back, I feel a mixture of gratitude, regret, and relief. Gratitude for 1720's initial belief in me, their investment in my talent, and the staff's hard work. I wouldn't be where I am now if not for the label. Regret for not speaking up for myself sooner, for allowing myself to be treated like a product rather than a person, for not recognizing my worth. Relief that I will NEVER be in that position again, that I will never allow myself to be taken for granted, to be used, or to sell myself short. I focus all these feelings into the artist advocacy work that I do now.

In 2019, the race question had resurfaced, thanks to Lil Nas X and "Old Town Road." Articles were being cranked out by Black and white writers who didn't seem to want to look deeper than Charley Pride, Darius Rucker, Mickey Guyton, Jimmie Allen, and Kane Brown for the BIPOC contributions to country music.

I understood them forgetting me, but how could you forget Linda Martell? DeFord Bailey? Lesley Riddle? Ruby Falls? Miko Marks? And the Black Country Music Association? I could go on and on. 2020 marked fifty years since the debut album of Linda Martell, the first Black woman to play the Grand Ole Opry and to chart a song on the *Billboard* Hot Country Singles chart. Her album, *Color Me Country*, was the foundation on which all women of color have built their careers.

I knew there were more stories that deserved to be told and preserved . . . so, with the encouragement of my dear friend Shellie R. Warren, and a ton of time on my hands, thanks to Covid-19, in March 2020, I began doing interviews for what would become "Color Me Country Radio," my radio show on Apple Music Country Radio, named in honor of Martell's groundbreaking album.

My friend Kelly McCartney brought the show to the attention of Apple Music, starting this wild ride. "Color Me Country Radio with Rissi Palmer" debuted on August 30, 2020, with the mission of telling stories of Black, Latinx, and Indigenous artists in country and Americana music. My life hasn't been the same since.

I had no idea that the spring of 2020 would also bring the deaths of Breonna Taylor, Ahmaud Arbery, and George Floyd, breaking the already cracked dam of race relations, causing us all to take an unflinching look at all its institutions and how they have been affecting people of color, especially Black people.

It lit a fire under me that said it was time to tell these stories, including my own, and no matter how painful or ugly, it was time for country music to see itself – complicated and omitted history and all.

In research for the show, I stumbled across so many artists with compelling stories. Artists like Sarge and Shirley West, who, as far as I know, were the first Black husband and wife country music duo. Contemporaries of Pride and Martell, they wrote with Tom T. Hall and toured the South in the Civil Rights era with a white band, playing regional oprys. Their music and lives were unknown to me but thanks to an old issue of *Billboard*, their son Joe West and his beautiful documentary about their lives, "A Song Can Change a Life," I was soon a fan. Their episode was the first time some of their music had been heard since the 1960s.

Ironically, this was the same month that Maren Morris stood onstage at the CMA Awards and said my name, along with Mickey Guyton, Brittney Spencer, Rhiannon Giddens, and Linda Martell, sparking a renewed interest in all of us.

Stories like the Wests are precisely why "Color Me Country Radio" exists; 2020 and 2021 showed me the power of just simply acknowledging someone. It can change the trajectory of someone's life.

I also found inspiration in Cleve Francis, a Black cardiologist-turned-country singer signed for a time to Capitol Nashville; and Frankie Staton, a singer-songwriter with an unsinkable spirit. Together, they created the Black Country Music Association. When the industry appeared to turn a blind eye to them, they built their own table, providing artist development through songwriting seminars and showcases for industry tastemakers. Their ingenuity and resilience moved the needle. If they had finances to back up their vision, who knows what else they could have achieved?

It blows my mind how much of this history is easily accessible but barely ever addressed or acknowledged by documentaries, books, and institutions of country music. With just a few Google searches and emails I figured it out. This is also true with finding artists of color. Trust me when I say there is no shortage of talent out here. Between social media and streaming services, I've found more compelling artists to interview and play than I have episodes for. Artists of color are absolutely thriving on both these platforms between followers and streams, so much so that it would almost appear to be an even playing field there . . . almost. Most of the artists doing well on these platforms remain unsigned. If millions of streams and reposts won't move the industry, what will? This leads me to believe that there is little care and effort put into changing the narrative and expanding the genre.

As we pass the one-year anniversary of the show, I'm absolutely blown away by the many victories and course corrections that have happened: Linda Martell being acknowledged and honored with the EqualPlay Award from CMT, the inclusion of six Black women in CMT Next Women of Country, Mickey Guyton's release of "Black Like Me" (a song I never could have imagined being written in Nashville, let alone released) and her subsequent Grammy nomination, activism, and career upswing, the influx of several BIPOC artists into the country music landscape, the many panels and discussions on race, and the completely unexpected inclusion of my show in the Country Music Hall of Fame's 2021 "American Currents" exhibit among them.

On the outside, this could very easily look like problems are being solved and everything is good. However, the work has just begun.

It's not enough for there to be, as syndicated radio personality Bobby Bones said in early 2021 (Levine 2021), a "vocal minority" fighting for change, this effort will take everyone. I've watched as a few artists found their voices this year, including myself, and used them to speak up about inequities, biases, and injustices within the Nashville system. It takes guts for someone who is currently in the thick of it to speak up and out against it. To all those who have said nothing, or whose activism is limited to simply posting a Black square on Instagram, or "haven't had the time to think about racism in the industry," it's not ok for you to rely on the work of a few.

Every effective movement in our history happened because there was a belief that all concerned parties were moving as one. The same rules apply here. If you want to be seen as a change agent, BE A CHANGE AGENT. Start with your circle. Who are you employing? Who are you writing with? Who are you working with? How are you looking out for those coming behind you? Are your statements or actions hindering those trying to do the work? Are you only looking out for yourself? If you aren't concerned with any of those answers, then step out of the way of those that are. Martin Luther King Jr. said, "A social movement that moves people is merely a **revolt**. A movement that changes both people and institutions is a revolution (my emphasis)."

What the industry needs is a revolution, not a revolt. It's not enough to see diversity onstage, it needs to permeate at every level.

And the biggest observation I've made is a toxic culture in fandom. I watched Rachel Berry – a Black elementary school teacher and country music fan – in 2020 talk about how much she loved country music but felt unwelcome at shows (Elasfar 2020). There was subsequent outpouring of support from fans and artists only to see in February 2021, Morgan Wallen's sales skyrocketed after being caught using a racist slur as a "playful" term for a friend.

For me, the hurtful part wasn't the slur. It was the reaction from fans. I have screenshots of people calling me everything but a child of God for saying it was wrong. They tell us to get over it because "it's no big deal" and "Black people use it all the time." The hate is downright demoralizing.

There have been days that take me back to my apartment in 2008, bracing myself to open hate mail, honestly wondering if the work is even worth it. It seems to be a disease of the heart that plagues the whole country, not just country music.

In moments of sadness and exasperation, I think about the good. The amazing work of writers like Andrea Williams, Amanda Marie Martinez, Holly G., and so many others who examine hard truths and ask hard questions; the proliferation of Black country content made from our unique points of view like the Black Opry, the work of my own home team, Apple Music Country Radio, and the intentionally diverse and varied programming they offer, and the long-overdue inclusion of Ray Charles in the Country Music Hall of Fame in 2021.

I think about the Color Me Country Artist Grant fund that Kelly McCartney and I started in 2020 that has given over fifty BIPOC artists grants to pursue their country music dreams and all the allies like Brandi Carlile's Looking Out Foundation, CMT, Newport Folk Foundation, Fiona Prine, Donald Cohen, and all the good folks that give monthly that made that possible. Race should never be the reason someone can't pursue their dreams, neither should money.

I challenge the entire industry to do more. For it to think about more lasting ways to truly transform the industry. Who are you including on your boards? Who are you hiring to run your record companies? Who are your A&R people? Who is writing and producing the hit songs?

It's great to see Black people on stage performing, hosting or in the audience at the awards, but if they can't win an award because they can't get signed in Nashville and can't get played on country radio – *what's the point?* Considering that Black people are foundational to modern country music, it's about time that this industry and its institutions begin to meaningfully consider and court Black audiences.

In the words of the multi-award-winning music producer (and one of the few Black Nashville music executives), Shannon Sanders: the industry is "leaving money on the table" when they don't consider people of color in their hiring, marketing, and signing practices.

This chapter of my life and career is my love letter to every artist whose names we'll never know or are pushed to the margins of history. To every Black or brown child that ever had a dream, only to be told they can't or shouldn't aspire to it because of the color of their skin. It's also a love letter to country music, from someone who believes that music built on "three chords and the truth" should include everyone's truth.

Bibliography

"29 of the Best Country Music Festivals Worth Traveling to This Summer." n.d. Vacationsmadeeasy.com. www.vacationsmadeeasy.com/TheBLT/ 29oftheBestCountryMusicFestivalsWorthTravelingtoThisSummer.html.

"60 Minutes II [60 Minutes Wednesday] Stories with Dan Rather." n.d. https:// danratherjournalist.org/sites/default/files/documents/60MinsII%20LIST.pdf.

"Henley, Love, Austin Testify to Limit Record Contracts." 2001. *The Lompoc Record.* September 6, p. 2.

"U.S. Sales Database." n.d. RIAA. www.riaa.com/u-s-sales-database/.

"The Women of Country Music Sing 'He Thinks He'll Keep Her.'" 2020. *Country Music Thang Daily.* May 4. www.countrythangdaily.com/he-thinks-hell-keep-her/.

Ahmed, Sara. 2014. "White Men." *feministkilljoys* (blog), November 4. https:// feministkilljoys.com/2014/11/04/white-men/.

——— 2019. *What's the Use? On the Uses of Use.* Durham, NC: Duke University Press.

All Things Considered. 2015. "You Know Exactly What These Six Country Songs Have in Common." NPR, January 9. www.npr.org/2015/01/09/376145745/ you-know-exactly-what-these-six-country-songs-have-in-common.

——— 2020. "Interview with 'Color Me Country' Radio Host Rissi Palmer." NPR, November 28. www.npr.org/2020/11/28/939737483/interview-with-color-me-country-radio-host-rissi-palmer.

Amiradakis, Mark Jacob. 2016. "Social Networking Services: A Digital Extension of the Surveillance State?" *South African Journal of Philosophy* 35 (3): 281–92.

Anderson, Carol. 2016. *White Rage: The Unspoken Truth of Our Racial Divide.* New York: Bloomsbury.

Anderson, Chris. 2004. "The Long Tail." *Wired,* January 10. www.wired.com/2004/ 10/tail/.

——— 2008. *The Long Tail: Why the Future of Business Is Selling Less of More.* New York: Hyperion.

Andsager, Julie, and Kimberly Roe. 2003. "'What's Your Definition of Dirty, Baby?': Sex in the Music Video." *Sexuality & Culture* 7 (3): 79–97.

Anzaldúa, Gloria, and AnaLouise Keating. 2009. *The Gloria Anzaldúa Reader.* Durham, NC: Duke University Press.

Appadurai, Arjun. 1996. *Modernity at Large: Cultural Dimensions of Globalization.* Minneapolis: University of Minnesota Press.

Arizona Rural Policy Institute, Northern Arizona University. n.d. "Demographic Analysis of the Navajo Nation Using 2010 Census and 2010 American Community Survey Estimates." Window Rock, AZ: Navajo Nation Planning and Development.

Askin, Noah, and Michael Mauskapf. 2017. "What Makes Popular Culture Popular? Product Features and Optimal Differentiation in Music." *American Sociological Review* 82 (5): 910–44.

Aspers, Patrik. 2006. *Markets in Fashion: A Phenomenological Approach.* London: Routledge.

Aspers, Patrik, and Frédéric Godart. 2013. "Sociology of Fashion: Order and Change." *Annual Review of Sociology* 39: 171–92.

Aspley, Janet. 2020. Hillbilly Deluxe: Male Performance Dress and Authenticity in Country Music 1947–92. PhD dissertation, University of Brighton.

Associated Press. 2007. "As a Black Woman, Rissi Palmer Is Country Rarity." *USA Today*, October 15. www.today.com/popculture/black-woman-rissi-palmer-country-rarity-wbna21307946.

———. 2017. "Sam Hunt Makes History, Explains Origin of Single 'Body Like a Back Road'." *Fox News*, July 31. www.foxnews.com/entertainment/sam-hunt-makes-history-explains-origin-of-single-body-like-a-back-road.

Auslander, Philip. 2006. "Musical Personae." *TDR: The Journal of Performance Studies* 50 (1): 100–19.

———. 2019. "Framing Personae in Music Videos." In *The Bloomsbury Handbook of Popular Music Video Analysis*, edited by Lori A. Burns and Stan Hawkins, 91–109. New York: Bloomsbury Academic.

Baker, Deborah. 2006. "Racism Fears a 'Simmering Pot' at N.M. Rez Border Town." *Arizona Daily Sun*, August 5. https://azdailysun.com/news/racism-fears-a-simmering-pot-at-n-m-rez-border-town/article_c74eab2c-54bb-5578-b2df-fd5df8babbaf.html.

Balaji, Murali. 2012. "The Construction of 'Street Credibility' in Atlanta's Hip-Hop Music Scene: Analyzing the Role of Cultural Gatekeepers." *Critical Studies in Media Communication* 29 (4): 313–30.

Banet-Weiser, Sarah. 2012. *Authentic TM: The Politics of Ambivalence in a Brand Culture.* New York: New York University Press.

Barlow, William. 1999. *Voice Over: The Making of Black Radio.* Philadelphia: Temple University Press.

Barrett, Frederick S., Kevin J. Grimm, Richard W. Robins, Tim Wildschut, Constantine Sedikides, and Petr Janata. 2010. "Music-Evoked Nostalgia: Affect, Memory, and Personality." *Emotion* 10 (3): 390–403.

Baumgartner, Hans. 1992. "Remembrance of Things Past: Music, Autobiographical Memory, and Emotion." *Advances in Consumer Research* 19 (1): 613–20.

Becker, Howard S. 1982. *Art Worlds.* Berkeley: University of California Press.

Bellamy, David, Howard Bellamy, and Michael Kosser. 2018. *Let Your Love Flow: The Life and Times of the Bellamy Brothers.* Dade City, FL: DarBella Publishing.

2022. "Diversity in Country Music." *International Country Music Journal*: 46–76.

Beltran, Mary. 2002. "The Hollywood Latina Body as Site of Social Struggle: Media Constructions of Stardom and Jennifer Lopez's Cross-over Butt." *Quarterly Review of Film and Video* 19 (1): 71–86.

Bender, Mark T., and Yongsheng Wang. 2009. "The Impact of Digital Piracy on Music Sales: A Cross-Country Analysis." *International Social Science Review* 84 (3/4): 157–70.

Bennett, Jessica. 2021. "The Working Woman's Anthem '9 to 5' Needed an Update. But This?" *New York Times*, February 7. https://www.nytimes.com/2021/02/07/business/dolly-parton-5-to-9-super-bowl.html

Bentham, Jeremy. 1791. *Panopticon: Postscript; Part I: Containing Further Particulars and Alterations Relative to the Plan of Construction Originally Proposed; Principally Adapted to the Purpose of a Panopticon Penitentiary-House*. London: T. Payne, Mews-Gate.

Bergman, David. 1993. Introduction. In *Camp Grounds: Style and Homosexuality*, edited by David Bergman, 3–18. Amherst: University of Massachusetts Press.

Berkvist, Robert. 2020. "Olivia de Havilland, 104, Who Starred in 'Gone With the Wind,' Dies." *New York Times*, July 26, p. 24.

Berlatsky, Noah. 2014. "The Racial Dynamics of 'Hick Hop'." *Atlantic*, July 15. www.theatlantic.com/entertainment/archive/2014/07/the-hick-hop-moment/374251/.

Bernstein, Jonathan. 2019. "Lydia Loveless Alleges Sexual Misconduct by Domestic Partner of Record Label Head." *Rolling Stone Country*, February 18. www.rollingstone.com/music/music-country/lydia-loveless-bloodshot-records-sexual-harassment-796005/.

Bernstein, Jonathan, John Freeman, Joseph Hudak, Brittney McKenna, and Marissa R. Moss. 2019. "Baby You a Song: Bro Country's 30 Biggest Bangers," *Rolling Stone*, December 3. www.rollingstone.com/music/music-country-lists/baby-you-a-song-bro-countrys-30-biggest-bangers-919249/.

Berry, Chad. 2008. *The Hayloft Gang: The Story of the National Barn Dance*. Urbana: University of Illinois Press.

Beyer, Alexa. 2021. "The Gay Songwriters Who Secretly Ruled the Country Charts are Ready for the Spotlight." *Mic*, July 26. www.mic.com/p/the-gay-songwriters-who-secretly-ruled-the-country-charts-are-ready-for-the-spotlight-82589639.

Blau, Jnan. 2009. "More than 'Just' Music: Four Performative Topoi, the Phish Phenomenon, and the Power of Music in/and Performance." Trans: *Transcultural Music Review*, 13 (January). www.sibetrans.com/trans/articulo/44/more-than-just-music-four-performative-topoi-the-phish-phenomenon-and-the-power-of-music-in-and-performance.

Bloodshot Records. 2019. *Too Late to Pray: Defiant Chicago Roots*. BS 273. Liner notes.

2020. *Pandemophenia*. BS 621. Liner notes.

Bonini, Tiziano, and Alessandro Gandini. 2019. "'First Week Is Editorial, Second Week Is Algorithmic': Platform Gatekeepers and the Platformization of Music Curation." *Social Media + Society* 5 (4): 1–11.

Born, Georgina. 2000. "Music and the Representation/Articulation of Sociocultural Identities." In *Western Music and Its Others: Difference, Representation, and Appropriation in Music*, edited by Georgina Born and David Hesmondhalgh, 31–37. Berkeley: University of California Press.

Bourdieu, Pierre. 1977. *Outline of a Theory of Practice*. Cambridge: Cambridge University Press.

——— 1984. *Distinction: A Social Critique of the Judgement of Taste*. Translated by Richard Nice. Cambridge: Harvard University Press.

Bowen, Dawn S. 1997. "Lookin' for Margaritaville: Place and Imagination in Jimmy Buffett's Songs." *Journal of Cultural Geography* 16 (2): 99–108.

Boym, Svetlana. 2001. *The Future of Nostalgia*. New York: Basic Books.

Brackett, David. 2016. *Categorizing Sound: Genre and Twentieth Century Popular Music*. Oakland: University of California Press.

Brady, Erika. 2013. "Contested Origins: Arnold Shultz and the Music of Western Kentucky." In *Hidden in the Mix: The African American Presence in Country Music*, edited by Diane Pecknold, 100–18. Durham: Duke University Press.

Breezy, Elle. 2016. "Beyonce Performs 'Daddy Lessons' with the Dixie Chicks at CMAs, Faces Backlash from Country Music Fans." *Singersroom.com*, November 3. https://singersroom.com/content/2016-11-03/beyonce-performs-daddy-lessons-dixie-chicks-cmas-faces-backlash-country-music-fans/.

Brothers, Eryn. 2020. "Is This the First Queer Country Song?" *Country Queer*, September 11. https://countryqueer.com/article/is-this-the-first-queer-country-song/.

Brøvig-Hanssen, Ragnhild, and Harkins, Paul. 2012. "Contextual Incongruity and Musical Congruity: The Aesthetics and Humor of Mash-Ups." *Popular Music* 31 (1): 87–104.

Brown, Dorothy A. 2021. *The Whiteness of Wealth: How the Tax System Impoverishes Black Americans – And How We Can Fix It*. New York: Crown.

Browne, David. 2020. "Country's Lost Pioneer." *Rolling Stone*, September 2. www.rollingstone.com/music/music-features/linda-martell-black-country-grand-ole-opry-pioneer-1050432/.

Browne, Simone. 2015. *Dark Matters: On the Surveillance of Blackness*. Durham: Duke University Press.

Brynjolfsson, Erik, Yu (Jeffrey) Hu, and Michael D. Smith. 2003. "Consumer Surplus in the Digital Economy: Estimating the Value of Increased Product Variety at Online Booksellers." *Management Science* 49 (11): 1580–96.

Bryson, Bethany. 1996. "'Anything but Heavy Metal': Symbolic Exclusion and Musical Dislikes." *American Sociological Review* 61 (5): 884–99.

Bufwack, Mary A., and Robert K. Oermann. 2003. *Finding Her Voice: Women in Country Music, 1800–2000.* Nashville: Country Music Foundation/ Vanderbilt University Press.

Bull, Michael, and Les Back. 2003. "Introduction." In *The Auditory Culture Reader,* edited by Michael Bull and Les Back, 1–14. Oxford: Berg.

Burns, Chelsea. 2020. "The Racial Limitations of Country-Soul Crossover in Bobby Womack's *BW Goes C&W,* 1976." *Journal of Popular Music Studies* 32 (2): 112–27.

Bush, George H. W. 1991. "Country Music Month, 1991, Proclamation 6358 of October 15, 1991." *Federal Register* 56 (201): 51969.

Burns, Ken. 2019. *Country Music: A Film by Ken Burns.* PBS.

Byrne, David. 2012. *How Music Works.* New York: Three Rivers Press.

Caplan, Lucy. 2020. "'Strange What Cosmopolites Music Makes of Us': Classical Music, the Black Press, and Nora Douglas Holt's Black Feminist Audiotopia." *Journal of the Society for American Music* 14 (3): 308–36.

Caramanica, Jon. 2016. "Review: Why 'Hero' is an Outstanding Country Music Debut." *New York Times,* June 1. www.nytimes.com/2016/06/02/arts/music/ maren-morris-hero-review.html.

———. 2017a. "Bye, Bro. In Country Music, It's the Year of the Gentleman." *Popcast,* September 22. *New York Times.* www.nytimes.com/2017/09/22/arts/music/ popcast-bro-country-gentlemen.html.

———. 2017b. "In Country Music, Nice Guys Finish First (For Now)." *New York Times,* September 21. www.nytimes.com/2017/09/21/arts/music/country- gentleman-thomas-rhett.html.

———. 2019. "Ken Burns's 'Country Music' Traces the Genre's Victories, and Reveals its Blind Spots." *New York Times,* September 12. www.nytimes.com/2019/ 09/12/arts/television/ken-burns-country-music.html.

Carlisle, Madeleine. 2020. "'Everything Has to Pass.' Why Dolly Parton is Optimistic About Life after Coronavirus." *Time,* May 28. https://time.com/ 5840666/dolly-parton-coronavirus-time100-talks/.

Carmean, Derek. 1999. "Reunited Knitters Play Benefit in San Francisco." *Rockabilly Central.* www.rockabilly.net/articles/knitters.shtml.

Carson, Charles D. 2012. "'Melanin in the Music': Black Music History in Sound and Image." *Current Musicology* 93 (Spring): 95–114.

Carter, Maria. 2017. "The Real-Life Love Story Behind Thomas Rhett's 'Die a Happy Man'," *Country Living,* November 8. www.countryliving .com/life/entertainment/a38112/real-love-story-behind-thomas-rhetts-die- a-happy-man/.

Casey, Jim. 2018. "Top 15 Best-Selling Country Albums of All Time, According to RIAA." *Country Daily,* March 14. www.thecountrydaily.com/2018/03/14/ top-15-best-selling-country-albums-of-all-time-according-to-the-riaa/.

Cash, W.J. 1941. *The Mind of the South.* New York: Alfred A. Knopf.

Castonguay, Roger. 2018. "Genettean Hypertextuality as Applied to the Music of Genesis: Intertextual and Intratextual Approaches." In *The Pop Palimpsest: Intertextuality in Recorded Popular Music*, edited by Lori Burns and Serge Lacasse, 61–82. Ann Arbor: University of Michigan Press.

Chalkley, Tony. 2012. "Surveillance: Why is Everybody Staring?" In *Communication, New Media and Everyday Life*, edited by Tony Chalkley, Adam Brown, Toija Cinque, Brad Warren, Mitchell Hobbs and Mark Finn, 201–14. South Melbourne: Oxford University Press.

Chang, Connie. 2002. "Can't Record Labels and Recording Artists All Just Get Along? The Debate Over California Labor Code 2855 and Its Impact on the Music Industry." *DePaul Journal of Art, Technology and Intellectual Property Law.* 12 (1): 13–24. https://via.library.depaul.edu/cgi/viewcontent .cgi?article=1239&context=jatip.

Chávez, Alex E. 2017. *Sounds of Crossing: Music, Migration and the Aural Poetics of Huapango Arribeño*. Durham: Duke University Press.

Cheng, William. 2018. "Black Noise, White Ears: Resilience, Rap, and the Killing of Jordan Davis." *Current Musicology* 102: 115–89.

Ching, Barbara. 2003. *Wrong's What I Do Best: Hard Country and Contemporary Culture*. Oxford: Oxford University Press.

Christenson, Peter, Donald F. Roberts, and Nicholas Bjork. 2012. "Booze, Drugs, and Pop Music: Trends in Substance Portrayals in the Billboard Top 100 1968–2008." *Substance Use & Misuse* 47 (2): 121–29.

Clarke, Betty. 2003. "The Dixie Chicks." *Guardian*, March 12. www.theguardian .com/music/2003/mar/12/artsfeatures.popandrock.

Cobble, D. 1991. *Waitresses and Their Unions in the Twentieth Century*. Urbana: University of Illinois Press.

Coe, Tyler Mahan. 2017. "Harper Valley PTA, Part 3: Tom T. Hall." *Cocaine and Rhinestones*, December 19. https://cocaineandrhinestones.com/tom-t-hall-harper-valley-pta.

Cohn, Nudie, and Petrine Mitchum. 1979. *Rhinestone Cowboy*. Unpublished.

Cole, Shaun. 2015. "Looking Queer? Gay Men's Negotiations between Masculinity and Femininity in Style and Dress in the Twenty-First Century." *Clothing Cultures* 2 (2): 193–208.

Coleman, Annie Gilbert. 1996. "The Unbearable Whiteness of Skiing." *Pacific Historical Review* 65 (4): 583–614.

Collins, Patricia Hill. 2000. *Black Feminist Thought: Knowledge, Consciousness, and the Politics of Empowerment*. New York: Routledge.

Cook, Nicholas. 1998. *Analysing Musical Multimedia*. New York: Oxford University Press.

Cottom, Tressie McMillan. 2018. "Reading Hick-Hop: The Shotgun Marriage of Hip-Hop and Country Music." In *The Honky Tonk on the Left: Progressive Country Music*, edited by Mark Allan Jackson, 236–56. Amherst: University of Massachusetts Press.

2021a. "Why I Keep Returning to Country Music as a Theme." *Essaying*, March 4. https://tressie.substack.com/p/why-i-keep-returning-to-country-music

2021b. "The Dolly Moment: Why We Stan a Post-Racism Queen." *Essaying*, February 24. https://tressie.substack.com/p/the-dolly-moment.

Country Music Association. 2016. "CMA Announces Key Consumer Research Findings During Member Webinar." May 4. www.cmaworld.com/cma-announces-key-consumer-research-findings-member-webinar/.

Country Music Hall of Fame and Museum. 2012. *Encyclopedia of Country Music*, 2nd ed. New York: Oxford University Press.

Cox, Julia. 2018a. The Protest Song: Bridge Leadership, Sonic Innovation, and the Long Civil Rights Movement. PhD dissertation, University of Pennsylvania.

2018b. "'Sing It So Loudly': The Long History of 'Birmingham Sunday'" *Southern Cultures* 24 (1): 62–75.

Craik, Jennifer. 2009. *Fashion: The Key Concepts*. London: Berg.

Crain, Zac. 2000. "Please Kill Me." *Dallas Observer*, January 20, 2000. www.dallasobserver.com/music/please-kill-me-6396524?storyPage=2.

Crenshaw, Kimberlé. 1989. "Demarginalizing the Intersection of Race and Sex: A Black Feminist Critique of Antidiscrimination Doctrine, Feminist Theory and Antiracist Politics." *University of Chicago Legal Forum* 1989 (1): 139–67.

Cunningham, Patricia A. 2005. "Dressing for Success: The Re-Suiting of Corporate America in the 1970s." In *Twentieth Century American Fashion*, edited by Patricia Cunningham and Linda Welters, 191–208. Oxford and New York: Berg.

Cusic, Don. 1993. "Comedy and Humor in Country Music." *The Journal of American Culture* 16 (2): 45–50.

2011. *The Cowboy in Country Music: An Historical Survey with Artist Profiles.* Jefferson, and London: McFarland and Company.

D'Ignazio, Catherine, and Lauren F. Klein. 2020. *Data Feminism*. Boston: MIT Press.

Daley, Dan. 1998. *Nashville's Unwritten Rules: Inside the Business of Country Music*. New York: Overlook Books.

Dansby, Andrew. 2001a. "Sony Sues Dixie Chicks." *Rolling Stone*, July 17. www.rollingstone.com/music/music-news/sony-sues-dixie-chicks-234848/.

Dansby, Andrew. 2001b. "Dixie Chicks Sue Sony." *Rolling Stone*, August 28. www.rollingstone.com/music/music-news/dixie-chicks-sue-sony-236628/

Davidson, Justin. 2019. "Rhiannon Giddens' 21st-Century Sound Has a Long History." *Smithsonian* 49 (10). www.smithsonianmag.com/arts-culture/rhiannon-giddens-american-music-history-21st-century-sound-180971449/

Davis, Fred. 1977. "Nostalgia, Identity, and the Current Nostalgia Wave." *Journal of Popular Culture* 11 (2): 414–24.

Denetdale, Jennifer Nez. 2016. "'No Explanation, No Resolution, and No Answers': Border Town Violence and Navajo Resistance to Settler Colonialism." *Wicazo Sa Review* 31 (1) (Spring): 111–31.

Densley, Rebecca Lin, and Eric Rasmussen. 2018. "Why Don't We Get Drunk and Screw?: A Content Analysis of Women, Sex and Alcohol in Country Music." *Journal of Popular Music Studies* 30 (3): 115–28.

Despres, Tricia. 2018. "Lauren Alaina Debuts 'Ladies in the '90s' Live in Concert [Watch]." *Taste of Country*, September 7. https://tasteofcountry.com/lauren-alaina-ladies-in-the-90s-concert-video/.

DiCola, Peter, and Kristin Thomson. 2002. "Radio Deregulation: Has It Served Musicians and Citizens?" *Future of Music Coalition*, November 18. http://futureofmusic.org/article/research/radio-deregulation-has-it-served-musicians-and-citizens.

Dijk, Teun A. van. 2006. "Discourse and Manipulation." *Discourse & Society* 17 (3): 359–83.

Donaldson, Lisa W. 2006. "Indian Rolling": White Violence against Native Americans in Farmington, New Mexico. PhD dissertation, University of New Mexico.

Donougho, Martin. 2016. "Hegelian Comedy." *Philosophy & Rhetoric* 49 (2): 196–220.

Douglas, Mary. 1966. *Purity and Danger: An Analysis of Concepts of Pollution and Taboo*. London: Routledge & Keegan Paul.

Drew, Rob. 2005. "Mixed Blessings: The Commercial Mix and the Future of Music Aggregation," *Popular Music and Society* 28 (4): 533–51.

Du Bois, W.E.B. 1903. *The Souls of Black Folk*. Chicago: A.C. McClurg & Co.
   1940. *The Dusk of Dawn*. New York: Harcourt, Brace & Co.

Dukes, Billy. 2018. "Remember When Garth Brooks Signed Autographs For 23 Hours Straight?" *Taste of Country*, June 15. https://tasteofcountry.com/remember-when-garth-brooks-set-autograph-record-fan-fair/.

Durrett, Deanne. 2009. *Unsung Heroes of World War II: The Story of the Navajo Code Talkers*. Lincoln: University of Nebraska Press.

Dyer, Richard. 1979. *Stars*. London: British Film Institute.

Edgar, Amanda Nell, and Ashton Toone. 2017. "'She Invited Other People to that Space': Audience Habitus, Place, and Social Justice in Beyoncé's Lemonade." *Feminist Media Studies* 19 (1): 87–101.

Edgers, Geoff. 2018. "Watch out, Country Bros. The Pistol Annies are Back." *Washington Post*, November 1. www.washingtonpost.com/entertainment/music/watch-out-country-bros-the-pistol-annies-are-back/2018/11/01/91ac4924-dc51-11e8-b732-3c72cbf131f2_story.html.

Edwards, Leigh. 2009. *Johnny Cash and the Paradox of American Identity*. Bloomington: Indiana University Press.
   2018. *Dolly Parton, Gender, and Country Music*. Bloomington: Indiana University Press.

Eicher, Ashley, and Hunter Kelly. 2019. "Lauren Alaina." *All Our Favorite People*, March 13.

Eidsheim, Nina. 2012. "Voice as Action: Toward a Model for Analyzing the Dynamic Construction of Racialized Voice." *Current Musicology* 93 (Spring): 9–33.

Elasfar, Dara. 2020. "Woman's Powerful Post on Being a Black Country Music Fan Goes Viral." *Good Morning America*, June 10. www.goodmorningamerica .com/culture/story/womans-powerful-post-black-country-music-fan-viral-71153147.

Ellis, Iain. 2010. "Resistance and Relief: The Wit and Woes of Early Twentieth Century Folk and Country Music." *Humor* 23 (2): 161–178.

Ellison, Curt. 1995. *Country Music Culture: From Hard Times to Heaven.* Jackson: University Press of Mississippi.

Enriquez, Sophia. 2020. "'Penned Against the Wall': Migration Narratives, Cultural Resonances, and Latinx Experiences in Appalachian Music." *Journal of Popular Music Studies* 32 (2): 63–76.

Epstein, Dena J. 1977. *Sinful Tunes and Spirituals: Black Folk Music to the Civil War.* Urbana: University of Illinois Press.

Estes, Nick, Melanie K. Yazzie, Jennifer Nez Denetdale, and David Correia. 2021. *Red Nation Rising: From Bordertown Violence to Native Liberation.* San Francisco: PM Press.

Estes, Nick. 2015. "Blood Money: Life and Death in Gallup, N.M." *Indian Country Today*, January 14. https://indiancountrytoday.com/archive/blood-money-life-and-death-in-gallup-nm-iH8U5802bE6gg_hKLuAYRw.

Fairchild, Charles. 2015. "Crowds, Clouds, and Idols: New Dynamics and Old Agendas in the Music Industry, 1982–2012." *American Music* 33 (4): 441–76.

Fanjoy, Trey. 2006. "The King and I." *Country Weekly*, June 5, pp. 26–28, 31.

Faris, Marc. 2004. "'That Chicago Sound': Playing with (Local) Identity in Underground Rock." *Popular Music and Society* 27 (4): 429–54.

Feiler, Bruce. 1996. "Has Country Music Become a Soundtrack for White Flight?" *New York Times*, October 20. www.nytimes.com/1996/10/20/arts/has-country-music-become-a-soundtrack-for-white-flight.html.

Feiler, Bruce. 2014. "Dreaming Out Loud: Garth Brooks, Wynonna Judd, Wade Hayes, and the Changing Face of Nashville (1998)." In *The Country Music Reader*, edited by Travis Stimeling, 280–89. New York: Oxford University Press, 2014.

Ferguson, Maeri. 2019. "Love Letter to Chicago." *No Depression*, November 7. www .nodepression.com/album-reviews/bloodshot-records-celebrates-25-years-with-musical-love-letter-to-chicago/.

Ferrandino, Matthew, and Brad Osborn. 2019. "Seeing Stories, Hearing Stories in Narrative Music Video." *SMT-V* 5.5. https://vimeo.com/357096231.

Filene, Benjamin. 2000. *Romancing the Folk: Public Memory and American Roots Music*. Chapel Hill: University of North Carolina Press.

Finn, Heather. 2020. "CMA Fest Host Thomas Rhett and His Wife Lauren Akins' Love Story Almost Never Happened." *Good Housekeeping*, August 10. www.goodhousekeeping.com/life/entertainment/a28591518/thomas-rhett-wife-lauren-akins/.

Fishkin, Shelley Fisher. 1995. "Interrogating 'Whiteness,' Complicating 'Blackness': Remapping American Culture." *American Quarterly* 47 (3): 428–66.

Fleming, Andrew, dir. 2019. *Dolly Parton's Heartstrings*. Season 1, episode 1, "Jolene." Aired November 22, 2019, on Netflix.

Fletcher, Michael A. 2017. "At American Legion Hall, Patriotism is Complicated by the Persistent Realities of Being Black." *The Undefeated*, September 25, 2017. https://theundefeated.com/features/american-legion-hall-patriotism-is-complicated/.

Ford, Jaclyn H., David C. Rubin, and Kelly S. Giovanello. 2016. "The Effects of Song Familiarity and Age on Phenomenological Characteristics and Neural Recruitment during Autobiographical Memory Retrieval." *Psychomusicology: Music, Mind, and Brain* 26 (3): 199–210.

Foucault, Michel. 1980. *Power/Knowledge: Selected Interviews and Other Writings*. New York: Pantheon Books.

Fox, Aaron A. 1992. "The Jukebox of History: Narratives of Loss and Desire in the Discourse of Country Music." *Popular Music* 11 (1): 53–72.

Fox, Pamela. 2009. *Natural Acts: Gender, Race and Rusticity in Country Music*. Ann Arbor: University of Michigan.

Fox, Pamela, and Barbara Ching. 2008. "The Importance of Being Ironic – Toward a Theory and Critique of Alt.Country Music." In *Old Roots, New Routes: The Cultural Politics of Alt.Country Music*, edited by Pamela Fox and Barbara Ching, 154–74. Ann Arbor: University of Michigan.

Fredriksson, Kristine. 2000. "Minnie Pearl and Southern Humor in Country Entertainment." In *Country Music Annual*, edited by Charles K. Wolfe and James E. Akenson, 75–88. Lexington: University of Kentucky Press.

Friskics-Warren, Bill. 2002. "Music: The Dixie Chicks Keep the Heat on Nashville." *New York Times*, August 25. www.nytimes.com/2002/08/25/arts/music-the-dixie-chicks-keep-the-heat-on-nashville.html.

Frith, Simon. 1996. *Performing Rites: On the Value of Popular Music*. Cambridge, MA: Harvard University Press.

Garber, Marjorie. 2009. "The Transvestite Continuum: Liberace-Valentino-Elvis." In *The Men's Fashion Reader*, edited by Peter McNeil and Vicki Karaminas, 210–29. Oxford and New York: Berg.

García-Quijano, Carlos G., and Hilda Lloréns. 2019. "Using the Anthropological Concept of 'Core Cultural Values' to Understand the Puerto Rican 2019 Summer Protests." *American Anthropologist*, October 29. www

.americananthropologist.org/2019/10/29/understanding-the-puerto-rican-2019-summer-protests/.

Garcia, David F. 2019. "When the Borders Crossed Us: A Latinx Musicology for Trumpism." Paper presented at Early American Music and the Construction of Race: An Interdisciplinary Workshop. Philadelphia, October 12, 2019.

Garcia, F. Chris. 1973. *Political Socialization of Chicano Children: A Comparative Study with Anglos in California Schools.* New York: Praeger.

———. 1995. "Mexican American Values in the American Southwest." SHRI Publications 56. Albuquerque: Southwest Hispanic Research Institute at The University of New Mexico Digital Repository.

Gebler, Leo, Joan W. Moore, and Ralph C. Guzmán. 1970. *The Mexican American People.* New York: Free Press.

Geczy, Adam, and Vicki Karaminas. 2013. *Queer Style.* London: Bloomsbury Academic.

Genette, Gérard. 1997. *Paratexts: Thresholds of Interpretation.* Cambridge: Cambridge University Press.

George-Warren, Holly, and Michelle Freedman. 2006. *How the West Was Worn: A History of Western Wear.* New York: Harry N. Abrams.

Giddens, Rhiannon. 2015. Liner notes for *Tomorrow is My Turn.* Nonesuch Records.

———. 2017. "Rhiannon Giddens' Keynote Address at IBMA Conference: Community and Connection." *Nonesuch Journal,* October 3. www.nonesuch.com/journal/rhiannon-giddens-keynote-address-ibma-conference-community-connection-2017-10-03.

Gilbert, Samuel, and Adria Malcolm. 2019. "Why Violence Persists in New Mexico's Indigenous Border Towns." *VICE Magazine,* September 9. www.vice.com/en_us/article/pa7ev9/why-violence-persists-in-new-mexicos-indigenous-border-towns-v26n3.

Ginell, Cary. 1994. *Milton Brown and the Founding of Western Swing.* Urbana: University of Illinois Press.

Glasrud, Bruce A., and Michael N. Searles. 2016. *Black Cowboys in the American West: On the Range, on the Stage, Behind the Badge.* Norman: University of Oklahoma Press.

Gnagy, Caroline. 2017. "Goin' Hillbilly Nuts: Fashion Culture and Visual Style in Country Music." In *The Oxford Handbook of Country Music,* edited by Travis D. Stimeling, 415–60. Oxford: Oxford University Press.

González-Martin, Rachel. 2020. "The Future of Folklore is Feminist: Intersectional Feminist Practice and US American Folklore Studies." Keynote Address, Ohio State University, Columbus, OH.

Green, Douglas B. 1976. *Country Roots: The Origins of Country Music.* New York, Hawthorn.

Grimshaw, Michael. 2002. "'Redneck Religion and Shitkickin' Saviours?': Gram Parsons, Theology and Country Music." *Popular Music* 21 (1): 93–105.

Gross, Emmeline. 2010. The Southern Gentleman and the Idea of Masculinity: Figures and Aspects of the Southern Beau in the Literary Tradition of the American South, PhD dissertation, Georgia State University.

Hall, Kristin M. 2021. "Album Sales Surge for Morgan Wallen after Racist Comment." *AP News,* February 8. https://apnews.com/article/morgan-wellen-album-sales-surge-3641ae1b0ac656e4af6445f226ffc8eb.

Hall, Stuart, and Paddy Whannel. 1964. *The Popular Arts.* London: Hutchinson.

Hamessley, Lydia. 2005. "A Resisting Performance of an Appalachian Traditional Murder Girl Ballad: Giving Voice to 'Pretty Polly.'" *Women and Music: A Journal of Gender and Culture* 9: 13–36.

———. 2020. *Unlikely Angel: The Songs of Dolly Parton.* Champaign: Illinois University Press.

Hammond, Angela D. 2011. Color Me Country: Commercial Country Music and Whiteness. PhD dissertation, University of Kentucky.

Handke, Christian. 2012. "Plain Destruction or Creative Destruction? Copyright Erosion and the Evolution of the Record Industry." *Review of Economic Research on Copyright Issues* 3 (2): 29–51.

Harvey, Eric. 2017. "Beyoncé's Digital Stardom." *Black Camera: An International Film Journal* 9 (1): 114–30.

Heidemann, Kate. 2016. "Remarkable Women and Ordinary Gals: Performance of Identity in Songs by Loretta Lynn and Dolly Parton." In *Country Boys and Redneck Women: New Essays in Gender and Country Music,* edited by Diane Pecknold and Kristine M. McCusker, 166–88. Jackson: University Press of Mississippi.

Hess, Amanda. 2020. "The Chicks Are Done Caring What People Think." *New York Times,* July 8, www.nytimes.com/2020/07/08/arts/music/dixie-chicks-gaslighter.html.

Hiatt, Brian, and Evan Serpick. 2007. "The Record Industry's Decline." *Rolling Stone,* June 28, 2007. www.rollingstone.com/news/story/15137581/the_record_industrys_decline.

Hickman, Susan E., and Charlene L. Muehlenhard. 1999. "By the Semi-Mystical Appearance of a Condom: How Young Women and Men Communicate Sexual Consent in Heterosexual Situations." *Journal of Sexual Research* 36 (3): 258–272.

Hight, Jewly. 2016. "Beyoncé and The Dixie Chicks Offer Up Lessons on Country Music's Past (and Future)." NPR, November 4. www.npr.org/sections/therecord/2016/11/04/500562813/beyonc-and-the-dixie-chicks-offer-up-lessons-on-country-musics-past-and-future.

———. 2018a. "Annies Return with Their Humor Intact." *New York Times,* November 1, 2018, C2.

———. 2018b. "How the Sound of Country Music Changed." NPR, March 20. www.npr.org/sections/therecord/2018/03/20/594037569/how-the-sound-of-country-music-changed.

Himmelman, Isaac. 2019. "Why is Country Music Considered So White?" *Huffington Post,* July 17. www.huffpost.com/entry/country-music-black-artists_n_5d2de760e4b085eda5a25516.

Hirsch, Paul M. 1972. "Processing Fads and Fashions: An Organization-Set Analysis of Cultural Industry Systems." *American Journal of Sociology* 77 (4): 639–59.

Hodak, Brittany. 2016. "Inside Country Radio's Gender Gap." *Forbes,* July 26. www.forbes.com/sites/brittanyhodak/2016/07/26/recent-pop-collaborations-highlight-country-radios-rampant-gender-problem.

Hoekstra, Dave. 1998. "The Three Decade Night of the Sundowners." *Journal of Country Music* 20 (1): 30–35.

Holbrook, Morris B. 1993. "Nostalgia and Consumption Preferences: Some Emerging Patterns of Consumer Tastes." *Journal of Consumer Research* 20 (2): 245–56.

Holson, Laura M. 2002. "Dixie Chicks and Sony May End Contract Dispute." *New York Times,* June 17. www.nytimes.com/2020/07/08/arts/music/dixie-chicks-gaslighter.html.

hooks, bell. 2004. *The Will to Change: Men, Masculinity, and Love.* New York: Simon & Schuster.

Hubbs, Nadine, and Francesca T. Royster. 2020. "Introduction: Uncharted Country: New Voices and Perspectives in Country Music Studies." *Journal of Popular Music Studies* 32 (2): 1–10.

Hubbs, Nadine. 2014. *Rednecks, Queers and Country Music.* Berkeley: University of California Press.

——. 2015. "'Jolene,' Genre, and the Everyday Homoerotics of Country Music." *Women and Music* 19 (August): 71–76.

——. 2020. "*Vaquero* World: Queer *Mexicanidad,* Trans Performance, and the Undoing of Nation." In *Decentering the Nation: Music, Mexicanidad, and Globalization,* edited by Jesús A. Ramos-Kittrell, 75–96. Lanham, MD: Lexington Books.

Huber, Patrick. 2008. *Linthead Stomp: The Creation of Country Music in the Piedmont South.* Chapel Hill: University of North Carolina Press.

——. 2013. "Black Hillbillies: African American Musicians on Old-Time Records, 1924–1932." In *Hidden in the Mix: The African American Presence in Country Music,* edited by Diane Pecknold, 19–81. Durham, NC: Duke University Press.

——. 2014. "The New York Sound: Citybilly Recording Artists and the Creation of Hillbilly Music, 1924–1932." *Journal of American Folklore* 127 (504): 140–158.

——. 2017. "The 'Southernness' of Country Music." In *The Oxford Handbook of Country Music,* edited by Travis D. Stimeling, 31–46. Oxford: Oxford University Press.

Hudak, Joseph. 2014. "Frankie Ballard Revels in Number-One Success of 'Sunshine and Whiskey'," *Rolling Stone*, November 21. www.rollingstone.com/music/music-country/frankie-ballard-revels-in-number-one-success-of-sunshine-whiskey-181844/.

———. 2020. "That Time Mary Chapin Carpenter Played the Super Bowl with Beausoleil." *Rolling Stone*, October 19. www.rollingstone.com/music/music-country/mary-chapin-carpenter-twist-and-shout-beausoleil-1077854/.

Hughes, Charles. 2015. *Country Soul: Making Music and Making Race in the American South*. Chapel Hill: University of North Carolina Press.

———. 2017. "'I'm the Other One': O.B. McClinton and the Racial Politics of Country Music in the 1970s." In *The Honky Tonk on the Left: Progressive Thought in Country Music*, 121–46. Amherst: University of Massachusetts Press.

Humphreys, Terry. 2007. "Perceptions of Sexual Consent: The Impact of Relationship History and Gender." *Journal of Sex Research* 44: 4, 307–315.

Hurtado, Ludwig. 2019. "Country Music is Also Mexican Music." *The Nation*, January 3. www.thenation.com/article/archive/country-mexico-ice-nationalism/

Hutcheon, Linda. 2000. "Irony, Nostalgia, and the Postmodern: A Dialogue." *Methods for the Study of Literature as Cultural Memory, Studies in Comparative Literature* 30 (6): 189–207.

Irons, Aaron. 2020. "Wherever We Have to Go: Bruce Robison on The Next Waltz & Finding Great Songs." *Sound and Soul*, November 18. www.soundandsoulonline.com/2020/11/18/wherever-we-have-to-go-bruce-robison-on-the-next-waltz-finding-great-songs/.

Isaac, Veronica. 2014. "Costume." In *The Oxford Handbook of Opera*, edited by Helen M. Greenwald, 553–81. Oxford: Oxford University Press.

Istvandity, Lauren, and Zelmarie Cantillon. 2019. "The Precarity of Memory, Heritage and History in Remembering Popular Music's Past." In *Remembering Popular Music's Past*, edited by Lauren Istvandity, Sarah Baker, and Zelmarie Cantillon, 1–10. London: Anthem Press.

Istvandity, Lauren. 2018. "Popular Music and Autobiographical Memory: Intimate Connections over the Life Course." In *The Routledge Companion to Popular Music History and Heritage*, edited by Sarah Baker, Catherine Strong, Lauren Istvandity, and Zelmarie Cantillon, 199–207. New York: Routledge.

Jackson, Mark Allan, ed. 2018. *The Honky Tonk on the Left: Progressive Thought in Country Music*. Amherst: University of Massachusetts Press.

Jacobsen, Kristina. 2009. "Rita(hhh): Placemaking and Country Music on the Navajo Nation." *Ethnomusicology* 53 (3): 449–77.

———. 2017. *The Sound of Navajo Country: Music, Language and Diné Belonging*. Chapel Hill: University of North Carolina Press.

Jameson, Fredric. 1991. *Postmodernism, or the Cultural Logic of Late Capitalism*. Durham: Duke University Press.

Jamison, Phil. 2015. *Hoedowns, Reels, and Frolics: Roots and Branches of Southern Appalachian Dance.* Urbana: University of Illinois Press.

Jenkins, Henry. 2006. *Convergence Culture: Where Old and New Media Collide.* New York: New York University Press.

Jensen, Joli. 1998. *The Nashville Sound: Authenticity, Commercialization and Country Music.* Nashville: The Country Music Foundation Press and Vanderbilt University Press.

Joannou, Cliff. 2020. "A Fine Bromance." *Attitude,* May, 2020, 31–43.

John, Emma. 2018. "'White People Are so Fragile, Bless 'Em' . . . Meet Rhiannon Giddens, Banjo Warrior." *The Guardian.* July 23. www.theguardian.com/music/2018/jul/23/white-people-are-so-fragile-bless-em-rhiannon-giddens-banjo-warrior-cambridge-folk-festival.

Jones, Loyal. 2008. *Country Music: Humorists and Comedians.* Urbana: University of Illinois Press.

Juslin, Patrik, Simon Liljeström, Daniel Västfjäll, Goncalo Barradas, and Ana Silva. 2008. "An Experience Sampling Study of Emotional Reactions to Music: Listener, Music, and Situation." *Emotion* 8 (5): 668–83.

Kaufmann-Buhler, Jennifer, Victoria Rose Pass, and Christopher S. Wilson. 2019. *Design History Beyond the Canon.* London: Bloomsbury Publishing.

Keane, Colleen. 2014. "Since Brutal Killings, Community Waiting for City and Tribe to Take Action." *Navajo Times,* December 31. https://navajotimes.com/reznews/homeless-community-innocent-victims-violent-assaults/.

Keel, Beverly. 2004. "Between Riot Grrl and Quiet Girl: The New Women's Movement in Country Music." In *A Boy Named Sue: Gender and Country Music,* edited by Kristine M. McCusker and Diane Pecknold, 155–177. Jackson: University Press of Mississippi.

——— 2015a. "Sexist 'Tomato' Barb Launches Food Fight on Music Row." *The Tennessean,* May 27. www.tennessean.com/story/entertainment/music/2015/05/27/sexist-tomato-barb-launches-food-fight-music-row/28036657/.

——— 2015b. "Tomato-gate Galvanizes Women in Country Music." *The Tennessean,* June 21. www.tennessean.com/story/entertainment/music/2015/06/18/tomato-gate-galvanizes-women-country/28936501/.

Kendrick, G. D., ed. 1981. *The River of Sorrows: The History of the Lower Dolores River Valley.* Denver: U.S. Department of the Interior Rocky Mountain Regional Office.

Kenney, Andrew. 2018. "Surprise, Colorado: The Guy Who Sold all Those 'NATIVE' Stickers is a Transplant." *Denverite,* May 25. https://denverite.com/2018/05/25/surprise-colorado-natives-inventor-beloved-bumper-sticker-utah/.

Kibler, Alison. 1999. *Rank Ladies: Gender and Cultural Hierarchy in American Vaudeville.* Chapel Hill: University of North Carolina Press.

Kierkegaard, Søren. 1987. "Concluding Unscientific Postscript." In *The Philosophy of Laughter and Humor*, edited by John Morreall, 83–89. Albany: State University of New York Press.

Killen, Buddy. 1993. *By the Seat of My Pants: My Life in Country Music*. New York: Simon & Schuster.

Kinder, Elizabeth. 2015. "Rhiannon Giddens: Turn for the Best." *fRoots*, May 2015, 28–33.

King, Stephen A., and P. Renee Foster. 2018. "'Leave Country Music to White Folk'? Narratives from Contemporary Africa-American Country Artists on Race and Music." In *Honky Tonk on the Left: Progressive Thought in Country Music*, edited by Mark Allan Jackson, 214–35. Amherst: University of Massachusetts Press.

Knight, George P., Nancy A. Gonzales, Delia S. Saenz, Darya D. Bonds, Miguelina Germán, Julianna Deardorff, Mark W. Roosa, and Kimberly A. Updegraff. 2010. "The Mexican American Cultural Values Scales for Adolescents and Adults." *The Journal of Early Adolescence* 30 (3): 444–81.

Krager, Caroline. 2020. "Lil Nas X's Stylist on Creating the Star's Most Iconic Looks." *i-d.vice.com*, January 28. https://i-d.vice.com/en_uk/article/v74bed/lil-nas-xs-stylist-hodo-musa-grammys.

Krumhansl, Carol Lynne, and Justin Adam Zupnick. 2013. "Cascading Reminiscence Bumps in Popular Music." *Psychological Science* 24 (10): 2057–68.

La Chapelle, Peter. 2001. "All That Glitters: Country Music, Taste, and the Politics of the Rhinestone 'Nudie' Suit." *Dress: The Annual Journal of the Costume Society of America* 28 (1): 3–12.

Lacasse, Serge. 2000. "Intertextuality and Hypertextuality in Recorded Popular Music." In *The Musical Work: Reality or Invention?*, edited by Michael Talbot, 35–58. Liverpool: Liverpool University Press.

——— 2018. "Toward a Model of Transphonography." In *The Pop Palimpsest: Intertextuality in Recorded Popular Music*, edited by Lori Burns and Serge Lacasse, 19–60. Ann Arbor: University of Michigan Press.

Lacasse, Serge, and Andy Bennett. 2018. "Mix Tapes, Memory, and Nostalgia: An Introduction to Phonographic Anthologies." In *The Pop Palimpsest: Intertextuality in Recorded Popular Music*, edited by Lori Burns and Serge Lacasse, 313–29. Ann Arbor: University of Michigan Press.

Lafrance, Marc, Casey Scheibling, Lori Burns, and Jean Durr. 2018. "Race, Gender, and the Billboard Top 40 Charts between 1997 and 2007." *Popular Music & Society* 41 (5): 522–38.

Lafrance, Marc, Lara Worcester, and Lori Burns. 2011. "Gender and the *Billboard* Top 40 Charts between 1997 and 2007." *Popular Music & Society* 34 (5): 557–70.

Laird, Tracey E. W. 2015. *Louisiana Hayride: Radio and Roots Music along the Red River*. American Musicspheres. Oxford: Oxford University Press. First published 2005.

Lakoff, George. 1987. *Women, Fire, and Dangerous Things: What Categories Reveal about the Mind.* Chicago: University of Chicago Press.

Landry, Alysa. 2014. "Teens Murder for Fun: Smash Heads of Homeless Men with Cinderblocks." *Indian Country Today,* July 24. https://indiancountrytoday .com/archive/teens-murder-for-fun-smash-heads-of-homeless-men-with-cinder-blocks.

Lange, Jeffrey J. 2004. *Smile When You Call Me a Hillbilly: Country Music's Struggle for Respectability, 1939–1954.* Athens: University of Georgia Press.

Laver, Mark. 2019. "Lil Nas X and the Continued Segregation of Country Music." *Washington Post,* June 20. www.washingtonpost.com/outlook/2019/06/20/ lil-nas-x-continued-segregation-country-music/.

Lavitt, Pamela Brown. 1999. "First of the Red Hot Mamas: 'Coon Shouting' and the Jewish Ziegfeld Girl." *American Jewish History* 87 (4): 253–90.

Leap, Braden. 2020. "A New Type of (White) Provider: Shifting Masculinities in Mainstream Country Music from the 1980s to the 2010s." *Rural Sociology* 85 (1): 165–189.

LeCompte, Mary Lou. 1985. "The Hispanic Influence on the History of Rodeo, 1823–1922." *Journal of Sport History* 12 (1): 21–38.

Lee, Elizabeth M., and Chaise LaDousa, eds. 2015. *College Students' Experiences of Power and Marginality: Sharing Spaces and Negotiating Differences.* New York: Routledge.

Lee, Stephen. 1995. "Re-Examining the Concept of the 'Independent' Record Company: The Case of Wax Trax! Records." *Popular Music* 14 (1): 13–31.

Lena, Jennifer C. 2012. *Banding Together: How Communities Create Genres in Popular Music.* Princeton, NJ: Princeton University Press.

Levin, Sam. 2016. "Rebel Cowboys: How the Bundy Family Sparked a New Battle for the American West." *The Guardian,* August 29. www.theguardian.com/ us-news/2016/aug/29/oregon-militia-standoff-bundy-family.

Levine, Daniel S. 2021. "Bobby Bones Defends Morgan Wallen After Racist Slur Scandal: 'Move On'." *Popculture,* July 18. https://popculture.com/country-music/news/bobby-bones-defends-morgan-wallen-racist-slur-scandal-move-on/#3.

Lewin, Kurt. 1947. "Frontiers in Group Dynamics II: Channels of Group Life; Social Planning and Action Research." *Human Relations* 1: 143–53.

Lewis, George H. 1991. "Ghosts, Ragged But Beautiful: Influences of Mexican Music on American Country-Western and Rock 'N' Roll." *Popular Music and Society* 15 (4): 85–103.

——. 1997. "Lap Dancer or Hillbilly Deluxe? The Cultural Constructions of Modern Country Music." *Journal of Popular Culture* 31, no. 3 (Winter): 163–73.

——. 2001. "The Color of Country: Black Influence and Experience in American Country Music." *Popular Music and Society* 25 (3–4): 107–119.

Lindquist, David. 2017. "Garth Brooks Lives Up To '90s Lore on Opening Night," *Indianapolis Star,* October 6. www.indystar.com/story/entertainment/

music/2017/10/06/garth-brooks-indianapolis-concert-keeps-it-country/727310001/.

Lipsitz, George. 1990. *Time Passages: Collective Memory and American Popular Culture*. Minneapolis: University of Minnesota Press.

——— 2018. *The Possessive Investment in Whiteness: How White People Profit from Identity Politics*. Twentieth Anniversary Edition. Philadelphia: Temple University Press.

Lizardo, Omar, and Sara Skiles. 2015. "Musical Taste and Patterns of Symbolic Exclusion in the United States 1993–2012: Generational Dynamics of Differentiation and Continuity." *Poetics* 53: 9–21.

Lorde, Audre. 1984. *Sister Outsider: Essays and Speeches*. Berkeley, CA: Crossing Press.

Lordi, Emily. 2020. "Working Girl: The Grit and Glory of Dolly Parton." *T: New York Times Style Magazine*, December 6, 70–75.

Lornell, Kip, and Anne K. Rasmussen, eds. 2016. *The Music of Multicultural America: Performance, Identity, and Community in the United States*. Jackson: University Press of Mississippi.

Lotz, Amanda D. 2017. *Portals: A Treatise on Internet-Distributed Television*. Ann Arbor: Maize Publishing.

Lugones, María. 1987. "Playfulness, 'World'-Travelling, and Loving Perception." *Hypatia* 2 (2): 3–19.

Luu, Christopher. 2018. "Post Malone Was Definitely Thirsty at the AMAs." *Instyle.com*, October 8. www.instyle.com/news/post-malone-amas-drinks.

Lynch, Kimery S. 2020. "Fans as Transcultural Gatekeepers: The Hierarchy of BTS' Anglophone Reddit Fandom and the Digital East-West Media Flow." *New Media & Society* (September).

Mack, Kimberly. 2020a. "'She's a Country Girl All Right': Rhiannon Giddens's Powerful Reclamation of Country Culture." *Journal of Popular Music Studies* 32 (2): 144–61.

——— 2020b. "'What Are You Gonna Tell Her?': The Power of Black Women's Narratives." *American Music Perspectives* 1 (2): 151–58.

Mackenzie, Mairi. 2011. *Dream Suits: The Wonderful World of Nudie Cohn*. Tielt, Belgium: Lanoo.

Madrid, Alejandro L., ed. 2011. *Transnational Encounters: Music and Performance at the U.S.-Mexico Border*. New York: Oxford University Press.

Mall, Andrew. 2018. "Concentration, Diversity, and Consequences: Privileging Independent over Major Record Labels." *Popular Music* 37 (3): 444–65.

Malone, Bill C. 1968. *Country Music, USA*. Austin: University of Texas for the American Folklore Society.

——— 2002. *Don't Get above Your Raisin': Country Music and the Southern Working Class*. Urbana: University of Illinois Press.

——— 2003. *Singing Cowboys and Musical Mountaineers: Southern Culture and the Roots of Country Music*, 2nd ed. Athens: University of Georgia Press.

Malone, Bill C., and Tracey Laird. 2018. *Country Music, USA*. 50th Anniversary Edition. Austin, TX: University of Texas Press.

Mann, Geoff. 2008. "Why Does Country Music Sound White? Race and the Voice of Nostalgia." *Ethnic and Racial Studies* 31 (1): 73–100.

Mann, Steve, Jason Nolan, and Barry Wellman. 2003. "Sousveillance: Inventing and Using Wearable Computing Devices for Data Collection in Surveillance Environments." *Surveillance & Society* 1 (3): 331–55.

Marshall, Lee. 2013. "The 360 Deal and the 'New' Music Industry." *European Journal of Cultural Studies* 16 (1): 77–99.

Martinez, Amanda Marie. 2019. "The Country Audience and the Fragility of Country's Whiteness in the 1970s." Paper presented at the International Country Music Conference, Nashville, Tennessee.

———. 2020. "Redneck Chic: Race and the Country Music Industry in the 1970s." *Journal of Popular Music Studies* 32 (2): 128–43.

———. 2021a. "As Country Music Faces a Racial Reckoning, a New Question: Where Are the Latino Artists?" *Los Angeles Times,* June 28. www.latimes.com/entertainment-arts/music/story/2021-06-28/country-music-nashville-latino-artists.

Martinez, Amanda Marie. 2021b. "Why Do We Need Dolly to Be a Saint?" NPR, August 20. –www.npr.org/2021/08/20/1029306864/dolly-parton-nashville-sevier-park-real-estate-why-need-be-saint.

Mather, Olivia Carter. 2017. "Race in Country Music Scholarship." In *The Oxford Handbook of Country Music*, edited by Travis D. Stimeling, 327–45. Oxford: Oxford University Press.

McCarthy, Tom. 2007. *Auto Mania: Cars, Consumers, and the Environment*. New Haven: Yale University Press.

McCusker, Kristine M. 2008. *Lonesome Cowgirls and Honky-Tonk Angels: The Women of Barn Dance Radio*. Urbana: University of Illinois Press.

———. 2017. "Gendered Stages: Country Music, Authenticity, and the Performance of Gender." In *The Oxford Handbook of Country Music*, edited by Travis D. Stimeling, 355–74. New York: Oxford University Press.

McCusker, Kristine M., and Diane Pecknold, eds. 2004. *A Boy Named Sue: Gender and Country Music*. Jackson: University of Mississippi Press.

McDonald, Paul. 2000. *The Star System: Hollywood's Production of Popular Identities*. London: Wallflower Publishing Ltd.

McKay, Mary-Jayne. 2000. "Dixie Chicks Not Whistling Dixie." *60 Minutes*. www.cbsnews.com/news/dixie-chicks-not-whistling-dixie/.

McKenna, Brittney. 2017. "Sam Hunt is Country Drake: Here are Eight Reasons Why," *Billboard*. February 4, 2017. www.billboard.com/articles/columns/country/7677943/sam-hunt-country-drake-eight-reasons-why-body-like-back-road.

McLaurin, Melton A., and Richard A. Peterson. 1992. *You Wrote My Life: Lyrical Themes in Country Music,* New York and London: Gordon & Breach.

McRobbie, Angela. 2002. "From Holloway to Hollywood: Happiness at Work in the New Cultural Economy?" In *Cultural Economy: Cultural Analysis and Commercial Life*, eds. Paul du Gay and Michael Pryke, 97–114. London: Sage.

Meier, Kennth J. 2018. "Looking for Meaning in All the Wrong Places: Country Music and the Politics of Identity." *Social Science Quarterly* 100 (1): 89–108.

Middleton, Richard. 2000. "Work-in(g)-Practice: Configurations of the Popular Music Intertext." In *The Musical Work: Reality or Invention?*, edited by Michael Talbot, 59–87. Liverpool: Liverpool University Press.

Miller, Karl Hagstrom. 2010. *Segregating Sound: Inventing Folk and Pop Music in the Age of Jim Crow*. Durham, NC: Duke University Press.

Miller, Rob. 1999. Quoted in *Poor Little Knitter on the Road: A Tribute to the Knitters*. BS 052. Liner notes.

Misztal, Barbra A. 2003. *Theories of Social Remembering*. Philadelphia: Open University Press.

Molina-Guzmán, Isabel. 2010. *Dangerous Curves: Latina Bodies in the Media*. New York: New York University Press.

Molina-Guzmán, Isabel, and Angharad N. Valdivia. 2004. "Brain, Brow, and Booty: Latina Iconicity in US Popular Culture." *Communication Review* 7 (2): 205–21.

Molinary, Rosie. 2007. *Hijas Americanas: Beauty, Body Image, and Growing Up Latina*. Emeryville: Seal Press.

Moody, Rebecca, and Paul Bischoff. 2021. "Surveillance Camera Statistics: Which City Has the Most CCTV Cameras?" *Comparitech*, May 17. www .comparitech.com/blog/vpn-privacy/the-worlds-most-surveilled-cities/.

Moon, Dreama G., and Michelle A. Holling. 2020. "'White Supremacy in Heels': (White) Feminism, White Supremacy, and Discursive Violence." *Communication and Critical/Cultural Studies*, 17 (2): 253–60.

Moore, Bobby. 2022. "Linda Martell Documentary Will Tell Country Pioneer's Crucial Story on Her Own Terms." *Wide Open Country*, March 23. www .wideopencountry.com/linda-martell-documentary/.

Moreno, Rosario. 2019. "Latinxs and Country Music." *The Medium*, January 8. https://medium.com/@rosariomorenocorona/latinxs-country-music-2bd449a0f226.

Moss, Marissa R. 2018. "Inside Country Radio's Dark, Secret History of Sexual Harassment and Misconduct." *Rolling Stone*, January 16. www.rollingstone .com/music/music-country/inside-country-radios-dark-secret-history-of-sexual-harassment-and-misconduct-253573/.

Moss, Marissa. 2019. "One More Scoop of Vanilla: A New Proposal Looks to Loosen Radio Ownership Rules." NPR, 7 June. www.npr.org/2019/06/07/730323196/one-more-scoop-of-vanilla-a-new-proposal-looks-to-loosen-radio-ownership-rules.

Muir, Peter C. 2010. *Long Lost Blues: Popular Blues in America*. Urbana: University of Illinois Press.

Murphy, Patricia. 2018. "Commander Quits Seattle Veterans Group over Harassment, Racism." *KUOW News and Information*, March 9. http://archive.kuow.org/post/commander-quits-seattle-veterans-group-over-harassment-racism.

Myerhoff, Barbara. 1982. "Life History among the Elderly: Performance, Visibility and Re-membering." In *A Crack in the Mirror: Reflective Perspectives in Anthropology*, edited by Jay Ruby, 99–117. Philadelphia: University of Pennsylvania Press.

National Indian Council on Aging. 2019. "American Indian Veterans Have Highest Record of Military Service." Albuquerque: National Indian Council on Aging. www.nicoa.org/american-indian-veterans-have-highest-record-of-military-service/.

Navajo Nation Human Rights Commission. 2010. "Assessing Race Relations between Navajos and non-Navajos, 2008–2009: A Review of Border Town Race Relations." St. Michaels, AZ: Navajo Nation Human Rights Commission. www.nnhrc.navajo-nsn.gov/docs/NewsRptResolution/0718 10%20Assessing%20Race%20Relations%20Between%20Navajos%20and%20Non-Navajos.pdf.

Neal, Jocelyn R. 1998. "The Metric Makings of a Country Hit." In *Reading Country Music*, edited by Cecelia Tichi, 322–37. Durham: Duke University Press.

——— 2006. "Dancing Around the Subject: Race in Country Fan Culture." *Musical Quarterly* 89 (4): 555–79.

——— 2007. "Narrative Paradigms, Musical Signifiers, and Form as Function in Country Music." *Music Theory Spectrum*, 29, 41–72.

——— 2016. "Why 'Ladies Love Country Boys': Gender, Class, and Economics in Contemporary Country Music. In *Country Boys and Redneck Women: New Essays in Gender and Country Music*, edited by Diane Pecknold and Kristine M. McCusker, 3–25. Jackson: University Press of Mississippi.

——— 2019. *Country Music: A Cultural and Stylistic History*, 2nd ed. New York: Oxford University Press.

——— 2020. "'Tennessee Whiskey' and the Politics of Harmony." *Journal of Popular Music Studies, Uncharted Country Special Issue* 32 (2): 214–37.

Neely, Emily C. 2004. "Charline Arthur: The (Un)Making of a Honky-Tonk Star." In *A Boy Named Sue: Gender and Country Music*, edited by Kristine M. McCusker and Diane Pecknold, 44–58. Jackson: University Press of Mississippi.

Newman, Melinda. 2020. "Dolly Parton Steers Her Empire Through the Pandemic – and Keeps It Growing." *Billboard*, August 15. www.billboard.com/articles/columns/country/9432581/dolly-parton-country-power-players-billboard-cover-story-interview-2020.

No Depression. 2012. "Peek Inside Gram Parsons' Notebook at the AMA Conference." NoDepression.com, September 3. www.nodepression.com/peek-inside-gram-parsons-notebook-at-the-ama-conference/.

Noble, Safiya Umoja. 2018. *Algorithms of Oppression: How Search Engines Reinforce Racism.* New York, NY: New York University Press.

O'Connor, Brendan H., and Gilbert Brown. 2013. "Just Keep Expanding Outwards: Embodied Space as Cultural Critique in the Work of a Navajo Hip Hop Artist." In *Indigenous Youth and Multilingualism: Language Identity, Ideology, and Practice in Dynamic Cultural Worlds,* edited by Leisy T. Wyman, Teresa L. McCarty, and Sheilah E. Nicholas, 74–95. New York: Routledge.

O'Neal, Jim, and Amy van Singel 2002. *The Voice of the Blues: Classic Interviews from Living Blues Magazine.* New York: Routledge.

Olenski, Steve. 2016. "Nostalgia Sells: Capitalizing on the Desire for Simpler Times." *Forbes,* August 4. www.forbes.com/sites/steveolenski/2016/08/04/nostalgia-sells-capitalizing-on-the-desire-for-simpler-times/https://www.forbes.com/sites/steveolenski/2016/08/04/nostalgia-sells-capitalizing-on-the-desire-for-simpler-times/.

Orosz, Jeremy. 2019. "'Straight Outta Nashville': Allusions to Hip Hop in Contemporary Country Music." *Popular Music and Society* 44 (1): 49–59.

Ortega, Mariana. 2006. "Being Lovingly, Knowingly Ignorant: White Feminism and Women of Color." *Hypatia* 21 (3): 56–74.

Osborn, Brad. 2021. *Interpreting Music Video: Popular Music in the Post-MTV Era.* New York: Routledge.

Parton, Chris. 2015. "Proof that all country music sounds the same? YouTube user strikes gold with six-song mashup." *CMT.com,* January 9. www.cmt.com/news/1747657/proof-that-all-country-music-sounds-thesame.

Parton, Dolly, and Robert K. Oermann. 2020. *Dolly Parton, Songteller: My Life in Lyrics.* San Francisco: Chronicle Books.

Parton, Dolly. 1994. *Dolly: My Life and Other Unfinished Business.* New York: HarperCollins.

Paterson, Kent. 2015. "Cowboy, Rabbit, and Border Town Violence." *NMPolitics.net,* July 24. https://nmpolitics.net/index/2015/07/cowboy-rabbit-and-border-town-violence/.

Paul, James. 2003. "Last Night a Mix Tape Saved My Life." *The Guardian,* September 25. www.theguardian.com/music/2003/sep/26/2.

Paulson, David. 2018. "Story Behind the Song: 'Body Like a Back Road'." *The Tennessean* March 23. www.tennessean.com/story/entertainment/music/story-behind-the-song/2018/03/23/story-behind-song-body-like-back-road/447282002/.

Pecknold, Diane, and Kristine M. McCusker, eds. 2016. *Country Boys and Redneck Women: New Essays in Gender and Country Music.* Jackson: University Press of Mississippi.

Pecknold, Diane. 2004. "'I Wanna Play House': Configurations of Masculinity in the Nashville Sound Era." In *A Boy Named Sue: Gender and Country Music*, edited by Kristine M McCusker and Diane Pecknold, 86–106. Jackson: University Press of Mississippi.

———. 2007. *The Selling Sound: The Rise of the Country Music Industry*. Durham: Duke University Press.

———. 2008. "Selling Out or Buying In? Alt.Country's Cultural Politics of Commercialism." In *Old Roots, New Routes: The Cultural Politics of Alt. Country Music*, edited by Pamela Fox and Barbara Ching, 28–50. Ann Arbor: University of Michigan Press.

Pecknold, Diane, ed. 2013a. *Hidden in the Mix: The African American Presence in Country Music*. Durham: Duke University Press.

———. 2013b. "Introduction: Country Music and Racial Formation." In *Hidden in the Mix: The African American Presence in Country Music*, edited by Diane Pecknold, 1–16. Durham: Duke University Press.

———. 2013c. "Making Country Modern: The Legacy of *Modern Sounds in Country and Western Music*." In *Hidden in the Mix: The African American Presence in Country Music*, edited by Diane Pecknold, 82–99. Durham: Duke University Press.

———. 2018. "Negotiating Gender, Race, and Class in Post-Civil Rights Country Music: How Linda Martell and Jeannie C. Riley Stormed the Plantation." In *Country Boys and Redneck Women: New Essays in Gender and Country Music*, edited by Diane Pecknold and Kristine M. McCusker, 146–88. Jackson: University of Mississippi Press.

Peel, Adrian. 2014. *Tequila, Señioritas, and Teardrops*. Jefferson, NC: McFarland & Company.

Petermon, Jade DaVon. 2014. Hyper(in)Visibility: Reading Race and Representation in the Neoliberal Era. PhD dissertation, University of California, Santa Barbara.

Peterson, Richard A. 1978. "The Production of Cultural Change: The Case of Contemporary Country Music." *Social Research* 45 (2): 292–314.

———. 1997. *Creating Country Music: Fabricating Authenticity*. Chicago: University of Chicago Press.

———. 2004. "The Dialectic of Hard-Core and Soft-Shell Country Music." In *Popular Music: Critical Concepts in Media and Cultural Studies*, edited by Simon Frith, 87–99. New York: Routledge.

Peterson, Richard A., and David G. Berger. 1996. "Measuring Industry Concentration, Diversity, and Innovation in Popular Music." *American Sociological Review* 61 (1): 175–78.

Peterson, Richard A., and N. Anand. 2004. "The Production of Culture Perspective." *Annual Review of Sociology* 30: 311–34.

Petrusich, Amanda. 2017. "Darius Rucker and the Perplexing Whiteness of Country Music." *The New Yorker*. October 25. www.newyorker.com/

culture/cultural-comment/darius-rucker-and-the-perplexing-whiteness-of-country-music.

Pew Global Attitudes Project. 2009. "Troubled by Crime, the Economy, Drugs and Corruption, Most Mexicans See Better Life in U.S. – One-in-Three Would Migrate." *Pew Research Center*, September 23. https://assets.pewresearch .org/wp-content/uploads/sites/2/pdf/266.pdf.

Philips, Chuck. 2001. "Stars Preparing to Rock the Boat." *Los Angeles Times*, March 29. www.newspapers.com/image/188243671.

Philips, Chuck. 2002. "Dixie Chicks, Sony End Feud with a New Deal." *Los Angeles Times*, June 17. www.latimes.com/archives/la-xpm-2002-jun-17-fi-dixie17-story.html.

Philips, John Edward. 1990. "The African Heritage in White America." In *Africanisms in American Culture*, edited by Joseph E. Holloway, 225–39. Bloomington: Indiana University Press.

Phillips, Stacy. 2018. "The Fiddling of Bob Wills." *Fiddler Magazine*, Spring, 4–11.

Pickering, Hugh, and Tom Rice. 2017. "Noise as 'Sound out of Place': Investigating the Links between Mary Douglas' Work on Dirt and Sound Studies Research." *Journal of Sonic Studies* 14: 1–14.

Pittelman, Karen. 2018. "Another Country: On the Relationship between Country Music and White Supremacy and What We Can Do About It." *Medium*, December 17. https://medium.com/@Pittelman/another-country-80a 05dd7fc15.

Pittman, Anne M., Marlys S. Waller, and Cathy L. Dark. 2005. *Dance a While: Handbook for Folk, Square, Contra, and Social Dance*, 9th ed. San Francisco: Benjamin Cummings for Pearson Education.

Purdie-Vaughns, Valerie, and Richard P. Eibach. 2008. "Intersectional Invisibility: The Distinctive Advantages and Disadvantages of Multiple Subordinate-Group Identities." *Sex Roles* 59: 377–91.

Quintero, Donavan. 2020. "Flagstaff Police Investigating Alleged Beating of Homeless Diné." *Navajo Times*, June 7. https://navajotimes.com/reznews/ flagstaff-police-investigating-alleged-beating-of-homeless-dine/.

Ramos-Kittrell, Jesús A., ed. 2020. *Decentering the Nation: Music, Mexicanidad, and Globalization*. Lanham, MD: Lexington Books.

Rasmussen, Eric E., and Rebecca L. Densley. 2017. "Girl in a Country Song: Gender Roles and Objectification of Women in Popular Country Music Across 1990 to 2014." *Sex Roles* 76 (3–4): 188–201.

Ratliff, Ben. 2016. *Every Song Ever: Twenty Ways to Listen in an Age of Musical Plenty*. New York: Picador.

Razack, Sherene, ed. 2002. *Race, Space, and the Law: Unmapping a White Settler Society*. Toronto: Between the Lines.

Reddin, Paul. 1999. *Wild West Shows*. Urbana: University of Illinois Press.

Reece, Erik. 2017. "Louisville Lip." *Oxford American*, November 21. www .oxfordamerican.org/item/1351-louisville-lip.

Renshaw, Simon. 2003. "Media Ownership (Radio Consolidation)." July 8. www
.commerce.senate.gov/2003/7/media-ownership-(radio-consolidation.

Reuter, Annie. 2018. "Listen to Chace Rice's Stripped Down 'Eyes On You' and
Chill." *Taste of Country,* August 5. https://tasteofcountry.com/chase-rice-
eyes-on-you/.

RIAA. 2020. "U.S. Recorded Music Revenues by Format." From the U.S. Sales
Database. www.riaa.com/u-s-sales-database/.

Ricci, Adam. 2017. "The Pump-Up in Pop Music of the 1970s and 80s." *Music
Analysis* 36 (1): 94–115.

Rodríguez, Richard T. 2017. "X Marks the Spot." *Cultural Dynamics* 29 (3):
202–213.

Rogers, Jimmie N. 1989. *The Country Music Message: Revisited.* Fayetteville:
University of Arkansas Press.

Roland, Tom 2019. "'Boyfriend Country' Brings Sensitivity to the Genre – And to
the CMA Ballot." *Billboard.com,* November 13. www.billboard.com/articles/
columns/country/8543442/boyfriend-country-sensitive-songs-trend-cma.

———. 2020. "Makin' Tracks: Morgan Evans' 'Diamonds' Mines Four Short Chords for
a Long-Term Goal." *Billboard.com,* January 7. www.billboard.com/articles/
columns/country/8547471/morgan-evans-diamonds-makin-tracks.

Rose-Redwood, Reuben S. 2006. "Governmentality, Geography, and the Geo-
Coded World." *Progress in Human Geography* 30 (4): 469–86.

Rosen, Jody. 2013. "Jody Rosen on the Rise of Bro-Country." *Vulture,* August 11.
www.vulture.com/2013/08/rise-of-bro-country-florida-georgia-line.html.

Ross, Andrew. 1989. *No Respect: Intellectuals and Popular Culture.* New York:
Routledge.

Rossman, Gabriel. 2012. *Climbing the Charts: What Radio Airplay Tells Us about
the Diffusion of Innovation.* Princeton: Princeton University Press.

Rourke, Constance. 2004. *American Humor: A Study of the National Character.*
New York: New York Review Books. First published 1955.

Rowe, Kathleen. 1995. *The Unruly Woman: Gender and the Genres of Laughter.*
Austin: University of Texas Press.

Roy, William G. 2004. "'Race Records' and 'Hillbilly Music': Institutional Origins
of Racial Categories in the American Commercial Recording Industry."
Poetics 32: 265–279.

Royster, Francesca. 2019. "Who's Your Daddy? Beyoncé, the Dixie Chicks, and the
Art of Outlaw Protest." In *Popular Music and the Politics of Hope: Queer and
Feminist Interventions,* edited by Susan Fast and Craig Jennex, 63–75. New
York: Routledge.

———. 2022. *Black Country Music: Listening for Revolutions.* Austin: University of
Texas Press.

Ryynänen, Toni, and Visa Heinonen. 2018. "From Nostalgia for the Recent Past
and Beyond: The Temporal Frames of Recalled Consumption Experiences."
International Journal of Consumer Studies 42 (1): 186–94.

Salinas, Brenda. 2016. "In Mariachi Music, a Distinctive Yell Speaks to the Soul." *Code Switch* (NPR), August 23. www.npr.org/sections/codeswitch/2016/08/23/488502412/in-mariachi-music-a-distinctive-yell-speaks-to-the-soul.

Samuels, David W. 2004. *Putting a Song on Top of It: Expression and Identity on the San Carlos Apache Reservation.* Tucson: University of Arizona Press.

Sanden, Paul. 2013. *Liveness in Modern Music: Musicians, Technology, and the Perception of Performance.* New York: Routledge.

Sanneh, Kelefa. 2015. "Bro-Country Grows Up." *The New Yorker,* June 22. www.newyorker.com/magazine/2015/06/29/mr-popular.

Savoy, Tammi. n.d. "Tammi Savoy and The Chris Casello Combo." *Miss Tammi Savoy.* https://misstammisavoy.squarespace.com/livemusic#/tammi-savoy-and-the-chris-casello-combo.

Scanlan, Sean. 2004. "Introduction: Nostalgia." *Iowa Journal of Cultural Studies* 5 (1): 3–9.

Scarry, Elaine. 1987. *The Body in Pain: The Making and Unmaking of the World.* New York: Oxford University Press.

Sedikides, Consantine, Tim Wildschut, and Denise Baden. 2004. "Nostalgia: Conceptual Issues and Existential Functions." In *Handbook of Experimental Existential Psychology,* edited by Jeff Greenberg, Sander L. Koole, and Tom Pyszezynski, 200–14. New York: Guilford Press.

Sexton, Tom. 2021. "Goodbye, Dolly: Mythmaking in Dolly Parton's America." *The Baffler,* February 8. https://thebaffler.com/latest/goodbye-dolly-sexton.

Shabazz, Sa'iyda. 2017. "20 Reasons Why the '90s Were the Best Decade to Grow Up In." *Scary Mommy* (blog), December 10. www.scarymommy.com/90s-were-best-decade-grow-up/.

Shaffer, Claire. 2019. "The Dixie Chicks' 'Fly' at 20: How the Country Group was Always Revolutionary." *Rolling Stone,* August 30. www.rollingstone.com/music/music-features/the-dixie-chicks-fly-at-20-how-the-country-group-was-always-revolutionary-878421/.

Sheehan, Rebecca. 2021. "'She Made Me Understand: How Lemonade Raised the Intersectional Consciousness of Beyoncé's International Fans." In *Beyoncé in the World: Making Meaning with Queen Bey in Troubled Times,* edited by Christina Baade and Kristin McGee, 165–190. Middletown: Wesleyan University Press.

Sheffield, Rob. 2018. "1990s Nostalgia: Why 2018 was the Year of the Nineties." *Rolling Stone,* December 14. www.rollingstone.com/culture/culture-features/90s-obsessions-nostalgia-charli-xcx-768664/.

Shelburne, Craig. 2005. "The Bellamy Brothers Are Still Country . . . In Many Nations." *CMT.com,* May 23. www.cmt.com/news/1502788/bellamy-brothers-are-still-country-in-many-nations/.

———. 2020. "Blending Her Latin and Rodeo Roots: Leah Turner Shares a Family Love Story." *CMT.com,* July 15. www.cmt.com/news/1823018/leah-turner-once-upon-a-time-in-mexico-video/.

Shiva, Negar, and Zohreh Nosrat Kharazmi. 2019. "The Fourth Wave of Feminism and the Lack of Social Realism in Cyberspace." *Journal of Cyberspace Studies* 3 (2): 129–46.

Shoemaker, Pamela J., and Tim P. Vos. 2009. *Gatekeeping Theory*. New York: Routledge.

Siapera, Eugenia. 2012. *Understanding New Media*. London: Sage.

Silversmith, Shondiin. 2015. "Border Town Violence: Who is to Blame?" *The Navajo Times*, February 5, https://navajotimes.com/ae/community/border-town-violence-blame/.

Simonett, Helena. 2001. *Banda: Mexican Musical Life across Borders*. Middletown: Wesleyan University Press.

Sisario, Ben. 2020. "The Dixie Chicks Change Their Name, Dropping the 'Dixie.'" *New York Times*, June 25. www.nytimes.com/2020/06/25/arts/music/dixie-chicks-change-name.html.

Skaggs, Rachel. 2019. "Harmonizing Small Group Cohesion and Status in Creative Collaborations: How Songwriters Facilitate and Manipulate the Cowriting Process." *Social Psychology Quarterly* 82 (4): 367–85.

Skeggs, Beverley. 2001. "The Toilet Paper: Femininity, Class, and Mis-Recognition." *Women's Studies International Forum* 24 (3): 295–307.

Smarsh, Sarah. 2020. *She Come By It Natural: Dolly Parton and the Women Who Lived Her Songs*. New York: Scribner.

Smith, Michael D., and Rahul Telang. 2016. *Streaming, Sharing, Stealing: Big Data and the Future of Entertainment*. Cambridge: MIT Press.

Smith, Stacy L., Marc Choueiti, and Katherine Pieper. 2015. *Inequality in 700 Popular Films: Examining Characters' Gender, Race, and LGBT Status from 2007 to 2014*. Los Angeles: University of Southern California Media, Diversity, & Social Change Initiative.

Smulyan, Susan. 2004. *Selling Radio: The Commercialization of American Broadcasting, 1920–1934*. Washington: Smithsonian Institution Press.

Solis, Gabriel. 2010. "I Did It My Way: Rock and the Logic of Covers." *Popular Music and Society* 33 (3): 297–318.

Southern, Eileen. 1971. *The Music of Black Americans: A History*. New York: Norton.

Spilker, Hendrik Storstein. 2017. *Digital Music Distribution: The Sociology of Online Music Streams*. New York: Routledge.

Staff of the Organized Crime and Gang Section. 2016. *Criminal RICO: 18:USC, 1961–1968*, 6th ed. Washington D.C.: United States Department of Justice. www.justice.gov/archives/usam/file/870856/download.

Stahl, Matt, and Leslie Meier. 2012. "The Firm Foundation of Organizational Flexibility: The 360 Deal Contract in the Digitizing Music Industry." *Canadian Journal of Communication* 37 (3): 441–58.

Stanzler, Wendey, dir. 2019. *Dolly Parton's Heartstrings*. Season 1, episode 2, "Two Doors Down." Aired November 22, 2019, on Netflix.

Stark, Phyllis. 2003. "Country Women Lose Hit Magic: Boom Turns to Drought for Even Top Acts." *Billboard*, July 5, 2003. 1, 73.

Stecker, Liv. 2018. "Walker Hayes' '90's Country': All 22 Song References, Explained." *The Boot*, August 30. http://theboot.com/walker-hayes-90s-country-song-references/.

Stephens-Davidowitz, Seth. 2018. "The Songs That Bind." *New York Times*, June 8. www.nytimes.com/2018/02/10/opinion/sunday/favorite-songs.html.

Stimeling, Travis D. 2014. Introduction to Bruce Feiler's "Dreaming Out Loud: Garth Brooks, Wynonna Judd, Wade Hayes, and the Changing Face of Nashville (1998)." In *The Country Music Reader*, edited by Travis Stimeling, 280–89. New York: Oxford University Press.

    2017. *The Oxford Handbook of Country Music*. New York: Oxford University Press.

    2020. *Nashville Cats: Record Production in Music City*. New York: Oxford University Press.

Stoever, Jennifer. 2016. *The Sonic Color Line: Race and the Cultural Politics of Listening*. New York: New York University Press.

Stoiko, Rachel, and JoNell Strough. 2017. "'Choosing' the Patriarchal Norm: Emerging Adults' Marital Last Name Change, Attitudes, Plans, and Rationales." *Gender Issue* 34 (4): 295–315.

Straw, Will. 2015. "Mediality and the Music Chart." *SubStance* 44 (3): 128–38.

Sullivan, John Jeremiah. 2019. "Rhiannon Giddens and What Folk Music Means." *The New Yorker*, May 20. www.newyorker.com/magazine/2019/05/20/rhiannon-giddens-and-what-folk-music-means.

Texas Commission on the Arts. n.d. "Little Joe Hernandez: Texas State Artist." www.arts.texas.gov/little-joe-hernandez.

Thomas, Tony. 2013. "Why African Americans Put the Banjo Down." In *Hidden in the Mix: The African American Presence in Country Music*, edited by Diane Pecknold, 143–70. Durham: Duke University Press.

Thomson, Jeffrey. 2019. "From Art School Dropout to Lil Nas X and Post Malone's Cowboy Atelier, Meet Union Western." *The Love Magazine*, December 5. www.thelovemagazine.co.uk/article/from-art-school-dropout-to-lil-nas-x-and-post-malones-cowboy-atelier-meet-union-western.

Tommy, Leisl, dir. 2019. *Dolly Parton's Heartstrings*. Season 1, episode 4, "Cracker Jack." November 22, 2019, on Netflix.

Tonks, Andrea. 2019. "Lily Allen Leaves Little to the Imagination in Eye-Popping Lace Top at Festival." *Express*, June 4. www.express.co.uk/celebrity-news/1135624/Lily-Allen-nipples-breasts-pictures-Governors-Ball-Music-Festival-2019-news.

Tosches, Nick. 1996. *Country: The Twisted Roots of Rock 'N' Roll*. New York: Da Capo. First published 1977.

Trading Economics. n.d. "Mexico Tourist Arrivals." https://tradingeconomics.com/mexico/tourist-arrivals.

Tran, Khanh T.L. 2020. "Grammys: Lil Nas X Turns Heads in a Hot-Pink Versace Outfit on The Red Carpet." *Los Angeles Times*, January 26. www.latimes .com/lifestyle/story/2020-01-26/la-ig-grammys-lil-nas-x-versace-red-carpet.

Trigger. 2015. "George Jones Explains What's Wrong with Country Radio." *Saving Country Music*, May 4. www.savingcountrymusic.com/george-jones-explains-whats-wrong-with-country-radio/.

Tuck, Eve, and K. Wayne Yang. 2016. "What Justice Wants." *Critical Ethnic Studies* 2 (2): 1–15.

Tyler, Paul L. 2014. "Hillbilly Music Re-Imagined: Folk and Country Music in the Midwest." *Journal of American Folklore* 127 (504): 159–190.

Tyrangiel, Josh. 2002. "The Dixie Chicks Get Serious." *Time*, August 19. http:// content.time.com/time/magazine/article/0,9171,338615,00.html.

United States Census Bureau. 2019. "QuickFacts: Colorado." Suitland: United States Census Bureau. April 27. www.census.gov/quickfacts/CO.

Unknown. "Hispanic Millennials Now Driving Country Music Growth." 2016. *Insider Radio*, October 7. www.insideradio.com/free/hispanic-millennials-now-driving-country-music-growth/article_5f1cd6ac-8c5a-11e6-bc1e-ebf398a0a4a4.html.

US Copyright Office. 2018. "Mechanical License Royalty Rates." Copyright.gov. https://copyright.gov/licensing/m200a.pdf.

Vander Wel, Stephanie. 2019. "The Lavender Cowboy and 'The She Buckaroo': Gene Autry, Patsy Montana, and Depression Era Gender Roles." *The Musical Quarterly* 95 (2–3): 207–51.

——— 2020. *Hillbilly Maidens, Okies, and Cowgirls: Women's Country Music, 1930–1960*. Urbana: University of Illinois Press.

Vargas, Deborah R. 2019. "On the Border with Maybelle Carter and Lydia Mendoza." *NPR Music*, August 15. www.npr.org/2019/08/15/748415123/ on-the-border-with-maybelle-carter-and-lydia-mendoza.

Vernallis, Carol. 2004. *Experiencing Music Video: Aesthetics and Cultural Context*. New York: Columbia University Press.

Wald, Elijah. 2001. *Narcocorrido: A Journey into the Music of Drugs, Guns, and Guerrillas*. New York: Rayo.

Waldfogel, Joel. 2017. "How Digitization Has Created a Golden Age of Music, Movies, Books, and Television." *Journal of Economic Perspectives* 31 (3): 195–214.

Warshaw, Nan. 2009. "Label Spotlight: Bloodshot Records." Interview by Corinne of pluginmusic.com. https://web.archive.org/web/20171021220828/www .pluginmusic.com/features/label.php?page=bloodshot.

Warwick, Jacqueline. 2007. *Girl Groups, Girl Culture: Popular Music and Identity in the 1960s*. New York: Routledge.

Watson, Jada, and Lori Burns. 2010. "Resisting Exile and Asserting Musical Voice: The Chicks Are 'Not Ready to Make Nice'." *Popular Music* 29 (3): 325–50.

Watson, Jada. 2019a. "Gender Representation on Country Format Radio: A Study of Published Reports from 2000–2018." *SongData.com*, April 26. Published in consultation with Woman of Music Action Network. https://songdata .ca/wp-content/uploads/2019/04/SongData-Watson-Country-Airplay-Study-FullReport-April2019.pdf

2019b. "Gender on the *Billboard* Hot Country Songs Chart, 1996–2016." *Popular Music and Society* 42(5): 538–60.

2019c. "Rural-Urban Imagery in Country Music Videos: Identity, Place, and Space." In *The Bloomsbury Handbook of Popular Music Video Analysis*, edited by Lori Burns and Stan Hawkins, 277–96. New York: Bloomsbury Academic.

2020a. "*Billboard's* Hot Country Songs Chart and the Curation of Country Music Culture." *Popular Music History, Special Issue on Popular Music Curation* 13 (1–2): 168–90.

2020b. "Inequality on Country Radio: 2019 in Review." *SongData.com*, February 17. https://songdata.ca/wp-content/uploads/2020/02/SongData-Watson-Inequality-Country-Airplay-2019-in-Review.pdf.

2021. "Redlining in Country Music: Representation in the Country Music Industry 2000–2020." *SongData.com*, March 12. https://songdata.ca/wp-content/uploads/2021/03/SongData-Watson-Redlining-Country-Music-032021.pdf.

2022. "Mobilizing the Demo Recording: Mickey Guyton's Advocacy and Protest for Equality in Country Music." In *Analyzing Recorded Music: Collected Perspectives*, edited by Mike Alleyne, Lori Burns, and William Moylan. New York: Routledge.

Webber, Bruce. 2014. "Donald S. Engel, Persistent Contract Lawyer to the Stars, Dies at 84." *New York Times*, January 31. www.nytimes.com/2014/02/01/business/donald-s-engel-persistent-contract-lawyer-to-the-stars-dies-at-84.html.

Weiner, Natalie. 2019. "Country Music Is a Man's World. The Highwomen Want to Change That." *New York Times*, September 3. www.nytimes.com/2019/09/03/arts/music/highwomen-country-supergroup.html.

Weinstein, Norman. 2003. "Secret Jazz: The Swinging Side of Western Swing." *All About Jazz*, October 14. www.allaboutjazz.com/secret-jazz-the-swinging-side-of-western-swing-by-norman-weinstein.php.

Weisbard, Eric. 2014. *Top 40 Democracy: The Rival Mainstreams of American Music.* Chicago: University of Chicago Press.

2017. "Country Radio: The Dialectic of Format and Genre." In *The Oxford Handbook of Country Music*, edited by Travis D. Stimeling, 229–47. New York: Oxford University Press.

Wells, Alan. 2001. "Nationality, Race and Gender on the American Pop Charts: What Happened in the '90s?" *Popular Music and Society* 25 (1–2): 221–31.

Whitaker, Sterling. 2019. "Kane Brown's 'Homesick' Finds Him Road Weary and Longing." *Taste of Country*, June 28. https://tasteofcountry.com/kane-brown-homesick/.

Whitburn, Joel. 2018. *Top Country Singles 1944–2017*. Menomee Falls: Record Research, Inc.

White, David Manning. 1950. "The 'Gate Keeper': A Case Study in the Selection of News." *Journalism Quarterly* 27: 383–90.

Wilkerson, Jessica. 2018. "Living with Dolly Parton." *Longreads*, October 16. https://longreads.com/2018/10/16/living-with-dolly-parton/#more-114881.

Williams, Andrea. 2020. "Why Haven't We Had a Black Woman Country Star?" *Nashville Scene*, August 6. www.nashvillescene.com/music/features/article/21142291/why-havent-we-had-a-black-woman-country-star.

Willman, Chris. 2005. *Rednecks & Bluenecks: The Politics of Country Music*. New York: New Press.

———. 2016. "CMA Awards as Grammy Auditions: How Country's Big Night Changed the Odds for Beyonce, Maren Morris & Maybe Even Dolly." *Billboard.com*, November 6. www.billboard.com/articles/news/grammys/7565707/cma-awards-grammys-beyonce-maren-morris.

———. 2020. "A Country Music Conference Dares Wonder: Could 2020 Be 'the Year of the Woman'?" *Variety*, February 24. https://variety.com/2020/music/news/female-artists-country-radio-seminar-1203514246/.

Witt, Stephen. 2015. *How Music Got Free: A Story of Obsession and Invention*. New York: Penguin Books.

Wittgenstein, Ludwig. 1968. *Philosophical Investigations*. New York: Macmillan.

Wood, Mikael. 2018. "Miranda Lambert's Pistol Annies Have Never Been More Important Than They are Right Now." *Los Angeles Times*. November 14. www.latimes.com/entertainment/music/la-et-ms-pistol-annies-interstate-gospel-interview-20181114-story.html.

Yahr, Emily. 2017. "Radio tour is not for the weak': Inside the First Step to Country Music Stardom." *Washington Post*, June 15. www.washingtonpost.com/lifestyle/style/radio-tour-is-not-for-the-weak-inside-the-first-step-to-country-music-stardom/2017/06/14/41feba42-4c60-11e7-9669-250d0b15f83b_story.html.

———. 2018. "Miranda Lambert is a Superstar. But Can She Get a No. 1 on Country Radio Only If She Sings with a Man?" *Washington Post*, November 12. www.washingtonpost.com/lifestyle/style/miranda-lambert-is-a-superstar-but-can-she-only-get-a-no-1-on-country-radio-if-she-sings-with-a-man/2018/11/12/6253c9d4-e63f-11e8-bbdb-72fdbf9d4fed_story.html.

———. 2020. "'There's a Problem with Sexism in Country Music': Why Samantha Bee's Late-Night Show Went to 'Investigate' Nashville." *Washington Post*, January 16. www.washingtonpost.com/arts-entertainment/2020/01/16/theres-

problem-with-sexism-country-music-why-samantha-bees-late-night-show-
went-investigate-nashville/.

2021. "How the Wives of Country Music Stars Created their Own Powerful –
and Sometimes Controversial – Instagram Empires. *Washington Post,*
February 1. www.washingtonpost.com/arts-entertainment/2021/02/01/
wives-country-star-instagram-social-media/.

Yazzie, Melanie. 2014. "Brutal Violence in Border Towns Linked to Colonization."
IndianZ.com, August 22. https://indiancountrytoday.com/archive/brutal-
violence-in-border-towns-linked-to-colonization.

Yoakam, Dwight. 1985. Interview by Paul Kingsbury, October 18, 1985. Country
Music Foundation Oral History Project, OHC336. Frist Library and Archive,
Country Music Hall of Fame and Museum.

Yotka, Steff. 2021. "The Local News: Indianapolis, Indiana Union Western Clothing."
Vogue USA. February 2021.

Young, Cate. 2014. "This is What I Mean When I Say 'White Feminism'." *Cate-
Young.com,* January10. www.cate-young.com/battymamzelle/2014/01/This-
Is-What-I-Mean-When-I-Say-White-Feminism.html.

Yucatán Magazine. 2019. "How Mexico Built Cancun from Scratch." https://
yucatanmagazine.com/how-mexico-built-cancun-from-scratch/.

Zentner, Marcel, Didier Grandjean, and Klaus R. Scherer. 2008. "Emotions Evoked
by the Sound of Music: Characterization, Classification, and Measurement."
Emotion 8 (4): 494–521.

Zhu, Kevin, and Bryan MacQuarrie. 2003. "The Economics of Digital Bundling."
Communications of the ACM 46 (9): 264–270.

Zoladz, Lindsay. 2019. "Is There Anything We Can All Agree On? Yes: Dolly
Parton." *New York Times,* November 21. www.nytimes.com/2019/11/21/
arts/music/dolly-parton.html.

Index

Printed in the USA
CPSIA information can be obtained
at www.ICGtesting.com
LVHW011524091123
763417LV00008B/327

9 781108 837125